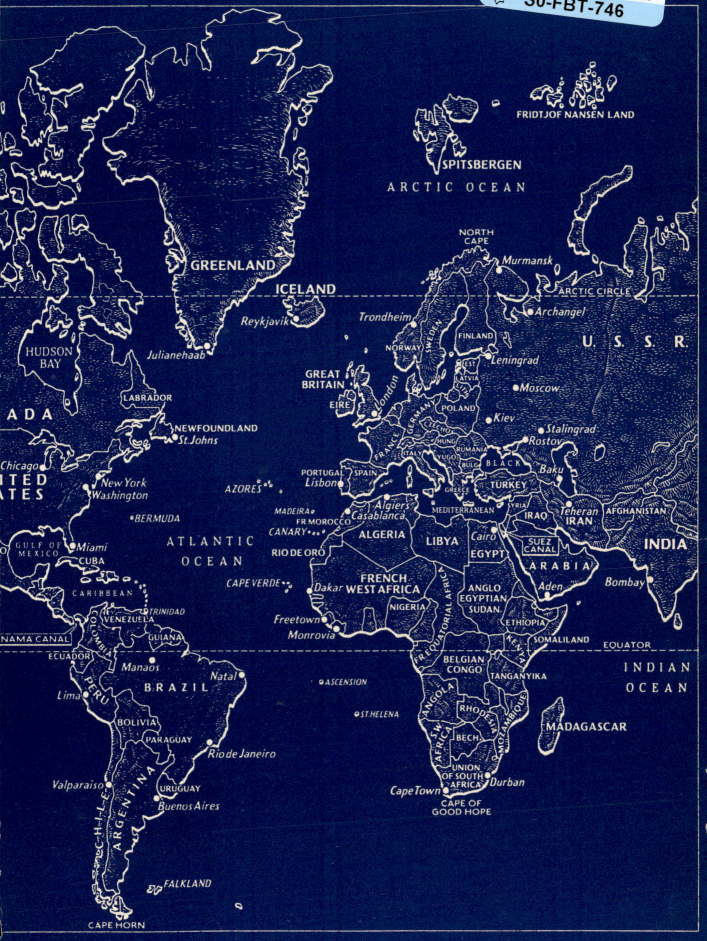

AN INTELLIGENT

AMERICAN'S

GUIDE TO THE

PEACE

AN INTELLIGENT
AMERICAN'S
GUIDE TO THE
PEACE

UNDER THE GENERAL EDITORSHIP OF

AND WITH AN INTRODUCTION BY

SUMNER WELLES

FORMER UNDER SECRETARY OF STATE

THE DRYDEN PRESS · 1945 · NEW YORK

PUBLISHER'S NOTE

THE PUBLISHERS wish to record their deep appreciation of the untiring labors of Mr. Sumner Welles, who, as the General Editor, gave unstintingly of himself at every stage in the preparation of this work.

The research and preparation of the material were entrusted to Mr. William J. Blake, who acknowledges the continuous services and aid of Mr. Joseph M. Bernstein, the untiring aid and cooperation of Mr. Stanley Burnshaw of The Dryden Press in the final presentation of the material, and the rewriting of several chapters by Miss Eleanor Sickels.

Thanks are owing to Mr. Samuel Guy Inman for his valued contribution on the peoples of most of the Latin American nations; to Mr. Lawrence K. Rosinger, of the Foreign Policy Association, for suggestions on the history of China; and to Mr. Randall Heymanson for suggestions on the history of Great Britain.

Where authorities on statistical data were in conflict and a choice was necessary, the sources used were, wherever possible, official.

The maps were prepared from PM base maps drawn by Harold Detje.

TABLE OF CONTENTS

Editor's Introduction

An Intelligent American's Guide to the Peace, 2

Europe

The British Commonwealth of Nations

The Western Hemisphere

The Far East

Near East and Mediterranean Orbit

Africa

International Organizations

AN INTELLIGENT

AMERICAN'S

GUIDE TO THE

PEACE

INTRODUCTION

THE PEOPLE of the United States are passing, in these years of 1944 and 1945, through one of the most critical periods in their national history. The future security of the Nation, and the course of events throughout the world, will be determined by the policies which they themselves decide their Government shall adopt after our victory is won.

The basic question upon which they must pass is one which vitally affects every citizen in this land. It is the question whether the United States shall bear its full obligations as a member of the family of nations, or whether it shall, once the war is won, return to the policies which the American people followed during the years between the two Great Wars, and wholly refuse to assume its proper share of responsibility for preserving peace in the world, and for cooperating with other powers in such a way as to make sure that in the years to come peoples throughout the earth may advance together in social and economic progress under the guidance of an enlightened civilization.

I am convinced that the vast majority of the citizens of this country have made up their minds that the policies of isolation have resulted in disaster to our national interest. I believe that the American mothers and fathers have long since reached the conclusion that the only assurance they can possess that their sons will not again be called upon to make the supreme sacrifice to preserve the freedom of this nation lies in the ability of the United States to join with other peace-loving countries in averting the origins of war, rather than through waiting until a world-wide conflagration threatens our own shores. I am confident that the taxpayers of the United States now see more clearly than they did before that the burdens which may result from our participation in a World Organization capable of preventing aggression will be infinitesimal compared to the cost of our present expenditures for war purposes as a result of which standards of living will inevitably be lowered for years to come.

On June 16, 1944, the President announced the broad outlines of the plan for International Organization which this Government would support in its negotiations with the other United Nations. This plan contained provisions for an Assembly in which all sovereign nations would be equally represented, a Council composed of permanent representatives of the Major Powers together with a small number of representatives of the smaller powers selected by "rotation" for brief terms, and a Court to which justiciable questions arising between nations would be referred.

Since that time preliminary meetings of representatives of the Great Powers have taken place in order that an agreement might be reached between them on a common plan. It is promised that before long all of the United Nations will be afforded the opportunity of joining in the framing of a final plan for International Organization.

Thereafter the Congress of the United States will undertake the consideration of this plan in order to reach a final determination whether or not this country will take part in the Organization that is so formulated.

Likewise the Senate will be called upon to approve, or to reject, the Peace Settlements in the negotiation of which this Government must participate.

The members of the Senate and of the House of Representatives must cast their votes of approval or disapproval upon these momentous issues in the knowledge that they act as the elected representatives of the American people.

In the grave months which lie ahead it is the obligation of every citizen of the United States to inform himself to the fullest extent possible concerning every aspect of the decisions which his country will now be forced to make. It is his duty to himself and to his family to study the problems with which our nation is confronted and to reach his own conclusions as to the course which should be taken. He should, whenever he deems it opportune, make sure that his representatives in the Legislative or Executive Branches of our Government are informed of the views which he thus reaches. Only in that way can he contribute toward making our Government the agency of an enlightened democracy, as it was intended to be by the framers of the American Constitution.

When the ultimate appraisal is made of the fundamental causes of the Second World War, such an estimate will undoubtedly maintain that by no means the least of the contributory factors was a lack of knowledge of, and interest in, the foreign relations of their country on the part of the peoples of the democracies. That charge will be peculiarly applicable to the people of the United States.

In so far as the United States is concerned, it cannot be denied that a measure of responsibility for the existence of these conditions over a period of many decades must justly be laid at the door of those leaders in both the Executive and Legislative Branches of our Government to whom the people had entrusted authority. In all but a few instances, they failed to persist in offering the people the light which they so greatly needed, and to which they were entitled.

The people of a democracy cannot reach wise decisions at the polls unless they possess both knowledge and understanding of the issues which they are called upon to decide.

It is a lamentable fact that to the vast majority of the people of the United States the whole problem of foreign relations has been something infinitely remote. It has appeared to be something shrouded in mystery. It has been a matter which they have for generations been willing to relegate to a handful of men designated for that function by their Government. Fortunately today, more than at any other time in the past, there exists a keener realization on the part of the citizenry of this country of the basic truth that the great question of whether this country can in the future remain at peace, or must once more find itself involved in war, will be settled by the foreign policy which this Government now adopts.

But there is as yet far too little appreciation of the fact that the daily life of every individual within the United States will be correspondingly affected thereby.

There is not yet apparently any full grasp of the inescapable corollary that not only will the lives of the youth of America be saved or sacrificed as the result of the decisions which the people of this country now make, but also that the standard of living, the economic opportunity, and the happiness of every one of us will be shaped accordingly.

The underlying truth of all of this must be hammered home again and again if the people of the United States are to achieve real security in the future.

It is imperative that the American people be shaken out of the slumber of complacency in which they have indulged during the past generations, and in particular during the past three decades, and be awakened to the stark truth that in the world of today and in the world of tomorrow the American democracy as we have inherited it cannot continue to function unless the people of this country fully comprehend that what we so blandly call the "American way of life" will no longer be conceivable unless they demand that their Government pursue a foreign policy which will safeguard it. Democracy within the United States will become a fiction unless the people of this country learn to know the truth, and determine their course in its light.

EVERY PEOPLE in their history come to crossroads — crossroads where one turning leads ultimately to disaster, and the other to national safety. In the 150 years of our national history the people of this nation have generally chosen wisely. In 1920, however, the decision which they made led inevitably to unparalleled danger for their country. Only the unflinching patriotism of the American people and the vast human and material resources which the nation had at its disposal saved us. We have learned, I think, that lesson. And the essence of that lesson is, that in the modern world geographical isolation is no longer possible. The overwhelming majority of the people of the United States have learned that there can be no security for this country, nor any safety for the liberties which they cherish, unless the United States plays its full part in some form of international organization which will keep peace in the world and which through international cooperation can make possible the gradual development of world stability.

Today the American people are once more at the crossroads. There was never before a greater need for full public understanding of the issues involved so that the choice before us may be wisely made.

There are at this time two outstanding objectives to be sought. The Government should make available to the people the fullest possible measure of information with regard to every aspect of the negotiations undertaken with foreign governments covering the peace settlements envisaged, and with regard to every feature of the discussions leading to the creation of an organized international society.

But the second objective is equally important. In order to be able fully to grasp the essential factors inherent in the information given to them by their Government, the citizens of this country must themselves personally study and discuss these grave problems and thereby be in a position to make a wisely reasoned choice when the time comes for their voice to be heard.

The people of the United States cannot afford to sit back and let these decisions be made for them. There is no family in this country which will not be directly affected by the decisions to be made. It is the obligation of every one of us, in our own self-interest, to think out for ourselves the issues with which our Government is concerned in the determination of its foreign policy. Only by so doing will we be in a position to detect the voice of the propagandists, speaking for the defeated Axis nations or because of their hate for one of our own Allies. (And we may be sure that the United States will be infested with these on an increasing scale during the months to come.) Only by so doing will we be in a position to reject as fatal to the true interests of this country the contentions still too frequently heard from the blind reactionaries who assert that recurrent wars are inevitable because they have always existed, that big fish eat little fish, and that consequently large nations will always destroy small nations. Only clear knowledge of the truth, a belief in the capacity of civilization to progress rather than to fall back, and an unwavering determination on the part of the people of this country to safeguard the nation, can counteract the effects of retrograde ignorance of this character.

Psychologists and many students of history will tell us that rivalry and antagonism are a part of the inherent nature of peoples, as they are of individuals. It may well be true that no power which the ingenuity of man can devise will eradicate the will to excel or to dominate on the part of members of the human race. So long as the spirit of nationalism prevails it cannot be denied that one country will always strive to outdo its neighbors.

But need we admit that this quality can find its outlet only in armed hostilities? Is the desire for peace on the part of men of good-will so feeble that they are willing to confess their inability to conceive of a world in which the determination of men to outstrip their fellows must inevitably lead to war? Is it not reasonable to assume, if peoples are willing to take as their premise that the greatest curse of the ages must be eradicated, that this quality of human nature can be canalized into new and constructive channels? Can we not fashion a world in which the peoples of the earth will keep the peace by force whenever law-breakers menace it, and confine man's innate determination to forge ahead beyond his companions to those fields of endeavor where benefits rather than destruction will result therefrom? Surely if the kind of new world which is envisaged is one in which men and women will gradually obtain freedom from fear and want as well as individual liberty, the rivalry between nations might well become a rivalry restricted to the social and economic realms.

In an address which Franklin Roosevelt delivered in 1926 at Milton Academy in Massachusetts, and which is today too little remembered, he said:

"Do not forget that Christ's greatest teaching was, 'Thou shalt love thy neighbor as thyself.' Certainly we are far from that goal. Yet we approach it little by little. This very future of complications, of change, will hasten our steps along the right path. The necessity of greater cooperation will put every individual into closer touch with every other. More and more we become interdependent. Communities merge into states, states into nations, nations into families of peoples.

"To take our part positively and not negatively is our underlying desire; to that end our education aims, and to that end the processes of the moment will work."

To take our part positively, is today more than ever the opportunity and the obligation of the American people. For the great end to which our education now aims, and the high goal to which the processes of the moment are now working, is the chance we are afforded of proving that the increasing inter-dependence of nations themselves can be utilized to end war and to increase the well-being of human beings in all the lands.

THIS BOOK has been published in the belief that it will facilitate the endeavor of the average citizen to obtain at this critical moment some of the basic and factual information which he will require in order to understand the major problems which this country now faces. This information is presented in no partisan spirit. It is wholly objective.

The book gives in summary form a brief picture of every independent nation and of every major dependent people of the world. It discusses their land and its inhabitants; their history between the two Great Wars; their economic life and their economic relations with other countries; and it finally emphasizes the salient factors which it is believed will determine the part each may play in the world of tomorrow.

In my judgment there is special need at this time for a wide dissemination of a book of this character.

It must be frankly admitted that the people of the United States in general have not in past generations thought well of the peoples of other countries. It is also true that in the melting pot which is America, large groups of United States citizens have inherited prejudices against other peoples which their forebears brought from the lands of their origin. In all of these cases, while these age-old hatreds may have been justified in the countries where they arose, they have no reason for existence in this New World. More than all else, the policies of blind isolationism current during the two decades after the First World War have been responsible for stifling a great part of even that normal instinct of interest in the affairs of other peoples which would be natural among a people who have enjoyed that high standard of public education prevalent in the United States throughout its history.

The people of the United States have consequently in past years been too prone to underestimate the virtues of other peoples. They have failed to recognize their special problems and to appreciate their social and cultural achievements. They have been too ready to view "foreigners" with general antipathy and with inbred suspicion of their motives. It would be futile to refrain from admitting that even now when our armed forces overseas return to this country, the friction engendered in war time between the members of the American Armed Services and the peoples of many of the countries where they have been fighting will create a feeling of antagonism which cannot lightly be brushed aside. Finally, as an outgrowth of all of these causes, public opinion will still tend to minimize the extent of the impact of other peoples upon the destinies of the peoples of the United States.

INTRODUCTION

The surest way to kill unfounded prejudice and suspicion between peoples through knowledge on the part of each concerning the other. It has already be come platitudinous to say that after the war the development of communications, and particularly the development of civil aviation, will bring every people of the world within forty-eight hours' distance of the people of the United States. The American people, whether they like it or not, will be next-door neighbors of every other member of the community of nations. For that reason alone, if for no other, it is the part of wisdom for us to learn what are the salient characteristics of other peoples and the chief problems with which they will be beset in the post-war years.

At the present moment there is every indication, as a result of the position taken by the two candidates for the Presidency, and by the leaders of the two parties in the Congress of the United States, that the transcendent question of the determination of American foreign policy has been removed from the sphere of partisan politics. It would seem to be equally clear that the overwhelming majority of the people of this country have already determined that the United States should assume its full responsibility in some kind of world organization.

I believe that an effective international organization can be constituted only through the creation of regional systems of nations charged with the primary duty of maintaining peace and of developing by cooperative methods economic and cultural relations within their respective spheres, under an over-all international body representative of all nations, great or small, and of all regions, and responsible for the maintenance of general world peace, as well as for general international progress.

Whether or not the United Nations ultimately determine upon the creation of an international organization of this character, I cannot overemphasize my conviction of the importance to every United States citizen of a far greater understanding on his part of the countries and peoples of the Western Hemisphere. It is in the New World that there lies the first line of security for the United States. Great strides have been made in recent years in achieving a greater measure of political and economic unity among the twenty-two nations of the Americas. But such unity can never pass the half-way mark unless the activities of governments, of colleges and schools, and of commercial interests are supplemented by the persistent determination of the individual citizens of all of the American countries. And this will come about only if it is made possible through a far greater measure of knowledge of the peoples of the neighboring countries on the part of the citizens of each American nation than that which has hitherto obtained.

Equal in importance is a more accurate understanding on the part of the people of the United States of the peoples of the Soviet Union and of China, and a fairer estimate than that which has always hitherto existed of the qualities and problems of the peoples of Great Britain and of France. For in the years to come, immediately after the war is over, the success of any international organization, and consequently, the fate of the entire world, will depend upon the ability of the people of the United States to cooperate harmoniously with the peoples of these four other great powers. Only through a friendly but realistic understanding on our part of their psychology and of their ambitions — both political and economic — can our egregious errors in appreciation, and our many unfounded suspicions of the past, be overcome.

The emphasis which I have laid upon these two important requirements is by no means intended to minimize the need for public opinion in the United States to obtain likewise fuller knowledge and understanding of the other nations and peoples of the world. For thereby is presented the surest way by which the people of the United States can truly become world conscious.

This book offers no suggestions as to what the peace settlements should be. It presents no blueprint for an international organization. It merely sets forth in easily assimilated form the chief factors in the national lives and economies of the other peoples of the world.

Our democratic institutions are founded upon the concept that the majority of the people are capable of determining their own destinies wisely. It is my hope that the information presented in this book will make it easier for an American citizen to obtain some of the facts upon which the decisions which he is now called upon to make must be based.

Europe

ALBANIA

The Land and the People

One of the smallest and most primitive countries in Europe, Albania in 1939 extended over 10,629 square miles — an area slightly larger than Vermont. Greece lies at her southern border, Yugoslavia at her north and east. Her western boundary is the Adriatic Sea, separating her from Italy about 100 miles away.

The Land. Albania is essentially a region of hills and mountains, with almost two-thirds wasteland. Not more than 10% of her area is cultivated, most of it crop land, the rest vineyards and orchards. The yield of Albanian earth per acre is one of the lowest in Europe, and yet the population that must be nourished by this small cultivated area runs to 1150 to the square mile! The only other source of food in this poor country is animal economy: there are 1,500,000 sheep, but only 400,000 cattle. Though statistics are not verifiable, Albania's food supply per person must be about the smallest in Europe.

Some fertile territory lies in the strip along the Adriatic and in the Koritza River basin. The government owns the land in the richest plain. Not only is Albania naturally difficult of access, but the few roads that existed have been torn up in the course of war and civil war. Travel facilities are primitive — the first railroad was built in 1940. A tenth of the people live in towns of over 10,000, but no city exceeds 31,000.

The People. More Albanians live outside their country than in it: about 250,000 in Italy, 50,000 in the U.S.A., and about 900,000 in the Greek province of Epirus, the Macedonian areas of Greece and Bulgaria, and the Kossovo district of Yugoslavia.

During the last decade the population was slowly increasing. The birthrate is about 28 per thousand, the deathrate about 17. No statistics on infant mortality are available.

The people are mostly mountaineers, strongly bound by tribal law, ready to avenge in blood the honor of their family, and resembling in their customs mountain folk in other remote highland regions of the earth. In the towns and fertile lowlands, however, these traits are mere memories as the population becomes modernized.

Although the law provides for compulsory education, only about a fourth of the children attend schools, most of which are located in the more fertile areas. Education is almost unknown in the mountain districts. Altogether no more than 5,000 Albanian children go to high school.

The 1,100,000 Albanians within the country proper divide into two important groups: the Ghegs, who live north of the Shkumbi River, and the Tosks, to the south of it. About 70% of the people are non-polygamous Mohammedans, the remaining 30% Christian. Of this minority, two-thirds are mainly Tosks (Greek Orthodox) and a third Ghegs (Roman Catholic).

The people have a picturesque history, marked by exploits of courage. Scanderbeg, Albania's "Lion of Christendom," was the hero of Christian resistance against the Turks. Albania's so-called "Sons of the Eagle," led in the 18th century by the celebrated Ali Pasha, defied the Ottoman Empire, with brilliant results.

The Nation's Economy

Agriculture. Albania's chief products are corn, tobacco, wheat, oats, and olive oil, the latter reaching an annual 4,000 gallons. The wool clip is about 2,100 tons. Very little meat is produced, religious injunctions preventing the Mohammedans from raising pigs. By force of circumstances, therefore, the people are largely vegetarians. Dairy products and cattle are important for export purposes, from the proceeds of which the Albanians buy manufactured goods from other countries.

Industry. Recently efforts have been made to stimulate industry, particularly petroleum production. Before 1935 there was no commercial exploitation of petroleum, but under Nazi occupation the annual figure of 200,000 tons was achieved. German attempts to establish a timber industry before 1939 were largely unsuccessful. The country has a good supply of several minerals, especially copper and chrome, which the Italians began to mine in 1940. Exploitation of these mineral resources may provide the foundation for Albanian industry.

Finances. The Albanian *franc* — on a gold basis — is nominally worth about 32¢. Its present value cannot be ascertained, as a result of successive Italian and German occupation. Money in circulation increased from 11 to 51 million *francs* immediately after Italy's seizure of the country in 1939. Taxation also mounted — from 28 million *francs* in 1938 to 74 in 1942. Albania's finances, never strong, are now in a well-nigh chaotic state.

Foreign Trade. The country's chief customer was Italy, who usually took two-thirds of her exports and supplied a third of her imports. Britain was next on the list. Albania's entire trade amounted to only $7,500,000 in imports and $3,200,000 in exports — with a chronic deficit. Her principal exports are cheese and eggs, hides, fur, wool, and petroleum; her principal imports are cotton and woolen goods, coffee, and sugar. Albania's foreign trade per citizen, $9, is by far the lowest in Europe.

History: 1914-1944

Origin of the State: 1913–1920. Albania had been part of the old Ottoman Empire that fell apart in Europe as a result of the Balkan Wars (1911–13). Convinced that the various peoples in the area now designated as Albania should be politically independent, the Great Powers constituted the country as a monarchy (1913), according the throne to a German prince, Wilhelm of Wied. Within a year he was expelled, and the new country was left without a settled government.

Struggle for Independence: 1918–1921. The Treaty of London (1915) provided for the partition of Albania. The Italians, however, having occupied most of Albania during World War I, declared it an independent state under Italian protection (June 3, 1917). In December of the following year a National Assembly of Albanians met at Durazzo and constituted themselves a Congress. A temporary government emerged as a result of their efforts.

Nevertheless, the Italians continued to occupy Albania, the Yugoslavs stationed troops in the northeastern part of the country, and the Greeks pressed their claims for the southern regions. Finally Albanian patriots formed a permanent government and compelled the Italians to leave in August 1920. Although Italy recognized the Albanian government, she retained possession of the island fort of Saseno off the port of Valona.

Albania became a member of the League of Nations in December 1920. President Woodrow Wilson had contributed his influence in sponsoring her independence and eventual recognition.

The following year, however, Yugoslavia invaded Albania. The League of Nations threatened the Yugoslavs with a boycott and forced them to withdraw. At last, on November 9, 1921, the Congress of Ambassadors of the Great Powers restored Albania to her 1913 boundaries, except for some small revisions; however, they confirmed the special position of the Italians with respect to Albania and charged them with the responsibility of maintaining the integrity of the small state.

The Rise of Ahmed Zogu: 1921–1926. Five Albanian governments had succeeded one another, as the country faced a succession of crises, invasions, claims to her land, and fluctuating relations with other states. But once the question of boundaries was settled, it became possible for a more enduring government to be formed (December 1921). Monsignor Fan Noli, a brilliant Catholic priest, was made Foreign Minister and Ahmed Zogu, a Mohammedan notable, Minister of the Interior. The clash of these two personalities became the dominant factor in Albanian politics for several years.

In June 1924, Ahmed Zogu was accused of reactionary policies. Following a popular uprising, he was exiled from Albania, and Fan Noli became the undisputed chief. Ahmed Zogu, however, enlisted the aid of Yugoslavia. Equipped with arms, he reentered Albania and compelled Fan Noli to flee. In January 1925 the country adopted a republican constitution and Ahmed Zogu was chosen President for seven years.

Internal difficulties in 1926 compelled him to seek the amity and assistance of Italy. The Italians responded with a $10,000,000 loan. They acquired a lien on Albanian revenues and the right to supervise taxes, and they in turn covenanted to equip the Albanian army.

Zogu proceeded to modernize the country. He abolished polygamy and supplanted Albania's tribal

See detailed map on pages 73, 141.

law with adaptations of the French civil and the Italian criminal codes. A common language, integrating the various dialects, was formulated for educational purposes. With respect to the land, an effort was made to distribute among the peasantry the large holdings of the once-dominant Mohammedan gentry.

In 1928 Ahmed Zogu was proclaimed King Zog I. The increasing influence of the Italians, however, continued without effective opposition. In 1931 Italy agreed to grant annual loans to meet the Albanian deficits and she governed the Bank of Albania from Rome. Aware of the poverty of Albania's economy, Mussolini insisted on lending sums that he knew could not be repaid, and thus he obtained control.

Italian Domination: 1926–1943. Italy had permitted King Zog the bauble of monarchy, but when he married in 1938 and a dynastic succession became a possibility, Italy's policy changed. Mussolini grew dissatisfied with a treaty of 1936 by which his government had acquired domination of Albania's economy. Without warning, Italy invaded Albania on Easter Sunday, April 7, 1939.

King Zog had already fled and popular resistance proved feeble. The Italians conquered the country within a week. Albania was made a puppet state and King Victor Emmanuel of Italy its monarch.

Great Britain, alarmed over the Italian advance into the Balkans, entered into unilateral pacts with Rumania and Greece, for a defensive alliance. The anxiety of the Yugoslavs was appeased by Count Ciano, the Italian Foreign Minister. He informed them that King Zog had requested troops to be used against Yugoslavia and that the peaceful government of Mussolini had naturally wished to restrain an aggressor.

The Italians proceeded to convert Albania into a stronghold, by constructing highways, bridges, and ports for the coming war. On October 28, 1940, Italian armies marched from Albania in an attack on Greece. In a brilliant five-month campaign the Greeks pressed back the Italian troops in southern Albania almost to the last ports. Their occupation, however, was soon terminated, as the German army, proceeding from its swift conquest of Yugoslavia, delivered a crushing defeat to the Greeks.

German Control: 1943–1944. The Italians reoccupied Albania, but with their reverses in 1943, effective administrative control of the country passed to the Germans. Three armies of Albanian resistance — two Moslem, one Christian — compelled four changes in the puppet government. With the fall of Mussolini (July 24, 1943), Albanian patriots vastly increased their numbers and the whole country blazed into rebellion. The Nazi forces of occupation faced tens of thousands of guerrillas. British officers arrived in Albania to guide the rebels.

Stakes in the Peace

Albania must organize herself internally. She must conquer her poverty, the worst in Europe. Her agricultural population must learn modern methods; her tribal population must be spurred to continuous industry instead of sporadic efforts. Better roads would diminish the "feud law," and improved education and communication would foster the feeling of community in place of family groupings. With a small area of cultivable land, Albania's prosperity appears to depend on animal husbandry and the exploitation of mineral resources, as well as industrialization.

But none of these prospects can come to fruition unless foreign capital is provided, unless there is peace in the Balkans, and unless the Albanian minorities within Greece and Yugoslavia are justly and intelligently handled.

With the loss of Italian power, Albania's safety depends upon an over-all Balkan settlement. A diminution in armaments in this whole area would reduce the prestige of the rifle and grant some dignity to the manual laborer, who has been far less glamorous hitherto than the gallant, wretched hill dweller. What the British accomplished with respect to the Scottish highlanders after 1746, in modernizing a tribal civilization, might serve as a rough precedent.

This little nation that, without resources or adequate nourishment, was able so long to maintain itself against powerful foes, gives promise of genuine accomplishment. Turkish feudalism is gone, tribalism is waning, and there are signs of modernization. An intelligent peace in Europe is probably all that Albania needs to make her beginnings as a modern state; for an intelligent peace presupposes economic assistance to the peoples who cannot possibly build up capital internally.

AUSTRIA

The Land and the People

Once the overlord of a great continental empire in southeastern Europe, Austria was reduced after 1918 to a small Alpine federal republic. Forcibly annexed by the German Reich in 1938, she ceased to exist effectively as a nation. Austria has not lost hope of revival, her restoration having been explicitly guaranteed by the Allied Powers.

The Land. Prior to the German annexation, Austria's 6,800,000 people inhabited an area about the size of Indiana, 32,369 square miles. Predominantly mountainous boundaries separated the country from Czechoslovakia (north), Yugoslavia and Italy (south), Switzerland (west), and the German province of Bavaria (northwest); a stretch of prairie land formed her frontier with Hungary on the east.

Austria contains five distinct areas: (1) The Arlberg, in the extreme west, is an Alpine region of high mountains with valleys opening toward Switzerland. (2) East of the Arlberg stands the Tyrol, a great forested Alpine mass with valleys running north and south; here the main direction of trade, like that of the valleys and rivers, is toward Germany. (3) The Klagenfurt basin in the southeast, a region of very fertile land with bitter winters and hot summers, looks toward Yugoslavia, with which it is bound economically. (4) Farther east, the Graz basin, also extending toward Yugoslavia, possesses coal and water-power resources and a soil favorable to intense cultivation. (5) The forested Bohemian plateau, on the north, leads to Czechoslovakia. Along the lower Danube, not far from Hungary, lies celebrated Vienna, long a cultural mecca and Austria's capital.

In terms of natural resources, the country's abundant water-power and deposits of coal and iron assume marked importance. The east is generally considered the best-cultivated agricultural region, while the west is the cattle-raising region. Almost the entire country is covered by thick forests, except for the broad Danubian plain.

The People. While the Austrians speak the German language and are ethnically related to the Germans of Bavaria, they rightly take pride in a distinct national culture expressed in music, architecture, and literature, as well as in daily manners and modes of life. The centuries-old historical tradition of Austria differs completely from that of Germany.

The country includes large admixtures of various

See also maps on pages 51, 99.

national groups, particularly in Vienna, once the center of an old empire composed of a multitude of races. Indeed, at one time non-Germans were so numerous in Vienna that infuriated ultra-nationalists put up signs: "Here German is spoken." It is chiefly in the western parts of the country, such as the Tyrol, that the population is as solidly Germanic as in neighboring Bavaria.

Austria's racial mixture has lent the country a rich and lively quality, particularly in Vienna, whose sprightliness bears little resemblance to the stodgier German cities. The gay, charming capital, a flourishing center of arts and sciences, was closer in spirit to Paris. Viennese women, justly famed for their beauty, were the product of intermingled Germanic, Slavic, Magyar, Rumanian, Italian, and even Ottoman blood. Here, too, during the late years of the 19th century, was the leading city of Jewish culture in the world.

Austria's birthrate was notoriously low, probably because of adverse economic conditions in her cities. By 1937 it had fallen to below 13 per thousand, and if this tendency, coupled with a high infant mortality rate, had continued, Austria's population would have declined from 6,800,000 to some 4,500,000 by 1970. After the Nazi occupation, however, the birthrate spurted to 21.8, one of the swiftest gains on record. The reason, of course, was that unemployment temporarily disappeared as the country engaged in an intensive rearmament program for the German Reich. With full employment, infant mortality likewise fell from about 92 to 72. Significantly, the deathrate increased under Nazi rule (from an average of 13.5 to 15.3), partly because of suicides and deaths in concentration camps. It remains to be seen whether the over-all population decline has been permanently arrested, for the Austrian birthrate is again tending downward.

Religion and Education. About nine Austrians out of ten are Roman Catholics, about one out of twenty, Protestants. The Jewish population, formerly around 3%, has been drastically and violently reduced. The Catholic Church is strongest among the peasantry, while in Vienna the working classes, though outwardly conforming, have often leaned toward free thought or religious skepticism. That the Catholic Church doctrines did not wholly prevail in the larger cities is strongly suggested by the declining birthrate. Religious liberty was complete under the Republic, which was set up after 1918.

Austria's educational level is high, though the school system hardly rivals that of Germany in technical efficiency or even in general diffusion. As in the country's ornamental army, Austrian "schlamperei" (carelessness), though charming in its expression, has led to inferior results. Still, education is compulsory, tuition-free, and largely decentralized; secondary education is widespread. Of Austria's three universities — at Graz, Innsbruck, and Vienna — the last-named has long ranked as one of the finest in the world, its medical faculty attracting physicians from all other countries.

Culturally, Austria has made splendid contributions in music, psychiatry, literature, and industrial design. To the famed music festivals at Salzburg came thousands of tourists every year. Vienna's workshops — the *Wiener Werkstätte* — have revolutionized modern designs in textiles, pottery, and furniture.

Before the Nazi conquest, Vienna blazed many trails as a progressive municipality; its model housing developments for workers, to cite one example, challenged the attention of the world. Reforms in public health, housing, and social insurance were all the more remarkable in view of the country's almost chronic poverty and economic distress after 1918.

The Nation's Economy

Agriculture. Until the collapse of the Austro-Hungarian Empire in World War I, Austria depended on a heavy tourist trade to get out of the beautiful landscape what the soil itself denied. Many Austrians, especially the Viennese (the largest consumers), obtained their food from the granaries of Hungary and the rich Bohemian land. Austrian farming itself was distinctly secondary to that in the outlying regions of the Empire.

Since 1918, despite laments about Austria's decline and despite the generally mountainous terrain, farm production has made remarkably strong advances. At present 27% of the country is under crops, 31% is good grassland, fully 40% is forested, and the rest is given over to horticulture and wine culture. The most highly cultivated areas are in the east, while in the west there is substantial cattle-raising.

Most Austrian farms are small (almost half are under 50 acres) and individually owned. In this respect the country is much closer to Switzerland than to Hungary, which retains her vast semi-feudal estates. Austria has clung to the system of peasant proprietorship that was fairly extensive even before World War I, and the strong trend toward federalism, or "states' rights," is explained by the peasants' tenacity in safeguarding their local rights and privileges.

In agricultural production per person, Austria ranks below Czechoslovakia but far above any other country in southeastern Europe. At the same time, yields per acre are not impressive — falling below the figures for Czechoslovakia and Hungary — even though they show a considerable advance over 1918.

About 32% of the people are engaged in farming, but the country has to import part of its food supply. Largest acreage is given over to rye, the basis of Austria's bread. Other important crops are potatoes, turnips, sugar beets, wheat, oats, and barley.

Cattle-raising is the chief branch of Austrian animal husbandry. But the 1,200,000 cows and 850,000 calves, while supporting a fair-sized beef industry, do not satisfy the country's needs. However, there is sufficient milk: Austrians are large milk-consumers, and dairy bars form a conspicuous feature of their cities.

Austria's agricultural economy is aided by fruit production: excellent grapes grow in the Vienna area, and apples abound in many regions, especially around Graz and in lower Austria. Heavy forests cover 38% of the land, a figure exceeded only in Finland and Sweden, and forestry as an occupation is encouraged under modern and efficient management.

Industry. Prior to 1938 about a third of those employed, some 1,500,000 persons, worked in industry; but since then, under the Nazi pressure for arms production, this figure must have risen substantially. The chief industrial centers are the large engineering and motor-car works at Steyr (about 70 miles west of Vienna) and the big aircraft factories at Wiener Neustadt (south of the capital).

Austria enjoys abundant natural resources in coal, water-power, and iron. Total production of coal, mainly brown, approaches 4,000,000 tons annually. Water-power is well utilized for electrical and chemical production. Annual iron ore production of about 900,000 tons represents a high point for central Europe, while the steel output of 1938 reached approximately the same total. Present estimates of iron and steel production double this figure, but some allowances must be made for Nazi propaganda. An additional resource, petroleum, has been found at St. Pölten, near Vienna, and is being exploited.

Vienna, like Paris an important center of luxury articles, was known for its skilled artisans in silks, embroideries, jewelry, chocolates, knitted goods, gloves, and musical instruments. During the old Empire, every ambitious artificer, it was said, from the Venetian lacemaker to the Galician folk embroiderer, found his way to Vienna. Although reduced by the sheer lack of markets, a surprisingly large number of artisans still remain active.

No description of Austrian industry is complete without reference to its unusually high rate of unemployment. Only a resolute overhauling of the nation's economy, after the amputations of 1918, could have overcome the chronic economic distress that plagued the country. But unlike the Swiss, the Austrians failed to make the requisite adjustments; sufficient capital was not available to expand the internal market. In 1933 the unemployed numbered 485,000: as late as 1938 they were still 320,000. In other words, for a period of six years, from a fifth to a fourth of Austria's workers were jobless.

National Income, Wealth, and Foreign Trade. In proportion to production, Austria is a large trader. Prior to Nazi occupation her annual imports were $240,000,000 and her exports $144,000,000 — a deficit of $96,000,000, or more than $15 per person. This deficit has been continuous for some twenty years. Even at the height of prosperity in 1929, with full employment, the deficit amounted to $150,000,000; and even at peak conditions only five-sixths of Austria's national income was provided at home, the remainder being made up largely by foreign investments and loans. When these were eaten away in 1931 the entire financial structure toppled over. At the time of her forcible annexation by Germany, Austria owed about $280,000,000 abroad and $220,000,000 at home.

Before the war principal exports were either in manufactured goods or in such raw materials as iron ore; food exports were insignificant. Chief imports were raw materials (especially cotton and wool), machinery, and a considerable amount of foodstuffs (reaching $45,000,000 yearly).

Austria traded mainly with her neighbors: Germany, Italy, and Hungary were her customers; Germany, Czechoslovakia, and Hungary her suppliers. She derived a large share of her income from foreign tourists who visited her mountains and mineral springs or who spent some time in Vienna and at the Salzburg music festival.

History: 1914-1944

When the Austro-Hungarian Empire collapsed in 1918, its lands were divided among the Republic of Austria, the Kingdom of Hungary, Czechoslovakia, Yugoslavia, Poland, Rumania, and Italy. From her former leadership of 53,000,000 people, Austria was reduced to a petty south German state of about 6,000,000. Vienna, the administrative, cultural, and military center of the old Hapsburg empire, lost its commanding position, for the new states created out of the territory put up tariff barriers and the country districts of Austria firmly opposed centralized government. After November 11, 1918, citizens of the industrial centers (Vienna and Linz) and the peasant Tyroleans and Carinthians were sharply opposed in politics.

The new Austria seemed to feel that unity with the Weimar Republic of Germany was only a matter of time. While Austrians were aware that they constituted a true nation, they felt bound to the Reich by economic and social ties — they had formerly composed the bulk of the strictly German section of old Austria-Hungary. However, the Allies specifically prohibited *Anschluss* (or annexation) and they undertook to support Austria's independence.

The Federal Republic: 1918–1920. The day after the 1918 armistice, Austrian members of the Imperial Parliament formed an assembly which declared Austria a democratic republic but also "a component part of the German Republic." From 1919 to 1921 Austria settled her boundaries with Czechoslovakia, Yugoslavia, Italy, and Hungary. On the whole, the boundaries were unfavorable to Austria; for example, Italy was granted undoubtedly Austrian populations in the Tyrol. But the Socialist Chancellor, Renner, was not a nationalist, tending rather to emphasize economic survival. Austria's situation was such that she depended on lavish generosity from abroad if her people were to revive.

In 1919 the first republican election took place. Forty-two percent of the Assembly were Socialists, 40% Christian Socialists, and only 16% Pan-Germans who insisted on annexation to the Reich. The Socialists were headed by two celebrated Marxian theorists of moderate tendencies, Karl Renner and Otto Bauer.

Regarding themselves as trustees for a workers' and peasants' state, they resisted the extreme revolutionary attitude of many industrial workers. But the resentful peasantry were not appeased. They opposed a centralized government, fearing the domination of Socialist and anticlerical Vienna; and they clamored for a Christian peasant society and a loose federal state. In 1920 a Christian Socialist government formed by Dr. Mayr replaced the Socialist-controlled régime.

Inflation and Foreign Control: 1921–1926. The loss of her pre-war market (through the division of her former territory) and the presence of tariff barriers in these areas in which she once traded freely, gravely affected Austria's economy. She found herself overindustrialized; she was a railroad center for an area she no longer served. Furthermore, insurance and banking revenues greatly diminished, because currencies were now diversified within the former empire. Income from tourists declined and tax payment from areas she formerly dominated no longer poured into Vienna. And the decline of her income classes was followed by a crisis in the luxury trades, which had largely supported the capital. But the needs of the people remained; and since Austria had no means of paying for them, she resorted to issuing paper money, in the vain hope that until it was wiped out, it would buy some imports.

The Mayr ministry, unable to master the inflation, combined with the German Nationalists. Czecho-

slovakia now offered to advance credit and urged the Allies to help Austria. The German Nationalists, however, wished to continue the economic chaos because it might provoke a clamor for unity with Germany. They quit the government. But a priest, Monsignor Seipel, united all anti-Socialists and called upon Europe to salvage Austria as an international duty. Recovery began when foreign control of finances was introduced and the currency was stabilized.

In 1925 Austria defined her constitution. The following year she achieved complete financial independence when foreign control over her revenues was withdrawn. The misery, dejection, and disorder of the inflation era gave way to temporary confidence. Indeed, two leading European economists, Sir Walter Layton and Charles Rist, were convinced that Austria could emulate Switzerland and that Vienna's size in the small Republic was not a permanent obstacle to prosperity.

But in 1926 a Christian Socialist bank collapsed. In the elections of 1927 the Socialists registered large gains, though they showed a majority only in Vienna, the "reddest" city in Europe outside the Soviet Union. Otto Bauer, their leader, announced that the masses might have to rely on other than parliamentary devices to assure their interests. Since Bauer had been a bitter opponent of extreme Leftists, this radical statement made Austrian capital apprehensive.

Organization for Civil War: 1927–1934. Two private armies formed: the *Heimwehr* (or Provincial Army), directed mainly against Socialists, and the *Schutzbund* (or Workers' Army). In 1927, when the police killed 89 people in a mass demonstration, the country grew dangerously tense. The *Heimwehr* leaders, including Prince Starhemberg, defied the government. For a moment these Rightist elements were calmed by the election of a Clerical, Miklas, as President. But this, in turn, inflamed the city workers. Although the *Heimwehr* now dominated the government, in the 1930 elections they obtained only 7 seats to the Socialists' 72.

The world economic crisis shook the always slight structure of Austrian recovery. By the spring of 1931 the economy verged on utter collapse. To avert this calamity, Austria negotiated a customs union with Germany, but France immediately objected, maintaining that this was *Anschluss* in disguise. In 1931 Austria's largest bank failed, precipitating a crisis that was to bring down the pound in London and ultimately the dollar in New York. To stop this disaster at its point of origin, the Allies loaned Austria $45,000,000, but she had to renounce a customs union with Germany for 20 years. The humiliation rankled.

In May 1932 a new government under Dollfuss accepted the Allied conditions. After the advent of Hitler, however, Nazism spread like wildfire among the conservative elements, and Dollfuss decided to rule by decree in order to maintain Austrian independence. The Hitler government of Germany countered by virtually putting a stop to tourist traffic, by propagandist browbeating, and by fomenting open disorder within Austria. The Reich formed a legion of Austrians in Germany along the Bavarian frontier. Dollfuss accepted Mussolini's support, which was given on condition that Austria become a Fascist state, destroy the Socialists, and practically break with the League of Nations. Dollfuss implemented this agreement by taking into his government a vigorous *Heimwehr* reactionary, Major Fey.

The Fascist State: 1934–1938. The Socialists had offered to cooperate against Hitler, but they opposed Dollfuss' Fascist state. In February 1934 they rose in revolution in Vienna and Linz. Their fierce battle ended in defeat, with the last shots fired in the imposing workers' dwellings (*Karl Marxhof*) in the suburb of Florisdorf. The government illegalized, jailed, exiled, and killed the Socialists.

Dollfuss did not long enjoy his triumph: a Nazi fanatic, Planetta, murdered the "Little Chancellor" on July 25, 1934. War seemed imminent, but Schuschnigg, the Clerical successor of Dollfuss, managed to stave it off. Hitler sent von Papen, his subtlest underminer, to Austria, while the Austrians continued to rely exclusively on Italian support. To insure this support, Austria adopted the constitution of a corporate Fascist state.

When Germany expanded her army, little Austria followed suit, also in violation of treaty limitations. But the Nazis enjoyed one continuing advantage: the economic contrast between the two countries. Germany's rearmament program had stimulated a boom, with full employment, and with a consequent population rise; but Austria saw only uninterrupted crisis, unemployment, and a dwindling birthrate. The Austrian did not stop to ponder the ultimate cost of Germany's apparent prosperity, and slowly sympathy with Nazism percolated under the surface of the Clerical and *Heimwehr* victory. However, Dollfuss' brutality had alienated any support that the city workers might have given the Austrian régime.

In July 1936 Austria woke up to find that Hitler and Mussolini had jointly agreed to guarantee her, provided she remained a Fascist German state. The Vienna government nursed the illusion that it would now be balanced for a long time between the contenders. Schuschnigg humbled the *Heimwehr* leaders, and by 1937 he was supreme chief of Austria. He had obtained support from the aristocratic class by restoring the domains of the old royal Hapsburg family. And he had assured some measure of economic recovery by resuming full payments on international debts, thereby retrieving Austrian credit.

But all these devices availed little. With no mass popular support, and with a hostile *Heimwehr*, the régime rested only on a disarmed peasantry and the "friendship" between Hitler and Mussolini. Nazi pressure became more intense. The Nazi leader Seyss-Inquart entered the cabinet, and Germany dictated antisemitic measures. All signs pointed to an early showdown.

The Nazis Take Over: 1938–1944. In February 1938 Hitler summoned Schuschnigg to Berchtesgaden, where the Austrian Chancellor agreed to still more concessions. Schuschnigg, once home, ordered a plebiscite for March 13 to determine whether the Austrians wished to join Germany. There was little question that however the plebiscite would be conducted, whether honestly or dishonestly, the people would reject *Anschluss*. Hitler moved quickly, ordered the plebiscite canceled, replaced Schuschnigg with

Seyss-Inquart. On March 12 Hitler entered his native Austria and the next day Miklas resigned as President. Austria, which had endured as a nation for nearly seven centuries, was extinguished. Hitler converted her into a mere German province, the *Ostmark*, or Eastern border district.

The Nazis rapidly organized racial and political persecutions, jailings, thefts, and murders. They ordered all former members of the Austrian government to be tried as criminals. Scorning the religion that had been so integral a part of the state, they stormed the palace of Cardinal Innitzer. At first the Cardinal and the Catholic bishops had supported the annexation, but the Vatican disclaimed responsibility for their action and summoned Cardinal Theodore Innitzer to Rome.

A spate of new investments in factories, oil works, and armaments broke up Austria's 20 years of unemployment, swelled her bank deposits, took "Aryan" business out of the doldrums, and dramatically raised the birthrate. The mind and heart of Austria were terrorized, but the stomach was somewhat satisfied. At first the people showed bitter resentment at the arrival of the hated *Piffke* (North German), but when he brought production up, they tolerated him, even though they continued to dislike him. Moreover, the former régimes had deprived the urban population of anything to fight for except a negative program: hatred of Nazism.

The outbreak of World War II found the once-independent Austria inextricably involved in the cause of German Nazism. Her manpower as well as her industry was pressed into service. And once Allied airpower began to destroy armament centers in the Reich, Austria's industries, remote from the bombing, were forced to work at feverish tempos. Meanwhile new groups had entered the population by transfer to Austria of Germans and enslaved workers from Nazi-occupied lands.

Foreign Affiliations. Since 1918 Austria has oscillated between Germany and Italy. When the Left was in power, the country was friendly to democratic Czechoslovakia. She has always been distant from Hungary, though rarely unfriendly. With Yugoslavia she has been on poor terms, never losing her resentment over the (south) Carinthian frontier. Basically, Austria was an economic orphan. Under the conditions imposed upon her during the years between the Wars a truly independent life for her was unthinkable.

Stakes in the Peace

The Moscow Conference of 1943 specifically stated that Austrian independence must be restored, but also that Austria must cooperate to this end. The degree of her cooperation would be a basis for consideration accorded Austria in the post-war period.

Austria is a logical center for a Danubian economic federation. An over-industrialized country, she needs customers. She must ultimately depend on free trade in the Danubian area; and her recent industrial development, even if based on armaments, has intensified that need. Considered economic opinion has always held that, given a large market among her neighbors, with whom alone she trades in volume, Austria can achieve a really high prosperity. She has ample resources for economic revival. An internal organization that liberates trade from self-sufficiency policies would benefit Austria more than almost any other commonwealth.

BELGIUM

The Land and the People

Called "the cockpit of Europe," because most European wars have been fought on her territory, Belgium is one of the richest, most populous, yet smallest countries in the world. Her area of 11,775 square miles (less than Maryland and Delaware combined) holds an estimated population of 8,400,000 (over 710 to the square mile) representing the greatest population density in Europe.

Belgium is bounded on the north by Holland (from whom she won her independence in 1830), and on the east by Germany — the nation that invaded her in 1914 and 1940, despite her neutrality. To the southeast, the Ardennes forest (Shakespeare's "Forest of Arden") separates Belgium from Luxembourg, with whom she shares a customs union. Her southern frontier is France.

The Land. Belgium's small coast on the North Sea, about 80 miles from England, lacks a good harbor. Indeed, much Belgian history is explained by the fact that her old harbors, Ghent and Bruges, have become silted up, and her great port, Antwerp, the busiest in Europe, can be reached only through the Scheldt River, which flows through Holland. However, Belgium is intersected by canals that bear a large traffic: those leading from the Rhine country towards Antwerp carry some of the heaviest shipping in the world.

The country consists of an upland and a marine plain, with the capital, Brussels, at their junction. Behind a seacoast of dunes, lie *polders* (low lands reclaimed from the sea by dikes), used largely for grazing. The sandy plain to the east is the most fertilized and cultivated stretch of earth in the world, a land so rich that it gave rise to a proverbial expression, "The magic of property turned Flemish sands into gold." This region contains the old cities of Bruges and Ghent, whose carillons and unchanged medieval aspect are the modern tourists' delight.

The rolling loam country rising from this sandy plain is given over to mixed farming. Though the Ardennes region is forested, much of it produces forage and cereal crops. Farming is secondary, however, along the Sambre and Meuse rivers, where Belgium's rich deposits and her large and busy factories are located.

The People. The country comprises two main groups: French-speaking Walloons, and Dutch-speaking Flemings. The Walloons for the most part occupy the industrialized uplands; the Flemings are largely farmers of the plains. During most of the 19th century, the Walloons dominated the government and education. From the 13th to the 17th centuries, however, Flemish civilization was one of the most flourishing in Europe, the cities of Flanders, together with those of North Italy, forming the centers of medieval wealth and population.

The birthrate, low enough before the Nazi invasion (about 15.3 per thousand), declined sharply to 12.1, then recovered to 12.9. Naturally, the exiling of large numbers of Belgian workers to Germany, together with malnutrition, have had their effects. The deathrate, which was 13.1 in 1938, rose to 16.1 in 1939 but has since dropped to 14.6.

The Belgian population actually declined under the Nazi occupation. Infant mortality is now about 80 per thousand as against the pre-war figure of 73. On the basis of peacetime figures, Belgium population in 1980 would have been about 7,400,000, a decline of a million from its present level; but the reproduction rate fell off even more sharply under the Nazis — from 0.86% to 0.67%. It is therefore difficult to forecast the growth of the Belgian population.

Religion and Education. All religions are treated equally under Belgian law and each of them receives a subsidy from the government in proportion to its active congregations. In practice, nearly all Belgians are Roman Catholics. But many of the workers are anticlerical, and among the middle classes, especially the Walloon element, skepticism is widespread. For all that, there are few countries in which the Catholic Church has so many devoted adherents and picturesque processions and costumes. The Catholic university at Louvain enjoys world-wide prestige.

With education compulsory, and with every commune, however small, obliged to support a local primary school, illiteracy is rare. There are numerous private and parochial schools as well, and high school education is widespread. The universities of Brussels, Ghent, and Liége maintain unsurpassed scholastic standards.

Belgium also contains a good many institutes of technology and higher learning; four Royal musical conservatories, 127 music colleges, an Academy of Fine Arts, and 62 schools of design. The Colonial School at Antwerp trains administrative personnel for the Congo.

The Nation's Economy

Agriculture. Producing the highest yield per cultivated acre of the entire world, Belgium also shows the highest cash yield per farm worker. Her varied products — "Brussels sprouts," endives, peas, carrots — are well known, and there is scarcely a branch of horticulture in which she is not supreme.

An extraordinary amount of labor is put into each small Flanders farm. The fields are often cut up into tiny plots, many of which are piped with hot water, sheltered by brick walls, covered by greenhouses and forcing beds. No sharper contrast to the American farm of the Middle West can be conceived.

Sixty percent of the country is cultivated. One-third is under cereal crops, one-seventh root crops, two-fifths forage; the rest is specialized, and the money yields of the specialized crops are by far the highest, since they involve the most labor. This small country produces fully 3,000,000 tons of potatoes, to take one instance. Potatoes are the only large crop that Belgium exports: the others, except for the garden products, are used domestically. But despite this intensive agriculture, the bulk of Belgium's wheat and flour must be imported; for no production yet devised could sustain a country so densely populated.

Industry. Belgium was termed the "paradise of capitalists" in the middle of the last century. Her Flemish population was nearly pauperized and the nation's standard of living as a whole was not high. This cheap labor, together with a free-trade policy for raw materials, extensive coal deposits, and a strategic location adjoining the most industrialized areas of Europe, determined Belgium's industrial destiny. Foreign capitalists invested, and, although labor became less cheap and the standard of living rose, the relatively low production costs long operated to favor the country's products.

Most of Belgium about Brussels and near the famed Borinage coal mines looks like one vast industrial city with miles of country roads paved with durable cobble stones and "Belgian blocks." Here amid the mines and along the rivers, canals, and an intricate system of rails, has grown up a production that gives rise to enormous trade. It consists in importing raw materials for transformation into finished goods for export. The resulting revenue is used for the purchase of food from abroad.

Coal production, averaging about 30,000,000 tons in good years, is one of the highest in the world in proportion to population. Although iron ore is imported mostly from France and Luxembourg, steel production is so extensive that Belgium is probably first among the nations of the world in per capita output of steel.

The country has extensive engineering works, especially about Liége and Antwerp. Her sugar refineries are large, and her brewing industry important, for the Belgian drinks 7 times as much beer as the traditional beer-drinking German.

About half the 2,000,000 employed population is in industry: 300,000 in metals, 160,000 in the mines, 225,000 in spinning and weaving, 100,000 in timber and furniture (the furniture-works at Malines supply a large part of Europe's cheap production). Some 600,000 people are employed in commerce, about 600,000 in farming.

Belgium's industry is highly mechanized, her investment in machinery per capita placing her fourth among the European nations, surpassed in this respect only by Great Britain, Switzerland, and Germany.

Money, Taxation, and Debt. The terrible economic effects of the war of 1914–18 did not easily wear off. Belgian money was severely devalued until, by 1936, the last devaluation brought it to merely a tenth of the 1914 gold value. Her present currency is curious: the *franc*, worth about 3.40¢, is the only money actually used; but five *francs*, called a *belga*, figure in international transactions. In September 1944 the *franc* was stabilized at 176 to the pound sterling.

In 1938 money in circulation amounted to about $740,000,000, but in 1942 the Nazi occupation had led to a 300% increase. The fate of this vast sum of money, created to pay Nazi occupation tribute and to enable the invaders to "buy" Belgian property, has not been determined, but a monetary treaty with the Netherlands assures orderly finances after the war. The gold reserve of the Bank of Belgium, about $800,000,000, is largely held in America, and this cover of $100 per person is ample for ordinary circulation needs.

Under the Germans, of course, everything was inflated; occupation costs in 1941 were assessed at $500,000,000, and in three years, this little country may have been mulcted of two billion dollars. Stock exchange speculation was feverish, prices rose 400% as a possible safeguard against inflation.

The national debt under the Nazis increased from about $1,200,000,000 to almost $3,000,000,000. It is now, assuming the *franc* as 3.40¢, about $400 per person. The fate of this debt is also not clear, since a large part of it was issued under duress for transfer to the Nazis.

Foreign Trade and Investments. Belgium's heavy per capita trade, though smaller than the Swiss, Dutch, and the Danish, is larger than Great Britain's and that of any other powerful country. She exports principally to France, Britain, the Netherlands, Germany, and the U.S.A. Her imports come mostly from France, Germany, Britain, and the Netherlands, although Argentine imports and American cotton are extensive. Chiefly she buys cereals, flour, and such raw materials for conversion as iron, cotton, wool. These converted products are then exported — as glass, brick, iron, steel bars, and yarns. Europe supplies Belgium with half of her imports and takes three-fourths of her exports.

She is extraordinarily dependent on foreign trade. Her life is bound up with world peace, prosperity, and liberal trade policies: whence her liberalism in political matters. Fifty-two cents out of every dollar Belgians take in derive from exports or from payments from abroad, and 50¢ out of every dollar they spend are for imports or for payments to foreigners. Hence Belgian industries rise and fall with world economic cycles. The difference is made up by investments abroad and in the Belgian Congo, about 11% of the national wealth being placed outside the country.

Belgium's one colony, the Congo, extends some 902,000 square miles with a population upwards of 10,000,000, all (except about 25,000 Europeans and Americans) native Negroes. In addition, Belgium holds a mandate over part of former German East Africa — involving 20,500 square miles and about 1,700,000 inhabitants.

History: 1914-1944

A constitutional monarchy since her foundation in 1831, Belgium hoped that Germany would respect her neutrality in 1914. But despite the Treaty of 1839, on which the Belgians relied, the Germans invaded the country at the outbreak of war. From then on, Belgium was in the French orbit. Her army fought valorously against the Germans, who occupied most of her land from 1914–18. Albert, the soldier-king of Belgium, earned tremendous popularity.

Reconstruction: 1918–1923. In the post-war period, the monarchy did not have to face the grave social disturbances confronting many other countries. To be sure, Belgium had over 800,000 unemployed and more than a third of her people lived on alms. But with astonishing speed she re-equipped her industry, restored communications and utilities, and channeled her domestic and imported foodstuffs to consumers.

These activities required enormous expenditures, however. An inflated debt and taxation hastened the collapse of a currency that had been sound for generations. Workers, now in demand for reconstruction, trebled the membership of the trade unions; farmers were enriched by high prices; industrialists could not satisfy the demand for sorely needed manufactures. But the classes that lived on savings, rents, fixed pensions, and annuities were ruined.

The country's social organization changed. The worker, who had not even had a full vote in the old days, now became a full citizen, and Socialism became a major tendency. In the first post-war election of November 1919, the government passed from the Catholics (who had held power for 35 years) to the intellectuals of the Liberal party and to the financiers. These had to cope with colossal difficulties engendered by almost total reconstruction, but they governed wisely.

Foreign Relations: 1919–1923. The Treaty of Versailles made Belgium sovereign. She could now make such allies or arrangements as she wished, unlimited by general guarantees; and in August 1920 Belgium negotiated a military alliance with France. She received the territories of Eupen-Malmédy, along her eastern boundary — the area contained many French-speaking people, but the Germans contested the population count. She also received Ruanda-Urundi, a rich cattle land east of the Congo in Africa, which she had conquered from the Germans.

Until 1923 Belgium had a favored position in regard to reparations payment. Her policy in this period was consonant with that of France, whom she joined in occupying the Ruhr in 1923. Belgium also sought to negotiate with England, but that country did not wish

See maps on pages 41, 91.

to be a party to French arrangements on the Continent. Largely at France's request, she made a customs and currency agreement with Luxembourg, which aided her economic expansion (1925). Her claims against the Netherlands — for the left bank of the Scheldt River and for a strip of territory along the Meuse River — were amicably settled without territorial revision.

Economic Revival: 1925–1931. The collapse of the Belgian currency under the strain of reconstruction resulted in a temporary truce among political parties. A Liberal-Catholic-Socialist government was formed. By this time the Socialists, led by the world-famous Vandervelde, were the most numerous party. However, the financial reconstruction was handled by E. Francqui, who recommended really severe taxation (socially popular because it was well graduated), a sinking fund to guarantee repayments of the debt, and the earmarking of railway revenues to service the debt.

Business revived as confidence returned and the Belgian franc was stabilized. These financial arrangements helped keep Belgium from feeling the severity of the world crisis until 1931. Other factors that helped were the development of technological research; the building of roads, ports, and canals; the spread of savings; and the greater purchasing power of the workers, once almost pauperized.

Once Germany had evacuated the Rhineland, Belgium's old animosity toward her diminished, and commercial exchanges with her became active. At home most of the parliamentary conflicts centered on the use of Flemish in the army or in education, for extremist Flemish movements had become an active minority.

The Crisis: 1932–1935. Belgium could not avoid the depression. As the largest exporter of finished goods in proportion to manufacture, she felt the impact of reduced purchasing power throughout the world. British devaluation of the pound in 1931 meant smaller receipts for Belgian exporters.

At first, Belgium depended on the unimplemented recommendations of the Oslo powers (Belgium, the Netherlands, Luxembourg, Norway, Sweden, Denmark, Switzerland) for a lowering of trade barriers. Later she made a working treaty with Luxembourg and the Netherlands for reducing tariffs. But when the self-sufficiency policies of other countries upset her expectations, Belgium generally raised her duties and imposed import quotas. She attempted to increase her credit by inducing her bondholders to accept a lower rate of interest. But none of these moves improved trade and employment.

The rise of Hitler revived agitation in Germany over Eupen-Malmédy, but for two years Belgium, like France, did not take Germany's rearming too seriously. In February 1934, when King Albert died in an accident, he was succeeded by his son, Leopold III, a quieter man of far less scope and capacity, but keen for new departures. He concentrated his attention on the rising power of Germany.

The continuing financial crisis, however, made the first year of Leopold's reign extremely difficult. Over-investment in the Congo, the fall in the price of colonial produce, and speculative excesses had damaged the banking structure. The *belga* (monetary unit of 5 francs) was overvalued in terms of the pound or the dollar. In 1934 the country lost $40,000,000 in gold. To offset the crisis, the government sought short-term credits to obtain reserves that might restore confidence. The ministry of M. Theunis, a man of great ability, sought to grant credit to the bankers against their threatening frozen obligations. In short, Belgium turned to the same remedies that President Hoover tried in the U.S.A. during 1931–33. Imports were cut, but the loss of British tourists (whose pound now bought so little in Belgian francs) more than offset the reduced expenditures.

The struggle was of no avail, and Belgium had to devalue her franc by 28% in March 1935. Immediately stock exchange prices rose, business increased, and the bankers escaped the penalty of their speculations and overoptimistic credits. But the consequent feeling of relief was tempered by the uneasiness of the people. For they suspected that there was a great deal of corruption in the state. They felt that the state was too direct an agency for high finance. This suspicion led to a gain in the extremist parties, in which money supplied by Hitler played a notable part.

The Abandonment of France: 1936–1939. With the Belgian franc devalued, Belgium moved out of the French financial orbit into that of Britain, who displayed a conciliatory attitude towards Germany. The Franco-Soviet pact of 1935 had disquieted wealthy elements in Belgium, who feared their own large Socialist movement and the rising power of the Popular Front in France. Within the Socialist party itself new tendencies arose. The older pro-French sentiment of a Vandervelde, to whom France was the land of Liberty, Equality, and Fraternity, was replaced by the cool isolationism of the Socialist Spaak, Minister for Foreign Affairs, and the quasi-Fascist banking policy of Henri de Man, the Socialist financial mentor.

Simultaneously, a young scoundrel, Degrelle, had begun a Fascist movement, attempting to give it a Catholic gloss by calling it *Rexism* (that is, the faith of Christ the King, *Christus Rex*). Catholics were horrified by the attitude of Degrelle, whose newspaper *Le Pays Réel* seemed almost translated from the Nazi press of the preceding week. By now, the older Nationalist parties in the Flemish-speaking areas seemed moderate compared to the VNV (Flemish People's Federation)

and the *Dinaso*, an imitation of the Brown Shirts. The atmosphere of corruption, Fascism, ultra-nationalism, isolationism, even racism, together with a more hectic tone in the extremist press, augured trouble. In this country of ancient liberties, raucous voices were unfamiliar but insistent. On the labor side, in the meantime, Communism also made gains.

In this supercharged atmosphere, King Leopold declared on October 14, 1935, that Belgium would go it alone, that she was affiliated with no other power, and that her policy would be determined solely by her own interests. His foreign minister, Spaak, reiterating the royal statement, announced that Belgium, who had been Europe's battlefield for centuries, now proposed to create fortifications and military equipment so strong that any aggressor would think ten times before assailing her might. In other words, Belgium, neutral and small, was stronger alone than with a General Staff and fortifications coordinated with France, a country with six times her power!

Belgium may have thought France a broken reed. The larger country had just devalued her currency and her Popular Front government was temporarily in difficulties over the Spanish Civil War. With her new and disquieting foreign policy, Belgium combined a promise of domestic reform. She sought to reduce rising discontent by projecting an imitation of the Roosevelt "New Deal" and French Popular Front laws. At the same time, an alarmed France considered fortifying her frontier with Belgium. For once, the French Chamber of Deputies dropped partisan debate to establish unity on this issue, but Marshal Pétain failed to carry out the mandate for which he had funds.

In 1937 Hitler unreservedly guaranteed the neutrality of Belgium. The isolationist faction considered this a confirmation of their policy. King Leopold paid a state visit to London, where he met the Chamberlain group — but his relations with the then government of Great Britain are still not exactly known.

In 1938 Belgium steered fairly easily through the Munich crisis. Rexism declined and moderation won increasing support. But the declaration of war in 1939 frightened the Belgian government headed by Spaak. It pleaded for neutrality. It had proposed frontier collaboration with Luxembourg, whom some circles appeared to regard as a more significant ally than France and Russia combined. It had as yet perfected no arrangements for joint defense even with the Netherlands. In the fall of 1939 Leopold visited Queen Wilhelmina, and both made academic pleas for peace.

Invasion and Subjugation: 1940–1944. On May 10, 1940, Germany invaded Belgium, under the pretext that the little country had arranged to help Britain invade the Reich. King Leopold cried for aid. France and Britain rushed it to him. Unwisely they engaged their troops in the very manner, time, and location that suited German strategy. There were other disadvantages to contend with. The French, for example, had never completed the Maginot Line to the North Sea, because they had feared this might offend Belgium, and because Marshal Pétain disapproved.

On May 28, King Leopold, disregarding the advice of his ministers, paid the price of his illusions by total capitulation. He consulted neither General Blanchard nor the Allies whom he had frantically called to his rescue. He said that he had no other option, that consideration for his soldiers and the weight of facts exceeded other obligations. Divested of royal power by the ministry, which retired ultimately to London, Leopold remained a prisoner at Laeken Palace at Brussels. Since then he is understood to have been imprisoned in Germany. His dignity in confinement and his refusal to aid the Nazis or legalize their acts have caused a popular reaction in his favor; even some ministers who deposed him speak of him sympathetically. But after the liberation of Belgium, those who had lived under the occupation proved more divided in their opinion of the king.

Following the invasion, the ultra-Nationalist Degrelle turned quisling and the "Socialist totalitarian" de Man became an expert for the Nazis. Most of the Flemings remained loyal, though some were seduced by the prospect of supremacy over the French-speaking peoples. The Belgian underground has resisted this second German occupation with admirable intelligence and consistency. The exiled government has conserved most of its liquid resources and has turned the Congo into an interallied war treasury of raw materials. The Belgians, worthy descendants of the heroes of *Till Eulenspiegel*, their epic of freedom, abandoned the doubts and vacillations of the pre-invasion period. The liberation in September 1944 revealed the scope and consistency of mass Belgian resistance. On September 8th the government of Belgium was restored at Brussels.

Stakes in the Peace

Like other small powers, Belgium will probably no longer rely on her traditional foreign connections. Her unilateral dependence on France, her only ally, is over. She had but one enemy: Germany; and the permanent reduction of Germany's capacity for harm would guarantee Belgium's security.

Belgium's stake in the peace is the healthful condition of the world as a whole. Her life is based on interchanges of commodities: she buys and sells more freely than any other land except some raw-material exporters like the Union of South Africa and New Zealand. She also has a unique function in that most of her imports are transformed by her into articles for export. Her stake is therefore freer trade, world peace, and stable organization.

Her only specific problem, apart from the universal questions of capital and labor, is the bilingual question that has tended to divide her people. But it is doubtful whether this question would play the same rôle in a peaceful world and in an expanding economy that it has played in the past world of fear, suspicion, and carefully nurtured hatred. The rise of education among the Flemings will take away the one-time cultural advantage of the Walloons. After that, equality can pave the way for fraternity.

BULGARIA

The Land and the People

If the Balkans are the political storm-center of Europe, Bulgaria, astride the Balkan Mountains and tense with Balkan passions, is the focal point of the storm. She is one of the little kingdoms we have a tendency to confuse with Graustark or Ruritania; but her history and her people and the problems of her future are very real — and very important for the peace of the world.

The Land. Bulgaria is a small country, with an area of 42,797 square miles (slightly under New York State's) and a population of 6,700,000 (slightly under New York City's). These figures include Southern Dobruja, a province on the Black Sea ceded by Rumania under Axis pressure in 1940. They do not assume that she will retain the 15,000 square miles and 1,700,000 people — parts of Yugoslavia and Greece, including Macedonia — "awarded" her during this war by her Axis partner, Germany. Leaving Nazi awards out of the reckoning, then, we may bound Bulgaria on the north by the Danube River (which separates her from Rumania), on the east by

the Black Sea and Turkey-in-Europe, on the south by Greece, and on the west by Yugoslavia.

The Balkan Mountains — the word Balkan means mountain — run from east to west to form the backbone of the country. North of the Balkans a country of high, bleak plateaus and fertile valleys, slopes gradually to the bluffs that rise high over the Danube overlooking the Rumanian plain. This is a great grain country. Easy passes cut through the mountains. At the eastern end of the range, where the elevation falls off toward the Black Sea, is pasture land.

South of the mountains lies the Maritsa Valley, famous in history from the time of Romans and Turks — a region of roses, tobacco, and mulberry trees, similar in appearance to parts of Greece and Spain. Sofia, the capital, a city of 300,000, stands at the northwestern tip of the valley; from it extends eastward the road to the chief Black Sea ports, Burgas and Varna. South of the Maritsa Valley tower the Rhodope Mountains, thickly forested, difficult of access, the home of the Macedonians, who spill over into Greece.

The climate of most of Bulgaria is continental:

winters are windy and cold, summers are hot, and the rains fall mostly in late spring and early summer. But south of the Rhodopes the whole landscape and climate are Mediterranean.

The People. The Bulgarians are typically stocky brunets. Although they have an Asiatic strain traceable to the Turks and the polyglot peoples of the old Roman and Byzantine empires, they are predominantly Slavic. Their language is very like the Russian; they use the Russian alphabet, and their state church, though autonomous, is Greek Orthodox.

The name Bulgar, meaning tenant farmer, was given to the mixed Slavic people who worked for the absentee Greek landlords of Constantinople and who developed in their rude mountains a society much like that of the Scottish Highlanders. The Bulgarian nation rose to great power in the 14th century, then was broken by the Moslem conquests. The Bulgars have never forgotten their imperial past. Frugal and honest, studious when they have the chance, democratic, dour but inwardly passionate, they have remained a volcanic force in Europe. Nowhere do political hatreds run deeper than in Bulgaria.

The birthrate, which was 39 per thousand in 1924, is now about 22; the deathrate about 13. Infant mortality, though still high, has dropped sharply (from 156 to 122). A generation hence Bulgaria should have some 8,500,000 people.

Religion and Education. The established Bulgarian church, of the Greek Orthodox rite (though expelled from the Orthodox Communion by the Patriarch of Constantinople because it declined to accept any but its own national authority), claims 80% of the people as communicants. There is a sizable minority of some 800,000 Moslems.

Education between the ages of 7 and 14 is tuition-free and compulsory, and the law is rigidly enforced. Illiteracy has fallen sharply: more than 40% in the 1920's, 30% in the early 1930's, and apparently below 20% today. There are nearly 2,000 high schools and junior high schools — a remarkable figure in view of the smallness and poverty of the population. There is one university, at Sofia, and ten other institutions of comparable standing.

The Nation's Economy

Agriculture. Forests cover 25% of Bulgaria. About 40% of the land is arable; every square mile of it must feed 370 people. The fertility of the soil is shown by the wheat yield, a sixth higher than Rumania's. But primitive farming methods and excessive subdivision of the land keep the yield of the other principal crops low — about the same as in southern Rumania, ahead only of southern Spain, Portugal, and Greece. Harvests are extremely variable: bad years are a calamity.

Of the employed population, 81% are in agriculture. The peasants own the land outright and are free from feudal levies or church tithes, though they pay a land tax. Pastureland and nearly all woodlands are held in common. Most of the farms are minute in size: six acres is above the average.

Bulgaria's principal crops, grown mostly north of the Balkans, are wheat (1,700,000 tons) and corn (about 1,000,000), then barley, rye, and oats. Most peasants sell their wheat and use their corn as the basic cereal food for the family. South of the Balkans crops are more varied: tobacco, exported for manufacture into "Turkish" cigarettes; fruit, especially prunes; wine; and silkworms. Farming in Bulgaria, with its wooden plows and other primitive tools, means backbreaking labor.

Bulgaria is a great sheep country. Her sour buttermilk and sheep's milk are famous and are even supposed by some to explain the unusual longevity of the people. Bulgarian cattle number approximately 3,000,000.

Industry. One of the least industrialized nations of Europe, Bulgaria employs only about 9% of her wage-earning population in mining and industry. Though the government has made serious efforts to encourage "infant industries," it has met with little success. Coal, of which over 2,000,000 tons (mostly brown coal) are mined yearly, is the chief mineral. During the war, coal production has been sharply increased.

National Income and Finance. With her undeveloped industry, backward farming methods, and small foreign trade, Bulgaria does not rate high in national wealth. Her per capita income of $43 is perhaps the lowest in Europe. Her national income — for a population nearly as large as New York City's — is less than that of such a city as Rochester, N.Y.

The *leva*, the Bulgarian currency unit, was stabilized at about 130 to the dollar before 1939. Savings were about $45,000,000 (less than $7 per person), and commercial bank deposits were $192,000,000. But Nazi domination since the outbreak of war has caused depreciation and inflation. While money in circulation has risen more than fivefold, the cost of living has more than doubled. Taxation too has more than doubled (from $16 to $36 per person), so that it amounts to nearly half the wartime national income.

Foreign Trade. Before the war, Bulgaria's exports were about $68,000,000, her imports $60,000,000. Since then, though exports have risen, imports have doubled, so that the balance is now adverse. Tobacco constitutes nearly half the exports in value. Apart from luxury goods, the only other large items are eggs, prunes, and wheat.

Bulgaria has long been a commercial dependent of Germany. In 1936, Germany supplied over 60% of her imports and took 50% of her exports. Shortly before the war Berlin offered a trade agreement which would have given Germany an absolute commercial monopoly. The only other large customers were Britain (for high-grade cigarette tobacco) and France (for the attar-of-roses used in perfumes).

History: 1914-1944

World War I. The constitutional monarchy of Bulgaria entered World War I deliberately to repair the territorial losses she had sustained at the close of the Second Balkan War (1913). About 7,000 square miles of her land had been taken from her by Greece, Serbia, and Rumania. She had lost all of Macedonia, some purely Bulgarian communities in Serbia, and her coast on the Aegean Sea, which deprived her of an outlet on the Mediterranean. Since Serbia was allied with Britain and France, Bulgaria joined the opponents, the Central Powers.

The Allied victory in 1918 brought added misfortunes to Bulgaria. The Treaty of Neuilly made her helpless against her well-armed neighbors, and she was saddled with a reparations debt of some $450,000,000.

Stambulisky: 1919–1923. The collapse of the old régime in 1918 had sent the Bulgarian King, Ferdinand, scurrying into exile. His son Boris succeeded, but he exerted little influence, for the people had chosen to follow a peasant leader, Alexander Stambulisky, a remarkable figure who had vigorously opposed the suicidal war.

He became Premier in 1919 and traveled to Paris to sign the Treaty of Neuilly. Accepting the terms in good faith, he returned to Bulgaria to cope with the problems of internal reconstruction. He assailed the traditionalists of the Right and the Communists of the Left, and manipulated elections — and swept his Peasant party into power.

From 1920 to 1923 Stambulisky governed as sternly as any modern ruler dared. He enacted a compulsory labor law whose provisions appear incredible today. All men and women between the ages of fifteen and twenty were forced to work for the good of the community and without compensation for an eight-month period for the first year and for a ten-day period every year thereafter until they had reached the age of forty. However, exemptions were obtainable by paying a tax; hence the wealthier groups were not affected.

Stambulisky's lasting accomplishment was his land expropriation bill, the most drastic in Europe. Lands belonging to the Church and the Crown and all private farms exceeding 75 acres per family of four were distributed to the peasantry, and only slight compensation was paid to their former owners. By 1929, some 93,000 families had received 810,000 cultivable acres. Thus the poorest tenth of the Bulgarians had a basis for livelihood.

Stambulisky levied income taxes only on the urban middle class. He jailed all members of former war cabinets; he revoked the freedom of the press. To him the professional class, the army, and commercial people were parasites living off the food-producer: the peasant. But in his exaggerated crusade in behalf of agrarians, he made the tactical error of restricting urban workers: hence, he lacked mass support in the towns.

His foreign policy rejected Bulgaria's historic feuds with her neighbor countries. He even tried to be truly friendly with the Serbs, his country's recent enemies. Under his régime, Bulgaria's indemnity to the Allies was substantially reduced and the term of payment extended.

The Macedonian Problem: 1923–1925. In 1923 the army and the wealthier classes overthrew the government and assassinated Stambulisky. A fanatical reactionary, Tsankov, became Premier. He excluded the Peasant party, then grossly manipu-

See maps on pages 73, 141.

lated the elections, and was triumphantly returned to power.

One of the most important groups in plotting Stambulisky's overthrow had been the Macedonians. These people were minority groups in three countries: Bulgaria, Serbia, and Greece. Some 260,000 refugees (mostly Macedonians) had been repatriated in Bulgaria from bordering nations; they formed a secret organization, IMRO (International Macedonian Revolutionary Organization), which became the most terroristic of the national-minority vengeance groups in Europe. Todor Alexandrov, their leader, maintained that the treaty stipulations assuring Serbia's just treatment of Macedonian minorities were a mere illusion. Stambulisky had tried to crush the IMRO and had failed. Upon his death, IMRO joined the reactionaries and became a power in Bulgaria.

Serbia, with her large, compact Macedonian minority, now became more hostile to Bulgaria for harboring the IMRO which was agitating within Serbia for Macedonian independence. "Macedonians were not Bulgarians, and therefore Bulgaria had no reason to encourage the Macedonian agitation within Serbia," the Serbians declared. "They believe they are naturally affiliated to Bulgarians," the Bulgarians contended. IMRO now demanded that the Macedonians within Serbia receive autonomy. The Serbians refused to grant it as the Greeks had refused a similar demand some time earlier.

In August 1924 the IMRO leader, Alexandrov, was murdered. In the terroristic reprisal staged by his followers in the IMRO, the peasants who had been loyal to the Stambulisky tradition suffered severely.

The Reign of Terror: 1924–1925. Both the peasants, who bitterly opposed Prime Minister Tsankov, and the wretched urban workers, who hated the army, the wealthier class, and some of the Macedonians, came to believe that Soviet influence would improve their condition. The developing philo-Russian movement included few Communists of the orthodox type, but the prestige of Russia had always been high in Bulgaria. The Tsankov government, fearful of the pro-Russian sentiment, branded all Leftists, Agrarians, and Liberals as Communists and resorted to mass terror.

In 1925, at the funeral of a murdered Bulgarian general, the Sofia cathedral was blown up, and over a hundred were killed and more than three hundred wounded. Tsankov declared martial law. Stating that the bombing was a Communist plot, the government jailed thousands and executed hundreds, usually without the pretence of a trial. Among those who escaped was a young Communist printer, George Dimitrov, who was later to emerge as the central actor in the Reichstag fire trial in Berlin (1933).

From now on assassination and kidnaping became normal in Bulgarian politics. No man could trust his own brother or father: the Dark Ages had returned. But once the bloodthirst was slaked, more conservative influences prevailed. The Allies permitted the Bulgarians to enlarge their army to cope with libertarian peasant and worker risings. Before long, a measure of "order" was restored to the country.

The Refugee Problem: 1925–1926. The Macedonian "Komitadjis" (or committees) had been constantly making forays into Greece from Bulgaria. In 1925 the Greeks invaded Bulgaria to suppress them. Greek occupation became so cruel that the League of Nations later forced Greece to pay a large compensation to Bulgaria.

Macedonians now poured into Bulgaria from Greece, where they were being persecuted. The ensuing refugee problem soon led to disorders. The costs of maintaining these people plus a devastating earthquake made it impossible for Bulgaria to meet her payments on the Allied indemnity. Lacking monetary assets, the Bulgarian government was forced to print money — which led to a wild currency inflation. The refugees now had to be settled permanently or anarchy would sweep the country. Bulgaria proceeded to mortgage her physical assets in order to meet the Allied indemnity payments. The government sold farms to 28,000 refugees on long-term credit, in an effort to ameliorate the condition of the Macedonian refugees.

Reconstruction: 1926–1931. In 1926 Liaptchev became Premier — a Macedonian but acceptable to most parties. His long tenure of office began with an amnesty for over 6,000 political prisoners. Political murders and kidnapings ceased, political exiles returned, and the press became relatively free. Though neither political liberty nor amnesty was complete, men could now walk about with at least reasonable safety.

In 1926 the League of Nations granted Bulgaria a loan to aid her refugees; Britain supplying $12,000,000 and the U.S.A. $4,500,000. The situation in Bulgaria thus changed for the better, but Yugoslavia, fearing that the funds might be abused, closed her Serbian border for a year to protect herself from a recurrence of Macedonian raids. Bulgaria declared martial law (1927) to control the internal situation and thus cooperate in Balkan peace. Hence, foreign relations improved, and in 1928, for the first time since 1911, Bulgaria did not feel that she was surrounded by enemies.

Beginning with 1930, the country's finances improved. Her war indemnities were reduced to $2,200,000 payable for 36 years, and the humiliating mortgage on her physical assets, held by the Allies, was removed. The following year, her World War I indemnity effectively ceased. In the meantime a second international loan of $25,000,000 ended the threat of inflation and soon stabilized Bulgaria's budget.

This economic stability encouraged larger freedom in elections. A new *bloc* took power from Liaptchev, in 1931, and granted three seats to the Agrarian party. But no sooner was this done than the Vienna banking system crashed and with it the Balkan economic situation as a whole fell into grave difficulties. With the prices of her products sinking to the lowest levels in the century, Bulgaria lay in the depths of a new crisis before she had dug out of the old one.

Army Plotting and Royal Power: 1934–1944. In May 1934 a new group, the "Zvenos," composed mostly of army officers, seized power under one Colonel Georgiev. They formed a one-party government and abolished Parliament. Despite their reactionary political philosophy, they entered into diplomatic relations with the U.S.S.R. in order to consolidate their position. They immediately suppressed the IMRO, reducing it to a small group of conspirators.

By 1935 King Boris had become a power in Bulgaria. When he saw that the Zveno group was inclining toward a republic, he proceeded to have Colonel Georgiev overturned and to form a new royalist government under General Zlatev. A whirl of ministries followed — of martial law, of alleged plots against the King, of the arrest of Zvenos on the Right and Socialists and Communists on the Left. Every act of terror led to a fresh ministerial crisis.

The royal government tried to bolster its shaky foundations with a nonaggression pact with Yugoslavia. In 1938, for the first time in four years, Parliament was convened — as a result of popular demonstrations. Instantly the government was defeated and the royal dictatorship threatened. New elections in 1939 showed that despite the terror, over a third of the people voted against a royal-sponsored government. In 1940 the government manipulated elections and made a better showing. Then it suppressed all parties and the new royalist Premier, Philov, reduced Parliament to a mere ratifying body.

When war broke out in 1939, King Boris decided to weigh the advantages of belligerency as against neutrality. He was of German origin and his wife was an Italian princess. Before long, however, Nazi patterns appeared in Bulgaria, including racial laws. In 1940 she received from Germany the Southern Dobruja section of Rumania, and in March 1941 she joined the Axis, believing its victory to be assured. The Germans used Bulgaria as a base for attacking Yugoslavia and Greece, and after the defeat of these countries, Germany awarded Bulgaria jurisdiction over large areas in the Macedonian parts of Yugoslavia and over Thrace (Greece). Although she was at war with Britain and the U.S.A., Bulgaria hesitated to become involved against the U.S.S.R., because of the strong pro-Russian sentiments of the Bulgarian people.

King Boris mysteriously died in 1943, and a regency governed for his son Simeon. By 1944 Bulgaria had become increasingly restive in her military venture. A "tolerated opposition" within the country became more vocal. With the death of Boris and the collapse of Italy, internal divisions multiplied. In no other country within the official Axis orbit was popular opposition to the government so strenuous. Antisemitic measures had been blocked by widespread rioting, and the attitude of the masses was unmistakable.

When Soviet armies marched into Rumania in the summer of 1944, Bulgaria's position became desperate. The U.S.S.R. declared war on Bulgaria. A pro-United Nations ministry was formed, and in September Bulgaria agreed to a cessation of hostilities.

Foreign Affiliations. From 1911 to the present, Bulgaria has been perhaps the most friendless nation in Europe. Commercially she lies within the German orbit; diplomatically she has been in perpetual difficulties with Greece and Yugoslavia. Strictly speaking, she has no permanent international associations, except for the strong feelings of unity with the Russians. Great Britain is on the whole well regarded by urban Bulgarians, and the old animosity toward Turkey and Rumania has largely declined.

Stakes in the Peace

As a defeated nation, Bulgaria will doubtless face the expiatory demands of Greece and Yugoslavia; but it is doubtful that the coming peace will permit these long-standing animosities to be perpetuated and thus recommence the endless round of punishment and its inevitable sequel, revenge. While Bulgaria's

crime in aiding the unconscionable assaults of the Nazis on Yugoslavia and Greece is inescapable and the cruelties of her ruling clique unpardonable, the complex situation of her people and the just basis of certain of her grievances will merit some consideration.

Bulgaria can become happy only if the per capita income of her people is, at the very least, doubled. The soil and the labor are available; the people are industrious and can easily increase productivity.

But this agricultural improvement can avail little unless Bulgaria's national and international situation becomes stable. Peace in the Balkans is the prerequisite — perhaps a Balkan federation of free commonwealths can succeed in focusing the mind of this region away from the past and upon the future. Only a development of this nature can serve to utilize the latent abilities of the Bulgarians. Sons of the middle class, who went into ill-paying army and government posts, can be directed into agricultural science or technology. The cruel military class, as absurd in its vanity as it appears in Bernard Shaw's *Arms and the Man*, can seek constructive channels or be eliminated. And the peasantry may come to recognize itself as one element in Bulgarian welfare rather than the total *raison d'être*. Macedonian cultural autonomy and a genuine respect for minorities, in a stable Balkan world, would enhance rather than hinder the growth of a healthy Bulgarian nationalism.

This country has shown the ability to make wise use of funds; under a democratic government it would deserve financial assistance from abroad. Until export markets are generally restored, Bulgaria should be able to expand her trade with the U.S.S.R. and Turkey.

CZECHOSLOVAKIA

The Land and the People

Woodrow Wilson was the godfather of the Czechoslovak republic, born at Paris in 1918, and Thomas Masaryk, her first President, and his close friend Eduard Beneš modeled their country's creed after our Declaration of Independence. The grateful Czechs commemorated American friendship in the names of railroad stations and public squares throughout their free land.

But German imperialists had long eyed this prize area whose independent nationhood America sponsored. Bismarck once said: "Whoever is the master of Bohemia is the master of Europe." And in the wake of the Munich Pact (September 1938) Germany finally seized the country.

Czechoslovakia was dismembered at Munich, but we shall here speak of the nation primarily in terms

of her original area, noting the post-Munich changes as they took place. From 1919 to 1938 Czechoslovakia (slightly larger than New York State) covered 54,244 square miles. The population reached 15,500,000.

The republic formed an island of democracy in central Europe. Created entirely out of land belonging to the former Austro-Hungarian empire, Czechoslovakia had complex boundaries, reflecting the desire of the Versailles peacemakers to group into a compact mass the largest number of Slavic peoples in the heart of Europe. Thus, Czechoslovakia was landlocked within five countries: Poland, to the northeast; Rumania, to the southeast; Austria and Hungary, to the south; and Germany, to the north and west.

The Land. The geographic complexity of a country so constituted is not easily described, but its chief divisions indicate the basic structure: (1) The beautiful Bohemian plain, surrounded by the forests of Bavaria, the Erz mountains and the Sudeten range, is fertile rolling country dotted with springs of volcanic origin. (2) Moravia, extremely fertile and picturesque, is separated from Bohemia on the southeast by mountainous, wooded, and sparsely peopled land. (3) Slovakia, a prairie land to the southeast of Moravia, is bounded partially by the Danube and the vast Hungarian plain. (4) Ruthenia (or Sub-Carpathian Russia) lies in the extreme east, a small forested mountainous province difficult of access.

The Versailles peacemakers deliberately gave Czechoslovakia a strategic and defensible frontier on the northwest facing Germany. This included the Sudeten land, with its German-speaking population, which had belonged to the Austrian empire before 1914.

In 1944 the country lay partitioned as follows: the Sudeten land had been annexed by Germany in 1938; Bohemia and Moravia formed a German "protectorate," Slovakia was an "independent" puppet state "under German protection"; the southern part of Slovakia and the province of Ruthenia were annexed by Hungary; and Teschen, an important mining district in the northeast, first taken by Poland, was absorbed by Germany.

Prague, the capital, located in the center of Bohemia, and on the Moldau River, has a climate similar to New York City's, though its summers are cooler. The climate in the rest of the country varies considerably. The country's rainfall, usually below 20 inches, is quite evenly distributed through the year.

The leading mineral resources, coal and iron, are found in abundance in the northeast, especially the Teschen district. Southwest of Prague there are extensive iron deposits, and some lead and copper in Slovakia.

The People. The Czechs (or Bohemians) and the Slovaks, both Slavic peoples speaking closely related languages, constitute 70% of the population. The Sudeten Germans number about 20%, the Ruthenians and the Hungarian minority about 10%.

The estimated 8,300,000 Czechs live chiefly in Bohemia and Moravia; the Slovaks, some 2,300,000, occupy Slovakia; the 3,400,000 Sudetens were never part of Germany but an important group in Bohemia and Moravia when the latter belonged to the Austro-Hungarian empire; the 600,000 Ruthenians, a people of Ukrainian origin, inhabit the Carpathian regions in the extreme east; and most of the 700,000 Hungarians live in Slovakia. Other groups were not numerous, the most sizable being the 186,000 who described themselves as Jews; the other Jews, until the advent of Nazism, considered themselves culturally either Czechs or Germans.

The population is predominantly "Alpine" in form, that is, round-headed, fairly short, stocky, and generally brunet. This is equally true of the Sudeten Germans, who do not differ so much in basic type as in language.

In Bohemia and Moravia the birthrate was extremely low (around 14.3 per thousand); in Slovakia, however, it was 23. The marked rise in the birthrate of the Sudeten Germans after their incorporation into the German Reich indicated that their economic

conditions were temporarily improved by employment in war industries. Only a moderate growth in population was permitted by the deathrate of 12.8 per thousand in Bohemia and 13.8 in Slovakia. Infant mortality was high (about 122) and was higher in backward Ruthenia and Slovakia than in the more industrialized areas of Bohemia and Moravia.

Religion and Education. Bohemia, traditionally a land of intense religious feeling, has witnessed great battles of religious doctrine. Until 1620, when the Bohemian nation was extinguished at the Battle of the White Mountain, Protestantism was closely identified with national aspirations. The Hussite heresy, too, bore a strong national imprint. But while Protestantism has exerted a powerful political force in the nation's past, the majority of Czechoslovaks (over 60%) are Roman Catholics who acknowledge Papal supremacy. There are also some 800,000 Catholics who subscribe to a "National" church that disavows Papal supremacy. The country includes 1,200,000 Protestants; 750,000 Greek Catholic and Orthodox adherents; 360,000 Jews; and at least 1,000,000 citizens who declined to specify any religious faith.

Before the war, Prague was one of the cultural capitals of Europe, a symbol of the high cultural attainments of the Czechs. The Slavs of Central Europe, headed by the Czechs, for centuries despised and ground down by arrogant Teutons, have proved a match for them in all the arts and sciences. What characterizes the Czechs is their intense modernity, their vivid comprehension of the contemporary world. Czechs rank high in Europe's poetry, fiction, and criticism; their painting and music are of the most modern type; their excellent translations, encyclopedias, and textbooks reflect the literary power of the country; their sports and mass singing have won merited fame.

While the Czechs are the most progressive and modernized group in the country, the Slovaks were making impressive forward strides under the republic. Widening opportunities for education contributed to this progress.

There were about 2,000 high schools, a large number of cultural and technical institutes, and four universities: two Czech (at Prague and Brno), one German (at Prague), and one Slovak (at Bratislava). Even a Ukrainian University was founded at Prague for the Ruthenians, but its fate under German occupation is uncertain.

In the schools, tuition-free and compulsory up to the age of 14, the language of instruction corresponded roughly to the proportion of population. It was Czech or Slovak in about 68% of the schools and German in 21%. Other minority languages were official for those minorities that formed compact groups. Czech was taught as a required second language in minority language schools.

In education as in government the Czechoslovaks succeeded admirably in welding together a Slavic nation based on democratic principles. They have proudly carried on the intellectual tradition of President Thomas G. Masaryk, certainly one of the outstanding political thinkers and statesmen of modern Europe.

Map labels: GERMANY, Dresden, ODER, Warsaw, COPYRIGHT, FIELD PUBLICATIONS, POLAND, Cheb (Eger), Breslau, Lublin, Praha (Prague), RUSSO-GERMAN BORDER AT START OF NAZI ATTACK JUNE 22, 1941, Nuremberg, Plzen (Pilsen), BOHEMIA, Krakow, VISTULA, Budejovice, MORAVIA, Brno, Mor. Ostrava, Cieszyn, Teschen, Munich, Lwow, Linz, SLOVAKIA, CZECHOSLOVAKIA, Vienna, Wiener Neustadt, Bratislava, RUTHENIA, AUSTRIA, DANUBE, Graz, Budapest, HUNGARY

See also maps on pages 51, 99.

The Nation's Economy

Agriculture. Enjoying agricultural abundance, Czechoslovakia is almost self-sustaining in food. Her crop-yields surpass the European average and are far higher than those of her neighbors, excepting Germany; yields of about $630 annually per man employed exceed the average for most of France. Production of potatoes, the chief crop, reached the striking figure of 7,500,000 tons, while the other leading crops — wheat, rye, barley, and oats — were extensive. Czechoslovakia ranks with the world's leading producers of sugar beets.

Even more impressive evidences of wealth are the figures for animal husbandry: 32,000,000 fowl, 7,000,000 geese, 2,000,000 ducks, and some 4,300,000 head of cattle and 2,800,000 pigs (source of the famous Prague hams).

Fruit production is also remarkable in this land of the cherry, peach, and plum, from which fine brandies are made. In her rich orchards grow the best apples and pears in central Europe. A large hops producer, she has been acclaimed for her Pilsner and Budweiser beers.

Of Czechoslovakia's territory, 42% is arable land, 33% forest, and 17% pasture and meadow land. Agriculture and forestry together employ about 40% of the people.

Industry. At the same time Czechoslovakia is one of the most highly industrialized countries for her area. Under a well-balanced economy, resembling that of France, about 37% of the working population were engaged in varied industries, ranging from superb Bohemian glass to highly developed coal-mining.

Annual production figures reveal large-scale activity: coal, 13,000,000 tons; brown coal, 16,000,000; iron and steel, 3,000,000. Industrial establishments included 1,700 textile mills, 2,100 glass works, 1,800 metal and machine shops, 600 chemical industries, 925 distilleries, 1,700 food-processing plants, 400 breweries, and 120 beet-sugar mills. World-famous are the Skoda armament works at Pilsen and the Vitkovice works.

Americans are well acquainted with Czech specialties, for the Woolworth type of store was largely stocked, before the war, with hundreds of their miscellaneous products, such as embroidered tablecloths, porcelains, toys, and musical instruments. Most of these industries require painstaking, chiefly semi-skilled, hand-labor. Unfortunately, many of the workers engaged were paid low wages, so that the products could be sold cheaply enough to overcome tariff barriers in other lands.

The Czechoslovaks know American tastes and the exigencies of the American market. Hundreds of thousands of them have come to the U.S.A., and Chicago boasts a sizable community of Czechoslovak origin. Returning immigrants seek to imitate this country, strengthening a bond that has existed since the creation of the republic.

National Wealth, Income, and Finance. Not rich by western European or American standards, Czechoslovakia easily led the countries of central and southeastern Europe. Her annual production per person ($725) far surpassed that of Austria, Hungary, Italy, Rumania, or Yugoslavia. She therefore occupies an intermediate position between the wealthy west and the backward southeast of Europe, though inclining to the former. Naturally, her over-all average is pulled down by the poorer, undeveloped areas of Slovakia and Ruthenia; Bohemia by itself is richer than most of Germany, having been one of the industrial centers of the old Austro-Hungarian empire. Yet income per person ($109) as against production per person ($725) dramatically suggests that low industrial wages and short earnings of the peasantry restricted internal consumption.

Obviously, it is difficult to assess the currency, debt,

tax, or savings situation in a land so tragically dismembered. But some facts are discernible, despite German plunder, terror, and "absorption." Money in circulation has more than doubled the 1938 (pre-Munich) figure, from $200,000,000 to $450,000,000. Despite the increased issue of paper money, commercial bank deposits and savings accounts have shrunk, indicating sizable hoarding of money through fear of German confiscation.

Peacetime budgets were around 10,000,000,000 crowns — approximately $230,000,000 — for central government expenditures. While the "protectors" of Bohemia and Moravia have not thought it expedient to publish figures of the current budget or rate of taxation, it is a plausible inference that the Nazi burden has been staggering. In Slovakia, one of the less developed parts of pre-Munich Czechoslovakia, the budget more than trebled under the Germans. In the rest of the country the situation is undoubtedly at least as bad and probably worse.

Foreign Trade. So highly industrialized a nation, with a population of only 15,500,000, requires foreign markets, and Czechoslovakia engaged extensively in foreign trade. Her exports and imports often balanced, but there were wide fluctuations from year to year. Assuming the value of the Czech crown (her national currency) to be 2.5 cents, exports averaged around $200,000,000 annually, imports $190,-000,000. Chief exports were iron and steel, cotton and woolen textiles, glass, leather, coal, and flour; chief imports: raw cotton, wool, machinery, chemicals, fats and oils, and fruits and vegetables.

Except for the cheap specialties exported to America, 90% of the business was with Europe, the leading customers being Germany, Austria, and Britain. Main supplier was Germany, followed by France, who accounted for only a third as much. Factors of geographic proximity explain Germany's prominent rôle in Czechoslovakia's foreign trade. The relative importance of Austria stems from the historical fact that the country's canals and railway systems were once an intimate part of the old Austrian empire. Czechoslovakian shipments by water went largely by way of Trieste, when that Adriatic port was Austrian, and later by way of the German ports. The Danube, Elbe, and Oder rivers were the leading transit routes to Germany, the latter two internationalized until 1935.

History: 1914-1944

The whole of Czechoslovakia belonged to the pre-1914 Austro-Hungarian Empire. The Czechs, subject to Germanic domination for centuries, had nearly lost their nationality and language. But national sentiment began to revive about a century ago, stimulated by the efforts of the Czech historian Palacky; and by the end of the 19th century Czech nationalism was extremely articulate and insistent. The Czechs gained steadily in education and government, but the all-powerful Sudeten Germans who owned the land and factories disdained them, considering them a race of servants, artisans, and peasants. Czech resentment of this treatment found a brilliant advocate in the university professor, Thomas G. Masaryk.

During World War I, both Masaryk and Eduard Beneš struggled abroad for recognition of Czech independence. The Allied leaders — one of whom, Woodrow Wilson, was a friend of Masaryk — grew increasingly aware of the justice of Czech demands. Accordingly, on June 29, 1918 the Pichon memorandum of the French Republic recognized the Czechoslovak committee, then resident in Paris, as a provisional government. After the Armistice of November 11, 1918, the Czech nation was formed at Prague. By Christmas of that year, it had incorporated the historic frontiers of Bohemia, including German-speaking districts.

The Republic soon absorbed the Slovak country to the south, formerly under Hungarian rule, but included a large, compact Magyar population, since otherwise land communications would have been rendered impossible. The Czechoslovaks then included the Ruthenians, a Ukrainian people who had suffered cruelty and neglect at the hands of their Hungarian overlords. Though the Ruthenians remained relatively backward under the Republic, their lot was far better than under the Hungarians.

The Formative Years: 1919-1921. Three centuries of domination had not given the former Germanic masters any appetite for submission to their ex-servants. Germanic demonstrations against the new government began and the Czechs, enjoying the first psychological release in generations, multiplied controls over the Germanic minority. And in one instance they used force, with resultant fatalities.

The boundaries of Bohemia formed a natural economic unit, but certain areas, like the Egerland jutting into Bavaria and a few other points, were completely and fanatically Germanic. Their inclusion in the republic proved most difficult, and many Czech patriots, foreseeing their explosive possibilities, did not approve their incorporation (1919), which had been undertaken largely for strategic reasons and in large degree upon the recommendation of French military technicians.

The principal change, however, was not so much in culture as in economics. The Land Law of April 10, 1919, marked the first step toward redistributing large holdings to the peasantry; while the Capital Levy Act of March 1920 fell most heavily on the wealthier people, mostly Sudeten Germans. These rich Sudeten Germans used every device to defame the Czechs and besmirch them in the eyes of the world. At the same time they sought to play upon and excite the racial prejudices of the poorer Sudeten Germans, whom they had oppressed equally with the Czechs.

The Treaty of St. Germain (1920) made Czechoslovakia assume the largest share of the debts of the defunct Austrian Empire. The Republic accepted this provision. On February 29, 1920 it adopted a constitution and language statutes. The constitution was liberal and democratic, providing for universal suffrage and proportional representation. The Sudeten Germans deeply resented the minorities statute, which allowed the official use of minority languages only where minorities formed a given percentage of the population.

On May 27, 1920, the Czechoslovak National Assembly met and elected Masaryk first President of the Republic. In the general elections, the Sudeten Germans polled almost 25% of the votes, thus indicating that no pressure was exerted against them. The census of 1921 showed that they were 23.3% of the total population of the country, but many of them, unable to tolerate their minority status, had emigrated. The Germanic minority cried out that the census had been falsified; but outside investigators found the highest possible margin of error was less than 1%.

The Boom: 1921–1923. The success of the Czechs in halting post-war inflation made their land the economic refuge of Central Europe. Capital fled Germany, Austria, and Hungary to seek a stable country. The export market soared. Bohemia had lost a share of her markets with the break-up of the pre-war free trade area of Austria-Hungary; but the 1920–23 boom concealed this threat from Czech eyes. In 1923, Germany's currency was stabilized, and the Czechoslovak boom collapsed. The Republic had to borrow abroad to stabilize its currency, receiving a $30,000,000 loan from London and New York at 8% interest.

Meanwhile, the land reform spread prosperity among the Czech farmers. Prior to 1914, 2% of the landlords had owned 25% of Bohemia and 1% had owned 33% of Moravia. More than half of all farm holdings had been a half acre or less in size. Now the Czechs supplemented the basic Land Law of 1919 with a series of land acts. One of the main provisions was that no estate could exceed 1,250 acres. By 1937 the government had redistributed fully 20,000 square miles, from rich Germanic landowners to poor Czech farmers. The forests, largely owned by the wealthy Sudeten Germans, were nationalized.

The Sudeten German landlords had employed numerous German-speaking personal dependents on their large estates; these now had to seek employment in the cities. Moreover, Czech immigrants returned from America with their savings and bought land from the impoverished Sudeten Germans. The dispossessed landowners set up a clamor, but despite their outcry, it appeared in practice that the great estates, though reduced, were not limited as drastically as the law provided. Prince Schwarzenberg, for example, retained an estate of 2,000 square miles, and the church lands remained for the most part nearly intact.

The Collapse: 1923–1925. Had these liberal land reforms merely transferred acreage from wealthy, feudal-minded Sudeten Germans and their flunkeys to hard-working Czech peasants, the hatred engendered by German propaganda might have fallen on deaf ears among the poor Germanic city-dwellers. But the collapse of the boom threw 450,000 workers out of work, mainly in the export industries in which Germanic labor predominated. Thus, most of the Sudeten German minority found a common cause against the Czechs and Slovaks.

In Slovakia, the treatment of the Magyar minority was not nearly as generous as the treatment of the Sudeten Germans by the Czechs in Bohemia. Conveniently forgetting that they had treated the Slovaks like animals for centuries, the Magyars made the most of their partially justified grievances.

In the midst of this unrest, the ultra-nationalist Czech Minister, Rašin, was assassinated. The government immediately passed a law for the "Defense of the Republic."

Recovery: 1925–1929. After 1925 world recovery set in. Conditions in Czechoslovakia speedily improved. As a result, the more sensible Sudeten Germans stopped perpetually complaining and collaborated with the Czechs in orderly economic programs. These Sudeten Germans came to be known as the "Activists." Significantly, their following grew as prosperity increased and shrank when a new economic depression appeared. Of the Germanic minority, however, only the German Socialist Party accepted the Czechoslovak Republic with permanent good grace. Several Sudeten German Activist ministers entered the government, and a period of social tranquillity seemed at hand. At the same time, however, certain Sudeten German sports and fraternal organizations continued a somewhat subdued opposition to the Republic.

Nearby Republican Germany was cooperative and, carrying out treaty stipulations, gave the Czechs an outlet to the sea by establishing free ports at Hamburg and Stettin and by internationalizing the Elbe and Oder rivers, permitting Czech boats and barges to ply freely with their cargoes. The German government disdained the nationalist agitation in Czechoslovakia considering that the Sudeten Germans had been a part of Austrian, but never of German, culture. By adopting the attitude that the Czechoslovak State was a permanent entity, the Germans made possible closer cooperation among the saner national elements within Czechoslovakia. Nevertheless, the Germans did resent the almost passionately pro-French attitude of the Czechs.

At any rate, by 1925 the Germanic minority had elected 24 Agrarian Party members to Parliament, 18 Socialists, and 12 Catholics — that is, 54 members favoring cooperation as against only 10 Nationalists and 6 outright Nazis.

The Economic Crisis of 1929–1933. The world crash again prostrated Czech economy. With the artificial stimulus of the recovery years removed, Czech industry, geared originally to the needs of the pre-1914 Austrian market, slumped noticeably. Importing nations, fearful of expending their final cash reserves, imposed high tariff barriers against Czech goods. The Japanese became dangerous competitors in all the low-priced miscellaneous articles for which Bohemia was famous. The factories, three-fourths owned by Sudeten Germans, were paralyzed. The crash of the Viennese banking system in 1931, with its serious repercussions on banks in Germany, carried some Czech banks down with it.

As a result, exports fell from $650,000,000 to under $160,000,000, far worse than the world average. More than that: the Germanic minority, not trusting Czech finance, had deposited their money in Germany and Austria and in German branch banks in Czechoslovakia. They lost almost all their deposits with the German banks. But the despised Czech banks, largely farmers' cooperatives and mutual savings institutions, had a more solid basis. Thus, the

Czech depositors, supposed to be "stupid" peasants, were solvent while the clever Sudeten Germans were ruined.

In 1933 Hitler came to power in Germany. His "success" in restoring employment by turning Germany into an armed camp contrasted with mass unemployment among the Sudeten Germans in Bohemia and Moravia. The Nazi leader lost no time in exploiting this situation.

The Nazi Agitation: 1933–1938. The Nazis' game in Czechoslovakia began more cleverly than elsewhere. They picked as "their" man an obscure gymnastics teacher from the Sudetenland, Konrad Henlein. At first, Henlein made a number of speeches emphasizing the need for cooperation with the Czechs provided certain conditions were carried out. Accepting Czech democracy as a basis and disavowing any idea of separatism, Henlein, in May 1935, obtained about 59% of all Germanic votes in Czechoslovakia for "cooperation." About 37% of the Sudeten Germans remained Activists, mainly Socialists, and 4% were Communists. The Czechs remained in the main faithful to the Agrarian and Socialist parties.

No sooner did Henlein receive a majority of the Sudeten votes than his tone changed. His followers fomented cultural struggles over schools, theaters, and opera performances. They charged the Czechs with discriminating against Sudeten Germans in the civil service.

For years many Sudeten Germans had accepted an "organic" or mystical view of society, as elaborated by a certain Professor Othmar Spann. Henlein took over this ideology, which asserted that all Germans were organic and possessed a "folk-soul" closely tied to the soil, whereas the Czechs were "rational" and therefore believed in the egoistic doctrine of democracy. Slowly the sports and nature-study organizations of the Germanic minority absorbed this Nazi ideology. The Czechs countered vigorously by further developing their own mass gymnastic organizations, the *Sokols*, which had begun decades before as a protest against the German *Turnvereins* (gymnastic societies).

The Sudeten Germans had a political object in their pratings about "organic" development. Henlein now announced that the Sudeten Germans in Czechoslovakia could not be treated as individuals, but as a group with their own "soul"; and that they must form a community within the state, to which every German must belong by blood and obey by blood, since "the individual does not exist in the German race-soul." In practice this meant handing over more than 40% of the Germanic minority who were anti-Nazi to the tender mercies of Henlein, without any protection in Czech law or the Czech courts. The game was, by this time, transparent.

Henlein now depended on the Nazi Party in Germany for funds. The recovery of 1936–37 having improved conditions among the Germanic minority in Czechoslovakia, Henlein's followers now feared that "activism" would again gain in strength. Hence he had to double his stakes. He demanded first that all Sudeten Germans within Czechoslovakia be aligned with German culture in Germany; second, that the Czechs compensate the Sudeten Germans in full for all the wrongs done them since 1918 (in short, restoration of the great estates to the large Sudeten German landowners); and finally, that the "Czechs must not drive us to desperation."

By this time, Czechoslovakia seethed with fear and hate. The Germanic minority lived in a state of perpetual frenzy and imaginary injustices. They invented atrocities on all sides, while across the border Dr. Goebbels orated on behalf of the "tortured Germans" in Czechoslovakia. The Germans kidnaped and murdered political refugees near the Czech-German border. At that very moment the Germans took away all rights from the tiny Slavic minority of Wends, who lived in Prussia; but that proved only momentarily embarrassing to the Nazi cry for "racial justice."

In 1935 Dr. Eduard Beneš succeeded the aged Masaryk as President of Czechoslovakia. Like all other forward-looking Czechs, Beneš realized that whatever restrictions, however slight, had been imposed on the Sudeten Germans, they must now be modified. Fearing that absolute equality might prevail and cut the ground from under their feet, the Nazis concentrated their fire on Beneš, whom they depicted as a satanic monster.

With the occupation of Austria by the Nazis in March 1938, Czechoslovakia found herself surrounded. The provincial government in Slovakia did nothing to aid Beneš and remained as violently opposed to liberalism as to the claims of its Magyar minority. The new Prime Minister, Hodza, a conservative professor, was not equal to the increasingly emboldened Nazi *provocateurs*.

Henlein, now openly a German agent, demanded an end to the Czech-Soviet alliance, the bulwark of Czechoslovak security. He formulated a lengthy list of demands, which Hitler publicly endorsed. On May 21, 1938, prompt action by the British and French averted war by Hitler against the Czechs on the Sudeten question. Neville Chamberlain, British Prime Minister, then sent Lord Runciman to Czechoslovakia to study the question of the Germanic minority; but at the same time he told American newspapermen confidentially that the Czechoslovak State as then constituted could not endure.

The Death Throes of the Republic: 1938–1939. Lord Runciman, in Czechoslovakia, spent most of his week-ends with the Sudeten German nobility, even giving the Nazi salute in answer to the crowds which gathered under his window. A lifelong Liberal in Britain, he probably thought it mere courtesy: it was interpreted otherwise.

Meanwhile, Goering, uncertain of Allied reaction, asserted that Germany had no aggressive designs; while Baron von Neurath, German envoy to Prague, stated that his country was "loyal to Locarno," that is, to international cooperation and honor.

On July 23, 1938, Georges Bonnet, the French Foreign Minister, had told the Czechs that French support depended in turn on British support, despite unequivocal French treaty commitments to defend Czechoslovakia. On September 7, the *London Times* suddenly advocated the annexation of the German-speaking areas in Czechoslovakia to Nazi Germany without a plebiscite, without any guarantees for the non-Nazi Sudeten Germans, and with no provision to protect the Czechs. Thereupon Hitler shouted that "atrocities" against the "Germans" were becoming intolerable and hinted at invasion. Henlein fled to Germany, an open traitor.

The crisis came to a head. To cope with the military menace, the Czechoslovak government named General Sirovy Premier. Soviet Russia, seeking to intervene, requested Rumanian cooperation to permit her troops to come to the aid of Czechoslovakia. France and Britain deliberately declined to act in concert with Russia, despite the French treaty of guarantee to Czechoslovakia and the Franco-Soviet pact.

British Prime Minister Chamberlain then humbled himself to make a series of "peace" pilgrimages to Hitler; but actually he capitulated outright to a series of Nazi ultimatums. Finally on September 30 the four powers, Germany, Italy, Great Britain, and France, met at Munich. Soviet Russia had been eliminated on German orders; while the victim, Czechoslovakia, was not even given a chance to plead the cause of her national existence. The four conferees at Munich agreed to hand over to Hitler at once the predominantly Sudeten German areas in Czechoslovakia, with additional areas to be defined by an international four-power commission. The ceded regions were such as to destroy the economic viability of the Czechoslovak Republic; moreover Hitler was now given all the Czech border fortifications. Thus Hitler became invincible — in the words of Bismarck: "Whoever holds Bohemia is the master of Europe." Britain and France declared that their complete surrender was justified because it guaranteed "peace in our time."

Within a week, German terror spread over Czechoslovakia. The liberal government of Beneš was ended and Hacha, a faint-hearted, reactionary jurist, became Premier. The Czech government began to ape Nazi racist and political ideas. And Germany treated with contempt the international commission appointed to define border areas.

Death and Resurrection: 1939–1944. In March 1939 Germany instigated an uprising of clerical Fascists in backward Slovakia. Stating that the Czech government could not deal with this "intolerable" situation, Hitler summoned Hacha. The Nazi army then invaded Prague and Germany took over the entire Czech area. The Nazis declared Czech territory a "protectorate" and Slovakia an "independent" state under German "tutelage." They then handed most of the Ruthenians over to the Hungarians.

Immediately the Nazis dropped all pretense of defending the Germanic minority. Flouting the slogan of "equal rights" for national minorities, the Germans declared the Czechs second-class citizens in their own country. The Slavs of Central Europe were again reduced to their inferior status of previous centuries. Henlein boasted that he had been shamming the whole time, that every move he had made had been part of an ordered and preconcerted plan. The Nazis roared cynically at the dupes who had accepted their pleas about the rights of minority peoples or the "injustices of Versailles."

Stunned at their betrayal by the Western powers, the Czechs felt that they could count on nobody and fell into abject despair. Collaborationists grew active, especially among the wealthier elements. But popular resistance was such that during World War II, the Nazis sent Heydrich, the most dreaded of the Gestapo terrorists, to discipline the people. When he was assassinated the Nazis answered with an act of unparalleled infamy: the utter annihilation of the small town that once was Lidiče.

A leading Nazi, Daluege, succeeded Heydrich as "Protector." The basic social change under the Nazis was the restoration of the landed estates to the nobility. Meanwhile Dr. Beneš set up a Czech government-in-exile in London. He obtained active support everywhere in the camp of the United Nations and concluded a permanent military and civil alliance with the Soviet Union. Thus the stage was set for the national resurrection of democratic Czechoslovakia.

Foreign Affiliations. Czechoslovakia's past is no longer material. Czech leaders have stated that a progressive Slavic Bloc, including the Soviet Union and Poland, is their country's first need for complete security. There is little doubt that Czechoslovakia will cooperate with special enthusiasm in a democratic world organization. Her past record showed her to be one of the most loyal and progressive members of the League of Nations.

Stakes in the Peace

Czechoslovakia's stake in the peace is, first, national integrity; second, the development of democratic "activism" among the Sudeten Germans with wide cultural autonomy, once they prove worthy of it; third, a rise in the material and cultural level of the Slovaks; and fourth, developing the Ruthenians as an intermediate "bridge" population serving as a cultural link with the Ukrainians in the Soviet Union.

Her principal economic needs are: free ports, a wide area of free trade in Europe for her remarkably varied and efficient industry, completion of the land reforms, an end to German supremacy in industrial production, and an integrated development of Czech economy with that of the old Austrian Empire, primarily those sections lying in the Danubian Basin.

DENMARK

The Land and the People

A tiny domestic kingdom today, Denmark once boasted a mighty empire, one of the great realms of Europe. Under famed King Canute she reduced England to a tributary in the 10th century, and up to 1814 her large empire included Norway as well as Iceland and Greenland. Birthplace of royalty, she gave a czarina to Russia, a queen to England. Renowned families of the German nobility — like the Moltkes, Bernstorffs, and Reventlows — stem from her southern provinces.

Yet modern Denmark is anything but haughty or aggressive. Unlike her German neighbor to the south, she is noted for a genuine devotion to democracy, religious tolerance, and peace. When the Nazis tramped into Denmark, they violated a vanguard nation of European culture. And the Danes gave their conquerors no rest.

The Land. Southernmost of the Scandinavian commonwealths, Denmark may be divided into the mainland — a tongue of land on the Jutland peninsula — and several fairly large islands to the east. Her single land frontier lies along the German province of Schleswig-Holstein (south). The Skagerrak and Kattegat waterways (north) separate the country from Norway and Sweden. The most important city, Copenhagen, commands the entrance to the Baltic Sea through a small strait (called the Sound), a strategic position that once earned Copenhagen the title of "Gibraltar of the North."

Denmark occupies 16,575 square miles, an area as large as Massachusetts, Connecticut, and Rhode Island combined. Of this territory, the mainland represents about 70%, the contiguous islands only 30%, but more than half the people live on the islands. The total population is 3,900,000. Over half live in the rural districts, a fourth in the metropolitan area of Copenhagen, which is overwhelmingly the cultural, political, and economic center of the nation.

One of Denmark's overseas possessions, Greenland, is of real importance for American hemisphere defense and was actively used by the U.S.A. for that purpose during World War II. The world's largest island, arctic Greenland has an ice-free area of 31,000 square miles and a population of 17,000. Denmark also owns the Faeroe Islands, north of Scotland. Until recently the King of Denmark was the titular monarch of Iceland, but even this nominal connection ceased in June 1944, when the Icelanders voted overwhelmingly in a plebiscite for an independent republic.

Denmark proper is almost entirely flat; the few hillocks rise to a maximum of 350 feet. Formed geologically by the Ice Age, this is the moraine country familiar to New Englanders. There are heaths and moors to the west and the west coast is lined with dunes, through which the sea has broken in some places, as in the Netherlands. Danish ingenuity has overcome the handicap of sandy soils.

Denmark has practically no mineral resources, with the exception of some brown coal in the south, and kaolin (used in porcelain work) from the island of Bornholm in the Baltic.

The People. Among the most highly civilized people in the modern world, the Danes have developed noteworthy techniques of economic cooperation, agriculture, and democratic procedure. Their ultra-modern cities surpass a good many American communities in the use of central heating, telephones, refrigerators, and household "gadgets." Their well-ordered civic sense is reflected in the low rate of crime and vagrancy. Excellent gardeners, the Danes take just pride in the beauty of their farms, villages, and cities.

They are a prosperous people who have proved their ability to overcome adverse circumstances. In the middle of the 19th century, when they had lost Norway and Schleswig-Holstein and their farmers were ruined by the competition of cheap grain production in America, the Danes were desperately poor and subject to recurrent crises. Their skill and resolution in coping with this situation form an object-lesson in human adaptation.

Since 99% of the people are of the same stock, unchanged for centuries, they may be called a "pure" northern people, tall, blond, long-headed. By contrast, the German "Aryans" look Alpine, but the Danes have no theories of racial superiority, having long ago adopted the best features of liberal thought.

Unlike other Scandinavian peoples, they are gay and talkative. Danish fondness for night life won for Copenhagen the reputation of "the Paris of the North." In their Tivoli Gardens the Danes invented the modern public amusement park that was to find its most famous American expression in New York's Coney Island.

The birthrate has averaged about 18; the deathrate of 10, and sometimes even less, is the best average showing in Europe (only Australia and New Zealand show comparable figures). Infant mortality averages around 55 per thousand. A steady gain in population is forecast for the next generation. To the U.S.A.'s varied racial stock, the Danes have contributed over 600,000.

Religion and Education. Since 1536 the established religion has been the Lutheran, with over 98% of the people professing that faith, but the Danes do not discriminate against religious minorities.

Among the extraordinary features of the national tradition is an avid interest in learning. Education has been compulsory since 1814. Literacy is very nearly universal. Danes read 9 times as many books per person as the Americans, 4 times as many as the British.

Denmark has two universities. Some 76,000 young people, or about a fourth of the population from 14–18, attend government high schools. Moreover, 300 technical schools and 100 commercial schools meet special needs of the 16–20 age group. When one adds 20 agricultural schools, 20 teachers' colleges, and a flourishing system of night high schools for adult education, it becomes evident that most Danes enjoy a good secondary education.

The Nation's Economy

Agriculture. Along with the Dutch and Belgians, the Danes are the top-flight farmers of the world. Consider, for example, the yields of the 8 most common heavy crops — hay, wheat, barley, rye, oats, sugar-beets, potatoes, and corn. These show relative yields of 168, as against 170 for the Netherlands and 178 for Belgium, an index 30% higher than in neighboring Sweden and Germany. If animal husbandry and dairy production are included, the Danes share (with the Belgians) first place in the world in cash production per man employed ($1,050). The corresponding average in the U.S.A., during normal good years, is $800.

Some 35% of the working population engage in agriculture, but by European standards the concentration of farmers per square mile is not dense. With 62% of the land arable, only 350 persons occupy each square mile of arable soil. Since yields per acre have doubled in the last 50 years, the population has not outpaced crops.

Danish law prohibits the land from being combined into large estates. The decided subdivision that results might well have proved excessive had each farmer been forced to supply his own capital, market his own goods, and in general meet his problems individually. But the cooperatives have been admirably developed to surmount these potential difficulties.

The cooperatives pool capital; buy machinery and fertilizer; store, market, and finance products until crop payments are made. Cooperatives handle over 90% of dairying, the country's mainstay; they market over 75% of Denmark's bacon, the second item of importance, proverbially "the Englishman's breakfast."

Danish butter production used to be Europe's highest — 190,000 tons — but it fell to 126,000 tons under the Germans. Similarly, under German occupation Denmark's high figure of well over 3,000,000 cattle and pigs and 34,000,000 chickens was slashed by an estimated one-fourth. Other indexes of Denmark's high level of production under her system of cooperatives were cheese (33,000 tons) and milk (55,000,000 quarts, the highest per capita output in Europe).

Industry. For a small agricultural country, Denmark has a remarkably well-developed industry which employs a third of her working people. In horse-power used per man, Denmark ranks with Germany. In machinery investment per person she belongs among the 7 highest nations of Europe.

Breweries are very important: Denmark's beer commands a quality price for export and the Danes are second only to the Belgians as beer consumers. Distilleries are active: Danish cherry brandy and *akvavit* are world known. Processed products like beet-sugar and margarine, no less than bicycles and machines, form a basic part of the country's industrial

See also detailed map on page 133.

activity. Her Diesel engine shipyards compete with the finest in the world, while production of brown coal and peat was intensified under German occupation.

National Wealth and Income. Denmark's national wealth has been estimated at about $1,255 per capita, about the same as France's, but a fourth less than Great Britain's. National income, at $190 a head, approximates Sweden's.

The unit of currency is the *krone*, or crown, normally valued at about 19¢. Under the Germans, there was only a moderate inflation. Money in circulation advanced from 600,000,000 crowns to over a billion, but the cost of living increased by two-thirds. Denmark's wealth in real terms has deteriorated significantly, and savings deposits have advanced less than the cost of living.

In the four years of occupation the internal debt, previously valued at about $162,000,000, increased to only $215,000,000, but fresh borrowing was larger than appears on the surface because of the extensive repayment of older debts. Foreign debts fell from $130,000,000 to $113,000,000, but this figure is difficult to analyze because of Denmark's forced financial ties with Germany and her inability to borrow from the Allied countries.

Foreign Trade. Denmark resembles Belgium in that half of her economy is bound up with foreign trade. Butter, eggs, and bacon account for two-thirds of all exports; vehicles and machines are the most important industrial exports. Leading imports are metals, coal, and textiles.

In 1938 exports totaled $340,000,000, imports $355,000,000, making Denmark the most active foreign trader per population in Europe. The principal customers in pre-war years were Britain, who took over 60% of the exports, and Germany, who took 20%. Chief suppliers of imports were Britain (about 36%), Germany (27%), Norway and Sweden

(11%), and the U.S.A. (6%). As a result of forced trading with Germany, the 1941 figures showed a drop of $80,000,000 in exports and $100,000,000 in imports, clearly indicating the serious consequences of the loss of the British market.

History: 1914-1944

1914–1940. Until 1940 Denmark virtually vindicated the old saying that that country is happy which has no history. In 1914 she was a constitutional monarchy under Christian X, her present king. The Danish royal family was considered the marriage market of Europe's monarchs, and her older aristocracy retained undue power and prestige — a circumstance wholly at variance with the high education and democratic maturity of her people. During World War I, Denmark maintained strict neutrality, though her pro-Allied sympathies were undisguised. Her real history, however, was internal, from 1914 until the Nazis invaded her territory 26 years later.

In 1917 she sold the Virgin Islands to the U.S.A. for $25,000,000, having taken a national plebiscite on this action. In 1918 she acknowledged the independence of Iceland, though her king was to be king of Iceland as well. Women were granted suffrage; the older aristocracy was shorn of its remnant of privilege; administrative and judicial procedures were modernized. The 1918 elections swung to the Left. The Socialists now insisted that army and navy expenditures were useless since Denmark was defenseless in any case; they urged that the funds be increasingly diverted to social benefits. Primogeniture was abolished in 1919; lands of the nobility could be sold freely; and in return for this concession some of their land had to be ceded for use as small holdings.

In 1920 the Danish population of the old duchy of Schleswig was reunited to Denmark after a plebiscite. Since some German minorities were included, they elected one deputy out of 140. Conservative circles, desiring to annex even German Schleswig, almost provoked a revolution; but the result was a new electoral law that extended proportional representation to country districts, actually strengthening parliamentary government.

In 1924 the Socialists came into power. Their majority in the lower house was opposed by the Conservative upper house: Socialist reforms were blunted. When the *krone* was stabilized at its old high level, falling prices injured trade and unemployment spread to 90,000. In 1926 a new government was elected. It undertook a complete deflation, reducing wages to the lower price level, and a new crisis ensued. When in 1931 Denmark followed Britain in abandoning the gold standard, Danish prosperity returned and eventually the urban unemployed found jobs.

Denmark had subscribed (1930) to the Oslo convention of the three Scandinavian commonwealths with the Netherlands, Belgium, and Luxembourg, which agreed on neutrality and common action. In 1934 she signed a nonaggression pact with Germany. Though the Socialists were in power in 1935 and 1936, their policy was cautious; and the following year Denmark, along with the other signatories to the Oslo convention, opposed using sanctions to enforce her neutral position.

1940–1944. The Nazis invaded Denmark (April 1940), taking over the country without real resistance. Ostensibly they permitted parliamentary government to function, although Communists were illegalized and Nazi racial laws invoked. The Danes resisted these barbarous decrees and helped over a thousand Jewish unfortunates to escape to Sweden. The king openly assailed the Nazi proclamation.

In March 1943 the Germans permitted an election, but the democratic parties, the great majority, could neither campaign nor print literature. Nevertheless the Socialist vote gained by 22%, the Liberals 24%, the Radicals 9% — and the Conservatives gained 29%, though the Nazis polled 3,000 less than in 1939. As a result of strikes and sabotage effected by the underground, the Nazis abolished Denmark's parliamentary government (August 1943). The Gestapo took over the country.

Meanwhile Britain stationed troops on Denmark's Faeroe Islands (north of Scotland) and the U.S.A. stationed forces on Greenland, both as wartime measures. In the summer of 1944, Iceland declared herself an independent republic, severing connections with the Danish royal family.

Foreign Affiliations. While she has been in the commercial orbit of Britain, Denmark's political affiliations have been with Norway, Sweden, and Finland and, to a lesser degree, with the Netherlands and Belgium. Thus, she has no political affiliations with any great power. Her royal family and her nobility have been related to German aristocrats and to the British court; but these affiliations must be regarded as minor.

Stakes in the Peace

World War II has demonstrated that Denmark can exist as a nation only if civilized rules prevail in international relations. Geographically she is indeed defenseless, and nothing short of utter German disarmament or the installation of democratic German régimes can assure her territorial safety.

Denmark's economic life has rested upon British fortune; the prosperity of Britain has been the cause of Denmark's prosperity. Overwhelmingly an exporter of dairy products, the country may find additional important markets if her other European neighbors arrive at new levels of prosperity. This diffusion of Denmark's exports thus presupposes a peaceful and thriving post-war Europe. In sum the country can be said to be without any creative future unless the coming peace assures a civilized and prosperous world.

FINLAND

The Land and the People

Named Finland by the Swedes, the country is known to the Finns as *Suomi*, "Land of Lakes." Her great forested areas are literally studded with thousands of bodies of water and the land is famous for great natural beauty. In the days when Finland belonged to the Czars, the country served the wealthy Russians as a summer vacationland.

Sharing frontiers with Sweden, Norway, and the U.S.S.R., the Finnish republic is one of the most northerly countries in the world. In winter her Arctic areas are darkened by almost perpetual night, and the winters are long and bitterly cold. Even at her southern extreme, in the sheltered regions on the Gulf of Finland, the months of cold are severe. Here the winter nights are extremely long — and the summer almost permanent day.

Today the Finnish-Soviet border extends some 900 miles, from the Gulf of Finland to the Arctic Ocean. To the northwest lies Norway, and to the west a sparsely settled area of Sweden. Finland's other borders are water: the Gulf of Finland separates her from Estonia, the Gulf of Bothnia from Sweden. Her only noncontiguous areas are groups of islands in the Baltic Sea, the most important of which are the Alands.

Finland's land area is large — 134,557 square miles, almost the size of Montana. But her population is about half that of New York City — under 3,700,000.

More than three-fourths of Finland is forested, and a good portion of this area is exploited as a gigantic commercial enterprise by both government and private interests. Her cities are small, the chief ones lying to the south, where the climate is relatively less harsh.

The People. The Finns are supposedly of Mongolian origin, though this widely accepted idea is probably true only insofar as a people once speaking a Mongolian language erupted into northern Europe and left its impress on the peoples conquered there. At any rate, the Finns speak a language that some scholars relate to the tongues of distant Turkestan in Asia. In physical appearance they are extremely fair, blond though roundheaded, fairly short, and blue-eyed, which indicates strong environmental influences and admixtures with neighboring peoples. In western Finland, however, most of the people are Swedes and they constitute a ninth of the total Finnish population. Once the dominant class, when the country was under Swedish rule, the Swedes still hold a high proportion of posts in the army and government service. In northern Finland, there are some Lapps, who are moving away from their primitive folkways under the impact of modern life.

The Finnish birthrate, though lower than it was a generation ago, is still higher than that in the Scandinavian countries, averaging about 20.5 per thousand. The normal deathrate is about 13.8. But in

See also detailed map on page 133.

one respect the country's population pattern is astonishing: wars reverse the trends completely, and are immediately reflected in a sharp decline in births and a sharp increase in deaths. Infant mortality (usually 66 per thousand) also rises rapidly in war. A population decline of about 5% within a generation was forecast, but this has undoubtedly been aggravated by the effects of two wars in rapid succession.

Many Finns have emigrated, mainly to Canada and the U.S.A., where they usually live in the lumbering sections and colder regions. Wars, emigration, and the difficulties of making a living have all slowed down the increase in population, which has risen no more than 5% since 1925. Yet the Finns are physically a tough, hardy people, accustomed to outdoor life and prominent in athletics.

Religion and Education. The Finns are Protestants of the Evangelical Lutheran faith, the national religion. Other faiths are tolerated. The only important religious minority adheres to the Greek Orthodox Church, about 2% of the people.

Illiteracy is practically nonexistent in this country of universal education. The number of high schools is large for the population, and there are 3 universities and several technical institutes of college level. For a country so poorly endowed with material goods, Finland has both a high quality of and a zealous regard for, education.

Newspapers, magazines, and books are widely read; and the Finnish people have two literatures, one in Finnish, the other in Swedish. Several Finns have distinguished themselves in modern architecture, while in music the country has been made world-famous by Jan Sibelius, whose symphonies are her national expression.

The Nation's Economy

Agriculture. With only a tenth of the land in use either as crop or pastureland and with a growing season reduced because of climate, Finland's agriculture obviously faces serious difficulties. And yet it engages about 65% of the people. The principal crops are rye, oats, potatoes, barley, and hay. Wheat is hardly known, the Finns being large consumers of rye bread. Butter production is fair, but a third less per person than in Sweden, where grazing conditions are more favorable. The yield of the eight leading crops per acre, though a fourth less than in Sweden, is larger than in neighboring Baltic countries to the south. Since there are only 320 people to a square mile of arable land, Finland is able to supply a large part of her own food requirements.

Landed property is very much "fragmented" or subdivided, the small farm being well-nigh universal. Two-thirds of all farms are less than 25 acres, and in all there are no more than 850 farms larger than 250 acres. Thus most farms operate on a family-subsistence basis. The people make up for the lack of capital and large-scale agriculture by an extensive use of cooperatives. In this respect, they rival the Danes: 85% of all Finnish dairy products are handled by these cooperative societies.

Annual agricultural production per worker is one of the poorest in all Europe — about $225 on a cash basis. Finland is thus only half as productive as Estonia, Latvia, or Sweden.

Industry. Wood, whether expressed in timber, sawed wood, pulp, or paper, is the great industry of Finland and here she ranks with the leading countries of the world. All industry engages about a seventh of the working population, of which the wood and paper industries employ about half. The remainder is absorbed in textiles and iron works and a small but growing chemical industry. Finland's production of wood-pulp per worker is the largest on earth, though normal production has decreased by two-thirds since 1939.

National Wealth and Income. The Finns are poor, the national income per citizen is estimated at $75. Although higher than in some Balkan countries and Poland, this figure contrasts with $195 in neighboring Sweden. Though statistics for national wealth are not available, Finland's savings figures are indicative. The year 1938 showed some $200,000,000 including accounts in cooperatives (less than $55 per person) and commercial bank deposits were about the same. These amounts become meaningful when we observe that in the same items Sweden's showing is three times as large. Though Finland is sometimes classed as the fourth Scandinavian country, her national economy has retained many features of the backward Russian development of Czarist days.

Foreign Trade. On the other hand, her foreign trade is brisk. About 46% of all Finnish national income derives from exports; imports or payments made abroad account for 47% of her national expenditure. In 1938 imports amounted to about $180,000,000 and exports nearly as much. This is a high figure, almost $100 per citizen, rivaling Germany's. Timber, paper, and chemical pulp constitute five-sixths of her exports, dairy products and minerals the remainder.

Britain, the principal customer, normally takes about 50% of these products, the U.S.A. and Germany about 10% each. Britain supplies about a fourth of Finland's imports, Germany a fifth. The Scandinavian countries together supply her with another fifth but buy only a tenth of her exports since most of their products are similar. Finland purchases chiefly metals and metal goods, machinery, and cereals. Trade with her next-door neighbor, Soviet Russia, has been negligible.

The war markedly affected Finnish economy. The British market was lost and Finnish exports sank to a mere third of pre-1939 figures. Imports from Nazi Germany, however, increased enormously. During World War II the cost of living doubled; the domestic debt increased tenfold (from $57,000,000 to $625,000,000), and the foreign debt fivefold (from $18,000,000 to $93,000,000). The national debt is now four times greater than the annual national income, a figure that is high even under adverse wartime conditions. Finland's impoverishment is striking.

History: 1914-1944

Finland prospered during World War I. Though ruled since 1809 as a Grand Duchy under the Czar she was not required to contribute men to the Russian armies. Instead, she sold Russia all that she could absorb, and the Helsinki stock exchange boomed. With the fall of Czarism (March 1917), the golden profits suddenly stopped. Orders were canceled, factories closed, and unemployment spread over the land.

White and Red Guards: 1917-1918. Masses of Russian workers, who had migrated to Finland during her war boom, struck fear in the wealthy Finnish classes who dreaded the possibility of a social revolution. Almost immediately after the end of the boom, they organized White Guards to protect their property. Finland had some social revolutionaries of her own, and when the White Guards were formed, the trade unions replied with an organization of their own, the Red Guards.

The elections indicated a gain by the Conservatives. Owing to the fear of revolution, the Socialist membership of the Finnish Diet (Parliament) declined from 102 to 92 (out of a total membership of 200). On November 15, a week after Lenin proclaimed the Bolshevik triumph, Finland severed relations with Russia. Lenin immediately recognized full Finnish independence on the ground that no country had the right to dominate another.

By this time Finnish unemployment was enormous and starvation was common. The working population and Red Guards seized power on January 28, 1918, adopting a constitution along western Socialist, rather than Bolshevik lines. Immediately General Mannerheim, a member of the Swedish aristocracy in Finland, organized the White Guard counter-revolution. Finnish "Hunter regiments" arrived from training in Imperial Germany, crushing the militarily inexperienced working groups at Tampere (Tammerfors). German armies arrived under the German General von der Goltz. Their victories enabled Mannerheim to enter Helsinki in triumph.

A rump parliament, convened by the conservative leader Svinhufvud, invited a German sovereign to take over the country. The Kaiser suggested Friedrich Karl of Hesse, who was chosen King (October 7, 1918), despite the certainty of Germany's defeat. The Kaiser's fall a month later interrupted the accession, which never took place.

White Guard Domination: 1918–1921. Meanwhile the Whites used the terrorist acts of the workers' armies (said to have killed 1,000 landowners) as justification for slaughtering 15,000 unarmed men, women, and children. The Whites also imprisoned 73,900 — equivalent for the U.S.A. of 3,000,000 political prisoners.

Mannerheim, opposing the pro-German Svinhufvud, advocated a big Finnish army. With the Kaiser's collapse, the German soldiers were sent home, and Mannerheim proceeded to woo the British. Forming a corps of 100,000 to maintain order, Mannerheim disenfranchised 40,000 Socialists and thus obtained an electoral majority. He calmly offered to join General Maynard (the British commander who was operating near Lake Onega as part of Britain's intervention in Russia) even though he had just been allied with the Germans against the British. General Maynard declined; Balfour, the British statesman, expressed his horror at the White atrocities in a speech in Parliament; and cooperation was thus rendered impossible.

But internally, the Conservatives apparently had crushed forever the landless peasants and newly industrialized workers. The Republic was initiated in June, 1919, and a month later a new constitution adopted. The anti-Socialist coalition held power until 1921 when an Agrarian and Progressive government replaced it.

Parliamentary Government: 1921–1923. By expelling the Communists from their ranks, the Socialists assumed their former parliamentary importance. The Communists promptly formed a Labor Party, winning 14% of all votes in 1922. Inevitably the common sense of the people returned: a general sentiment arose for democratizing farm holdings so that a secure social order could be built on the welfare of the masses of the people, instead of depending on the will of the determined, wealthy Swedish minority.

By a peace treaty with the Soviets (1920), Finland had obtained an outlet on the Arctic (Petsamo). Following her dispute with Sweden on the control of the Aland Islands, she was awarded them by a League of Nations decision (1921). Finland turned from violence. When the Karelians revolted against Russia, the Finns refused to aid them despite their Karelian affiliations; and when other Baltic states invited them to join in arrangements clearly aimed against Russia, the Finns declined.

Under their leader Kallio, the Agrarians formed a new government and passed the basic land law of Finland, the Lex Kallio, which enabled the poorer peasantry to acquire land. (By 1929, $5,000,000 had been loaned to the peasants; by 1934, 65,000 had acquired land and 53,000 more had become cottage and small allotment owners. One Finnish family in three now owned land, however small, and 2,000,000 acres were added to cultivation. The per-acre yield increased; cereal crops gained; and milk production augmented by 45% between 1920–1937.) Not only agrarian reform, but also the encouragement of the cooperative movement (by Agrarians and Socialists alike), became a dominant political tendency, despite a determined opposition.

Quasi-Authoritarian Government: 1923–1928. By a coup in 1923, the Communist party was dissolved, its 25 members of Parliament arrested, its press suspended. Finding itself without a complete Parliament, the Kallio ministry dissolved, and was succeeded by a government of bureaucrats, who in turn gave way to a Socialist ministry. Tanner, who had managed the cooperatives efficiently, became Prime Minister in 1925. A final amnesty bill for survivors of the Civil War passed in 1927. Thereafter Kallio (Agrarian), Cajander (Bureaucrat), Tanner (Socialist), and others alternated in power. In 1932, Prohibition, a fanatical belief of large numbers of Finns, was abolished. Alcoholism, which had once threatened the country, soon diminished.

World Crisis: 1928–1931. Graver questions than Prohibition agitated Finland. She suffered her economic shock in 1928, a year before the world crisis. The fall of receipts from wood exports brought an unfavorable trade balance of $50,000,000 ($16 per person). By 1930 trade declined even lower. The press attributed the loss to the "slave labor and dumping" of the Soviet competitor. The pastors repeated this theme in their sermons and Finland was in a ferment.

Lapua: 1931–1933. The Socialists were defeated, and a wave of terrorism, lynch law, and Fascist ideology swept Finland like her forest fires. The movement originated in Lapua, hence this name was given to the Fascists. Parliament voted 134–66 for penal laws against radical activities. Military leaders entered into liaison with Poland. General Wallenius, a Lapuan, led the terrorists; Stahlberg, a Progressive but not allied with the Socialists, was kidnaped. In the parliamentary balloting for the presidency Svinhufvud, the permanent pro-German leader, won over the "missing" Stahlberg, 151–149. Meanwhile Britain's suspension of the gold standard forced Finland to follow suit.

Recovery and New Problems: 1933–1939. Economic recovery came swiftly. A British building boom, unprecedented in European history, made Finland's timber a leading British import. The government wisely concentrated on stimulating wood products, so that when the timber boom ended it would have another string to its bow. Lapua

objected, and progressive forces reasserted themselves.

However, the gulf between rich and poor widened
during the recovery and real wages declined. The
workers gravitated back to Socialism, while the
Lapua movement remained fixed (7%), largely aided
by clerical oratory. Average weekly wages (about
$6) could not cope with rising costs. The workers
insisted on unemployment insurance available in
the Scandinavian lands. The trade union movement, split into two hostile sections, was impotent to
bring pressure (in many places it was terrorized by
Lapua). In this poverty the tuberculosis rate rose to
what may have been the highest in Europe.

In 1934 a nonaggression pact was made with the
U.S.S.R. Progressives assumed power and their
leader, Kallio, succeeded Svinhufvud as President
in 1937. In 1938 the government banned the
Fascist party, but the courts invalidated the decree.

The Finnish–Soviet War: 1939–1940. The outbreak of World War II led the Russians to demand a
retrocession of Finnish areas near Leningrad and the
port of Hangö, in the southwest tip of Finland. Recognizing the Soviet Union's need for security, Finland
at first was complaisant, but was adamant about
Hangö. The Soviet Union's offer of territorial,
population, and financial compensations was felt
to be irrelevant to the weakening of Finland's
position, even if these compensations were quantitatively considerable. Upon the rejection of her
demands, the U.S.S.R. invaded Finland (December
1939).

The Soviet Union justified her action by averring
that Finland's resistance was the signal to transform
the "phoney war" into an all-European anti-Soviet
alliance. She asserted that Finnish airdromes and
other equipment were excessive for Finnish finances.
Replying that these assertions were false, Finland
insisted that a small people was being sacrificed to
the necessities of a powerful state.

The Soviet government declared the Helsinki
Ministry to be nonexistent and made a treaty with a
"Finnish People's Republic" installed at Terijoki, a
frontier town. Finland appealed to the League of
Nations, which convened at once, condemning Soviet
Russia as an aggressor and expelling her.

A year earlier the Finns had rejected a guarantee of her integrity from Britain, France, and the
U.S.S.R. German promises undoubtedly inspired
this rejection, but Germany was not yet ready to
attack Russia. Britain and France, however, offered
Finland aid. Norway and Sweden refused to allow
their armies passage, but they aided Finland in legal
ways.

After the Russians had broken Finland's defenses
(the Mannerheim Line), General Mannerheim decided to cease fighting. The March 1940 peace gave
the Soviets the large eastern city of Viipuri (Viborg),
much territory in Karelia and about Lake Ladoga,
as well as Hangö. The terms were much harsher
than those originally offered by the Russians. Finland lost many of her hydroelectric installations and
part of her cellulose industry.

The Second Finnish–Soviet War: 1941–1944.
Finnish relations with Germany grew closer. In
June 1941, disregarding her new nonaggression pact
with the U.S.S.R., Finland joined in the Nazi assault
on the Soviet Union. Three years of war are understood to have undermined her economy.

Great Britain declared war on Finland on December
7, 1941, but the U.S.A. remained neutral. The
American decision was based on the close traditional
relations between the two countries and on the reasonable hope that by continuing official relations with
Finland, the U.S.A. could more effectively exercise
influence in terminating Finnish collaboration with
Germany. With the expulsion from America of the
Finnish Minister Procope (summer of 1944), the
situation became strained.

In September 1944, Finland withdrew from the
war. Under the peace terms offered by the Soviet
Union and Great Britain, Finland returned to her
1940 borders; she lost her Arctic port of Petsamo
(and its nickel mines); she regained Hangö, but
granted a 50 year lease of the peninsula of Porkkala
(near Helsinki); and she agreed to pay an indemnity
of $300,000,000 (payable over six years and in kind)
to the U.S.S.R.

Foreign Affiliations. The Finnish wealthy classes,
largely of Swedish origin, naturally are friendly to
Sweden but they dislike her liberalism. The outlook
of these groups is basically pro-German, and they
have shown unmistakable sympathy for the Nazi reaction. Progressive forces rely on Great Britain, of
whom Finland is almost an economic dependency.
There is a pro-Russian element, but it has been
small and feared, and did not cope with the
hatred of Soviet Russia spread wide among large
elements.

Finland has often shown a tendency to affiliate
with the Scandinavian bloc and the Baltic bloc, but
neither has materialized. The Finnish people incline to the Estonians who are of similar stock and of
related speech.

Stakes in the Peace

Finland's economy will be prostrate at the end of
the war, for her markets have been gone for years, and
nourishment and clothing are doubtless at their worst
levels. Relief is the first necessity for the Finns, whose
quasi-starvation has been vouched for by Scandinavian sources. After the wounds are healed, the
country must arrive at workable relations with the
U.S.S.R.; and the Soviets in turn must assist Finland
in improving her economic existence.

Finland still depends on the sterling *bloc* for her
economic life, because of her trade with Britain.
But the basis of her export — wood and lumber —
must be varied by the introduction of other industries. So long as she depends on her forests, Finland's economy will be basically contingent on
Britain's. Similarly, her agriculture must be improved, so that crop-yields can approximate Swedish
levels and thus assure a better food supply to the
people.

What kind of government will rule Finland? To

begin with, the power of the pro-German clique must be ended, and a government installed whose practical efforts will be directed toward a stable post-war Europe. Finland's experience in the cooperatives has been an invaluable democratic training. Among

peasant, worker, and merchant, progressive attitudes have exhibited marked virility. In a world organized for peace and prosperity, Finland can become a serene country, at last freed from her neurosis of insecurity.

FRANCE

The Land and the People

Ever since the tenth century, France has been one of the great nations of the world. For many centuries, she was indisputably the greatest nation of continental Europe, focus of the culture of the West. In the coming peace France will speak as the second largest country in Europe and the second largest empire in the world.

The Land. France in Europe, with her island of Corsica, has an area of about 212,600 square miles; if fitted into northeastern U.S.A., she would cover all New England, New York, New Jersey, Pennsylvania, Maryland, and part of Virginia. The French Empire outside Europe occupies 4,617,000 square miles. All told, a tenth of the world's surface is French. There were 42,000,000 people in France in 1939 and over 67,000,000 in her Empire — some 109,000,000 inhabitants in all.

A compact state in western Europe, France extends from 43° to 50° North Latitude; her breadth (from Strasbourg to Brest) is about 600 miles. Brest is at the tip of the Brittany peninsula, between the English Channel and the Bay of Biscay; this great Atlantic bay forms the western boundary. Southward, the boundary turns inland to follow the Pyrenees, which separate her from Spain. The 300 miles of Mediterranean coast on the south give France her "window on Africa." As the boundary turns inland again, for 200 miles France faces Italy to the southeast across the Alpine Divide. In the center east rises the mountainous boundary with Switzerland.

To the northeast France faces Germany across the Rhine — whenever France is in possession of the hotly disputed provinces of Alsace and Lorraine, most of which are in the Rhine valley. The boundary then turns west, skirting the hilly Saar country and the small state of Luxembourg, whose iron deposits continue those of French Lorraine. The boundary with Belgium on the northeast is at first hilly and forested (the Ardennes), but later it enters rolling country with coal seams, then crosses the flat Flemish plain to the North Sea. On the north, France faces Britain across the English Channel, which varies in width from 21 to 83 miles.

Thus everywhere France is protected by water barriers or by mountains with passes leading outward — everywhere except for the open frontier with western

Belgium, which has been the traditional invasion route to the heart of the country, the region of Paris.

Lying in the north temperate zone, France has the marine and Alpine climate of western Europe, except for her Mediterranean coastal strip. No comparable area has a year-round climate so mild and favorable to human activity. The plentiful and regular rainfall, the abundant sunshine, the fat loam covering the limestone in most of the country have made France a land where men have thrived since long before the Romans. If the population of modern France does not seem commensurate with her possibilities, it is not for lack of advantages of location, climate, and soil.

The country divides into well-defined areas, each with its own economic advantages. Brittany (northwest) with its rocky coasts and mournful interior, is peopled by fishermen. Central France is a series of plains, some (like the Beauce) as flat as Illinois, but most of them gently rolling, perfect for vineyards and intensive cultivation. Normandy, the most northern province, is a rich orchard and dairy country, noted for its apples, cider, cattle, butter, and fine cheeses. Picardy, in the northeast, is swampy but ideal for beet sugar and root crops.

The country rises into uplands as it approaches the old volcanic center of France, a land of extinct craters, called the Auvergne. Most of this soil is infertile, but the valleys are rich and long, and intersect the highlands so thoroughly that communication among them is easy. Moreover, the Auvergne is served by some of the best roads in Europe, built by Napoleon and pleasantly shaded by the trees he planted to conceal military movements. This volcanic region has many medicinal springs and watering places, the most celebrated of which is Vichy.

The Alpine country to the southeast, although cold in winter, is famous for its poultry. To the southwest, in the low coastal area of the Garonne river near Bordeaux, lies the pine-covered sandy plain of the Landes, a great sheep country, abounding in orchards and vineyards, which have made the region populous since long before the Christian era.

South of the dreary upland known as the Causse, through which flow canyon rivers like those in the American Rockies, lies the Mediterranean coastal region. This idyllic land, though hot and dry in summer, enjoys for the rest of the year a lingering spring. Its strawberries, melons, and flowers are the winter delight of northern Europe. It is the classic country of wines, perfumes, and intoxicating sunlight.

In short, there is no part of France, except the high Alps and small sections of the Cévennes Mountains, which does not invite human life and human enterprise. Small wonder that this beautiful land has tempted an age-long succession of invaders.

The People. The French are an ancient people: except for some Roman colonists and a constant trickle of immigrants who have been completely absorbed, they are racially the descendants of the Gallic people Caesar found in Gaul. The older view that their racial composition was altered by the Germanic invasions has been largely abandoned. France's extraordinary assimilative powers are cultural, not racial.

Although it is true that, after the First World War had left France biologically weakened, foreigners came to number about 7% of the population, most of these are either French-speaking Belgians, Catalonians speaking a language much like southern French, or North Italians easy to absorb culturally. Other foreign elements include an important Polish immigration to the mining districts of the north, and (in peacetime) many residents from Britain and the Americas who came to France out of personal preference rather than economic necessity.

Population Prospects. France's population is slowly but steadily declining. The low birthrate now characteristic of Western nations showed itself first in France, beginning about 1820, a generation after the French Revolution had shattered feudalism and given land to the peasantry. We may measure the effect of this trend by a series of percentages: in 1800 France had 16% of the population of Europe; in 1890, 10.7%; in 1930, 8.8%. The French birthrate is no longer so conspicuously low as it was, because other birthrates have fallen. But the process has been going on in France for a long time, and, taken in conjunction with her tremendous losses in World War I, not to mention the devastating effects of World War II, it has unquestionably weakened her as compared with her neighbors.

The French birthrate before the war was under 15 per thousand, it is now estimated to be 13; the deathrate has reached 18, for the first time surpassing the birthrate. Even before the war the deathrate was high, because the French population is older than most: in 1936, 15% were over 60 years old. When we consider that in the same year the corresponding percentages were: U.S.S.R. 6%, Germany 12.5%, and the U.S.A. 10.4%, it becomes clear that French longevity — however flattering to French living standards — holds no bright augury for the future. Infant mortality was not especially heavy, 63 per thousand, but during the war it has averaged 70. All this means that by 1970 the population of France will probably be only 37,000,000, as against 42,000,-000 in 1939.

The great strength of the French people is that, despite geographical diversity and a wide variety of human types — representing the three main European groups, Nordic, Alpine, and Mediterranean — they have perhaps the firmest and most enduring sense of national unity on the continent. This national unity has time and again overcome violent factionalism and crushing disaster. Writing of France in the 18th cen-

tury, Montesquieu pointed to "the supreme facility with which she always recovers from her losses, diseases, casualties, and the resilience with which she always withstands or even overcomes the vices of her various governments."

One element in this strong sense of nationality is the prestige enjoyed by the French language. For centuries French was not only the diplomatic language of Europe but the second language of every educated European. French is spoken in Haiti and the province of Quebec, throughout the French Empire, in southern Belgium, and in western Switzerland, and is widely used in the Near East in commerce and education. The Catalan of Spain and Ligurian of northwestern Italy are closely related to Provençal, the language of southern France. Before 1940, French books were an essential leaven in the culture of Latin America and many of the smaller European nations.

Religion and Education. In the 1906 census over 60% of the French described themselves as Roman Catholics, but since that time we have only estimates, based on baptisms, marriages, burials, confirmations, and, most important of all, the Easter confessional. And these estimates, because of the widely different views of the estimators as to who should be counted a Catholic and who not, vary from 16% to 62%. In most of France, at all events, Catholicism is the prevailing faith, though the degree of its influence varies from the intensely religious atmosphere of Brittany to the skepticism of Normandy. Parish churches attract only moderate congregations, mostly feminine. In recent years a militant anticlerical movement has spread throughout France. Many monastic orders, required to apply for special permits (which were often denied), preferred to go abroad.

Protestant congregations number about 1,000,000, concentrated in Alsace and in the extreme south, home of the Huguenots. French Jews, the first in Europe to be given complete equality (in 1791), have been so thoroughly assimilated that estimates of their number vary; the best guess is about 250,000, over nine-tenths in Paris and Alsace. Many temporarily emigrated during the Nazi-Vichy terror.

French education in peacetime is tuition-free, compulsory, and militantly secular. All schools are part of the University of France, and there are ministries of education and of the fine arts. The rule that every *département* (state) of France must have two normal schools is rarely waived. The Ecole Normale Supérieure, at the head of the system, has an almost unrivaled position in international education.

Lycée education (equivalent to our high schools and junior colleges) formerly required payment of partial tuition, but was recently made entirely free. The latest figures give 197 *lycées*, 324 communal colleges, and 30 special secondary schools for girls.

Some of the 17 French universities (whose normal enrollment is 83,000) have been famous for hundreds of years. The University of Paris has been the leading European university since the 11th century, when the "nations" gathered there to listen to Abelard, as later they listened to St. Thomas Aquinas. The medical school at Montpellier dates from the 12th century, and fully ten other French universities were founded during the Middle Ages or the Renaissance.

France has long been the center of multifarious in-

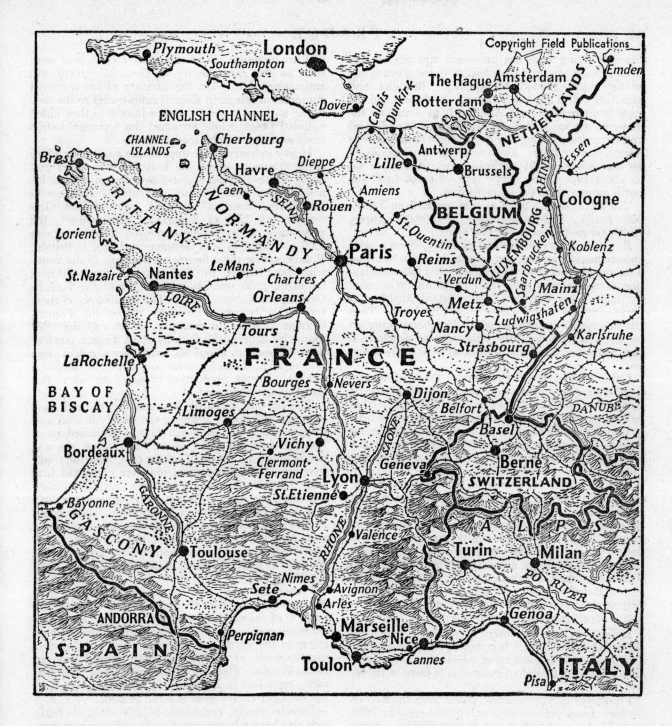

The map shows France and surrounding regions with many labeled cities.

tellectual activities in philosophy, science, and the arts. For eight hundred years Paris has had more book and art stores than any other city. Hundreds of advanced institutes specializing in arts, colonial lore, languages, archaeology, ethnology, sciences, medicine, mathematics, artillery, political science, as well as innumerable studio art schools have flourished in France. Several of these enjoy international eminence: the Ecole des Hautes Etudes (Higher Studies), the Institute of France, the Ecole des Chartes (Documentary Science), and the Ecole des Beaux-Arts, the world's leading art and architecture school.

It is of course impossible in our discussion to give even a hint of the complex and powerful impact of French art, literature, and general culture on the modern world.

The Nation's Economy

Agriculture. France is an intensively agricultural nation, with fully 46% of her land under crops, 30% grassland, meadow, and pasture, and 19% forest. Most of the pasture land is in rugged mountainous areas; the plains, even the area around Paris, are almost entirely under cultivation. Thus very little of the land is unused.

In good years she produces practically all the wheat, oats, rye, barley, and beet-sugar she needs. France is famous for many fruits, nuts, and vegetables, especially apricots, peaches, walnuts, cherries, and above all, Anjou and Commice pears. She has the largest and most lucrative wine production in the

41

world, varying from the unrivaled vintages of Bordeaux, Burgundy, and Champagne to the crude wines of the south around Montpellier. Brandies and sparkling ciders are also profitably produced, and the local beers brewed from Alsatian hops dominate the domestic market. From the south come fine olive oil and citrus fruits, though by no means so abundantly as from Spain or Italy. Flowers are grown extensively for themselves and for perfume. Indeed, France has in abundance nearly every type of crop, from the north temperate to the semi-tropical.

The farms have a large animal population: 3,000,-000 horses, 16,000,000 cattle, 10,000,000 sheep, 7,000,000 swine, and 1,300,000 goats.

But, for all its richness and diversity, French agriculture has its troubles, the greatest of which has been a manpower shortage. With the partial industrialization of the country after the First World War came a "flight from the land," rural youth drifting in great numbers to the cities, especially Paris. Thus the decline in population which had been going on in some regions for fifty years was so accelerated that some farming communities were actually dying out.

Other difficulties fed the trend. Production costs were high, many farms were too small to be worked profitably; tariffs and quotas were weak protection against the cheaper production of the great grain belts of Canada and Argentina. It was a costly and losing battle. Though on the eve of 1939 half the people were still living in the country, only 38% of them were in agriculture.

The French farmer is reputed to be the best in the world. No other, surely, is more devoted to the land, more zealous in cultivating it. And if the whole range of crops — from string beans to exotic fruit — is averaged in, the French yield is still the best per acre, per dollar, and per man. But in the large field crops, the French yield both per man and per acre is less than that of Germany, Denmark, the Netherlands, or Belgium. Based on small holdings and diversified crops, French agriculture meets with difficulty the competition of large, mechanized production.

Industry. French economy is based on a delicately maintained equilibrium between agriculture and industry, the relative weight of which, formerly about equal, has recently shifted somewhat in favor of industry.

France has sought industrial power since the days of Colbert, Louis XIV's minister, who as early as 1670 realized the potentialities of manufacturing. Until the rise of Germany after 1870, she was the second manufacturing country in Europe, though so far behind England as scarcely to be a competitor. Most French manufactures have been for the domestic market, only the luxury goods being destined for export.

But this luxury trade is financially so important that a mere statement of France's comparative lack of industrialization does not tell the whole story. Skilled labor rather than machinery goes into the making of the silk and brocade of Lyons, the tapestries of Aubusson, the laces of Calais, of such fine comestibles as *pâté de foie gras*, the sales of which (before the war) ran into millions, or of those modish *articles de Paris* — jewels, fans, smart clothes and hats, fine bookbindings,

and art furniture. Even the more mechanized work such as the manufacture of Grenoble gloves still emphasizes skill. Yet the pressure of international competition relegated these famous trades to the rear of the national economy except insofar as they aided national prestige and attracted the immense tourist trade and the wealthy foreign colony.

Heavy industry made appreciable gains after 1919, when France acquired the Lorraine iron mines and began to develop her water-power to compensate for a shortage of coal. French per capita investment in machinery, however, was still only 40% of Germany's and 27% of England's. Furthermore, the percentage of her people employed in industry was 33% as against 41% in Germany and 51% in Britain. If we examine these figures on the basis of the countries' populations, we find that the French-British industrial ratio was about 1 to 2, and the French-German ratio about 1 to 3. The significance of these ratios can be appreciated by taking the French-German ratio as an example. If we call the 1929 industrial figures 100, then by 1939, French production had sunk to about 80, while German had risen to over 130. French production, of course, sought a market, German production prepared for war. But the disparity increased.

The pre-war disparity between French and German heavy industry is shown specifically in iron and steel production. Although France produced more iron ore than any other country in Europe, she was handicapped by a lack of coking coal, with the result that her 11,000,000 tons of ore were converted into some 7,500,000 tons of pig iron annually. Germany, however, had only 3,000,000 tons of iron ore, but produced 18,000,000 tons of pig iron. Nor could France's 6,000,000-ton steel production, large as it was, compare with Germany's 18,000,000 tons. It was the same story in coal: annual French production 50,000,000 tons, German 186,000,000, British 236,-000,000.

France, however, was the leading European producer of bauxite (for aluminum) and (through her control of Algeria) of phosphates. She has large potash deposits in Alsace. Her textile industries, centering in the north, are important, and as a pre-war manufacturer of woolens she was second only to Great Britain. Her automobile production (200,000 cars), once first in Europe, had sunk to third place, but on a per capita basis was still second.

French fisheries, employing 145,000 men, are fairly well mechanized; the average annual catch is normally worth some $35,000,000. French shipping totaled 3,000,000 tons in 1940, but has been reduced by the war — the fate of the *Normandie*, queen of the merchant fleet, is only the best-known example. The intensive wartime shipbuilding programs of Britain and the U.S.A. have further worsened the competitive position of France.

French industry has been greatly strengthened by the work of many inventors, such as Claude's in air reduction, Houdry's in oil refining, de Lavaud's in iron pipes. French proficiency in glass manufacture has also been a sustaining factor.

National Wealth, Income, and Finance. Of the countries whose economy is not based on heavy industry, France is the richest in the world. Her pre-war national income, estimated at $1,250 per capita, was about five-sixths that of highly industrialized Britain and half that of the U.S.A. — or more, if we accept the argument of French economists that estimates of American wealth are exaggerated by capitalization of stocks and farmlands. In the accumulation of physical goods — furniture, carpets, porcelains, works of art, and the like — the French were the richest people in the world, but in automobiles, home conveniences, and quantity of clothing they could not rival the Americans. As a non-industrial nation, France had a less favorable record: her per capita income of $176 yearly, while fair, was far below Great Britain's $270, not to mention the U.S.A.'s $525.

In 1929, a sizable proportion of French capital (some 15%) was placed abroad. Fear of social disorders at home increased this percentage, and it may well exceed 20% today. In fact, after 1934 wealthy Frenchmen consistently preferred the pound and the dollar to the French franc. The large deposits outside France, coupled with the considerable invisible income from tourists, made for a useless accumulation of capital which, instead of enriching French industry and agriculture, assisted the industrial growth of foreign competitors. As much as 3% to 4% of the national pre-war revenue was net income from prior accumulation abroad.

This *rentier* tendency has existed for several decades. Prior to 1917 the figure for French funds abroad was much higher because the bulk of French investment was in Czarist Russia, especially in Russian bonds. Practically all of these enormous investments were lost, and France never recovered financially from the blow. Her money, which had been stable for a century, collapsed under the strain.

Before this débâcle, French finances were conservative and French money rates the most stable in existence. Decades would pass without alteration of more than ½% in the discount rate of the Bank of France, the central bank of the country. And this stability was accomplished without any resort to a deliberate cheapening of interest rates.

But the loss of the pre-1917 Russian investments, the staggering financial burden of the First World War, and the dependence in national financing on loans rather than direct taxation, had by 1928 brought the franc down from 19.3¢ to 3.9¢. This rate rose to 6.7¢ when the U.S.A. devalued the dollar in 1934, but in 1936 the financial crisis provoked by fear of the Popular Front government sent the franc down again. The present nominal rate of exchange is 2.0¢. But the German occupation has thrown French finances into confusion. Among the problems of reorganization, not the least will be the disposition of the francs issued by the invaders for use in "paying" for their plunder.

Foreign Trade. Pre-war France had a brisk foreign trade, which, characteristically, stood halfway between the enormous activity of such great traders as Britain and the Netherlands and the comparative inactivity of the agricultural nations. It was above the European average — $100 per person as against Britain's $200 and Germany's $98. France exported 24% of the national production (the corresponding figure for Britain is 25%). She imported

nearly 24% of home consumption (the corresponding figure for Britain is 32%). While Germany, preparing for war, consciously pursued a policy of self-sufficiency and resorted to barter schemes, France persisted in the classical methods of foreign trade. She was not as self-contained and self-sufficient as was commonly believed.

The leading French exports, in order of importance, are chemical products, raw wool, cotton textiles, iron and steel, fine wine, silk textiles, perfumes and soap, and jewelry. Her leading imports, in order, were coal and coke, raw cotton, cheaper wine, cereals, wool, oil seeds, and petroleum.

The French colonies, the U.S.A., Britain, Germany, and Belgium, in order of importance, supplied the imports; and the exports were purchased by the French colonies, Britain, Belgium, Switzerland, the U.S.A., and Germany, in the order named.

History: 1914-1944

1918–1919. A democratic republic since 1870, France emerged from World War I as its great victim and great victor. Of her total population of 12,000,000 males of military age, 1,500,000 had been killed and 3,000,000 seriously wounded. For years the streets of France were crowded with crippled veterans — men who limped, men with "reformed limbs," and men with *gueules cassées* (broken faces, *lit.* "smashed mugs"). The ten richest *départements* (states), with over 12% of the population, had been occupied by the Germans, and enslaved and depopulated.

With the lowest birthrate in Europe since 1840, France's future looked dark. Her acquisition of 1,800,000 people in Alsace-Lorraine did not compensate for her population losses. Not merely had a tenth of her national wealth vanished, but she had lost, by reason of the Russian Revolution, over $5,000,000,000 in investments abroad (which would be the same as America's suddenly losing $17,000,000,000). With her gaping cities, hundreds of miles of smoking and desolated villages, with populations ravaged by tuberculosis, France's single preoccupation was never to see an invader again. In the eyes of the French, the detached attitude of the Americans and British was the coolness of peoples who had not suffered — the objectivity that comes from safety.

French manpower had been reduced. The shortage was made up by drafting natives from the colonies into the armed forces; the shortage in field and factory labor, by the then welcome immigration of Belgians, Spaniards, Italians, and Poles along with some Arabs. Despite the common notion that this influx imperiled France, the fact is that three-fourths of the immigrants were either Catalonians (Spain), Piedmontese (Italy), or Walloons (Belgium), all of whom spoke dialects akin to French. France is the absorber of peoples: children of immigrants are rarely distinguishable from French of old stock.

The soil had been injured. To Americans and Britons this seemed a temporary misfortune, but to the French, with whom the soil is a passion and among whom even statesmen and society women are farmers part of the year, the injury was close to sacrilege. To men of the border regions, like Poincaré, it was a personal hurt. Indeed, the "liberated soil" from Germany was the heart of French policy. In this mood France shaped the Treaty of Versailles.

Not only had the Germans enslaved the people and looted machinery and even personal belongings: Germany had just imposed two crushing and predatory treaties — Brest-Litovsk, with Soviet Russia (March 1918), and Bucharest, with Rumania (March 1918) — Germany had not shown the slightest inclination to be generous to these defeated nations. The precedent for taking territory without consent and for imposing harsh indemnities had been set by Germany in her victory over France in 1871. In view of Germany's historic record, her pleas for mercy went by the board. Clemenceau, the grand old man of France, the "Tiger" and the artisan of victory, regarded the terms of the Versailles Treaty as mild (See *Germany, History*). France had been bled white and stripped of her equipment while every square mile of Germany had been spared and her equipment left intact. For Poincaré and Clemenceau, these facts were enough.

It was agreed that the Rhineland would be occupied for 15 years, that the rich Saar region would be under French mandate for 15 years, and that Alsace-Lorraine would be restored to France. At last the black veil on the statue of Strasbourg in the Place de la Concorde was taken off. "Justice had triumphed." The lost provinces had come home to their mother, *La France!*

Readjustment Period: 1919–1922. The exaltation of victory did not last long: France is the country of the most acute class and factional conflict. During the war, the Sacred Union had been nominally imposed, for the invader was at the gates. Once the danger was removed, the struggle recurred between the Socialist workers and their unyielding employers. Class struggle was more bitter than before the war. To soothe it while the maimed nation still rejoiced in victory, Clemenceau ordered a general election, which resulted in a Nationalist triumph and the formation of a "Right" majority in the government, the first such since 1877 when the Clericals had been crushed.

France, always on the Left, was surprised at her own choice. The trade unions, over 2,000,000 members, protested. They demanded the 8-hour day and the "English Week" (half-holiday on Saturday). By 1920 French admirers of Soviet Russia challenged the older leadership and the struggle became all the fiercer as France was practically at war with Russia. She sustained the White Russian armies who were fighting the Reds and egged on Poland to attack the Soviets; she saved Poland from collapse. Only the mutiny of the French fleet in the Black Sea served to reveal the danger of the government's anti-Soviet policy in a country with an overwhelmingly "Marxist" working class. Clemenceau had once collaborated with the Paris Commune; being a realist, he quit. France suddenly found that she had lost her investments in Russia and the expense of her interventionist expeditions, to boot.

She proceeded to frame a new system of national defense. Since Germany no longer had a frontier with Russia, she was now potentially stronger against France than in 1914. Clemenceau therefore cemented two alliances: one with Poland; the other with the Little Entente — Czechoslovakia, Rumania, and Yugoslavia. Thus Europe was equipped with a "sanitary zone" against the Bolsheviks and Germany was outflanked in the east, west, and south. Belgium was also a faithful ally. These arrangements gave rise to a decade of French supremacy in Europe, when it appeared that French civilization would become as dominant as it had been in the 18th century. French victories in Morocco and the acquisition of Syria as a French mandate fortified this illusion.

Industrially, too, France made impressive moves. From her previous position as a basically agricultural state, she shifted to become the leading iron producer in Europe; she developed a large industrial population, became the leading European maker of automobiles and glass; she engaged in engineering works that were the first in scope in Europe until the Soviets built the hydroelectric plant at Dneprostroy. The mutilated population of France showed a new energy that flowed out not only in her traditional cultural supremacy but also in football, tennis, swimming, marathons, and even jazz bands.

Paris was the political and financial center of Europe, again the Mecca of tourists, the mystical center of Western civilization. But all along the French knew that Germany was inherently stronger and that American industrial technique could never be rivaled. No people are more prone than the French to describe themselves as others see them: a sense of the ridiculous has been as everpresent in them as it was absent in the German and Italian Fascists.

Currency Crises: 1922–1926. The war had cost France more than her current resources. Too much of the expense had been met by loans, too little by taxation. Taxation had to be sharply increased. But since the new mass of taxation exceeded the liquid reserves of the banks, the government had to issue money in excess of a proper gold backing. As a result, the franc, which had resisted every misfortune from 1802 to 1919, at last collapsed.

The world-wide industrial and price collapse in 1921 at first helped France. Her depreciated franc enabled her to export; tourists arrived in droves. But the pressure of the 1921 crisis resulted in eventual unemployment. By 1922 trade unionism sharply declined; the Socialist movement split into Socialists (led by Léon Blum) and Communists. The unions were broken in a railway strike, by the Premier Millerand, an ex-Socialist who knew their vulnerable points.

The "Right" majority in the Chamber of Deputies forgot that they were usually in a minority and became arrogant with victory. Royalist groups (*Action Française*) began to demonstrate and assail the "Leftists." The illness of President Deschanel resulted in the election of the man most hated by the workers, "a traitor," their former leader Millerand. The latter was made President of France and the Right had forced Clemenceau from the premiership.

Another ex-Socialist, Briand, known for his deftness in appeasing conflicting elements, finally became Premier. He encouraged the rise of the navy, and although at the Washington Conference he agreed to limit capital ships, he expanded the building of destroyers and submarines. "It is easy to sink ships but difficult to drown admirals," was his wry comment on a policy that still further alienated Britain from France. In the meantime, the Nationalist press hurled its rare treasure of invectives at Britain for her policy of the "balance of power." She was again "perfidious Albion," the one country that never kept her word and always betrayed her friends.

A consequence of this situation was the rise to power of Poincaré, a Lorraine lawyer, a Hannibal pledged to life-hatred of Germany — whose every provincial newspaper he read to study the motivation beneath the "sleek" diplomatic phrases. When the Germans failed to deliver timber as reparations, he moved into their richest province, the Ruhr, which he occupied for 9 months against world protests. France had demonstrated her power; but she lost British sympathy, and engendered furious nationalism within Germany. And at the same time the Allies permitted Germany to rearm in order to quell the social disorders within the Reich. The moneyed groups in France deposited their funds abroad as the franc declined in consequence of Franco-German policy. Poincaré fell from power.

France resumed her ordinary behavior in 1924, the Left winning the elections with big majorities. The new parliament forced Millerand to resign and a genial Protestant mediocrity, Doumergue, was selected for the presidency, a position now regarded as a mere sinecure. The dominant Socialists and Radicals tried to force Alsace to accept the French anticlerical laws, and this roused an autonomous party in the region. Premier Herriot tried to cope with the fall of the franc, but he was worsted by the Regents of the Bank of France, an almost hereditary board of custodians of the national currency. He then sought to impose a national assessment on assets, whereupon the currency crisis became too sharp. The Left still held political power but the Right had economic power; and the economic power won. Briand and the multimillionaire (in francs) Loucheur tried to reorganize the finances. But it was hopeless: the cost of living had risen 700% since 1913. The life savings of the thriftiest Europeans were almost wiped out.

Poincaré Achieves Recovery: 1926–1931. By 1926 the franc had dropped to under 2¢. Enormous foreign loans at high interest rates had failed to rescue it. German speculators attacked it, selling it short. Into this situation Poincaré was recalled to power. With billions in francs having been sold by foreigners who never actually owned them, Poincaré calmly announced that he now had resources to maintain the franc. By driving up the price of the franc by more than 100%, he ruined France's enemies in every financial center. Flushed with prestige as the savior of (what was left of) the franc, he formed a new government of Center parties.

France now recovered completely from the war. Some 2,700,000 people were settled in the devastated areas. Livestock, which had diminished by 90% in these regions, was more than replaced. Some 800,000 houses were built or rebuilt. Millions of damaged acres smiled again. But the general farm crisis persisted. About 6% of the arable land had been abandoned between 1913 and 1926 as farmers flocked into the better-paying industries. Prices of farmland had

not risen to match the fall of the franc, but farm products did rise in price under Poincaré and the farmers rallied to his support. In conservative areas like Normandy and Lorraine, his power was complete. Rural French bought automobiles and radios and began to dress and think like city folk. The blue blouse and *sabots* (wooden shoes) began to disappear.

Aluminum plants arose in the central districts rich in bauxite. Modernization of housing became widespread. Workers' cities grew up. An apartment house boom made Paris and the larger cities advanced in comforts and superior in beauty. As a result of this industrial and building boom France suffered no serious unemployment until three years after the American crash of 1929.

Meanwhile Briand had established friendly relations with Germany through the Locarno agreements (1925), and with the German Stresemann, he planned to evacuate the Rhineland four years in advance (1930). The Nationalist press declared that France had committed suicide; students paraded the streets, demanding Briand's death. But Liberal feelings prevailed. When General Sarrail bombed Damascus to quell a Syrian revolt (1926), he was recalled: such conduct was deplored, whatever the provocation. Marshal Lyautey's victories (1925) in Morocco were criticized rather than endorsed; whereupon the piqued pro-Consul encouraged imperialist attitudes. Not only had the U.S.S.R. been recognized by Herriot, but the Czarist embassy, a princely palace of architectural splendor, was restored in full pomp as the Soviet embassy.

The era of good feeling was enriched by prosperity and expansion, which arose from French thrift and confidence. No one wished to dislike anybody. Even the perennial conflict of classes was at low ebb.

Rise of Hatred: 1931–1934. In 1929 a capable reactionary, Tardieu, and an ex-Revolutionary Socialist and ex-political suspect, Laval, were installed in power. The ministry congratulated itself on the fact that while the rest of the world lay economically prostrate, with the pound and dollar declining, France had found the solution to crises in a "harmonious balance" between agriculture and industry. Laval took over the premiership in 1931 and the following spring the world economic crisis finally hit France.

Meanwhile Communism began to gain. Communists not only controlled many towns, but they were zealots for new schools and housing schemes and were therefore popular as such municipal councillors would be anywhere. When President Doumer was assassinated by a White Guard Russian, the traditional enemy of Communism, the Communists were able to whisper that the President had been murdered in order to provoke an election slogan. Nevertheless Tardieu proclaimed that the unique issue was Communism — "Communism is the enemy!" Briand died during the campaign, and with him went the last "conciliator."

The Left outnumbered the Right by 3–2, and the Center drew small support. With the depression and the rising threat of Hitlerite Germany, France became a veritable inferno. Brawls, quarrels, hot speech, the refusal of people in restaurants, offices, anywhere to be normally polite articulated the intense divisiveness of the country.

Popular Front Is Formed: 1934–1936. Unemployment was extensive. The internal price structure was too rigid, for the franc, now at a premium of 70% over the pound and dollar, was too high in terms of world prices. Frightened of any further devaluation of the franc, the government clung to the gold standard, preferring to reduce wages and costs to protect it. On the other hand, armaments had to be increased. Immigration was stopped and foreign workers were even asked to leave.

With deficits of $400,000,000 and the country in a state of insane hatred, Herriot gave up. He had been hurt when parliament refused to pay the American debt. He held that even though France risked ruin, she had given her word and must keep it, unless the U.S.A. forgave. He was right. If France had waited a few months, the debt probably would have been forgiven and she would have kept her reputation. But Herriot's attitude provoked suspicion that he was not "practical." Daladier, an honest Radical, son of a baker, succeeded him, and he in turn was succeeded by Chautemps. Then the storm broke.

One Stavisky, a Russian, had been engaged in shady municipal financing with the aid of certain Radical politicians. When the corruption was publicly revealed, the Right exploited the scandal in order to convince the people that the Republic was in the hands of thieves. For six weeks bands patrolled Paris, tearing up benches, burning buses, terrorizing Leftists. Their campaign culminated in an attempt to enter the Chamber of Deputies, February 6, 1934. The government fired on the demonstrators. They fled. Martyrdom was on their side, but the Republic had broken its enemies.

All factions of the workers' parties united for once, indicting the demonstrators as Fascists and claiming that their indignation over corruption was feigned, that their leadership included almost every financially suspect person in France, and that unworthy as the government was, it had to be sustained against Fascist attacks. The result was something close to civil war. Finally old President Doumergue was recalled to office as Prime Minister and a coalition government formed to calm the nation. The "leagues" were ordered to stay out of politics: the "Patriotic Youth," the "King's Peddlers" (*Camelots du Roi*), the "French Solidarity," the "Francists," and most powerful of all, "The Fiery Cross" (*Croix de Feu*) led by Colonel de la Rocque. The workers were also kept calm as orderly government resumed control.

The murder of Foreign Minister Barthou with King Alexander of Yugoslavia (October 9, 1934) showed that the Fascists would stop at nothing, for it was Barthou who had been organizing Europe against Hitler. (By unifying France with Russia and the other Slavic nations, he tried to frustrate Hitler's program.) France needed a strong policy: Doumergue resigned; Flandin, a weak and vacillating tool of the industrial combines, became Premier.

A succession of ministries followed, but they brought forth the Franco-Soviet pact that surprised Europe (May 1935). France had despaired of Britain's steadfastness after the Anglo-German naval

negotiations had been made without her consent; and while she sought to retain British friendship, she was determined to secure peace by enlisting all Europe except Germany and Italy. Though the pact was approved by Right and Left as a matter transcending parties, many Rightists (like Laval) actually began to sabotage it and others (Radicals like Bonnet) really disliked it.

Meanwhile all the Left parties, from Radicals to Communists, were engaged in forming a *Front Populaire* (Popular Front) to combat Fascism. France saw two Bastille Day demonstrations on July 14, 1935: the Rightists' on the Champs Elysées, and the Leftists', ten times as large, in the Place de la Bastille itself. This division went through every town. There was no France any more; there were two nations.

Popular Front Régime: 1936–1938. The May 1936 elections took place in an atmosphere charged with the news of Hitler's rearmament and of the triumph of the Popular Front in Spain. The Left won overwhelmingly. The Socialists gained (under Blum), the Radicals lost many seats, and there were now 72 Communists instead of the 10 in the previous parliament. Socialists and Communists polled 44%, and with the Radicals they were close to 72%. No country in history has ever shown so Left a vote in a free contest.

Panic swept the wealthier people of France. They began to sell their francs in huge amounts, and since the franc was still 70% above the dollar and the pound, they received many dollars and pounds. The government encouraged the sit-down strikes. Appointed Premier, Blum began the long overdue social reforms but without securing the financial structure. When a conflict arose over the Bank of France, the Leftists raised the battle cry: "Down with the 200 Families," by which they meant the hereditary grand fortunes of private bankers and industrialists. The Bank was democratized; Jouhaux, leader of the trade unions, entered its council of Regents. Business declined, production sank. Some people whispered a phrase that was later to spread through the country: "Better Hitler than Stalin."

Inept as it was, the Blum government did a great deal of good. It created workers' camps; great resorts on the Riviera were opened to people who for the first time got paid vacations, Saturday afternoons free, and a 48-hour week. In short, the French worker at last arrived at the point which the British worker had reached twenty-five years before. *Maisons de Culture* (cultural institutes) were also opened for workers interested in educating themselves. Social improvements, however, have their source in production; and the Blum government never managed to get production firmly under way.

When the Spanish Civil War broke out in July 1936, Blum announced, to the astonishment and chagrin of his following, that he was prepared to suggest that all countries refrain from shipping arms to Spain. Republican Spain was virtually the religion of the Left: Blum had to defend himself. He pointed to Britain: if France opposed the desires of Britain with respect to Spain, British pressure might ruin the franc and the savings of the French people be wiped out. Blum maintained his policy, but the franc was not saved. The wealthy classes began to deposit even greater sums abroad, and the franc collapsed. Blum's Spanish policy continued despite the fact that everyone knew that nonintervention was a farce.

The weakening of Blum's position also resulted in a division within the country that was by now unbridgeable. The franc had dropped 30%, but although business improved, it was not spectacular. A grandiose exposition was projected for 1937 to show the world that France was still the leader of civilization. Recriminations from the Right and Left caused such difficulty that the exposition opened late and its effect was spoiled. By now, if one side favored anything, however minute, the other was bound to injure its success. On only one point was there agreement: the length of military service had to be increased.

Even the Right was divided on the Spanish war. Some Catholics held General Franco to be a crusader; others, like Maritain, Mauriac, and Bernanos, leading Catholic thinkers, maintained that the Loyalists were the true Christians. Conservative Catholics were the core of the reaction; liberal Catholics multiplied their newspapers, magazines, youth organizations, and supported the Popular Front.

Blum dissolved the *Croix de Feu*, which immediately reorganized as the French Social Party. An ex-Communist, Doriot, replaced de la Rocque as the Fascist leader. This man knew the arts of demagogy, of achieving reaction by the use of ultra-leftist language. Blum, frightened, asked for a "pause." He was answered by a great surge of strikes. Throughout 1937 the franc sank to 39 to the dollar, business improved, strikes increased, cultural activities flourished, and disorders multiplied. Such contradictions were unique even for France, home of political drama. Finally Blum was overthrown and the Radicals took power.

Appeasement and Static War: 1938–1940. A degree of unity slowly took shape. Patriotic Rightists (like de Kérillis and Buré) and Leftists began to join: France was in danger and her divisions would prove fatal. Meanwhile a new group of Fascist terrorists, the *Cagoulards*, outfitted secret arsenals. Then in September 1938 Daladier joined with Chamberlain in sacrificing Czechoslovakia, despite the solemn guarantees that France had given to this struggling republic. Mortified by this Munich pact, one French general sent back his medals to the French government and broke his sword over the dishonor of France. Though Daladier was showered with flowers by a group of wealthy women at the Madeleine church, he returned home to a generally silent Paris. Two months later French labor declared a general strike against the "Men of Munich." It was swiftly suppressed. Pro-Hitler factions now felt that they had little to fear from the Left.

Throughout the summer of 1939 French foreign policy was indistinguishable from that of Chamberlain in Britain. But whereas British Conservatives, like Churchill and Eden, could assault the Chamberlain policy, in France everyone's foreign politics seemed to be combined with his views on capital and labor. Meanwhile Foreign Minister Bonnet suggested to the German Foreign Minister Ribbentrop

that France did not take her pact with the U.S.S.R. too seriously. And the Comité des Forges (iron and steel cartel) now became demonstrative in its principle of appeasing the Nazi régime.

The announcement of a pact between the U.S.S.R. and Germany, August 23, 1939, stunned the French. Their government immediately outlawed the Communist party, suspended its newspapers, and issued special decrees suspending Communist parliamentary deputies. Within a week a crisis confronted France, as a result of Franco-British guarantees to Poland. When it became certain that Hitler intended to march into Poland, Britain and France had no alternative but war. On September 2, 1939, Britain and France were officially at war with Germany, but the conflict was a nominal affair in the west until the following May. The Russo-Finnish battles and the expected adhesion of Italy to France were the chief topics of discussion; and it was not until Germany invaded Norway that the French awoke to the grave realities of their plight.

In the meantime, armament and aircraft production lagged, and Nazi decisiveness contrasted with French lassitude. The long series of domestic disputes and the continued retreats of France before the dictators had drained French soldiers of enthusiasm. The Gallic spirit, once a synonym of martial glory, seemed to have vanished. The French General Staff had begun to think like the old Chinese: it believed in walls (the Maginot Line) and in waiting for the attack. Daladier's government expected fundamentally that Germany would fall apart from economic weakness before any actual battle with France.

His régime was replaced by the more energetic Reynaud government (April 1940), but it was too late. The Germans attacked in the west on May 10th. Their breakthrough at Sedan (May 13th), twice the grave of France, opened the way to a breach of French defenses that was never repaired. A month later France was prostrate.

German Occupation and French Resistance: 1940–1944. The old Marshal Pétain counseled surrender. The Chamber of Deputies, hurriedly assembled, for the most part agreed to end the Republic and to delegate its powers to Pétain. He agreed to an armistice that allowed nearly two-thirds of France to be occupied. France was divided into Occupied and Unoccupied zones, which everyone recognized as a German device to divide the French people even more deeply.

Pétain retained a shadow of independence. The British, now left alone to fight the Nazis, demanded that the French fleet remain independent of German control. When the armistice was signed, only about a third of the French navy remained in French ports and was consequently subject to German pressure. Some ships entered British ports; others were interned at Alexandria. The bulk, however, were stationed in North African ports. It was regarding this latter portion of the French fleet that British policy was so largely concerned. The British, fearing an evasion of these demands, fired at the French fleet at Mers-el-Kébir near Oran (July 4, 1940), and Franco-British feelings of antipathy deepened.

Pétain proceeded to take over certain German patterns. "Liberty, Equality, and Fraternity" were removed from government edifices and "Family, Labor, Fatherland" substituted. The whole of France grew increasingly totalitarian, though this had not been necessary, even under the armistice terms. It was either servility on the part of Vichy or it indicated an inclination, long dormant, to shape France in the Nazi pattern. The whole French empire remained in Vichy control, except that Eboué, Negro governor of a French Equatorial province, raised the flag of revolt at Lake Chad.

General Charles de Gaulle, whose advice on mobile warfare had been ignored by Pétain, refused to accept the surrender. Appealing to all France to resist, he declared: "France has lost a battle, she has not lost the war." He proceeded to build the Free French resistance from his headquarters in London.

Within France herself, two years were needed to organize an underground movement. The remarkable fighting machine that emerged, under the name of the Maquis and later known as the F.F.I. (French Forces of the Interior), contributed substantially to German defeats. Resistance was far more difficult for the 1,500,000 French war prisoners and the hundreds of thousands of other Frenchmen who had been sent to work in German factories by the collaborationist Premier, Laval.

Early in 1941 the French in Indo-China yielded to Japan's demands, thus giving the latter her naval foundations for later victories in Malaya. But the tide turned for France in November 1942 when the Americans and British landed in North Africa. Darlan, a leading Vichy power, came over to the Allies; but he soon was assassinated, and a temporary French government arose in Algiers under the sponsorship of Generals Giraud and de Gaulle.

Pétain denounced the Americans and British as invaders. On November 11, 1942, the Germans canceled the armistice and occupied all of France. Though the Germans had violated the armistice, Pétain held that France was still bound by her signature. Finally the Germans moved toward the great French naval base at Toulon. Since the fleet stationed there lacked enough fuel to escape, French officers and sailors blew up many vessels in the harbor — the greatest naval suicide in history, even surpassing the German scuttling of their fleet at Scapa Flow in 1919. The French fleet had the courage to die though it had lacked the will to resist.

By 1943 the entire French Empire, except for Indo-China where the Japanese were stationed, had passed out of Vichy control. Following the brilliant Allied invasion of northern France, June 6, 1944, the F.F.I. multiplied their activities. At this time the U.S.A. and Britain, who had declined to consider the Committee of National Liberation at Algiers as a permanent government, now modified their attitude; they made working agreements in Metropolitan France *pro tem* with the de Gaulle régime. Wherever Allied troops penetrated, it became clear that the control of Vichy had been only nominal.

On August 19–23, 1944, Paris was liberated by a popular rising, as American troops surrounded the city. The French now joined the attack on Germany, with organized army units of their own.

Stakes in the Peace

Though France has prided herself on the balance between her agricultural and industrial economies, this balance has proved to be a weakness. Much of her agricultural organization is outdated and expensive. Her industries, on the other hand, could be developed much more intensively if she had a greater supply of coking coal and if technical education were more diffused. The latter requirement could be easily attained in so advanced a nation; and coking coal is obtainable from Germany. If France could make satisfactory arrangements for coking coal from an internationally administered western Germany the Northern French and German Rhineland area could become the first industrial producer, for its size, in the world. A good deal of French industry needs to be modernized; unit costs of production have been too high, owing to antiquated machinery and methods.

The industrial enrichment of France would not adversely affect her artisans. On the contrary, the wealth arising from such a development would strongly increase the purchasing power for fine arts, crafts, and the innumerable refinements of French ingenuity. She can remain the world's fashion center, even if most of her designs are used abroad in mass production. Her perfumes, silk prints, paintings, and similar products enjoy markets only insofar as there is a world surplus of income. Just as the French Revolution of 1789, by creating a luxurious middle class, really developed French cuisine more than the old nobility had done, so France has steadily gained in artisan skills as the world became industrially richer.

Certain reforms are bound to occur in farming. Centralized cultivation and extensive planning can easily increase yields and reduce costs in the giant "ordinary wine" areas, wheat districts, beet-sugar estates, and cattle ranges. On the other hand, it would be difficult to think of basic improvements in the more specialized crops — garden vegetables, fruits, melons, fine wines, flowers; and these workings will doubtless remain small units.

France's economic crises have originated in world price fluctuations of her basic crops and her large industrial production. Her potentialities in both are such that she could easily expand these productions on a cost basis that would enable her to compete when prices declined.

France must abandon her idea of self-sufficiency: that because she can make herself economically independent, she can be freed from foreign pressures. World War II has demonstrated that the very organization of French "harmony" — her balance between agriculture and industry — precludes industry from developing into the decisive factor; and therefore that instead of being protected by this "harmony," she is actually weakened by it. France cannot ignore the twentieth-century economic reality — her industry must dominate her agriculture.

French colonies have recently gained in importance. While she has come to use her North African empire as part of her own economy, France will have to make greater concessions to the native populations. The best solution for the rest of her African empire would seem to lie in some international organization, since France has failed to provide sufficient capital for satisfactorily increasing the welfare of the natives.

Once France is freed from recurrent invasions and enormous armament expenditure, the workmanlike, thrifty, and intelligent French nation would be much better off even with small industrial and agricultural change. France seeks no conquests; she is an ideal candidate for world organization. She who has seen five bloody invasions in the last 150 years, needs it more than any other power.

GERMANY

The Land and the People

Germany was the last of the leading Western powers to be industrialized, but once this was achieved (1850–1900) the nation rose swiftly to a dominant position in Europe. Her political unification was progressively undertaken by the German Empire (from 1871); its final form was imposed by Hitler himself (1934). Her aggressive rulers chose war as their instrument of national policy; and twice within our century a highly militarized Germany has been the focal point of world conflagration.

We shall consider Germany primarily in terms of her peacetime boundaries, before her forcible conquests of Austria and parts of Czechoslovakia in 1938–39. Occupying 181,700 square miles in the heart of Europe, Germany's population in 1938 was about 69,-000,000. Before 1914, her somewhat larger territory contained nearly 67,000,000. Her increase in population is thus much smaller than is commonly believed. Nevertheless, Germany has more people than any other European country except the Soviet Union.

With 370 inhabitants per square mile, and about 860 persons to every square mile of arable land, Germany is thickly populated; but her repeated claims that she is "a people without room" do not square with the facts. She has actually more *Lebensraum* (living space) than many other European nations. (The density of Germany's population as compared with her arable land is less than 40% that of Belgium, 37% of the Netherlands, 28% of England and Wales, less than 50% of Switzerland.)

The Land. Germany consists mainly of lands that form part of the North European Plain. Thus the whole of Germany bordering on the North and Baltic Seas and the Jutland peninsula is a plain. Western Germany is not distinguishable physically from neighboring Holland, nor eastern Germany from adjacent Poland. But the southern third of Germany presents a sharply contrasting physical appearance. Although only a tiny section is truly Alpine, the uplands rising from the northern plain to flank the Alps constitute the beautiful hilly districts of the southern area: the former kingdoms of Bavaria and Württemberg.

The two sections of the country — the northern plain and the western and southern regions of high-lands and valleys — correspond to marked differences in religion, customs, and political and cultural traditions. Temporarily overridden by a unifying power imposed from above, these regional differences cannot be erased.

In western Germany, the fertile Rhine river valley is bounded by the Vosges mountains and the hills of Luxembourg and Belgium; for a hundred miles the Rhine itself, the leading commercial river of Europe, forms the boundary with the French provinces of Alsace and Lorraine. The valley of the Moselle, west of the Rhine, is famed for white wines and for fruits, while the Ruhr valley, once farming land, is now the very symbol of heavy industry. East of the Rhine as it approaches Switzerland lies the celebrated Black Forest. The Swiss frontier is hilly and intersected with lakes, including the large Lake of Constance. The boundary with Austria on the south is truly Alpine, with thickly forested mountains and hills. A natural mountain chain, the *Erzgebirge*, separates Germany on the southeast from the square tableland of Bohemia, the heart of Czechoslovakia.

Northeastern Germany, a region of swamp and fen, lakes and sandy farms, is the homeland of the hereditary Prussian aristocracy. The population, especially in East Prussia, a German island wedged into Polish and Lithuanian areas, is mixed and largely non-German.

The famous moors of the Lüneburg Heath are in the north, around Brunswick, and west of this area stands the ancient Teutoburger Forest, once considered impenetrable, where the Roman legions experienced their first significant defeat (9 A.D.). The river mouths of the Weser and the Elbe, on the North Sea, though flat and muddy, have contributed to the development of the giant ports of Hamburg and Bremen. In the center of Germany stretches the Altmark plain, the region once called Brandenburg, later Prussia, and then Germany.

But the true strength of Germany lies where the Northern Plain and the southern and western uplands meet. Here fertility of soil and abundant mineral resources conjoin to form the real centers of German power: the industrialized Rhineland, Westphalia, most of Saxony just north of Bohemia, and Silesia wedged in between Bohemia and Poland. Coal resources of good quality abound in the Ruhr valley, the nearby Saar basin in the northwest, and Upper

Silesia in the extreme southeast. Some zinc, lead, graphite, iron pyrites, and copper are found in Silesia; iron ore and manganese in the Ruhr valley. Potash, invaluable as a fertilizer, is mined in large quantities at Stassfurt in central Germany.

Germany's extensive and scientifically husbanded forest resources cover about a quarter of the country's total area. Her water-power resources, while not large, are developed to full capacity.

The German uplands with their rolling hills, cultivated valleys, and rich cities are among the most physically attractive regions of the civilized world. Prussian power began when the Junkers came out of their large but unfertile estates in the northeast to dominate these wealthy areas.

Germany's capital and administrative center is Berlin (population 4,332,242), and her leading seaport Hamburg (1,682,220). Other cities of over 500,000 population are Munich (828,325), Cologne (768,426), Leipzig (701,606), Essen (659,781), Dresden (625,-174), Breslau (615,006), Düsseldorf (539,905), Frankfort-am-Main (546,649), and Dortmund (537,000).

The People. Notwithstanding the myths disseminated by their Nazi leaders, the Germans, like most peoples, are of diverse racial origins. Only near the Baltic and North Seas in the Northern Plain do blonds predominate; in central Germany blonds and brunets are about evenly divided; and toward the Alpine south, most of the people are brunets. Hence the German people show both Nordic and Alpine influences.

Historically, the Germanic tribes — the Teutons, the Quadi, and the Marcomanni — were not numerous, and the degree to which they overwhelmed the Celtic-speaking peoples of the Rhine or the long-established Alpine races in southern Germany is open to question. In eastern Germany, Slavic influence is widespread. Though the boundaries of German speech have been pushed eastward to Poland in ten centuries of battles, the conquered Slavic peoples have to some extent absorbed the conquerors. The "truest descendants" of the old Germanic peoples are the Angles and the Saxons, who are found not in Germany but in southeast England.

Thus, the German people, with multiple origins, are a fusion of outstanding European types. To what extent the relatively recent political unification of Germany has brought about racial and cultural cohesion is a highly debatable question.

The survival of serfdom in Germany has been remarked upon by students of society, for serfdom persisted in Germany centuries after it had disappeared from Western Europe. In the 18th century the Hessians were sold like cattle by their princes to fight the American colonists; and the Prussian serfs were not emancipated until the Wars of National Liberation after 1813. Only in the free cities (especially cities in the north, like Lübeck, or Imperial guild cities like Nuremburg) were the inhabitants as free and enlightened as in western Europe.

The peoples of present-day Germany retain great diversity in their habits. The typical Prussian peasant is either a sharecropper on a large estate or a tenant of the old landowning nobility; but the Rhineland fruit-and-vegetable farmer is practically indistinguishable

in outlook from his French counterpart. Until the advent of the Nazis to power in 1933, the workmen of the Ruhr were as socialistic as workers in heavy industry throughout Europe; and politically, pre-1933 Berlin was strikingly similar to Paris. Hence, facile generalizations cannot be applied to the whole of this numerous people.

The language of the south Germans is the old "High" German; that of the northern plains people is closer to Dutch; and though they have all been taught standard German in excellent schools, the common people of each province find it hard to understand the dialects of the other provinces.

German Minorities. In Europe, the main centers of German diffusion are in Austria, whose people are largely Germanic in origin, in the Sudeten areas of Czechoslovakia, and in Transylvania (a province claimed by both Hungary and Rumania). In the three Baltic States, long under German cultural domination, the Germans are few indeed — less than 4%. Actually, therefore, there are non-Reich Germans along some of Germany's frontiers and small clusters elsewhere, but no large islands of German culture in foreign lands.

Before 1939 there were no sizable national minorities in Germany, apart from a trickle of Polish and Italian immigration into the Ruhr district and a Jewish population of about 600,000. Many Jewish settlements in the Rhineland date back to the occupation of these formerly Celtic areas by the Teutons. In pre-Nazi Germany many German Jews had emigrated or become assimilated; moreover, their birthrate had been low, so that their proportion of the population had been declining markedly for over a century. Today, as a result of Nazi persecutions, only a handful of Jews remains.

German emigration has long been active, and some authorities estimate the proportion of Americans of Germanic stock as high as a seventh. In Latin America too there are some German groupings, especially in Brazil and Chile. But despite intense preoccupation with this "Germany Abroad," there is no island of German culture outside Europe remotely comparable in numbers to French Canada, for example.

Population Prospects. From 1918–1933 the consistently low birthrate sank below 16 per thousand and for three years in the 1920's it was under that of France. Employment in armament industries and Nazi premiums for large families raised the figure to as high as 20.4 in 1939, but war reduced it to 14.9 for 1942, and in view of the probable loss of millions of adult males, a declining birthrate seems likely. The peacetime deathrate has been around 12, so that normally there has been a natural increase. Infant mortality at 63 to 74 per thousand is the same as in France, but a much poorer showing than in Britain, Sweden, Norway, or Switzerland.

The net reproduction rate was calculated at 0.698 in 1933, forecasting a decline of 30% a generation hence. Intensive efforts raised it to 0.996 in 1940 (according to a "revised method" of calculation by the Nazis), but it has since fallen to about 0.750. It is certain, then, that the Germans will not be as numerous in 1970–90 as they are now. And they may even decline to under 50,000,000.

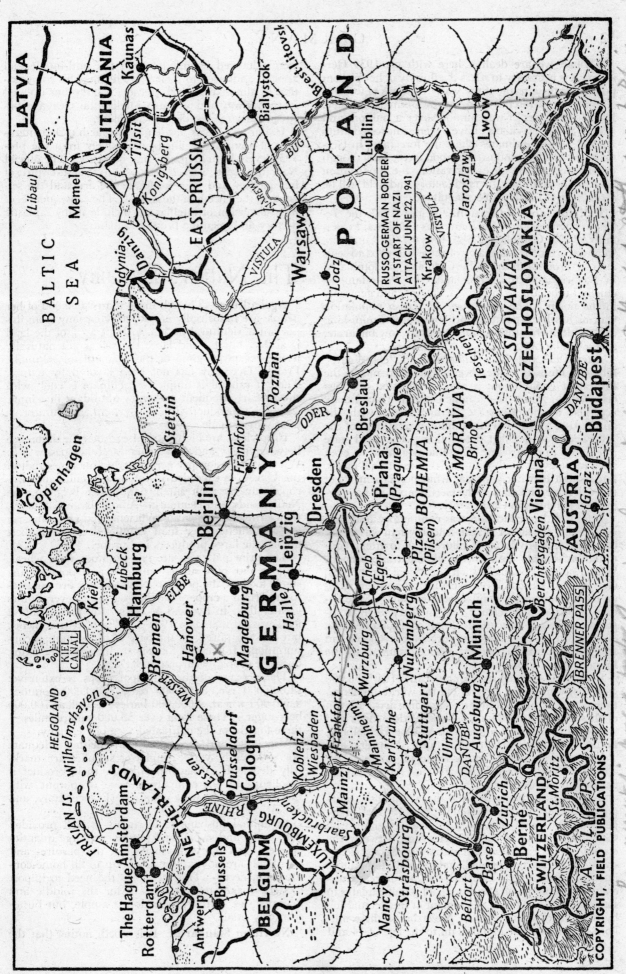

RUSSO-GERMAN BORDER
AT START OF NAZI
ATTACK JUNE 22, 1941

KIEL
CANAL

BRENNER PASS

COPYRIGHT, FIELD PUBLICATIONS

51

Though we are dealing here with pre-1939 Germany, it is necessary to stress the fluidity of her present population as a result of the war. Millions of foreigners have been forcibly enrolled in German industry. French prisoners of war number over a million, and many Soviet civilians have been impressed into service. Some estimates place the foreigners in Germany at half the industrial labor force, and though this figure may be an exaggeration, the repatriation of the millions of foreigners in factory and field will be a problem of incalculable magnitude.

Religion and Education. Before 1933 the religious composition of Germany was as follows: Protestants 62.7%, Catholics 32.5%, Jews 0.7%. Some 4% were unclassified, but many of these belonged to sects akin to Protestantism. The Catholics predominated in Bavaria and the Rhineland; the Protestants — chiefly Lutherans — in Prussia, Saxony, and generally in the north. The percentage of Jewish population was, as has been pointed out, constantly diminishing as a result of emigration, intermarriage, low birthrate, and assimilation.

After 1933 the State undertook to "coordinate" religious life. It made several efforts to nazify the Protestant communion; it often humiliated and discriminated against the Catholic Church, which finally accepted a new *Concordat* (arrangement) with the authorities; and its harshly inhuman treatment of the Jews needs no detailed description. The Nazi state attempted to reintroduce Teutonic paganism or even Nazi ideology as a substitute for the traditional faiths, but though it is not yet clear what permanent effect this will have, the mass of the German people have remained believers in Christianity.

Before Hitler, education was compulsory and universal up to the age of 14; the school system was partly centralized, partly local. Children had to attend continuation schools until 18, or choose trade schools. With 1,300,000 pupils in such vocational institutions, Germany surpassed all other countries; and this stress on technical training may account for some of the triumphs of German science and industry — by comparison, French education remained fundamentally classical. Germany's advanced technical schools had 180,000 students, secondary schools (similar to the French *lycées*), 673,000.

Until 1933 Germany's 25 universities (with 88,000 students) were in the forefront of the world of science, though not paramount in letters and fine arts. Eleven of these universities date from the Middle Ages and the Renaissance, and some of them, like Heidelberg, Bonn, Göttingen, Halle, Freiburg, Leipzig, and Tübingen, were world-famous leaders in many fields. The book trade in Leipzig was the most thoroughly organized in the world.

Yet it must be borne in mind that German learning and reading were concentrated in about 10–15% of the people. Nowhere else in an advanced industrial society was there so wide a cleavage between the classes. The extensive circulation of books exclusively for a "learned public" indicates that the large intellectual class remained isolated and bureaucratically aloof from popular culture. This gulf explains to some degree the fanatic resentment of intellectual life by millions of young Nazis. Nevertheless these millions had all attended schools up to the age of 14 and were educated enough to read the anti-intellectual appeals addressed to their prejudices. This combination of almost universal literacy, a large but isolated learned class, and a sharp intellectual cleavage between classes is peculiar to Germany.

Under the Nazis academic scholarship and literature of any sort declined impressively from the pre-1933 levels, both in quality and quantity. The official Nazi ideologists worked zealously to stifle the spirit of free inquiry and to subordinate the arts and the sciences to the "needs of the state." The consequences of this subversion of intelligence include many fantastic literary and scientific pronouncements.

The Nation's Economy

Agriculture. Though more than 9,000,000 of her people are industrially employed, Germany is an important agricultural nation. About 40% of the land is arable, but by and large the soil is not naturally fertile except in some of the rich uplands — unlike France, Germany has not been favored by nature. Though rainfall is ample, the climate is cool, with storms fairly frequent and snow abundant in winter. Thus the productivity of German agriculture is mostly man-made.

Crop yields are high and quite stable: the difference between good and bad years rarely surpasses 8%. Wheat production per acre, nearly four times that of the U.S.A., is exceeded in intensively cultivated Europe only by such small nations as Belgium, the Netherlands, and Denmark. Among large producers, the Germans are the most efficient, and German cash farm-production per man employed is the highest among the large producers in Europe.

The principal crops are rye, potatoes, oats, wheat, barley, and beet sugar, with rye and potatoes the staple foods of the people. Nowhere else are potatoes so important a crop — the total output is several times greater than in the U.S.A. Domestic production of food was estimated in 1932 at 87% of requirements, but this was purely on the basis of direct human consumption. If livestock fodders are included, the figure does not probably surpass 80%.

The acreage of the principal crops is extensive: 11,000,000 rye, 8,000,000 oats, 7,000,000 potatoes, 5,500,000 wheat, 4,000,000 barley, as well as 700,000 beet-sugar. These total over 53,000 square miles — three-fourths of the cultivated area of Germany.

Vegetable and fruit crops are neither adequate nor sufficiently varied, and egg supplies are markedly deficient. Vineyards, though their product is excellent, do not compare in size or output with those of the great wine countries (France, Italy, and Spain).

In animal husbandry, Germany is well provided with cattle and swine, and produces a large quantity of meat and dairy products; but the pasture- and grasslands are not extensive enough to fill home-consumption needs. This fact, plus the need to import fodders, makes meat expensive for the middle and lower classes. Milk production is ample, but butter relatively small.

Nutrition Standards. It is worth noting that the

ratio of home-grown products to domestic needs is so high only because Germany's nutrition standards are well below those of other advanced nations. Hence, self-sufficiency has been easier to attain than in Britain, for example. For adult males, annual consumption (per pounds) of leading foods are as follows: bread and cereals: Germany 294, Britain 310; meat and fish: Germany 91, Britain 106; dairy products: Germany 286, Britain 315. British averages run about 10% higher, but if comparisons are made with a younger country like Australia (whose averages are: bread and cereals 313 pounds, meat and fish 207, dairy products 484), the contrast with Germany is impressive. And compared with her immediate neighbors (the Belgians, Dutch, and Danes), the average German is not well nourished. Workers in heavy industry, storm troops, Gestapo employees, soldiers, and Nazi officials are all extremely well fed; but these are, obviously, the privileged groups. (A relevant index is beer, traditionally considered the German beverage: Germany consumes far less beer per capita than Belgium or Denmark.)

While it is abundant in cheap and coarse foods, German agriculture is deficient in medium-priced articles of diet. The largest meat product is pork, not beef or veal. Even the fish consumption is less than half the per capita figure for Britain; and here too, the main catch of Germany's fisheries is the cheap herring. In food consumption as a whole, therefore, Germany occupies an intermediate position between countries like Belgium and Denmark, and those bordering her on the south and east, which are industrially less advanced.

Two facts are essential to an understanding of German agriculture. (1) The northeastern section of the country, poorly cultivated, consists of the vast estates of the Junker landowners, on which semi-feudal conditions still prevail. These farms are uneconomical; were it not for exorbitantly high protective tariffs and government subsidies, the owners would have to give them up. However, these lands provide the economic basis for the hereditary caste of Prussian officers and government officials, and for this reason they are sustained. (2) Secondly, the price of this land is extremely high in view of its cash yield. Land in the fertile southwest, where farming is modernized and individual holdings predominate, is priced fairly; but in the great farming areas of Pomerania and East Prussia the high price of land is artificially maintained on the basis of a class monopoly.

In view of our findings, German agriculture emerges as efficient, extensive, maintained at the cost of inadequate nourishment of the people, and subsidized where it is uneconomical. It must be clearly divided into (a) satisfactory farming regions where the land is subdivided (the south and the west), and (b) the unsatisfactory Junker regions (the east). All regions that were Prussian before the Battle of Waterloo (1815) fall into the latter deficit class, which deficit explains why Prussia had to extend her domain over richer areas.

Industry and Mining. The growth of German industry in the second half of the 19th century startled the world. In 1870 it was far behind Britain's and even inferior to France's. Between 1870 and 1930 the approximate ratio of growth in industry was from 1 to 5.5 (Britain's during the same period was only 1 to

2.3). Yet while this transformation was striking in terms of European development, it could not rival the 1 to 13 ratio that obtained in the rapidly expanding U.S.A. One must remember that rates of growth depend on the size of the base, for as countries grow older, their rates of increase diminish. Hence, the relative growth of German industry, while impressive, has not been so spectacular as it appears to be on the surface.

Contrary to popular belief, German industry, undoubtedly efficient and technically in the front rank, does not surpass the efficiency of Britain. The ratio of horse-power used per worker was 6.65 hours in Britain, 6.04 in Germany (13.38 in the U.S.A.). Germany's figure is impressive compared with France's and that of other nations that trail far behind; but it is the lowest among the most industrially advanced Western countries.

In another index of industrialization — machinery investment per capita — Germany ranks as follows: Germany $9, Britain $13.50, Switzerland $13.40, U.S.A. about $31. In percentage of population engaged in industry, the comparisons are: Germany 41%, Switzerland 44%, Britain 51% — and the Netherlands 38%, Czechoslovakia 37%, France 33%.

World War II, of course, has altered these figures, but they afford a sound peacetime basis for understanding. We do not know (it is a military secret) whether foreign hand-labor has been used to supplement Germany's deteriorating machines, or if, on the contrary, Germany has built uneconomical machinery to press the struggle. On this point outside investigators are unclear and German sources deliberately confusing. It is therefore difficult to estimate Germany's present economic industrial plant.

Normally, about 13,000,000 Germans are employed in heavy industry and 1,900,000 in textiles. Based on abundant coal, her heavy industries lost some of their supremacy when the Lorraine iron fields were transferred to France and when Luxembourg entered the Belgian customs union. But with roughly 10% of Europe's population, Germany produced 14% of the world's steel; 15% of its machinery, 17% of its chemicals, and 46% of its synthetic dyes.

Her annual production of 15% of the world's coal is her strong point. Were Germany to lose the Saar basin or yield Silesia to Poland, her industrial power would be appreciably weakened. Frederick the Great once said of Silesia, "This is my Peru!" considering this region as vital to Germany as were the Peruvian mines to the grandeur of 16th century Spain.

In most mineral resources Germany is deficient. Iron, copper, lead, zinc, bauxite (for aluminum), manganese, and chrome (for ferro-alloys) — for these strategic minerals she must depend on outside sources. She has an ample supply of potash (for fertilizer), but minor resources of phosphates. The creation of synthetic nitrogen (1913) by the German-Jewish scientist Haber made Germany independent of Chilean nitrates, and the development of both synthetic rubber and the liquefaction of coal into hydrocarbons have lessened her dependence on imports of rubber and petroleum. But since she lacks oil fields and is not overendowed with water-power (though her existing resources are fully utilized), Germany's fuel position must remain based on her ample supplies of coal.

She is notably deficient in textiles, her dependence on cotton imports being a permanent necessity. Indeed, industrial raw materials constitute 60% of Germany's imports, and without them she would be a second-rate state unable to keep her industries going.

However, Germany possesses certain undeniable industrial advantages: the largest nation in the heart of Europe, she is crisscrossed by a network of rivers, canals, and railroads, unparalleled in the world. In the sciences, especially chemistry, she has made startling advances. And she is technologically ahead of her southern and eastern neighbors. So long as most of these nearby lands remain agrarian states, Germany will be able to apply strong pressure on them for barter; and political penetration will follow closely on commercial influence. But if these countries also become industrialized, she will not be able to retain her paramount position.

A key problem of German industry is the excessive accumulation of capital in relation to the country's internal market. Germany has paid her workers less in proportion to their output than has any other European nation. In 1913 real wages per worker were only 75% of the British figure. The wages paid to German workers were 44% of their output — much the worst showing among advanced industrial nations, and this ratio was steadily declining, whereas in other countries the level remained more constant. Since Germany produces mostly capital goods, and since her workers, compared with those in other countries, were less able to buy consumers goods, the domestic market has been more restricted than that of other industrial nations. The over-rapid accumulation of German industrial capital has also been based on the weakening of the middle classes by deliberate cartel and inflation devices.

National Wealth and Income. In terms of per capita *wealth*, Germany belongs to the intermediate rather than advanced nations. At the peak of business conditions, the comparison was: Germany $935, France $1,250, Belgium $1,000, Switzerland $2,000, Britain $1,620. Surprisingly, the German figure was lower than Argentina's and Spain's.

Because she was an industrial state, Germany's *income* per capita made a better showing: Germany $191, Switzerland $252, the Netherlands $268, Britain $270. In comparing Germany with France, if we take into account that Germany is far more industrialized, her per capita income did not much exceed that of France ($176).

Moreover, variations in income are as marked in German economy as in American. Until 1933, when the government instituted rigid controls and production bore no relation to markets, Germany suffered more than any other European country from cyclical economic crises in income, wealth, trade, production, and prices (though not more than the U.S.A.).

Finances. In dealing with prevailing German finances, we must remember that the Nazi government has resorted to so many statistical distortions that comparable figures with the past or with other nations are difficult to establish. The investment in armaments has been consistently underrated and figures for the national debt carefully disguised. The national debt as of June 1943 was given as about 216,000,000,000 gold marks (nominally $86,400,000,000), but certain items totaling several billion marks were excluded from this statement. The 1939 figure was given by the Nazi government as 30,000,000,000 marks: thus it has risen sevenfold, despite Germany's plunder of some 300,000,000 Europeans. In the same period (1939–1943) the budget increased from 28 to 91 billion gold marks (from approximately $11,200,000,000 to $36,400,000,000).

Money in circulation has risen steadily, from about 6,000,000,000 marks in 1934 to 27,400,000,000 in 1942. Though there is no report on savings accounts since 1939, the last clear figure (1937) reported 23,000,000,000 marks ($9,200,000,000). If the mark is accepted at 40¢, this is an impressive figure, not much below the per capita savings in Britain.

Government control has effectively prevented any steep rise in stock-exchange prices. At the end of 1942 they were only 50% above pre-war levels, despite a more than fourfold increase in money. The government thus puts a brake on any stock-market speculations that might betray a popular fear of an impending catastrophic fall in German currency.

It is not easy to determine the true value of the *Reichsmark*, the currency unit. In 1943 it sold in neutral Switzerland at 6¢, while the German "tourist mark" sold at 19¢ and the German "trade-savings mark" at 3¢. In actual purchasing power within Germany the mark seemed worth about 18¢ (summer of 1943), but mark notes were hawked in Basel (Switzerland) for less than 2¢.

Foreign Trade. Germany's drive for foreign trade was for a long time as dynamic as her industrial growth. In 1880 her exports were 11.4% of the world total, her imports 11.3%. By 1910 exports were 12.6%, imports 13.5%. But in 1930 the German Republic, diminished since 1918, had only 10.9% in exports and 8.7% in imports. Thus Germany's relative peak had been reached before World War I.

But since most of her losses in percentage had been taken up by the U.S.A., Germany continued to make a good showing in Europe. At the height of peacetime prosperity (1928) her per capita trade was 3% below that of France. But France exported luxury goods while Germany exported mainly capital goods — metal goods and machinery, which were strategically more important.

In 1938 German exports approximated $2,000,000,000 and her imports $2,100,000,000 — amounting to 9.5% of world exports and 9% of world imports. She did not exceed this modest proportion despite her blackmailing of the many economically weak nations whose trade she practically monopolized.

German exports vary widely according to political exigencies. Steel exports have fallen by three-fourths when armament policy so dictated; machinery exports have increased when they were needed to reduce another country to dependence on Germany for repairs and replacements. In short, Germany's foreign trade policy has been governed by other than purely market considerations: it has always borne some relation to her political strategy.

The Netherlands have long been her principal customer; then follow Britain, the U.S.A., Italy, France, Czechoslovakia, and Sweden. Although the proportion of her Balkan exports is enormous, the quantities involved are not comparable to those sent to the seven larger countries. The leading export items have been iron and steel products; cotton, woolen, and silk fabrics; beet-sugar, paper, chemicals and dyes, coal and coke, and leather-goods.

Her main sources of imports have been the U.S.A., Britain, and the Netherlands. The chief items: petroleum; cotton, wool; iron ore, other ores, and metals; vegetable oils and such foodstuffs as butter, eggs, meat, fruits.

The amount of German shipping in 1937 (3,700,000 tons) did not correspond to her position in world trade. Not much larger than it had been in 1910, her tonnage in relation to world shipping was much reduced. Since neither her shipping nor her fisheries are proportionately adequate, she has been unable to develop a maritime strength capable of challenging the nations she has sought to dominate. Undoubtedly Germany will be a minor factor in shipping after World War II, especially if she is required to make restitution for her destruction of vessels belonging to such victim nations as Norway and the Netherlands.

History: 1914-1944

Before her defeat by the Allies in November 1918, Germany was an empire governed by an Emperor (Kaiser) whose powers were broader than those of most constitutional monarchs. He had the right to name the Imperial Chancellor and his cabinet without interference from the legislative body. Parliamentary government as we understand the term did not exist. The German Empire was a centralized federation of 26 states, 4 of which were kingdoms: Bavaria, Saxony, Württemberg, and Prussia. Prussia, the largest kingdom, embracing about 60% of the empire's population, was also the domain of the Kaiser himself.

This empire was recent, dating from 1866 and given imperial expression in 1871. Up to that period, Germany had consisted of a congeries of petty states and principalities, not having been effectively united since the imperial period of the 13th century. Hence the phrase "the Third Reich," later used by Hitler.

The First Year of the Republic: 1918-1919. Military defeat stunned the Germans. A mutiny of the sailors at Kiel gave the signal for revolt, and the people overthrew the Kaiser (November 9, 1918). Proclaiming a Republic, they chose Ebert as President, a former saddle-maker and a Socialist. The Socialists assumed control of the government, but carefully preserved the hostile Civil Service and the equally hostile General Staff and officers' corps.

Since the Germans had surrendered on French soil, two legends began to circulate: — among the German liberals, that they had surrendered only because they trusted President Wilson's Fourteen Points; among the conservatives, that they had been stabbed in the back by Socialists and "democratic Jews." The simple fact that the nation surrendered because it was militarily beaten was too banal to be accepted.

Within two months, the Spartacists (*Spartakus-Bund*) led by the fiery Leftists, Karl Liebknecht and Rosa Luxemburg, rose up to establish a Workers' Republic.

These two revolutionaries were not Bolsheviks, but they had fought tooth-and-nail against the war and would not trust the German Socialists who had accepted it. They were murdered and their bodies thrown into a Berlin canal; and the Socialists called in the army to repress the rising workers' revolt. From that time on every government in Germany required the support of the army.

The first elections gave 45% of the votes to the Socialists, with the Catholic Center Party the leading opposition group. Since the Catholics favored liberal domestic policies, a coalition government of Socialists and Catholics became possible.

The German armies slowly withdrew from Russia and the Ukraine, and, most laggardly of all, from the Baltic States. By the summer of 1919 Germany was confined to her own shrunken borders. The Treaty of Versailles (June 1919) imposed severe penalties on her: she had to restore to France, Alsace-Lorraine, subjugated in 1871; to Denmark, Danish Schleswig, stolen in 1864 by Bismarck; to resuscitated Poland, large areas inhabited by Poles, whose long subjugation resulted from the criminal partitions of the 18th century.

The Germans, with the adroit talent for propaganda that never fails them, then centered their protests on minor border rectifications, forgetting that substantial justice had thus been done to some 6,000,000 people, and that, at the most, some injustice was done to 300,000 Germans. Germany insisted that the loss of 6,000,000 inhabitants to whom she had no right, deprived her of "her" valuable economic resources.

In addition, the victorious Allies insisted that she pay reparations for her wanton acts in France and Belgium and that, having plundered French and Belgian coal for several years, she allow a 15-year period in the coal-rich Saar region, during which the victims might replenish their stocks. At the end of that period, when economic satisfaction had been granted, the Saar would be free to rejoin Germany, if it so desired.

The Germans balked at the corridor of Polish population in the east, that separated them from the Junker stronghold of East Prussia with its 1,500,000 Germans — they were oblivious of the fact that if they held the Polish peoples of the corridor, they would be blocking 30,000,000 Poles from the sea. Ratios of the interests of 20 Poles to 1 German did not interest them; they were the "superior" race.

The Allied reparations figures were astronomical, but they were never paid. The Germans borrowed the first payments from London and later payments from international banking circles throughout the world. Indeed, it is doubtful whether the net burden (after receipts from loans) imposed on defeated Germany, even making allowance for her lost colonies and merchant shipping, was not the lightest in reparations history. From the very moment of the Versailles Treaty, however, the rulers of Germany, who had just dictated the far more brutal Treaties of Bucharest and Brest-Litovsk, clamored for justice and mercy. Exploiting the world sympathy thus aroused, they began to rebuild their army for world conquest.

In the autumn of 1919, the newly founded Weimar Republic framed a Constitution, which on paper was the most advanced in the world. Politically and socially progressive, it aroused hopes everywhere that the new Germany would be unlike the old.

Military Power Reasserts Itself: 1920–1923. There were, however, other portents. The government had confined the recent repression of a Soviet uprising in Bavaria to a special corps of reactionary officers rather than to a popular militia. In 1920 the older Junker elements, contemptuous of verbal assertions of republicanism when accompanied by truckling to their class, attempted an army rebellion in Berlin. The leader of this *putsch* was a civil servant named Kapp, whose father had been a Socialist in America. The workers met this threat by calling a general strike and forming a people's militia; and the rebellion collapsed.

The General Staff then began to finance criminal groups of officers, called the *Feme*, who resorted to assassination. In 1922 the *Feme* murdered Foreign Minister Rathenau and the Catholic leader, Erzberger. Throughout the 1920's frequent assassinations, ambushes, and bomb-throwings occurred in Germany — they were the work, not of Anarchists, but of Junkers. Between 1920–23 the Junkers had a field day. With social disorders rampant, especially in Saxony, Hamburg, and the Ruhr, the Republican government entrusted the repression of these disorders to the most brutal army leaders, like von Epp.

These disturbances resulted in the formation of various private armies. A young Austrian-born police-spy and ne'er-do-well in Munich, named Adolf Hitler, became member Number 7 of one of these army-sponsored groups. This was the Nazi Party (National Socialist German Workers Party) founded in 1919.

The success of Mussolini in Italy caused the budding Nazis to imitate him slavishly, without any pretence of originality. In 1923 Ludendorf, the old head of the German army, joined with Hitler in attempting the "beer-hall rebellion" in Munich. The authorities quickly subdued it and sent Hitler to Landsberg Prison. Installed in a comfortable special cell, the Nazi "martyr" wrote *Mein Kampf*, a *pot-pourri* of Pan-German, racist, and Fascist concepts expressed in bad and ungrammatical German. His following, at first small, rose to importance in 1924, then shrank to a tiny group, until it was suddenly resurrected in 1930.

The Inflation: 1919–1924. By the Versailles Treaty, the Germans had been allowed an insignificant army (100,000 men), no navy, and no air force. The sums saved on the once-crushing expenditures for armaments were earmarked for reparations. But in 1919 the Allies, rightly mistrusting the good faith of the Junkers, committed a serious blunder: they extended the blockade after the armistice, fearing that any supplies from abroad would be used to implement military resistance. This led to German economic weakness, the mark falling from 24¢ to 6¢. But inasmuch as the French franc had also fallen from 19¢ to 7¢, the drop did not seem catastrophic.

The Germans early glimpsed the value of inflation as a national weapon. They used every crisis in politics and economics as proof that a ruined country could not behave otherwise. Money began to flood from the printing-presses. The mark fell to 2¢, at which point the middle classes faced ruin. Then it fell

even lower, and the Allies, to bolster German economy, reduced the reparations figures. The mark sank even further. German factories worked overtime, flooding world markets with cheap exports and fully employing labor. Thus the only class that could revolt — the working class — was stymied, and the middle classes looked obediently to the army and the government bureaucracy for salvation.

The German financiers, industrialists, and Junkers built up enormous deposits in dollars and pounds and *guilders*, while they paid their own people in worthless marks. Then in 1923, when reparations shipments were defaulted, Poincaré marched the French army into the Ruhr basin, the heart of German industry. Inflation now attained fantastic heights, the mark reaching 6 trillion to the dollar in Cologne. Disorders broke out everywhere in Germany.

The frightened Allies permitted the Germans to double their army so as to restore order. Thus the Old Guard had gained all along the line: the wealthy Junkers were free of debt, the peoples' savings had been rendered worthless, the industrialists had re-equipped German industry out of export profits and built up ample reserves abroad, farm prices were high, the drastic shortage of consumers goods had led to rioting and thus to an increase of armed authority, and the ruined middle classes were psychologically ready for a Messiah.

Foreign Loans: 1924–1929. When the drama was played out, the government initiated a solid currency, the *Rentenmark*. Under the Dawes Plan (1924), the Allies scaled down reparations to reasonable figures, and a plethora of American, British, Dutch, Swiss, and even French loans poured into the country. With the aid of these funds, Germany modernized her industries and public works. Warnings by far-sighted Germans that these loans would never be repaid and would be used for sinister ends were swept aside; instead still more grants of short-term credits to German banks were forthcoming. The Dawes Plan yielded to the more generous Young Plan (1929). Everyone seemed anxious to hand over as much money as possible to a group that had shown itself extremely adept at defaulting in 1919–24.

Germany's failure to repay these loans and credits finally caused the pound and the dollar to devalue. (Moreover, it led to a new series of devices whose object was to default while appearing to pay — Dr. Schacht's multiple marks schemes, 1933–38 — and to German domination of agricultural Europe by an ingenious barter system, 1934–40.) At any rate, from 1924 to 1929 Germany seemed restored. The first fruits of recovery were (1) a referendum to restore the properties belonging to the Kaiser, who now lived in exile in Holland and (2) the election of the Junker, Marshal von Hindenburg, as President of the Republic (1925). The Allies, however, allowed Germany to reenter the concert of Europe and to join the League.

Despite these portents, liberal sentiments were superficially widespread under the Weimar Republic; and while foreign money poured in, it seemed to the uninformed as though Germany, despite the terrorism of her officer clique, was essentially democratic.

With the beginning of the world depression in 1930, the flow of foreign money into Germany ceased. As if by magic, Hitler's vote rose eightfold and his Nazi Party obtained over 100 seats in the Reichstag (Parliament). Nazi armed bands roved the streets, terrorizing those who dissented from their ideas. The police were slack, and the judges almost invariably acquitted Hitler's Storm Troopers, and usually fined and jailed their victims. This pattern almost never varied. By the autumn of 1930 the real challenge of Nazism, not the formal façade of the Weimar Republic, dominated Germany.

The Rise of Hitler: 1930–1933. The Junkers had grown prosperous. But so uneconomic were their great estates and so extravagant were the officers in gambling casinos and night-clubs, that after two years of low farm prices the Junkers were again in financial need. They plundered the Treasury for subsidies. Their scheme, called the *Osthilfe*, was a direct steal from the State to keep their class solvent. The *Osthilfe* proved such a scandal, however, that the government strove with all its might to conceal its abuses. Now the army began to move closer to the despised Nazis. Fear of Socialism served as the pretext. Soon they consummated that dread union which Germans call *Roggen und Eisen* (rye and iron) that is, the fusion of the powerful industrialists and the landed estate-owners of Prussia. The Junkers looked upon the Nazis as a terrorist scum, to be used and then later discarded.

But the reactionary army elements, organized into the *Stahlhelm* (Steel Helmets), recoiled from the Nazis, so that it was not easy to effect the fusion. The Hindenburg clique thought it cleverer to play on the fear of the Nazis and thus force the Socialists to accept Hindenburg as "the lesser evil." Others, like the wealthy "press magnate" Hugenberg, remained obdurate and undisguisedly backed only reactionary army officers. Still others, like the Rhineland nobleman, von Papen, relied on devious intrigues to set up an aristocratic dictatorship. The Communists, on the extreme Left, saw in the general breakdown the possibility of a social revolution. Such was, in brief, the alignment of forces at the depth of the depression in 1932.

In 1931 Germany's banking system fell apart. The creditors made various stopgap arrangements and the banks resumed operations haltingly. Industrial production sank to pre-1900 levels. The Reichstag refused aid to the Bruening government (a Catholic-led coalition); it floundered in financial chaos and then issued a series of "emergency decrees" (January 1932) which smacked strongly of Fascism.

In the spring elections of 1932, Hitler received 38% of all votes for the presidency, as against Hindenburg, who won a majority, thanks largely to the support of the Socialists. Once in office, Hindenburg turned his back on those who had voted for him and appointed von Papen Chancellor, without even the pretence that von Papen was responsible to or desired by the Reichstag. The new Chancellor immediately issued decrees for tax-anticipation notes and other financial devices to enrich his group and free them from taxation.

At this show of arbitrary insolence, popular discontent mounted, and forced the dismissal of von Papen in the late autumn of 1932. Von Hindenburg then appointed von Schleicher, "the social General," an officer with a curious mixture of feudal and liberal ideas. The November 1932 presidential elections showed a significant drop in the Nazi vote to under 32%, while the Communist vote rose to 18%. At this juncture, the Hindenburg group, the Papen group, the Hugenberg Nationalists, and the *Stahlhelm* agreed to call in Hitler as Chancellor of a Nationalist government. They relied on their compact class organization to "tame" Hitler whenever it suited them, as they had always done in the past.

A transport strike in Berlin in January 1933 revealed acute divisions among the parties of the Left, the Socialists and the Communists. Hitler and the Nazis cunningly took the side of the strikers even more fanatically than did the Communists. The Junkers, realizing what was afoot, dismissed the incompetent von Schleicher and appointed Hitler Chancellor of the Reich (January 30, 1933). Hitler appeared before the senile Hindenburg, whom he had previously ridiculed and assailed, and acknowledged his appointment by kissing the old Marshal's hand.

Hitler in Power: the First Phase — January 30, 1933 to June 30, 1934. At first, the shock of the accession to power of the vulgar, ranting Hitler was such that it was considered merely a barbarian interlude. The parties of the Left were still bickering over the details of a Popular Front movement, as though they still had time. The government called new elections for March 5. When the Nazis realized that, despite street riots, terror, and a gagged radio and press they conceivably might not win, they seized providentially on the "Reichstag fire." They declared it was a Communist plot and the beginning of the "Red terror" in Germany.

Hitler arrested five men in connection with the Reichstag burning: a drugged Dutch youth, a German Communist deputy, two Bulgarian workmen who scarcely knew German, and a leading Bulgarian Communist living in exile in Germany, Dimitroff. The outside world soon became convinced that the Nazis themselves had fired the Reichstag, as a pretext for their persecution of the Left.

The March 5 elections took place in this highly charged atmosphere. The Nazis polled 44% of the vote, the Nationalists 8%, so that Hitler had a majority for a Nazi-Nationalist coalition. But this bare majority, the result of pressures, terror, and fraud, did not deceive Hitler. Even the Communist vote remained at about 15%. It was clear that the Nazis could not rely on the parliamentary façade to sustain their rule.

A quick succession of edicts settled the fate of the anti-Nazi opposition. First the Nazis attacked the Jews as the authors of Germany's miseries. Although the German Jews numbered at most 1% of the total population, plundering them promised to provide an excellent source of income for the Nazi party leaders. The Jews in other countries retaliated by defensive actions usually by boycotting German goods. Thereupon, Hitler thundered that the Jews desired nothing but Germany's destruction, and their possessions were expropriated.

Meanwhile Hitler obtained the Reichstag's endorsement of his foreign policy. He had to force the pace because the Lausanne Conference of 1932 had really ended reparations and the Nazis could no longer exploit them to explain Germany's previous woes. The Socialists in Parliament servilely endorsed Hitler's "patriotic" policy (he had already expelled the elected Communist deputies, jailing or exiling them). Thus certain that they would never resist, he proceeded to declare the Socialists illegal, jailed or exiled most of them also, and confiscated all the funds of the trade unions and other workers' organizations.

With these funds seized from the Jews, Socialists, Communists, trade unions, and cooperatives, Nazi finances improved considerably. Hitler then went to work on the Freemasons, prohibiting, plundering, and arresting them. Ultimately he banned the Seventh Day Adventists and Christian Scientists. And despite a *Concordat* with the Pope (1933), he pillaged and expropriated convents and monasteries, and degraded priests and nuns.

Still, his situation was not too brilliant. The Junkers suspected him of being more than their servant; while his own Nazi followers watched him with mingled feelings. Hitler had promised that, once Chancellor, he would close the Stock Exchange and large department stores, distribute the chain stores to loyal Nazi merchants, nationalize the banks and insurance companies, and put an end to "the slavery of interest" on loans. He had built up a following among the middle classes on these pledges.

No sooner was Hitler in power than he put the banker, Dr. Schacht, in charge of finances. Every move of Hitler strengthened German banks; and by an ingenious system of special currencies, he outwitted the foreign bankers. Instead of smashing the monopolies (many of whom had secretly financed the Nazi Party), he canceled their debts to the government and rewarded them with free distribution of stock, amounting in value to hundreds of millions of marks. Interest remained as before. True, the workers had "Strength through Joy" and other glittering organizations, but the dazed Nazi rank-and-file began to suspect that they had been fooled.

Such Nazis as Roehm, the chief of the Storm Troopers, Ernst, Heines, and others were blackguards, but they were also dupes. They saw that they were socially unwelcome at Berlin, and that the Junker Goering and the opportunist Goebbels enjoyed special favors. Roehm, Ernst, Heines, and others had considered themselves National *Socialists:* now they began to agitate for "the second revolution." They plotted to gain power for the Nazi Storm Troopers, who were to rank with the army.

Meanwhile secret rearmament had begun in Germany. Though constantly denied, the outside world knew that it was going on. France and Britain took it lightly, feeling that Germany could be easily handled so long as the Rhineland was demilitarized and no conscription existed in Germany. By 1934 rearmament reached such proportions that Nazi Germany's economic recovery began to compare with Britain's. The Nazi barter system did not increase exports as a whole, but directed them according to political exigencies; German exports soon dominated the trade of southeastern Europe. This was the lever with which Nazi Germany pried apart the small, economically depressed states from their alliance with France.

Rearmament: 1934–1936. In June 1934 Hitler staged a party "purge," murdering several hundred Storm Troop leaders. Others who found death at the hands of the Nazis included General von Schleicher. Thus Hitler made common cause with the army, the Junkers, the leaders of finance and industry, and the government bureaucracy as against the plebeian Storm Troopers who had followed their Fuehrer through thick and thin since 1920. For a time, the ferment in the ranks of the Storm Troops jeopardized Hitler's rule.

But the "second revolution" proved abortive. Luckily for Hitler, Hindenburg died; and the Nazi leader ostentatiously attended his funeral in the East Prussian swamp-lands. The burial ceremony was reminiscent of a gathering of Gothic barbarians. Now President as well as Chancellor, Hitler humbled the aristocrats who had planned to use him as their tool.

He consolidated his power as a result of three far-reaching moves: (1) increase in employment with no increase in real wages, so that both labor and capital were satisfied — the workers with jobs, the employers with higher profits; (2) savage repression of all dissenters, so that night descended on the human mind in Germany; (3) administrative unification of all Germany, abolishing the old particularist states, duchies, kingdoms, and free cities. Thus the Nazis left open no available avenue of opposition to their régime except the remote possibility of total opposition throughout the entire Reich.

In foreign affairs, Hitler took Germany out of the League of Nations and unilaterally denounced one treaty after another. Several times, when his fortunes seemed to ebb, he received a friendly gesture from governing circles in Britain. In fact, newspaper proprietors like Lord Rothermere in London exalted Hitler as a model for Great Britain. German national pride was duly flattered.

Nazism went hand-in-hand with terror. Such acts as the murder of Chancellor Dollfuss of Austria, kidnapings and murders in Czechoslovakia, the assassination of King Alexander of Yugoslavia and French Minister Barthou at Marseilles, and the murder of Premier Duca of Rumania were either Nazi deeds or committed by Nazi-inspired groups.

Within Germany, the "coordinated" newspapers invented an uninterrupted series of grievances, denunciations, and crises, until hysteria replaced normal behavior. The Nazi régime kept the Germans politically busy much of the time by consulting them on plebiscites and ratifications. Moreover, the radio broadcasts to the people were what the Nazis wanted them to hear, and little information was allowed to percolate from abroad. The stock device for silencing opponents became the concentration camp.

By the spring of 1935 Hitler reestablished military conscription. No foreign nation seriously protested. Now the army enjoyed prestige again and had work to do.

In the spring of 1936 the Nazis reoccupied the Rhineland and proceeded to remilitarize it. This was not only the first overt violation of the Versailles Treaty but also the first move toward the creation by force of the "Greater Germany." Though the French seemed willing to intervene, the British sought peace; and so the French, themselves divided and worried by their own elections due in six weeks, abstained from action. This move of the Germans constituted the acid test. The failure of France and Great Britain to prevent it persuaded Hitler that he could safely go ahead. Hitler had previously proposed an armament treaty by which Germany would have 300,000 regular army soldiers plus millions of Storm Troopers and *Stahlhelm* veterans. Now he ceased to emphasize these para-military formations and built up the regular army without let or hindrance.

But he retained the Storm Troopers for a special purpose. At the colossal Nuremburg rallies of the Nazi Party every September, the Storm Troopers marched with shovels and other insignia of labor, while Hitler fulminated against the Jews, Bolshevism, internationalists, and the plutocratic democracies. In 1936 he concluded the Anti-Comintern Pact with Japan and Italy.

"Germany Must Expand!": 1936–1939. By 1936 all Germany was a workshop humming with war industry. The country's capital was almost exhausted. She had accumulated hoards of essential fuels, chemicals, and metals, but this "recovery" did not create adequate new purchasing power, since the goods manufactured were not useful either in production or consumption. Super-combines, initiated in heavy industry, largely redounded to the benefit of Nazi overlords like Goering: the party leadership plundered enterprises over which it exercised increasing control. The time was fast approaching when mere newspaper "episodes" would not suffice. Germany must soon, as Winston Churchill declared, expand or explode.

Hitler tested the democracies in the Ethiopian crisis (1935–36) and the Spanish Civil War (1936–39): he found them as soft as butter. By the spring of 1938, Germany possessed a superb, highly mechanized army and the best air force in Europe; she even had submarines again, as a result of an Anglo-German naval agreement (1935). Now Hitler felt that he could seize as much plunder as he wished whenever he so desired. His seizure and annexation of Austria (March 1938) met with only perfunctory protests from abroad. At the same time, he revealed the basic weakness of his "Axis" and "Anti-Comintern" partner, Mussolini, who allowed him to act as he pleased in Italy's "sphere of influence," Austria.

After the Munich pact of September 1938 (See *Czechoslovakia, History*), the Nazis began their mutilation of Czechoslovakia. At the same time, the revelation of French weakness cut the ground from beneath the Franco-Soviet pact. Then in the spring of 1939 Hitler destroyed Czechoslovakia altogether. Though he was roundly condemned, he met with no effective opposition.

Carefully watching the protracted negotiations between Britain and Soviet Russia in the spring and summer of 1939, he waited for an opportunity to blackmail the Western powers into giving him power over Poland. He had always shouted that he was the guardian of Europe against Bolshevism, and since 1933 he had enjoyed considerable sympathy abroad because of his anti-Communist imprecations. Now he sent his Foreign Minister, Ribbentrop, to Moscow to treat with the despised Bolsheviks! On August 23, 1939, Germany and the U.S.S.R. signed a nonaggression pact.

Since Poland had declined Soviet help under any circumstances, Poland's position was not materially changed. But to Hitler, the main object of the pact with the U.S.S.R. was to frighten the Western allies into granting him still more concessions short of war. If, he calculated, Britain and France had not resisted him when they had Soviet Russia as a potential ally, they would certainly do nothing now.

Germany Unleashes World War II: 1939–1944. Hitler's calculations were both right and wrong. When Germany invaded Poland, Britain and France gave no effective aid to the Poles. But when Polish resistance collapsed, Hitler found that Soviet Russia had occupied eastern Poland and all of the three Baltic States. Russia had come nearer to Germany's industrial centers than the Germans had penetrated to the heart of the coveted Soviet Ukraine. Hitler outwardly accepted this new state of affairs, though, as he later revealed, Russia's actions rankled.

For six months thereafter the war took on a strange character. The naval war was slight, the war in the air almost nonexistent, and artillery exchanged only occasional salvoes. While the Allies waited for the economic collapse of Germany, the Nazis invaded Norway, Denmark, and a month later Belgium, Luxembourg, and the Netherlands and, in a six weeks' war (May-June, 1940), subjugated France. Germany's plunder in the prostrated areas was so great that it became a major factor for the next three years in sustaining the German war machine.

Later Nazi excursions into the Balkans contributed vital foodstuffs and raw materials to Germany. In varying degrees and in nominally different forms, Rumania, Hungary, Bulgaria, Yugoslavia, and Greece fell under Hitler's control. Italy, once an ally, became an appendage of the Reich. On September 27, 1940 Japan became a formal ally.

Flushed with victory, and confident that Britain had been desolated by the aerial "Blitz" and the submarine blockade, Hitler launched his sudden invasion of the Soviet Union in June 1941. The initial German penetrations were deep; but despite the conquest of a territory nearly four times that of Germany, and one of the richest on earth, the costs of acquiring and holding this western area of Russia far exceeded the benefits. For the first time in Hitler's career, a series of territorial gains had not yielded an increment.

Meanwhile, the strain on German manpower compelled the Nazis to rely increasingly on forced labor for industry. Foreign slave laborers within Germany soon became indispensable to her armament production. No gambler in history has ever attempted to achieve so much on the basis of a state like Germany, relatively small in territory and natural resources, with an internal social organization compounded of terror and slavery.

The Nazis had not, however, lost their cunning. They followed a conscious policy of weakening France biologically by tearing some 2,000,000 Frenchmen from their families, and by starving, massacring, and depopulating large populations in many other countries, while the Germans themselves were better nourished and thus biologically better prepared for a third world war. The canker of Nazism lodged in the heart of civilization, Europe. Jews were exiled, starved, murdered, cremated; Poles enslaved by the millions and over a million martyred; the very Serbian people seemed doomed as were the Greeks; and a village, Lidiče, razed to the ground and its inhabitants massacred or enslaved, manifested to the Czechs that the day of the Assyrian flayer had returned.

But German over-extension began to reveal itself in reverses in Africa (winter of 1942–43) and particularly on the Soviet front, after the Nazi defeat at Stalingrad (end of 1942). The alliance with Japan did not fundamentally alter the Nazi position in Europe. By 1944 it grew clear that, as in 1917, Germany had to contend with the aroused industrial might of the U.S.A.; that she had underestimated British resiliency and courage; and that, as before, she had wholly failed to understand the new Russia. The specter of military defeat loomed over Germany. By September 1944 the Russians had penetrated East Prussia and the Anglo-American forces were in Germany. Rumania, Bulgaria, and Finland deserted the ramshackle structure. France, Belgium, and Luxembourg rose from the dead.

Stakes in the Peace

Germany's stake in the peace is not of her choosing. In her case, the query is, rather, what shall be done with Germany?

The suggestions are innumerable. Some contemplate the restoration of Germany to something like the Weimar democracy (1919–1933) with the added burdens of reparations and territorial adjustments and the punishment of proven overt war criminals, the "re-education" of the people by their own experience, and the disarmament of the country. This solution is popular with pacifists.

On the other extreme are the exterminators, who insist that the Germans have been invaders and desolators of mankind since the Teutonic tribes hurled themselves on the superior peoples of Roman culture to send them into the Gothic night. Less extreme are those who would allow this generation of Germans to live but would make sure that they can have no children. Others wish to deprive them of crucial territories, such as Silesia and East Prussia, so as to weaken their future war potential. Others wish to compel German labor to repair the ravages of the Nazi crimes in the lands they invaded. Some wish to limit their punishment to depriving Germany of the Ruhr and Rhineland areas, which would then be assimilated to Western democratic culture. The Englishman, Lord Vansittart, and his following clamor for their permanent secondary position and some kind of inherent overseership by superior civilizations.

For some time Soviet opinion held that the German worker might show an unsuspected manhood and that once he destroyed his rulers he would have the right to shape his own destiny, but, of course, after he had compensated the Nazi victims. Soviet opinion seems less sanguine today.

Some favor mere re-education, holding that the *psyche* and not external or political agencies are at the source of German behavior and that the German can be redeemed. Some, especially among formal intellectuals, see the Germans as merely an intensified example of reactionary attitudes, lamentably too

commonly diffused. Others, still more cynical, regard the Nazis as the agents of other and more powerful abettors, and hold that their thinking is by no means confined to Germany. Many scholars have favored short-term supervision of Germany by a League of Nations capable of enforcing decisions, and their gradual reintegration into the commonalty of mankind.

It would not be profitable to examine all the plans, of which there are many, some ingenious and critical, many well-documented but capricious, and others simply the honest emotional products of the passion for justice among innocent victims.

All plans for the future of Germany may be subsumed under two headings: (1) those which hold that specific forms of German social organization, with their historic impact, are the cause of the many instances of German aggression; (2) those which hold that the Germans (whether by inherent nature or by historic factors so deep as to be equivalent to inherent behavior) are so constituted that they can never be permitted equal responsibility with other nations. The first seek to analyze, control, remedy, and slowly re-establish the German people as part of world culture; the second deny that possibility.

The constructive course is one which will tend to make of the future generations of Germans something which will be capable of cooperating with the rest of humanity rather than one which assumes at the outset that no improvement in the German people can ever be brought about.

The editor of this book has suggested in *The Time for Decision* that a reading of German history shows that the General Staff, as the embodiment of the military class, is the perennial force that dominates Germany, whatever its political vesture or economic appearance. The General Staff regards defeat as only a temporary setback. It always connives at the restoration of German armed might. It uses nationals within other countries as the carriers of its power and the agency for enfeebling resistance. It used central government within Germany and complete "Statism" as its lever for control. Therefore, any peace arrangement that enables the occult power of the General Staff to reassert itself, must fail of its purpose.

The editor has suggested a plan for the decentralization of Germany, which, after depriving her of the principal seat of the Junkers, East Prussia, divides her into three states. The first is made up of Bavaria, Württemberg, Baden, and Hesse-Darmstadt, together with the Rhineland and the Ruhr — predominantly Catholic, and liberal in political outlook. A second state in North Germany consists of upper Hesse, Thuringia, Westphalia, Oldenburg, and Hamburg, basically Protestant, but freed from the old Prussian class basis. The third state is the Northeast, consisting of old Prussia, Mecklenburg, and Saxony, with its capital at Berlin.

The editor has, of course, considered the objections that may be urged against this plan. He has analyzed Germany's centrifugal tendencies, pointing out that the unity of Germany is imposed, rather superficial, and recent (*The Time for Decision*, pp. 351 ff.). The proposed tri-partite Germany would not, of course, possess a unified military organization nor a centralized financial and commercial economy, yet it would retain internal Germanic cultures and permit of a humane and democratic unfolding. The editor also suggests that the intransigent German militarists may even try to carry out their plan under the disguise of revolutionary ideals. These Protean possibilities require United Nations' supervision, until the healing process is made manifest in the Germans' now indurated spirit.

Germany has exhibited two central tendencies, both unique in Western society. One, the economic, is an excessive accumulation of industrial capital, so great that it has impelled German industry to economic adventure instead of to the ordinary pursuit of business. The second, the social, arises from the holding of large, unprofitable landed estates, whose owners constitute a hereditary military caste.

The cultural gap between classes is extreme. Hence, an enormous industrial technique and a docile people are harnessed to a nearly feudal social order. Indus-trial power, elsewhere associated with liberalism, is here combined with military power, to create the most explosive social situation in the Occident. And no solution of Germany's difficulties is worth while that ignores these fundamentals: the union of landed militarists and industrial overlords.

The Germans have a great talent for organization, for science, and for industry. They show a perseverance which could work wonders if it were socially directed, instead of being misdirected by aggressors. Fortunately, by 1970 German population should stabilize or decline and this may aid a peaceful state of mind.

But no solution of the German problem can be perfect: no payment of reparations in money, commodities, or toil can atone for the shame, humiliation, and torture that the Germans have inflicted on others nor the wanton injury they have done to their own better nature.

GREAT BRITAIN
THE UNITED KINGDOM OF GREAT BRITAIN AND NORTHERN IRELAND

The Land and the People

Since the middle of the 18th century until recent years, Great Britain has been the foremost nation of the world in political influence. Her home population and area would not, of course, confer this importance upon her. But Great Britain is the seat of the British Empire, or British Commonwealth of Nations, whose territory and population are at least a fourth of the world's. Until recently, Britain was undisputed "mistress of the seas," that is, she had a navy without peer, and as such, dominated the oceans of the earth. No discussion of the peace in almost any area of the globe can be meaningful without taking into account Britain's important position there.

Area. Great Britain is an ancient kingdom, founded in the 9th century and incorporating the equally ancient realm of Scotland. Her area is 94,663 square miles in the homeland (England, Wales, Scotland, Northern Ireland, the Isle of Man, the Channel Islands), but the empire area, including dominions, protectorates, mandates, and condominiums is estimated at 13,355,426 square miles — more than four times the area of continental U.S.A.

Population. The people of the homeland are estimated at 47,907,000. The British Empire as a totality may now number as many as 572,000,000. Although it is difficult to arrive at the precise world percentage of the Empire population, owing to uncertainties of the population of the world, a fair figure would appear to be 26.5 per cent.

In addition to her officially reckoned population, Britain has special interests in Egypt, whose inhabitants exceed 16,000,000. The principal British dominion in North America is Canada; in Africa, the Union of South Africa; in Oceania, Australia and New Zealand; and the crown jewel in Asia is the compact realm of India, which, with Ceylon and Burma, totals over 400,000,000 people.

Britain's Island Position. The rise of Great Britain has fascinated and mystified historians. How did this small island come to achieve such historic supremacy? Explanations vary all the way from the geographic to the psychological and political; but since geographical data can be measured and the facts are undisputed, this is the safest point of departure.

Britain is nearest Europe across the shallow Strait of Dover, about 21 miles wide, and facing the northeast corner of France. This is the location of the famed "chalk cliffs of Albion," for which the Romans named England "Albion," the white country. The Channel to the south varies from 21 to 83 miles, and in the east the British coast faces the North Sea (across which the Angles, after whom England was named, sailed from the German lowlands in the 6th century). To the west, the coast of Scotland faces a stormy sea rolling on to Iceland. Southward, the mountainous coast of Wales is separated from Ireland by a channel averaging under 80 miles. Ireland, the western island, extends over 32,000 square miles, but most of it is constituted as Eire (See *Eire*).

The insular position of Britain was no protection until she possessed an adequate navy. In the early days, invading Celt and Roman, Pict and Saxon, Dane and Norman, found Britain's water boundaries no obstacle to swift conquest. The increased wealth of the country at the end of the 13th century plus the dissensions on the European continent enabled Britain to shape her destiny with only rare dangers of invasion.

In the 16th century the modern British navy was born, and with the establishment of British naval superiority over the Netherlands, France, Spain, Portugal, and Denmark, Britain's security was achieved. Not until 1914 was this security again threatened — this time by the rising commercial power of Germany.

While England's island position unquestionably explains her maritime development, Britain's privileged history must be based on other sources than geography. Free from the virtually incessant land wars on the European continent, Britain's economy could develop more rapidly. Except for the Dutch cities, the feudal system died earlier in England than in any other land. Intermarriage of noble and commoner left her the only country without a genuine aristocracy — a country in which even royalty married commoners and in which the aristocracy was re-recruited largely from traders and manufacturers. The absence of a stratified *noblesse* led to the growth of a fluid society; and religious dissent led to an absence of uniformity in social attitudes.

The struggle between landowner and merchant eventuated in political *parties* in England before any other land, and this small country has exemplified continuous parliamentary government for centuries. England has taught the world the acceptance by the minority of defeat in elections; the questioning of authority — even of royal authority; the common law as against the Roman law; the *habeas corpus;* religious toleration; and the use of science by industry. Britain was the first land in which contract largely replaced status and money relations rivaled those of class. However much her conservatives have sought to arrest the process of democratization, they have always failed in the end. The English view of the world reached its ultimate in the American Revolution, with Washington and Jefferson. In France in 1789, British liberal views (the "Whiggish" view) developed into dogmas and shaped Western history for a century and a half.

The Land. Great Britain is not a fertile land. A large section consists of fens, moors, Scottish heather, unproductive highlands, or stony valleys of Wales. The rainfall is average in the east and excessive in the west. There is little sunlight; only in the south and southeast is it sufficient for rich crops. The climate is generally mild. Snows rarely visit London and the south, and the summers are not hot. London's summers average 63°, winters over 37°. Despite legend, fogs are not common in England, but in the humid cities, hundreds of thousands of chimneys and uncontrolled factory smoke result in the well-known "peasoupers."

The small quantity of good soil, the inadequate sunlight, and the modest area of land free from drenching rains mean that the north and west of England and Scotland are mostly pasture- and grasslands. Some of the small area that is good for farming is encroached upon by city and town dwellings, and, as the British are devoted to the one-family house, miles of "ribbon dwellings" occupy what could have been vegetable farms around her large cities.

The most abundant natural resource in the country is coal, a fourth of the estimated reserves of Europe, enough to last at least 700 years at the present rate of mining. The main coal centers are South Wales, Yorkshire, Northumberland, and the Clyde near Glasgow. Iron ore, mostly low-grade, is distributed widely throughout the country. The tin mines of Cornwall (southwest England) were for centuries the world's chief source of supply, but now produce less than 2% of world output. The country has few petroleum resources, apart from oil shale.

The People. Great Britain has been peopled by successive waves of conquest and settlement. Hence, the composition of her population is one of the most mixed in Europe, chiefly of Celts, Saxons, Danes, and Normans. After 1500 there began a continuous inflow of Flemings, Huguenots, and other peoples in search of refuge from persecution.

The British are a fair people near the North Sea and brunet in the western part of the island. Their stature cannot be considered as a mean figure because the wealthier classes average over 5 feet 8 inches and workers average under 5 feet 5 inches. The average height of the British army in World War I was slightly less than that of the French, although the number of tall men was much greater.

The British are an urban people, the city dwellers of the world *par excellence*. Nearly 9,000,000 live in "greater London," and four of her cities (with their immediate suburbs) number over a million inhabitants: Liverpool, Birmingham, Glasgow, and Manchester. Actually, however, whole areas are practically continuous cities. It can be said that 4 Britons out of 5 are town dwellers.

Population Prospects. This people has one of the lowest birthrates: England under 15 per thousand, Scotland about 17. The deathrate is also quite low, having averaged about 12 during the last decade. Infant mortality is only 53 in England, but 69 in Scotland. The forecast for England, however, is for a sharp decline in population within a generation, the probability being that by 1980 the people will be less than 40,000,000 — some estimates put it as low as 38,000,000.

Britain was once a land of emigrants, but that outflow has been much reduced. She has populated most of Canada, Australia, New Zealand, has contributed nearly half the white inhabitants of South Africa. In the U.S.A., emigrants from Great Britain and Northern Ireland outnumber those from Eire two to one. Large numbers of Britons lived abroad for trade, administration, or, frequently, for pleasure.

Language. Britain is the center of diffusion of the English language, the principal commercial speech of

SHETLAND IS.

ORKNEY IS.

NORWAY

HEBRIDES

SCAPA FLOW

Inverness

SCOTLAND

Aberdeen

Glasgow

Edinburgh

NO.
IRELAND

Belfast

Galway

Newcastle

NORTH

SEA

Dublin

EIRE

Cork

Liverpool

Hull

Birmingham

WALES

Coventry

ENGLAND

Bristol

London

The Hague

NETHERLANDS

Plymouth

Southampton

Dover

Dunkirk

Brussels

Cologne

ENGLISH CHANNEL

Cherbourg

BELGIUM

COPYRIGHT, FIELD PUBLICATIONS

mankind. Spoken today by 200,000,000 people, it is understood by many more. It dominates more than half the commercial exchanges of the world. Its enormous, profound, and varied creative literature, its large technical vocabulary and its reference works, together with its two points of view — British and American — have assured it a secure position against rival tongues.

Religion and Education. The established Church of England is the Protestant Episcopal, the head of which is the King. A large number of Englishmen, however, profess the nonconformist Protestant faiths, the principal ones of which are the Baptist, Wesleyan (Methodist), and Congregational. These have all become more important in the U.S.A. than the Church of England. The established Church of Scotland is Presbyterian. But there are also many dissenters. Roman Catholics in Britain, numbering almost 5% of the population, are found largely among the Irish

immigrants. Great Britain is the most important of the Protestant countries of Europe. Religion is free; the few vestiges of early restrictions are not observed in practice, although the King must always be a Protestant.

Elementary education is tuition-free, compulsory, and universal. High schools enroll about 560,000, and the "public schools," as the large, historic private schools are called, have a large attendance. The names of Eton, Harrow, and Winchester are typical: from their graduates come an extraordinary proportion of ministers of the Crown, diplomats, and high military men. The universities have about 55,000 students — some 11,000 in residence at the ancient seats of learning at Oxford and Cambridge, and the rest in the newer urban universities. There are numerous higher scientific and technical institutions, as well as specialized schools for colonial and military training.

The education of the people is on a fairly high level,

but neither in the diffusion of books nor in the pursuit of serious literature can the mass of the British people be compared with the Scandinavians, Dutch, French, or Swiss. Czechoslovakia and pre-Nazi Germany were also superior. Formal education has been largely a middle- and upper-class affair, although in recent years labor groups have shown zeal in fostering the Workers' Education Colleges, and these are becoming widespread.

The Nation's Economy

Agriculture. Agriculture in Great Britain, unlike that of any other country, is not important except in time of war. Only 7% of persons gainfully employed are in farming — the smallest proportion in the world, while 51% are employed in industries — the highest relative proportion in the world. In Britain, 1,200,000 people are engaged in agriculture, as compared with 7,700,000 in France, whose total population is smaller. Britain is thus the most crowded country in the world — there are 3,000 people to every square mile of arable land — even more than in Japan.

British farmers put up a valiant battle to feed this teeming mass, and their yield per acre and per man is the first among the important countries. But not even a wheat yield a third higher than that of France can do the impossible. Britain's 17,500 arable square miles compare to more than 80,000 in France or to more than 500,000 square miles in the U.S.A. Obviously, Britain must always import a large part of her food. The arable area is, of course, capable of some extension, and recent efforts to increase the food supply during wartime suggest that British crops can be augmented. If the large estates are more economically utilized and the excessive pastoral areas are returned to crops, Britain may possibly be able to raise half of her domestic requirements.

The animal economy produces a good supply of meat and wool, although not enough for domestic consumption. Britain produces 50,000 tons of wool clip a year, by far the largest output in Europe except for the Soviet Union. This wool is of excellent quality as is almost all the agricultural and pastoral production of Britain. Meat production is characteristic — fully 50% is prime beef.

Poultry and dairy products, though celebrated, supply only a part of domestic consumption. Food produced in Britain commands the highest prices. Actually Argentina and Australia supply the beef, and Denmark and Ireland the bacon and eggs for most middle-class families in Britain. Fortunately the fish catch, a fourth of Europe's, is abundant and cheap.

Land ownership is excessively concentrated. It has been estimated that about 2,500 families own more than half of Great Britain. Even the large majority of the productive area is tenant-farmed. From the Norman Conquest of 1066 to the long series of land enclosure acts (ending in 1832), the nobility and the "squirearchy" have taken the land away from the yeomanry. The surplus population flowed into the towns or went abroad — and built Britain's industry and empire.

Mining. Britain's coal production, the foundation of her industry, is the highest per capita among the large nations. She averages about 236,000,000 tons per annum, as against 186,000,000 for Germany and 400,000,000 for the U.S.A. In steel, British production is tending to stabilize at about 12,500,000 tons, although in crises it has sunk to less than half. Its proportion to the American production, however, is almost always the same, the two rising and falling together. It is about a fourth of the United States' and two-thirds of Germany's production. In pig iron Britain produces only a third as much as Germany, but in copper and tin smelting she is supreme.

Industry and Employment. Great Britain is the most important industrial area in the world for her size and population. Over half of the people are engaged in industry. In use of horsepower per man and in machinery investment and mechanization, she is first in Europe (though second to the U.S.A. and Canada). However, in production per man, Britain is slightly behind Germany.

She has an enormous body of skilled artisans, the true capital of a country. The Britons excel whether as shipwrights, wool-carders, fine cotton spinners, engineers, or tailors. Like the French, they have gone over increasingly to quality production, leaving the cruder markets to Germany and Japan.

By the 1930's the shift from heavy to light industry had become a permanent trend, but the pressing need for armaments changed the emphasis back to England's one-time supremacy — heavy industry.

Great Britain was the first country in Europe to be industrialized. The Industrial Revolution took place there seventy years before it occurred in France. Britain was the first to exploit the use of water-power, coal, and steam. She was the first to transform herself from a land of peasants into a land of industrial townspeople. She was the first to use the railroad — even today her railway system is the densest of any important country — and the first to employ the steamship on a gigantic scale. While she later found a sharp competitor in the U.S.A. in industrial inventions, until 1860 her use of them so far exceeded that of other nations that she became known as "the workshop of the world."

In order to obtain cheap food from other countries and to import the cheapest raw materials, which she transformed into exports, Britain adopted a free-trade policy (1846). Her ships en route for imports carried British coal when they lacked export cargo. Every inch of space on every boat and every trip of Britain's shipping were utilized whenever possible — which helped considerably in building up this industrial supremacy. Until the rise of the U.S.A. and Germany in the last third of the 19th century, Britain's lead was uncontested.

Today her rôle is more modest. And yet Lancashire is still outstanding for textiles, Glasgow and Newcastle for engineering and shipbuilding, industrial London for diversified manufactures, Birmingham for light industries and hardware. South Wales, as a coal, iron working, and smelters region ranks as the industrial rival of the Ruhr in Germany and the Pittsburgh area in the U.S.A.

She has 50,000,000 cotton spindles as compared with 10,100,000 in France, 9,800,000 in Germany, and 9,200,000 in the U.S.S.R.

Ordinary peacetime factory employment exceeds 8,400,000 persons. American factory employment in peacetime numbers under 8,000,000. The mere statement of these ratios shows that Britain must export to live, for she has no domestic market comparable to that of the U.S.A., for her large industrial production.

The occupational distribution of the British people shows a high ratio of persons in trade and finance (3,400,000), thus confirming Napoleon's epigram that the British were a "nation of shopkeepers." But most striking is the number of domestic servants — 2,700,-000, as against only 900,000 in nearby France. The ratio of domestic servants to persons employed is 1 to 8. Owing to the socialization of public utilities in many cities, the rise of social services, and the normal naval and colonial armed services personnel, there are 1,700,000 people in government service in normal times. (This would be equivalent to 5,000,000 in the U.S.A.)

The British factory workers and persons engaged in transport and mining are almost all members of large trade unions, which are also politically articulate.

Wealth. In per capita national wealth Britain has two-thirds that of the United States. On a population basis of 48,000,000 in Britain to 133,000,000 in America, Britain would thus be a fourth as rich as the U.S.A. But in Europe her relative position admits of no dispute. She is wealthier than Germany, per capita, by 5 to 3; than France by 5 to 4.

Income. In national income she is also first in Europe, exceeding even the prosperous Netherlands and Switzerland in income per person. Since her per capita income is half that of the U.S.A., on a population basis, Britain has under a fifth of America's income.

Of Britain's national wealth, in 1939 about 17% to 18% was invested abroad. Apart from the Netherlands, no country exceeds this ratio, and only France, with 16%, approached it. The figures of British foreign trade confirm this: Her exports have generally been about $1,800,000,000 a year *less* than her imports.

This enormous deficit points to other sources of income than exports with which to pay for imports. These are (1) dividends and interest received from investments abroad, (2) profits from shipping the cargoes of other nations, (3) insurance premiums received in London and Liverpool from foreign lands, (4) profits from direct British enterprise abroad, (5) receipts out of taxation, such as pensions of civil servants paid from abroad, (6) profit from international banking transactions. In normal times the profits out of "invisible income" exceed those from foreign trade by 5 to 1. As a counter-expenditure there must be reckoned the large tourist spendings of Englishmen abroad.

The flow of capital out of Britain, which made her the largest creditor nation on earth, diminished after 1928 and dried up effectively during the 1930's. Home-building and the development of light industries, together with the modernization of heavy industries and preparations for defense replaced the centuries-old export of capital.

During the recent war-years, Great Britain has been compelled to liquidate most of her holdings abroad. We shall observe later (See *Stakes in the Peace*) that this necessity has altered the trade and income basis of the kingdom.

Banking and Government Finance. Since 1693 and until World War I, London had been the international banking capital of the world. As late as 1911, more than half of all the world's commercial bills of exchange were drawn in pounds sterling on London. As late as 1937 London bank deposits exceeded those of New York.

The British pound sterling was valued at $4.86 in United States currency from 1836 to 1916. During World War I, it was stabilized at about $4.75, by arrangement; and later it slid to $3.18. In 1924 it was again established at $4.86, but in 1931 it fell to $3.12. When the American dollar was devalued, the pound rose to $5.50 — only to fall to about $4.90, which became a long-term rate of exchange.

During the present war, the pound fell to the panic level of $3 when France surrendered in May 1940; but in the autumn of the same year it was re-established at $4.04. Its prestige, as expressed in the phrase, "as safe as the Bank of England," is not what it once was. It is not unshakable. The gold pound is selling today officially for 2 pounds in paper money, or twice its face value. If there were a free market in gold, it would sell at a still higher figure in paper pounds.

The financial position of England during World War II is not as yet definite, but one thing is certain: India, to take the leading instance, has been transformed from a debtor into a creditor. In 1939–1943 Great Britain's payments in excess of income reached some £3,000,000,000 ($12,000,000,000, assuming the pound to be worth $4 for the present). She also faces short-term claims on her of £1,500,000,000. Since it is manifestly impossible for a country that has restricted the manufacture of civilian goods in wartime to pay for these claims in goods, Great Britain has been compelled to "block" these payments, that is, the creditor nations have these deposits in London, but cannot draw on them except to use them internally in Britain; but they cannot be paid externally in either cash or goods.

The national debt has increased during the war. The domestic debt, $36,000,000,000, rose to $86,000,-000,000 by the end of 1943 (taking the pound at $4.04). The foreign debt increased from $4,800,000,000 to $6,000,000,000 (exclusive of lend-lease). This burden of $92,000,000,000 is equivalent to $2,000 per person, or $10,000 per average family of five. It is more than two-and-a-half times the peak wartime income of Great Britain. It is more than 4 times her peak peacetime annual income. However, as Winston Churchill has asserted, there are few families in Britain that do not hold $1,000 worth of war bonds.

Government budgets have reflected wartime needs. Great Britain has always been a severely taxed country. For a long period, income and estate taxes were about the highest in the world. In 1938 the government spent $5,500,000,000, in 1943–44 about $25,-000,000,000. This is equivalent to over 60% of national wartime income and actually exceeds peacetime income. If the service of the debt is added to pre-war government activities, and to this are added the burdens of war pensions and reconstruction costs, permanent government costs must rise to more than half the peak peace income.

Price controls during World War II have prevented a runaway inflation, but the stock market has risen as a hedge against ultimately higher prices. Interest rates are low, but this is largely the result of deliberate Treasury policy.

Foreign Trade. Great Britain is the largest trader in the world. In 1938 her imports were nearly $4,200,-000,000 and her exports $2,350,000,000. She accounts for nearly 18% of the world's imports and 10.4% of its exports. About 32% of all she consumes comes from abroad.

Her importance as an import nation became strikingly clear in 1931 when she departed from the gold standard. By this action, she was unable to buy as much as she had bought before, for she had cheapened her currency (the pound sterling) as against the sound money of other countries. In order to keep Britain as a customer, the "sound money" countries had no alternative but to sell to Britain at lower prices or face a serious loss in exports. In order to alleviate the contingent effects of declining prices, the U.S.A. ultimately devalued the dollar.

Britain's immense trade, exceeding that of the U.S.A. by more than half, is largely carried in British bottoms. Her gross tonnage of over 17,200,000 in steam and motor vessels (with the British Empire, 20,100,000) was almost a third of the world's peacetime marine power. However, this proportion has declined since 1914 when the tonnage of Great Britain and her Empire amounted to 44% of the world's.

A British White Paper, issued in London in October 1944, revealed that between 1938 and 1943 Britain's export trade declined by 51% in value and by more than 70% in volume.

History: 1914-1944.

The November 1918 armistice found Great Britain very much changed from the country that had entered the war in 1914. The foundations were the same: a monarchy the symbol of imperial unity, a House of Lords socially exalted but historically secondary, and a House of Commons that was the true lawmaking body. But in the course of the war the sacrifices and labor of the common man had changed the emphasis from class to commonalty.

Victorian manners, values, and literature were dead. The U.S.A. had risen to surpass the British Empire in wealth; the British dominions were now free of any dependent colonial feeling; royal houses had tumbled in many lands, as a wave of democracy flooded Europe; and in the old Russian Empire, perennial rival of Britain in Asia, the historic rôle of social classes was now threatened at its source. At the same time, patriotism in Britain had risen to its highest pitch since the victory at Waterloo.

David Lloyd George, then Prime Minister of a coalition government, struck while the victory bells were still ringing: he called for an election. During the war, the electorate had been trebled. Property qualifications and plural voting had both been abolished. British women over thirty years of age were given the ballot. Lloyd George had been the man most hated by British Conservatives (Tories), for he had been the pre-war author of the Land Taxes and the propositions to humble the House of Lords. Hence, before they would agree to join with him in the coming election (1918), the Conservatives imposed harsh demands: he had to concede them enough seats in Parliament to become a majority.

The "Khaki Election" and the Coalition Government: 1918-1922. The election proved a landslide for Lloyd George and the Tories. Labor and the Liberal party were almost smothered. The Irish elected extreme Nationalists who refused to enter the Imperial parliament (See *Eire*, *History*). Labor, however, succeeded the old Liberal party as "His Majesty's Opposition."

The British economist Keynes characterized the new Parliament (1919) as "hard-faced men who looked as if they had done well out of the war." They backed Lloyd George's reparations demands of Germany, accepted the Treaty of Versailles, and they were even content that Britain receive almost no territorial acquisitions, except League of Nations mandates. Great Britain entered the League, expecting President Woodrow Wilson to bring the U.S.A. into that world organization. But America's refusal to join turned Britain back to her older pattern in Europe — the "Balance of Power" — although she still favored France as against Germany.

In 1918–19 she joined France in armed intervention against revolutionary Russia, but the resistance of workers' "councils of action" throughout Britain and the poor showing of the counter-revolutionary (White) Russian armies finally caused the British to withdraw from this costly venture. She also backed Greece against Turkey (1921), with disastrous results and a weakening of her prestige in the Near East.

Her attitude toward France grew less sympathetic as France extended her alliances through Europe; and as France undertook many moves directed against Germany, Britain became critical and even distant. For Britain, the restoration of European industry and commerce was the guiding principle, whereas reparations and, above all, security were primary for mutilated France.

Britain faced other difficulties. In Egypt, nationalist agitations became insistent and in India, the war had stimulated enough mature nationalism to require Britain to liberalize considerably her administration under the Montagu-Chelmsford reforms (See both *Egypt* and *India*, *History*).

But these external situations were secondary to internal developments. Once the bitter struggle with the Irish was concluded in 1921 (See *Eire*, *History*) discussion turned to the industrial position of Britain. From 1918–20 there had been a fantastic boom. Prices rose to an index of 323 (as against 100 in 1913); there was full employment and lavish spending. Men spoke in terms of hundreds of millions of pounds, because budgets bore no resemblance to the pre-war expenses of the state. The national debt had risen from $4,000,000,000 to ten times that figure (or to $5,000 per family). Profits had been enormous.

In 1921 the bubble burst. Prices fell by 53% within a few months, and Britain entered a period of permanent mass unemployment, with vast "depressed areas." Shipping, her commercial foundation, now far exceeded the needs of trade. Coal, Britain's industrial basis, could not meet French and German competition, for currencies had collapsed in both these countries and they could therefore sell at lower prices abroad. The British pound dropped from its normal price of $4.86 to $3.18. To restore international confidence, the U.S.A. and Britain cooperated to restore it nearer to parity. Nevertheless, the stronger it was, the less was the pound able to compete with the inflated currencies on the continent of Europe.

During the 1918–20 period of full employment, trade unionism had risen nearly threefold, to embrace some 6,000,000 British workers. But, once unemployment exceeded a million, trade union membership dramatically declined. The Lancashire cotton mills, faced with international competition, cut wages. Labor retaliated with widespread strikes. The coal miners, accusing the government of bad faith and insisting that the Sankey report (1919) had agreed to nationalize the mines, embarked on a strike that paralyzed British industry. Finally, after acute struggles, coal profits and coal-miners' wages were both deflated; and the country turned from prosperity to retrenchment.

She felt that three moves were necessary to assure recovery: (1) the reduction of German reparations and the reduction or cancellation of war debts; (2) a cut in armament expenditures; and (3) the imposition of protective tariffs to counter the recent tendency of the U.S.A. to high protection. In line with these objectives, Britain concluded various agreements. The Washington Naval Conference (1922), with the United States and Japan concurring, limited the building of capital ships. Reparations were scaled down after the French occupied the Ruhr in Germany (1923), and an agreement was made in Washington to pay the war debt to the U.S.A. over 62 years, with annual payments rising to $175,000,000 (1922).

The Conservatives Take Power: 1922–1924. Great Britain had been a Free Trade country since 1846. It was her boast that any foreigner who could produce more cheaply than an Englishman had the right to outsell him in England. To Free Traders, this was the source of British greatness. No coalition dared to espouse Protection; hence, the Conservatives had to get rid of Lloyd George, since they were swinging toward Protection. They enjoyed the support of the rising monopolies, a new phenomenon in Britain, once the citadel of free competition.

The Conservatives, in control, desired a truly Conservative cabinet and prime minister. Lloyd George's position had been weakened as a result of his almost continuous posturings at international conferences. Moreover, his manipulation of foreign policy had not proved advantageous for Britain. Finally, his temperamental vagaries and the growing belief that he lacked the qualities of character required for the "long pull," made inevitable his departure from government.

Bonar Law, a Glasgow businessman of Canadian birth, succeeded to the premiership. However, the great personalities among the Conservatives did not approve: Balfour, Austen Chamberlain, and Lord Birkenhead followed Lloyd George out of office.

In the November 1922 elections, the Conservatives gained a majority over all other parties combined, but Labor rose to 144 seats (a fourth of Parliament). Soon after his triumph, Bonar Law died; and it was fully expected that his successor would be Lord Curzon, who had served as Viceroy of India. But to the surprise of England, he was bypassed in favor of another businessman, Stanley Baldwin. It was felt that Labor would have found a winning issue in the appointment of a prime minister who was not a member of the House of Commons. As many Conservative leaders had created a strong prejudice against Lord Curzon in the mind of King George V, the latter could constitutionally choose either Curzon or Baldwin, and he chose the second.

The age of the Patrician was over, the age of the Industrialist was here. Conservative leaders who had refused to abandon Lloyd George, returned to the fold.

By now unemployment had reached 1,300,000 (equal to 3,500,000 in the U.S.A.). This was a new and disturbing phenomenon. The government had spent $2,000,000,000 on the "dole" and still sought a solution. The Tories went all out for Protection — they called it "safeguarding" — and appealed to the voters. The Conservatives won 40% of Parliament, Labor polled over 30%, and the Liberals polled nearly 30%. Since the government had been defeated, Labor, as the leading opposition party, was called into office. However, Labor depended on Liberal support. In January 1924, Ramsay MacDonald, the son of a servant girl, became Prime Minister and constituted a Labor government. Some Liberals, like Lord Haldane, consented to serve in the new ministry.

Labor and Conservative Alternations: 1924–1929. British workers did not make the task of their government easy: strikes broke out everywhere. Social legislation was delayed, and when the budget was introduced, Philip Snowden, Chancellor of the Exchequer, based it on Free Trade and economy, with social expenditures secondary. Furthermore, Free Trade was further advanced by the repeal of the temporary tariffs that had been imposed during the war.

Britain recognized the Soviet Union (1924) but difficulties arose when the Soviets refused to repay private investments and debts voided by the Bolshevik revolution unless Britain agreed to pay the U.S.S.R. for the damages caused by British intervention in 1918–20. Anglo-British relations became embittered. The Liberal supporters of the Labor government opposed the treaty, and in October 1924 the government appealed to the voters. At this point the British Foreign Office made public a letter from a leader of the Communist International (Zinoviev) urging the British people to revolt. Prime Minister MacDonald wavered: he wished to claim credit for its publication yet he would not endorse its authenticity.

The Soviet government protested. Lord Rothermere, owner of the powerful *Daily Mail*, claimed that he had forced the Foreign Office to publish the Zinoviev document. His public confession of power did not strike the country as unusual, for a new generation of "Press Lords" had come into being — men who issued daily pronouncements as though they were the arbiters of Britain's fate. The London press, whose circulation is, relative to population, many times that of leading American newspapers, had grown to be an extra-governmental power.

In the October 1924 election, the Labor party was defeated, the Liberals almost obliterated, and the Conservatives rode into power on the national dread of revolution. Prime Minister Baldwin appointed Winston Churchill, Chancellor of the Exchequer. Churchill now arranged to restore the pound to its traditional parity of $4.86 and to make London again the banking and investment center of the globe.

Baldwin's watchword was recovery. At Locarno (1925), Germany was taken back into the family of countries and she agreed to enter the League of Nations. World economic recovery prevailed. American business was booming. It looked as if nothing could go wrong.

But things did go wrong. The pound proved to have been stabilized above its value. Exports dropped. Unemployment rose. Wages were again cut in the coal mines; but this time the government wanted uninterrupted production. So it gave the mineowners a subsidy of $100,000,000 and thus the miners lost no income. Confidence reappeared. When Austen Chamberlain returned from Locarno, he was welcomed as the creator of perpetual peace and awarded the Knighthood of the Garter, usually reserved for royalty.

The industrial crisis, however, persisted. With coal subsidies running out, the miners struck in the spring of 1926. The strike lasted for months and prevented Britain from sharing in the world revival of trade. In May the Trades Council decided on a sympathetic strike of all workers in basic industries. The resulting General Strike, the nearest approach to total stoppage that had ever been seen anywhere, lasted about a week. Firm government action combined with the substitution of volunteer workers (from the middle and upper classes) combined to break the strike — which had inconvenienced the poor more than the rich. However, the coal strike lingered on until winter. It ended with the defeat of the miners, and Labor was bitter.

Second Labor Government: 1929–1931. The continuing crisis led to a general election in the spring of 1929. This time Labor swept into power with 289 seats, against 260 for the Conservatives and 59 for the Liberals. But this result derived from the antiquated division of electoral constituencies. In percentages the voting showed: Labor 38%, Conservatives 38%, Liberals 24%. The Liberals therefore demanded Proportional Representation. The Conservatives objected, for the prevailing system usually favored them; and the Laborites objected because they felt that it might prove advantageous for them as well.

The workers expected Socialism, but the men they had chosen to represent them had no such illusions. It was a standing joke in London, the day after the elections, that as Labor came within 4% of a clear Parliamentary majority, its leaders blanched and said: "My God! We haven't a majority, have we?" Mythical or not, the purport of the story was exact.

As Labor now undertook to govern by itself, Ramsay MacDonald chose the four most conservative leaders of Labor for his cabinet: Thomas, Clynes, Henderson, and the Labor party's fiscal expert, Snowden. Not long after (September 1929), Snowden, Chancellor of the Exchequer, made a speech in which he predicted that the collapse of the booming American stock market was in the offing. He refused to base his treasury policy on assumptions of perpetual prosperity. A month later Snowden's sober economic sense was vindicated as the stock market in New York collapsed on October 24.

In social legislation, the Labor government proved even more timorous than the Conservatives had been. In 1930 it faced a panic, with unemployment at 3,000,000 (equivalent to 8,000,000 in the U.S.A.) and with trade at precipitously low levels. The country clamored for economy. The "May Committee," formed to examine governmental expenditures, recommended a cut of $400,000,000 in the social services (unemployment relief, old-age pensions). The budget deficit by now had reached $850,000,000.

Foreigners withdrew funds from British banks. The Bank of England, once mistress of the world, asked for credits from the Bank of France and the Bank of the Netherlands. It borrowed $250,000,000, which went speedily, then another $400,000,000, which went even faster. The situation became unmanageable when the Viennese Credit Anstalt institution failed and no one trusted anything but gold.

Britain had to take decisive action. In this extremity, the Labor government split: MacDonald and Snowden favored a National government to save the state, but the majority of Labor ministers refused to reduce payments to the workers (in accordance with the May Committee's recommended cut in social services). The government resigned in August 1931.

A National government took power, composed of Conservatives, most Liberals and a handful of Laborites, but important ones. It appealed to the country to save the pound, and initiated economies, even in the pay of the armed services. Disorders broke out in the Royal Navy at Invergordon (Scotland). Though the extent of this outbreak has not been given, estimates range from localized protests to widespread mutiny; and whatever the truth, the effect was significant. Money was withdrawn from London in massive amounts — more than the country could face. Britain had no choice but to abandon the gold standard. Although the pound lost a fourth of its value by this action, Britain herself hailed it as the harbinger of recovery.

The National Government and Recovery: 1931–1932. In the coming election, virtually the entire press denounced the Left wing of Labor. Every other element was, however, united and the government won by the most crushing victory ever seen: 562 to 52. Confidence was reborn. But the popular vote revealed that Labor had polled 34% as against 38% in 1929. With a broken party and no press, Labor demonstrated a cohesive strength that surprised trained politicians. This showing convinced the Conservatives of the need for truly constructive measures and for long-term prosperity.

The Conservatives, who had the majority in Parliament, utilized the crisis to bring in their favorite device: Protection. The Free Traders were trapped. If they deserted the government, Labor would take over power. Hence, they accepted defeat, but bitterly; and they hoped that the facts would vindicate them.

Their hope was futile: Britain purchased over 17% of the world's exports. By lowering the value of the pound, she compelled the selling countries to lower their prices — either they had to reduce prices to meet Britain's reduced buying capacities or they continued to store their unsold surpluses which were threatening to choke their economies. Deflation throughout the world became severe. In the U.S.A. the economic crisis deepened. As the world crisis steadily grew worse, Britain's situation remained static. By June 1932 the pound had fallen by nearly a third; and yet stock exchange prices, even expressed in the now depreciated pound, were at the low point of many decades. It seemed as if nothing could save the economy.

Neville Chamberlain, the new Chancellor of the Exchequer, then converted the War Loan; that is, government bond interest was reduced from 5% to $3\frac{1}{2}\%$. The country cheerfully accepted the reduction and the government thereby saved $150,000,000 yearly.

Once investors were willing to accept only $3\frac{1}{2}\%$ on government bonds, they rushed to buy good common stocks yielding up to 9%. Finance revived. Banks became liquid and credit flowed again. By the spring of 1933 Britain was enjoying full recovery, while the U.S.A. faced a bank holiday. The lesson of Britain was learned throughout the world. The British adopted the philosophy of "cheap money" (low interest rates), since it had overcome the worst of all crises in a country that had been depressed for ten years.

In 1931 the Statute of Westminster had converted the Dominions of the British Empire into a free association of self-governing commonwealths. The following summer the Ottawa agreements were made, by which practically every member of the British Empire received preferential duties. Ultimately the Ottawa agreements proved a deterrent to world recovery. However with imperial solidarity and prosperity, and with war debts and reparations virtually ended (in accordance with the Lausanne agreement, summer of 1932), Britain had impressively shown to the world that the inherent strength of the "tight little island" had been amazingly underrated.

The Industrial Boom: 1933–1935. Hitler's rise in 1933 did not unduly disturb London. Britain was absorbed by her housing boom that was based on "cheap money." By 1935 a million new houses had been erected. Miles of London suburbs looked as brand-new as the environs of Los Angeles. Household comforts replaced the archaic kitchens with which British housewives long had struggled. Unemployment decreased by a million. Though there were still nearly two million unemployed, the National government boasted about the increase in employment.

Meanwhile Britain modernized her industrial equipment. The previous boom at first had left the depressed areas as black as ever, for recovery had concentrated on light industry and building. Now heavy industries were also called upon for armaments. Britain turned from accumulating capital to increasing the expenditures of her consumer population. Foreign loans to other countries had ceased in 1928, so all the money formerly used to fertilize the world was now reinvested in the British Isles. The local boom was slowly undermining the international position of Great Britain.

To cope with these implications, the government embarked upon planned production and price regulation. The old reliance on Free Trade was now over and Trade Associations, or cartels, were accepted as normal — and the Conservative party came to rely increasingly on the support and assistance of these new economic institutions. For the time being, all differences were forgotten in the Jubilee of King George V (May 1935).

Conservatives in Power: 1935–1937. In the spring of 1935, Britain grew uneasy over Italy's planned attack on Ethiopia and Hitler's rearmament program. A more determined policy was demanded than that of the pacifistic Ramsay MacDonald: Stanley Baldwin succeeded him as Prime Minister immediately following the Jubilee. The National government was now merely a coalition of Conservatives with Liberal and Labor fringes. The Labor party issued a program in which it declared that British recovery had consisted of a series of showy expedients, fraught with possibilities of disaster. Labor demanded nationalization of basic industries, transport, and finance.

Baldwin branded the Labor party as threatening prosperity by its revolutionary programs. He appealed to the voters, as he pledged a program of collective security for world peace as well as reliance on the League of Nations. His Foreign Secretary, Sir Samuel Hoare, pledged resistance to foreign aggressors. British opinion expressed itself overwhelmingly in favor of world organization and of resistance to the dictatorships in Italy and Germany.

Baldwin was swept into power, although Labor increased its representation to 154 seats. Actually Baldwin obtained only 52% of the country's vote — the electoral constituencies were still "loaded."

On December 7, 1935, Britain woke up to a shock. Foreign Secretary Hoare and Prime Minister Laval of France had signed an agreement with Italy for partial Italian acquisitions in Ethiopia. Aggression was not being stopped but rewarded! British indignation was profound and would not listen to pleas of "realism." The pact was not implemented. Soon after, King George V died and party strife was hushed.

In 1935 British popular opinion became puzzled by the Anglo-German Naval Treaty by which Britain, without consulting her former ally, France, had agreed to allow Germany to build submarines. The Italian conquest of Ethiopia and Britain's behavior during the Spanish Civil War in 1936 caused popular resentment at the complaisance with which the British government was accepting tyranny. The French Premier, Léon Blum, made it appear that

British pressure forced France into her policy of a Nonintervention Committee with respect to the Spanish Civil War. This Committee came to be regarded as a tragic farce, in view of the active intervention against the Spanish government by German and Italian Fascists.

But these issues were brushed aside as the country became preoccupied with a picturesque controversy — over the desire of King Edward VIII to marry an American, Mrs. Wallis Simpson. The King was asked to abdicate, which he did. His brother, the Duke of York, succeeded him as George VI and was crowned at the time planned for his brother's consecration.

Neville Chamberlain: 1937–1940. Following the coronation, in May 1937 Neville Chamberlain succeeded Baldwin as Prime Minister. Chamberlain was the idol of the "City" of London, that is, of the financial elements. Slackening trade was compensated for by armaments expenditures — they rose from $570,000,000 in 1934 to $2,030,000,000 in 1939.

The rise of Sir Oswald Mosley and his "Blackshirt" organization had led the government to pass a Public Order bill prohibiting para-military formations.

However, in foreign affairs, the German occupation of Austria in 1938 was declared as not requiring British action. But Britain took a firm stand on the first crisis resulting from Hitler's demands on Czechoslovakia (May 1938). Chamberlain privately stated that he had no belief in the viability of Czechoslovakia as the republic was constituted, the last step in a policy of "appeasement" that had begun seven years before with acquiescence in Japan's seizure of Manchuria. Verbal condemnations and acceptances of accomplished facts went hand in hand. Chamberlain dismissed Foreign Secretary Anthony Eden, Italy's antagonist, and visited Mussolini in Rome.

Later, in an effort to arrive at a solution of the Czechoslovakian crisis, Chamberlain flew to Berchtesgaden to "appease" Hitler. Then he made a second trip to Godesberg and a third trip — this last to Munich, where in collaboration with Premier Daladier of France, he agreed to terms that resulted in the evisceration of the Czechoslovakian state (See *Czechoslovakia, History*), by the terms of the Munich Pact of September 1938. When he returned to England, Chamberlain was greeted with flowers tossed by suburban housewives. He declared that he had guaranteed Czech independence and obtained "peace in our time."

Churchill and Eden protested the eternal incidence of dishonor, but most of the Conservative party looked upon them as trouble-makers. "The lights of Europe are going out, one by one," Churchill warned. But his talents were not allowed to be placed at the service of his country at this critical moment. At the same time, the Anglo-German Fellowship, one of the most powerful organizations in Britain, including influential aristocrats and parliamentarians, urged friendship with Hitler and entertained his emissaries.

On March 15, 1939, after launching a provocation against the Czechs, Hitler added the provinces of Bohemia and Moravia to the Reich as "Protectorates." Chamberlain denounced Hitler as a treaty-breaker and expressed Britain's determination to block any further German attempt to change the map of Europe. Hitler then demanded the return of Danzig and a readjustment of the Polish Corridor, and took over the port of Memel. Britain proceeded to extend her offer of protection not only to Poland but to Greece, Rumania, and Turkey. Chamberlain began to sound out Soviet Russia on a military alliance and sent Mr. William Strang of the Foreign Office to Moscow.

On June 29, Lord Halifax warned Germany that Britain was ready for war, and the following day the Poles informed Germany that any act of aggression would be considered a cause of war. By July 31, an Anglo-French military mission went to Moscow to engage in staff talks with the Soviet High Command. The length of the negotiations led to mutual mistrust.

On August 23 the German-Soviet nonaggression pact was announced. The British warned Hitler of their readiness to blockade Germany, and on August 25 they announced an even more binding treaty to defend Poland. Ambassador Sir Neville Henderson brought Hitler's proposals to the Chamberlain cabinet; these were rejected on August 29. Hitler invaded Poland on September 1, and when he ignored the Franco-British ultimatum, the British declared war on September 3.

During the quiet phase of the war, from September 1939 to April 1940, Chamberlain commanded his majority; but when Germany invaded Belgium and the Netherlands, despite his almost pathetic cry, "I will not resign," he was ousted (May 10, 1940).

Churchill and National Resurrection: 1940–1944. Churchill and Eden, the true prophets, assumed office; and Britain began to rise to her destiny with that power that has so often confounded her ill-wishers from the days of Queen Elizabeth. The British army evacuated Dunkirk and France abandoned her in June 1940. The little island faced a continent mobilized by the Germans, from Sicily to the North Cape. Not in her worst days, when she alone faced Napoleon, did her situation seem so hopeless. She was compelled to attack the French fleet at Mers-el-Kébir (July 4, 1940) and disaster followed disaster. Churchill, resolute, pledged "blood, sweat, and tears" and years of misery, while his all-party government symbolized unity. When the Germans launched their "air Blitz" in September 1940, there were no parties — only Britons. During this chronicle of misfortune, Britain became an object of scorn from those who considered her vanquished. She had backed Poland, Norway, the Netherlands, Belgium, France — her alliance was the kiss of death. She backed Yugoslavia and Greece. Her tattered legions were thrown back and disaster was complete in Crete (May 1941).

Not only was she militarily defeated, but her foreign investments were nearly all sold to provide resources, partly because the "cash and carry" legislation of the U.S.A. denied her credit possibilities. In June 1940 Churchill stated that the Old World would have to be held by Britain until Europe's slavery was righted by the New World. In September the "destroyer-bases" arrangement with the U.S.A. aided these perspectives. In March 1941 the passage of the American Lend-Lease Act stopped the bleeding of British assets that had threatened her with economic death.

With Hitler's attack on Russia (June 1941), Britain acquired forthwith a giant ally, capable of coping with German military power. In the meantime, her situation in Africa grew perilous. It appeared that she might lose the Suez Canal and the road to India. At the nadir of her misfortunes, Japan attacked the U.S.A., and two days later (December 9, 1941) Britain suffered the loss of two of her greatest battleships in the Malayan area, and the beginning of a long series of defeats that cost her Hongkong, Malaya, Singapore (February 15, 1942), and, for a space, all Burma. Japan was poised at the gates of Australia and her navy could scour the seas almost to Ceylon.

'In November 1942 the years of misery began to turn. Following the British attack at El Alamein, the whole of French North Africa returned to Allied control, and on January 26, 1943, the German army at the gate of Stalingrad surrendered to the Soviets. Since that time, reverses have been few and the United Nations have moved in a steady tide of success against the Germans. Only the fearful attack by robot bombs for a time dampened the exaltation roused by the Allied invasion of France (June 6, 1944).

After ten years of chronic depression (1921–31) followed by seven years of appeasement and three years of defeat, the British people have not only overcome their foes, but their political life has been lighted up by constructive studies of long-term recovery (the Beveridge and Woolton plans for a democratic, socially integrated people). Externally, the Moscow, Teheran, and Cairo agreements, and the Dumbarton Oaks conferences, affirmed Britain's resolve to work with her allies for world security and an enduring peace.

Stakes in the Peace

Britain's position at the end of the war will bear little resemblance to that in 1939. In that year she held half the foreign investments of the world. Today her foreign debt greatly exceeds the remnants of her foreign investment. Revenues from shipping are sure to be proportionately less than in 1939. The entire British Empire accounted for about 30% of world trade in 1939, but Great Britain is not the British Empire, and it seems doubtful that at the end of the war she can resume her former proportion — and yet she must.

Great Britain has imported about $1,900,000,000 more than she exports per year. This deficit has been made up by her "invisible" receipts from foreign investments and other sources; and it is safe to reckon that about $1,500,000,000 of this revenue has vanished. On the other hand, her imports cannot be reduced. If Sir John Orr's calculations are correct, with respect to the inadequate nourishment of large parts of the British population, the imports should be increased. Home agriculture cannot contribute more than a small part of the additional food required.

If Britain is to maintain her pre-war standard of living, she must export per year $1,500,000,000 more than she did in 1939 (that is, in pre-war values). This can be put another way: her gross exports must rise from $2,400,000,000 to $3,900,000,000. But they must increase even more because she must import raw materials with which to manufacture much of the increased exports. Britain must double her exports, or her standard of living must appreciably decline. Since no people will consent to decreased standards after years of privation in food, clothing, housing, and the like, the problem of Great Britain is enormous.

The difficulty is complicated by the existence of the "blocked sterling" credits. Britain cannot usefully export to those who now hold claims on her "blocked sterling" balances, for such exports would merely cancel some of these credits: they would not create in Britain a fresh capacity for purchasing needed imports.

It has been suggested that the only possible solution to this gargantuan problem lies in the industrialization of the backward areas of the world by the joint enterprise of the advanced nations. As an alternative, Britain might resort to barter methods. She must, in any event, resist world inflation, because she is primarily a buyer and therefore cannot worsen her situation by having to pay high prices for raw materials and for food. Her interest indubitably is in sound finance and freer trade — but these will not, by themselves, provide her with sufficient exports.

Internal finances have been excellently managed. Note circulation and bank deposits are at reasonable levels; the debt is not an excessive burden (despite the dramatic figures); and interest rates have risen less in Britain than in any other belligerent nation. Under rationing, real wages have increased somewhat. The British people may be said to have a more equally distributed prosperity than ever before. There are abundant surpluses for capital investment. Physical capital, in the form of factories and machinery, is perhaps even excessive for the needs of the domestic market.

Britain's problems, therefore, are primarily external. If her level of exports can be sustained so that she can afford to purchase the imports she requires, the needs for domestic rebuilding and consumers goods should stimulate her domestic economy for many years.

In international relations, Britain must become part of the world organization. Since 1907, when Sir Percy Maxwell warned Britain of the possibilities of the submarine, and since 1909, when Bleriot crossed the Channel by plane, Britain has abandoned all thought of isolation. The rocket bomb is the latest in a long series of innovations that have transformed the "islander" psychology. Moreover, rising nationalism throughout the world will undoubtedly reduce the colonial supremacy that Britain once possessed.

Britain is a populous European country — but she is inferior in agriculture to France, in industry to Germany, in basic power to the U.S.S.R. As one of a family of nations, her safety and prosperity are assured. As an island off Europe and looking far away toward imperial destiny only, the contradictions have already become too profound. The remarkable powers conferred upon the island in the past by naval supremacy and industrial primacy can no longer be sustained without collective international action. Whether it is in currency, trade, investment, standard of living, security, or empire, Britain's fate is no longer subject to her own will. The "balance of power," Britain's guiding principle in international relations since 1688, cannot assure her safety and greatness in the future.

GREECE

The Land and the People

"The glory that was Greece" lives in the grateful memory of all Western peoples, since ancient Greece was the fountainhead of our civilization. Somewhat over a century ago when freedom was reborn among the Greek people, Lord Byron thought the cause well worth dying for. In our own day the tragic heroism of the people has made many revise Poe's phrase and speak of "the glory that *is* Greece." So, although Greece, like any other nation, must be set down here in statistics, the reader with an historical sense will find the dry facts strangely alive.

The Land. With an area of 50,270 square miles (about a fifth in islands), Greece is larger than New York State. This figure includes the large slice of territory in the north recently seized by Bulgaria, but here considered an integral part of the Greek land. Under Nazi occupation, exile and starvation reduced the population to an estimated 7,200,000.

Greece forms the tip of the Balkan peninsula, jutting into the Mediterranean with her islands about her. To the north and northwest stand mountainous frontiers with Albania, Yugoslavia, and Bulgaria. On the east, she faces Turkey-in-Europe and the island-studded Aegean Sea (across which lies Asia Minor, itself once Greek). On the south, the Peloponnesos thrusts land-fingers into the Aegean, Mediterranean, and Ionian seas. Southeastward lies the large Greek island of Crete. Off the northwest coast, where the boundary line turns inland, the Ionian Sea lies with its famous islands such as Corfu and Ithaca, legendary home of Ulysses.

Greece is a mountainous country with a mild Mediterranean climate. Though most of the land is sterile, fertile valleys slope down to the sea, ending in bays guarded by rocky promontories and islets. Between these isolated valleys the Greeks have from time immemorial communicated by water: with the Phoenicians they were the great seafarers of antiquity.

High, bare mountains cover northwestern Greece — a region of poor roads and poverty-stricken shepherds. In the northeast lie Macedonia and Thrace, and the Macedonian city of Salonika (Thessalonike, population 260,258), situated on a perfect bay, the gateway to the Vardar valley leading through Yugoslavia to the Danube. Of the Greeks repatriated after the Greek-Turkish war of 1922, a half million settled in the moderately fertile valleys of this region.

Fertile Thessaly lies in the east-central region, and southwest of it Boetia, once malarial but now drained and fertile. To the south is the capital, Athens (population 483,330), whose port (Piraeus, population about 250,000) is in normal times the busiest shipping center in the country. The Peloponnesian peninsula, jutting southward, is a land of limestone threaded by fertile valleys.

Greece's once-dense forests have been practically denuded, but recent attempts have been made to encourage reforestation. Minerals abound — iron, pyrites, copper, chrome, silver, lead, manganese, nickel, and brown coal — mostly in Thessaly, Euboea, at the southern tip of the Attic peninsula, and in several of the Aegean islands.

The People. When the Turks ruled Greece, they had to engage Greek administrators, for the modern Greeks did not lend themselves to subjugation. In the century and a quarter since the Turks were expelled, the people have raised their cultural level at an amazing rate. Still a maritime people, inclined to commerce and as politically minded as in the days of Pericles, the Greeks have spread over the world — whether in flower shops and restaurants in the U.S.A. or among the merchant princes of London and Marseilles. From Australia to Scotland, Greek sailors are known in every port; and wherever they are, both rich and poor gather in coffee-houses to study newspapers and talk politics.

The origin of modern Greeks is a subject of scholarly controversy, many authorities in the 19th century having argued that the ancient Greeks had been extinguished. The present view is that the ancient strain persists beneath the Gothic, Slavic, Turkish, and other admixtures through the centuries. When one now encounters the famous profile of the Greek statues, it is rarely accompanied by golden hair and blue eyes; and in certain regions, notably in Macedonia, racial admixtures are extreme. However, most of the people in British-held Cyprus and the Dodecanese Islands are unmistakably Greek.

Before the war the birthrate, though varying between 23 and 30, averaged 25 per thousand; the deathrate had declined from 15 to 13, and infant mortality, from 122 to 99 in less than a decade. The population increased from 1,400,000 to 7,200,000 in less than a century. It is difficult to estimate the effect of the war on this rising population curve.

Religion and Education. The official religion and the prevailing faith is the Greek Orthodox, but

minorities — 2% Mohammedans, 1.2% Jews, 0.5 Roman Catholics, and a scattering of Protestants — enjoy complete religious liberty. The Holy Synod, governing council of the Greek Orthodox Church, is seated in Athens. In the famous monastic retreat on the rocky promontory of Mt. Athos — where no woman may set foot — are 20 Greek Orthodox monasteries with 4,800 monks.

Cultural standards in pre-war Greece were high. Compulsory education for 7 to 12 year-olds was strictly enforced, except in remote rural areas. At least 80% of the children appear to have received instruction; 70,000 went to high school. Greece supported 150 professional schools, 34 music conservatories, some 40 technological institutes, and 3 universities (at Athens and Salonika). Most university students prepared for professions: in a typical year, at the University of Athens, 20% for medicine and over 50% for law. Much effort was given over to the preservation of Greek antiquities, in which many foreign institutes were also engaged.

The Nation's Economy

Agriculture. Less than 18% of the country is arable. About 8,500 square miles must support 7,200,000 people — 850 people to the cultivable square mile. Only high crop-yields could meet this situation, and Greek yields are about the poorest in Europe (a third under Bulgaria's). The annual production per farm worker is only $220, the lowest in Europe. Part of the trouble is that much land on each tiny farm (few families have over 10 acres) must lie fallow because the topsoil is thin and easily blown away. Sufficient capital and modern techniques could solve these problems. As it is, the scarce farmland is worth less than $30 an acre.

Wheat, barley, corn, and oats are raised, though in inadequate amounts, as well as wine-grapes, currants, olives, and many oranges, lemons, and figs. None-too-successful attempts have been made to raise enough cotton and rice for home consumption.

About 54% of the people are required to produce Greece's scanty food supply.

Animal husbandry yields considerable cheese but almost no butter or cow's milk. Milk and cheese come from the 5,000,000 goats and some meat as well as wool from 8,000,000 sheep. Fisheries are inconsequential. In short, even in normal times the Greeks do not overeat.

The food situation, always precarious, became catastrophic under German occupation. Greece had been importing a fourth of her food — half of her wheat — and when the Germans came, the import sources were cut off and the scanty home production fell sharply — wheat by more than 60%. The wonder is not that so many Greeks have starved but that so many have survived.

Industry and Mining. One of the less industrialized nations, Greece had a per capita machinery investment of less than 60¢; only a sixth of the working population was in industry. The older industries were olive oil, wine, and other food products, but after the transplantation of a million Greeks from Turkey, beginnings were made in textiles and chemical works. Pre-war industrial production, centering in Athens and Salonika, was valued at about $100,-000,000.

Greece's varied mineral resources yielded a pre-war average of 200,000 tons of brown coal, 175,000 of pyrites, 22,000 of chrome, 150,000 of iron ore, and smaller quantities of at least 10 other strategic metals. With proper exploitation, the production could be considerably greater.

National Income and Finance. Greece has had a history of recurrent financial crises. The currency unit, the *drachma*, worth nominally about 115 to the dollar, actually was about 150. Under Nazi occupation, it was inflated by more than 100 to 1, until it sold at well over 30,000 to the dollar. It has been effectively wiped out, and discussion of Greece's internal debt is useless, since no one knows at what rate the currency will be revalued after the war. The people's wretched savings, valued at $10 per capita, are gone unless there is revaluation of the *drachma* on an agreed basis. Taxation in terms of pre-war *drachmas* now yields about 40% less; there is no production or trade to sustain it. The foreign debt of $300,000,-000, always a delicate problem, can now be serviced only by a reconstructed Greece.

Foreign Trade and Shipping. The Greeks are still active traders, some 8% of them are in commerce. Although low by western standards, their per capita normal trade is normally twice that of the other Balkan countries (Rumania, Bulgaria, Yugoslavia) and only a sixth less than Italy's and a tenth less than Spain's. Pre-war Greece imported food, textiles, yarns, raw materials and machinery for manufactures, coal, and petroleum. She exported mainly horticultural products such as currants and olive oil.

Germany dominated Greek trade before the war, as she dominated all agricultural countries in southeastern Europe. By 1935 she had more than a fifth, by 1939 more than a fourth, with Britain the second supplier and the U.S.A. the second customer, and the U.S.S.R. rapidly increasing her trade with Greece. When the Germans moved in, Greek economy crashed and Greek foreign trade with it. Imports fell from $130,000,000 in 1938 to $39,000,000 in 1941; exports from $90,000,000 to $30,000,000.

The Germans also destroyed, damaged, or captured probably half of the great 2,000,000-ton merchant fleet — which almost rivaled Britain's in proportion to population, and which was Greece's richest asset. Since the country depended largely on shipping revenue to compensate for her unfavorable trade balance, this loss is a severe obstacle to post-war recovery.

History: 1914-1944

In 1917 Greece was a monarchy under King Constantine, a brother-in-law of the Kaiser. When Constantine refused to allow the Allies to land in Greece and use Salonika as a base, the Allies disregarded him. Sure of popular support, especially of the dominant political party led by the Cretan statesman Venizelos, they occupied Salonika, dethroned Constantine, bestowed the monarchy on his son Alexander, and obtained Greek cooperation in the prosecution of the war. In 1917–18 Allied armies in the Balkans were based in Greece. Venizelos converted his country into a staunch ally.

The Allied victory in 1918 crowned Venizelos' policy with success and Greece entered the peace with high hopes. The Greeks felt that they would receive the Aegean coast in Europe, the Aegean Islands, and the city of Adrianople in European Turkey; and perhaps even Constantinople and the Straits from the Black Sea to the Aegean, as well as the western part of Asia Minor, including the Greek-populated seaport of Smyrna. Had Greece obtained these territories, her population and area would have more than doubled. And the treaties of Neuilly and Sèvres (1919 and 1920) appeared to confirm the most optimistic hopes of Venizelos.

Defeat and the Refugee Problem: 1920–1924. In 1919 King Alexander died. At the subsequent election Venizelos was defeated and King Constantine recalled to the throne. The Allies cooled at this show of popular fickleness and refused to recognize Constantine, insisting on a reconsideration of the Treaty of Sèvres. France and Italy held aloof; Britain still backed the Greeks but cautiously and with some misgivings.

The Greeks, in possession of a sizable British loan, sought to retrieve the situation by conquering Asia Minor from the Turks. Unluckily for them, the Turkish nationalist movement led by a young patriot, Mustapha Kemal Pasha, had produced Turks of a far different caliber from those of the corrupt old Sultanate. A Greek army, inflamed by visions of a Greater Greece, marched from Smyrna to overcome Kemal's ragged levies. At Eskishehir, the Turks routed the Greeks and the campaign was over. Greece lost Smyrna and became again a small state.

In September 1922 King Constantine was again dethroned. Finally, the Allies reduced Greece practically to her pre-1914 boundaries by the Treaty of Lausanne (1923). Venizelos, displaying rare political courage, signed for his country. Moreover, the pact provided for the wholesale exchange of populations between Greece and Turkey. Mohammedans in Greece were to be repatriated in Turkey and Greeks in Turkey resettled in Greece. This transfer of populations was perhaps the largest-scale transplantation of minorities in history. Since such resettlement was beyond Greece's means, the League of Nations in 1924 raised a $50,000,000 loan to assist her. Slowly over 1,000,000 refugees entered Greece and wrought profound changes in her population and economy.

Political Disturbances: 1923–1929. Constantine's eldest son, George II, was nominally king, but real power lay with General Pangalos. When in 1923 suspicions arose that George was attempting a monarchist *coup* to affirm his rule, republican feeling flared up. In March 1924, George went into exile and a republic was proclaimed. Venizelos had meanwhile returned as prime minister but left after the people voted more than 2 to 1 for a republic. Admiral Condouriotes became provisional president.

At this juncture, Greece suffered further humiliation. Reacting violently to the killing of an Italian on a boundary mission in Greece, Mussolini bombed the defenseless island of Corfu, forcing Greece to pay him damages after this wanton act. Exasperated, the Greeks invaded Bulgaria on the charge that the Bulgarians had abetted atrocities inflicted by the Macedonian minority in Greece. Here too Greece was compelled to pay damages.

General Pangalos then proceeded to overthrow the Republican government and declared himself dictator. A true *opéra-bouffe* dictator, he assailed the press, attacked the monasteries, suspended the Constitution, irritated his neighbors, and regulated everything down to the length of women's skirts. A revolution in 1927 drove him from power and into prison.

The new government, fearful of the liberal tendencies of the Republican Guard, dissolved it. For a time there was terror and civil war in Athens. But soon the disturbances ceased and honest elections took place. Following the usual pattern in Greece, republicans and royalists were virtually balanced. An all-party government (except for Communists) was formed under Zaimis, but he soon gave way to Venizelos. In September 1928 Venizelos signed a treaty of amity with Italy and began friendly relations with Turkey and Yugoslavia, thus burying historic feuds. From that year to 1932 Venizelos guided Greek affairs.

Stabilization and Restoration of the Monarchy: 1929–1935. The government restored the Constitution and made efforts to placate even Bulgaria. In November 1932 the moderates under Tsaldaris triumphed at the polls. Gradually the monarchists regained hope and sought to restore the throne, vacant since 1923. In 1935 the republicans, convinced of an imminent monarchist restoration, staged an uprising that was suppressed. Venizelos, the leader of the abortive rebellion, fled abroad. Thus power again shifted from the republican Venizelists to the monarchist groups. The marriage of a Greek princess, Marina, to the Duke of Kent in England enhanced the prestige of the monarchy.

In the 1935 general elections, Tsaldaris won 287 out of 300 seats in Parliament, whereupon General Kondylis led a monarchist revolt. A subsequent plebiscite returned King George II, who entered Athens and agreed to a broad political amnesty.

The Metaxas Dictatorship: 1936–1941. The first elections under the restored King resulted in an almost equal division of pro- and anti-Venizelist deputies, the balance of power resting with the Communists. In the meantime, Venizelos, for forty years Greece's outstanding statesman, died.

Faced with a snarled parliamentary situation, the Conservative General John Metaxas struck. Declaring that the Communists were about to seize the factories, army, and police force, he proclaimed a dictatorship on August 4, 1936. He justified his action by asserting that he had thus saved the country from being drenched in blood. His rule was drastic, assuming the typical characteristics of a Fascist régime; but many Greeks, wearied by the long cycle of changes and disorders, accepted the new state of affairs.

During the Metaxas régime, commercial and intellectual relations with Germany grew closer. German leaders, like Goering, flattered the little country and her German-educated chief of state with their attentions. But Italy's seizure of Albania in April 1939 ended Greece's illusions; and she then received a unilateral guarantee of her independence from Great Britain and France.

On October 28, 1940, without the remotest shadow of an excuse, Mussolini attacked Greece. The Fascists invaded from Albania but were driven back by the valiant Greek army, which almost achieved total victory over the incompetent invaders. At that point, however, Nazi Germany intervened to save the Axis by attacking Yugoslavia on April 6, 1941. The Germans soon sped down the Vardar valley to Salonika, defeating the Greeks and combined British-New Zealand forces that had been thrown into the struggle at the last moment. The Germans then occupied Greece and handed over some authority to the Italian Fascists. In May the Germans took the island of Crete, and punished the Greeks for their superb courage by inflicting unspeakable indignities upon the entire people. Metaxas had died during the Italian War in January 1941; his successor, Koryzis, committed suicide.

Greece under Quisling Rule: 1941–1944. The Germans established a quisling government under General Tsolakoglu. The Greek government-in-exile functioned in London with Tsouderos as Premier, but King George still governed by royal decree. Guerrilla warfare sprang up in Greece, with two major factions fighting each other as well as the Germans. One group, said to be Communist-led, inspired the E.A.M., or National Liberation Movement (its army is called E.L.A.S.); the rival group was led by an officer, General Zervas.

In 1944 mutiny broke out on the Greek ships in Alexandria harbor, spreading to some Greek army units. Long political discussions ensued, after which King George II agreed to maintain the Constitution and abide by a plebiscite concerning his fate. Radical Greeks insisted, however, that George's support of the Metaxas régime proved that he could not be trusted. Protracted negotiations occupied most of 1944, without any definitive agreement between the Greek underground movement and the government-in-exile, until August when a unity pact was signed.

Foreign Affiliations. Since 1824 Greece has been in the British orbit. The royal family has been related either to German or Russian royalty, but as a rule British influence has been unchallenged. Culturally, though not politically, French influence has been paramount. Under the Nazis, German pressure increased but was never decisive. Common adherence to the Orthodox faith caused a great many Greeks to look toward Czarist Russia, but after the Bolshevik Revolution the Greek Church cooled toward the new Russian régime.

Greece is no longer at odds with Turkey and is quite friendly to Yugoslavia. She is cold, however, to Albania and has extensive claims against Italy. Bulgaria, as constituted before September 1944, was an antagonist, as is the Macedonian minority within Greece.

Stakes in the Peace

The first and all-compelling stake of Greece is sheer physical survival. Whatever régime prevails, she will need far-reaching financial assistance to keep her people alive. Her second need is an effective guarantee of security. The manner in which the German armies overran the country within a month proves that only solid international organization can shield this country.

With greater attention to their subsistence crops, the Greeks could improve their agriculture, but their small over-all amount of cultivable land indicates that light industry is their principal hope. If freer trade replaces the crippling policies of self-sufficiency in the 1930's, the Greeks, with their maritime gifts, their trading skill, and their intellectual agility, may be able to play a larger part in world commerce.

Given a reasonable treatment of national minorities in the north, Greece should have no enemies. Indeed, there is little to covet in her domain. And if measures of international security eliminate strategic considerations, her possibilities improve immeasurably. The development of the port of Salonika would greatly aid recovery, while an increased Soviet market for her food specialties would stimulate exports. Political disturbances might decrease if many middle-class Greeks turned away from careers in the liberal professions, especially the law, in favor of scientific and industrial techniques. Finally, the lowering of barriers to emigration would give many Greeks a chance to utilize their native talents in overseas countries.

In view of their land's limited natural resources, Greeks can hope for nothing too spectacular; but they have wrestled successfully with an unfavorable environment in the past and may be expected to overcome their present tragic adversities.

THE HOLY SEE

Organization and Jurisdiction

The Pope, Pontiff, and Bishop of Rome is the center of Catholic Unity and the head of the Roman Catholic Church, the most numerous body of Christians in the world. His official residence is Vatican City, in Rome, which is also the seat of the College of Cardinals, a body of not more than 70 leading Catholic prelates of various nationalities who represent Catholics the world over. A vote of two-thirds of this College elects the Pope, and when the Papacy is vacant, the College functions in its place. The Church itself is administered by 12 Congregations; and there are other commissions, three tribunals, and diverse offices.

For many centuries, and until the unification of Italy in the 1860's, the Pope ruled over 16,000 square miles in Central Italy and a population that finally reached 3,200,000. The Church refused to accept the abolition of its temporal power by the Italian government in 1871. The situation was settled in 1929 (Lateran Treaty) when the Church received a territory of 108.7 acres to be known as Vatican City.

This city has the full rights of a sovereign state. With a population of some 1,000, Vatican City has its own coinage, customs officers, radio broadcasting station; and 13 of its buildings have extra-territorial status. The Governor of Vatican City is appointed to deal with purely secular matters; its law is based on canon law and ecclesiastical procedures, and not on the Italian Civil Code. The Society of Jesus administers the university within its bounds.

Diplomatic Relations. Even when it had no territory of its own, the Papacy enjoyed diplomatic status. Today, the Papal Secretary of State carries on diplomatic relations with some 35 important countries; unofficial relations are maintained with other countries through the Vatican's Apostolic Delegates. The Papacy maintains diplomatic relations not only with Catholic countries but with Protestant, Greek Orthodox, and secular states as well. It does not, however, maintain relations with the Mohammedan states. The Vatican has undertaken compacts, termed *Concordats*, with a number of nations for the purpose of regulating the internal relations between Church and State.

History: 1914-1944

In 1918 the Pope, Benedict XV, was confronted by a Europe widely different from the Europe that had prevailed when he was elected in 1914. World War I had resurrected Poland as a new state, which was predominantly Catholic, as well as the Catholic state of Lithuania. In southern Ireland a Catholic people was reaching toward autonomy. In the Netherlands, the cabinet was headed by Catholics, a religious group long regarded as minor in importance. At the same time, the greatest Catholic empire in Europe, Austria-Hungary, no longer existed as an entity. Catholics in Croatia had become affiliated with a state under the domination of the Orthodox Church of Serbia. Catholics in Transylvania had become a minority in a Rumania now dominated by the Orthodox Church. And in Germany, smaller Catholic monarchies, like Bavaria, had become secularized.

The Vatican's international relations were correspondingly modified to deal with the new Europe of 1918. The descendant of an aristocratic Genoese family, Pope Benedict XV exhibited remarkable suppleness in his understanding of the new social forces. Arrangements were made with Czechoslovakia (where religion and nationalism were closely allied), with Austria (where a large anticlerical party functioned), and with Hungary (whose Catholic crown was declared in abeyance). Outside Europe, the Papacy faced in Mexico a rising anticlericalism and in the Philippines a National Church that had been founded by an ex-Catholic bishop. Benedict XV labored incessantly in behalf of the Catholic populations throughout the world.

His death, in 1921, was followed by the election of Achille Ratti, Archbishop of Milan and lately *Nuncio* (envoy) to Warsaw, where he had served during the Polish war with Russia. Descended from a family of weavers, Pope Pius XI, as he was named, differed from his predecessor. He was a bibliographer and a scholar; nevertheless he possessed large practical abilities. In 1929 he concluded the Lateran Treaty with Italy which gave the Papacy extra-territorial status and which also reinstated Catholicism as the state religion of Italy. A number of other *Concordats* were concluded, many of them advantageous to the Vatican, though not all were faithfully observed by the signatory government, as for example, Germany after 1933. In 1931 the new Republican government in Spain altered the age-old position of the Church in that country, but during 1939 the alteration was canceled.

Cardinal Pacelli, Secretary of State and a statesman of steadily growing importance in Papal affairs, succeeded Pius XI upon the death of the latter in 1939. He was named Pius XII. His reign has witnessed World War II, the loss of Church sovereignty in Poland, the decline of Church influence in other European states fallen under the domination of the anti-Christian Nazis. In Japan the Church was forced to accept the law requiring all Christian denominations, whatever their doctrines, to fuse. The Catholic Philippines came temporarily under Japanese control. The U.S.S.R. absorbed Lithuania. Furthermore, Croatia's status as an independent nation appears transitory, and the restoration of Transylvania to Hungary is not assured — both nations being of importance to Catholic policy. In certain other regions, such as Eire and Quebec, the spiritual authority of the Church has become increasingly important in shaping political ideals. In France, the Pétain régime restored prestige to the Church, but certain Church dignitaries regarded this as unwelcome because of the relationship of the Pétain government to the German government.

The Papacy has repeatedly and eloquently exhorted the combatant nations against continuing World War II, but in this, as in all such efforts since the 16th century, its voice has not been heeded.

HUNGARY

The Land and the People

Which Hungary? The Hungary of 1938 or the Hungary of 1940 as swollen by the Nazis? That is the first question to be faced in a discussion of this country and the peace.

For Hungary would be a major European state *with* her forced acquisitions at the beginning of the war, a secondary agrarian power *without* them. In 1938 she numbered about 9,000,000 people and extended over 35,855 square miles; her population has since been enlarged to 14,700,000 and her area to 66,472 square miles. She has snatched 2,400,000 inhabitants from former Rumanian territory, 1,700,000 from Czechoslovakia, and 1,100,000 from Yugoslavia.

But since most, if not all, of these huge acquisitions will have to be surrendered, we shall consider Hungary as of 1938.

The Land. Hungary faces Czechoslovakia (north), Rumania (east), Yugoslavia (south), Austria (west).

A vast plain, Hungary includes some of the flattest country on earth. So flat are some parts of this plain (or *puszta*) that the traveler sometimes imagines he is on the sea, and on hot summer days the desert phenomenon of the mirage is common. A sweep of mountains virtually surrounds this plain, the Carpathians on the north and east, the Alpine system on the west. The land is 60% arable, the highest percentage of any important country in the world. A few lakes, such as Lake Balaton (largest in central Europe), remind one that in remote geological time Hungary was a great inland sea.

The immense Bakony forest separates the country's two well-defined regions: the small plain in the northwest, and the Great Hungarian plain in the southeast. The Danube River, an important channel of trade and communications, cuts through the heart of Hungary in a north-south direction. The only other important river is the Tisa in the northeast.

Hungary's mixed climate shows the usual seasonal extremes of the continent, despite some Mediterranean and marine influences, mainly in the west. Since rainfall in the summer is not abundant, most of the country is a grassy plain resembling the famed steppes of Russia. But the soil (most commonly the *chernozem*, or black soil) is generally superb.

Hungary's principal minerals — coal, iron ore, manganese, and bauxite (for aluminum) — are found chiefly in the areas around Pecs, in southern Hungary, and Miskolc, northeast of Budapest.

The People. The Hungarians, or Magyars as they call themselves, are considered by many to be descendants of an Asiatic Mongolian rather than a European people. Certainly their language, related to Turkish, does not belong to the Indo-European family of speech. But various factors, notably physical appearance, seem to point to the Hungarians' basically European origin. While a Mongolian strain has persisted, it is not paramount. Very likely the Mongolian horsemen who dominated the Hungarian plain in the 10th century imposed their language on an older Slavic stock.

Nevertheless, this people, living in the heart of a Europe that is basically either Slav, Latin, or Teuton, or mixtures of these components, is immeasurably proud of its racial uniqueness. So intense is this pride that almost all who have come within the Hungarian orbit have succumbed to a pressure to "magyarize" their names. The Magyars are efficient assimilators, and many Germans, Slavs, Latins, and Jews in their midst have become as fiercely patriotic as the Magyars themselves. On the other hand, compact ethnic groups under their rule have hated them with a virulence that has plagued European politics. Hungarian-Rumanian relations have been particularly embittered during recent decades in the disputed region of Transylvania.

The Hungarians claim that they number over 8,000,000 of the 9,000,000 in Hungary proper and some 3,500,000 outside the country's borders. But this claim is violently disputed throughout central and southeastern Europe; and the figures have of course radically altered because of Hungary's acquisitions as an ally of Nazi Germany. One fact is clear: to the other peoples under her domination Hungary does not grant equal rights, considering their cultural status inferior.

Most Hungarians live in overgrown villages, often the size of cities, from which they go out to till the fields. Small vegetable patches usually adjoin the individual houses in these extensive settlements. The Hungarian landowning gentry ape the English gentry in their manners and mode of life; but unlike their British models, they have remained feudal-minded, adamantly opposed to even the mildest land reforms.

The low birthrate average of 20 per thousand has declined still further during the war, contrary to the general trend in central Europe. The deathrate averages around 14 and infant mortality (usually around 130) is extremely high. Though no rapid growth is likely, the population seems able to reproduce itself for the next generation.

Hungarians are emigrators. With wealth distributed very unevenly, dire need has forced many to wander afield, mainly to the U.S.A., where they work mostly in heavy industry. Hungarians in the U.S.A. number 300,000, but with their families their contribution to American stock must be approximately 1,000,000.

Religion and Education. The following religions are recognized by law: Roman Catholics, 64.9%, Greek Catholics (Uniates) 2.3%, Calvinist Protestants 20.9%, Lutheran Protestants, 6.1%, Jews, 5.1%, and smaller Greek Orthodox, Unitarian, Baptist, Armenian, and Mohammedan groups. Until recently Hungary was a land of toleration, but lately antisemitic laws have been severe.

Only about 9% of adults are illiterate. School is compulsory up to 12, and children must attend continuation schools until the age of 15. There are hundreds of schools for apprentices in agriculture and commerce, and 19 training schools for teachers.

Secondary education is extensive. *Gymnasia* (or superior high schools) enroll over 70,000 pupils (four-fifths are boys). There are 5 state universities and one technical university, with an attendance of about 12,000.

Hungary's culture is famed: her high position in international drama, mostly of the *boulevard* type of play, and clever topical journalism are well known. Her serious scholars are spread far and wide, many in other lands.

The Nation's Economy

Agriculture. With 60% of her land arable, and about 58% of all employed laborers engaged in farming, Hungary is basically an agricultural nation. The country is not overpopulated for its agricultural resources; about 420 people per square mile of arable land, well below the European average.

Cereals are the principal crops: wheat alone yielding 2,400,000 tons annually, and corn about the same (though variability in corn-yields is almost two to one between good and bad years). Other important crops are potatoes, rye, barley, sugar beets, and oats. The famous Tokay wine grape is extensively cultivated in the uplands.

Hungary's per acre yields of corn are the highest in Europe, but because the country is given over to low-priced products and feudal conditions still persist in land relationships, farm cash yields are low, about $440 per man annually, almost a third less than in

See also maps on pages 51, 99.

neighboring Czechoslovakia. In such staple articles of diet as rye and potatoes, Hungary lags well behind Poland.

Landowning System. No account of Hungarian agriculture is complete without reference to the backward, near-feudal system of land tenure. Alone among the nations of central Europe she has stubbornly resisted all tendencies to land reform. Before 1914, a handful of the landed feudal-minded nobility owned a third of Hungary. In 1925, after defeat in war and revolutions, these 1,100 families still owned a third of the country. Below them, the squires or "gentry" own another sixth. Latest figures show that these landed "magnates" still own over half the farms, a situation paralleled only in Junker-controlled East Prussia. The one land "reform" that did take place was the confiscation in the 1920's of land owned by the nobility or middle class who had espoused liberalism or the cause of the Allies. And these farms went to the already dominant nobility! It may be said that the chief source of income for this landowning class is neither wheat, corn, cattle, nor grapes, but *rent*.

Thus, Hungarian farm economy is based on large estates and tenant farming, with only a small number of independent farm owners. At least two million landless farm laborers completely depend on haphazard employment, and a million others own little more than glorified Victory gardens.

For a country that has been called "the European Texas," Hungary has only a moderate cattle population: about 1,000,000 head, only 800,000 horses, and 2,500,000 pigs. Although 12% of the country is forested, timber production satisfies domestic needs only. Among the minor food sources, the excellent lake and river fish of Lake Balaton and the Danube and Tisa rivers must be mentioned.

Industry. Hungary's industrial development remains minor, except for extensive coal mining in the Pecs area in the southwest and highly skilled electrical machinery manufacture in the region around the capital, Budapest. Of the employed population 19% is engaged in industry and mining,

chiefly the latter, and most of the industries are based on agriculture: sugar refining, flour, hemp, flax, and fruit products.

Coal production usually reaches 1,000,000 tons annually, brown coal 8,000,000, but during the war the latter has risen to 12,000,000. Bauxite (for aluminum) has been mined in increasing quantities, so that Hungary has become one of the leading bauxite producers in the world. The iron and steel industry, though it has made some progress, remains small.

Skilled workers received about $9 a week in 1933, unskilled from $2 to $4. Inasmuch as the cost of living is not proportionately low, the real wages of the industrial population are even further depressed. The resulting poverty is graphically reflected in Budapest. Lying on the Danube, the capital is scenically one of the most beautiful cities in Europe, but the housing of workers has been disgraceful compared with conditions in progressive Vienna.

National Wealth and Income. Since excessive concentration of landholdings and low industrial wages do not make for a high degree of comparative wealth, Hungary's per capita assets are below those of Rumania, Yugoslavia, and Czechoslovakia.

The unit of currency is the *pengö*, normally worth 17¢ though it was "pegged" at 28¢. The last report on the people's savings, in 1938, gave $68,000,000, an extremely poor figure. At the same time, taxation in 1938 amounted to about one-third of national income, a very high peacetime percentage.

Since 1939, Hungarian economy has been closely tied to Nazi Germany's. Foreign trade has increased considerably, through territorial growth and arrangements with warring Germany. Taxation has risen from $260,000,000 in 1938 to $730,000,000 in 1943, a sharp rise even making allowances for the increased size of the country. And currency has multiplied more than sixfold from 1937 to 1942, while the cost of living has gone up by more than 50%.

Foreign Trade. Peacetime figures gave $122,-000,000 in imports and $153,000,000 in exports. Normally, 80% of Hungary's imports were manufactured goods, thus emphasizing the relative backwardness of her home industries. The chief exports were foodstuffs: wheat, flour, meat, poultry, lard, and hides, and the only manufactured product exported to any extent was electrical machinery. Hungary sold chiefly to Germany, Austria, and Italy, and bought mainly from Germany, Austria, and Rumania. Trade with the large Western powers was negligible.

The export of Hungary's chief farm product, wheat, has been based on cheap labor, which has enabled it to hold its own against Canadian and Argentine competition. If, on the other hand, the landed proprietors introduce modern machinery and techniques to compete with other wheat-exporting nations, they will throw millions of farm workers into unemployment. Fear of the social consequences has prevented this, and the dilemma of Hungarian agriculture is unresolved.

History: 1914-1944

For two centuries the kingdom of Hungary was one of the two sections of the Dual Monarchy of Austria-Hungary. Her status was that of an autonomous kingdom of this Hapsburg empire, and not a subject nation. She ruled over some 23,000,000, largely Magyars but including sizable minorities.

When in October 1918, King Charles promised to convert his realm into a federation of peoples, the Hungarian nobility protested. They threatened to cut off all food supplies from Austria if the "integrity of the lands of the Hungarian Crown" was violated. A week later, however, the Hapsburg régime collapsed with the defeat of the Central Powers by the Allies.

Radical Governments: 1918–1919. Count Michael Karolyi, a member of a wealthy landowning family, but himself a liberal with Socialist leanings, became Premier. His minister for nationalities (Oscar Jaszi) urged equal rights for all the peoples within Hungary and envisaged a federation similar to the Swiss. But this generous proposal came too late: the national minorities within Hungary's borders (Slovaks and others) were demanding independence, and the country was too weak to resist.

The revolutionary ferment continued. In the spring of 1919 a young Communist, Bela Kun, took power and proclaimed Hungary a Soviet republic. Instituting a "dictatorship of the proletariat," he sought to socialize industries in a country that was little industrialized and ill-prepared for such speedy and drastic transformation. Resistance to the Soviet régime increased, as its zealous young protagonists rushed to carry through their program. Kun, increasingly unpopular, sought to reorganize the army, drove the Czechs out of eastern Slovakia, and led a campaign against the invading Rumanians. The latter defeated his hastily formed levies and the Hungarian Soviet Republic fell apart. Bela Kun fled the country. Once in Budapest, the Rumanian armies indulged in an orgy of plunder.

The Counter-Revolution: 1919–1920. Meanwhile the Conservative elements, who had long dominated the country, prepared a counter-blow. They formed two armies: one under Rumanian command,

the other under French. When the Rumanians withdrew, and the Hapsburg Archdukes failed to regain power, a Conservative leader, Admiral Horthy, entered Budapest to restore the old monarchical order.

Accusing the Bela Kun government of having killed "585 persons," Horthy gave the signal for the "White Terror," which soon raged throughout Hungary, inflicting wholesale reprisals against the "Reds." Hungarian historians have claimed that this terror has been exaggerated; nevertheless, moderate trade unions throughout Europe proclaimed a long boycott against Hungary. At any rate, the effect was powerful enough to minimize Socialist agitation within the country for a long period.

Treaty of Trianon: 1920. The Treaty of Trianon effected the most thoroughgoing amputation suffered by any of the Central Powers, except Austria. By it, Hungary lost 67% of her pre-1914 area, about 57% of her arable land, more than half her population, and over half her factories and workers.

Hungary reverted to the former monarchical constitution. But the throne remained vacant, and Admiral Nicholas Horthy exercised the functions of a Regent.

While internal affairs were grave, external problems were even graver. Three neighboring nations, Czechoslovakia, Rumania, and Yugoslavia, organized themselves into the Little Entente, to defend their acquisitions from Hungary. Hungary, without a single friend among her neighbors, soon found herself in bitter conflict with the Czechs over Slovakia and Ruthenia, with the Austrians over Burgenland, with the Yugoslavs over the Voivodina province, with the Rumanians over Transylvania. More than that: while Austria patiently accepted her losses, Hungary clamored for justice and the revision of treaties. Her enterprising historians and propagandists sought assiduously to influence British financial and journalistic circles; and one influential publisher, Lord Rothermere, became a vehement champion of "justice for Hungary."

Reconstruction: 1925–1929. This campaign soon stood her in good stead. The attempt to rebuild the country from 1919 to 1924 had resulted in a runaway inflation, followed by economic collapse. In July 1924 London bankers subscribed 80% of a $50,000,000 loan floated for Hungary's revival. The government established a new unit of currency, the *pengö*, in July 1925; and by 1926 Hungarian recovery was complete. The League of Nations assisted generously with further loans of $250,000,000, of which Britain furnished $95,000,000 and the U.S.A. $100,000,000. Benefiting in addition from a further $90,000,000 extended in short-term credits, Hungarian foreign trade rose spectacularly.

Economic Crisis: 1929–1934. The fall in world export prices not only affected Hungary's grain market; it also damaged her small but specialized manufactures for export. By 1932 she had contracted the highest per capita foreign debt in southeastern Europe (about $85). For the first time since 1919, economic needs rather than patriotic or chauvinist pride directly shaped political demands, and an Agrarian *bloc* came into existence. The development of policies of autarky (self-sufficiency) throughout

Europe throttled exports, and Hungary defaulted on her debts. Even private business loans had to undergo long-term readjustments.

However, by 1934 the old chauvinist attitude reasserted itself. The cry again arose that Hungary's salvation lay in the restoration of her lost populations, and that with their return national welfare would gain immeasurably.

Foreign Relations: 1927–1935. As early as 1927 Count Bethlen, then Premier, sought the friendship of the rising star, Mussolini. The Allies countered at once with the Franco-Yugoslav Pact. Italy now backed "revision": that is, the demand for the reincorporation into Hungary of her lost territories. Hungary now entered fully into the Italian orbit. In 1932 Gombös became Premier, a man of amorphous Fascist tendencies, who represented the landed "gentry" as against the huge "magnates" or estate-owners.

In 1934 the Yugoslav government charged Hungary with maintaining a terrorists' camp at which the murder of the Yugoslav King Alexander had been plotted. It also declared that Hungary was equipping Croatian nationalists (the Ustachi) for acts of terror. This controversy, ineffectually handled by the League of Nations, dragged on for years.

At this time the rising power of Nazi Germany impressed the Hungarians. Although they feared that Germany might annex Austria and thus expand to their very frontiers, economic expediency required them to court the Nazis. Moreover, Hungary's ally, Italy, had proved a disappointment as a buyer of Hungarian exports.

Rise of German Influence: 1935–1944. Barter arrangements with Germany soon came to dominate Hungary's economic life. Slowly, her political life conformed to the new state of affairs. Despite some vexatious restrictions, Jews had been well treated in Hungary, but in May 1938 official antisemitism began in earnest. The avowedly pro-German Imredy took over the ministry.

The Imredy cabinet began with a show of national authority, imprisoning some Hungarian Nazis. The two small Nazi parties then united, confident that these measures were but window-dressing. After making unsuccessful overtures to the Little Entente, Imredy resigned; but Regent Horthy refused to accept his resignation. The government then proceeded to enact new racial legislation. Thus, while the surface policy of her government was always conciliatory, basically Hungary moved closer to Nazi Germany. Few countries have followed a more consistent policy of diplomatic double-dealing.

In 1937 the Upper House of Parliament voted itself wider powers and reduced the Lower House, once popularly elected, to the status of a consultative body. The Upper House proceeded to confer almost total power on Regent Horthy.

From 1939 on, Germany allowed Hungary to share in some of her booty. Hungary profited from the dismemberment of Czechoslovakia; she obtained a slice of Rumania; and she participated in the invasion and subsequent partition of Yugoslavia (1941). In June 1941 she declared war against the U.S.S.R. at Germany's behest — the Hungarians alleged that Soviet airplanes had flown over their territory. In December 1941 they formally entered the war against Britain and the U.S.A.

During the battles on the eastern front, Hungary's armies suffered considerable losses. But on the whole, the country was less affected by the conflict than any other land in southeastern Europe. On the surface, at least, she appeared prosperous. At the same time, she took pains to garrison her southern frontier with Rumania, though both nations were ostensibly allies and brothers-in-arms of Germany.

As signs of a German defeat multiplied in 1944, Hungary grew plainly restive and searched for some face-saving solution. Hitler, acting decisively, ordered the German Army to occupy the country. In April 1944 the Nazis swept away all pretenses of Hungary's position as an independent ally. In September 1944 she was at war with her erstwhile "ally," Rumania, and by the next month the Russian army was on her soil.

Foreign Affiliations. Hungary has nothing but "foes" on her frontiers. She has cultivated the friendship only of the Fascist states and of certain extreme reactionary elements in Britain. Owing to the sizable Hungarian population in the U.S.A., she has diligently courted American public opinion, but with indifferent success.

Stakes in the Peace

Hungary is primarily a grain-exporting agrarian state. Her industrial development, though somewhat expanded during World War II, is still small. Thus she entirely depends on a brisk foreign trade for a rising standard of living and future economic well-being. Foreign loans have failed to remedy her difficulties because a proper basis of foreign trade has been lacking. Reabsorption of the populations taken from her by the 1920 Treaty of Trianon has in no way seriously altered this fundamental fact. Indeed, it is difficult to avoid the conclusion that the Hungarians have constantly harped on "revision" of boundaries to divert public opinion from their backward, semi-feudal land system.

Hungary's primary stake in the peace, therefore, is friendship with her neighbors. But she can never achieve this until her land system is at least as democratic as theirs. The manufacturer and merchant are entitled to a higher status in her social and political life, replacing the landed nobility; and the workers to a higher standard of living, such as prevailed in free Czechoslovakia. Furthermore, Magyar minorities in other lands should receive genuine cultural autonomy.

Some of Hungary's demands for "revision" were perhaps justified, but they were used to promote a reactionary, bellicose policy. But once she has an agricultural system more closely resembling the French or the American, these national demands will become less of a threat to European peace and security, and she may reach suitable accommodations with her neighbors. The eclipse of the landed magnates and gentry and the rise of the farming and industrial groups would lay a solid basis for internal welfare and international amity.

ITALY

The Land and the People

For many centuries it was scarcely an exaggeration to say that all roads led to Rome. Hub of the Western world both in a secular and a spiritual sense, the Italian capital dominated the greatest empire of ancient times. Italy was mistress of the Mediterranean for over 500 years. In the Middle Ages and Renaissance her commercial and artistic supremacy was uncontested. As the center of the Roman Catholic Church, with over 300,000,000 members, she has occupied a position unique in the religious life of the Occident.

Yet from the fall of the Roman Empire until as late as 1870, Italy was not a unified country. Her cities were distinguished for their intensely local allegiances. Milan and Venice, Genoa and Florence, Palermo and Cagliari, had little in common. The barriers separating her regions, politically as well as geographically, long prevented the molding of Italy into a modern unified state.

Today this kingdom of southern Europe, most populous of the countries centering on the Mediterranean Sea, covers an area of 119,714 square miles inhabited by over 45,600,000 people. While the country is thus smaller than New Mexico, her shape is so long and narrow that she extends 650 miles from southern Sicily to the Tyrol. Her main regions, each quite different, are: (1) the Alpine northern mountains; (2) the level plain of the river Po, the country's most highly developed industrial and urban area; (3) the thin bootlike peninsula, mountainous in the spinal center, with short rivers running to the sea and narrow coastal plains; (4) the rocky island of Sardinia and the mountainous mass of Sicily.

Before World War II, Italy also possessed a colonial domain that was large in area but sparse in population and resources. This empire included Libya and Tripolitania, across the Mediterranean, populated by only 700,000, but with an area of 420,000 square miles, not to speak of adjacent deserts of 212,000 square miles. Italy's domain also embraced less important countries like Eritrea in East Africa and Somaliland, with a combined area of 239,000 square miles and a population of 1,600,000; in addition, Italy held some islands in the Aegean Sea, populated by about 130,000 Greeks, and occupied Ethiopia.

The Land. Two-fifths of the Italian people live in the Po valley, which, with its principal cities of Milan and Turin, forms the industrial center of the country. In the absence of coal resources, the abundant Alpine water-power has been used to promote manufacturing. Here the stormy climate ranges from extreme heat in summer to freezing points in winter. With abundant and fairly steady rain, the soil is exceptionally fruitful and intensely cultivated, producing in only one-fifth of Italy's area almost a third of the country's wheat, most of the corn, all of the rice, and nearly five-sixths of the beet-sugar. The Po valley is also the only center of silk production outside the Orient.

The Alps, curving about Italy's northern boundary, cut her off from Europe, only a few passes permitting the movement of traffic. In the eastern part of this sweeping range, limestone mountains, sparsely populated, separate Italy from Yugoslavia. The natural barrier formed by these hilly chains has accentuated the special national characteristics of the country.

Italy's long boot-like peninsula, dominated by the central Apennines range, which does not exceed 10,000 feet, is strewn with fertile valleys, quite isolated for the most part. The only excellent harbor, Naples, is surrounded by the most fertile and densely populated agricultural area in Europe. Two crops a year are common in this region of the olive and citrus tree. The warm Mediterranean Sea makes the climate wholly different from the continental Po basin and the cooler Alpine valleys, the winters being rather damp and cool, the summers dry and hot. Rainfall is abundant but not evenly distributed; snow is practically unknown in the lowlands.

Sicily, granary of the ancient world, is the classic land of lemons and oranges, though much of its soil, especially near the great mass of Mount Etna, is sterile. It is a warm island, with the winter temperature rarely averaging under 53°.

Italy's lack of trees — less than a tenth of her area is forested — has caused severe landslides in the wake of torrential rains, especially in the Apennine Mountains.

The country is generally deficient in mineral resources, but most seriously lacking are coal and iron, a lack which handicaps Italy for industrial competition with any of the great powers. On the other hand, she has important assets in sulfur (mostly in Sicily) and mercury. Italy furnishes half the world's supply of mercury, but the mines from which it is produced are located near Trieste and may be lost in boundary rectifications with Yugoslavia. The country's marble quarries are a continuing source of wealth.

The People. The Italian people are little changed, on the whole, from the days of Julius Caesar. The Lombards and Goths who poured in from the north did not basically affect the fairly homogeneous population of Roman days, and subsequent immigration into the country has been negligible. Italians remain primarily of Greek origin in Sicily and Naples, of Latin origin around Rome, and Etruscan around Florence. Their language is an altered Latin with few foreign admixtures.

Italians, however, have emigrated in astonishing numbers all over the world: in proportion to population, no people has emigrated more. Some estimates of emigration in a single generation reach more than 9,000,000! The countries most favored by Italy's emigrants are the U.S.A., France, Argentina, and Brazil.

The Fascist government pursued an active population policy aiming at an increase in numbers for

SWITZERLAND

AUSTRIA

HUNGARY

COPYRIGHT, FIELD PUBLICATIONS

Berne

BRENNER PASS

Bolzano

Trento

Udine

Ljubljana

Zagreb

Treviso

Vicenza

Goritza

Trieste

Susak

Fiume

Brod

Novara
Vercelli

Milan

Brescia

Verona

Padua

Venice
Chioggia

Rovigno

Pola

SAVA

Turin

Pavia

Mantova

PO RIVER

Ferrara

YUGOSLAVIA

Asti
Alessandria

Piacenza
Tortona

Parma

Reggio

Modena

Bologna

Imola

Ravenna

Cuneo

Genoa

Chiavari

Faenza
Forli

Cesena

Rimini

Zara

Sarajevo

Savona

San Remo

La Spezia

Carrara
Massa
Lucca

Pistoia

SAN MARINO

Pesaro

FRANCE

Nice

Imperia

Monte Carlo

MONACO

Pisa

Florence

Arezzo

Ancona

Spalato

Leghorn
(Livorno)

CAPRAIA

Perugia

Dubrovnik
(Ragusa)

Piombino

ELBA

PIANOSA

MONTE CRISTO

Grosseto

GIGLIO

Pescara

Calvi

Corte

Bastia

Sulmona

Termoli

Ajaccio

CORSICA

Vatican City

Rome

I T A L Y

Campobasso

Barletta

Bonifacio

MADDALENA IS.
CAPRERA IS.

Foggia

Bari

ASINARA

Tempio

Terranova

PONZIANE IS.

Benevento

Altamura

Potenza

Martina Franca

Brindisi

Porto Torres

Sorso

Sassari

Otieri

Nuoro

Naples

Salerno

ISCHIA

Sorrento

CAPRI

Taranto

Otranto

SARDINIA

Sorgono

Capri

Gallipoli

Oristano

Sibari
Corigliano

Rossano

Iglesias

Cagliari

TYRRHENIAN SEA

Cosenza

Crotone

SAN PIETRO

Catanzaro

SAN'ANTIOCO

USTICA

EOLIE ISLANDS

Palmi

MEDITERRANEAN SEA

Barcellona

San Giovanni

Scilla

Reggio Calabria

Trapani

Palermo

Partinico

Patti

Messina

EGADI IS.

Alcamo

Cefalu

Taormina

STRAIT OF MESSINA

Marsala

Castelvetrano

Menfi

SICILY

Enna

Mazara del Vallo

Ribera

Catania

STRAIT OF SICILY

Sciacca

Agrigento

Augusta

Bizerte

Porto Empedocle

Gela

Syracuse

Bone

La Calle

Sedjenane

Mateur

GULF OF TUNIS

CAPE BON

Ragusa

Vittoria

Modica

Tabarka

Beja

Tunis

Kelibia

PANTELLERIA

ALGERIA

Nebeur

Medjez el Bab

Laghouan

Nabeul
Hammamet

Souk Ahras

Le Kef

Pont du Fahs

Enfidaville

GOZO

Valletta

TUNIS

Maktar

Ousseltia

Sousse

MEDITERRANEAN SEA

MALTA

Kairouan

Monastir

LONG ISLAND
DRAWN TO SAME SCALE

RAILROADS

0   50   100   150 Miles

military enterprise. Despite this effort, the net increase diminished. The birthrate, 29.7 per thousand when Mussolini took power, declined to 23.4 in 1940 and 20.2 in 1942; the deathrate sank from 17.3 to 14.1 in the same period. Thus the annual increment was 6.1 per thousand when Mussolini fell, as against 12.4 when he became dictator. Infant mortality at 108 per thousand has not decreased in the last decade, so that the net reproduction rate had sunk to 1.13 in 1935-37. On the basis of statistics, one can forecast that Italy's population will be a little more than 50,000,000 a generation hence.

Religion and Education. Practically all Italians (an estimated 99%) follow Roman Catholicism, the state religion. Nevertheless, in the north there has been an anticlerical attitude in politics as well as a rather indifferent performance of religious duties among large segments of the people. In the south, religious practice is strict and practically universal.

Other religious faiths are tolerated, though some restrictions were made against the Jews but not against the practice of their religion. Upon Mussolini's fall, these restrictions were repealed.

Education is tuition-free and compulsory to the age of 14; and yet there is a great deal of illiteracy among adults of the south, especially of Apulia, Calabria, and Sicily. About 150,000 attend advanced schools and 55,000 study at the 5 free and 22 private universities. Many of these institutions are among the most ancient in Europe. Bologna was founded in 1200, Perugia in 1276, Pavia in 1300. In the pre-Fascist period, the universities were the true centers of erudition and liberal culture: even under Mussolini much time was required before these schools could be made to conform to political expediency. Italian books on politics never sank to the levels of German distortion, even in the worst periods of Fascist tyranny.

The Nation's Economy

Agriculture. Italy is intensively farmed, as a whole, with 42% of the land under cultivation — a high figure, considering the mountainous character of the country. Nevertheless, some yields are inadequate: wheat, for example, despite governmental encouragement, yields less per acre than in France. The yield of corn is the best in Europe, however, and it is the base of the staple dish of the poor — called *polenta*.

The draining of swamps has added a little to the arable area, but a change from the *latifundia* system (great estates worked by poor tenant farmers) in the south might raise farm yields to the higher average of the Po valley. The crop production per man is quite low: 46% of the population is engaged in agriculture — far too many for the yield. Not only is the productivity per acre below most of France in even the most progressive areas of Italy, but the annual farm production amounts to only $244 per worker as against $340 in Spain, $305 in Yugoslavia, $583 in southern France — to consider merely Italy's Mediterranean neighbors! As compared with the $800 in northern France, it is actually pitiful. The capital wasted by Mussolini in futile conquests could have been better devoted to solving this central problem of Italy.

The principal crop is wheat, of which the country now produces four-fifths of her requirements; but durum wheat, the base of spaghetti and macaroni, must still be imported (from Russia and the U.S.A.). Wine production is large, averaging over two-thirds that of France. Olive oil production is the second in Europe, usually reaching about two-thirds of normal Spanish production. Crops have been adversely affected since 1939 by the war, and the continuous shortages that have been accumulating now constitute a serious deficiency. With a population of 1.4 persons to every acre of arable land, Italy requires a more progressive system of agriculture.

The animal economy of Italy is not satisfactory. She has half as many horses as France, and she is adequately supplied only in sheep.

Industry. About 25% of gainfully employed Italians are in industry. The country is not very well mechanized, with machinery investment per capita approximately $2.40 (as against $3.50 in France, $8.75 in Germany, and $31.70 in the U.S.A.). The principal industries are textile manufacturing (cotton, silk, and rayon), sugar-refining, and cheese-making. Chemicals are important, especially the Montecatini sulfur works. Turin manufactures automobiles and machinery, and the country has a fair-sized aviation industry. Production of food specialties, particularly macaroni and tomato paste, continues to play a large part in the nation's economy.

Shipping. With a merchant marine estimated at 4,500,000 tons, Italy has made a bid for maritime power. For a time, her luxury liners were prominent in transatlantic traffic. Submarine sinkings may not have been compensated for by new shipbuilding, but Italy's merchant marine is ample for her carrying trade.

National Wealth and Income. Italy is an astonishingly poor country, when her historic position is taken into account. Wealth per capita approximates $405, a fifth under Yugoslavia's, and two-fifths of Spain's. Although she is somewhat more populated than France, her wealth is only a third. The national income of about $103 per capita is also low, but in this respect the comparison with Spain and France is better, 6% less than the first and 60% that of the second country. Clearly then, Italy wants accumulated capital more than she wants industrial activity.

Although Italy is an old European banking state, 3% of her net national wealth was owned by foreigners. She paid out about 1% net of her national income to foreigners, without receiving compensation in goods. But, of course, the large receipts from tourists and pilgrims to the Vatican City, and from emigrant remittances, must have made up for this loss.

Foreign Trade. Exports approximated $550,-000,000 in 1938, imports about $590,000,000. An unfavorable trade balance was chronic, and later estimates show it as aggravated. Foreign trade per capita was half that of neighboring France, and a fifth of Britain's.

In normal times she exported principally to Germany, Switzerland, and Britain; and her imports were primarily from Germany, the British Empire, and the U.S.A.

History: 1914-1944

1915-1918. Italy, a constitutional monarchy consolidated in 1861, entered World War I as an Allied power in May 1915, nearly ten months after France and Britain. Since 1882 she had been a member of the Triple Alliance with Austria and Germany. The Allies, seeking to detach Italy permanently from this grouping, offered her (1915) the secret Treaty of London, which granted her large territorial gains in the Balkans and the Near East. But when the war ended, it became clear that the Treaty of London could not be fulfilled short of another war. The new nationalities arising out of the ruins of the old Austrian Empire, together with a modernized Turkey, would resist Italian expansion. Hence Italy felt that she was a victim of bad faith.

This sense of betrayal explains much of her postwar thinking, especially in foreign affairs. As it was, she received the Trentino district in Austria, 250,000 Austrians of German speech in Southern Tyrol, the port of Trieste, and adjacent areas largely populated by Slavs. The Allies, moreover, confirmed her possession of the Dodecanese Islands, Greek in population. Nevertheless, Italy considered herself cheated of the fruits of victory.

Industrial Disorders: 1919-1920. Though a victor in the war, Italy resembled a defeated nation. Unemployment was widespread, especially among the returned veterans. A depreciated currency, a large debt, rising prices, a feeling of historic futility, all combined to fan discontent and disorder in the country. Revolutions throughout Europe affected Italy's workers, the mass of whom were Socialists. The middle classes in the north, largely agnostic and republican, despised the government at Rome. The intellectuals fell under the spell of "futurist" poetry and of hard, Nietzschean doctrines.

The poet D'Annunzio, from whom Mussolini later stole most of his ideas, whipped up the spirit of expansion and martial glory. In 1919 D'Annunzio formed a body of young men (called the *Arditi*) to sweep down upon Fiume, a Yugoslav city with an Italian population. These young men acted like *banditti*, wore black shirts, howled bombastically, swore obedience to an inspired leader. At this time, Mussolini, formerly a violent Leftist Socialist, was editing a newspaper in Milan. This political renegade held no positive doctrines. The French Foreign Office had paid him to agitate for Italy's entrance into the war. During the war itself he was enthusiastically pro-Ally and republican, violently anti-Catholic. Friendly to the D'Annunzio group, he quickly absorbed their passion for glory, personal expansion, and their inchoate but grandiloquent dogma.

In 1919 vague movements called *squadre* (mostly of ex-soldiers) were sweeping north Italy. Bitter and sanguinary conflicts divided the social classes. In this atmosphere, the cry arose that Italy must succeed France as the mother of the Latin peoples. The expansionists shouted that Italy was the heir of Rome.

They claimed Savoy and Nice in France, as well as Corsica and Tunis.

The old politicians who composed the government could see no new forces arising. Typical liberal statesmen of an earlier day, they were good Europeans, skilled negotiators, with a nicely balanced sense of possibilities and limitations, of give and take. The ardent, unemployed youth hated them. And in the north young veterans were becoming municipal bosses, called *Rases* (a Ras is an Ethiopian chief). In addition, the fear of Bolshevism played havoc with old-time arrogant manufacturers, to whom the idea of a labor union, however mild, was abhorrent. They were glad to subsidize a counter-revolutionary guard.

The Italians, born originators, invented the "sit-down strike." When the workers occupied the factories in May 1919, hoisting the Italian flag, Mussolini endorsed the sit-down as a manifestation of "will." But when the workers raised the red flag and formed "Red Guards," Mussolini joined the employers. He demanded direct action. The *squadre*, the *Arditi*, the *Rases*, were ready at hand. Soon the disorders spread to the peasantry. They began to reach southern Italy, always decades behind the modern, educated North.

On March 23, 1919, the Fascist Party was founded. The Socialist Party, meanwhile, was split between Maximalists (sympathetic to Soviet Russia) and Moderates. Prime Minister Giolitti carefully reduced the sit-down strikes until in 1921 the number of industrial strikers declined by 50%, agricultural strikers by 90%. Mussolini was later to claim that he had put an end to this serious problem. Actually the strikes were over long before he entered office.

Transition to Fascism: 1920-1922. In April 1921 Giolitti dissolved Parliament. He asked the young, fluid section of disciplined terrorists to help him defeat the Catholics (Popular Party) and the Socialists. After their services to Giolitti, the Fascists returned only 35 members to Parliament and their movement began to decline. They now became Monarchists, even Clericals; they demanded a few paltry ministerial jobs. But Facta, the new Prime Minister, treated them with contempt. Then four fanatical leaders, de Bono, de Vecchi, Balbo, and Bianchi, gathered 50,000 of their following and marched them into Rome to demonstrate. It was a "march against politicians," a march of 50,000 unemployed middle-class young men hungry for government jobs and apparently incapable of passing civil service examinations. King Victor Emmanuel refused the government's request to sign a "state of siege" declaration. Suddenly he telegraphed Mussolini to form a ministry. Mussolini arrived on a Pullman sleeper. Such was the "Revolutionary march on Rome" of October 1922.

No sooner was Mussolini in power than he rudely kicked the Fascists out of Rome and immediately formed a coalition government with the hated "politicians." Four Fascists received posts, ten non-Fascists. Mussolini thereupon asked for "special powers." These were granted his ministry by a vote of 215 to 80, even the Catholics wishing to give him, as they thought, an opportunity to fail. Socialists and Communists voted "No."

Mussolini was the prisoner of the Popular (Catholic)

Party and its astute leader, Sturzo. Unless he could break the Catholic hold, he was their messenger boy, although nominally Prime Minister. He therefore framed an election law under which the plurality party (not the majority) was to have two-thirds of the parliamentary seats — another original Italian idea that was later copied in many countries. The Catholics resigned, furious at betrayal. The electoral law passed, and in 1923, Mussolini's party won a clear majority of votes by the lavish use of cudgels and "castor-oil persuasion" (another innovation). The government declared a million ballots invalid because they were "mutilated by illiterates."

Parliament assembled, but to Mussolini's amazement, the opposition would not down. Socialist leaders, above all Matteotti, continued to expose him. The country showed its moral disgust. Satirists, cartoonists, intellectuals opened fire. When Matteotti was murdered, Italy recoiled in horror from her "Balkanized" government. Mussolini promptly laid the blame on some associates. He reconstructed the cabinet, relied on Nationalists, promised to stop violence, and reform his unpopular Fascist party. The opposition refused to believe this "perpetual coward and liar," as they termed him. They left his Parliament and adjourned to a hall on the Aventine Hill — and became known as the Aventine opposition. Mussolini solicited their return, but they refused. Every man who counted for anything in Italy was with the Aventine, including the former premiers. Realizing that he must act alone or perish, Mussolini carried on with only 300 deputies chosen by his election system. On December 27, 1924, the opposition, under Rossi, charged Mussolini with being Matteotti's murderer, and demanded his arrest as a common assassin. Mussolini answered by creating "the Fascist State."

Fascism: 1925–1927. On January 3, 1925, he disciplined and muzzled the press. It took a year before he shackled the great conservative newspapers, but opposition organs went at once. Even when he was dictator, however, he watched his step. Not until 1926 did he declare that only rich countries could afford free speech and that Italy was too poor to afford more than one opinion, a cry parroted by Hitler in 1935. Mussolini abolished Freemasonry because it was pro-French and devoted to the "obsolete principles of liberty and equality." In November 1926, after the most nearly successful of the many attempts to take his life, the dictator passed a law for the defense of the State. After this, any trace of liberty was dead. It had taken him four years to round out the new doctrine.

Still, Fascism had no fixed principles. The party was divided. Its leaders, hungry for graft, were corrupt, quarrelsome, disobedient, like the cupbearers of Al Capone. To assure them posts, Mussolini deprived the 125 Parliament deputies of the Aventine opposition of their seats. He jailed thousands of opponents without trials. He formed a secret police, the "Ovra," inspirer of the "Gestapo" in Germany. He banished thousands more to the islands, especially Lipari. The most brilliant men fled into exile, braving the secret police in the Alps. Thus was bred the Fascist plague, later to sicken Europe through the Nazis, imitators of Mussolini.

The Italians originated the Nazi pattern: street brawls, violence by degradation (castor oil), the shirt (black in their instance), uniform style of dress, the salute (the Roman upraised hand), strutting parades, worship of war as "the only male activity," mental poisoning of youth (from children of four in the "wolf cubs," of around eight in the "Balillas," and of sixteen in the "Young Guard"), the jailing of intellectuals and dissenters, deprivation of the seats of elected deputies, refusal to grant trials, suppression of free speech and free press. The Fascists emphasized youth — their song was *Giovinezza* (Youth), sung even by greybeards. They developed artistic "futurism." They prated of the "poor state" and the "have-not states."

But they needed more: a unified party, discipline, a doctrine, some reason for being. Hence in 1927, they welded the party under the "Duce" or Leader (the German *Fuehrer*) who was infallible. Society was to be "organic"; classes were to be superseded by the unity of the nation; labor, capital, and the professions were to be formed in "corporations"; free speech was "analytical" whereas obedience was "synthetical"; equality was an insult to facts. Mussolini's philosopher, Gentile, created an elaborate theory of "Hierarchy."

The Fascists drew up a charter of labor and created a "Corporate State." Then Mussolini forced the weary and oppressed to become joyful at night in Fascist-sponsored recreations (*Dopolavoro*). (The Germans copied every item, the last as "Strength through Joy.") For all this elaborate nonsense, there was not even the trace of the functioning of the "Corporate State" until late in 1931, although pro-Fascists everywhere pointed to its glittering success when it did not even exist.

Consolidation of Organized Fascism: 1927–1935. In the meantime Mussolini had become the maverick of foreign affairs. He had entered Albania. He bombed refugees in Corfu, and as a reward for his mass murder of these innocents, the League of Nations forced Greece to pay him damages (1924). He threatened war, drilled reserves on the French frontier, and began the technique, later used by Hitler, of keeping the world in everlasting turmoil and fear. But all this did not produce bread and employment. In 1925 Il Duce found himself with a crashing currency and a deep industrial crisis — and this when all Europe and America were recovering without his philosophy. To the U.S.A. he sent a conservative, Count Volpi, who returned with a handsome loan that year. Then followed a sizable number of American loans, for industrial, and above all, hydroelectric enterprises. The confidence given by these Americans to his régime greatly aided his cash box and his prestige; the currency was stabilized and economic recovery slowly matured (1926–27). Mussolini used the funds partly to subsidize the Fascist militia. Even one American poet, Ezra Pound, was later subsidized to betray his country.

Mussolini still fulminated. In 1925 he charged that the banks had destroyed the *lira*; he promised to cope with these "parasites." They told him to keep quiet and he cringed. He even restored freedom of speculation on the notoriously manipulated Milan stock exchange.

Italy's greatest need was land reform. The large estates in the south were comparatively unproductive and the people had been forced to emigrate in large masses. In 1924 the U.S.A. restricted this emigration. Fortunately, France remained, as did Argentina. But the reduction of emigration outlets was quite serious; it became necessary to cope with the problem.

Of all Balkan, eastern, and southeastern countries, only Hungary did less than Mussolini to redistribute land holdings. Instead he publicized a scheme for draining the Pontine swamps. The amount involved in such showy public works with which foreigners were beguiled, was at best not 5% of what democratic France was spending without swaggering. When it became clear that neither pleasantry nor public works could beguile the people, Mussolini opened the "Battle for Wheat." Italy obtained a larger wheat production, but at the cost of raising more expensive garden and fruit produce. Hence, the farmer was further impoverished to make the country self-sufficient for war. The last straw was the statement that the trains now ran on time. While this was true of the luxury expresses used by foreigners, other train schedules did not appreciably violate their established levels of punctuality. However, the Fascists drove beggars from the streets so that they might not annoy tourists, and they cleared some of the worst slums of Naples.

In 1930 the crisis hit Italy. It prostrated the land after a feeble recovery. The banks had to be salvaged by a new institute which took over their frozen loans. Industrial unemployment rose to over a million. (It remained over 600,000 even in 1935 with war preparations going on.) The Fascists never solved the crisis. As late as 1938, industrial activity per capita had not recovered to the 1929 level, itself only a poor recovery from the chronic crisis of the 20's.

Hitler's advent to power (1933) both fortified and threatened Mussolini's position. He was strengthened by the conversion of Europe's most powerful industrial state to his Fascism and by Germany's aping of all the forms and slogans Mussolini had developed. He was threatened by the fact that a powerful Germany could never be countered by an industrially weak Italy. Mussolini had slowly built up Balkan power, especially by championing reactionary Hungary against the "Little Entente." A paramount Germany would jeopardize his dominant position in Hungary and Austria. His only other tenuous hold was in Bulgaria and in almost worthless Albania.

The Fascist dictator had only one domestic triumph, the Lateran Treaty of 1929, which had ended the 58 years of cool relations between the Vatican and Italy. He flirted with France, but increasingly relied on Germany. After the murder of Dollfuss in Austria showed him that Hitler was intent on conquest in his own orbit, Mussolini signed a treaty with Germany for division of "spheres of influence" (1936).

The Ethiopian and Spanish Wars: 1935–1938. The overshadowing rise of Germany and the continuing crisis, which he could not overcome, led Mussolini to an adventure in Africa. Italy had long coveted Ethiopia. In an attempt to conquer that country in 1896, she suffered defeat at Adowa.

Mussolini spoke constantly of wiping out the "shame of Adowa." Between 1934 and 1935 the Fascists carefully worked up provocations while the Italian General Staff planned war. An incident at Walwal (early 1935) provided the occasion for a belligerent press campaign, and in September, Italy launched her invasion. The League of Nations, after dallying, imposed sanctions on Italy (November 1935). But the sanctions were so arranged that they afforded the maximum of irritation and the minimum of practical results. Italy conquered Ethiopia in May 1936 and the Italian King was designated emperor.

It soon became clear that conquered Ethiopia could not aid Italian employment or trade for many years. A new diversion occurred. The Italians aided General Franco in his attempt to establish Fascism in Spain. For two years Italy poured far more than she could afford into a bloody venture so cynical that the last shreds of decency were gone. Italy's humiliating defeat at Guadalajara in 1937 made her the mockery of Europe.

Guadalajara had an effect on Hitler. Having jointly guaranteed with Mussolini the independence of Austria in 1936, he now expressed his contempt by taking Austria without consulting his co-guarantor. Mussolini swallowed the pill. Germany now had taken away his last sphere of influence, the Balkan regions. His power was gone.

It flickered briefly when he was made the instrument for appealing to the four powers of Europe to seek peace in the Czechoslovak question. Hence at Munich the rôle played by Mussolini appeared to be significant. It masked his historic futility.

World War II and Mussolini's Fall: 1939–1943. At the outbreak of the European war, Italy, the second member of Hitler's "Axis," remained neutral. She did not wish to drain her feeble resources until a quick victory was assured. On June 10, 1940, when France lay at the feet of the Nazi conqueror, Mussolini entered the contest. In 1939 he had conquered King Zog of Albania; in 1936, the poverty-stricken Ethiopians. This time he reckoned poorly. France went down and he had the satisfaction of policing Nice, birthplace of Garibaldi. But the Germans granted him nothing, not even Corsica or Tunis. They preferred to play with a weak, but far richer France than with a proven nullity.

Mussolini sought to retrieve his tarnished fame (for his small loot led to much ridicule, even in suppressed Italy). In October 1940, he attacked Greece, a state with a tenth of Italy's strength. The Greeks soundly trounced him and brought him close to destruction. At this point the Germans, who had enjoyed his discomfiture, came to the rescue and conquered Greece for him. He then entered Africa, but the inconsequential campaign of his general, Graziani, led to the Germans' unmistakably taking over under Marshal Rommel. Mussolini then lost Tripoli, his last colony (the British had already restored Ethiopia to her Emperor and taken Italy's other African colonies). The Allies took his last legions in Tunis, and then invaded Sicily. In July 1943 the palace revolution in Rome, engineered by the king and Marshal Badoglio, eliminated the wretched conqueror. Mussolini was imprisoned, but later rescued by German aviators.

On September 8, Badoglio concluded an armistice with the Allies. Mussolini then formed a shadow government at Verona, called the Workers' Fascist Republic (October 1943). In 1944 he was an exhibit in Hitler's cinema appearances, his health impaired, a bloated, aged man, whose mental balance was even questioned. In Milan and Turin the workers were reoccupying factories and battling the Fascists. In the peninsula, Allied troops took Rome and advanced to the valley of the Po. By August 1944 the former dictator had a shadow authority, invalidated by popular revolt and completely subject to the Nazi military.

The Aftermath: 1943–1944. Neither Marshal Badoglio nor King Victor Emmanuel excited popular enthusiasm. The many parties of the old Aventine opposition, considered long dead by the Fascist police, revived with amazing speed. Leading the Liberals were Benedetto Croce, the intellectual glory of the kingdom, and old-line diplomats of the great tradition, like Count Sforza. There were exiles who insisted on an anti-Vatican policy, like Professor Salvemini of Harvard University. The Communists were led by Togliatti ("Ercoli"). The older Socialists were active, as was the Catholic Party. All these various groupings managed to reduce their differences and arrive at a common program. As a result of popular pressure, the king agreed to relinquish power to his son, Umberto, when Rome was regained. This was achieved in June 1944.

Under the armistice agreement with the Allies, however, military government prevailed, with civil government as a cooperating agency. This led to bickerings and discontents, but none sufficient to alter the social bases of the kingdom. A new civil government under Bonomi, who had been premier in 1921, replaced Badoglio. There was a constant regrouping of parties, but criticism, free speech, and intelligence were reborn. The terror had ceased. In 1944 the kingdom, bereft of factitious grandeur, poor, desolated by a régime that had ignored every vital problem to center on every showy avoidance, found herself face to face with almost baffling difficulties. Italy's fleet was at the service of the United Nations, however, and her volunteers and guerrillas proved that the spirit of Garibaldi, long dormant, could be roused when liberty was once more a possibility.

Stakes in the Peace

Italy is the poorest of the major powers, primarily because she lacks natural resources. Her poverty is accentuated by her lack of capital in agriculture and by her antiquated landholding system in the south, especially in Sicily, Calabria, and the Abruzzi. In the more fertile areas the subdivision of land is excessive, cooperation feebly developed. Even a superficial study of Italy's agricultural yields shows that her dairying could be doubled with ease both as to cattle population and milk, that yields per acre of basic food crops could be advanced a third.

Italy requires free trade. This will enable her to export high-priced specialties (berries, olives, citrus fruits) and greens (lettuce, romaine, broccoli, asparagus). Intensive culture in the dense areas and organized farming in the extensive cultivation areas could effect a great increase of yield. Together with larger capital and better farming methods, this would increase per capita national income by more than a half and raise Italy to a level rivaling southern France.

In industry, Italy cannot so easily overcome the handicap of shortages in coal, oil, and iron. Outside of rayon and cotton, Italy's products do not occupy too brilliant a competitive position. Here too, it would seem as if the artisans might be better organized, with chambers of commerce seeking to market high-priced items. The widespread arts and crafts in Italy are still pursued on an uncoordinated basis, their principal outlet being the tourist market.

In heavy industry, Italy might stress aluminum transformation and electro-chemical enterprise. After all, Switzerland, with much the same assets and liabilities industrially as northern Italy, has a per capita production in industry twice that of the Milan area. To achieve this, Italy needs more widespread technical knowledge. Though she has superb engineers and mathematicians, their achievements have been rather abstract. The production of an encyclopedia so beautiful, rich, and learned that it shamed America and England — but at a price that only the very wealthiest can afford — is only too typical of Italian enterprise.

Since "glory" is gone, the waste of money on army, navy, and bogus public works could go into education, rebuilding, and farm machinery. Italy requires capital (from a world organization) and the services of farm experts. Her colonies are important neither for her nor for any other country; their disposition is almost a psychological matter of Italian pride. She has already agreed to yield the Dodecanese Islands to Greece.

Italy was, until the Fascist shame, a liberal country, almost first in the world in humane penology, social science, and intellectual maturity. She was always a decent member of the family of nations. She can resume that position tomorrow.

LUXEMBOURG

The Land and the People

The grand duchy of Luxembourg, tucked away between France, Belgium, and Germany, has developed a spirit of patriotism remarkable for a country so tiny and so involved in frequent diplomatic machinations. A vestige of the numerous principalities that constituted the old Holy Roman Empire, Luxembourg lost her western half (which is now a Belgian province), passed through a series of sovereignties that read like a romantic novel, and finally, in 1867, became an independent, neutralized state. Although the Prussian garrison was withdrawn at that time, Luxembourg remained a member of the German Customs Union, predecessor to the German Empire. But after the Germans violated her neutrality in the First World War, unable to function alone, she voted for an economic union with France; and when that was declined, joined a customs and currency union with Belgium (to endure until 1971). She is, therefore, economically in the Belgian area, and has shared Belgium's fate. When the Germans occupied the country in 1940 they incorporated her into their own customs area again.

The Land. Luxembourg has an area of only 999 square miles (a fifth less than Rhode Island's). Yet, small as she is, she has two distinct types of country and climate: in the north, raw winters and infertile uplands which are part of the great Ardennes Forest; in the south, the fertile Lorraine slope, where the sunnier climate permits grape-growing. The whole country lies at a fairly high altitude.

The People. Wedged between southeast Belgium, French Lorraine, and the German district of the upper Moselle, Luxembourg combines all three in her people and culture. The language is a German dialect, but French is widely known and largely employed in official communication. This sort of Franco-German culture has been characteristic of the Lorraine region since the days of Charlemagne.

The rate of natural increase of the people is very low, but the level of intellectual attainment is high. Education is tuition-free and compulsory; illiteracy is unknown. With a population about the same as that of Akron, Ohio, Luxembourg has approximately equal educational facilities: 24 high schools, 5 advanced high schools, 13 specialized colleges, and an academy of music. Luxembourgers are almost unanimously Roman Catholic.

The Nation's Economy

Agriculture. About a third of the people work on farms — some 450,000 acres are under cultivation. Cattle, pigs, and poultry are numerous, and the yields, especially of the main products — potatoes, oats, and rye — are far above the European average. Indeed, Luxembourg's general prosperity in normal times is surpassed only by that of the most intensively cultivated areas of Belgium, Denmark, and the Netherlands.

Industry. Before the war, the country mined annually about 5,000,000 tons of iron ore (the iron content of which was as high as a third) — more for her size than any other country in Europe. Her production of cast iron (1,800,000 tons) and of steel (2,000,000 tons) was impressive not only relatively but absolutely. Iron and steel production together were valued at some $42,000,000, or $140 per person.

One of the richest and most industrialized parts of the famous Lorraine ore fields, Luxembourg has been included in a series of cartel arrangements that have dominated European iron and steel production since the 1900's. Of course, nearly all Luxembourg production is normally exported.

Finance. Practically the entire adult population (60%) had savings accounts before the war, at the rate of $76 per capita, $23,000,000 in all. Taxation came to about $10,000,000 (approximately $33 per citizen), and the national debt was about $16,000,000 domestic and $7,000,000 foreign. How much the Germans have added to this burden is not clear.

History: 1914-1944

Although German armies occupied Luxembourg during World War I, her mining economy was not seriously affected because she had been a member of the German Customs Union. Upon the annulment of this membership (in 1918) Luxembourg was given five years of customs-free export quotas to Germany equal to her average pre-war trade. Thus, she was able to manage through the interim period.

In 1920 a plebiscite called for economic union with France, 60,000 favored it against 22,000 for Belgium. But the French government, solicitous of Belgian friendship, asked Luxembourg to form an economic union with Belgium. Though the Belgians were piqued by the preference shown France, Luxembourg and Belgium entered into an economic union for fifty years and proper customs and currency alignments were effected.

Meanwhile, Grand Duchess Marie Adelaide had abdicated in favor of her popular sister, Charlotte. The dynasty was victorious in a popular referendum (1919), though the constitution was liberalized in some important respects.

Luxembourg followed Belgian policy in foreign relations, and adhered to the Oslo Convention (1930) with the Scandinavian states. In 1935 her currency conformed, though not fully, to the Belgian devaluation. The following year, when the Belgian king withdrew from a military alliance with France, Luxembourg and Belgium undertook plans for common frontier defense.

Internally the political situation remained static. Some 45% adhered to the Conservative Catholic Party, in power; about 33% to the Socialist Party, which was aggressively anticlerical; and 11% to various liberal and radical groups.

Germany occupied the country on May 10, 1940. The bitter people expressed their hostility through common strikes and demonstrations. The Germans then incorporated the country into the Reich. About a tenth of the male population had meanwhile been deported to Germany. In September 1944, following the Allied drive against the Nazis, the government-in-exile returned to its duchy.

Luxembourg's stake in the peace cannot be basically differentiated from that of Belgium; which is also true of her foreign relations. (See *Belgium*.)

THE NETHERLANDS

The Land and the People

The Kingdom of the Netherlands, unofficially called Holland, is rich out of all proportion to her size in money, empire, and fame. Her empire almost girdles the globe. The names of her cities — Delft, Leiden, Haarlem — the dikes, windmills, balloon-trousered skaters, and milkmaids of her traditional landscape; and even many of her family names — such as Van Buren, Roosevelt — are comfortably familiar to Americans.

The Dutch are the only people in the world who have literally made their land.

> *Holland that scarce deserves the name of land,*
> *But as the offscouring of British sand,*
> *And so much soil as was contributed*
> *By British pilots when they heaved the lead,*

sneered a 17th-century British poet, when the two nations were at war. But what better compliment could he have paid to the ingenious industry which reclaimed Holland from the sea? It is an old Dutch saying that the principal manufacture of Holland is Holland.

The Land. This reclaimed land lies on the northeastern coast of the European mainland, about 100 miles east of Britain at the nearest point. To the north and west is the North Sea, to the south Belgium, to the east Germany; the inland boundaries follow no natural features of topography.

The present area of the country is 12,692 square miles, about as large as Connecticut and New Jersey combined. When the project for filling in the Zuider Zee is completed, there will be about 13,500 square miles of land, and further reclamation may increase this figure. Meanwhile the 9,000,000 people live 700 to the square mile.

Ever since the Middle Ages, Holland has been densely peopled. The land is low and flat. The great cities — Amsterdam, Rotterdam, The Hague — lie below sea level, protected by dikes or by high dunes along the coast. Three-quarters of the people live below sea level. Only in the little tongue of land called Maastricht, between Belgium and Germany, is there any point higher than 300 feet.

Back of the coastal dunes lies a region of sandy soil where flowers and vegetables flourish. Behind the sand stretch grassy lowlands known as the *polders*, everywhere crisscrossed by ditches and canals (Amsterdam has been called the Venice of the North). The landscape of the polders, with its pastures, thin gray skies, and ancient windmills (used in the old days as a primitive source of power), is familiar to American museum-goers from the faithful paintings of the Dutch masters. Through this country, from Germany to the sea, flows the Rhine. At its estuary is the great port of Rotterdam, which, with Antwerp in Belgium, in normal times leads the continent in shipping tonnage.

This tiny, flat, water-intersected land boasts the third-largest colonial empire in the world. In the Pacific lie the Netherlands East Indies: the storied Spice Islands, Netherlands New Guinea, and Java, Sumatra, part of Borneo, fabulous Bali, the Celebes. In the Caribbean region, on the opposite side of the globe, lie Surinam (Dutch Guiana), and the West Indies islands of Curaçao and Aruba. The Empire of the Netherlands comprises in all 790,000 square miles, with over 70,000,000 people. It contains almost 8 times the population and over 60 times the area of the mother country.

The People. The Dutch are Germanic in origin and speak one of the numerous Low German dialects, but across the centuries, as they developed their own rich tradition, they have become sharply differentiated from the other Low Germans. North of the Rhine the people are predominantly blond, south of it mixed. They are a tall people, well above the European norm, averaging nearly 5 feet 7, both men and women. There is some slight admixture of Javanese blood, as many middle-class men have gone out to Java and married Javanese women.

The Netherlands is unique among Western industrial nations in that the birthrate has not fallen off in recent years. This fact is not to be explained by any government-sponsored or other organized campaign: on the contrary, birthcontrol information has been encouraged. Nevertheless the annual birthrate has remained between 20 and 21 per thousand, an average distinctly higher than that of any neighboring country. The deathrate is equally remarkable:

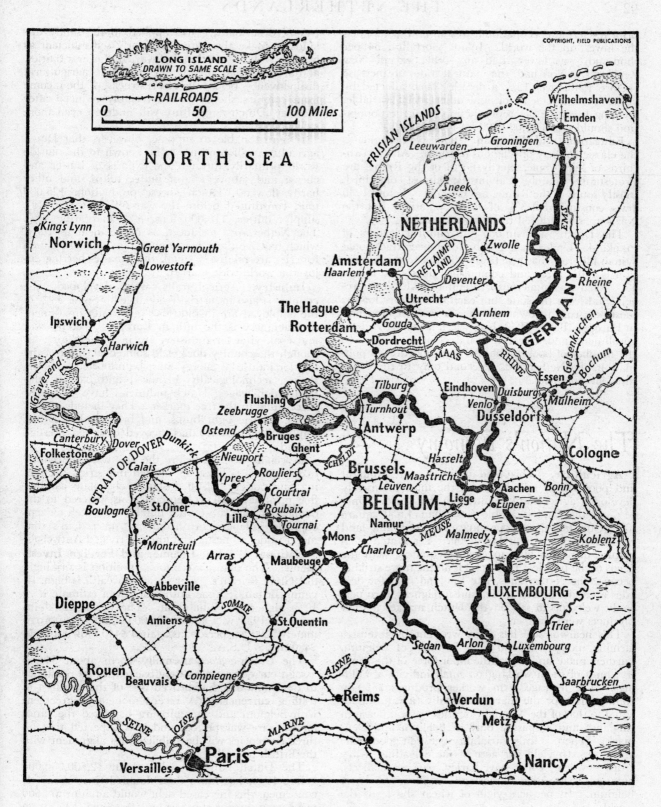

LONG ISLAND
DRAWN TO SAME SCALE

— RAILROADS —

0   50   100 Miles

NORTH SEA

FRISIAN ISLANDS

Leeuwarden   Groningen

Wilhelmshaven
Emden

King's Lynn

Norwich   Great Yarmouth
             Lowestoft

Sneek

NETHERLANDS

Zwolle

Amsterdam
Haarlem   RECLAIMED LAND

Deventer   Rheine

Ipswich

Harwich

The Hague   Utrecht   Arnhem
Rotterdam
             Gouda   GERMANY
Gravesend   Dordrecht   Gelsenkirchen
                              MAAS
                                    RHINE   Bochum
Canterbury   Dover   Tilburg   Eindhoven   Essen
Folkestone   Dunkirk   Flushing   Duisburg   Mulheim
                    Zeebrugge   Turnhout   Venlo
             Ostend   Bruges   Antwerp   Dusseldorf
                    Ghent
STRAIT OF DOVER Nieuport   SCHELDT   Hasselt
Calais   Ypres   Roulers   Brussels   Maastricht   Cologne
Boulogne   St.Omer   Courtrai   Leuven   Aachen   Bonn
                    Lille   Roubaix   BELGIUM   Liege   Eupen
Montreuil   Tournai   Namur   Malmedy   Koblenz
             Arras   Mons   Charleroi   MEUSE
Abbeville   Maubeuge
                                          LUXEMBOURG
Dieppe   SOMME   St.Quentin
       Amiens   Trier
                                    Sedan   Arlon   Luxembourg
Rouen   Beauvais   Compiegne   AISNE   Saarbrucken
       SEINE   OISE   Verdun
                    MARNE   Reims
                                          Metz
Paris
Versailles   Nancy

THE NETHERLANDS

BELGIUM

LUXEMBOURG

prior to German occupation it was around 8.5, among the lowest in the world. Infant mortality, 34 per thousand, was lower than any other except New Zealand's. Nor had the natural rate of increase (before 1940, over 12% a decade) been affected by crisis, unemployment, or any other social variable. Judging from the net reproduction rate, the population should reach 11,000,000 by 1970.

Education and Religion. The Netherlands is the classic country of religious freedom. Almost two-thirds of her people, mostly north of the Rhine, are Protestants (mainly Calvinists); almost one-third, mostly south of the Rhine, are Catholic. Before 1940 Jews constituted 1.3% of the population, but the Nazis greatly reduced this figure.

The Dutch rank among the cultural leaders of mankind. Under their highly developed educational system illiteracy has practically disappeared. Education is tuition-free and compulsory up to the age of 13. Even the numerous denominational schools receive aid from the state, but each community for the most part runs its own schools — a rare phenomenon in Europe. Before 1940 there was a large high school enrollment, and over 10,000 university students. In the number of books published in proportion to population, the Netherlands is second only to the Scandinavian countries.

The Nation's Economy

Agriculture. This land of inadequate sunlight and poor clayey soils is one of the most intensively developed agricultural countries in the world. Only 31% of the land is arable (less than 4,000 square miles); the population per square mile of arable land reaches the high figure of 2,300. Yet Dutch agriculture has been able to cope adequately with the needs of the people. Its success is all the more striking because the Netherlands, like England, was for decades a citadel of free trade, and foreigners were perfectly welcome to sell on the Dutch market if their products were cheaper.

This near-miracle has been wrought by intensive farming methods second only to those of Belgium. Farmers make up 24% of the labor force of the country, most of them working on small individual holdings. The average farm worker produces $850 in commodities for the market annually (a ratio about equal to that of the "Home Counties" in southeastern England, and surpassed only in Belgium and Denmark). There is little variability between good years and bad. In yield per acre of the 8 leading heavy crops — wheat, corn, hay, barley, oats, sugar-beets, potatoes, rye — the Netherlands is second only to Belgium. In per-acre yield of wheat she leads the world.

After the world depression of 1929–1933, when the country was glutted with cheap imports, emphasis on these basic crops steadily increased. The process was accelerated as the policy of economic self-sufficiency (or "autarky") developing in other countries narrowed the market for flower bulbs and dairy products, the country's chief agricultural exports.

Intensive agriculture was applied to the sandy uplands to make the nation as nearly self-sufficient as possible. Thus the land of varied flowers, dairies, and orchards had already lost some of its agricultural distinctiveness before the Nazis struck. If the income from colonies should be appreciably reduced after the war, Dutch agriculture will undergo even more radical changes.

It is reasonable to suppose, however, that Dutch agriculture will continue to be known to the outside world primarily through the exports of butter and cheese and, above all, of bulbs, tulips, and other hardy flowers. Dutch cheese production, 125,000 tons, constituted before the war 6% of the world's supply; butter, 110,000 tons, 3%; margarine, 6%. The Netherlands produced as much meat as Italy, which has five times her population. Though Dutch fisheries are relatively small, the Maatjes herring enjoyed a world-wide market.

Industry. Agriculturally well developed, the country is also industrially advanced. Some 38% of the employed are in industry; per capita investment in machinery is the fifth in Europe. Water-power and coal, vital for industry, are insufficient and, although the country does yield some coal, most of the fuel for industrial energy must be imported. Nevertheless, technologically advanced and paying relatively high wages, Dutch industries have competed successfully in the free market. They include radios, cocoa, electric light bulbs, and bricks. The Dutch shipbuilding industry has enjoyed deserved prestige abroad.

Especially notable before the war were the Dutch luxury trades. These specialized industries, producing fine pottery, distilled spirits, chocolate candies, fine printing, and art reproductions, catered to the demands of the substantial number of Dutch citizens enjoying independent incomes. Amsterdam's diamond trade, domestic and foreign, rivaled Antwerp's.

National Wealth, Income, and Foreign Investments. The nation's economic position is strikingly like Great Britain's. Her national wealth is high, rivaling Britain's; some authorities even estimate it at 10% higher per inhabitant. The net national income in 1938 was about $2,600,000,000 — approximately $290 per person, as against $440 in Britain and $480 in the U.S.A.

The Dutch *guilder*, normally worth about 54¢, is a solid currency, adequately backed; in its resistance to devaluation it has proved one of the sturdiest of trading currencies. A recent monetary agreement with Belgium and Luxembourg has fixed the ratios for the post-war period, and it is expected that all three currencies will be stabilized by alignment with the British pound sterling.

The Dutch national debt, about $2,500,000,000 before 1940, has more than doubled since then. If confirmed, this increased debt would amount to $600 per person, but its status is undetermined. Taxation in normal years was approximately $500,000,000 ($58 per head).

Bank deposits before the occupation were enormous for so small a country, and the leading banks were world famous. Savings in 1938 were about $700,000,000, or nearly $80 per person, as against $90 in the same year in the U.S.A. And this does not take into account the resources of private banks and investment associations.

Foreign Trade. The Dutch are among the greatest traders on earth. Their experience and prestige in commerce go back 400 years. Before the war, annual imports amounted to about $800,000,000, exports to about $570,000,000, giving an adverse balance of about $230,000,000 — a per capita trade varying from $200 to $250 a year. The Netherlands Empire as a whole enjoyed 5% of the trade of the world.

The leading exports have been butter, cheese, margarine, tin, and finished metals. Seventy-five percent normally go to Europe, mainly Britain and Germany. Typical imports are grain, cotton, textiles, iron and steel, petroleum, and fertilizers. Most of these came from Germany, yet enough key items (such as tin) came from the Netherlands East Indies to reflect the position of the Dutch as a leading imperial power. The great mercantile fleet which carried Dutch trade all over the world was large (3,400,000 tons) and efficiently administered. How much it has been weakened by war and the Nazi occupation no one can say.

But it would be hard to exaggerate the extent to which the Netherlands must depend on flourishing world trade for the restoration and continuance of her high economic standing. In normal times, she exports about 34% of all she makes and imports about 37% of all she uses. Her stock exchanges and lively commodity futures markets were international. American stocks, for example, were prominently quoted on her exchanges, and at the outbreak of war she owned $600,000,000 in American investments. But most striking — and precarious — in her pre-war position was that some 23% of her national wealth lay in the Netherlands East Indies and 6% of her national income was derived from overseas possessions. As in Britain, dividends, profits from colonial factories and plantations, pensions, insurance, shipping, and transshipping make up the deficit in foreign trade. No country, not even Britain, is so dependent on income from abroad.

It is not surprising, therefore, that the Dutch are intelligently concerned with world affairs, that their newspapers are remarkably well informed on international matters of all sorts, cultural, political, and economic. If the high economic and cultural standards of the country are to be restored, it must be in a free and prosperous world.

History: 1914-1944

The Netherlands, a liberal constitutional monarchy, was a neutral during World War I. However, as the Allies restricted imports into the country, for fear that they might reach Germany, a serious food shortage developed and industrial activities almost ceased. Despite her difficulties, the Netherlands succored a million Belgian war-refugees.

1918-1929. Yet upon the conclusion of peace, relations with Belgium became strained. The Belgians asserted that their frontier with the Netherlands had made Antwerp helpless before the invaders. They claimed, moreover, that because the Dutch Maastricht area jutted between Belgium and Germany, it was difficult for Belgium to defend her eastern border. After rather prolonged negotiations, Antwerp was given a larger share of the Rhine trade, to the detriment of Rotterdam. In the meantime, the refusal of the Netherlands to give up the ex-Kaiser Wilhelm, who had sought refuge on her soil, gave rise to prejudice abroad.

In the 1918 elections, for the first time in Dutch history, the premier was chosen from the Catholic party. Strangely enough, he was supported by the two orthodox Protestant parties, which joined with the Catholics against the older Liberal party and the Socialists. (In few countries do religious affiliations play so large a political rôle.) The Protestant parties were: the Christian-Historical party, representing the Orthodox Calvinists of the Dutch Reformed Church; and the Anti-Revolutionary Party, representing those Protestants who belonged to dissenting sects. The Liberals were composed largely of upper- and middle-class agnostics.

The 1919-1921 post-war boom had ended in a depression, recovery from which did not begin until late in 1924. The three-year crisis resulted in a demand for public works to engage the large number of unemployed. Simultaneously, however, a cry arose for economies to stabilize the budget and thus generate confidence. In 1925 the country held new elections under compulsory voting and proportional representation. But the bickerings among the parties prevented any of them from obtaining a majority in Parliament. Hence cabinets were formed outside Parliament, and the inconclusive 1925 elections resulted in executive control in which the monarchy recovered importance. The royally designated de Geer government soon faced nationalist revolts in the East Indies, which it overcame. The de Geer government retained popularity so long as it participated in the world boom of 1925-29.

The Seven-Year Crisis: 1929-1936. The world crash of 1929 severely affected the country. Prices of her colonial products fell sharply. Income from abroad was curtailed. The Netherlands, long a citadel of free trade, now imposed quotas on imports. Instead of relying exclusively on a free market, the government made trade agreements with several countries.

But other shocks came to the Netherlands, the nation most devoted to orthodox finance and currency. When the British suspended the gold standard in 1931, the Dutch lost heavily, for they had large deposits in England. They demanded compensation, insisting that Britain had given assurances that she would not devaluate. The British, however, denied their demands.

Despite these losses, the Dutch held firmly to the gold standard. With nearly all the world turning to monetary devaluation, they preferred to endure falling prices, hoping that supply and demand would restore an economic balance. However, from 1931 to 1936 there were constant alarms about the parity of the Dutch *guilder*. Every few weeks witnessed immense withdrawals of bank deposits, most of which returned when confidence was restored, but only to be withdrawn soon after. And these perturbations did more harm than devaluation.

The Netherlands stood firm on the gold standard. World recovery, by improving her commerce, aided her economy somewhat after 1933. Her leading colonial products, rubber and tin, advanced in price. The results of strict governmental economy, however, disturbed the people — a revolt broke out on a cruiser in the East Indies in protest against pay cuts. Unemployment, an unrelieved curse, increased. For the first time, the Royal Family was jeered at in the States-General (Parliament), and while this demonstration was followed by a loyal outburst, it registered the rising irritation.

In 1934 the provincial elections showed a Nazi vote of 8% and a large Communist vote in Rotterdam and Amsterdam. In 1935 unemployment reached its peak in the Netherlands (384,000, or about 5% of the population), while it declined markedly elsewhere. In 1936 the social strain of maintaining the *guilder* became apparent in strikes and stagnant markets. When the French abandoned the gold standard, the Dutch followed suit, the very last people to yield; even then, the Netherlands devalued less than any other country. In addition, she who hated subsidies, had to subsidize her high-cost merchant marine.

The War Shadow: 1936–1940. At once business boomed, but the recovery did not last long. The country feared German invasion, and Germany's hunger for Dutch colonies. Moreover, losses from Germany's repudiations and barter systems proved too large for the country easily to absorb. Certain elements in the very highest circles were pro-Nazi, for example, Sir Henri Deterding, a power in the Royal Dutch oil interests, was avowedly so.

In 1939 the Mendelssohn bank crash led to further financial fears. The ministry of Dr. Colijn, the sagacious financier, fell. Unemployment was again up to 400,000. It seemed as if no policy could cope with these recurring economic difficulties. Seventeen out of 22 years since the 1918 peace had seen high unemployment. For all that, the Nazi vote sank to a mere 4% and extreme Leftism tended to decline.

In 1938 Premier Colijn had extended the term of military service and arranged a mobile water-based defense against German invasion. But as the Netherlands had never accepted any collective security or even arranged for military conversations with other powers, such belated preparations could be merely stopgaps. Meanwhile, it was hoped that economic difficulties would be diminished by the successful drainage of the Zuider Zee, adding 520,000 acres of prime farm land to the country's assets. In 1939, the government announced great canal and shipping projects.

Invasion and Occupation: 1940–1944. All this went by the board when war came. King Leopold of Belgium and Queen Wilhelmina of the Netherlands met to coordinate plans and to make pleas for neutrality. When the Germans assailed the Dutch in 1940, Nazi paratroopers canceled the water defenses, as German residents fired into the backs of Dutch defenders of their country. This large Nazi Fifth Column soon made Dutch resistance useless. The country surrendered in less than a week, and the ministry and Royal Family moved to London.

The Dutch were restive under Nazi control. In few countries has student resistance been so striking. Since racial and religious intolerance are alien to the Dutch, they took the side of the underdog at great risk to themselves. There were some collaborators, but never more than an infinitesimal percentage of the people.

The huge loss of overseas trade impoverished the economy. The Germans had largely destroyed Dutch shipping and had gutted the port of Rotterdam. They packed off Dutch workers to the Reich. Under the presidency of the Austrian quisling, Seyss-Inquart, they turned Dutch factories into German arsenals.

Dutch afflictions did not end here. In 1942, Japan's assault on their colonial possessions swept them away in less than three months. The Netherlands lost a large part of her East Indies fleet. It was not until 1944, in New Guinea, that the Dutch flag again floated over a town in Dutch territory. By September 1944 the homeland was being redeemed.

Foreign Affiliations. The Netherlands is the gateway of Germany's industrialized area. Hence the interchange of Dutch and German civilizations is continuous and important. Psychologically, however, there is almost a gulf between them.

The relations of the Netherlands with her other neighbor, Belgium, until recently were cool, even hostile. The Dutch took a long time before they ceased to regard Belgians as rebels, and certainly as economic and spiritual inferiors. Their common sorrow has ended this old antagonism.

Although the Netherlands has been partly dependent on Anglo-American goodwill for the preservation of her empire, her neutrality has been deep-rooted. While she has had some intimate contacts with the three Scandinavian democracies, these have been largely superficial. She has for centuries relied on free trade as her weapon and her salvation rather than upon political alignments.

Stakes in the Peace

World War II has demonstrated that the Netherlands is utterly helpless without international protection and international organization. It has also proved that such a country, more dependent than any other on revenues from abroad, requires world financial stability. Her history since 1914 shows that every world crisis and involvement has her at its mercy.

Without a surplus of income, her standard of living must diminish. Her colonies, however rich, in view of rising nationalism among the native peoples, require some international cooperation to maintain their position as sustainers of Dutch welfare. Recognizing that greater concessions to the native peoples are required, the Dutch have recently promised them dominion status.

The Netherlands, the international commonwealth *par excellence*, would be the first beneficiary of a world organization.

NORWAY

The Land and the People

Norway, home of the ancient Vikings, and now a progressive Scandinavian democracy, has long been a land of sturdy, seafaring men. This long, narrow country, marked by mountains and deep bays (fjords), is so rugged that travel from one part to another is often more easily accomplished by sea than over land. Much of Norway lies north of the Arctic Circle, and the country has little sunlight in the long winter nights which, in the north, almost preclude days, while in summers the "midnight sun" and the white nights make darkness almost unknown. Yet the coastal waters are warm, and despite a latitude that would indicate polar weather, the winters in the north are quite endurable.

On the east Norway faces Sweden, from whom she is separated by a fairly continuous mountain range. Her western boundary is the north Atlantic over which the Vikings made their forays on Iceland and Scotland. Norway shares a boundary with Finland in the Arctic north, near Petsamo, where both countries are almost uninhabited.

The Land. One of the least populated nations of Europe, Norway numbered 2,937,000 people in the pre-war estimate — less than the population of Chicago. For a land area of 124,588 square miles, this figure seems extremely low, unless one bears in mind that almost three-fourths of this mountainous country is unproductive and almost a fourth forested, with barely 3% either grass- or farmland. The valleys near the capital, Oslo, and the Trondheim depression account for the arable areas. Here the soil is satisfactory and rainfall abundant.

Norway's well-developed water-power resources furnish the highest per capita figure in the world. The country possesses aluminum and iron ore deposits mainly in the north. On the whole, however, Norway is among the most poorly endowed of European countries in natural resources.

The People. Typical Scandinavians, the Norwegians are predominantly blond and tall, their average height for both sexes surpassing the figure for Europe. Norwegians have emigrated extensively, especially to the U.S.A., where they have settled mostly in the Wisconsin-Minnesota area (numbering 347,000 in 1939). If their children are included, it may be said that a fourth of the Norwegian people have settled in the U.S.A.

Norway's birthrate and deathrate, both low, average 16 and 11 per thousand respectively, and her infant mortality rate of 37 is among the lowest in the world. The people are very healthy and long-lived, but a population decline to under 2,500,000 by 1980 is forecast, and if emigration increases to anything like past proportions, the figure may be even lower. Norway must and does rely for her destiny on the quality, not the numbers of her people.

Religion and Education. The Norwegian King

See also detailed map on page 133.

nominates the bishops of the Lutheran Church, which is the established faith of the country. Ninety-seven per cent of the people follow this faith, but religious tolerance prevails, except for Jesuits.

With education compulsory until the age of 14, illiteracy is practically unknown. Though there is only one university (Oslo) with some 4000 students, secondary education and technical schools are widely diffused.

A country of well-developed culture, Norway has made significant contributions to science, literature, the theater, and music, out of all proportion to her scanty population. Names such as Ibsen, Grieg, Nansen, Amundsen, and Björnson, are universally known.

The Nation's Economy

Agriculture and Fishing. Though Norway is basically a nation of seafarers, fully 35% of her people live by agriculture and forestry. A mere 2,500 square miles is the theater of this farming and pastoral activity, and however sparse Norway's population, the scarcity of good soil means that the land is really densely peopled: about 880 Norwegians must subsist on every arable square mile.

Part of their living, therefore, must come from the sea, and 16% of Norway's employed are in her fisheries. The fish catch is the largest in Europe (by weight), about 7% of the world supply. Meat,

100,000 tons yearly, is ample for the population, which needs a high caloric intake to live in the damp, inclement winters and to withstand the exacting demands of lumbering, fishing, grazing, and summer farming. Their occupations are pursued intensively to take advantage of the short sunlight season.

In the southern river valleys the production per acre of such basic crops as wheat, barley, hay, and oats is higher than in most of France and Germany. Only in the far north does it thin out, and even there it exceeds that of Rumania, Bulgaria, or Spain. Few farmers have rivaled the Norwegians in overcoming an adverse situation. The annual cash value of crops per capita is not very high, largely because they are forage and cereals; nevertheless, it is twice that of Italy, for example.

Industry and Shipping. Industry engages about 28% of the gainfully employed. Norway's abundant water-power is exploited in her aluminum plants, dynamite factories, and calcium carbide works. Electrochemicals and chemicals, machinery and metals, are leading industrial activities, but her industries are less mechanized than those of nearby Sweden and Denmark. Food products, especially packed fish, are important; manufacture of oils and soaps is increasing; and the whaling industry is the world's largest.

Since her shipping exceeds 4,000,000 tons per year, in proportion to population Norway far surpasses every other country. She has, for example, 2½ times the shipping of Great Britain on a population basis. This seaborne trade, which was steadily growing before 1939, had nearly doubled since 1914, producing a yearly income of about $120,000,000 (equivalent on a per capita basis to $5,500,000,000 for the U.S.A.), thus illustrating the relative weight of shipping in Norwegian economy.

Foreign Trade. In foreign trade, Norway is sixth in world rank for her population. Her exports were about $190,000,000, imports $315,000,000; the annual deficit, $125,000,000. Chief exports were fish, forest products, aluminum, and nitrates. After the German invasion, her trade, which was largely with the Western Allies, fell off markedly and most of the shipping that could be salvaged was placed at the service of the United Nations.

National Wealth and Foreign Exchange. A moderately wealthy country, Norway has per capita assets amounting to about $900; but she is poorer than her neighbors (Sweden $1,135, and Denmark $1,225). Both of her neighbors are, of course, much more favored by nature, so that Norway has done at least comparably well in accumulating national wealth. National income of about $225 per person exceeds both Sweden's and Denmark's by about $40.

In the 1920's Norway made up the deficit of her exports partly by borrowing capital abroad or inviting foreign capital to invest in the country. As she received 38% of her national income from exports, dividends, and the return of capital invested abroad, and paid out 41% for imports and foreign financial payments, this provision of fresh capital (amounting to 4% yearly) eased her difficulties. But since the deficit of exports is chronic and not improving, it is clear that she must either expand her services (such as carrying cargoes), borrow abroad, or obtain new capital investments.

Finance, Taxation, and Debt. Money in circulation prior to the 1940 invasion was about 600 million *kroner* (about $133,000,000). It had increased by 67% since 1933, but was still adequately covered by gold (about 50%). Under the Nazis it must have seriously depreciated: the stock exchange index rose from 115 to 185, despite a marked falling-off in trade, indicating a preference for shares rather than currency. Before the invasion, commercial bank deposits were about $105 per person, and savings deposits about $125 per person. The savings exceeded the per capita average in the U.S.A. by a wide margin.

Norway's debt amounted to about $330,000,000, of which about 38% was owed abroad. Interest and fixed charges on this debt had to be paid, despite an adverse balance of trade, but it was being redeemed at a good rate. This financially responsible policy is being carried out by the Norwegian government-in-exile.

Taxation was about $62 per capita. Under the Nazis it was spectacularly increased under the heading of "occupation costs."

History: 1914-1944

1914–1939. The constitutional monarchy of Norway was neutral in World War I. In 1918 the abrupt stoppage of her war-engendered prosperity led to grave social disturbances. Norwegian trade unions were closely linked with the Labor party, whose aims were avowedly Socialist. Following Lenin's success in Russia, this party joined the Communist International, while right wing elements of the labor movement formed a Socialist party. For two years major strikes agitated the country. They were finally overcome by the unyielding Conservative government.

At the same time, Norway's economic crisis was aggravated by a Prohibition law that caused the loss of valuable trade with wine-producing countries (Spain, Portugal, and France). The serious internal abuses of Prohibition paralleled those in the U.S.A. At last the harried government restored trade by permitting wines to enter freely. All other alcohol was assigned to a monopoly which turned over profits above 6% to the government.

A Left coalition government was formed by the Farmers party and the Labor party after the latter group had withdrawn from the Communist International. In 1928 a Labor government came into power, declaring that it must prepare Norway for a Socialist society. However, after the 1929 crisis, all parties combined to save the economic system, which was seriously threatened by the flight of capital from the country. The new coalition government inspired confidence; withdrawal of capital ceased and the gold standard seemed assured. Once more Norway enjoyed prosperity. But it was short-lived, coming to an end in 1930.

Largely dependent on her financial relations with Britain, Norway devalued her money to conform to the pound in 1931. But this step did not curb unemployment, which continued to mount until 1935. As a result, Labor returned to power. The Nygaardsvold government was formed and then popularly endorsed in the 1936 elections, and a period of fair economic improvement ensued.

In 1937 the Norwegian government joined the other "Oslo Powers" in an attempt to make trade freer. But Denmark protested that Norway still resisted food imports, and thus was deflecting Danish trade from nearer markets to Britain. Norway replied that the Oslo Seven-Power Pact (See *Denmark, History*), having lost its significance, should expire in 1939. Defense discussions, however, were to be continued with other Scandinavian states.

Neutrality: 1939-1940. Like most smaller neutrals, Norway was dominated by fear when war broke out in 1939. By April 5, 1940, she had lost 54 ships of 120,000 tons and the lives of 392 sailors. Her protests to Germany were moderate, however, and when she received no acknowledgment, she acquiesced. Her protests to Britain against breaches of neutrality were firmer, since she knew that the British were more responsive to law and diplomatic procedure. But public opinion increasingly favored England, especially after the British raided the German ship *Altmark* in Norwegian waters and revealed the treatment of captives on the vessel. Nevertheless, the Norwegian government vigorously protested the British raid. Disregarding Churchill's warning that Norway would soon be attacked by Germany, the Norwegian government went so far as to escort German ships carrying contraband (particularly iron ore from Narvik) through Norwegian waters, without receiving any guarantees for the safety of its own seamen.

German Invasion and Occupation: 1940-1944. On April 9, 1940, Germany invaded Norway on the pretext that imminent British invasion had to be forestalled. Actually the Germans had planned an invasion long before the British had blockaded iron ore shipments from Narvik. Major Quisling, whose name has since become a byword for treachery, was ready with a Nazi government. Carefully prepared occupation troops sprang from German vessels. German children who had been succored by Norwegians during World War I, now grown men, rewarded their benefactors with a subjugation at which they were all the more expert because they could speak Norwegian.

King Haakon and the Labor government, refusing to yield, waged a hopeless struggle for several weeks and inflicted naval losses on the Germans. Once the die was cast, the Norwegians were roused to fury. Their dauntless resistance to the Nazis and their brave support of commandos have immortalized Norway's heroes.

As their pretense of a Norwegian government, the Germans relied on the National *Samling* or Nazi party, which had demonstrated its popularity in the 1936 elections by failing to obtain a single seat in Parliament. The real dictator was Terboven, a German Nazi. Under his rule, Germany plundered Norway. Two billion dollars were stolen in the first three years of occupation, or nearly 75% of Norway's annual income. She lost 40% of her merchant fleet. Forced labor drafts took many of her young people to Germany. But as the Nazi myth of Norway's "independence" became steadily thinner under martial law, church and school combined with laborer and farmer to oppose the Nazis by every means. In London, meanwhile, Norway's government-in-exile prepared a complete juridical system ready to function against traitors and collaborators on the day of liberation.

Foreign Affiliations. Before Germany's designs on her, Norway did not have a single enemy. Especially cordial were her diplomatic relations with the two other Scandinavian countries, but her reliance rested ultimately on British sea power. Her friendships did not avail her in 1940.

Stakes in the Peace

Norway has been severely shaken, terribly impoverished. Her merchant fleet, foundation of her commercial status, has been weakened. Yet neither her chemical nor hydroelectric installations have been damaged much, and the restoration of her fleet may not be too expensive or difficult if she can take advantage of the indicated world surplus of shipping tonnage at the end of the war.

Norway will require swift and adequate relief. Otherwise the dislocation and poverty of the country may result in a social situation resembling the one that existed from 1919 to 1921. She will definitely need temporary credits, but it is doubtful that she will have to be burdened with a large long-term debt.

POLAND

The Land and the People

Poland, an ancient state of eastern Europe, has had a proud and tragic fate. A great power in the late Middle Ages, she was extinguished as a nation in the last quarter of the 18th century. The indomitable spirit and undying passion for independence of the Polish people resurrected their state in 1918. The Allied Powers simultaneously ratified Polish independence. But it was again extinguished 21 years later at the hands of the Nazis. The United Nations have agreed that Poland will be reconstituted as a great nation under the coming peace.

The Land. The country's boundaries, today in sharp dispute, were fixed from 1918–1939 as follows: on the west, Germany; on the southwest, Czechoslovakia; on the southeast, Rumania; on the east, U.S.S.R.; on the north, Latvia, Lithuania, and the German province of East Prussia. Between East Prussia and the rest of Germany stood the "Polish Corridor," connecting Poland with the Baltic Sea.

None of these boundaries was stable. Russia disputed Poland's eastern region, maintaining that it was not basically populated by Poles and that Poland suppressed the non-Polish inhabitants, the Ukrainians and White Russians. Lithuania remained unreconciled to the loss of her richest province and city, Vilna. Germany hotly contested the Corridor, asserting that it degraded her by cutting her off from her people in East Prussia. She also insisted that part of Polish Silesia in western Poland was truly German. The Czechs claimed that Poland had robbed them of the coal-mining area of Teschen in the southwest. Only the corner at Rumania was free from dispute, except that the Russians claimed it — from Rumania. The Free City of Danzig, created by the Allies to serve the landlocked Polish state as a port on the Baltic Sea, was also resented by Germany, who claimed it as a German city. In the period between the two world wars, the Poles built a modern seaport of their own, Gdynia, which drew away much of the shipping traffic that had formerly passed through Danzig.

A country whose major parts are threatened with amputations and drastic readjustments is difficult to delimit. Poland indisputably held 150,052 square miles in 1938, and the 1931 census showed a population of 32,100,000. In population, therefore, she ranked sixth in Europe (exceeded only by the great powers: Soviet Russia, Germany, Britain, Italy, and France).

The land, about the size of California, is a gigantic plain with wide areas of marsh and forest. Except for the uplands and the crest of the Carpathian Mountains to the south, Poland lies at less than 1,000 feet above sea level. There are no natural boundaries, except in the mountainous south, and the frontiers of the country fade imperceptibly into the territory of her neighbors.

Western Poland is industrialized, especially about the coal deposits in Polish Silesia and in the textile center of Lodz. She has large cities — Poznan, Kracow, the ancient capital, and the modern capital, Warsaw, on the Vistula river. Eastern Poland, however, is exclusively rural, sparsely populated, and industrially backward.

The land is studded with lakes and pine forests, swamp and fen and moor. In the east, the Pripet marshes, fabled source of the Slavic peoples, divide the farm lands to the north and south of it. Rich black soil runs through the center of Galicia, the long strip of upland north of the Carpathians.

Poland's climate is typical of continental Europe. Winters average about 25°, summers, 66°. Rainfall is fair and regular; snow is heavy, and the snow season long.

The People. This essentially Slavic people has had closer historical ties with the West than with the East. Under the Czars the Poles exhibited more Western traits than did the Russians. Polish is written in the Latin and not the Russian alphabet. Polish Catholicism is Roman and not Greek, and Poland has been the eastern outpost of Roman Catholicism in Europe. Polish universities, even in the 14th century, looked to Bohemia and north Italy, not to Constantinople and Kiev, for their cultural affinities. Poland's social system also was closer to European feudalism than to Slavic tribal forms. Although in appearance, language, and folklore the Poles are decisively Slavs, their Western European ties and inclinations must be borne firmly in mind, for they explain to a large degree Poland's special position.

How many of Poland's inhabitants are Poles, is hard to determine. According to official Polish figures, they number about 70% of the total population — about 22,000,000 out of 31,000,000. According to spokesmen of Poland's minority peoples, however, the Poles number about one-half.

Political oppression, social restrictions, and poverty induced waves of emigration that took on mass proportions after 1880. Poles number over a million in the U.S.A.; with their children, they may equal 3,000,000 Americans. Large sections of northern France contain thoroughly Polish villages, as does the Ruhr in Germany. If we take into account these emigrants, people of Polish stock number more than 26,000,000 today.

Before World War II, the birthrate of this prevailingly blond people was about 25 per thousand, a notable drop from the figure of 37 that was maintained before 1914. The deathrate was not high (about 14), but infant mortality was severe (140 per thousand). On a long-term basis, however, Poles are increasing; in 1970 they should number 30% more than in 1940.

But all such calculations, significant for most countries, are tragically academic for Poland. The Nazi terror has murdered nearly 2,000,000 Polish Jews,

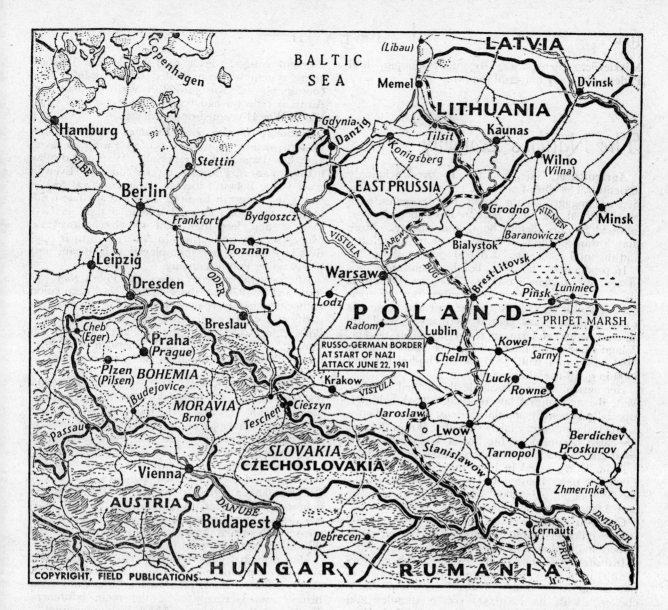

Map labels:
BALTIC SEA · (Libau) · LATVIA · Copenhagen · Memel · Dvinsk · LITHUANIA · Hamburg · Gdynia · Danzig · Tilsit · Kaunas · Konigsberg · Wilno (Vilna) · Stettin · ELBE · EAST PRUSSIA · Berlin · Frankfort · Bydgoszcz · Grodno · NIEMEN · Minsk · VISTULA · NAREW · Baranowicze · Poznan · Bialystok · Leipzig · ODER · Brest-Litovsk · BUG · Dresden · Warsaw · Pinsk · Luniniec · Breslau · Lodz · POLAND · PRIPET-MARSH · Cheb (Eger) · Radom · Lublin · Kowel · Praha (Prague) · RUSSO-GERMAN BORDER AT START OF NAZI ATTACK JUNE 22, 1941 · Chelm · Sarny · Plzen (Pilsen) · BOHEMIA · Luck · Budejovice · Krakow · VISTULA · Rowne · MORAVIA · Cieszyn · Jaroslaw · Brno · Teschen · Lwow · Berdichev · Proskurov · Passau · SLOVAKIA · Stanislawow · Tarnopol · CZECHOSLOVAKIA · Zhmerinka · Vienna · DANUBE · AUSTRIA · Budapest · Cernauti · PRUT · DNIESTER · Debrecen · HUNGARY · RUMANIA

hundreds of thousands of Polish Catholics, and has dispersed unnumbered others to the ends of Europe. Though trustworthy figures are unavailable, there can be no doubt that Poland's population has been cruelly reduced, perhaps by as much as 15%.

Education and Religion. The people are diverse in culture, having been for a century and a half partitioned among Germany, Austria, and Russia. Those under Austrian rule enjoyed political and cultural liberty. Poles under Prussian control, however, were persecuted and became politically active in the struggle for independence. The Poles who lived under Czarist Russia knew no freedom at all and their economic condition was tragically oppressive. If we bear in mind this disparate background, we may appreciate how difficult it has been to fuse the peoples of Poland into a stable, homogeneous state.

In religion, however, there is essential unity, since the mass of the population closely observes the Roman Catholic faith. The Greek Uniate and Greek Orthodox churches prevail among Ukrainians in Poland and those living in White Russian areas are Greek Orthodox. Protestants number about 3% of the population. Around 10% of the people of Poland were Jews, who also accounted for a fourth of the city-dwellers. This large proportion reflects the fact that Poland was for centuries the Jewish homeland, and since 1880 the source of more than two-thirds of all Jewish immigrants to foreign countries.

The educational system in Poland has been complicated by the demands of national minorities and religious minorities. Ukrainians and White Russians have insisted that they have been culturally neglected and oppressed. The dominant Poles, on the other hand, have vigorously denied these contentions.

Elementary education has been free and compulsory. Illiteracy, however, is high among adults, except in areas once governed by Germany. Polish universities are ancient and well regarded. Kracow's dates from the 14th century, Vilna's from the 16th, Lwow's from the 17th. The others have similarly high standards. Poland has also been known for her large number of specialized technical, art, commercial, and other institutions, and for some 47,000 advanced students.

In science, literature, and music, Poles have achieved high distinction. Such names as Copernicus,

Mickiewicz, Sienkiewicz, Reymont, Chopin, and Paderewski enjoy universal renown.

The Nation's Economy

Agriculture. The country is overwhelmingly agricultural — three-fourths of her working population are engaged on the land. Rye, potatoes, oats, barley, wheat, and sugar beet are the principal crops, followed by flax, hemp, hops, and chicory. More than a third of the land is given over to agriculture, and the total arable area is 70,000 square miles.

In productivity, however, Polish agriculture stands in an intermediate position. Western Poland is about as productive as central France, but the great bulk of Polish agriculture (in the east and center) is about a third below central Germany. Similarly, in cash value of farm products per farm worker, Poland's position is intermediate: her figure is about $480, compared with $630 in Czechoslovakia and $400 in quasi-feudal Hungary.

Her agriculture is geographically divided. In the west, the agricultural law of 1920 limited holdings, especially in heavily populated areas; land was better divided, the peasantry fairly well off. But in the east (the area occupied by the Soviet Union in 1939), great estates and semi-feudal conditions prevailed.

Animals are raised in large numbers. There are 7,000,000 pigs (Polish ham is world famous), 10,-000,000 cattle, 4,000,000 horses. Sheep number only 3,000,000.

One-fifth of Poland is forested — some 30,000 square miles of standing timber. Forty percent is owned and exploited by the state.

Industry. Although only 9% of Polish employment is in industry, textiles are an important part of the country's economy. Lodz, "the Polish Manchester," with its 1,870,000 cotton spindles and 800,000 wool spindles is one of the world's leading textile cities.

Apart from agriculture, Poland's principal employment is in mining. Her coal production, 38,-000,000 tons in 1938, ranked her immediately after France in Europe. Her zinc deposits were sufficiently valuable to have interested American capital.

Among the other industries, are steel (1,500,000 tons) and rolled iron (1,000,000), both in Polish Silesia. Though these figures are small compared with those of powerful industrial nations, they are large for an agricultural state. Moreover, they were rapidly expanding in the years before 1939.

Worthy of mention also are Poland's salt works near Kracow and the refineries established at Lwow to process the petroleum from the small deposits in the Carpathians. Sixty-one plants refine some 500,000 tons of beet-sugar.

Before 1917 Polish industry was organized either to supply the Russian market (which collapsed in 1917) or to be integrated with German or Austrian economy. As a consequence, her industrial development has been largely disbalanced or arrested by political events. Note, in this connection, that Russian and German-Austrian railway tracks were of different gauges. Prior to 1914 Russian Poland's entire system was coordinated with Russia's. The coordination of Russian-Polish with German and Austrian railways had barely been completed when World War II erupted on Polish soil.

National Wealth and Income. Although her western section approaches central European levels and her large cities, especially Warsaw, display luxury quarters, Poland is a poor country. Even in good years, Poland's income per person was $53 — one of the lowest in Europe. It is actually one-tenth of the American income, less than a third of Germany's, and less than half of Czechoslovakia's. Money sent by immigrants in America to their relatives in Poland at one time played a significant part in sustaining Polish economy.

After several currency crises, the Polish *zloty* was stabilized in 1928, at about 11.2¢. Nazi occupation authorities, however, fixed its value at the nominal parity of 20¢. Immediately before the 1939 invasion, Polish prices were 58% of the 1929 level, when British were 85%, German 78%, and American 79%. Actually, Poland had the most deflationary policy in the world.

Her national debt was not large: domestic, $300,-000,000; foreign, $270,000,000. Per inhabitant, her debt was only $15, one of the lowest known. At the same time her savings, per inhabitant, were extremely low: in 1939, about $7.70, as compared with $40 for the French.

Foreign Trade. In the troubled year of 1938, Poland imported about $252,000,000 and exported only $222,000,000, a serious deficit of $30,000,000 for a debtor country. Her trade per capita was only $22, less than a fourth of the European average. About one-seventh of her production was exported, and of this, all except 3% went to Europe.

Her principal exports were coal, coke, timber, zinc, chemicals, petroleum products, metal products, and rye, barley, flour, pigs, bacon, butter, and eggs. Britain and Germany were the main customers. Trade with the neighboring U.S.S.R. was minimal.

Her imports were chiefly ores, metals, cotton, and wool — supplied by Germany, Britain, and the U.S.A.

Under German occupation, some war industries were developed, but reliable information about them is not available. Moreover, Polish economy, never too well-balanced, will undoubtedly emerge from more than five years of war in a state approaching chaos.

History: 1914-1944

For hundreds of years Poland's powerful neighbors had dismembered her ancient kingdom. Between 1772 and 1793 Russia, Austria, and Prussia thrice partitioned the country. In 1816 the Congress of Vienna again divided her. In 1846 Austria annexed the free state of Kracow, an historic survival.

Prussia had acquired Poland's western and northwestern area (centering around Poznan, with some 4,000,000 people); Austria the south and southwest (around Kracow and Tarnow, with some 6,000,000); and Russia the central region (around Warsaw, with about 20,000,000). The Prussians were tyrannical: they sought to humiliate the Poles, colonize their lands with Germans, and reduce their language schools. Austria, far more liberal, even gave the Poles control of Ukrainian minorities in Galicia. The Russians, who made their Czar, King of Poland, after a rebellion in 1831, imposed a tyranny that scandalized the world.

The crime of suppressing one of the leading European peoples agitated the conscience of Europe. The thunder of Chopin's patriotic compositions gave a universal character to the resentment of the Polish people. But it was not until 1914 that the Poles, who had often risen for freedom, found their great opportunity for revival.

Liberation Currents Prior to the 1918 Armistice: 1914–1918. Perhaps no country suffered more devastation and misery than Poland from 1914 to 1918. To win the Poles from Russia, the Austrian and German Emperors on November 5, 1916 guaranteed the creation of an independent Polish state. Establishing a regency until the monarch was designated, they held elections for a state council, or upper parliamentary chamber, that was to sit at Warsaw. Josef Pilsudski, a moderate Socialist and an able soldier, judged that Austria's record entitled her most to Polish confidence; he formed a Polish legion to fight for Austria. On the other hand, the celebrated pianist, Paderewski, treated with the Allies for an independent Poland, a demand supported by Woodrow Wilson. After the Russian Revolution of 1917, Lenin announced that Russia had no right to subjugate Poland. Thus, with all major powers declaring for Poland's independence, the country appeared certain to be free, no matter how the war might turn.

The harsh German-Austrian peace terms at Brest-Litovsk required the Russians to renounce Poland. Once Russia was eliminated, all pretence of restoring Poland was cynically abandoned. When the deceived Pilsudski protested, he was sent to prison in Germany. The summer disasters of 1918 left Germany and Austria without any following in Poland.

Austria collapsed in October 1918, Germany in November. Pilsudski, liberated, hastened to Warsaw, and Poland was reborn. Poles in the former Austrian and German territories now rallied to Warsaw, which became the capital of the new republic. In January 1919 the old pro-Austrian and pro-Allied groups reached an arrangement. Pilsudski was to be President, Paderewski Prime Minister and Minister of Foreign Affairs. A constituent assembly was to be formed by universal suffrage.

The New Poland and the Wars with Russia: 1919–1921. The new state began with an intoxicating sense of rebirth. But it had almost no assets. The people were ragged, starving, and diseased. Poland possessed neither rolling stock, factories, nor farm equipment. Relief poured in but it could scarcely cope with the horrors of the situation.

Poland had to seek recovery despite the obstacles of three factory systems built for wholly different markets, three types of land tenure, three kinds of law, three separate railway systems. She faced large minority problems, especially in the distressed condition of the Jews. Boundaries remained unfixed. The peasantry clamored for land. The Poles in the former Russian areas had little civic experience; a large part of technique and professional skill had been supplied by the Germans and Austrians.

In this plight the reborn country went to work with a will. She adopted a democratic constitution in 1921. She accomplished an astonishing revival of industry and commerce, of transport and land reform, though improvements were confined in the main to the completely Polish areas. The jeers of the Germans about "Polish economy" proved to be arrogant snobbery. Few countries have done so much, in so short a time, on so poor a basis, and with so complex a problem.

The treaties of 1919 gave Poland access to the Baltic Sea. They established a Corridor separating the Germans from East Prussia, an area that was to be composed of populations either Polish or akin to Polish. Danzig was to be a Free Port in which Poland would have special rights. In addition, the treaties provided for plebiscites in Prussian Silesia and among the Masurian peoples in East Prussia (from whom the dance, *mazurka*, derives). At the suggestion of Britain's Lord Curzon, the eastern boundaries were fixed at a point where the White Russians, Lithuanians, or Ukrainians began to predominate.

Poland was in no condition to fight new wars, but Polish nationalists urged the country into a contest against the Soviet Union. At this time the French, under Clemenceau, were fearful of the rise of the new Soviet state, which had already cost them their position as a financial power by having canceled the colossal French investments in Czarist Russia. The French were also aware of the anxiety of Polish nationalists to recover the great estates of the Polish nobility, which lay east of the line drawn by Lord Curzon. Hence, the French government was by no means averse to the Polish campaign against the Russians; and they both advised and assisted Poland throughout its duration (1920–21).

The Soviet army, however, delivered crushing blows to the Poles, and in 1920 the Russians had advanced to the gates of Warsaw. At this point, the French General Weygand kindled a flame of military determination among the Poles. By the "Miracle of the Vistula," the Polish troops drove back the Russians and achieved victory.

The Russians were more concerned with their civil war, poverty, and famine than with boundaries or glory. They signed the Treaty of Riga in March 1921, by the terms of which Poland extended about 100 miles beyond the boundaries assigned her by the Allies. Poland insisted on acquisitions deep in White Russia and the Ukraine, and the Soviets were too beleaguered to resist.

France had failed in the object of restoring her investments, but in Poland she had an ally beholden to her for her very life and her new territory. Thus Poland became the central knot in the "Cordon Sanitaire" which was to protect Europe from Bolshevism. This position governed Polish foreign policy for fifteen years. Fear of Russia was paramount. The French subsidized Poland as the rearguard of their European interests. In 1934, when France sought to reverse this attitude, the pattern had already been set. The Franco-Polish alliance was buttressed by liberal loans; French engineering firms were entrusted with building the new port of Gdynia, which was ultimately to supersede German-populated Danzig; French money poured in steadily (private investment was over $55,000,000, large for Poland's investment possibilities).

Parliamentary Government and Territorial Changes: 1921–1926. In 1922 the Upper Silesia plebiscite led the Allies to divide the disputed area. Most of the coal-mining lands fell to Poland, but there is little doubt that the district divisions basically followed ethnic lines. In East Prussia, the Mazurs voted overwhelmingly to remain German. The Teschen district was absurdly divided: Poland received the town, the public utilities were divided, and the coal mines went to the Czechs. In the north General Zeligowski expelled the Lithuanians from their capital of Vilna; the Poles repudiated his *putsch* (1920) as "disobeying orders," but they retained the territory. Lithuania suspended all relations with Poland.

In the east, Pilsudski, on the demand of the Allies, guaranteed autonomy to the Ukrainian population ceded by the Treaty of Riga. All these arrangements were to cause far-reaching, historic results much later. In the meantime, antisemitic tendencies, often exhibited, reached violent political expression as mass boycotting was applied to Jews. Other minority faiths, however, fared better. Pope Pius XI took a special interest in Poland, where he had served as Nuncio, and a *Concordat* with the Vatican was established in 1925.

The proportional representation system multiplied sub-sections of parties and made parliamentary cabals active. Many bizarre combinations arose. However, monetary inflation created a spurious prosperity that made the political issues less urgent. The Conference of Allied Ambassadors ratified all Poland's territorial acquisitions, however gained. In 1923 the State appeared stable. The minorities received assurances that their cultures would be respected, and at first these concessions appeared to be workable.

Land reforms began in 1919. But since the government lacked funds to compensate large landowners properly, it was decided in 1925 to distribute only 50,000 acres a year for 10 years. In the border districts near Soviet Russia and Germany, the government permitted large estates; in the center of Poland it assigned lower size limits, but these were only partly effective. Despite this unsatisfactory redistribution, farming grew more prosperous for many years. In the industrial sphere, Poland permitted labor unions to operate freely under the act of 1919.

It took more than two years to frame the constitution, which was a compromise: although enacted in 1921, it did not operate until 1922. In that year elections were held for the first constitutional parliament. The Nationalists, Peasants, Socialists, and National Minorities Bloc were the four leading groups, while many Ukrainians boycotted the polls. Pilsudski refused to run for president. The new President, Narutowicz, was almost immediately assassinated, and an old Socialist, Wojciechowski, elected to fill the vacancy. But the real power was in the Premier,

General Sikorski. His régime failed because of the inflation, which by now had ruined the country and led to rioting.

A non-party government under Grabski reorganized the finances. In 1924 it established the gold *franc* as the currency under the name of the *zloty* (19.3¢). Immediately, however, this over-valued currency caused an industrial collapse. Exports declined, and a wave of bankruptcies threatened to engulf private business. The *zloty* fell to 10¢, at which level it was fairly valued. The government obtained foreign loans to stabilize the perilous situation. But these loans were inadequate, and the interest on them burdensome.

Forced to pledge one resource after another, the government drained the treasury. In November 1925 Grabski resigned. The country was in economic chaos, and no solution proposed could withstand the sabotage of any given private interest. The very existence of the nation was dubious on the dark New Year's Day of 1926.

Pilsudski's Coup and the Authoritarian Régime: 1926–1934. On May 12, 1926, Pilsudski entered Warsaw at the head of his troops. The government declared him a rebel. He fought in the streets for two days, having planned his *coup* for the day when a railway strike would make difficult the movement of troops into the capital. The government was overthrown, and the victor proclaimed his friend Moscicki, a scientist, as President. The *Seym* (or Parliament) hastily agreed to this designation.

Pilsudski became Premier and Minister for War. He created a strict authoritarian government (though not as extreme as in Italy), which seriously curtailed liberties. World prosperity put a gloss on Pilsudski's Cromwellian policies and a deft revision of the constitution gave him about a fourth of the deputies in 1928. The proportion of his following was no longer material, for the Executive determined everything; Parliament had become an ornament.

The world crisis shook Poland severely and her weak economy declined proportionately more than the world average. Slowly Pilsudski inclined toward the Fascist states. When Hitler came to power (1933) Poland was obviously more sympathetic to his Germany than to the former democratic Weimar republic.

Friction with the West increased. Poland's treatment of minorities had not fulfilled treaty obligations. So far were the Ukrainians from the autonomy promised them that their schools in Galicia had fallen from 2,200 under Austria in 1911 to about 750 under Poland in 1928. Peasant leaders were in marked disfavor. The 1932 nonaggression pact with the U.S.S.R. had increased the feeling of security but it was the 1934 nonaggression pact with Hitler that marked a real change in orientation.

France, alarmed, backed Russia for membership in the League of Nations, now that she was unsure of Poland. In September 1934 Poland bluntly stated that until a general minority system of supervision prevailed, she would not permit inspection or review of her treatment of minorities under the treaties to which she was a party. By this time, Pilsudski had come to feel that authoritarian government of the old type was not enough and that Poland must adopt a quasi-Fascist system.

Totalitarian Constitution: 1935–1939. In 1935 the government illegalized all parties except one, the "Camp of National Unity." Furthermore the 1921 constitution was annulled by a body which was not qualified to do this under the constitution's provisions. The new Parliament was to be named out of candidates picked by "corporations," as in Fascist states. The President was all-powerful; he could even designate his successor. Thus the need for popular approval effectively ceased. Liberal elements at once declared the 1935 constitution illegal, but the present Polish government-in-exile seeks proof of its legitimacy in that constitution's provisions, which, it insists, must be judged as having actually functioned.

The new government decided on an aggressive policy of "Polonization" to compel minorities to accept Polish culture. Soon after Pilsudski's death (May 12, 1935) his designee, Marshal Rydz-Smigly, Inspector General of the army, became "first citizen after the President." Colonel Josef Beck, the Foreign Minister, and Rydz-Smigly represented Poland to the outside world.

At the collapse of Czechoslovakia in 1938, Poland moved to seize areas in Teschen from the stricken nation. These areas were much larger than those to which Poland had any ethnic claim. Such enthusiastic participation in Nazi plunder diminished confidence abroad in Polish policy. In the spring of 1939 Poland compelled Lithuania to renew diplomatic relations with her despite the smaller country's reluctance. Mobs of hooligan students, aping the Nazis, acclaimed the use of "force" as the sign of a virile people. However, the demands of the peasantry for land and credit became so insistent that action was initiated to distribute large estates, mostly owned by influential Germans resident in the area.

German demands on the Polish Corridor followed. They speedily roused Poland, who now realized that her very life was in peril. In March 1939, however, she rejected Russian aid. Great Britain immediately gave the country her unilateral guarantee. The Polish "Colonels," as the highly vocal military clique was called, were adamant against any passage of Soviet armies on Polish soil, even to fight Germany. Rather than permit Russian soldiers as allies, they relied on their own forces. The British Prime Minister Chamberlain's continued discourtesy to the Soviet Union encouraged the "Colonels" in their stand. Poland stated that she was adequately prepared to face Germany alone.

On August 23, Germany and the U.S.S.R. signed a nonaggression pact. The Germans began their usual whirlwind of crises, threats, and "atrocities." They forced the pace and declared war (September 1, 1939) on Poland. The Polish armies were scattered to the four winds: in less than a fortnight the government had fled abroad and only the heroic citizens of Warsaw continued to resist, in one of the most remarkable exhibitions of courage in modern annals.

The Germans expected to take all Poland within the week. There was no longer any effective military opposition. On September 17 the Soviet armies entered eastern Poland on the ground that no government existed in Poland and that 10,000,000 White Russians and Ukrainians had to be protected. Soviet armies moved west and faced the Germans. Confronted by demands that would have taken away three-fourths of Poland, the Germans stiffened. After sharp negotiations, Russia obtained over half the Polish territory, roughly corresponding to the frontiers assigned her by Lord Curzon. Germany obtained the lesser area, but more than two-thirds of the population and certainly more than three-fourths of the national wealth.

The Aftermath: 1939–1944. Whatever sorrows Poland had experienced in the past were as nothing compared to her fate under the Nazis. The Germans almost annihilated Poland's Jews; some figures estimate their dead at two millions. The invaders killed a million other Poles. They dragged millions, slaves in effect, into German factories and fields. They annexed most of Poland, designating a small central area around Warsaw as the Government General, administered by a German governor. The Nazis set up a small ghetto state about Lublin. But underground rebellion was rife. No quisling government could be formed.

In the Russian areas, the Soviets redistributed the land, carrying out, as Sir Arthur Keith observed, long-delayed and necessary agrarian and other reforms. The Soviets encouraged White Russian and Ukrainian culture and sponsored Polish schools and culture for that minority. They restored Vilna to the Lithuanians. A plebiscite was held which favored Russia, but, of course, the Poles contest its validity, and this is true even of many Poles who ardently favor friendship with the Soviet Union. There was no comparison, however, between the treatment accorded populations under the German and Soviet occupations, whatever may be the judgment on the ethics of Russia's initial action. In 1941, Germany's attack on Russia soon wrenched away these Polish territories and their conditions became the worst in all Poland. They were not recovered until the Soviet campaigns of 1944.

The Exiled Government and the Moscow Committee: 1944. At first there was a *rapprochement* between Moscow and the Polish government-in-exile domiciled in London, but suspicions deepened. The Polish army in the U.S.S.R., declaring that its treatment did not inspire confidence, asked to be withdrawn. It was evacuated through the Middle East. Certain commanders of the army remained within the Soviet Union and formed a Polish army to fight by the side of the Russians. Each side accused the other of espionage. The Polish army, removed to the Near East, did excellent service, later, in the Italian campaign; and Polish sailors and airmen proved valuable allies throughout the European naval and air war and in the French campaign of 1944.

The chief of the Polish government-in-exile, General Sikorski, died in an air accident near Gibraltar (July 1943). His great talents were sorely missed. It was he who had conducted the successful initial negotiations at Moscow with Marshal Stalin in order to reach an agreement with the Soviet Union. It is probable that Polish-Soviet difficulties in 1944 would never have reached dangerous proportions if Sikorski had been on hand to treat with the Soviet government.

The newly constituted Polish government-in-exile

was more inclined than its predecessor to be conservative in policy, although Socialists participated in it. Both the Soviets and the Poles remained adamant on the question of their common eastern border.

After strain and bitter recrimination, the Soviets sponsored, or benevolently regarded, the formation of a rival government-in-exile, the Polish National Liberation Committee in Moscow. They denied the legitimacy of the London government, declaring that its powers had been arbitrarily delegated by the "Fascist" constitution of 1935. The Moscow committee had the advantage of having several divisions in the field, and in the occupation, *de facto*, of Polish territory, with its seat established at Chelm in Poland (July 1944).

The London government was divided in counsels: some sought an understanding with Russia, while others, like General Sosnkowski, its military chief, insisted on full recognition and the pre-war Polish boundaries as essential before any negotiations could take place. The Soviet government persisted in recognizing the Chelm committee (installed in Lublin, near the notorious Nazi "murder camp") only as a provisional government (August 1944). It guaranteed a strong, independent Poland, and it declared that such a Poland must absorb East Prussia and become a Baltic power. The London government refused to credit the good faith of these affirmations, but Mikolajczyk, its Premier, entered into negotiations with the Lublin committee.

Foreign Affiliations. Poland's foreign affiliations of the past, like her long alliance with France, are meaningless today. She has to live in a Europe where Germany is beaten and yet where France does not hold the military hegemony. Her past assumptions must be changed.

Stakes in the Peace

With the Vilna area now part of the Soviet Baltic republics, Poland's eastern boundaries will depend on an understanding with the Soviet Union. The Czechoslovak government will be close to the Soviet Union. In this Slavic constellation, Poland must find a place.

The outbreak of war in 1939 showed that Western guarantees, by themselves, are ineffective. The Poles, as an important and endowed people, will find their reciprocities with their two Slavic neighbors, within the framework of an international organization.

Poland must first be rebuilt and nourished, for her biological condition is desperate. Her first stake in the peace is the destruction of the German landed interest. No sooner did the Germans enter in 1939 than they restored princely domains to their aristocracy, whatever the gibberish about the Nazi soldier fighting for a "folk community." The true democratization of land ownership is the first major need of her national life. But this must be on a cooperative basis (Poland is a land of extensive culture), and not on the multiplication of poverty through "dwarf holdings." More than two-thirds of the people are engaged in agriculture. It would be easy to increase crop-yields by a third with proper capital and organization. The acquisition of East Prussia would aid food production considerably.

Polish industry had for two decades operated under the loss of its natural market, the immense Soviet hinterland. Poland's second major need, therefore, is a system of reciprocal arrangements for the exchange of manufactured goods. Trade agreements would diminish those recurrent crises, from 1921 to 1926, and from 1929 to 1937, which have plagued her industrial development. Without such changes it is not easy to see how Poland can overcome her heartrending poverty. It is notable that the twin demand for democratization of land and good industrial relations with her neighbors is the limit of the program advanced by the Polish army under the Lublin committee. The Peasant party and its exiled leader, Witos, would have dominated Polish politics if the strong hand of Pilsudski had not interposed. Hence it is doubtful if this party's basic influence can much longer be denied.

PORTUGAL

The Land and the People

Once the world's leading maritime nation, Portugal (ancient "Lusitania") still retains an overseas empire 23 times larger than her home territory. The farflung colonial possessions of this little Latin state have for centuries enjoyed the protection of the British imperial shield, the intimate alliance of Portugal and Great Britain dating back to the 14th century.

Situated on the Iberian Peninsula in Europe's southwest corner, Portugal is bounded by Spain and the Atlantic Ocean. To her continental area of 34,254 square miles (approximately the size of Indiana) should be added the 1,146 square miles of her Azores Islands in mid-Atlantic and Madeira Island off the coast of Africa. The colonial territory in Africa and the Far East totals 808,000 square miles. The mother country's population of 7,702,000 is also exceeded by the colonial population of 9,400,000.

The Land. The Portuguese climate, with rainfall above the average, favors agriculture, though the soil is fertile only near the coasts and in the north, where vineyards are abundant. Nevertheless, about half of the country is cultivated. A fourth is forested with a predominance of chestnut and oak trees, whose nuts and acorns are widely used for animal fodder. Portugal's plentiful cork and olive trees are an important source of the nation's wealth, as are her mineral resources located in the southeastern area, near Spain.

The People. The population derives basically from the Iberians encountered by the Romans in the pre-Christian era. But across the centuries there have been considerable infusions from other peoples: Celts and Goths, Moors and Jews, some of whom came as conquerors, others as settlers. The importation of Negro slaves led to some admixtures in the extreme south, while in the north the people are racially related to the Spaniards of Asturias and Galicia (where the people still speak a Portuguese dialect).

With a fairly high birthrate of 24 per thousand and a deathrate fluctuating between 16 and 17, Portugal's natural gain would be about 6% per decade, but this net increase is reduced by heavy emigration. While emigrants have overwhelmingly settled in Brazil, the U.S.A. has some 215,000 Portuguese, most of whom live in New England.

Religion and Education. Roman Catholicism, though not the official state religion, prevails among most of the people, and under the 1940 *Concordat* with the Vatican, the Catholic Church enjoys many distinct advantages. At the same time, religious freedom for other faiths exists. The Portuguese have been familiarized with Protestantism by the British, long established in Lisbon and in Oporto, where they dominate the port-wine trade.

Some estimates place illiteracy as high as 60%, but official figures are 50% lower. Despite a nominally tuition-free and compulsory school system, Portugal's educational budget of about $7 per capita is one of the smallest among modern nations. Students number 6,000 in the three universities of Lisbon, Oporto, and Coimbra, the last-named (founded in 1290) being a traditional center of learning with high standards. Portugal's former literary fame has dwindled with the passing of her leadership to Portuguese-speaking Brazil, of whom she was the cultural mother country.

The Nation's Economy

Agriculture. Engaging 58% of the working population, agriculture centers about olive oil and wine. Portugal ranks as the third-largest olive oil producing country, with a yearly volume of 12,000,000 gallons. Wine production, annually 150,000,000 gallons, concentrates on expensive port wines. These major industries, however, depend on crops that vary considerably between good years and bad. Portugal also produces fair amounts of rice and corn, a wheat crop inadequate for domestic needs, and an extremely deficient supply of dairy products.

Animal economy does not suffice for home needs. Though horses, mules, donkeys, and oxen are widely

See detailed map on page 321.

used in farm work (modern tractors and farm implements being virtually unknown), they number only about 1,300,000.

On Portugal's typically small farms annual production per worker amounts to some $400 a year in the port-wine area and $340 elsewhere, figures that are below the average for western Europe. Deficient crops (resulting from the backward rural economy, primitive methods, and poor fertilizers) and a fairly dense population in the countryside compel emigration overseas.

Industry. Portugal's poorly equipped industry employs 22% of the working population, chiefly in the production of consumers goods: china, porcelain tiles, lace, and embroidery. No other European country shows so many people engaged in industry on a level so primitive. Machine investment per capita does not reach even two-thirds that of neighboring Spain (by no means a well-industrialized nation), and Portugal ranks twentieth in Europe in this respect.

The textile industry in Lisbon and Oporto employs some 50,000. In Portugal's important fishing industry, some 55,000 fishermen average an annual catch worth about $10,000,000, mainly of sardines — for export.

The country profits greatly from the mining of her mineral resources, chiefly pyrites and wolfram (tungsten), both of strategic military value. Few countries surpass her in the production of wolfram; she supplies some three-fourths of Europe's production. From 1937 to 1941, Portuguese wolfram production advanced 300% to fill German war requirements. Coal, on the other hand, fails to meet even the domestic needs of the country, and potential electric- and water-power resources remain largely unutilized.

Finance and Foreign Trade. During World War II, neutral Portugal, following an extremely conservative financial policy, has reduced her national debt and increased her budget only slightly. Although bank deposits, like prices and stock-exchange quotations, have risen, and while money in circulation has doubled, the rise has not been abnormal. These facts show good management when one considers that for three years the flow of refugees through Lisbon made that city the most crowded cosmopolitan center in Europe whereas before it had had few visitors. For a time these refugees purchased *escudos* (monetary unit of Portugal, fixed at about 25 to the dollar), and the sudden demand for consumers goods threatened the country with inflation.

Exports and imports have maintained an active pace, exports totaling about $106,000,000, imports $97,000,000. Government-controlled agencies handle 70% of the exports, the chief being wolfram, sardines, cork, and wine. The principal imports, revealing Portugal's deficiency in home-grown food and industrial raw materials, include codfish (staple food of the poor), wheat, machinery, and metals.

Main supplier and customer in foreign trade is Great Britain, though during the war Germany received a large share of Portuguese wolfram.

Foreign Relations. As has been stated, Great Britain's close relations with Portugal date back to the 14th century. For several centuries a common opposition to Spain created bonds of interest and after the Methuen Treaty (1703), these ties became even closer. In the Peninsular War of 1808–1814 Britain's efforts to liberate Portugal from the rule of Napoleon cemented the alliance, and during the 19th century Britain stood guard over Portugal's important overseas possessions.

History: 1914-1944

Early in World War I, the young republic of Portugal became a belligerent, in fulfillment of her old alliance with Britain. Owing to the high prices commanded by her exports, Portugal prospered during the war, but the mass of her people remained poor and the war left no lasting change in her economy.

Portugal had become a republic in 1910 after long experience as a monarchy. Her republican history from 1918–1925 reads like a chronicle of assassinations, revolutions, and abrupt ministerial changes. Finally, the army attempted to seize control in 1926, provoking a workers' uprising in 1927 which was supported by the marines and part of the élite Republican Guard. The following year General Carmona, who had helped suppress this revolution, was elected President.

Fascist System: 1933–1936. In March 1933, Portugal adopted a new constitution, providing for a Fascist type of state. Under the active sponsorship of Antonio Salazar, a professor of economics, the country was transformed into a virtual dictatorship, with Salazar as the effective ruler and Carmona the traditional, though largely nominal, head. With the ballot limited to "educated heads of families," both male and female, about 60% favored the new constitution, 35% abstained, and 5% opposed.

Theoretically the dictatorship based itself on "corporations"; in practice, the major interests represented were merchants, bankers, and landowners, corresponding to their status in the nation's economic life. Strikes and lockouts were forbidden.

Salazar imposed rigorous economies to balance the budget and launched a public works program for economic improvements. Having assumed power at the depth of the world depression, he was fortunate to have world recovery soon aid Portugal's exports and help him carry out his program. In foreign policy, however, he was forced to act with agility. Portugal was haunted by the idea that her African colonies might be

taken to satisfy German and Italian demands for expansion; hence she placated both Germany and Italy as well as her traditional ally, Britain.

Internal discontent, however, remained active and the government had to put down a soldiers' and workers' uprising in 1934. To give an appearance of popular control, the government ordered an election. Boycotted by the "legal opposition" groups — such as the Republicans and Socialists — the election automatically returned the "National Union" party of Salazar to power. Thereupon, Salazar demanded that the unions nominate a labor representative to the "Corporate Parliament." When they refused, he named a labor delegate of his own and increased restrictions on Liberal and Leftist groups.

By 1935 the dictatorship was complete. Censorship of the press, of publishing houses, and of every other form of public expression was imposed even more drastically than in Fascist Italy. To compensate for this lack of liberty, the government proposed a fifteen-year program of economic development to cost $265,000,000. It summoned a council of the Portuguese colonial empire to inquire into the reasons for its economic stagnation.

In order to maintain the goodwill of Britain, who alone preserved the Portuguese colonial empire, the Salazar government sustained Britain in her quarrel with Italy over sanctions to be imposed on Mussolini for his invasion of Ethiopia.

The Spanish Civil War: 1936–1939. The success of the Left in the Spanish elections of February 1936 disquieted the Portuguese régime. The latter entered into intimate relations with Rightist Spanish political leaders; and a conspiracy against the Spanish Republic, headed by the exiled Spanish General Sanjurjo, was hatched on Portuguese territory. When General Franco rebelled against the Spanish government in the summer of 1936, Portugal made little effort to disguise her active cooperation with the Spanish Insurgents. British pressure forced her to join the Nonintervention Committee but once a member, she used the same cynical and temporizing tactics as Italy and Germany, refusing to allow her frontier with Spain to be supervised.

These actions led to a naval insurrection in Lisbon, which was quickly suppressed. Every officer of the army and navy had now to take an oath of allegiance in which he pledged support to the Corporate State and declared that he had no radical ideas. Realizing the paramount influence of Germany in neighboring Spain, the government began a long flirtation with the Nazi state, as a counterpoise to Portugal's traditional alignment with Britain.

In 1939 the mask of neutrality was dropped. At the end of the Spanish Civil War, General Franco agreed to compensate Portugal for the services of her "volunteers" and the two countries concluded a nonaggression pact. The "volunteers" were publicly decorated in 1939 in Lisbon.

World War II: 1939–1944. Fearful of possible German vengeance striking at her through nearby Spain, Portugal did not enter World War II despite the terms of her alliance with Britain. Lisbon meanwhile had become the center of tens of thousands of refugees from Central Europe, the Low Countries, and France, as well as a strategic point for air travel between Europe and the Americas. The country entered upon a boom period. Shipments of wolfram to the Germans rose sharply, replacing her diminished exports of port wine and sardines.

After four years of war, however, the gains of the United Nations brought about a decided change in Portugal's attitude. She renounced wolfram exports to Germany and permitted Great Britain to utilize the Azores as a naval and air base, thus assisting the anti-submarine war in the Atlantic. In the spring of 1944, however, Salazar declared that even if Fascism should fail everywhere else, he could not envisage a return to democracy in Portugal.

Foreign Affiliations. Portugal has been an ally of Britain since the 14th century; she has been bound to Britain commercially by the Methuen Treaty of the early 18th century. Britain restored her independence from Napoleon's rule in 1811; and upon Britain rests her colonial and sea power. She is a "have" power, yet the proximity of a Spain in the thrall of Nazi Germany and the succession of victories by the "have-not" nations, forced her for a time to hedge. Now she is slowly returning to the alliance with Britain.

Stakes in the Peace

Portugal requires: (1) active trade, primarily with Britain; (2) the development of her really backward colonies, especially in Africa; (3) safety from an aggressive Spain; (4) growth in democratic freedoms at home; and (5) an economic program that can genuinely exploit her astonishing advantages of soil, climate, and geographic position. Not one of these objectives can be attained on a purely national basis; hence her stake in international organization is well-nigh decisive.

RUMANIA

The Land and the People

How large is Rumania? Few modern lands have gone through so many territorial revisions as has this kingdom in southeastern Europe. Today Rumania extends over an area of 74,888 square miles, about a fourth larger than she was before World War I. In terms of American area, Rumania today is slightly smaller than South Dakota.

The country consists principally of two provinces: (1) Walachia, to the north of the Danube River and bordering on Bulgaria, and (2) Moldavia, inclining to the south and bordering on the Soviet area of Bessarabia. The broad Danube, at the southern boundary, provides a natural avenue for trade.

The Land. Rumania's two great natural resources are the basis of her national economic existence: her fertile soil and her petroleum deposits. In both she is remarkably endowed. Her soil is among the most fertile in the world, her petroleum fields are the largest in Europe.

Because of the richness of her earth, Rumania has been one of the granaries of Europe since the days of the Romans. Rich river deposits extend through Walachia, whose plains are given over chiefly to cereals, primarily wheat. The crops are diversified in the fertile hilly area of Moldavia; and in the mountains and plateaus of Transylvania (to the north of Walachia) orchards and vineyards are plentiful. Cattle-raising and sheep-raising are characteristic of the plains and hilly lands of Dobruja (to the southeast). Extremely hot summers and bitter winters define the country's climate. Although the annual rainfall is about the average for the temperate zone (25 inches), summer drought in some years severely reduces the harvest.

Rumania's petroleum deposits, situated chiefly in Walachia, became known to Americans in the course of World War II. The refineries centering about Ploesti were a target for United Nations airplane attacks, because of the strategic importance of Rumanian oil to the Nazi military machine.

The People. Rumania's population today is estimated at 13,500,000 — roughly as many people as there are in the state of New York. According to Rumanian government sources, the population is overwhelmingly Rumanian (83.5%), the balance being composed of various minority groupings: some 500,000 people of German speech, long settled in Transylvania; (2) about 500,000 Hungarians; (3) about 200,000 Slavs; (4) a Jewish population variously estimated but possibly between 500,000 and 900,000; and (5) Gypsies, whose numbers are not reliably estimated, but whose music and folklore color and deeply impress Rumanian civilization.

The people assert that they are primarily descended from the Romans who settled in Dacia (now Walachia) about 120 A.D. Whether or not this is wholly true, the Rumanian language is Latin in most constructions as well as in other respects, and it also shows a strong Slavonic and some Turkish admixtures. Being thus a balance of two basic elements (in which respect it resembles English), the Rumanian tongue has proved a rich medium for literary expression.

Except for German merchants and salesmen, immigration into Rumania has been almost nonexistent. Emigration, however, has been a factor, particularly in two instances: Rumanian Jews, who came to the U.S.A. in large numbers (prior to the closing of the gates in 1923), and middle-class Rumanians who emigrated largely to France, where they were readily assimilable.

The high birthrate and deathrate (26 and 19 per thousand, respectively) would have given Rumania a crude natural population increase of 7%, were it not for the astonishingly high infant mortality — 180 per thousand. This rate is not only the worst in Europe; it is even higher than that of India.

Education. Except for a few large centers — notably, the capital city, Bucharest, whose metropolitan area approaches a million inhabitants — Rumania is overwhelmingly rural. About four-fifths of the population are peasants. Although primary education became officially free and compulsory following World War I, the program remained circumscribed in practice, with the result that even today the population (particularly the older generation) is largely illiterate.

The universities, however, are large and well administered, and follow the French educational model. So strong is the French influence in all cultural pursuits that for all practical purposes Rumania has been regarded as a French cultural colony. In scientific education, however, Vienna provided the model.

Religion. Religious influences and controls occupy a special position in Rumanian life. Both the Greek Orthodox and the Greek Catholic (Uniate) churches, are supported by the state, but the Greek Orthodox stands in a position of unique authority. Its Patriarch acknowledges no superior anywhere; hence the Greek Orthodox Church of Rumania is independent of the Russian Patriarch as well as of the former head of the church at Constantinople. The effect of this religious independence has inevitably been a fact of importance, and the established clergy is extremely active politically.

Minority religious groups have been variously and unreliably estimated. The pre-1940 boundaries would include some 1,200,000 Roman Catholics, as many Protestants, some 200,000 Moslems, and between 500,000 and 900,000 Jews. Of these four sectarian communities, the Jews have been severely burdened. Despite Rumania's guarantees to the Great Powers under the Treaty of Berlin (1878) and despite the nominal provisions of her 1923 Constitution, antisemitic regulations have been characteristic of Rumanian law. Nevertheless, until the nazification of Rumania, the Jews managed to live tolerably in the country, despite the discrimination and the special burdens placed on them. Roman Catholics, Protestants, and Moslems for the most part were permitted to live normally.

The Nation's Economy

Grain and petroleum are the two mainstays of Rumania's economy. Her other industries — flour milling, brewing, steel production — are inconsiderable. The 1933 estimates show that her investment in machinery was the smallest in Europe, markedly less than that of her poorest neighbors. The amount of horse-power utilized per worker was also the lowest in Europe. Rumania, then, apart from her petroleum, must be viewed basically as a country specializing in grain exports.

Agriculture. Nearly four-fifths of the population are engaged in agriculture, with about 320 people to every square mile of arable land. Because of primitive methods of farming, the yield per acre is about 17 bushels for wheat — well below the average for Europe. The yield per person engaged in agriculture is far below the American level — actually, Rumania's agricultural productivity per farmer is about one-fifth that of our Middle West. These low averages, produced despite Rumania's excellent soil, help to explain the nation's poverty.

Cattle, swine, and horses are also produced in quantities insufficient for the country's internal needs. Yet the shepherd is the hallmark of Rumania; his 7,000,000 sheep yield a wool clip of 25,000 tons. But again, despite the fact that the Danubian and Dobruja plains are naturally indicated for stock-raising, the increase is well below the European average.

Basically Rumania is dependent for her agricultural income on the export of grain, for grain constitutes five-sixths of the entire crop. This excessive dependence on one market — if the price of wheat declines, the nation's entire economy is seriously hurt — has inevitably led to intensified political crises.

The peasants, constituting 80% of the population, and living in an economy subject to recurring crises, articulated their discontent by demanding land reforms (beginning with 1921). The large estates were diminished and offered for sale on easy terms to small holders and landless peasantry; but the reform was never wholly accomplished. The new landholder was in debt for the price of the land and required capital to develop them. Hence, though landholding was nominally democratized, the new owners were unable to produce as much per acre as were the well-financed larger estates. The peasants were thus subject to usurers where before they had been subject to the nobility. In sum, shortage of capital and credit and primitive farm methods, together with less orderly marketing, gave rise to a long series of internal political disturbances, flaring into violence; and these became characteristic of recent Rumanian history.

Petroleum. Europe's largest petroleum fields, situated chiefly in the heart of Walachia, occupy the activity of a very small percent of Rumania's population in peacetime. It is generally estimated that Rumania's oil production has been about 5,600,000 tons per year. Despite its declining yield, the importance of this fact can scarcely be overemphasized, for a country possessing so great a reservoir of petroleum commands the concern of every industrialized European nation.

National Wealth and Income. In her most prosperous year (1928), Rumania's per capita *national wealth* was estimated at about $500. This was higher than that of Hungary or Bulgaria and equal to that of Yugoslavia. However, the *national income* per capita was only $68 in the same year, when Britain's per capita national income was $270. Today Rumania's wartime total national income is estimated at about one billion dollars a year. This is one-fourteenth of what it is, *per person*, in the U.S.A.

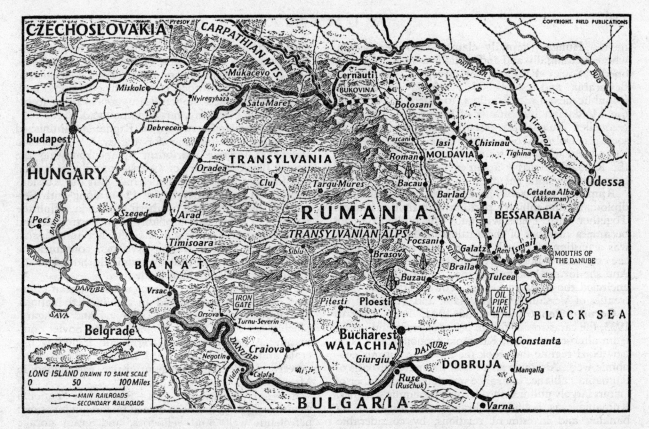

The map shows Rumania with surrounding countries: CZECHOSLOVAKIA, HUNGARY, BULGARIA, and the BLACK SEA. Regions labeled include TRANSYLVANIA, MOLDAVIA, BESSARABIA, BANAT, WALACHIA, DOBRUJA, BUKOVINA. Cities shown: Budapest, Belgrade, Bucharest, Odessa, and others. Inset: LONG ISLAND DRAWN TO SAME SCALE 0 50 100 Miles. Legend: MAIN RAILROADS, SECONDARY RAILROADS. COPYRIGHT. FIELD PUBLICATIONS.

The enormous inflation in Rumania since 1939 reached such a degree that the cost of living in 1942 was estimated at three times the pre-war figure.

Furthermore, despite the loss of a third of her population, the government budget had risen from $150,000,000 in 1938 to $900,000,000 in 1943. A large part of this governmental expenditure, of course, was made to sustain the Nazi army of occupation.

Although the war interrupted the flow of statistical data, certain facts are discernible. As a result of the serious territorial losses sustained in 1940, Rumania's wheat production sank from 4.8 to 1.8 million tons; corn from 6.0 to 3.6 million tons; potatoes from 2.0 to 0.6 million tons. If we bear in mind that the population was lowered by one-third, it is apparent that the most productive territory had been lost. Soya production had been cut by 90%. The nation's level of poverty had thus been deepened. The only constructive change of which we know was the increase in wool production, doubtless as a necessary compensation for the absence of the cotton and flax imported in peacetime.

Rumania's imports and exports present a curious picture, compared with pre-war figures. Her imports dropped from $90,000,000 to $45,000,000; her exports from $105,000,000 to $75,000,000. However, her exports — grain and oil — were not paid for by the Nazis; they remain as book credits in Germany!

History: 1914-1944

Rumania had been governed since 1866 by a branch of the German Hohenzollerns, related to the last German Kaiser. Because millions of Rumanians living in Hungary had been mistreated under the old Hapsburg rulers, hatred of the Austro-Hungarian monarchy was intense. Russia, on the other hand, was favorably regarded, for although the Czars held Bessarabia with its large Rumanian population, Imperial Russia had for generations been the liberator and protector of Rumanian areas.

World War I. Rumania's entry into World War I in 1916, on the Allied side, met with a speedy and crushing defeat. The German General von Mackensen demonstrated the weakness and military ineptitude of the decorative Rumanian generals in a series of sharp strokes that have become military classics. Humiliated and reduced, Rumania made peace with the Germans in 1917; but with the collapse of the Central Powers a year later, Rumania suddenly emerged as one of the victor states. The militarily defeated country thus obtained Transylvania, northern Bukovina, Bessarabia, all Dobruja, and part of Banat, a fertile land near Belgrade. She was unrecognizable, having more than doubled in area and population.

Rumania deftly used every incident to continue to increase her territory. When she defeated the Hungarian Communist Republic (1919), she seized the lands along the Tisa River in Hungary. And she extended her sovereignty over Bessarabia (1919) when the new Soviet state was too feeble to resist.

Her case for these acquisitions was not implausible. Rumanian peoples are gathered in a vast circle, reaching almost to the limits of these new domains, and within that circle are large compact islands of minorities — Hungarians; Germans who migrated from Saxony in the Middle Ages; Unitarian survivors of the 16th century; and other diversified groups. But except for southern Bessarabia and southern Dobruja, the rim of the circle was always Rumanian.

None of her neighbors accepted this aggrandizement. Hungary proudly clamored for her people, who educationally and industrially were more developed. Soviet Russia never accepted the loss of Bessarabia and established a Moldavian People's Republic next to its frontiers, to assert her claim to the Moldavian inhabitants of Bessarabia. The unreconciled Bulgarians, resenting the acquisition of southern Dobruja, bided their time. Only with the Yugoslavs, who had some claims to Banat, could the Rumanians arrive at an understanding; because both had the same enemies.

Rumania undertook in 1920 to consolidate her diplomatic and military position with that of France. Together with Yugoslavia and Czechoslovakia, she became a member of the Little Entente (1926) that was a bastion of French power. She served to limit the extension of Bolshevik influence in the Slavic areas. And she formed one link in the chain of nations that encircled the defeated Central Powers after the 1919 treaties of Versailles, St. Germain, and Trianon.

German Penetration: 1933–1941. From 1929 to 1933, the catastrophic fall in prices of grain and petroleum almost prostrated Rumania economically. The new Nazi régime then took the kingdom into its economic web. Although as a result the material basis of Rumania's alliance to France was shaken, a number of factors largely nullified the German economic schemes. Rumania was bound to France and England by banking and investment relations, by considerable trade, and by historic gratitude for national aggrandizement and territorial increase.

Fascist groupings in Rumania soon resorted to assassination. The pro-Ally Prime Minister Duca was their first victim; and when the French Minister Louis Barthou, sponsor of the Little Entente, was murdered along with King Alexander of Yugoslavia (Marseilles, 1934), it became clear that German-Hungarian influence would stop at nothing to achieve its Fascist aims in the Balkans. Foreign Minister Titulescu, however, remained unshaken. Relying upon France, he managed to hold Rumania to her historic policy until 1937. Though his adroit and subtle diplomacy was in the classic tradition of Talleyrand, in the end, he could not resist the historical trend, and was forced to resign (1937).

Fascist groupings, such as the "Iron Guard," and other quasi-military organizations, had already undermined the kingdom. King Carol II, by changing the Constitution, creating totalitarian parties, and nullifying the results of an election (1938), paved the way for his own ruin. The weakened kingdom could not resist the Soviet ultimatum to surrender Bessarabia and northern Bukovina (June 1940). The fall of France left her without a friend, and under German pressure she yielded North Transylvania to Hungary and southern Dobruja to Bulgaria.

By 1940 Fascism was dominant: Carol was forced to abdicate and flee. His son, Michael, was proclaimed king, and Gen. Ion Antonescu became the dictator. Actually, he was the puppet of the Nazis, who soon took over the Rumanian state in all but name.

World War II. When the German armies invaded the Soviet Union (June 1941) Rumania entered the war to retrieve territories lost to the Soviets the previous year. Under Nazi pressure, she was compelled to accept the loss of part of Transylvania to Hungary, who was also on the side of the Nazis. Rumania and Hungary were uneasy allies. They continued to maintain armies on their common frontiers; and both countries exploited the tense situation to bring feeble pressures on Germany, but all to no avail.

This anomalous position of Rumania diminished the nation's enthusiasm for the war. Antonescu sought to inflame patriotism by incorporating the Soviet Black Sea port of Odessa into the kingdom, naming that area Trans-Dniestria. But the Russians recaptured it in the spring of 1944, along with Bessarabia, Bukovina, and northern Moldavia. Half the Rumanian army had probably been destroyed, and the country had nothing to show for her anti-Russian adventure. United Nations aviators, concentrating on the oil fields and railway terminals, added to the miseries of the Rumanian land.

In August 1944, after a tremendous Russian offensive, Rumania surrendered to the United Nations. She also declared war upon Germany and Hungary, placing her army at the disposal of the Soviet command. A new coalition government, including liberals and hitherto proscribed Leftist elements, took power. In September, an armistice was signed in Moscow.

Foreign Relations. Of Rumania's national wealth, some 7% has been owned by foreign investors: petroleum wells and refineries, and grain storage facilities, viz., elevators, docks. These holdings have been the most profitable enterprises in the country. In normal times, 5% of the national income has been exported as dividends and interest to foreign investors, chiefly British and French; and this does not take into consideration the large additional sums exported to foreigners in the form of profits from trade with Rumania.

The British owned the major part of Rumania's petroleum industry: the French, the grain installations. These investments were temporarily "acquired" by the Nazis in the course of World War II. The present production of petroleum is about 5,600,000 tons per year, of which one-third was consumed at home and the remainder exported — to Germany, of course, for the use of the Nazi military.

Germany had always been an important customer, but since 1933 Rumania's economy had been so intimately intertwined with the German needs that her economy was, for all practical purposes, dictated by the Ministry of Economics in Berlin. The drastic fall in agricultural prices after 1929 and the surplus of grain in world markets brought about Rumania's dependence on German barter schemes. Except for what remained of British and French investments, Germany became the master of the kingdom's economy.

Stakes in the Peace

What can be done with this country when the New Europe is constituted? What materials does she offer to the powers who will construct the peace?

Rumania depends on two exports (grain, oil). Her agriculture has been excessively concentrated on one crop: grain. Her farm areas are overpopulated; her farming methods extremely backward; her productive yield peculiarly low. And yet she possesses some of the richest soil in Europe. Will her great potentialities be exploited? If so, by what means?

Her petroleum industry, owned chiefly by foreign investors, has been inadequately utilized. And yet her fields are the richest in continental Europe, although her production is one-thirtieth of the American. What countries will obtain this oil, and by what arrangements? Will it be used to industrialize Rumania itself — a land whose per capita machinery investment is, save for Albania's, the smallest on the entire continent?

Her people are newcomers to education; illiteracy is widespread; superstition is still more important than science in planting and harvesting. Her churches have been supported by the state, are independent of international controls, and play an active part in politics. Her population is divided. Sections of her own countrymen now live under the flags of the U.S.S.R. and Hungary. Will these areas be returned to Rumania? Will the Moldavian People's Republic surrender Bessarabia, or will this republic extend its sovereignty to include the Moldavians in the ancient kingdom of Rumania? Soviet Foreign Minister Molotov has stated that the Moldavian People's Re-

public will not attempt to encroach on Rumanian land.

What of Rumania's future political alliances? With her German affiliations removed, will she be returned to her former alliance with France — and will France have the capacity to make such alliances? Will she be transformed from her traditional monarchy into a democracy along Western lines? along Soviet lines?

Eighty percent of the Rumanians live on farms. The impoverished Rumanian peasantry face two poles of attraction: the American, with its investment and machinery for individual Rumanian farms, or the Soviet *kolkhoz* system, with its tractors, machinery, fertilizers, in centralized installations. The Soviet advantage is proximity; the American, the higher level of personal consumption. The American system calls for credits, the Soviet system for a protracted period of diminished consumption while building up a capital investment.

Will the future of Rumania be worked out as part of the solution of the entire Balkan problem, through a Danubian or Balkan federation? Will the Rumanian people themselves have a large voice in this future, or will their rich land of oil and grain be returned to its pre-war precarious condition of a buffer state?

THE SOVIET UNION

The Land and the People

World War II has dramatized the immense human and natural potentials of the Soviet Union, officially termed the Union of Soviet Socialist Republics. A sixth of the globe, Russia is bounded on the north by the Arctic Ocean, on the east by the Bering Straits (which separate her from Alaska) and the Pacific Ocean, on the south by Manchuria, China, Afghanistan, Iran, Turkey, and the Black Sea. On the west, the Soviet Union faces Rumania, Poland, the three Baltic States (which she claims), and Finland. This immense perimeter of over 25,000 miles encloses more than 8,000,000 square miles.

The land dominates eastern Europe and northern Asia, and confronts, within a distance of less than a thousand miles from its land frontiers, more than half the human race. Its strategic position with regard to air routes is decisive, but, on the other hand, its maritime position is astonishingly small compared to its immense bulk.

In Europe, Russia faces the landlocked Baltic and Black Seas; in Asia, the inland Caspian Sea; in the Arctic, she looks to the icebound ocean. Only in the Pacific, near Japan, does she have some harbors onto

the open ocean, which can be used the year round; but these are immensely distant from her industrial centers: here her population is sparse and her industry small.

The river systems of the U.S.S.R., although apparently among the greatest in the world, are curious in that they run either to landlocked or to Arctic seas. The Volga, Russia's greatest river highway, ends in the Caspian Sea which has no outlet at all. The Don and Dnieper rivers flow into the locked Black Sea. The Siberian rivers, such as the Ob, Yenesei, and the Lena, however large they may appear on the map, are frozen most of the year. These waterways serve as inland arteries only, and then for only part of the year.

Natural Resources. The area of the Soviet Union (over 8,000,000 square miles) is larger than the U.S.A., Canada, Alaska, and Mexico, combined. The population (about 190,000,000) exceeds the total of the U.S.A., Canada, Alaska, and Mexico by 20,000,000. The arable area is enormous: about 900,000 square miles, as against 500,000 square miles in the U.S.A. The climate of the U.S.A., however, is on the whole more favorable to agriculture.

For the most part, the Soviet Union is a vast plain. Her northern area is forested, the southern areas contain the famed steppes (endless grasslands) on which the celebrated Cossacks ride their horses. The Ukraine, the great plain in her southwest, is perhaps the largest single fertile tract in the world, excepting, perhaps, America's Middle West. In Asiatic Russia, called Siberia for the most part, the climate of a large section of the country is too cold for important agriculture. The swampy tundras diffused through Siberia are large and also fairly useless. To the south, in Turkestan, part of the country is a true desert. As it stands, therefore, about 3,500,000 square miles of huge domain of the Soviets may be cultivated intensively some day. The other 4,500,000 square miles can support only a relatively sparse population: mainly foresters, fishermen, and miners. But although geographers think the use of this land is limited, intensive exploration, planning, and irrigation conducted by the Soviet government have indicated possibilities that were lightly esteemed heretofore. The pioneer attitude of the Russians toward these neglected areas recalls the covered-wagon era in American history.

In minerals the U.S.S.R. is second only to the U.S.A., and these resources are widely diffused through the land. She has large deposits of iron and oil, and in many minerals (such as platinum) and fuels (such as peat) she is first in the world. But in relation to the size of the settled area, the U.S.S.R. is not so richly endowed in mineral resources as are some smaller countries in western Europe; and by this test, she is far poorer than the U.S.A. Yet the coal deposits of the Donets basin near the Black Sea are now rivaled by newly discovered Siberian fields, and during World War II, the shift of heavy industry to areas whose mineral resources were formerly little known indicates that many surprises are possible.

The winters are exceedingly cold in most of Russia. Moscow's temperature averages only 13.3° in January and 66° in July — an annual average of but 39°. North of Moscow, the skies are cloudy five days out of six. In the Ukraine (to the south), however, the climate is similar to Ohio's; and farther south the winters are even milder, especially in the beautiful Crimea and the Caucasian-Black Sea coast where semi-tropical vegetation grows and cotton and tea plants flourish. In other words, the Soviet Union, by reason of her extension from 40° to 75° latitude, and her breadth of over 5,000 miles, has almost every variety of climate, with the colder areas predominating.

In the south, the *chernozem* (or black soil), given good rainfall, should be about the best in the world for abundant crops. Most of agricultural Russia has an average rainfall of about 25 inches, fairly well distributed; but the northern and Siberian areas are deficient in rainfall, the average for 4,000,000 square miles being 10 inches or less.

Outside the great central plain, where the population is densest, the mountain ranges rise. The Caucasus Mountains (in the extreme south) are the highest in Europe, and the Pamir plateau, bordering Afghanistan, has been termed the "roof of the world." The Ural mountains, however, are actually low, hilly, low-strung masses. This range, conventionally separating Europe from Asia, contains considerable mineral and petroleum resources.

The People. The populations of the U.S.S.R.

are among the most diverse known, but Slavs overwhelmingly predominate. The "Great Russians," radiating from Moscow (these are the people usually meant by the term "Russians"), constitute the absolute majority. With the "Little Russians" (Ukrainians), and the "White Russians" (in the extreme center-west), and other Slavonic groups, they amount to nearly four-fifths of the population. Tartar influence is strong in the southern desert country; Mongolians are found near China; the Georgians (Stalin is one) are important in the Caucasus, as are the Armenians and Jews. There were numerous German farming colonies, principally about the Volga, who have been recently shifted inland; and, in the newly acquired territories in the west, the Letts, Estonians, and Lithuanians, together with the Moldavians in the south, are significant elements. Many Soviet peoples of mixed origins, such as the Cossacks, have adopted a Russian culture.

Differences in nationality are emphasized by the Soviet government, which regards them as valuable and significant. Native literatures, dress, dance, customs, and cuisines are vigorously encouraged among the more than 150 peoples, under the cultural slogan: "Socialist in content, national in form." Nevertheless, the Russian language enjoys such prestige that it gains despite this nationalist emphasis. The minority peoples are largely grouped into separate commonwealths, corresponding to the British Dominions. But central control is firmer than in the British Commonwealth.

Population Prospects. The population is estimated at 193,000,000 in the territory claimed. This includes the Soviet Union as it existed before 1939, the territories formerly in Poland, Rumania, and Finland in the west, and also the three small Baltic republics. It was estimated in 1943 that if the Soviet population maintains its rate of increase (which though steadily lessening is still impressive), it will have 250,000,000 in 1970, and if the new territories are included, it will have 285,000,000. War losses are assumed in this calculation. It is expected that the population of the U.S.A. in 1970 will be about 160,000,000.

Granting these estimates, the proportion of the Soviet Union's population to that of Europe and the Soviet Union combined will rise from 30% in 1930 to 40% in 1970. If her agriculture and industry increase in proportion, she will be the paramount economic power of continental Europe. Germany (that is, the old Reich, as of 1937), at that time, will not number more than 70,000,000. It is this possibility that may explain the haste of the German assault — a last battle to subdue a people whose impending population superiority as an independent state would be too large to be contested a generation from now.

The majority of the northern Russians are blond; in the central plain also blonds predominate. Brunets are the majority only in the Ukraine and other southerly regions. The head form of the Russian people, however, is not long; it is intermediate between long- and round-headed peoples. Their height is about the average for Europe, but large sections of the population are extremely tall and strong. The women are exceptionally energetic and can perform tasks in field and factory that astonish foreigners. This has been true for centuries.

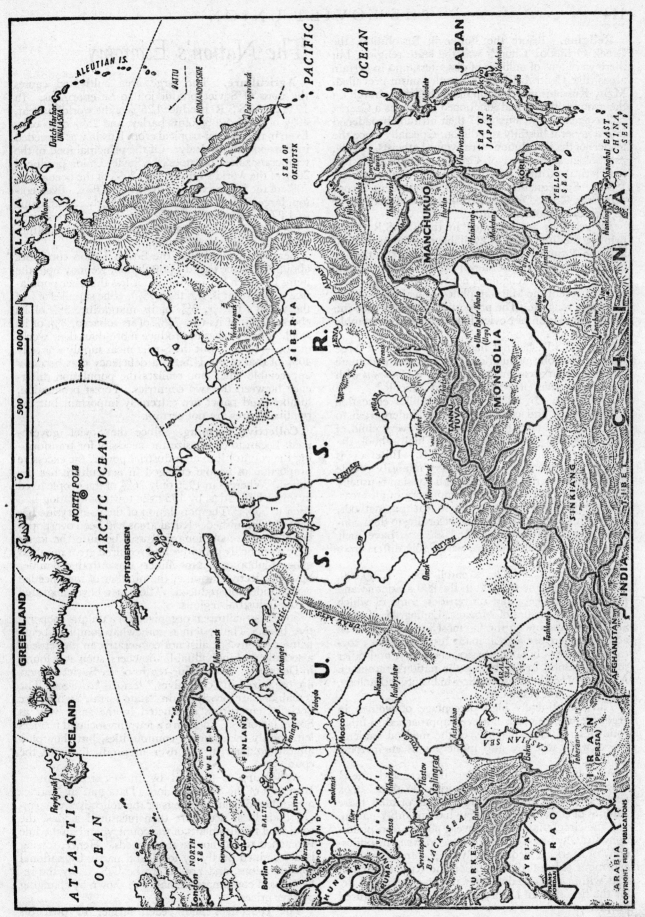

ALEUTIAN IS.

Dutch Harbor
UNALASKA

OATTU

KOMANDORSKIE

PACIFIC

OCEAN

JAPAN

Petropavlovsk

Hakodate

Yokohama

TOKYO

Osaka

ALASKA

Nome

SEA OF
OKHOTSK

SEA OF
JAPAN

Vladivostok

Sovetskaya
Gavan

KOREA

YELLOW
SEA

Shanghai

EAST
CHINA
SEA

Arctic Circle

SIBERIA

Verkhoyansk

Niko

Khabarovsk

MANCHUKUO

Harbin

Hsinking

Mukden

Peiping

Tientsin

Nanking

C
H
I
N
A

1000 MILES

500

0

180

S.

Taishet

Chita

Ulan Bator Khoto
(Urga)

MONGOLIA

TANNU
TUVA

SINKIANG

Sian

Lanchow

TIBET

NORTH POLE

ARCTIC OCEAN

S.

YENISEI

ANGARA

LENA

Kirensk

ALDAN

120

S.

Novosibirsk

OB

IRTYSH

U.

SPITSBERGEN

URAL MTS.

Tashkent

ARAL
SEA

AFGHANISTAN

INDIA

GREENLAND

Murmansk

Archangel

Vologda

Kuibyshev

Kazan

CASPIAN SEA

Teheran

ATLANTIC

OCEAN

ICELAND

Reykjavik

NORWAY

SWEDEN

FINLAND

Leningrad

MOSCOW

Smolensk

Kiev

Kharkov

Rostov

Stalingrad

Astrakhan

VOLGA

Baku

CAUCASUS

Batum

Tiflis

IRAN
(PERSIA)

NORTH SEA

London

Berlin

DENMARK

NETH.

BALTIC

ESTONIA

LATVIA

LITH.

POLAND

Warsaw

CZECHO-SLOVAKIA

HUNGARY

RUMANIA

UKRAINE

Odessa

Sevastopol

BLACK SEA

TURKEY

SYRIA

IRAQ

ARABIA

TRANS-
JORDAN

COPYRIGHT, FIELD PUBLICATIONS

113

Religion. Before the Bolshevik Revolution, the Greek Orthodox Church was the state religion, but there were tens of millions of dissenters, and in certain areas (like Central Asia) Mohammedanism prevailed. Many Russians violently opposed the state church on the grounds that it had functioned largely as a Czarist police agency; and after 1917 their attitude broadened into a general hostility to religion, especially since the leaders of the Revolution were avowed atheists. As the psychological residues of Czarism disappeared, this anticlerical attitude became politically irrelevant (by 1936). Subsequently the Soviet government recognized the Greek Orthodox Church Synod because of its loyalty to the new régime.

All religions are tolerated in the U.S.S.R. State printing facilities are now available to religious bodies, and the Protestant faith has even made spectacular gains throughout the Bolshevik régime. Nevertheless, among the youth, religion is not widespread, for most of them accept the Marxian philosophical view, which precludes religion. The proportion of believers to the entire population of Soviet Russia seems to resemble that of France.

The U.S.S.R. has not had the problem of a large Roman Catholic population. Should this eventuate in her western areas, negotiations for a *Concordat* with the Vatican may prove delicate and difficult.

Education. In all 16 Soviet republics education is tuition-free and compulsory from kindergarten to high school. Latest figures show that every child of normal faculties attends primary or high school, the number exceeding 40,000,000 pupils. Illiteracy is rare except among the aged. Every minority people teaches in its own language; though Russian is usually an accessory tongue, it is not compulsory in all areas. The republics differ considerably in teaching methods, approach, or stresses in subjects, according to their concrete needs. Trade unions and *kolkhozes* have their own educational institutions, whose rôle differs from that of other schools.

Higher technical colleges enroll about 1,300,000, and there are some 600,000 in the 800 academic and professional colleges and universities, some of which (like the Universities of Moscow, Leningrad, Kazan, and Kiev) are among the foremost in the world. In addition, there are a great many institutions for geography, geology, botany, physics, chemistry, and other subjects helpful in developing the nation's resources. A system of academies specializes in history, ethnology, diplomacy, and aesthetics.

The exceptionally high percentage of women in graduate institutions is not even approached in other countries. A clear majority of the medical students are women, who are also numerous as engineering students.

With her tradition of ballet, theater, and music, Russia is studded with conservatories. With her book trade sponsored by the state, she has printed more editions of classic literature than has any other nation, and the circulation of new novels, poetry, and philosophy (usually based on *dialectical materialism*, the philosophy of Marx) is incomparably large. In view of this enormous cultural dissemination the Russians expect that within a generation after the war there will be, for the first time in history, a nation of fully cultured people.

The Nation's Economy

Agriculture. The large area cultivated causes the mass of Soviet production to be enormous. In 1938 the U.S.S.R. produced 25% of the world's wheat, 40% of its rye, 20% of its barley, and 25% of its oats. Even in rice, a semi-tropical crop, Russia was exceeded in Europe only by Italy. Of the principal food of the temperate zones, potatoes, the Soviet Union produced 20% of the world's supply, also 20% of the beet sugar, 70% of the hempseed, and 70% of the flax. Even cotton, large-scale planting of which is fairly recent, came to 14% of the world crop. The U.S.S.R. produced 25% of all the phosphates for the world's agriculture and 14% of the world's milk.

Bearing in mind that the Soviet Union comprises about 9% of the world's population, we may note the items in which her production is less than her population quota (that is, less than 9%). She supplies 6% of the world's butter, 3% of its margarine, 3% of its cheese, $2\frac{1}{2}$% of its tea, $7\frac{1}{2}$% of its tobacco, 8% of its wool. Soviet fisheries produce more than their world quota — 12% — but the Soviet meat supply was only 40% of that of the U.S.A., a deficiency that becomes appreciable when one realizes the population difference between the two countries. Forest production, lumber, and paper are extremely important but the relative figures are not certain.

Collective Farming. Since the Soviet government began to emphasize the necessity for transforming the country into an industrial power, the excessive proportion of people engaged in agriculture has declined. Whereas in 1926 only 26% of the people lived in towns and cities, by 1939 the town population had risen to 56%. The population of the countryside has actually diminished. Rural areas had been overpopulated in pre-revolutionary Russia because the farms were wretchedly primitive and required great numbers of hand-laborers. As machinery was introduced under Soviet collective farming, the number of men needed was considerably reduced. These men have emigrated to the industrial regions.

Soviet agriculture is organized on a unique cooperative basis. The system is somewhat complex, being neither wholly Socialist nor cooperative in the sense of associations of individual landowners, such as is found in Denmark. About nine-tenths of the Soviet farmers are organized in "collectives," termed *kolkhozes*. The remainder are nearly all in "state farms," which are Socialist enterprises conducted in the same way as Soviet factories. There are a few unassociated farmers left, mostly in primitive communities, but they play almost no part in the over-all productivity of the country.

Agriculture is planned by the Central Planning Institutes of the Soviet Union. Data and suggestions are gathered from meetings of the collectives of farmers, their local needs are then measured against the total food requirements of the country, and a schedule is reached to harmonize these needs. Hence, sowing is determined partly by local and partly by national considerations, and not, as in the U.S.A., by the reflections of consumers' demands as shown by changing market prices.

The collectives allow each farmer to own his

own home, vegetable and flower patch and lawn, some poultry, pigs, fruit trees, and berry patches; but the "instruments of production," — that is, farming machines, tractors, fertilizers, and other large equipment — are owned in common, as are the fields and cattle used for general production. No farmer can hire another and pay him wages or in any other way make a profit out of another man's work. His individual property is for him and his family to work; all other work is collective and the financial rewards are assessed by elected representatives. In addition, the central government sends "Agronoms" (or county agents) to advise the collectives on methods of soil conservation and of increasing yields. The "agronom" is paid by the collective if it has a surplus, or by the government if the collective is still in a process of development.

Among the many changes resulting from farm collectivization, at least two must be mentioned because of their long-term effects. In economic planning, there has been a tendency to shift from an excessive dependence on cereal crops to "technical" crops — silk, cotton, and other items used as sources of chemical materials. In the personal life of the farm worker, there has been a tendency to convert the collective into a community center of cultural interests, thus counteracting the former rural isolation — and reminding one of the best features of the American "grange."

Collectivizing the farms was a bitter process. The wealthy peasantry resisted with all its strength and the contest with the "kulaks" ("fists," as these rich farmers were called) became a veritable civil war. The "kulaks" slaughtered far too many animals, with a consequent serious loss in livestock, and food shortages reached famine proportions in certain areas. The livestock shortage had been almost completely remedied by 1941 when World War II exposed the country to the Nazi invaders, whose plunder can scarcely be estimated. The struggle for collectivization of the farms is considered a glory by the Russians; but many critics have deplored its cost and suffering. Whatever the cost, the collective farm is permanent in the Soviet Union of today. When the scarcity of animals is remedied, the collective farm should be able to show an increasing yield in every product.

Though the Russian farm economy exceeds the American in *yield per acre* by about 45%, it is well below the American economy in crops *per man-hours worked*. Until this latter ratio equals that of western Europe, let alone that of the U.S.A., the Russian farmer has far to go. However, since 1933, when collectivization was completed there has been a tendency to higher yields per man-hour, which seems to have continued even during the war.

Industry. The Soviet government inherited a wreckage. In 1921 the capital available to industry per capita was almost as low as in the African Congo. Seven years (1914–1921) of catastrophic foreign and civil war had reduced production to a trickle and had wrecked, rusted, or made obsolete all existing machinery. The "Nep" (New Economic Policy) of Lenin was then formulated. Individual capitalists were allowed to rebuild the structure while the government patiently worked out plans to supersede private initiative. This mixed system came to an end about 1928 when the First Five-Year Plan, mother of all planning schemes, was introduced.

National production was projected for five years: so much labor-time was awarded to producers' goods, such as machinery and railroads, and so much to consumers goods. A deliberate choice was made in favor of producers' goods on the ground that the Soviet Union would be militarily attacked some day, and that she must be able to resist on the basis of her own production. The result was an enormous increase in industrial productivity, in factories, machinery, and (after 1936) transportation.

But the production of consumers goods lagged, and for three chief reasons. The over-all population had enlarged. Great numbers of rural people who had flocked to the cities suddenly demanded goods that they had never "needed" before. In addition, the government's vigorous educational program had raised the level of the workers' demands.

This contrast between shortages in basic necessities and factories rivaling the most modern on earth, was striking. But the ensuing years have shown that in concentrating on national defense, the Soviet government had wisely calculated the proportions of production — particularly in view of the industrial inexperience of Russian workers, and the short time at their disposal. The U.S.S.R. sought to achieve in a decade what industrial Germany had done in 40 years.

The total results appear to be as follows. With 9% of the world's population, the Soviet Union exceeds its quota in the following: iron ore 15% of world production, manganese 40%, chrome 18%, petroleum 11%, gold 15% (estimated). Steel products, the index of industrial maturity, are 14% of world output. Coal is about 13% of world production and water-power utilization is large.

It is difficult to state the ratio of Soviet production to that of the United States. In a depression year, 1938, it was 65% of American production; but today, under war conditions, it would appear to be less than half. In terms of world industrial production the U.S.S.R. holds third place, following the U.S.A. and greater Germany.

The index of Soviet industrial production, which was 100 in 1929, reached 535 in 1940 according to Soviet sources and 430 according to hostile German calculations. Since it is in a growth phase, its increase naturally exceeds the American, which rose from 100 to 105 in capital goods, and from 100 to 122 in consumers goods in the same period. Production in 1928 in the U.S.A. was $7,000 per worker in industry, in Britain $2,050, in Germany $2,250, and in the Soviet Union, only $1,150. Nine years later, the estimate was $7,050 for the American worker, $2,900 for the German, $2,750 for the British, and $2,900 for the Russian. Russian productivity, then, had reached the average for western Europe by 1937. There are no later comparative data available, but war production indicates that the Russian worker is well ahead of his 1937 levels.

In 1913, Russia (including Poland, her most industrialized sector) accounted for 2.6% of world industrial production; in 1937, without Poland, for 13.7%. In 1913 Russian production was one-fifth of American, today it is about one-third. Per capita, this means a fourth, so that the Soviet Union is still not America's industrial rival. However if the Soviet post-war rate of growth continues relative to other countries, in about a generation its importance may be such as to parallel any of the older countries in technical development.

The consumer goods industries, never too flourishing before the war of 1941, must by now be in considerable arrears. In clothing, housing, and comforts, the level of the Soviet worker is still well below the British. But against this must be reckoned such invisible income as free nurseries, paid vacations, and free medical care, in which both countries compete. The housing situation in the Soviet Union is still acute because of swift gains in urbanization. There is not enough labor to build heavy industry and housing and it is housing that has failed to keep pace.

The cultural industries — books, newspapers, radios, phonographs, records, sheet music, art reproductions, the building of concert halls, theaters, cinemas, and schools — have gone ahead faster than industrial production, this being a fixed policy of the Soviet government. Although these cultural industries employ relatively little labor, the impact of their products on the people is, of course, enormous.

The wear-and-tear of the war on Soviet industry must be almost incalculable and the devastation wrought by the Germans will be a severe burden on the country for many years. The distortion of industry for war purposes, as well, must create similar problems for the Soviet Union as for other belligerent nations.

Finance. Since the U.S.S.R. is a Socialist federation of republics (not Communist, except in aspiration), her finance basically differs from that of all other countries. All enterprise is socially owned and private profits do not exist. Capital is provided, not by individuals, but by the State, and the State exclusively manages all foreign trade. The State also controls the currency in foreign exchange. Within the country, the *rouble* is the unit of currency, worth about 19.3¢ — the same as the French gold franc before devaluation.

Soviet budgets are stupendous because they constitute almost the total economic life of the country. Peacetime budgets exceeded $45,000,000,000, for example. The internal debt, some $8,000,000,000, is mostly held by collective farms, cooperatives, trade unions, and State savings institutions. The total savings, which take diverse forms, such as trade-union funds, collective farm funds, etc., are not strictly comparable in character with those of other countries. Before the war, State savings accounts of private depositors were about $1,000,000,000.

Commercial banks exist in order to clear accounts between branches of state industry or cooperatives. Owned by the State, they also effect ordinary banking operations, such as draft payments.

Private property is permitted in the following items: homes, furniture, personal belongings, plots of land for daily needs, cottages in seashore, mountain, and country areas for rest. Soviet citizens can bequeath in full their savings, government bonds, and private property, and such bequests are tax-free. No citizen can export funds or hold property abroad.

Foreign Trade. Soviet trade, at $3 per capita, is one of the smallest in the world and incomparably the smallest for a country of such enormous produc-

tion. The 1938 figures were $260,000,000 for imports and $250,000,000 for exports. Principal customers, in order of importance: Britain, U.S.A., and Germany; principal suppliers: Germany, Britain, the U.S.A. Russia exported principally timber, minerals, furs, and canned fish. Machinery and metals, textiles and textile raw materials constituted two-thirds of her imports.

History: 1914-1944

Basically the Soviet Union occupies the territories ruled till 1917 by the "Autocrat of all the Russias," the Czar. Before 1905 Russia had been an absolute monarchy; in that year a constitution was granted, though its effect was largely nominal. In 1917 the Czarist state was overthrown as a result of the political, economic, and military weakness it displayed during World War I. During this year of upheaval three different governments took power. In March, the Conservatives and "Constitutional Democrats" organized the first ministry headed by Prince Lvov. From May to November, Kerensky headed a government based on a Socialist orientation but relying on a national democratic front, comprising the propertied classes. On November 7, Lenin led the Bolsheviks (left-wing of the Social-Democratic Party) in a social revolution which gave power to the Soviets, that is, to a "Council of Workers and Soldiers."

Lenin, founder of the Soviet Union, was a disciple of Karl Marx (1818–83), who introduced "Scientific Socialism" to modern thought. Lenin created a "Workers' and Peasants' Government" which assumed that, as the wealthy enemies of the workers and poor peasants were proved to be not amenable to democratic control, the revolution of the poorest class could be assured in a transition period only by the "Dictatorship of the Proletariat." It assumed, moreover, that Socialist dictatorship would turn into the purest democracy ever known and that ultimately, when the last stage, or Communism, was reached, men would at last have learned to live harmoniously. Thereupon, the State, regarded as the instrument for compulsory association, would wither away — its army, officials, and police become things of the past, "like the battle-ax."

The First Days of the Soviet Revolution: 1917– 1918. At first Lenin met with comparatively little armed opposition inside Russia. Soon after, he dissolved the Constituent Assembly (or Parliament), contending that it was largely chosen before the swift revolutionary changes presented the country with new issues. This decision led to a split with the older Socialist elements and especially with idealistic terrorists and anarchists.

Meanwhile, the Germans had been camped on Russia's western frontiers awaiting social dissension, and now that it had come, they began to advance against Russia. At Brest-Litovsk, in March 1918, they imposed as harsh a peace as modern history has witnessed. Lenin accepted this peace to permit bleeding Russia to revive and prophesied that the arrogant Kaiser, who dictated its terms, would lose his power long before mutilated Soviet Russia would; he proved right within eight months. Lenin acknowledged the independence of the border areas of Russia: the autonomous Grand Duchy of Finland, and Estonia, Latvia, and Lithuania. He granted the independence of Poland in keeping with the principles that had animated all radicals in the Czarist Empire, "the prison of nations."

A striking innovation of the Bolsheviks was the stress on national culture and autonomy, proposed by the Commissar of Nationalities, Joseph Stalin, who came from Georgia, in the Caucasus. This emphasis was a departure from a traditional Socialist belief that nationality was a *bourgeois* fiction and that the only fatherland of a worker was his class.

The Soviets, meanwhile, were kept busy by intervention and armed insurrection. They had issued a decree distributing all the arable land to the peasantry; they had confiscated the mines, factories, and banks without compensation; and they had repudiated all foreign and domestic debts. The time had come when the former propertied class must accept these decrees or fight them. They chose to fight.

The Civil Wars: 1918–1921. There were many phases of the effort to smash the new régime. The following were the principal counter-revolutionary moves: the invasion of the Ukraine, first by General Denikin and then by Wrangel; the invasion of Petrograd (now Leningrad) by Yudenich; the civil war in Finland (See *Finland*); British and French intervention in Murmansk, Archangel, Odessa; dissenting Socialist risings in Georgia (the rest of the Caucasus was chaotic); Greek and Italian intervention in the Ukraine and German occupation of both the Ukraine and the Don Cossack country; the occupation of Siberia by Semenov and Admiral Kolchak; and the American and Japanese occupation of Vladivostok — among a host of others. Fourteen countries joined in the assault, and twenty-two major insurrectionary armies were organized. In addition there were countless bands led by adventurers and brigands as well as by prisoners of war, like the Czech legions.

No country, not even the revolutionary France of 1793, had ever faced so many enemies and lost so much territory. At one time Lenin commanded only 250,000 square miles, centering about Moscow, while the enemies of the Soviets occupied over 8,000,000 square miles of Russia. With a perseverance that startled the world, Lenin drove out every one of the enemy armies and reconquered an area nearly three times the size of the U.S.A. Resistance to the intervention grew among the people of Britain and France, while the American General Graves urged that his troops be withdrawn from Siberia.

In 1920 Poland was the last to attempt an invasion; the Poles were driven back to Warsaw, but the French General Weygand, who came to their aid, eventually defeated the Soviet army and the Russians had to cede part of White Russia and the Western Ukraine to Poland. In 1922, when the Russians ousted the Japanese from the Far Eastern Provinces, the Soviet Union became mistress of her entire territory, except for the part ceded to Poland.

The Price of Revolution: 1920–1923. Victory was attained at a tremendous cost. The people were ragged; cholera and typhus ravaged the country; food rations, even in the great centers, were below those of the worst afflicted Balkan countries. The industrial capital that remained scarcely surpassed, per person, that of the Congo. Czarist Russia had been in the rearguard of European industry, but in 1920 the production of iron and steel was only 3% of Russia's poor 1913 figure. Industry turned out only 14% of what it did in 1913, and agriculture, always deficient, produced under 50% of the wretched 1913 figure. No such collapse had been seen in Europe since the 17th century. When armed intervention ceased in 1921, Europe anticipated the imminent collapse of the ramshackle edifice.

In 1919, Lenin had taken a leading part in organizing the "Third International" of Communist parties in various lands. Lenin, anticipating that Russia would be joined by other important commonwealths, placed high hopes on social revolution in Germany and Austria, most of whose workers were under Marxist influence. When the conservative forces triumphed, Lenin realized that most of the uprisings in other countries lacked a sufficient popular basis. He condemned "infantile Leftism," that is, any attempt to bring about Socialism prematurely. The Soviets now had to reappraise their situation; by 1921 they could not make plans on the assumption that revolutions would take place in other countries. Lenin stated that he had faith that Socialism could, nevertheless, be built in Russia.

The New Economic Policy: 1921–1926. Lenin pointed out that the Socialist transformation of industry in Russia had proceeded without an adequate technical base. Engineers, technicians, managers, hostile to a revolution that had deprived them of their former status, either fled the country or remained to sabotage. The workers were inexperienced and largely uneducated. The peasantry would not produce because its crops were taken away to sustain the wars of defense, and the city had no goods to give the farmer in exchange. Hence, to stimulate industry, private enterprise and the profit motive would have to be restored; to encourage farm production, peasants would have to receive payments for their crops — payment that would enable them to purchase goods. Lenin consequently introduced the New Economic Policy (N.E.P.), which produced a group of well-to-do businessmen called Nepmen.

Lenin was assailed from every quarter. Some accused him of treason to Socialism, others of abandoning workers everywhere in order to salvage Russia, while capitalists abroad saw in the N.E.P. the end of an experimental government, now compelled to return to the old system. Lenin insisted that this was a time-saving expedient to lay the bases for a Socialist industry by training a new generation of technically skilled workers. He also wished to hold the peasant problem in abeyance until a large-scale Socialist industry was established from which farmers could obtain tools, machines, fertilizers, and consumers goods.

Lenin's ideas prevailed, but not without opposition. Two "deviations" appeared: the "rights" held that only an arrangement with foreign capitalism could facilitate recovery; the "lefts" declared that Socialism could not endure in Russia unless revolution spread widely outside the country. Lenin clung to his New Economic Policy, even welcoming foreign investment. In January 1924 he died. Today he is venerated above all men by the Soviet peoples.

Stalin and Trotsky Battle on Basic Policy: 1924–1927. No sooner was Lenin dead than the conflicts that simmered during his life came to a boil. Trotsky, a fluent orator and journalist, skilled in many languages, had joined the Bolsheviks on the eve of their triumph in 1917. In the minds of many his name was coupled with Lenin's as the co-creator of the Revolution; Stalin, by contrast, had received no attention in the foreign press. Hence, the outside world was surprised to learn, after Lenin's death, that Stalin had become Secretary of the Communist Party — in effect, the most influential post in the country. Stalin continued the internal development directed toward the establishment of Socialism in one country. Trotsky opposed Stalin's program, but was overwhelmingly defeated; in exile, he carried on a relentless battle against the Soviet government, which he claimed, had "betrayed" the Revolution.

Stalin's Industrial and Peasant Policies: 1927–1933. By 1927 Russia had restored pre-war industrial production. The Nepmen, as Lenin had predicted, remained a small group of speculators, while industry passed slowly into the hands of the Soviets. By 1928, all industry, except for a few artisans, was socialized. Then Stalin created the Five-Year Plan, holding that the time had come for the first stage of Socialism; that is, for a planned economy that did not have to reckon with individual interests but only with the physical problems of production. Stalin's plan aroused the gentle amusement of professional economists; the Institute for Cooperative Economics in Geneva obtained critical, statistical studies by the world's greatest experts, all of whom agreed that the enormous rate of capital investment envisaged by Stalin could never be realized. By 1933, when the rest of the world had sunk into a slump, the Five-Year Plan was a spectacular success.

With all industry socialized, in 1930, Stalin decided that the cooperatives and communal land organizations were a proper basis for a change-over to collective farming, for which the industrial basis had now been laid. In order to sustain collectivization, the Soviet government decreed that there were to be two systems of farming. One was the State Farm (*Sovkhoz*), limited to extensive cultures of one very simple type (like the oceans of wheat in the Volga basin), where mechanization was easy. The other, the system of *Kolkhozes* (or cooperative farming), was worked out for the great mass of the peasantry who engaged in mixed farming. Under this second scheme the basic central production for any given area was worked collectively; machinery was owned by the cooperative; marketing and financing were pooled. But in addition, every farmer was guaranteed a vegetable plot, poultry, some livestock, and some fruits; in short, most of his subsistence was to be personal, rather than collective.

Poor and middle-class farmers rallied to the *Kolkhoz* idea; the rich farmers, or "Kulaks," not only opposed it but nearly wrecked the Soviet economy with their opposition. There was famine in the Ukraine during 1932, and many years later some livestock categories were still very deficient. The Soviets considered the collectivization achievement well worth this high price, which was in effect a minor civil war. In 1933 the Soviets won completely.

The Rise of Nazism and the New Diplomatic Policy: 1933–1940. In 1933 Hitler's advent to power in Germany indicated that the danger of military attack, long feared, had at last become imminent. The Soviet state was directly threatened by an industrially powerful Germany now controlled by a man who proclaimed Soviet Russia's extermination to be his cardinal reason for existence. Nevertheless, diplomatic relations with Germany were retained. As early as 1925, Stalin had begun the policy of maintaining normal diplomatic relations with other countries, and by 1933, having been recognized by the U.S.A., the Soviet Union was on diplomatic terms with almost all countries. She now joined the League of Nations (1934), where her representative, Litvinov, proposed world disarmament and later vigorously advocated collective security.

In 1935 the Soviet Union urged the punishment of aggressors and refused to recognize Italy's conquest of Ethiopia. She formed a military alliance with France and Czechoslovakia, following her policy of opposing Fascist aggression. In 1936 Russia accepted membership on the Nonintervention Committee for Spain, but would not consider herself bound while Italy and Germany obviously sustained Franco. In 1938 she stood ready to back Czechoslovakia, as Dr. Beneš has confirmed, but France refused to cooperate. Excluded from the parley of Munich (September 1938), the Soviet Union still urged collective action against the Fascist "Axis." But months of dilatory action made her fearful and she entered into a nonaggression pact with Germany (August 23, 1939).

Germany had planned to conquer all of Poland, which would have put her close to Moscow and Kiev. She had thought that by the German-Soviet pact she had allayed Russian watchfulness. When Poland collapsed before the swift Nazi advance, the Soviet Union entered Poland from the east and occupied the areas of which she had been deprived by the Polish victory of 1921, and which, the Soviet Union asserted, were overwhelmingly White Russian or Ukrainian in population. Immediately after compelling the nettled Germans to accept this unwelcome arrangement, she requested the Baltic States near Germany to permit her to station troops and use bases in the three Baltic republics. They acceded to the demand, but continued in intimate relations with Germany.

The Soviet Union also demanded that Finland yield her territory near Leningrad and the naval base of Hangö, in exchange for which Finland was to receive other territory and compensation (See *Finland, History*). The resistance of the Finns led to a three-month war, after which Russia imposed terms more stringent than her original demands (March 1940).

In June 1940 Russia demanded the cession of Bessarabia from Rumania (Russia had never accepted the inclusion of Bessarabia into Rumania as justified) and also insisted on the cession of Ukrainian populated areas in the Rumanian province of Bukovina. Both were granted.

The Soviet Union stated that the three Baltic States were in relations with Germany, seeking to nullify their defense arrangements with the U.S.S.R. of the previous year. She occupied Estonia, Latvia, and Lithuania, and plebiscites were conducted which ratified her occupation.

Internal Developments: 1933–1940. A second Five-Year Plan projected a shift in emphasis from capital re-equipment to production of consumers goods. The Soviet worker in 1933, compared with the Londoner or Parisian, was poor in clothing and many amenities. The Soviets were beginning to solve the housing problem, and they contended that the average citizen had other benefits: culture, rest, vacations, sanatoria, a guaranteed job, protection against costs of sickness and old age. These imponderables weighed heavily with the Russians in assessing the "standard of living." Nevertheless, it was clear that consumers goods must be stepped up. This goal was partially achieved by 1938.

However, the development of education always means an increase in the need for quality and variety in products, and the expansion of consumers goods could not cope with this growing need. After 1937 the obvious Axis preparations for total war caused a reversion to the former emphasis on capital goods and armaments, but this was no longer a uniquely Soviet, but a world tendency.

In 1934 it was broadly hinted that while Soviet production figures were impressive, they were uneven, that transportation was defective, factories misplaced, statistics over-optimistic. In part such weaknesses were attributed to poor coordination and to old habits of laziness so hard to eradicate when a people have for centuries sought to evade a tyrannical monarchy. The Russians, however, accused the "deviationists," or those who opposed Stalin's policy, of also sabotaging industrial life. With the murder, in December 1934, of Kirov, a leading advocate of Stalin's views, these charges became more emphatic. For over two years there were three separate groups of trials of those charged with seeking to overthrow the state by murder, sabotage, arson, and with conspiracy, internally and abroad, to defeat the industrial and farming program. The Soviets denounced Trotsky (exiled since 1929) as a leading instigator of this conspiratorial activity.

In 1937 one of the heads of the Red Army and seven other generals were executed on the ground that they had plotted with foreign powers to overthrow their country. There was world-wide skepticism concerning these trials, but it was maintained in Moscow that World War II had been scheduled to begin in 1937 with an attack on the Soviet Union, who was to be betrayed by her own generals. Since these trials the examples of traitors in other lands like Quisling, Neditch, and hosts of others have made these charges seem less melodramatic and far-fetched than they did in 1935–37. The Russians persist in attributing their survival in 1941 to the preventive measures taken against a Fifth Column within the country.

The Constitution (1936). In 1936 the Soviet government concluded the drafting of a constitution guaranteeing freedom of speech, press, worship, and franchise. The Constitution guaranteed the right of employment, an adequate standard of living, health and old-age benefits, participation in industrial decisions and planning. The Constitution permitted savings, private ownership of plots of land, inheritance of private belongings; it did not oppose inequality of earnings rising out of differences in skills. The Soviet Constitution was hailed in Russia, but the skeptically minded abroad saw it as mere declamation.

Far Eastern Developments. The Soviet Union had often been provoked by the Japanese, particularly after their conquest of Manchuria in 1931, when they blocked the Chinese Eastern Railway, a short cut to Vladivostok. Once the Japanese held Manchuria, the Soviets could either attempt to drive them out or come to terms. The Five-Year Plan was still in the balance at this time. At last, after prolonged negotiations, Russia sold her majority interest in the Chinese Eastern Railway (1935).

Now the Soviets played for time. They built up an independent industry in Siberia east of Lake Baikal, improved railway transport to the Pacific, and defeated the Japanese in several border skirmishes. Today the Russians have a large autonomous army in eastern Siberia with its own armaments and supply bases nearby; and this army ties up the élite of the Japanese (Kwantung) army on the border.

In China, the relations between Soviet Russia and Chiang Kai-Shek's régime, though workable, are often strained because of Russia's insistence that the Generalissimo stations too many troops near Chinese Communist areas rather than using them against Japanese invaders. As a gesture of goodwill, the Russians withdrew (in 1942–43) from Sinkiang, or Chinese Turkestan, long within their sphere of influence.

The War with Germany: 1941–1944. After the fall of France, relations between the Soviet Union and Germany grew increasingly chilly. The German moves in Rumania were clearly aimed at the U.S.S.R. and the Reich had begun intimate military relations with Finland. Russia countered by signing a treaty with Yugoslavia, displaying a hostile attitude towards German expansion in the direction of the Balkans and Turkey. On June 22, 1941, Hitler suddenly attacked the Soviet Union, using the pretext that he was protecting himself and Europe from Russia's early design to "Bolshevize" other countries.

The Germans marched to the gates of Leningrad, Moscow, and the Caucasus; they reached the key to the Volga, Stalingrad. They slew and enslaved millions, demolished whole cities, and committed mass atrocities. The Russians, developing a magnificent defense, "scorched the earth" and transported machinery in huge quantities to factories set up in the east. In the rear of the German armies, the Russians depended systematically on vigilant guerrilla organizations ("partisans").

After a valorous resistance, they rolled the Germans back as much as 1,200 miles in 18 months (January 1943 to August 1944). While their own figures of soldier dead are appalling (over five millions), the Red Army inflicted more staggering losses on the German armies. At Stalingrad (January 1943) they turned the Nazi tide. During the war, the Soviet Union displayed an industrial power, facility in supply, and firmness of morale that refuted the gloomy predictions of many foreign observers.

In the spring of 1943 the Communist International was dissolved. Another evidence of changed relations was the official recognition of the Synod of the Greek Orthodox Church.

On February 1, 1944, the Soviet government announced another fundamental change. The Soviet

Union was thenceforth to consist of sixteen independent Soviet republics, each controlling its own army and foreign relations (much like the relation of Canada and Australia to Great Britain). This decentralizing tendency was especially welcome as a demonstration of increasing self-determination of the many nationalities in the U.S.S.R.

In 1941 the Soviet Union signed a twenty-year alliance with Great Britain; and in December 1943, at Teheran, the U.S.A., Great Britain, and the Soviet Union agreed to cooperate for an enduring peace, inviting other nations to participate in the creation of an orderly world. It was clearly implied that world recovery was a greater need and peace a greater boon than insistence on differences in their internal social systems.

Stakes in the Peace

The Soviet Union can scarcely need territory. But she will probably delimit her boundaries or approximate boundaries, as they existed in 1914. Overlying all other issues is the insistence of the Soviet Union upon what she regards as her essential security. Moreover, it is likely that she will also require the assurance that "friendly" governments will be installed in all of the adjacent European countries. She needs many years of peace to bind up her wounds, to rehabilitate masses of disabled, to restore separated families, to bring masses of citizens back from slave labor in central Europe. She has to rebuild factories, railroads, mines, houses, and must make the scorched soil fertile again. Disorder can have no attractions for the Soviet Union and war certainly none.

In addition, the country is consecrated to the idea that if a Socialist society were at peace and had no armaments to consider in its planning, it would demonstrate by example the superior merits of the system. Whether this passion for success in peaceful emulation is well-founded or is an illusion, it is certain that until Socialism provides creature-comforts greater than that of advanced countries, its appeal will not be universal. Hence the Teheran declarations embody the objective needs of the Soviet Union. Her recent decentralization is an index of a feeling that this security will be attained.

The Soviet Union's need for credits is obvious. She has an immense terrain to develop. Her population increment, without war, is spectacular. She can have none of the territorial needs that have been held up before peoples in Germany and in Italy. Naturally, as the leading state of the Asiatic-European land area, Soviet Russia's weight for peace is enormous. Two devastating struggles in less than twenty-five years on her soil have been enough.

The Soviet Union is implacably hostile to Japanese militarist adventures in Asia, but the specific form of that resentment is not as yet definite.

THE BALTIC REPUBLICS

Originally parts of the old Russian Empire, the three Baltic States, Estonia, Latvia, and Lithuania, were separated from Russia during the Bolshevik Revolution in 1917, and then reabsorbed into the Soviet Union in 1940 as constituent republics of the U.S.S.R., after plebiscites whose permanent validity has not been officially accepted by the U.S.A. The Soviet Government has made it officially clear that these countries will remain component parts of the U.S.S.R. They are separately discussed here only because their new position has not as yet been internationally ratified.

ESTONIA

The Land and the People

The Land. Lying on the western edge of the U.S.S.R., Estonia is bounded on the north by the Gulf of Finland, on the west by the Baltic Sea, and on the south by Latvia. Including the large Baltic islands of Dagö and Oesel in the Gulf of Riga, she has an area of 18,353 square miles (about the same as Vermont plus New Hampshire).

The land is flat and fertile only in certain areas: the ice sheet of the Glacial Age having scraped off the soil in much of the country and left bare rock. The climate, ordinarily cold in winter (average below 30°) and only moderately warm in summer (about 62°), varies so much that crops are unreliable. The only important mineral resource is oil shales.

The People. The Estonians, who make up seven-eighths of the population of Estonia, are a blond people, more closely related both racially and culturally to the Finns than even to the Latvians just south of their border. Most of the remaining eighth of the people are Russians. The so-called German "Balts" are only 1.5% of the population, but their influence has been out of all proportion to their numbers. For centuries they diffused German culture through the University of Dorpat, dominated the professions and the bureaucracy, and ruled the country as landed aristocrats. Bitterly resentful of the loss of their great estates, they played a large part in the transformation in 1934 of the Estonian Republic to a dictatorship.

The Estonians number about 1,126,000, of whom

some 140,000 live in the capital city, Tallinn (formerly Reval). Since the birthrate has been about 16 per thousand and the deathrate about 15, no appreciable change in population is forecast for the next generation.

Religion and Education. At least five-sixths of the people are Lutheran in religion, most of the rest are Greek Orthodox. Education is widespread. An interesting feature of the excellent pre-war system was instruction of minorities — Russians, Germans, Swedes, Letts, and Jews — in their own tongues.

The Economy

Agriculture. The Estonian land is 46% grass, 20% forest, with only 18% arable — and 16% waste. Some 70% of the people are engaged in farming, mostly oats, barley, and rye. Yet Estonia has to import grain. For, although the crop value per person before the war was twice Finland's to the north and 15% more than Latvia's to the south, yields per acre of these and other northern grains were less than half those of the advanced agricultural countries of Europe, and about 15% under Poland's.

Besides staples like wheat and potatoes, Estonia also normally produces flax (10,000 tons) and is well stocked with cattle, sheep, pigs, and poultry. Great efforts have been made to develop a dairy industry, in imitation of Denmark's, especially for butter. Before the war, practically all the dairy farmers worked in cooperatives.

Industry. Apart from a few textile mills, Estonia's small industries, which employ only 56,000 people, arise mostly out of local farming and forestry. Her pre-war production of shale oil, which reached 180,000 tons, was the greatest in Europe, and it was probably increased considerably under the German occupation to help meet the Nazis' crying need for oil.

Finance. Prior to the Soviet régime, Estonian commercial and cooperative bank deposits were about 122,000,000 *kroons* (a kroon was worth about 24¢) or $29,000,000. The surprisingly low figure for savings (about $2,600,000) may perhaps be explained by a tendency on the part of wealthy Estonians to deposit in Swedish banks out of fear of the neighboring U.S.S.R. Taxation under the old régime came to $25 a person. The internal public debt was practically zero, the external about $27,000,000. The whole financial structure was exceedingly simple.

Foreign Trade. As a rule, before 1940, Estonian exports exceeded imports by a good margin, although in 1938 the two balanced at about $28,000,000 each. The chief exports were butter, timber, flax, and cellulose; the chief imports raw cotton, iron and steel, sugar, wool, and fertilizers. Most of the imports came from Britain (58%), Germany (31%), and the U.S.A.

History: 1914-1944

Formerly a part of the Czarist Empire, Estonia proclaimed her independence on February 24, 1918, five months after the Soviets took power. The Allies recognized her independence almost immediately, but on April 21, 1918, Germany annexed the country. The collapse of Germany (November 1918) restored Estonia's independence. Meanwhile, Finland backed a new Estonian army (under General Laidoner) against the Bolsheviks; and a British fleet (under Admiral Sinclair) blockaded the Gulf of Finland and landed arms. Combined Anglo-Finnish-Lettish contingents then wrested eastern Estonia from the Soviets. A peace treaty followed, by which Russia recognized Estonia's independence and remitted the latter's share ($7,500,000) of Russia's gold holdings.

Temporary Stabilization 1920-1934. During the treaty negotiations, Estonia passed a Land Reform bill by which the great landed estates of 750 acres or more, covering over half the country, were subdivided into farms not exceeding 50 acres. This was the most thoroughgoing agrarian reform in the three Baltic nations. Estonia also adopted a democratic constitution, with the secret ballot, proportional representation, initiative and referendum, and universal and equal suffrage. For three years genuine democracy prevailed, and the fury of the German governing class knew no bounds. Numbering slightly over 1% of the population, this group of descendants of the "Baltic barons" held democracy in contempt. One of them, Alfred Rosenberg, later became the "philosopher" of the Nazi Party; and all of them plotted ceaselessly to regain their lost power.

In 1923 the government declared Communism illegal. In December 1924 a Red revolt flared up and was suppressed; thereupon the government formed a White Guard, similar to that in Finland. Despite this internal struggle, Estonia signed a nonaggression pact with the U.S.S.R. In 1926 the League of Nations granted Estonia a loan of some $6,800,000 at 7% interest. With internal tranquillity restored, the national minorities acquired fuller cultural autonomy. In the meantime, Estonia had concluded an alliance with Latvia, but Finland held aloof from a similar tie.

Dictatorship Established: 1934-1939. In January 1934, the country adopted a new constitution, centering power in the executive. Two months later the Diet (Parliament) was dissolved, martial law proclaimed, and an "authoritarian" state established with Paets as dictator. A plebiscite voted by a large majority for a new constitution in 1936, but the dictatorship was continued "for a year." In 1938 a new corporative Fascist constitution came into effect, the dictator Paets naming himself president. On September 10, 1938, the country again came under martial law, with suspension of civil rights.

Estonia and World War II: 1939-1944. In the summer of 1939, Estonia declined guarantees against indirect aggression, preferring that no Soviet guarantees enter into any British arrangements for Eastern Europe. After the outbreak of war in September 1939, the Soviets demanded Estonia's collaboration in defense; she acceded, and a ten-year mutual assistance pact was signed. In accordance with treaty provisions Russia used Estonia as a base of military operations during the Soviet-Finnish War (1939-1940).

In June 1940, the Soviet government asserted that the Estonian government was sabotaging defense arrangements. A plebiscite followed under Soviet auspices and in September 1940 Estonia became a Soviet republic. The exiled Paets government protested both the sponsorship and implications of the plebiscite.

Later in the same year, as the Germans drove back the Russians, Rosenberg entered his native city of Tallinn (Reval) to become Nazi administrator of the "Ostland." A puppet government of Germans and pro-German Estonians ruled the country until 1944, when Soviet armies re-entered Estonia, repulsing the Nazi army of occupation.

Foreign Affiliations. Estonia has been friendly to Finland and Latvia, and has enjoyed intimate political and economic connections with Britain. Only the small cluster of Baltic barons of German origin and a few of their satellites have been pro-German.

LATVIA
The Land and the People

The Land. Latvia, the central Baltic state, lies on the western border of the U.S.S.R. between Estonia to the north and Lithuania and Poland to the south, with the Baltic Sea and the Gulf of Riga forming her western boundary. Her area is 20,056 square miles, or 25,395 including her lakes. Besides some Russian districts in the east, the country comprises the historic duchies of Courland, long a focus of Western civilization in Eastern Europe, and Livonia, whose great port of Riga was a cultural capital of the old Russian Empire and the center of German culture east of the Reich.

Like Estonia, Latvia is a flat land, but her soil is better, for here the glaciers of the Ice Age left deposits of loam. There are no important mineral resources. Forests, many owned by the state, cover about a third of the land. The cool, forested beaches on the Gulf of Riga were celebrated summer resorts before the war. For here on the coast the climate, bitter cold in the interior, is tolerable even in winter. The ports of Windau (Ventspils) and Libau (Liepaja) are ice-free all the year.

The People. The Latvians (Letts) are an ancient people, prevailingly blond, mostly long-headed though with a round-headed minority, and taller than the average European. They speak an old Indo-European language with many analogues to Sanskrit. The ancient stock has, however, been much intermixed with neighboring peoples — Swede, German, Pole, Russian, and Finn. Important minorities are Jews (over 5% before the war, in Riga and the trading cities about 18%) who make up the small commercial and artisan class; Russians, over 10% (more than 16% if the Russian count is correct), who are in the majority in the eastern areas about Dvinsk; and the Germans.

The Germans are only about 4% of the population now, but in Czarist times they were more numerous and still ruled the country as they had for centuries, since the time of the Teutonic Knights: they constituted the nobility, owned the land in great estates, followed brilliant careers in St. Petersburg, and

treated the native population with arrogant brutality. Riga, the Hansa city, was their citadel; its central section looks as German as Lübeck. The agrarian revolution of 1920 dispossessed the German landlords and distributed most of the lands to the Lettish farmers. During the German occupation, of course, the old ruling class temporarily reasserted itself.

The pre-war population of Latvia was 1,950,000, 75% of it rural. Riga, the capital, had fallen off to 400,000 from 500,000 in the days when it was an important port of Czarist Russia. Until recently it looked as if the population of the country as a whole were on the decline, but stability has set in with a deathrate of about 15.5 per thousand, a birthrate of 19, and infant mortality at about 70.

Religion and Education. More than half (56%) of the Latvians are Protestants, 24% Roman Catholics (concentrated near the Lithuanian and Polish frontiers), 15% Greek Orthodox (concentrated near Russia), and 5% Jews. Religious liberty prevailed before the German occupation.

Education in normal times is tuition-free and compulsory, and illiteracy, unknown among the young, is rare even among adults. As in Estonia, every minority had a right to instruction in its own language, even up to the university. Higher education centers in Riga, where there are a celebrated Academy of Music, an Academy of Fine Arts, and a University (formerly the Polytechnic School).

The Letts have proved themselves an intellectually active people. In Czarist days their cities were centers of revolutionary thought and action. Riga is famous among scholars as the city which dared to publish Kant's philosophical thunderbolt, *The Critique of Pure Reason.* And though of late years the importance of book publishing has diminished, there was before the war a lively press in Yiddish, German, and Russian, as well as Lettish.

The Economy

Agriculture. About 28% of the land is under cultivation, 30% each in forests and grassland, and 12% unproductive. A high proportion of the people (68%) lives by farming. Since the great estates of the old régime were run as units, breaking them up into small farms of 100 hectares (250 acres), or less, for a time lowered their productivity, especially as the peasants found themselves without equipment or capital. The consequence was a yield as poor as that of any Balkan country. But before the war cooperatives were slowly remedying the situation, especially in dairying. With proper education and modernization Latvia can easily double both crop yields and dairy production — and become prosperous.

As things stood before the German occupation, Latvia still had to import grain, though her principal crops were rye, barley, oats, potatoes, wheat, and flax. Except that 400,000 horses were not enough to work farms so lacking in mechanization, farm animals were fairly numerous: 1,300,000 cattle, 1,300,000 sheep, 700,000 pigs. Butter production had increased rapidly to over 30,000 tons.

Latvian fisheries are known for the world-celebrated smoked whitefish and sprats of Riga.

Industry. Latvian industry suffered considerable decline with the loss of the Russian market after the Revolution, then made a partial recovery. Before the war, however, it employed only 11% of Latvian manpower. Machinery investment per capita, though lower than in Western countries, was higher than in Estonia, Lithuania, or Poland, and nearly equaled Finland's. Large technical schools, some of them first-rate, contributed to this result. Production, however, was small and unvaried, consisting largely of textiles (especially linens), metals, chemicals (largely forest products), and woodworking.

Finance. The currency unit was the *lat*, worth about 18.5¢. About $35,000,000 in this currency, or nearly $18 per person, was outstanding when the U.S.S.R. absorbed the country. Commercial bank accounts stood at about $37,000,000, savings at $26,000,000 (not much more than $13 per person). Taxation, which before the war came to $35,000,000 or the high sum of $85 per year for a family of five, was doubled just before the Soviet intervention in 1940. The domestic debt was small, $9,000,000, the external debt still moderate, only $26,000,000.

Foreign Trade. In 1938 Latvia's exports and imports balanced at about $45,000,000, a per capita trade of $45. She sent out timber, flax, and butter, chiefly to Britain, Germany, and Belgium. She received manufactured goods, raw materials for textile mills and metal products, and some grain, coffee, and sugar, chiefly from Germany, Britain, and the U.S.A. (mostly cotton). But the movement of merchandise was a ghost of what it had been before the Revolution, when 57% of Russia's Baltic trade went through Latvia.

History: 1914-1944

The area now known as Latvia belonged to Czarist Russia at the beginning of World War I, and the Russians formed Lettish army units to be sent to fight against Germany. When revolution broke out in Russia in 1917, these Latvian units joined with the Bolsheviks. Germany proceeded to form a Baltic militia. While Britain and Germany fought each other in the west, a British officer commanded this German-sponsored army aimed at destroying the Soviet régime in the east.

The Bolsheviks were driven from Riga on May 22, 1918, and on November 11, the Allies recognized the German-backed Latvian government. Nevertheless a military corps under the German officer Bermondt continued to plunder the Latvian province of Courland until the end of 1919.

Post-war Difficulties: 1920–1934. Economically, independence proved disastrous for Latvia. Not only had she been ruined by war, but Riga, Libau, and Windau, her leading ports, no longer served as outlets for Russia's extensive Baltic trade. For years their empty docks, decaying port installations, dead factories, and deserted railroad yards bore witness to the difficulties of substituting new markets for the lost hinterland of 150,000,000 Russians. The popula-

tion of once mighty Riga declined; and the surplus of industrial plant and labor seemed to promise only disaster. Moreover, political hostility to the U.S.S.R. required Latvia to divert her trade from its natural channels and to seek export markets in distant lands.

In 1922 Latvia made commercial treaties with the other Baltic states. Hope for economic reconciliation with the Soviet Union improved, and the belief was held abroad that Russia was reserving special commercial privileges for Latvia in the future. Extensive land reforms initiated a slow economic recovery. Redistribution of the great German-owned estates, together with the stimulation of timber and flax exports and the development of dairy farming, partially compensated for the loss of the Russian market. With a nonaggression pact with the Soviet Union (1932) and the establishment of the Baltic Federation (1934) Latvia moved toward a healthy economic basis.

The Ulmanis Dictatorship: 1934–1939. In May 1934, Prime Minister Ulmanis suspended the Diet (Parliament) and increased his executive power. By 1936 Latvia became an authoritarian dictatorship on a "corporative basis"; parliamentary government was ended. The executive alone wielded legislative powers; and the people were deprived of even a nominal voice in government, such as still technically persisted in Italy. As Fascism developed in Latvia, relations with Soviet Russia cooled noticeably. The small minority of German aristocrats gained in influence, and Latvia's orientation became unmistakably pro-German.

In April 1936 the Latvian Chief of Staff visited Russia along with the Estonian and Lithuanian chiefs of staff, but prompt German threats ended any idea of collaboration with the U.S.S.R. The Nazis grew extremely active, insisting upon privileged treatment for the small German minority in Latvia. In practice, this amounted to free rein for the German minority to organize within the Latvian state. Nevertheless, by March 1938 the Ulmanis dictatorship thought itself secure enough to suspend martial law, which had prevailed for years.

World War II: 1939–1944. Germany had refused to guarantee either the neutrality or the inviolability of Latvia in 1934. Despite this implicit warning, the Latvian government refused in 1939 to permit an Anglo-Russian guarantee of her integrity on the ground that it was an affront to her independence.

In September 1939, after the German invasion of Poland, the U.S.S.R. demanded of Latvia certain facilities for defense, which were granted. The following June, however, the Soviets charged Latvia with acting in the interests of Germany. Thereupon the Latvian government (together with many German nobles) fled to the Reich. In July, Latvia held a plebiscite which ratified her new status as a Soviet republic. The exiled government denounced this action as an election held under duress.

The following year Nazi armies occupied Latvia, and Riga became the capital of the Nazi-designated province of "Ostland." German colonists moved in, and violently pro-Nazi Latvian noblemen recovered their lost lands and social importance under the new German puppet régime. It was not until 1944 that Soviet armies reconquered the region from the determined Nazi occupants.

Foreign Affiliations. Latvia had close relations with only one country, Estonia; with her other neighbor, Lithuania, they were less satisfactory. Owing to a powerful minority, German influence was important; but among the Latvian merchant class, pro-British attitudes were pronounced — because of Britain's important shipping trade, the Baltic Mercantile and Shipping Exchange in London, and the influence of the English Club in Riga. Urban Jewish elements and even some German merchants in Latvia shared this pro-British sympathy.

LITHUANIA

The Land and the People

The Land. The boundaries of Lithuania, southernmost of the three Baltic states, are still in dispute. As they stood in 1939, the little country was bounded on the north by Latvia, on the east by a tongue of Poland separating her from the U.S.S.R., on the southeast and south by Poland (which had taken the Lithuanian capital, Vilna, by a military *coup* in 1920), on the southwest by the German province of East Prussia and the League of Nations mandate of Memel (which was, however, under Lithuanian sovereignty), and on the west by a small stretch of Baltic coastline without a port. As thus constituted, Lithuania was best described geographically as an enclave in northern Poland. Vilna (Wilno), however, was restored when Soviet armies occupied it in 1939; and if her claims to the Vilna area are upheld, Lithuania will be twice as large as in 1939 and important in her own right.

The 1939 boundaries enclosed 21,500 square miles of territory with a population of about 2,400,000. Addition of the Vilna district brings the figures to over 24,000 square miles and 2,900,000 people. But the old Lithuania claimed much more: Memel (her only port) and the surrounding territory, with 1,100 square miles and over 150,000 people; 10,000 square miles in Poland with 1,000,000 people; and some territory in Latvia. If all these claims were allowed, the population would be nearly 4,000,000.

Lithuania is hilly, not a monotonous plain like Estonia or Latvia, and her soil is more fertile than that of the two more northerly states. The marine climate is rigorous in the interior but not at all severe on the coast. Kovno (Kaunas) and Vilna, on the great river Niemen, are well-known cities; but 87% of the Lithuanians live in the country — this is the most rural of the Baltic states, although also the most densely populated.

The People. The Lithuanians speak a language related to Lettish but differing markedly in vocabulary. Like the Letts, they are prevailingly blond, but unlike the Letts are nearly all round-headed; the coast-dwellers are taller than the people of the interior. Jews have constituted about 8% of the population as a whole, but almost half of the town population.

Many Jews from Kovno and Vilna joined the flood of 400,000 Lithuanians who emigrated to the U.S.A.

(This sizable group, larger than that from either of the other Baltic states, is depicted in Upton Sinclair's celebrated novel of the Chicago stockyards, *The Jungle*.) Now that this emigration has declined, a large decennial population increase should show itself in Lithuania as a result of the high birthrate (22.5 per thousand) and the much lower deathrate (13), despite the shamefully high rate of infant mortality — 122 as compared with 70 in Latvia.

Religion and Education. Over 80% of the Lithuanians profess Roman Catholicism. Protestants numbered 10% of the population before the annexation of Memel by the Germans, probably 5% after it. The only other important religious minorities are the Jews and a few Greek Orthodox communicants.

Before the German occupation, education was tuition-free, compulsory, and general, though about 15% of the adult population was still illiterate. High schools and normal schools were beginning to show large attendance, and there were over 30 institutes of higher learning, technology, commerce, and the arts. Besides the ancient University of Vilna, another university had been established at Kovno.

The Economy

Agriculture. In contrast to Latvia and Estonia, fully half of Lithuania is arable, only 28% is grassland, and 17% (mostly near the Latvian border) is forested, with a mere 8% unproductive. The pine forest takes a fair section of the rurally employed, but even so over 77% of the people engage in farming. The number of people to the arable square mile, about 240, is not excessive. The principal crops are potatoes, rye, barley, oats, and wheat.

Although the agrarian reforms of 1920 were less widespread in Lithuania than in her two Baltic neighbors, there was considerable subdivision. Pre-war crop yields, however, were 15% higher than Latvia's, nearly equal to central Poland's; cash income per farmer, on the other hand, was slightly less than in Poland or East Prussia. As in Latvia, the growth of cooperative dairying had increased the output of butter, but Lithuania's 20,000 tons was still only two-thirds Latvia's production.

The country had a fair supply of farm horses (about 600,000), of cattle (1,100,000), and of sheep (1,200,000), an especially high number of pigs (1,300,000), and poultry in excess of 3,000,000. Compared with other East European holdings, these are good figures.

Industry. Pre-war Lithuania had little industry. Only 6% of the people were industrial workers, and per capita investment in machinery was by far the lowest in Northern Europe. The 40,000 workers produced $80,000,000 worth of goods, or only $40 worth each per week, not allowing for the cost of raw materials. The principal industries were smoked meats and fish, wood products, textiles, metals, and some leather goods.

Finance. The *lit*, Lithuanian monetary unit, was worth about six to the dollar. For a small rural country, Lithuania had very respectable bank deposits, (over $100,000,000) and although savings were small ($17,000,000), the farmers' investment in cooperative accounts should be added. Lithuanians paid about $58,000,000 in taxes, or $24 per person; the public debt, $10,000,000 external and $10,000,000 internal, was inconsequential.

Foreign Trade. In 1938, the last year of the peace, when Lithuania still controlled the port of Memel, her exports amounted to $40,000,000 and her imports to about $39,000,000. Half the exports — butter, meat and meat products, flax fiber, pig products, eggs — went to Britain, only a tenth to Germany. Britain also supplied most of the imports — cotton and woolen yarn and thread, cotton and woolen textiles, coal, and fertilizers — with Germany ranking fourth.

History: 1914-1944

Lithuania had been a part of the Czarist Russian empire for over a century. In the course of World War I, the invading Germans promised the Lithuanians independence, and the Lithuanian Clerical party in 1917 invited a German prince to become king of their land. Following the collapse of Germany in November 1918, a Lithuanian Council of Independence met at Vilna and proclaimed itself a provisional parliament. Among its leaders were two men who subsequently ruled the country — Valdemaras and Smetona. In December 1919, Lord Curzon's suggested boundaries in Eastern Europe gave Vilna to the Lithuanians; and when the Soviet armies evacuated Vilna, they ceded the city. In addition, the young Soviet republic ceded the city of Kovno (Kaunas), paid Lithuania an indemnity, and turned over to her some valuable forest lands. Thus constituted, Lithuania made an agreement with Poland to ratify Lithuania's acquisition of Vilna, but in 1920 the Polish General Zeligowski violated the pact and occupied the city. And three years later the Allies endorsed this action, since it appeared irreversible.

Thus greatly shrunken in area, Lithuania moved her government to Kovno. Having learned that aggression, once successful, could be ratified, the Lithuanians proceeded to occupy the Baltic port of Memel, renaming it Klaipeda. In 1924 the problem of Memel became a concern of the League of Nations. And though the German majority within the port remained permanently hostile, Lithuania retained control.

Dictatorship Replaces Democracy: 1926-1938. In 1926 Lithuania was governed by a duly elected coalition of Liberals and Socialists. Upon their signing of a nonaggression pact with the U.S.S.R., a military coup took place. Power passed into the hands of Valdemaras, backed by a Fascist organization called the "Iron Wolf." Though he was nominally president, Valdemaras became a virtual dictator; and he refused to alter the continued state of undeclared war with Poland over the Vilna question (since 1920). Land-reform bills had been introduced and implemented in the meantime, but they were far less thorough or comprehensive than similar reforms in Latvia and Estonia. In 1929 he became the victim

of a bomb attempt, and anti-Fascist groups tried to govern the country.

From this point on, Lithuanian history is characterized by three basic tendencies: internal authoritarian régimes, conflict with Poland over Vilna, and conflict with Germany over Memel. From 1927 to 1930 martial law prevailed in Memel. Incidents multiplied as the Germans charged oppression and the Lithuanians countercharged German conspiracy. One fact is certain: in the Memel Assembly, the Germans always elected 24 representatives to the Lithuanians' 5.

In 1933 Hitler's advent to power frightened Lithuania, who rushed to conclude a nonaggression pact with the Soviet Union. Realizing that she had no friends, she sought to enter into a Baltic pact with Latvia and Estonia. But these two Protestant states, dissimilar in culture from Catholic Lithuania, feared possible entanglements in the Memel and Vilna controversies. Finally, Lithuania joined the Baltic Federation (1934), but it was agreed that she would be henceforth friendlier to Poland. Soon she set up an all-Lithuanian directorate to rule over Memel, thus irritating Germany. Much of Lithuania's assurance rested on the fact that, unlike Latvia and Estonia, she was an almost self-supporting agrarian country.

On December 28, 1935, all opposition parties were dissolved as another dictatorship, headed by Smetona, now took control of the country. Poland charged that Lithuania was now aiding Ukrainian "terrorists," and the atmosphere grew tense. Meanwhile the Lithuanian government refused to follow Poland when the latter devalued her currency; even after France devalued the franc, Lithuania held to the gold standard. The contrast between her comparative economic stability and Poland's recurring crises offered an effective propaganda point in Vilna, which she exploited.

Humiliation of the Dictatorship: 1938-1940. This period of national truculence was rudely interrupted by Poland's ultimatum (1938) to be friendly or else suffer the military consequences. Lithuania deferred to the Poles and rigorously curbed criticism of them in her public press. She dissolved the "Association to Liberate Vilna," proclaimed emergency laws in Kovno, and gave her dictatorship constitutional form. The more patent the government's weakness became abroad, the more stringent grew its domestic controls.

In the spring of 1939 Hitler seized Memel, allowing the Lithuanians to retain some minor port facilities. Thus, after twenty years of struggle, the isolated little nation was deprived of her historic claims to a Baltic port.

In the autumn of 1939, when Germany and Poland were at war, the Soviet Union demanded that Lithuania afford her facilities for defense. Lithuania yielded. But in May 1940, the Russians charged that the Lithuanian government had connived at the kidnaping of Soviet soldiers; and in June their troops entered the country. On July 21, 1940, a popular plebiscite declared Lithuania a Soviet republic. The members of the former Smetona government, who had fled to Germany, denounced the plebiscite as fraudulent and not binding.

When the Germans invaded the U.S.S.R. (June 1941) they made Lithuania a district of the "Ostland," governed from Riga. The former chief of staff of the

Lithuanian army headed a pro-German puppet régime, which was immediately faced with fierce opposition. Everywhere Lithuanian guerrilla bands formed, some pro-Soviet, others not. Finally in 1944, Soviet armies reconquered the country.

Foreign Affiliations. Apart from a wholly nominal arrangement in 1934 with Latvia and Estonia, Lithuania had no friends abroad. She had been embroiled with her two powerful neighbors, Poland and Germany, and had been basically hostile in sentiment to the Soviet Union, despite her nonaggression pact with the Russians.

SPAIN

The Land and the People

Once the owner of an empire rivaling Britain's, Spain is today a totalitarian state in southwestern Europe, whose territory, save for small segments in Africa, has shrunk to her homeland on the Iberian peninsula.

Her area, 190,607 square miles, is about a fourth larger than the state of California. If we include her Balearic Islands in the Mediterranean and her Canary Islands off Africa, the total is 196,507 square miles.

The Land. Bounded by Portugal on the west and separated from France by the almost impassible Pyrenees Mountains, Spain's geographic position is significant. Her relative remoteness from Europe, coupled with her far-flung expanse of seacoast, has impelled her historically to expand outward, a tendency similar to that of England. Washed by the Bay of Biscay on the north, the Atlantic on the west, and the Mediterranean on the south and east, Spain thus dominates strategically three of the most traveled sea routes in the modern world.

The country is a plateau with the highest mean elevation in Europe, except for mountainous Switzerland. Three rivers, the Tagus, Duero, and Guadalquivir, flow downhill from this plateau to the Atlantic, and the Ebro cuts through to the Mediterranean. Broad, fertile valleys spread out along the rim of the sea; most of them are irrigated, and this is where the majority of the people live.

Some geographers regard Spain's soil as naturally infertile; but others, pointing to the historic fact that Spain was one of the most populous and fertile parts of the Roman Empire, assert that the land has been neglected and denuded by man, and that it can be restored by afforestation, liming, and consistent care. There is little doubt, however, that a plateau like the celebrated La Mancha in the center of the country and most of rocky Castille can never produce very much.

Spain's northern rim, facing the Bay of Biscay, is flanked by the high Cantabrian Mountain range, which gives the seacoast a temperate, marine climate like that of Brittany or Wales. The plateau, however, is hot and dry. The Mediterranean and south Atlantic coastal regions enjoy typical Mediterranean climate throughout. In the south, winters average 50°, summer about 80°; in Andalusia, winter temperatures are over 60° and the climate resembles southern Florida's, though it is less humid. Here, the Moors, who once dominated Spain, built excellent irrigation works and produced two large crops a year, making it the richest province of Europe. In the north, the climate is like England's, with as little direct sunshine; while in the central plateau the summers are dry and stifling, the winters as cold as those of northern Europe. Climate has played an important part in forming the variety of human types that Spain can show.

But climate is only one of the factors that has encouraged and perpetuated regionalism. Topography too has accentuated this tendency; notably, the separation of the people living on the Bay of Biscay from the rest of their countrymen by the Cantabrian Mountains, and the wide, almost desert-like expanse that divides the north of Spain from the south. In fact, this country is the outstanding example in Europe of a land in which regionalism — that is, the persistence of deeply rooted local interests, habits, and pride — has remained powerful within the framework of the national state.

The People. The Spanish call their country "The Spains," as if to underline these regional differences among the people. Present population is about 26,000,000, and not even the desperate civil war that raged for more than two years (1936–1938) has had much effect on the net rate of population increase. The birthrate is high normally, but as a result of civil war and the attendant sufferings, it has fluctuated violently between the two estimated figures of 16.2 and 25.6 per thousand. The deathrate is fairly high, varying between 16.5 and 18.6, and seriously affected by war, famine, and large-scale exile. Infant mortality is extremely severe: one baby out of seven does not live to see its first birthday.

In peacetime, however, the natural rate of increase would have been 20% per decade, had it not been for the constant drain of emigration, mostly to Latin America. Argentina has been the favorite destination, but Spanish settlers are active and fairly numerous throughout the South American continent. Here too they band together in their local regional societies as Basques, Galicians, Asturians, and Catalonians, rather than as Spaniards. Successful migrants often return to resettle in Spain; and these *Indios*, as they are called, become an invigorating element, inasmuch as they have outgrown the closed and often stifling tradition of old Spain.

There are 5 main divisions of the Spanish people. The Galicians in the northwest (General Franco is one), a mountain and fishing people; the Catalonians, centering around Barcelona, more familiar with modern industry; the Basques in the north, who speak a language apparently unrelated to any other European tongue, and are politically divided between mountain people and seaboard people; the Andalusians in the south, of mixed Moorish, Berber, and Jewish blood; and the Castilians, proverbial for their pride and almost fantastic personal courage.

In addition to these major groupings, there are such minor survivals as the Aragonese, the Navarrese, the Leonese, and the Asturians. Most Spaniards are of old Iberian stock, only the nobility having been affected to any extent by the German invasion in the early centuries of the Christian era. Archaeological remains show that, except in Andalusia, Spanish facial types and body build have been constant for over 2,000 years.

Education and Religion. Roman Catholicism dominates the country and nearly all who profess a religious belief hold to that faith. The republic, which came to power in 1931, separated Church and State, but the Franco régime reconstituted Catholicism as the established religious institution, returning its vast holdings and restoring the monastic orders.

Many Spaniards, however, are anticlerical or agnostic in religion, though their number is difficult to estimate. Protestantism is tolerated but scarcely well known. The dominant religion in Spanish Morocco is Mohammedanism.

During the last few decades, efforts were made to increase the spread of popular education, and after 1931 a wave of educational reform swept Spain. High schools became fairly widespread, and university education enrolled over 35,000 students. But the disorders of the 1930's halted whatever progress had been made. In 1930 about half the population was unable to read and write, and there is little reason to believe that this proportion has substantially diminished. Since 1939 the Catholic Church has resumed control of the country's schools, thus again linking education tightly to the established religion of the country.

In general, despite a rich heritage of culture and an admirable body of imaginative literature, Spain has lagged far behind Western Europe in science and learning. Moreover, the cleft between conservatives and radicals is far deeper than in most other lands. This gulf is spiritual as well as economic, social, and political. Spain is known for her bitter, uncompromising civil wars that have rent the nation at intervals from 1836 to 1939 and that have impeded her material and social progress.

The Nation's Economy

Agriculture. Spain is a large wheat producer, with more than 10,000,000 acres devoted to this basic food. But yields are only half those of neighboring

See detailed map on page 321.

France, largely because of deficient rainfall and the primitive methods of farming rather than any intrinsic deficiency of the soil. Despite these handicaps, Spain's arable area is fair — 31% of the territory. With nearly 63,000 arable square miles, the proportion is not much below that of fertile France.

Other important crops are corn in the north, barley in the south, and rice in the irrigated Mediterranean areas. Rice, an essential ingredient of Spanish cooking, corn, barley, olive oil, and salted cod are basic foods of the masses.

Spain is an important producer of good wines, and the famed *huertas*, or gardens of Valencia, grow more oranges than any other part of Europe. Since the days of the Moors, Spanish horticulture has been the envy of other countries. In the dry south, the olive tree is a distinguishing feature of the landscape.

The agricultural system varies regionally in Spain. In the center and south, the estates of the grandees and *hidalgos* are like little, self-enclosed countries, with the peasants living in villages and going out in the fields to till the vast estates. In the north, especially in Catalonia, peasant proprietorship is more diffused; hence the farming population is richer. In some parts of Estremadura in southern Spain, rural wages were as low as $25 per working year; while in the north, the average was about 8 times greater.

But this static picture of Spanish agriculture does not depict the present situation any more than a description of our South before the Civil War would reveal its condition after 1865. Spain's average yield of wheat, formerly 4,000,000 tons, has declined to 2,800,000; and meat production now stands at 64,000 tons as compared with a former figure of 150,000. Rice has fallen to half of pre-1936 production; barley to two-thirds; and potatoes and wine are each down by a fifth. Olive-oil production has dropped 25%, and milk production per capita is a fourth that of France. Fisheries, though less affected, produce only half the per capita amount of neighboring Portugal. In short, the mass of the population is seriously underfed; and, what is worse, the deficiencies have continued over a number of years with cumulative effect.

Industry. Of Spain's total working population, 56% are engaged in agriculture and 21% in industry. There is some modern industry, chiefly in Catalonia, and long working hours serve to increase industrial output somewhat. Apart from minerals, the leading industries are cotton spinning, lace and knitting mills, woolen textiles, paper, and glass.

But it is in mineral resources that Spain is exceptionally rich. Iron from Bilbao has been noted for its high quality since the Middle Ages. Spain is the leading European producer of copper, has rich pyrites and quicksilver deposits, commercially important lead and zinc, and abundant coal in the Asturias.

Demands from Axis Europe have kept the production level of these industries much higher than that of agriculture. Coal has reached a new production high, about 8,000,000 tons (compared with the great French production of 50,000,000 tons). Steel at 600,000 tons and iron ore at 800,000 have maintained their pre-war levels; copper and lead are off a third. Significantly (for Axis needs), mercury production has more than doubled and tungsten (wolfram) has trebled, though the increase in the latter metal does not compare with the hectic rise in its Portuguese production. Pyrites has fallen to a third of pre-war production, but these deposits are mostly British-owned.

National Wealth and Income. Paradoxically, Spain is a nation that still benefits from her former empire, notwithstanding that she lost Mexico in 1822, most of Latin America before 1824, Cuba, Puerto Rico, and the Philippines in 1898, and now owns no colonies of value apart from a few minor territories in Africa. This paradox arises from the fact that the private wealth invested by Spaniards in estates and real property in the important cities of the former Spanish colonies is still extant, so that there is a sizable income from rentals and profits flowing back into Spain, particularly from such cities as Manila, Havana, and Mexico City. Moreover, returning emigrants often retain substantial investments abroad.

These factors explain the apparent contradiction between Spain's national wealth and national income. The figures are illuminating: while her average per capita wealth is about $1,030, the average per capita income is a mere $108. This ratio of under 10% is the lowest found anywhere, and compares with 20% in the U.S.A., 17% in Britain, 22% in Germany, and even 25% in Italy. Wages in Spain are low and a disproportionate share of the national income goes to investors or landlords who favor a safe, low rate of return on their investments. These facts point, in other words, to a class of investors who are extremely hesitant about investing venture-capital at home and who still cling to the economic doctrines of a bygone feudal society with an overseas empire.

Foreign Trade. Spain's foreign trade has not been helped by World War II. Before 1935, when the *peseta* was worth about 14¢, imports were about 875,000,000 *pesetas*; and in 1941, they were 549,000,000 *pesetas*, the *peseta* having dropped to less than 10¢. Inasmuch as prices are considerably higher, this shows a serious falling-off in volume. Exports fell in the same period from 593 to 520 millions (*pesetas*).

The Civil War (1936–38) almost depleted the reserves of the Bank of Spain, taking away nine-tenths of its gold cover. Meanwhile, paper money in circulation has quadrupled. Despite this dangerous inflationary movement, the average of share prices has only risen from 90 to 135. Unemployment is still high in Spain, at a time when it is almost nonexistent elsewhere.

History: 1914-1944

Spain was a neutral during World War I. From 1914–18 she developed her industries, strengthened her finances, and modernized her entire outlook. The war raised wages in Spain almost to western European levels and strengthened the industrial and merchant class.

From 1919–21 Spain participated to the full in the post-war boom. But the 1921 crash brought her back to pre-1914 levels of business and wages. There was, however, one significant difference: the newly emerging classes of businessmen and wage-earners now had a wholly different consciousness of their position, and each group henceforth insisted more vigorously on its own demands.

Steps toward Dictatorship: 1921–1923. Internal politics showed many divisions, two of them regional. The Catalan and Basque peoples demanded autonomy. Among the working class, Socialists and Anarchists competed for leadership, each having their own trade unions. (The Anarchists, being Syndicalists, are somewhat akin to the American I.W.W. movement before 1914.) In the rural districts of Castille, *caciques* (local bosses) herded the peasants to the polls; in Galicia, the peasants were as conservative as those in Brittany or Quebec; while in Andalusia, the peasants employed on the great estates had, until then, voted as the grandees ordered, but the towns were radical. Most of the intellectual class were liberal republicans, without Socialist tendencies.

None of these factions could command an outright majority. The police, the army, and the church were the conservative pillars; while in the opposing camp, the extremist Anarchists often followed a terrorist policy. To allay public discontent, the government sought in the usual manner to win glory: in foreign adventures. But its campaign, begun in the Riff mountains of Spanish Morocco against the Berber chief, Abd-el-Krim, soon came to an inglorious end. The Moors crushed the Spanish army in July 1921, killing 10,000 and capturing 15,000. The Anarchists commented on this adventure by murdering 160 employers in Barcelona alone in 1922 and 1923. The whole country rang with cries for the punishment of the *Responsables* — for those who had brought about the crisis and military shame. Civil war loomed.

General Primo de Rivera then seized his opportunity. As Captain-General of Catalonia, he had a large following in that province. Now that King Alfonso had forbidden the *Cortes* (National Parliament) to meet, Primo succeeded in having the King name him "Director" of Spain. This move, on September 14, 1923, ushered in the dictatorship.

Primo de Rivera's Dictatorship: 1923–1929. Although he immediately suspended the Constitution, unlike other dictators, Primo declared that this was a temporary expedient. Throughout his rule he never declared his régime permanent. He went in for a grandiose program of public works to reduce unemployment. He ordered magnificent and useless roads, economically unwarranted railways, and ambitious buildings erected next to huts. Despite the absence of coordination, general world recovery assisted his plans for economic expansion.

In 1925 the French, alarmed at the effect of Spanish incompetence on their rising colonial empire in North Africa, defeated Abd-el-Krim in battle and restored Spanish Morocco to the Spaniards. With the Moroccan disaster repaired, Primo established high protective tariffs and state monopolies (in petroleum, for example). Somehow he managed to collect overdue land taxes from the grandees, obtained loans from abroad, and balanced the budget, a rare accomplishment for Spain even in her best days.

In an attempt to imitate Italian Fascism, he formed "the Patriotic Union of Young Men," organized 27 "corporations," or representative bodies of business and labor, suppressed newspapers, banned clubs (these were the centers of political discussions in Spain), and fulminated against the League of Nations, withdrawing Spain from membership for two years. Striking against the autonomists, he prohibited the teaching of the Catalan language.

Despite these moves, he remained an old-line reactionary, lacking the energy of genuine totalitarian dictators. When an artillery corps of discontented officers rose against him, he suppressed them and established an out-and-out police state. Then the *peseta* collapsed in 1929; the tired "Director" resigned his post and left for Paris to haunt the French cafés where he had spent a happy youth. He died there shortly thereafter.

Last Days of the Monarchy: 1929–1931. Another general, Berenguer, succeeded Primo de Rivera and proclaimed the Constitution. But Berenguer's policy was that of the hated monarchy. From one end of Spain to the other, army officers and intellectuals conspired and declaimed against the régime. In October 1930 a premature rebellion of the army at Jaca in the Pyrenees Mountains revealed the scope of the discontent. Two exalted young revolutionary officers were shot: now the revolution had its martyrs. While an army rising was postponed, a large number of political prisoners formed a republican government in the "Model Prison" at Madrid.

The municipal elections in the spring of 1931 showed that King Alfonso had no following in the cities. He abdicated and was allowed to go abroad peaceably. So without bloodshed, the whole of Spain proclaimed the Republic on April 14, 1931.

Honeymoon of the Republic: 1931–1933. The new republic set out with high hopes and lofty ideals. Born in the depths of a world economic depression, it nevertheless refused to adopt pessimistic views. In December 1931, Republican Spain adopted a Constitution, which in many respects was one of the most progressive documents of its kind. It kept intact the older forms of capitalism but it declared Spain a "Workers' Republic." It concentrated power in a single house of Parliament, the *Cortes*, and provided practically unlimited powers to the legislative body. This was in sharp contrast to past experiences, for Spain had previously always relied on the executive (even under the first republic of 1868 and the Castelar Republic of 1874).

The conservative republican Alcalá Zamora, was "kicked upstairs" to the Presidency, and Azaña, a liberal republican, became prime minister with widespread powers. The government prohibited the Catholic Church from the field of education and cut off all state subsidies to religious groups. It did not, however, disturb the religious orders (called the *Friars* by the Spaniards). It allowed the Jesuit order to remain but confiscated 30% of their large investments, leaving the remainder intact in the names of designated individuals.

Despite some Leftist opposition, which insisted that the women would vote as the Church directed, the government gave women the vote. It recognized regional autonomy and in 1932 declared Catalonia a "Generality," that is, a semi-independent state with its own language and culture. The exiled Catalan leader, Maciá, returned to Barcelona, where he was publicly honored. Tackling the military problem, the government retired 10,000 of the 22,000 officers of the over-staffed army, but gave them ample pensions. For the first time the military were not allowed to rank above civilians.

The government opened 10,000 new schools, encouraged public works on a planned basis, and introduced industrial arbitration to replace the often bloody conflicts between capital and labor. It grappled with the fundamental land problem. In the north, farm holdings were too small for subsistence, in the south too large and sparse to be worked profitably. The government therefore established "communities" in the north, where the farmers could voluntarily pool their resources, and granted them a credit of 15,000,-000 *pesetas* (then $2,500,000) for voluntary collectivization. In the south, it confiscated Crown Lands and some of the giant estates of the grandees.

The republican government even showed military power by crushing the rising of a reactionary, General Sanjurjo, in Seville in August 1932. The persistence of large-scale unemployment and the slow tempo of land nationalization, however, led to Anarchist outbreaks, which the régime soon mastered. By August 1933 the Republic, thinking itself secure, ended its temporary laws for the "Defense of the Republic" and ordered the restoration of full civil liberties. With all its faults and inadequacies, the Republic, as the English historian Jackson observed, "did more for the people in eighteen months than the Monarchy in fifty years."

The Conservative Reaction: 1933–1936. Yet the Republic, despite all its reforms, remained content with half-way measures. Every move it made earned the hatred of the conservative elements, while it failed to satisfy the sharp hunger of the peasantry or provide jobs and more generous wages for the city workers. Most of the leaders of the Republic were of the intellectual class, with an unlimited faith in reason and persuasion. They left almost inviolate the foundations of the old economic and social order.

The opposition gathered all its forces. Lerroux, a politician who had made his career in Barcelona by mocking the Catholics and appealing to the café loungers, now joined hands with Gil Robles, the talented reactionary leader of the Right, with the Carlists of Navarre, for whom even King Alfonso was too modern, and with every other conservative group. They all united in an "Anti-Marxist Coalition." In the ensuing elections, the women's vote proved the factor that defeated the Republicans and restored the Rightist groups to power.

Lerroux, the onetime atheist, restored Church subsidies. The government again entrusted education to the priesthood and the monastic orders. It ordered workers to be moved from one province to another in gangs, so that they would have no voting residence and could be transferred in the event of strikes. The commercial classes were not too happy at these manifestations: they favored a conciliatory rather than a repressive policy toward the workers. But the men who constituted the government were firm in their belief that authority was the source of Spain's national character.

In September 1934 the Leftists combined. All groups, from mildly liberal academicians clear over to extremist Anarchists, decided to join in common resistance. Revolution broke out in October. In Barcelona, the government put down the uprising in a few days; but in the Asturias mining province of the north, the struggle was ferocious and sanguinary, occupying the attention of all Europe. Though the revolt was suppressed in a month, thousands of rebels hid their guns in the wild Cantabrian mountains. Thenceforth "Asturias" became the rallying-cry of the Left.

The year 1935 witnessed the gathering of forces on both sides. Ideological struggles were mounting in Europe but Spain, the land of extremes, was to become the most contested battleground between the Rightists and the Leftist Popular Front. In February 1936 the conservative government held an election. The results showed a decisive parliamentary victory for the Popular Front.

The Road to Civil War: 1936. The incoming government was moderate Left, mainly composed of liberal republicans. It began with a policy of temporizing. Although the Communist element was very small, having won only 4% of the electoral vote, the newly organized Fascist party, the *Falange*, seized on this 4% to denounce the mild Madrid administration as Moscow-dominated.

But whatever the government's attitude may have been, the mood of the people was inflammatory. Falangists and workers, groups fought each other everywhere. Spain became a theater of strikes, lockouts, raids, assaults, burnings, and shootings — both sides insisting that they were defending themselves. But the crucial problem was the peasants' strikes. In Malaga province they struck for increases of from 2 *pesetas* (26¢) to 15 *pesetas* a day and refused to accept less. The city workers insisted on wage increases ranging as high as 300%. Strikes had become the extra-governmental method for altering the basis of society.

At this threat, the conservative elements, prompted by the German and Italian governments and winked at by the Portuguese dictatorship, united for counter-revolution. They set a tentative date for September 1936, but had to advance it. In the early summer, Rightists in Madrid murdered Lieutenant Castillo of the Assault Guards, faithful to the Republic. Leftists retaliated by murdering Calvo Sotelo, a traditionalist leader from the Basque country and a prominent member of the Right.

On July 17, Francisco Franco, a general who had been removed as head of the General Staff and retired to Morocco, led a rebellion from Spanish Morocco. The next day his army groups rose everywhere throughout Spain, but in Madrid and Barcelona the poorly armed people drove them from the barracks. It looked as if the uprising would soon dissipate, when Italian airplanes began to transport Moorish troops *en masse* from North Africa to Seville. Within a week civil war was under way: the dress rehearsal of World War II had begun.

International Situation and the Spanish Civil War. No legal government resisting rebellion had ever been deprived of the right to import arms for its own defense. Such an action would be tantamount to placing a premium on rebellion. But in July 1936 all Europe was so tense that Léon Blum, Socialist Prime Minister of France, feared that if the Spanish Republic received arms, the champions of the Insurgents, Germany and Italy, would use that as a pretext for unleashing a world war (See *France, History*). Waiving precedent, therefore, the French suggested that both sides be deprived of outside aid by a nonintervention committee. Great Britain endorsed this move, as did nearly all the other powers. Germany and Italy accepted, but of course, with no intention of abiding by its decisions.

The Powers then constituted the Nonintervention Committee. Soviet Russia joined it but insisted that she would sustain the Spanish Loyalists if Germany and Italy were found sustaining the Insurgents. What actually happened was that Germany and Italy sent large-scale aid to General Franco's Insurgents, cynically denied it, then later boastfully admitted it, while the Nonintervention Committee engaged in protracted inquiries and "research" rather than a determined effort to face the issues squarely. The Committee attempted several steps, such as a submarine patrol, but basically nonintervention aided only the Insurgents. It doomed the Loyalists.

Meanwhile, thousands of volunteers made their way to Spain from Leftist groups throughout the world and fought to defend the Spanish Republic, while the Fascist powers, Germany and Italy, sent detachments of their regular armies, properly equipped and officered.

The Conduct of the War: 1936–1939. Atrocities prevailed, each side accusing the other violently. The Loyalists stated that whatever atrocities were committed on their side were either reprisals or the work of fanatical, irresponsible groups in the heat of passion, who were soon disavowed and eliminated; but they accused the Insurgents of indulging coldly and systematically in terror. The Insurgents retorted that the beast of Bolshevism had been unchained. Among the Insurgents, the Falangists, a Fascist group, acted as a sort of special police force under General Franco.

The war began with the Republic holding the Mediterranean and Basque coasts, as well as the Madrid-Valencia triangle. By February 1937, the Insurgents had captured Malaga on the Mediterranean, and by October the Basque coast. However, the Loyalists inflicted a stinging defeat on the Italian forces at Guadalajara. By the spring of 1938, the Insurgents had broken through to cut off the Mediterranean coast, and by the early spring of 1939, the Loyalists had lost everything, including Barcelona. But so determined was the Loyalist resistance that only a *coup d'état* within Madrid forced a surrender in March 1939.

From the outset (November 1936) Germany and

Italy had recognized the Franco régime. Soon an increasing number of other nations recognized Franco; and upon the fall of Madrid in 1939 his régime gained almost instant recognition everywhere. Only Mexico and Soviet Russia refused to recognize it.

The Spanish Civil War was a testing ground for military tactics, new weapons, and new explosives. Nazi Germany, above all, regarded it in this light. Upon the conclusion of the conflict, General Franco admitted his indebtedness to Germany, Italy, and Portugal and made arrangements to repay them impressive sums of money.

At the end of the war, hundreds of thousands of Spaniards fled abroad, mainly to France and French North Africa, where they were put in concentration camps. Others obtained refuge in Mexico and Soviet Russia. How many Spaniards Franco has imprisoned since the Civil War is not known, though some estimates are well above a million. Numerous executions also marked the aftermath of the war.

1939–1944. Whatever may have been the sympathies of Spain, her enormous losses made it impossible for her to do more than connive at Axis successes during World War II. German influence was paramount in Spain: indeed, even the control of the Gestapo was only thinly disguised. Despite the sympathies of the Spanish government with the Axis and its constant provocations, such as the seizure of Tangier in North Africa, Britain and the U.S.A. followed a careful policy in the expectation that Spain would not thus become an avowed belligerent. Both the British and American governments resisted constant and often vehement criticism of this policy, though no one substantially questioned the friendliness of Franco's government to the Axis. In November 1942, the Americans landed in French North Africa. The Allies watched Spain carefully and garrisoned the border of Spanish Morocco.

Within Spain, unemployment remained staggeringly high and food supplies scanty. Even World War II did not bring about a revival until 1942; and this revival, despite large-scale Axis purchases of vital raw materials, remained relatively modest. The Franco régime has not restored civil liberties, nor has the veneer of authoritarian rule put an end to internal conflicts. The older aristocracy, especially the Duke of Alba and the monarchists, mostly friendly to Britain, still pursue independent paths; while the pro-Axis jingoism of the Falangists has begun to look absurd.

Foreign Affiliations. Spanish public opinion has long been divided: in World War I the Court circles, related to the Bourbons and Hapsburgs, favored the Central Powers, Germany and Austria; while the merchant and industrial groups, as well as the workers, were pro-French and pro-British. At present, however, a similar classification is perhaps too neat: the grandees have turned increasingly toward Britain as they have watched Hitler's fortunes wane. At the same time, the Franco government has sponsored *"Hispanidad"* (Spanishness) and actively encouraged the *Falange* to spread sentiments favoring the present Spanish régime in Latin America, with intimations that its social system is more naturally suited to Latin America than democracy.

Stakes in the Peace

Spain's economy is based on agricultural exports, mainly from large estates. Until 1936 she possessed a sizable wealthy class who, if they had been more capitalist in outlook, could have used their capital to modernize the country. It is clear that Spain could rival France at the height of the latter's well-being, if she abolished her traditional feudal outlook. Few countries are so blessed in mineral resources, none endowed with better climate or geographic position; and the history of Spain is almost a roll-call of energies and achievements.

Spain's greatest needs are irrigation, modern farm machinery, more subsistence farming, less emphasis on "cash crops" for export, and a much higher degree of industrialization. The great estates in the south must be put to better social uses, while in the north some form of cooperative agriculture seems to be indicated.

The Spanish people, except for scattered feudal survivals and some pastoral folk in Navarre, are very prone to European and world cooperation. There are no basic obstacles to Spain's participation in a world organization as an honored and active member.

SWEDEN

The Land and the People

Sweden has played a part in European history altogether out of proportion to her size. In the 17th century she was one of the world's leading military and political powers. Today this ancient monarchy, neutral in war, is given over to the arts of peace and the democratic "Middle Way," and she has accepted her position of diminished importance.

Largest of the three Scandinavian commonwealths (which include Norway and Denmark), Sweden is 173,347 square miles in area — not much smaller than Germany and a sixth larger than California.

The population is estimated at about 6,400,000. The land faces the Baltic; only the port of Göteborg looks out to the western seas.

Facing the Baltic Sea, Sweden is bounded by Finland (northeast) and Norway (west). Towards the south, the narrow straits of the Kattegat and Skagerrak set her off from Denmark.

The Land. Sections of Sweden resemble parts of each of her Scandinavian neighbors. The south is similar to some of Denmark in fertility, being mostly level land and subject to a more southerly marine climate. A little to the north is an area of colder, hilly country, largely forested, whose timber and match industry have become a source of national wealth. Central Sweden is a region of many lakes and rolling glacial plains, where the soil is reasonably good for farming. Stockholm, the capital city of 556,954, stands in the heart of this area.

This countryside looks familiar to many Americans, with its red barns, white church steeples, and isolated farms, except for many castles of the nobility, which are of the true fairybook type.

Near the mountains that separate Sweden from Norway in the north, lie the Kiruna iron mines, whose quality is unrivaled. There are also iron mines in central Sweden, not far from Stockholm. Northern Sweden is bitterly cold in the long winter and the nearly freshwater sea is ice-covered. This is the region of timber, sawmills, and paper factories.

The People. The Swedes are a classic "Nordic" people; longheaded, blue-eyed blonds predominate, though there are some settlements of dark people, like the Danesmen. They are among the tallest men in Europe.

Swedes have emigrated in large numbers, especially to the U.S.A., where whole areas of Minnesota, for example, reflect much of Swedish culture. They numbered 595,000 in 1930 and 445,000 in 1940, immigration having diminished and the older stock having died off. But over the years they must have contributed from a million and a half to two millions to the American population.

In the homeland, they show little tendency to increase. The birthrate averages 14.7, the deathrate about 11.4. The rate of natural increase is small, and the infant deathrate very low. But since the proportion of adults is increasing, the population of Sweden should decline to about 5,600,000 by 1980.

Religion and Education. The country is overwhelmingly Protestant (99.8%), the Lutheran faith being the established church. Though there are some legal disadvantages for the tiny minority that does not accept the state religion, in practice these are forgotten, and religious liberty is a fact.

The democratic Kingdom of Sweden has had tuition-free, compulsory education for over a century. Hence illiteracy is unknown and the educational level high. There are two ancient universities (at Upsala and Lund) and numerous advanced schools for commerce, science, and technology. The nation is celebrated for her scientists (Berzelius, Linnaeus) and for her engineers, one of whom, Ericsson, invented the *U. S. S. Monitor*, that so well served the American Union cause in 1862. Sweden has a large and serious bookreading population; bookshops are numerous, the public press on a high level. The names of August Strindberg and Selma Lagerlöf are, of course, eminent in world literature.

The Nation's Economy

Agriculture. About 9% of Sweden is arable — 15,000 square miles. The country is not over-populated, yields are high, and with 32% of the people engaged in farming, food is ample. The cash value of farm production per man is slightly below the average for progressive European countries.

The principal crops are those of most northern countries. Oats are first, then wheat, rye, barley, potatoes, sugar beets, forage-roots, and, above all, hay, in which Sweden is one of the great producers of Europe. The value of the crops was $270,000,000 for 1938, for which year the crops of the U.S.A. were $3,200,000,000. Since Sweden's population is one-twentieth of ours, her farming seems about a third more prosperous.

The cattle population is large, about 2,600,000 head; nearly as much, proportionately, as in the U.S.A., but distinctly less so than in neighboring Denmark. Swine number 1,300,000, but other animals seem to be inadequate for domestic needs.

Since four-sevenths of the people live in rural areas, and these areas are consistently prosperous, the basic well-being of this large percentage of the population cushions the country well against the shocks of depression.

Industry. Though begun relatively late in the last century, Sweden's industry has made up for lost time, today engaging more than 35% of the employed. The machinery investment per person, $5, is the highest in Scandinavia, and this figure must have been exceeded during the present war. Though she has to import coal for fuel, her industries, both large and small, are found in every province, but principally around Stockholm and Göteborg. They are among the most modern, highly specialized, and efficient in Europe.

Swedish ball-bearings and high-grade steel are in a class by themselves, and the nation ranks high in complex mechanical manufacture such as telephone equipment, electrical machines, precision machine-tools, and cream separators. From Sweden came the gas refrigerator. In fine metals and machinery, she seems determined to assume leadership and under her present sound financial system she is extremely attentive to the costs of production, which are exceptionally low per unit. Swedish glass is famed for quality, and her porcelain ranks high. As most of north Sweden is a forest, timber and wood products are extremely important. Planed boards and furniture are national specialties. Woodpulp and paper are also produced in quantity. Over 100,000,000 trees are felled each year, and some 55% of the national territory is forested. Her match industry at one time so dominated the world market that its financial crash, which came with the death of Ivar Krueger (1932), proved the leading financial calamity of the 'thirties.

But Sweden's industry took the post-1929 depression in its stride. The nation's ability to survive world economic collapse as well as her own Krueger crash startled skeptics and pessimists, and led to innumer-

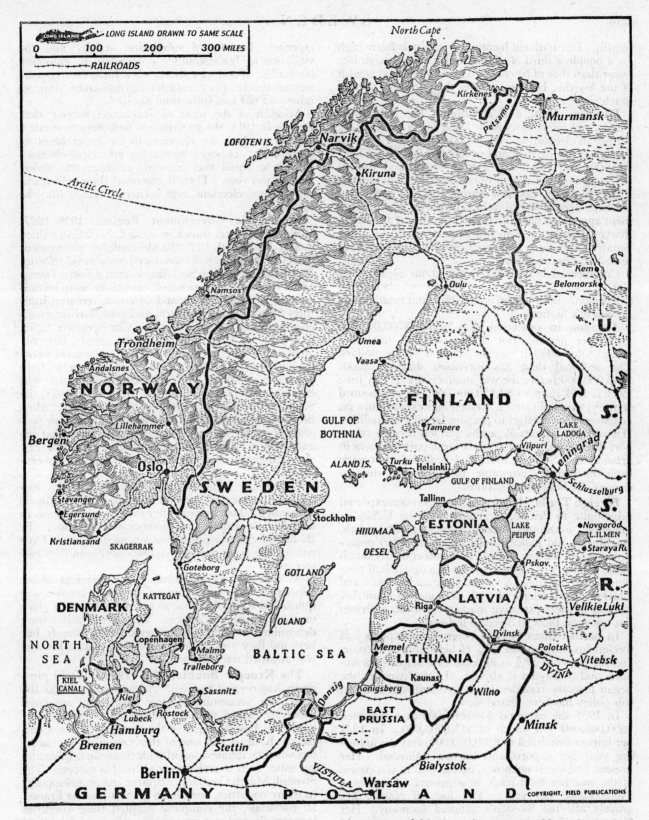

able attempts to fathom her industrial secret. "The Middle Way," that is, the system midway between individualism and Socialism, between private and state enterprise, soon came to be widely extolled. Whatever the secret, after the 1928–29 boom, Swedish industrial production, at its worst moment, went down by merely 11%, and by 1939 was 65% greater than in 1929. Armament orders accounted for only a small percentage of this rise. As a matter of fact, diminished foreign markets have hurt Sweden more than Nazi demands for munitions have benefited her. Industrial production in 1944 was 15% below the 1939 level.

National Wealth and Income. Sweden is one of the wealthiest countries in Europe. She ranks just after Britain, Holland, Switzerland, and Denmark, exceeding all other European countries in per capita wealth. Her national income per capita is fairly high for a people a third of whom are farmers, though it is lower than that of Norway. The accumulated wealth of the Swedes, however, makes their country appear much richer.

Finances, Debt, and Taxation. The established currency of the country is the *krone*, worth about 23.8¢. Money in circulation, 708,000,000 *kroner* in 1934, was 1,400,000,000 in 1939 and over 2,000,000,000 ($476,-000,000) in 1942. But gold holdings and foreign currency reserves rose proportionally. The cost of living, however, doubled during the war — Sweden has been careful to maintain neutrality. The government appears to have intervened to prevent any stock-market speculation of such a scope as would lead to a runaway inflation, and stock exchange prices have remained almost static.

Commercial bank deposits are about $1,300,000,-000, or about $200 per person, and savings about $160 per person. Both figures are striking and rank among the world's highest.

Taxation in peacetime was about $700,000,000 ($110 per person), but in the watchful neutrality period after 1939 it rose to about a billion dollars. The national debt has increased sharply: about $640,000,000 before the war summer of 1939; in June 1943 it had risen to $2,150,000,000. For a neutral country, this indicated a tremendous expenditure on armaments in an effort to prepare for all eventualities. Her wartime industrial production fell because of export difficulties. Apparently a large part of it was in armaments. Sweden, though neutral, did not escape from the primary economic difficulties and dislocations of the belligerent nations.

Foreign Trade. In normal times, Sweden exported principally to Britain, Germany, and the U.S.A. — minerals, woodpulp, wood, manufactured metals, machinery, and paper. Fully two-fifths of her peacetime exports were to countries not subsequently dominated by the Axis. Since Sweden's geographical position placed her under a virtual German blockade and allowed only a trickle of trade to non-Axis countries, the loss of these extensive markets has been a serious but not fatal blow to Swedish industry.

In normal times Sweden depends on exports and foreign investments for 29% of her national income, and she pays out 29% of national expenditures for imports and in payments abroad. In the 'twenties, she began to make considerable investments abroad, but this policy has been abandoned.

In 1939 she exported $450,000,000 and imported $600,000,000 — a deficit of $150,000,000. In 1941 her import deficit fell to $100,000,000, and the following year her exports and imports balanced. Her present position is unknown, except that in the course of the war her total trade as a neutral fell by some $400,000,000 per year. This loss, of course, has gravely affected Sweden's national economy. Her future prosperity depends on a resumption of world trade.

History: 1914-1944

Although she remained neutral, Sweden suffered from World War I. Her trade dropped considerably,

especially because of submarine activity and the vigilance of both military contenders in enforcing blockades. Food ran short; class bitterness became aggravated in this constitutional monarchy that retained an old and influential nobility.

Mindful of the wave of revolution surging over Europe in 1918, the government took steps to create a democratic basis for elections to the lower house of Parliament. It began by making municipal elections subject to equal and universal suffrage and giving women the vote. Then it extended these reforms to the national elections, and invited Socialists into the cabinet.

Democratic Government Begins: 1919-1927. With the electoral franchise trebled, Socialism gained apace. In March 1920 the old coalition government fell, even though it had introduced some social reforms. Branting, the leading Socialist, formed a Social Democratic cabinet. He was adroit enough to begin investigations into monopolies and to create research institutes for socializing industry, and then, having awakened criticism, to resign. The Conservatives again took power. They appealed to the people, but only after lavish relief measures and unemployment benefits had been instituted. To court the electorate, both parties now agreed that constitutional reform was essential to liberalize the state. In October 1921, the Socialists triumphed. But two years later, when Branting failed to obtain support for his extensive program of coping with a chronic industrial crisis and unemployment (which Europe suffered in 1920–22), the Conservatives once more took over the government.

Conservative, Liberal, and Socialist cabinets succeeded one another with alternating administrations. The sum total of changes, after these ministries, was to liberalize education and democratize taxation. In the face of strong popular pressure, no party could have resisted this basic progressive tendency, even the Conservatives.

At first the Conservatives were skeptical about joining the League of Nations, but their interest was quickened when the League granted Sweden a place on the Permanent Council. The Conservatives were determined to obtain the strategic Aland Islands, but here too they yielded with good grace when Finland was awarded the islands.

The Krueger Bubble: 1927-1932. World prosperity had revived Sweden. As the country forgot the crisis, she accumulated great investment surpluses which she placed abroad. Master-mind of this movement was Ivar Krueger of the Swedish Match Company. Krueger was one of those astonishing characters who can inflate a world-wide financial bubble and get sober men to stake their all on his success. The Swedish Match Company acquired match monopolies in many countries, even in so great a land as France. In exchange, the company granted these countries large credits and cash payments, against which it issued bonds. Conservative banking opinion in Sweden regarded the whole venture with suspicion. They felt it was beyond Sweden's capacity, and they took precautions against a collapse.

By 1929 Krueger had made it appear that Sweden was one of the crucial financial centers of the world. In his schemes he had tied up a large part of Swedish industrial organization. Since his chief competitor was Soviet Russia, he organized a campaign to punish the U.S.S.R. for her "slave labor and dumping." Krueger was close to White (anti-Soviet) Russian and Fascist groupings everywhere.

The world crisis of 1931, by restricting credits, put an end to Krueger's system, and in 1932 he committed suicide. The shock of the financial collapse, at the very bottom of the general economic crisis, seemed to threaten the survival of Swedish economy. However, the responsible Swedish bankers who had anticipated this dreadful end of the Krueger world trust, acted with decision and intelligence. Six months before the financier's death, Sweden had abandoned the gold standard. She had joined in the British currency trend, following her "cheap money" policy. In 1932 Sweden was able to ride through a crisis so grave that it would have prostrated any other economy. When the country discovered that a large part of the Conservative leadership had been involved with Krueger, power virtually fell into the laps of the Socialists, led by Hansson.

Recovery on an Unstable Basis: 1932–1939. Socialists and banking elements worked together for recovery. An American, Marquis Childs, was to celebrate this effort as "the Middle Way." Actually it was a slow process. Unemployment was widespread, reaching fully 22.8% in 1932 and consistently remaining proportionately larger than Britain's throughout the decade, and in fact never ceasing to be an important problem. However, industrial production picked up steadily as productivity per worker dramatically rose. But the domestic market could not match the increased production, since so many potential buyers were unemployed. The effect of this chronic unemployment of labor and capital was aggravated by World War II, which deprived Sweden of her world markets.

In the meantime, the Agrarians had succeeded the Socialists. Wartime necessities, however, led to a coalition government of Agrarians and Socialists.

World War II: 1939–1944. Sweden was neutral almost to excess. During the Finnish war (1939–1940) her sympathies lay with Finland against Russia, but though she aided Finland she would not be involved in technical breaches of neutrality. When Norway was invaded, Sweden continued to supply Germany against her sister state, being fearful of resisting the Reich. Though most of the population remained pro-Ally, pro-German sentiment was more widespread in Sweden than in Norway and Denmark. The Nazis had many articulate friends, such as the explorer Sven Hedin.

During the war against Russia, Sweden permitted German troops and supplies to cross her country for several years. On the other hand, her humane service in transferring civilian refugees is a badge of honor. She made some arrangements with the Allies to permit foreign supplies and food to reach Sweden and pass through the German blockade. Nevertheless, the war

has been a difficult period for the country, and the events of 1918–19 seem to have a similar contour today.

During the war Sweden held an election (September 1940) which gave the Socialists a large majority over all other parties combined. In spite of this, an all-party government was formed, only Communists were excluded. The government initiated a tremendous armament policy (the quality of Swedish armament production holds high rank in the world).

Under continued British and Soviet protests against her aid to the enemy, and as a result of her own constant friction with Germany, Swedish policy hardened towards the Reich. Nazi transit of troops ceased. When the Nazis expelled the Jews from Denmark, Sweden rose to the occasion and offered them asylum and relief. The Swedes trained Norwegian exiles as riflemen. Throughout 1944 popular hatred of Germany became increasingly vocal and government reaction to Germany more hostile.

Foreign Affiliations. Politically, Sweden's only affiliations have been with the "Oslo Powers," that is, Scandinavia, the Low Countries, and Switzerland. Actually she has been very sympathetic to Finland, who has a large Swedish minority. Though her aristocracy and conservative elements have been friendly to Germany, they have not taken any serious risks in behalf of that sentiment.

The old trade relations with Britain have built up a friendship for that country, but this is also not strong enough to influence policy. The large Swedish immigration to the U.S.A. has promoted really intimate knowledge of American life and problems, but this has not had political results.

From 1700 to 1919 Sweden was haunted by Czardom. The Swedes considered Russia almost the ultimate conqueror. Although the people fear Soviet Russia less than Czarism, the more conservative elements have added social distaste to national interest and probably are more suspicious of Russia today than before. For them the Finnish conflicts are evidences of Russia's absorptive intentions. The presence of the skilled Soviet ambassador, Madame Kollantay, has done much to dispel these fears.

Stakes in the Peace

Although the strongest of the four Scandinavian states, it is doubtful that Sweden could resist a powerful enemy for more than a few weeks. Hence she must rely, like the other northern countries, on a world peace organization for her independence.

No other country has a greater interest not merely in freer trade, which is the primary need of her two sister commonwealths, but in the free investment of capital abroad. As with Britain and the Netherlands, this is an integral part of her prosperity. Should her chronic surplus of capital continue, Sweden may have to face drastic internal social alterations.

SWITZERLAND

The Land and the People

The sturdy Swiss, a democratic-minded mountain people, wrested their independence from Austria in the 14th century and later expanded into a miniature League of Nations. Cherishing their independence and developing local habits, costumes, and legends, the Swiss permitted all sorts of differences among the inhabitants of the various cantons (or counties) without affecting their national unity. This unique quality has long made them the envy of civilized Europeans.

In the 18th century and until the beginning of manufacture, Swiss people — mostly shepherds or cowherds or farmers — were so poor that many of their youth were forced to emigrate and join foreign armies. Swiss guards became part of many foreign armies and still are used by the Vatican. Since the advent of industry in the 19th century, Switzerland has become rich and the current is reversed: about a tenth of her population are foreigners. These consist of political refugees in large part, for the Swiss have clung to their tradition of hospitality to victims of persecution.

The international character of Switzerland has given rise to such movements as the Red Cross (which uses the Swiss flag in reverse) founded by a Swiss, Dunant, as well as to the use of Switzerland as the seat of the League of Nations and other international bodies.

The Land. The distinctive geographical character of Switzerland, mecca of tourists, is probably too well known to require detailed description. Most of her 15,944 square miles are in the high Alps. One-third is rocky mass, the greater part over 10,000 feet high. Another third, less elevated but still extremely high, is dotted with picturesque lakes and valleys. Cities like Zurich and Lucerne lie in the uplands of partly Alpine character. Only along the German frontier, toward the extreme north, is the elevation moderate.

Four countries bound Switzerland: Germany (north), Austria (east), Italy (south), and France (west).

The largest part of Switzerland's 4,200,000 people lives in the lower elevations, where there is ample summer rain and where the winters, though very snowy and long, are not as severe as in the high Alps. In these lower areas cattle-raising is an important industry.

Mineral resources are scanty, with some iron and manganese concentrated in St. Gallen canton. The soil is thin, for the most part, and only in a few valleys does it pay to farm. Owing to numerous falls and mountain rivers, water-power is abundant, but on the whole, few lands offer so slender an economic basis for their population. Yet Switzerland is rich. Fundamentally she owes her development to her determined and industrious people.

The People. The Swiss speak several languages; 70% use a German dialect, about 21% speak a quaint French (Swiss Romande), and about 6% Italian. The Germans occupy the north and center, the French the west, the Italians mostly one region, the Ticino, just north of the great Lombard plain of Italy. A fourth group, the Grisons, living mostly in one canton, speak *Romansch*, a strange survival of Latin. French-, German-, and Italian-speaking Swiss, the three chief elements, live in harmony under their federal system.

Switzerland's peacetime birthrate of about 15.2 per thousand has risen during the war. The deathrate averaged about 11.8. Infant mortality was very low (about 34 in 1939) but it has since risen to 40. The rate of natural increase is small, and since the adult proportion is growing, it seems likely that the Swiss population will decline somewhat in the next generation.

Religion and Education. Switzerland allows absolute liberty of religious conscience. However, there are certain restrictions on the creation of bishoprics, and the Jesuit order is prohibited, and so are additional convents and monasteries. Furthermore, any religion hostile to the government or preaching hatred of other faiths may be banned. The population numbers about 57% Protestants, about 41% Catholics, the rest being Jews, agnostics, and sects found among the numerous immigrants.

There is almost no illiteracy. Primary learning is compulsory and tuition-free, each canton being responsible for its own educational system. The high schools enroll 100,000 and there are numerous advanced private schools for foreign children, Lausanne being famous for such institutions. Switzerland has 7 universities as well as a technical school at Zurich, one of whose students was Albert Einstein. Foreigners have attended Swiss universities in large numbers, notably the old Russian *intelligentsia*. In learned societies, laboratories, research institutes, and the like, Switzerland is almost first in the world, considering the size of her population.

The Nation's Economy

Agriculture and Stockraising. The arable land is well under 2,000 square miles, for fully 22% of the country is unproductive, mostly high mountains. Some 23% is forest, 26% under grass, and 22% thin pasturage. About a fifth of the population engages in farming and cattle-raising.

With dairying universal in this land, milk alone accounts for 35% of Swiss production. Much of the milk is canned or used in the milk chocolate which Swiss makers, who also have cattle farms in other countries, have made popular everywhere. Milk production per capita is three times the U.S.A. figure, and cheeses like Gruyère and Emmenthaler ("Swiss") have a world market. The value of cattle and pigs slaughtered accounted respectively for 17% and 13% of all agricultural receipts, fruits and poultry for 10%. The yield of wine is also very high (16 gallons per head). Ordinary farming thus plays only a small part in rural life; indeed Switzerland's agriculture cannot feed her own people — food ranks high among her imports.

Industry. Swiss industry is best known to outsiders by its watches and clocks, and to our fathers by its delightful music boxes. Actually, watches and clocks continue as the principal industry of French Switzerland, while cheese, condensed milk, and chocolate are highly important in the German districts. Some iron ore and manganese are mined in St. Gallen canton.

Switzerland's 10,000 factories, ultra-modern and efficient, employ 46% of the working population. Investment in machinery per capita equals Britain's; that is, Switzerland is first in continental Europe. The high cost of labor does not work out as a disadvantage, owing to the high output per worker. The Swiss are celebrated for embroidery manufacture and laces; their dyes and drugs are the best made. The electrical machinery, motor installations, and electro-chemical products of its leading firms loom high in this industrialized nation.

Finance, Taxation, Currency. The Swiss unit of currency, the *franc*, is worth about 23.2¢, but actually sells for more. So cherished is Swiss money that in "black markets" it enjoys a considerable premium over every other. The whole of Europe wishes to protect itself in this money. Nazis, disguising their names and affiliation, opened accounts in Swiss banks, and Frenchmen who wished to conceal their wealth from the Nazis did the same. The inflow of refugee money has been encouraged by the fact that this traditionally neutral country has always been a haven.

As Europe's leading tourist country, Switzerland has been described not as a country but as "a cross between a café and a safe-deposit vault." Though this ignores her superb industry and stockraising, in an international sense it is true, for the Swiss banks with their fine organization, and Swiss laws, with their intelligent hospitality, have conjoined to obtain an amazingly high level of commercial banking deposits.

About 12,000,000,000 *francs* (at the actual rates of exchange, about $3,600,000,000) or $900 per person is an extraordinary figure showing the importance of foreign deposits. The proof is the comparison with the savings bank and cooperative bank savings: these are a mere 15% of the commercial bank deposits.

The federal government budget (excluding the government-owned railway system) reaches about one billion francs ordinarily, and has been doubled to take care of dislocations caused by the war. A great part of the taxation is effected by the cantons, which have broad local powers.

Exclusive of the railway debt, the Swiss national debt is about 5,800,000,000 *francs* ($1,400,000,000 at par, or $1,350 per capita) — a considerable burden should there be an economic decline. Stock exchange speculation is sane. At the close of 1942, prices were only 12% above pre-war levels, reflecting the slow increase in money in circulation, perhaps the most conservative in the world. But the cost of living has gone

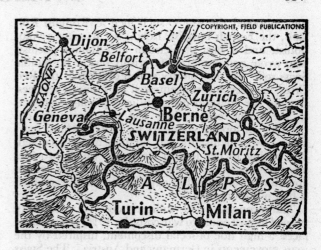

up by some 45% during the war. This may be accounted for by specific shortages in consumers goods, since all the countries around Switzerland were involved in war.

Foreign Trade, Wealth and Income, Foreign Investments. Foreign trade is enormous, ranking with the Danish and the Dutch. Fully 43% of the national income derives from exports and revenues from abroad, and the Swiss pay out 40% of their income for imports and payments abroad. Not only does this rich country have a surplus of cash receipts despite a surplus of imports, but it has invested an eighth of its national wealth abroad and these investments have been productive. Six per cent of the national income comes from dividends and interest from other lands.

The Swiss banks, international in character, are staffed with statistical and economic experts who go abroad for long periods and protect Swiss interests.

Switzerland exported $300,000,000 in 1938 and imported $360,000,000. During the war her foreign trade increased by $40,000,000 in exports and $100,-000,000 in imports.

Her exports were principally clocks and watches, machinery, dairy goods, silk and rayon, and dyes; her imports: grain, minerals, fruit, meat, chemicals, cotton goods. Germany has always been her largest supplier, followed by France and Italy. The U.S.A. and Britain usually are fourth and fifth. Among her customers, the best is Germany, then France, followed by Italy and Britain, with the U.S.A. usually fifth. During the war, Switzerland, geographically surrounded by the Nazis, traded chiefly with Germany and German satellites.

Switzerland is rich, her per capita wealth of about $2,000 being a fourth higher than Britain's and twice Germany's; and less than a fifth under the American figure. Zurich is said to be the richest city on earth in per capita wealth. Though national income per person is slightly below the British, the frugal Swiss accumulate more out of these receipts in the shape of savings and investments.

History: 1914-1944

A neutral in World War I, Switzerland gave asylum to citizens of other countries who, for differing reasons, opposed the war — such men as Romain Rolland, the French novelist, Lenin, the Russian revolutionist, and a host of German and Italian pacifists who wrote and organized feverishly on the hospitable Swiss soil. As the country which originated the Red Cross, Switzerland concentrated on humane services. Despite her constant difficulty in explaining her acts to the belligerents — since she was unusually dependent on foreign countries for materials and markets — Swiss neutrality was fundamentally accepted. But, owing to her federal structure, which provides large powers to the cantons (states), the Swiss central government often had to explain cantonal acts which it had not sponsored.

The economic and military costs of neutrality proved almost equal to war costs: by 1918, Switzerland faced a high tide of social discontent, inspired by the mass movements in Germany and Austria. The Swiss mobilized their army to defend the social order.

Between 1918 and 1922, a one-year spurt of prosperity was succeeded by nearly three years of acute depression, with more than a fifth of the whole population and more than a third of the city population, unemployed. Various efforts were made to improve matters. Finally, after a proposed capital levy was defeated (1922), confidence was reborn and business revived. By 1924 world recovery had absorbed the Swiss unemployed. Meanwhile (1920) Geneva was chosen as the seat of the League of Nations.

Minor Events: 1922–1932. Most of Switzerland's problems were small: attempts to introduce protective tariffs, which were modified; an arrangement for a free customs zone with France; absorption of little independent Liechtenstein into the Swiss customs union; final determination of Swiss-Italian boundaries; and one drama, the murder of a Soviet delegate and a jury's acquittal of his assassin, which led to bitter relations with the Russians. But, until 1929 when the world crisis peculiarly affected Switzerland, because of her international interests, Swiss history was very quiet.

The Seven-Years Crisis: 1929–1936. The crisis shook Switzerland. She had considerable investments in America. Her banks were involved in German industries and had granted German credits to an inordinate extent. When the English pound went down in 1931 and America's depression continued, the loss of tourist trade proved enormous (some estimated that it had declined by four-fifths). This simultaneous loss of her principal investments (Germany), her principal visitors (Englishmen), and her principal outlet for liquid funds (the U.S.A.) called for the utmost in Switzerland's age-old adaptability. The hotel industry was subsidized; "standstill" agreements with German bankers held the line; import quotas prevented a drain of funds; food imports were cheapened by the world agrarian crisis; and American stock exchange values rose after the 1933 devaluation. Although by 1934 recovery seemed to be on the way, the carryovers of depression were considerable and in French Switzerland they proved quite serious. The Swiss watchmaking trade had suffered. In Geneva, Nicole, an ardent Left Socialist, grew powerful and for a time it seemed as though property itself was threatened. There were riots and some workers were killed. It took much

statesmanlike behavior to appease spirits, but by 1936 this had been achieved. In the meantime, in the German sections of Switzerland every difficulty was exploited in order to build up Nazi influence.

Switzerland, like every member of the gold *bloc*, was subject to chronic rumors of devaluation, sudden withdrawals of funds, and a price level too high for her exports. As Switzerland had eliminated double taxation and was thus the prize refuge of capital in all Europe, these perturbations were enormous in relation to the internal economy of the little country. When 4,000,000 people lose $170,000,000 in gold (as Switzerland did) it is the same as though the U.S.A. had lost over $5,000,000,000. Despite these losses, the struggle to maintain the gold standard was continued; but when France abandoned the gold standard in September 1936, Switzerland, along with the Netherlands, followed suit. Once there was no further fear of devaluation, capital poured back into the great Swiss banks.

Preparations for Neutrality: 1936–1939. In 1936 the Nazi leader of Switzerland, one Gustloff, was assassinated by a Jewish youth. The government prohibited all Nazi organizations and rigidly supervised all organizations of Germans in Switzerland. In order to assure neutrality, military service was extended in 1938, armaments largely increased, gold transferred into mountain depths unknown and inaccessible, every person compelled to hold a food hoard (for which loans were granted if they were poor), and full preparations made for many years of a "siege economy," so that Switzerland might not be starved out of neutrality. On December 15, 1938, fearful of the results of the Munich pact, the Swiss passed a law for the defense of the Republic and the Constitution, conferring extraordinary powers on the Swiss Federal Council.

During the period of the devalued *franc*, both tourist business and employment had revived; social tensions relaxed. Import quotas became liberalized. A fourth national language was recognized, Romansh, peculiar to the canton of Grisons.

The War: 1939–1944. Switzerland lost most of the League of Nations, which left for Lisbon in 1940, though some of the services, such as its statistical organization, remained at Geneva. The Bank for International Settlements, retaining German and Allied directors, continued to function at Basel.

Despite some friction about airmen crossing the frontiers, Switzerland, as in World War I, remained primarily a refuge. While the Nazis raged, Jews and Italian anti-Fascists by the tens of thousands crossed into Switzerland, as did streams of French refugees; and the country, despite its tight food situation, managed to cope with their arrival. While democracy was proclaimed dead by Hitler, in every Swiss canton men met inspiringly in the open fields, even in sight of Germany, freely elected their cantonal governments, debated without fear, petitioned for initiating legislation, and conducted their referendums for direct legislation. Nevertheless, unless Switzerland did business with Axis countries completely surrounding her, she faced economic death. Hence she was compelled to grant the Germans over $300,000,000 of wartime credits, the repayment of which is dubious and the loss of which may have serious consequences.

Elections were held in October 1943. The Socialists gained considerably, and they are now almost a third of the Assembly. The anti-Socialist groups formed a coalition government.

Stakes in the Peace

The federal republic of Switzerland has absolutely no foreign associations or sympathies. Although a member of the League of Nations, she demanded a neutrality so complete that it was in juridical contradiction with her membership obligations in the League. Her French population is not pro-French, very few of her Italians were pro-Italian, and only a small minority of her Germans, pro-German. She has a large foreign population glad to be "away from it all." Switzerland depends on her tenacity, the difficulty of conquering her, and the historic sympathy for her survival. Also, and most important,

citizens of every belligerent country have a considerable part of their cash reserves in Switzerland.

Switzerland will have to face tremendous economic losses from Axis business, but the sums do not seem sufficient to induce a major crisis. On the other hand the revival of tourist business, almost ended for five years, will bring in additional foreign money. Export trade will be conducted on a better basis than by accepting Axis promises to pay. Social variations in Europe may increase the flow of funds to Switzerland. But whatever difficulties Switzerland may have, none appear to be dangerous.

Nevertheless, international organization will relieve her of the burden of armaments, of an army too large for Swiss resources, and of the constant cost of fear: that is, regulations and withdrawals which disturb confidence and injure business and employment. Switzerland's historic position in international organizations and her hospitality, as well as the fact that she is her own miniature League of Nations internally, make her adhesion to international organization practically certain.

YUGOSLAVIA

The Land and the People

Yugoslavia, the tripartite land of the Serbs, Croats, and Slovenes, was created after World War I out of the independent kingdoms of Serbia and Montenegro and the regions of Croatia and Slovenia, formerly under Austrian rule. Contemporary Yugoslavia has an area of 95,558 square miles (as large as New York, New Jersey, and Pennsylvania combined). Her population of Yugoslavs — the word means South Slavs — is estimated at 15,900,000, with almost five million more people than there are in Canada.

Yugoslavia is a typically Balkan land of many boundaries. To the north, she faces her former masters, Austria and Hungary; to the east, Rumania and Bulgaria; to the south, Greece and Albania; and to the west, the Adriatic Sea and Italy. Farther up on her western border, where Yugoslavia touches Italy, this frontier has given rise to impassioned, historic controversies. Indeed, every land boundary of this country has been the object of conflicting claims and counterclaims.

Yugoslavia was constituted as a country, not because she was a complete geographical unit, but because of the common origins, language, and sentiments of the mass of the inhabitants. The Serbs, Croats, and Slovenes are ethnically all South Slavs and speak closely related Slavic tongues. In fact, Serbian and Croatian are dialects of the same language. About half the population inhabits the northern plains, which are part of the Danube basin, while a small section (around 7%) lives along the Adriatic coast. Between lies a wild, mountainous area covering fully half the country. The people of the plains turn to the other nations of the Danube basin for trade, while only the small minority on the Dalmatian coast, facing the Adriatic, has a Mediterranean outlook.

The Land. Slovenia, in the northwest, is a grassland, with abundant water-power and timber supplies. Utterly different is Dalmatia, in the southwest, with its jagged coast-line, rocky islands, and no back country except steep mountains. Though this "Illyrian land" has magnificent natural beauty and was the vacation spot of the old Roman emperors, the region is almost inaccessible to travel and there is practically no cultivable land in the thin small valleys. Back of Dalmatia's sunny coast stand the towering Dinaric Alps and a high limestone area of heavy rain and wretched soil. East of this region is Bosnia, well-cultivated, with many river valleys and rich loam, and a continental climate of the classic type — cold winters and hot but tolerable summers. A rich grain country lies to the north of Bosnia. In the south a labyrinth of highlands and broad fertile valleys spreads out toward Bulgaria and Greece. Here the land produces vegetation similar to that in the most favorably endowed regions of Greece.

With almost a third of the country forested, the

total amount of arable land can be estimated at no more than 47%. This would signify about 510 Yugoslavs to every square mile of cultivable land. Most of the working population is engaged in agriculture.

Yugoslavia's mineral resources suggest the possibility of important development. Her copper, antimony, chrome, lead, and brown coal — for the most part found in northern Serbia and Croatia — account for such industrial productivity as she has already achieved. But most of her other mineral resources have not yet been exploited. Of potential importance in the future industrial evolution of the country is the Danube River that flows through Yugoslavia from Hungary, passing through Belgrade on its way to Rumania. It is, of course, the country's most important artery of commerce and shipping.

The People. Three peoples constitute the bulk of the Yugoslavs; the Serbs in the eastern areas, the Croats in the north, and the Slovenes in the northwest. Most of the inhabitants of Dalmatia are Serbs, but they are mixed with Albanians, people of older Latin stock, and, in Bosnia, with Turks of the Moslem faith, survivors of the old Ottoman Empire that once controlled this entire area. In the lower valleys, to the south, there are peoples of Macedonian and Bulgarian stock, fighters for centuries and, at times, redoubtable terrorists. In the north are Germans and Hungarians, left over from the old Austro-Hungarian Empire, who look down on the Slavic majority. There is also, in Serbia, a considerable population of Gypsies.

Despite this seeming crazy quilt, the three principal peoples — all South Slavs — constitute five-sixths of the total population. In the past they have differed in material prosperity and culture as well as in religion. The Croats, mostly Roman Catholics, were better educated and wealthier largely because under Austro-Hungarian rule, industry had been developed in Croatia. The Slovenes, also Roman Catholic, have shown a much slower response to the stimulus of modern industry. The Serbs, followers of the Greek Orthodox faith, have been far less prosperous than the Croats. Much of their energy has been spent in the struggle for national survival, which has been a Serbian tradition for centuries.

There have been many points of conflict among these peoples, but the recent Partisan war against Germany has helped to cancel most of the facile generalizations about "inherent racial differences among the Yugoslavs." Some Croats have proved exemplary guerrilla warriors; some Serbs have been accomplices of Fascism. Pavelitch, the Croat, and Neditch, the Serb, have both collaborated with the Nazis. In the battle against the invader, national unity has nearly been achieved among the peoples of Yugoslavia; and where differences persist, they largely cut across national or racial lines. Furthermore, whatever differences exist could doubtless be overcome in a Federal Commonwealth which granted autonomy to the principal groups.

Yugoslavia's chief cities are, in a real sense, the "capitals" of her various population groups. Belgrade, the center of Serbian culture, and the nation's official capital, numbered 238,775 people in 1931. Zagreb (Agram), in the heart of Croatia, is a city of 185,581. Next in size is Sarajevo, in Bosnia (78,182 people), historically famous for being the eruption point of World War I. The Slovenian center is Ljubljana, a city of 59,765 inhabitants.

Religion and Education. Yugoslavians follow three principal faiths, all of which are recognized. The Greek Orthodox Church comprises 50% of the people, chiefly the Serbs; the Roman Catholic, 37%, chiefly Croats and Slovenes; and the Mohammedan, about 11%, mostly inhabitants of Bosnia. The Greek Orthodox religion enjoys a government subsidy; the Catholic Church is bound by a *Concordat* with the Vatican; the Mohammedans have a Grand Mufti, who deals with the government. Other faiths, though minor, are provided for in the government's ecclesiastical budget.

Education is nominally tuition-free and compulsory from the ages of 5 to 14, and is carried on in the prevailing language of the region. Illiteracy is still widespread among adults, but more so in Bosnia and Old Serbia than in the former Austrian-dominated sections of Croatia and Slovenia. There are three universities (at Belgrade, Zagreb, and Ljubljana) and some institutes.

Though newspapers are not widely read, except in Croatia, the people everywhere are politically alert and have a rich vein of traditional folklore and literature. The Serbs possess the richest literary traditions, both oral and written, while the Croats are more advanced in the fields of science and technology.

The Nation's Economy

Agriculture. For few countries do the estimates by competent authorities as to arable land vary so widely as for Yugoslavia. As we have observed, the most probable figure is about 47%, which would signify about 510 persons to every square mile of cultivable land. Primitive methods of cultivation are in use everywhere except in Croatia; but with more modern farming methods, the entire people could be adequately nourished. About 85% of the working population is engaged in agriculture.

Though Yugoslavia is below western European agricultural standards, she is not as backward as is frequently supposed. In terms of the cash value of produce per man employed, she ranks ahead of Italy, Greece, and Bulgaria. In the north the 8 leading farm crops show a good yield, rivaling that of southern France and central Italy; and even in the bleak mountainous regions, productivity is greater than in neighboring Bulgaria and Rumania.

The principal crops are corn, in which Yugoslavia is second only to Rumania in Europe, high-quality wheat, and grapes. Animal production is even more important: this is a land of sheep and, as in all countries once dominated by Moslems, lamb and mutton are almost the only meats consumed. The sheep population is over 9,000,000, about half that of Spain or England, Europe's leading sheep-breeding nations; and the wool clip reaches an annual figure of 15,000 tons. There are also some 3,000,000 pigs, 20,000,000 poultry, and 1,200,000 horses — figures that are high for southeastern Europe. Plums are

the outstanding fruit crop, with some 50,000,000 plum trees in the country.

Farm production has been hard hit by the war, corn having fallen off by a half and wheat by a third, with other crops suffering a less drastic reduction. Unlike Hungary, Yugoslavia has had extensive land reforms and is predominantly a country of small farms. Hence, although misery is at present undoubtedly widespread, the outlook for the future of agriculture is not too bleak because feudal conditions no longer exist and there is a sizable class of independent farmers in the country.

Industry. One of the least mechanized countries on the continent, Yugoslavia ranks only above Rumania in machinery investment per person. Only 15% of her workers are employed in industry and mining. Light industries: flour, brewing, distilleries, and shoes, so characteristic of all arrested industrial states, predominate. Expertly handwoven and dyed carpets are the pride of handicrafts workers in Old Serbia.

The foundations for modern industry, however, are complete. Yugoslavia has varied and extensive mineral resources, with sizable amounts of copper, lead, chrome, bauxite, antimony, pyrites, iron, cement, and even some gold. These resources are chiefly in northern Serbia and Croatia, with iron ore in Bosnia.

She produces more than half of Europe's antimony, a fifth of the chrome, a fourth of the lead, a sixth of the copper, and has a good supply of brown coal. The Bor copper mines in north Serbia make Yugoslavia the first copper-producer in Europe.

About 30% of the country is forested and forest products are beginning to be exploited, especially in the young paper industry. Further exploitation, however, will require intensive development.

Finance, Taxation, Debt. For her section of Europe, Yugoslavia is not a poor country. Surprisingly enough, her wealth per person is $500. In this she exceeds Italy and Hungary and equals Rumania. Her per capita income is also similar to Rumania's, some $70 per person.

The unit of currency is the *dinar*, worth normally about 2.25¢. A sharp deflation in prices occurred after 1929, and even in 1939 prices were still a fourth lower than in 1929. But during the war both the cost of living and the money in circulation have doubled.

An agrarian country based on small subsistence farms does not have large banking deposits, so that the figure of $125,000,000 in commercial deposits is not unusual. Savings, however, were astonishingly small, a mere $80,000,000 (or $5.60 per person).

Taxation, about $12 per person or about one-sixth

of the national income, was not too severe. Under German occupation, however, these figures have risen sharply. The national debt is a complex affair, difficult of analysis, because of the many boundary changes in the past three decades.

Foreign Trade. In 1938 Yugoslavian imports were $112,000,000 and exports $115,000,000. Principal imports were cotton and cotton textiles, wool and woolen goods, iron, machinery, and silk. Principal exports were copper, lead, bauxite, chrome, wheat, pigs, timber, meat, and eggs. Germany was by far the largest customer and supplier, her share in Yugoslavian trade increasing sharply after the depression years of 1929–1933. Subsequent "clearing" arrangements eliminated the need for Yugoslavia to make cash payments and thus brought her more securely within the German economic sphere. The other suppliers and customers of importance were Austria and Czechoslovakia. Clearly Yugoslav commerce is central European. Trade with Britain and other Western nations was minimal. In terms of trade the country is oriented towards the Danube and not the Adriatic.

History: 1914-1944

Prior to 1918, the land now called Yugoslavia was composed of (1) the Kingdom of Serbia, which was at war with Austria-Hungary, (2) the Austrian provinces of Bosnia and Herzegovina, (3) the former Hungarian provinces of Croatia and Dalmatia, and (4) the independent Kingdom of Montenegro, an ally of Serbia in her war against Austria-Hungary. The Treaty of London in 1915 stipulated that steps be taken to ensure the unity of the peoples within this area. Two years later, at the conference of Corfu, their representatives agreed to form a "Kingdom of Serbs, Croats, and Slovenes," under the Serbian royal family. Other peoples were also to be comprehended in the proposed kingdom wherever they could not easily be separated from these three leading southern Slav groupings.

Formation of the Tripartite State: 1918–1922. No sooner was the federated state of Yugoslavia born (1918) than it faced a special difficulty. The coasts of Dalmatia had also been promised to Italy in 1915. The fiery, nationalistic poet, D'Annunzio, seized Fiume (1919), an Italian-speaking city with a Slavic countryside. His early ejection led to diplomatic maneuvers with Italy culminating in the Treaty of Rapallo (1920) which made Fiume a free port. In 1922, however, the advent of Italian Fascism complicated matters. It was not until 1924 that the question was resolved by designating Fiume Italian but its environs Slavic.

In 1920 Yugoslavia sought protection by joining the Little Entente as a charter member with Rumania and Czechoslovakia. For her situation was perilous; she had begun her independent existence with the enmity of six nations. Italy was a powerful and inimical next-door neighbor. Hungary was hostile because Yugoslavia had acquired the Voivodina with its Hungarian minorities. Acquisition of refractory Macedonian populations led to the hostility of Bulgaria. Conflicts with the Albanians, whom the Yugoslavs invaded and maltreated, brought League of Nations' punishment and also increased friction with Italy (1921). Relations with Greece were not cordial as yet, owing to clashes over the use of the port of Salonika, the Serbian outlet to the Mediterranean. Austria insisted that her minorities were severely treated in the Croatian and Slovenian regions. Even with an Allied land like Rumania, acid differences developed over frontiers.

Yugoslavia's main reliance was on the continued friendship and support of France. Alexander, her powerful monarch, insisted on a constitution that would centralize this state so hastily compounded. The Centralizers (Unionists) were nearly all Serbs, led by the veteran statesman Pashitch; the Federalists, or "States Rights" groups, were mostly Croats led by an adored tribune, Stepan Raditch. The Centralizers won a complete victory in the Constitution of 1922.

The Croat Opposition: 1922–1928. Raditch would not participate in the forming of the constitution. By abstention he felt that he would always be able to question its legality, and his supporters refused to participate in Parliament. Though Raditch was exiled, nothing shook the fidelity of his party. The Serbian Unionists soon realized that, whatever their passion for domination, a country with six neighbors, none absolutely sure friends, could scarcely afford the luxury of internal strife. Hence, in 1925, the government pardoned Raditch and issued a general amnesty. In turn, he ordered his Croat party to participate in Parliament, and he even took office in the cabinet.

In 1924 the government also attempted an arrangement with Italy, Rumania, and Greece. But, despite British requests to grant autonomy to the clearly Macedonian population of southern Serbia, the government was unrelenting, and a long series of terrorist campaigns and border forays with Bulgaria began to poison the life of the country.

The strain on friendship between Serb and Croat was always great and parliamentary debates grew vicious in tone. In 1928 an enraged Serb deputy fired his revolver at random in the direction of members of the Croat party. He killed three deputies, one of them the Croat leader Raditch.

The Royal Dictatorship and Compulsory Unity: 1928–1934. Croat resentment at this insane massacre could have destroyed the fabric of the state. King Alexander, faced with the boycott of the Croat people, met the emergency, on January 6, 1929, by establishing himself as dictator, suspending the constitution, and forming a non-party cabinet. He prohibited all parties and jailed and exiled opposition leaders. The dreaded secret police, the *Glavtchina*, resorted to the refined tortures of the Middle Ages.

In order to diminish the memory of the threefold origin of the state, the name was changed to Yugoslavia, the Kingdom of the South Slavs; that is, Serb, Croat, and Slovene, were no longer specifically named. Alexander terminated historic divisions such as Bosnia and Dalmatia; he substituted nine *Banovinias*, or new provinces, to replace the past. He also reformed and unified education, imposed and collected taxes, simplified and improved administration, took vigorous economic measures to combat the dire effects of the world depression of 1929, and, in fact, did everything but trust the will of the people.

On September 3, 1931, he proclaimed a new constitution under which the Crown was dominant. The constitution prohibited all parties that were based on either religious, racial, or regional groupings. It recognized three dialects, but they were not to be considered separate languages as the autonomists insisted. No candidate for parliament could represent a party that did not have adherents everywhere in the kingdom. Two-thirds of the seats in parliament automatically were to revert to the party commanding a plurality, irrespective of whether or not it had a majority.

The elections were boycotted. Alexander faced new opposition, especially from the 600,000 Begs (Moslems), mostly landholders. The Montenegrins were indignant at their suppression. It was clear that apart from the 79% of the population who were of the three major peoples, the 21% scattered among other nationalities would play a disintegrating rôle.

Despite this rigorous royal dictatorship, Alexander was highly regarded by large numbers of people in Western Europe. The British writer, Rebecca West, almost deified him in her famous *Black Lamb and Grey Falcon*.

In the face of Germany's growing menace, Alexander decided to visit France. On October 9, 1934, he was murdered in Marseilles, along with Louis Barthou, the French Foreign Minister, by a Macedonian terrorist thought to be connected with the Ustachi, or Croat Fascist group. The Yugoslav government openly charged Hungary with abetting the murder.

The Regency of Prince Paul: 1934–1940. King Alexander had once flirted with the idea that Germany should acquire Austria, since this would reduce Italy to a secondary rôle in Europe. In 1934 he had even visited Sofia in Bulgaria, a truly courageous act. Following his assassination, his young son, Prince Peter, succeeded and the regency was granted to Alexander's cousin, Prince Paul, and two Croats, Drs. Stankovitch and Perovitch. The centralizing tendency, however, though less violent, remained dominant.

A new Prime Minister, Yevtitch, ordered an election in May 1935. Opposition was allowed, but the conduct of the elections was disappointing. Yevtitch was soon followed by Stoyadinovitch, a Conservative statesman who was to dominate Yugoslavia for a long time. Certain small concessions were now made, but none of a basic nature. In view of the electoral showing of the Opposition (38%, distributed among Serbs and Croats), Stoyadinovitch formed a government of Slovene Clericals, Bosnian Moslems, and Croat "Radicals" (not radicals in our sense), in addition to the older Centralizers. He sought a *Concordat* with the Vatican to ensure Croat support, but the Serb Orthodox priesthood relentlessly fought any arrangement with the Vatican.

In the meantime foreign policy shifted. Prince Paul, a connoisseur of the arts and a reactionary, surrounded himself with White (anti-Soviet) Russian exiles, who were basically pro-German. As the government moved toward friendlier relations with Bulgaria and Italy, its engagements with the Little Entente and France receded in importance.

Attempts to patch up the state continued. Stoyadinovitch met with Matchek, the martyred Raditch's successor among the Croats. The government ratified the Papal *Concordat* but the Orthodox priesthood again suspended it. The Croats then joined with three Serb opposition parties. Thus the basic authoritarian nature of Yugoslavia was threatened by a rising refusal to accept its implications.

In the spring of 1939 a new government was formed in which Croats became an important force and in which their leader, Matchek, participated. The elections prior to this change had shown that the opposition could poll over 40%, and the stiff-necked Centralizers were compelled to yield.

Foreign policy began to shift to even closer friendship with Italy, Hungary, and even Bulgaria, but without any yielding on territorial questions. Germany was now a northern neighbor, having absorbed Austria, and the fall of Czechoslovakia made German domination appear inevitable. The Italian occupation of Albania seemed to outflank Yugoslavia and threaten her everywhere. She thereupon obtained British guarantees. The fall of France in 1940, and the domination of Rumania by the Germans, emphasized Yugoslavia's weak position. The older internal divisions now became a luxury that this imperiled commonwealth could not afford.

German Occupation: 1941–1943. In the spring of 1941 the German government insisted upon the alignment of Yugoslavia with Axis policy. The government acceded, but a wave of national resentment swept the country. King Peter II was declared of age, the complaisant regency ended, and a government of national resistance constituted in Belgrade.

On April 6, 1941, Germany invaded and in three weeks the state was no more. The Germans formed puppet governments, installing the Fascist terrorist Pavelitch in Croatia. The apparent anti-German fire-eater, General Neditch, proved to be the leading quisling in Serbia. Whole areas were seized by Hungary, Italy, Bulgaria. The country was parceled out, the Serbian population decimated. An Italian prince was invited to become king of puppet Croatia. He consented but never reigned, owing to Mussolini's fall (July 1943).

Resistance Movements: 1942–1944. A government-in-exile was constituted and it disposed of a few forces. But within Serbia a General Mihailovitch utilized a group called the Chetniks, who were resisting German aggression. Soon, in the mountainous areas of the west, a veteran trade union leader, Josep Broz, formed a large guerrilla army, the Partisans. Broz soon became known as "Marshal Tito." His following came to exceed that of Mihailovitch, who, he asserted, was not fighting Germany at all, but was primarily interested in fighting Yugoslavs of radical politics.

Slowly, British diplomatic and military investigators, without wholly endorsing Tito's view, came to regard him as the true instrument of Allied progress in Yugoslavia. Mihailovitch continued to assert that Tito was a Communist and that he (Mihailovitch) alone represented a true anti-German opposition for exclusively national objectives; he pleaded that he required more equipment before his opposition could produce results. Many critics asserted that Mihailovitch was an old-line Pan-Serbian.

A long series of negotiations with the exiled Yugoslav government resulted in its moving from distant London to Cairo, and a formula was sought for unity. Tito, in the meantime, formed his own government on Yugoslav soil. Despite a welter of contradictions and hatreds, it is obvious that large elements, if not all, of the contending groups, recognize the necessity for serious concessions. Tentative arrangements were made between Tito and King Peter II, though of a tenuous nature. In the meantime, the Croat leader, Dr. Matchek, though not vocal, did not accept Axis domination and his following remained large in Croatia.

The Partisan campaign in the Bosnian and coast areas has had some spectacular successes and is among the most brilliant guerrilla activities of the war. By tying up nearly as many German troops as the more organized Allied campaign in Italy, it greatly harassed the Nazi invader. Its example heartened Balkan resisters in the southeastern lands of Europe; by October 1944 much of Yugoslavia was liberated from the Germans.

Foreign Affiliations. Basically Yugoslavia depended on France from 1919 to 1935, and, while she sought "reinsurance" with the Axis grouping, her main reliance was always on Anglo-French association. Her hostility to six neighbors was never much attenuated. She had no friendship for Soviet Russia, the kinship of Slavic speech not playing the historic rôle assigned to it in Czarist days.

Stakes in the Peace

Yugoslavia, despite her coast line, is a Danubian valley commonwealth. Nevertheless, her Mediterranean ports and her outlet to the east by way of Salonika may prove important for large areas of the country. She suffers from primitive communications, and, in the uplands, from primitive poverty, though the richer farming areas are up to the European average. Nevertheless, the backwardness of agriculture as a whole, compared to the most advanced countries, placed Yugoslavia at the mercy of Germany. For the larger nation was willing to accept her products on a barter basis, when Yugoslav products were not salable on a cash basis.

Since Germany is still the largest natural market, there is no easy way of reorienting Yugoslavia's agricultural outlets. The Partisan movement indicates, however, that in lands of extensive culture, socialized farming may prevail, and with a more intensive industrialization, the local market may be greatly extended.

Ending the power of the Moslem gentry would be a constructive step in the mountain country where they dominate. However, the nation primarily needs industry and a steeply accentuated rise in mining and transportation. This is feasible with comparatively modest capital investment. Industrial employment would diminish the redundant rural and pastoral population and raise the general standard of living.

It is clear that today the Serbian unifiers have lost their historic primacy. The Partisan movement ignores the national differences that, under the surface, were already diminishing in the late 1930's. The federalization of the 16 Soviet republics will tend to become an example to Slavic peoples. Once the menace of an ever-threatening Italy, Hungary, and Germany is removed by international cooperation, Serb insistence loses much of its basis.

Certainly the oppression of the Macedonians must be remedied if the land is to enjoy tranquillity, and it would also assure the fraternal sympathy of Bulgaria — and both states are essential to a southeastern European political and trade grouping.

The British Commonwealth of Nations

AUSTRALIA

The Land and the People

Australia, a self-governing Dominion of the British Commonwealth, is the world's largest island and smallest continent. Lying "down under" in the southwest Pacific, she is 12,000 miles from the centers of European industry and population and 7,000 miles from the west coast of the U.S.A.

Australia's history has been shaped by several factors: the predominantly British origin of her population, her distance from world markets and dependence on sea routes, her sparse population yet near one of the most densely settled areas of the world (southeast Asia and the Dutch East Indies), her high standard of living compared with almost the lowest in existence in the nearby lands of Asia, and her vigorous pioneering rôle in progressive social reforms and democratic government.

The Land. Occupying an area of 2,974,000 square miles, almost equal to that of the continental U.S.A., Australia's population is estimated at 7,184,-000, less than that of New York City or London. Nearly half of the people live in the six state capitals: Sydney (population 1,279,000), Melbourne (1,024,-000), Brisbane (318,430), Adelaide (318,190), Perth (215,700), and Hobart (65,000). The settled area is primarily along the southeastern seaboard, where some 5,000,000 inhabit a strip from Brisbane to Adelaide.

Rainfall and climate strongly influence this surprisingly low population figure. Primarily a great basin with a low average altitude (the only elevations being some moderately high mountains in the southeast), most of the country is either rainless or has an annual rainfall under 20 inches; in fact, nearly half of this vast expanse forms one of the great deserts of the world. North and northeast of this desert extends a tropical grassland with poor rainfall, while on the north coast, facing the Timor Sea, the extremely hot tropical savanna has excessive seasonal rainfall. Along the Pacific coast from Brisbane to south of Sydney lies a humid, subtropical area with a climate well-adapted to Europeans. Here is the famous sheep country of the state of New South Wales; and here an extensive wheat and fruit crop is grown. Here too is Australia's only important river, the Murray River. At the extreme southeastern tip of the country the climate approximates that of Mediterranean Spain and Italy. Tasmania, Australia's southern island, has cold winters and produces abundant northern fruit in her fertile valleys, Tasmanian apples resembling those of New York State.

The flora and fauna of Australia are picturesque and unique. The kangaroo, lyre bird, bower bird, cockatoo, koala ("teddy bear"), emu, and above all the platypus — a "missing link" between bird and mammal — have enriched the science of zoology. The leading tree, the eucalyptus, has been adapted for decorative purposes in other warm lands; and the mimosa, which as the "wattle" is a symbol of Australia, is far more fragrant there than in the south of France.

The trackless stretches of the Australian bush country or "outback," prevailingly brown in color, contrast with the rich green of New Zealand's countryside. Moreover, giant wheat farms and sheep ranches ("selections"), some of them larger than the state of Connecticut, are a feature of the country; while the Great Barrier Reef, off the Queensland coast, is perhaps the most exquisitely colored coral reef on earth.

Mineral resources abound. Gold is mined in Western Australia, Northern Territory, Victoria, and Queensland; and it was the discovery of the precious metal in Western Australia in 1851 that led to a "gold rush" similar to California's. Coal is found in New South Wales especially, but also in Victoria, Queensland, Western Australia, and Tasmania; iron in New South Wales and South Australia; silver, lead, and zinc in the extreme west of New South Wales and in Western Australia; copper in South Australia; and wolfram (tungsten) in Northern Territory.

The People. Over 99% of the Australians are of European stock, and of these over 97% are of British origin. The native population has been very much reduced, but efforts are being made to preserve the totem-worshiping aborigines on reservations because, despite their low material culture, they have one of the most elaborate tribal organizations known. One device of theirs, the boomerang, has entered the English language.

The Australians are perhaps the best-fed people on earth, consuming far more milk, butter, and meat on the average than Americans. They are a new pioneering people, with none of the traditional British reserve: generally tall, athletic and fond of outdoor life, hospitable, ready spenders, good-natured, and genuinely democratic. They originated the Australian ballot in elections, were pioneers in women's suffrage, and, with the New Zealanders, have been far ahead of Britain and the U.S.A. in their social experiments. Their slang is perhaps even more original and colorful than the American.

Unlike Britain, Australia has no rigid social classes, the wealthy being too few to constitute a distinct class. Wages for workers, like the cost of living, are high, and per capita national income approximates that of the U.S.A., though it is slightly less in money terms. The strong labor movement has become a major political force in the country, at present governed by the Labor Party. The country has abolished hereditary titles and even regards knighthoods with disfavor. The Church of England has the most adherents but it is no longer a state church.

The Australians' passion for horse-races, cricket, tennis, and soccer, though it has been overstressed, exists nonetheless; as does their passion for tea and the long history of independent spirits — "swaggies" — who have gone to live in the bush. The Australian "cobber" (or chum) has often been depicted in the literature of English-speaking peoples.

The country has a low birthrate: during the world economic depression it sank to 16.6 per thousand and with full employment rose to 18.4. The deathrate has been about 10. Infant mortality (only 38) is, apart

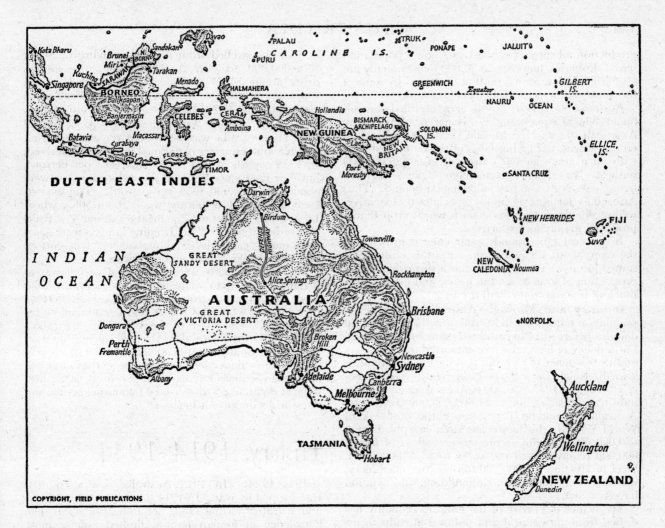

from New Zealand whites, the best average showing on earth. Life expectancy is as high as among American whites. During the depression a decline in population was forecast for the next generation, but it now appears that Australia will at least hold her own.

Nevertheless, the country is still underpopulated. The "White Australia" policy, barring all Asiatic immigration, principally out of fear of "cheap labor" flooding the country, is strictly enforced; and European immigration is carefully regulated. The tropical sugar areas in Queensland are worked mostly by immigrants from southern Italy, who have been relegated to a somewhat inferior social status. Since Australia was built up by immigration and can still, according to competent authorities, absorb several more million people at the very least, the immigration question is one of the most acute facing the country.

Education and Religion. With education tuition-free and compulsory, adult illiteracy (under 4%) is found largely among immigrant groups. School attendance is universal and the standards are high. Australia has eight universities with 15,000 students; the outstanding two are at Sydney and Melbourne.

Over 75% of the population are Protestants, around 20% Roman Catholics. Of the Protestant groups, more than 40% subscribe to the Anglican faith.

Culturally, Australia is subject to three "pulls": the first is the British, largely because of tradition and the paramount position of London in the book world; the second is the American, which centers around period-

ical literature and the movies; and the third, gaining fast, is the native Australian. Formerly, Australia lost much of her talent to Great Britain, but this tendency has diminished.

Australian literature has impressively matured, and music and the fine arts have made notable gains. Many Australians have become world-famous, like Nellie Melba, the opera-singer, Gilbert Murray, Percy Grainger, Griffith Taylor, the geographer, and John Hunter, the physiologist. Australians are often distinguished by extreme originality and pugnacity in upholding their theories.

The Nation's Economy

Agriculture and Animal Husbandry. Australia is basically the land of wool and wheat. She has 125,-000,000 sheep, almost 18 per inhabitant, and her annual wool clip of 550,000 tons approaches 30% of world supply — no other land produces even half that amount. Her 13,500,000 cattle exceed the American figure on a per capita basis by more than 3 to 1; and her supply of horses, 1,600,000, is large. The only marked deficiency in animal economy is in swine.

Annual meat production is over 1,000,000 tons, of which 53% is beef and veal, 40% mutton and lamb, 10% pig. Per capita production of meat is more than twice America's, butter, milk, margarine, and cheese production all surpassing the U.S.A. on a population basis. Fisheries, however, at 30,000 tons annually are astonishingly low for a land that is washed by some of the most prolific ocean-fish areas known.

Australia's relatively small area of tilled land — about 33,000 square miles — is exceeded by many American states in the Middle West. The principal crop is wheat, occupying 60% of the cultivated land with an average annual output of over 125,000,000 bushels. No other crop remotely compares with this figure, oats, corn, and hay following far behind. Thus Australia's farming is highly specialized, extensive, well-mechanized, and based on a wheat crop that is produced mainly for export.

In tropical Queensland, sugar cane is grown and the crop, about 4.5% of world output, is mostly consumed locally. The southeast has a surprisingly high production of grapes, apples, pears, and citrus fruits, much of it going to the British Isles.

Industry and Mining. Australia's large urban population reflects her industrial growth. For several decades before 1914 industry was slow in developing, but a policy of high tariffs for imported manufactures and the existence of plentiful coal for fuel fostered this growth, which the exigencies of World War I accelerated. In 1935, 450,000 workers were engaged in industry with an output of $1,800,000,000 (taking the Australian pound at par). Since the outbreak of World War II, this figure has risen sharply to over 650,000 workers with an output in 1940–41 of £644,-000,000 (equivalent at par value to $3,200,000,000). Steel production is 3,000,000 tons yearly; machinery, machine tools, munitions, shipbuilding, and aviation have boomed.

The center of gravity of the nation's economy has shifted from agricultural and pastoral pursuits to industry. Though many figures have been withheld for military reasons, the trend is unmistakable. Australian statistics give the following percentages in cash values of national production: manufactures 49%, livestock 20%, agriculture 13%, dairy and poultry 11%, mining 7%.

In mining, Australia has been an important gold producer since the discovery of gold in Western Australia in 1851. Annual output is valued at about $40,000,000. Peacetime figures for coal production give 14,000,000 tons, with 4,000,000 of brown coal, and 2,000,000 of iron ore, and 1,300,000 of pig iron. These figures have all risen during the war. In the absence of oil, an abundance of good-quality coal supplies the natural fuel for heavy industry. Australia also contributes 16% of the world's lead, 12% of its zinc, 2% of tin, 3% of wolfram (tungsten), 5% of silver, and 1.6% of antimony.

Transport facilities remain inadequate for a country so vast. Moreover, each state has its own railway-gauge system, thus unduly complicating freight and passenger travel. But the leading centers of population are well linked, and air travel is being resorted to on a large scale both for passenger travel and goods.

Finance. The unit of currency is the pound, valued at one-fifth under the British pound. The wartime ratio has been fixed at $3.22 to the pound. Prices have risen over 40% and the cost of living by about 23% during the war, and government controls appear to be working quite successfully. The budget has swelled from a pre-war figure of about $300,000,000 to over $2,200,000,000; the foreign debt, about $1,900,000,000, has remained almost stationary while the domestic debt has risen from about $1,100,000,000 to more than double that sum.

Foreign Trade. Until the outbreak of World War II, Australia was dependent on exports, from which about a quarter of national income was derived. In 1938 exports were $518,000,000 ($83 per person), but they have since declined somewhat; imports were about $455,000,000 ($65 per person). The exports were constituted as follows: wool, about 50%, wheat 13%, gold 11%, butter 9%, meat 8%, flour 4%, fruits 3%, ores and metals 2%. Leading imports were gasoline, motor cars, electrical machinery, tea, cotton, silk, steel, books, drugs, and chemicals.

Peacetime exports were distributed as follows: to Britain 60%, Japan 12%, Belgium 6%, France 5%; while imports came from Britain 41%, U.S.A. 16%, then Japan, Dutch East Indies, and Canada, all under 10% each. The share of the U.S.A. in Australia's foreign trade, substantially increased during the war, now begins to approach Britain's.

Australia's dependence on seaborne trade has encouraged the development of large coastal ports; and some of them, like Sydney and Melbourne, are among the world's important harbors.

History: 1914-1944

1914–1924. In 1918 Australia was a country transformed by war. In 1914 she had been a pastoral and wheat-exporting land, her industries small, her knowledge of foreign nations limited among most people to mere memories of the mother country. In 1918 she had a large army with a record of heroism and tragedy on the battlefields of Asia, Africa, and Europe. Australia now had a large industry. She had entered the war without debt and had come out of it with an indebtedness of nearly $2,000,000,000. She had been governed before 1914 by men immersed in local problems; in 1918 her Premier, W. M. Hughes, was a rampant imperialist and nationalist who aggressively opposed Woodrow Wilson at Versailles.

Hughes had been head of the Labor Party, but he was expelled in 1917 because he favored conscription, an issue that split the party. Joining his remnant of the Labor Party with the Liberals, Hughes came back as Prime Minister, heading a new Nationalist Party (which in 1932 was to take the name of the United Australia Party). He clamored for Australian mandates over Pacific areas. He did not favor separation from Britain, but rather combined a passion for British imperial power with an insistence that Australia get a more advantageous position within the Imperial arrangement. At Versailles he obtained mandates as well as immense phantom reparations from Germany. Hughes had won the war and the peace, and he came back to an overwhelming victory in the 1920 election. Under him, Australia won admission to the League of Nations as a sovereign commonwealth.

In 1919, however, a cloud loomed on Hughes's golden horizon. The Country Party was formed, based on the farming interest, and by 1922, with 14 members out of 75 in Parliament, it began to hold the balance of power. Led by a country physician, Dr. Earl Page, it worked hard to doom Hughes, whose demagogy and overbearing tendencies had provoked profound antagonisms; and it agreed to arrangements with the Nationalists (1923) for the joint purpose of removing Hughes. The Prime Minister was succeeded by his temperamental opposite, an exceptionally able and broad-minded business man, Stanley Melbourne Bruce. Since Hughes was an active machine politician who "got out the vote" while the others rested on their dignity, a compulsory voting law was passed for federal elections in 1924, thus assuring Bruce and Page a full turnout of their supporters. Hughes continued a maverick career in politics, but the glamor of the "Anzac" period was over. Economics now dominated all thinking, except for effective unity on the "white Australia" population policy.

Economic Issues: 1924–1939. In 1924–25 a period of labor disorders reached levels that even Australia, paradise of unionized labor, had never known. The American I.W.W. had a large following in the mining areas; in the ports, the seamen and dockers were extremely militant. The great harbor strike of 1925 not only paralyzed Australia, whose entire economy is based on exports, but also aggravated the difficulties of the importer, Great Britain. Sydney, where the strike centered, inspired British seamen with the idea of the General Strike, which was to take place in the mother country a year later. To break up the strike, Page and Bruce united, the first representing the farmer who had to export, and the second reflecting a conservative social philosophy. The strike was broken, but it increased the militancy of labor for many years: it became Labor's legend as Gallipoli had become the national legend.

However, prosperity prevailed, and there was a bout of borrowing and confident speculation. The Wool Realization scheme and the compulsory wheat pool benefited from world recovery. But in 1927, while the world was at the peak of prosperity, Australia faltered and a commission of the most eminent British industrialists and bankers was sent out in the spring of 1928 to study the threatening situation. They turned in a report so patronizing, so full of the counsel of ancient wisdom to young profligates, that resentment became nearly universal. That they were objectively right was not noted because of their unfortunate manner.

In 1928 Australia showed the first symptoms of the world crisis and the deterioration of sound currencies, the Australian pound slumping in relation to the British pound. By 1930 the whole question of debt was in the balance and clever local politicians like Theodore in Queensland got quite a following for unorthodox finance. In the meantime, Bruce, representing the protectionists, had traded off his needs with Page, who wanted fixed agricultural prices, so that protectionism grew apace. With it arose local, high-cost manufactures, which, though they would collapse under free trade, led to an industrialization of the land.

In 1927 the Federal government took a great step towards centralization by assuming state debts at the price of Federal control. Thus Australian federation, which had begun in 1901, was truly consummated. The Federal Capital of Canberra was the physical symbol of a country that wished to transcend the old (and continuing) jealousies of New South Wales and Victoria.

In 1931 England abandoned the gold standard. Australian prices rose once more and a gentle recovery set in. Unemployment had been rife and the general *malaise* in labor and finance was remedied just in time to prevent more extreme alignments in politics. The Bruce-Page government had triumphed in 1928, but Labor was reviving. Such astute politicians as Lang in Sydney and men of extraordinary learning and force like Evatt were giving the Labor Party a new tone, although cautious leadership, like that of Curtin, set the basic approach. In 1933, too, the Civil Service, owing to nationalization of key utilities, employed about a ninth of the people. It was calculated that, allowing for every one dependent on government disbursements, a fifth of the electorate was on the receiving end of taxes.

National pride remained intense. For example, the Statute of Westminster of 1931, welcomed throughout the Empire as confirming dominion quasi-independence, was not ratified by Australia. However, for Imperial Preference agreements, concluded at the 1932 Ottawa conference, there was protectionist enthusiasm, and only slight criticism.

In 1934 the Labor Party was split wide open between the regulars and the Lang faction in New South Wales. An election took advantage of this split and J. A. Lyons, a Catholic from Tasmania, headed the government, representing the United Australia Party. The Country Party, as always, traded its balance of power to great advantage, but within the United Australia Party new men were rising, like Menzies, more forceful than Bruce or Lyons.

There were new problems too. Great Britain might not forever be the principal customer; local manufacturing might alter the entire economic base. There was, for the first time, an internal accumulation of capital, with almost no dependence on London; and the country would have to rely largely on herself for her defense, since Britain's resources were too thinly spread against too many dangers. The older Australia with her traditional party slogans, was dead.

In 1938 Australia forgot politics for the great Sesquicentennial celebration of the founding of the country, which led to an outburst of national pride and, among the cynics, of a debunking literature. In the midst of rejoicings, Australian labor refused to load cargoes for Japan, but it was disciplined by the government. Then the government embargoed exports of iron ore, on the ground that Australia's supply was deficient for home defense. The Ottawa agreements began to irk Australia, and attempts were initiated to revise tariff schedules and to make arrangements with the U.S.A.

1939–1944. In 1939 Menzies became Prime Minister. When war between Germany and Britain broke out, Australia immediately stood by the mother country. The war seemed remote, however, and did not, at first, much affect Australia. Nevertheless, Asiatic danger loomed large. Diplomatic relations were established with the U.S.A. in January 1940; R. G. Casey became the Australian and Clarence E. Gauss the American Minister. In February 1940 "Anzacs" landed in Egypt.

Australia was transformed into a modern industrial state and an arsenal, as the country engaged in ship and airplane manufacture. Everyone was employed. Menzies asked for a National government of all parties, but Labor refused. In September 1940 all non-Labor groups buried the hatchet, and even Hughes came back into the national union, as a symbol of past victory. The government defeated Labor by a small margin.

There was no conscription for overseas service. The country was agitated by large Australian losses, as in World War I, and the generalship of the campaigns in Greece, Crete, and Egypt did not inspire much enthusiasm. A critical country required new leadership, and A. W. Fadden of the Country Party replaced Menzies. For him there was one enemy, Communism, and he raised the Communist issue against all Laborites. The September 1941 elections defeated him and returned Labor to power, after two decades, with Curtin as Prime Minister. The Labor Party demanded increasing nationalization and State Socialism.

Before it could begin its domestic program, however, Japan attacked and, by March 1942, when Java fell, Australia, for the first time in her history, was in mortal peril. The Australians valiantly fought back the menace which reached Port Moresby, facing north Queensland, in the spring of 1942. By the fall of 1942 Australian tenacity and American naval aid had changed the situation. From then on, the perimeter of Japanese power was steadily reduced. Large American forces, under General MacArthur, were stationed in Australia and intimate associations between the two nations began.

In August 1943 Labor captured control of both the Senate and the House of Representatives, for the first time since 1914. Labor defeated its combined opponents by 51 to 23, and the Country Party of Fadden and the United Australia Party of Menzies, both humbled, dissolved their old, but uneasy alliance.

Stakes in the Peace

An industrialized though still underpopulated Australia faces the future. At the same time, she has certain older difficulties: the wool clip and carryover will undoubtedly be excessive soon after the war. Yet this problem, which would have been Australia's national preoccupation in 1919, is today secondary in importance.

Australian steel production, if developed for local needs may, for example, reduce the market for her wool in England, since Britain would lose her steel exports to Australia, with which to pay for the wool. If Australia seeks to replace the importation of fabricated goods in exchange for her raw material exports, she has two alternatives: one is to diminish the production of such exported raw materials as wool, wheat, butter, and lamb, and turn to a more intensive agriculture. But this would still further increase the costs of national production, thus making higher protective tariffs necessary.

On the other hand, she might seek to reduce her trade with Britain and export to the closer Far Eastern countries (when they have higher living standards), thus retaining both her export basis and her industrial advances. She might also increase her exports to a nation like France, accepting luxury goods in return. But if she wishes to retain manufactures that compete with those of Britain, she must either realign her trade or vary the raw materials she produces.

Her basic problems have radically altered since pre-1939 days; her reduced dependence on British capital, the striking change in her debtor relationship to Britain, and the swelling accumulation of local capital all underline this change. The classic dilemma of protection or free trade has now a different direction, if not significance. At bottom, of course, all these problems are contingent on the fact that Australia, with her 7,000,000 inhabitants, is still in a growth phase of population; and only the remote future can tell whether the "white Australia" policy will be maintained.

In the political sphere, World War II has shown that Australia is one of a constellation of nations, her security being contingent on the cooperation of larger states. Her undoubted valor would not otherwise have sufficed to guarantee her national security in the southwest Pacific. Australia was enthusiastic for the pre-war League of Nations and will undoubtedly join wholeheartedly in any post-war world organization for peace.

CANADA

The Land and the People

The 3,000-mile unfortified border between the U.S.A. and the Dominion of Canada is eloquent testimony to the friendly relations between the two countries since the War of 1812. When the thirteen colonies broke away from the British Empire the Canadian provinces refused to join them, but gradually they attained not only a federal union but a practically complete independence within the British Commonwealth of Nations. Today the Dominion of Canada's diplomatic status is equal to that of any other sovereign state in the world.

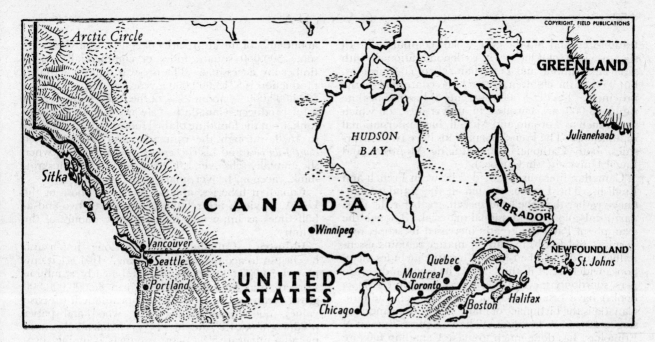

The Land.

Canada covers the whole of the continent north of the U.S.A., excepting Alaska (northwest) and Labrador (east). Her vast expanse of 3,466,000 square miles is 15% greater than continental U.S.A., but the inaccessibility and Arctic cold of the north greatly reduce the habitable area. Hence nine-tenths of the estimated 11,812,000 population (less than New York State's) live in the region near the southern border.

The land extends from the Great Lakes and the northwestern American plain to the polar sea. Its configuration is similar to that of the United States: the warm, damp coastal strip along the Pacific, the high Rockies, the great prairie, the farming lands about the Great Lakes, a fertile strip along the St. Lawrence river, excellent farming lands in the warmer oceanic stream areas of Nova Scotia. Our Adirondacks are a southern spur of the Laurentian mountains in the Province of Quebec.

Canada is a land of lakes, of enormous forests, of rich mineral deposits, of trappers, miners, and fishermen. Though only about 92,000 square miles have so far been found arable (U.S.A. has 500,000 arable square miles), Canada's resources could support a much greater population.

The People.

The two basic racial stocks are British and French. Canadians of French origin exceed 3,500,000. Canadians of British origin include some 3,000,000 English, 1,400,000 Scottish, and 1,300,000 Irish. Among the minor strains are about 500,000 German, 230,000 Scandinavian, 250,000 Ukrainian, 170,000 Jewish, 150,000 Dutch, and 150,000 Polish, besides some 150,000 aboriginal Indians and Eskimos, and many other nationalities. In short, Canada's experience with the fusion of peoples has been similar to the U.S.A.'s, though on a smaller scale.

The birthrate varies from 30 per thousand in French-Canadian to about 20 in English communities, the Dominion average being 23.4. The deathrate is low, about 9.7; infant mortality is average, about 60 (somewhat higher among the French). In peacetime a natural increase of 10% was forecast for the next generation; in this the French-Canadians play a disproportionate part, and any diminution of immigration would increase the French proportion.

The English-speaking Canadians are more like Americans than any other people. In national wealth and standard of living, in industrial investment and efficiency, in manner of life in the city and on the farm, the two peoples are closely akin. But Canadians are not Americans — far from it — in spite of cafeterias, drug-stores, ice cream sodas, hot dogs, movies, and comics. They are a distinct nationality, in form, American, certainly British, but above all Canadian — shapers of a new culture, convinced of their own national destiny.

The French-Canadians are another story; they add another flavor to that new culture and national destiny, but at present, except for an assimilated minority, they are a people within a people. One may observe the best of their world, which centers in the St. Lawrence region of Quebec, in the novel, *Maria Chapdelaine*: the antique French speech, which knows none of the cultural or political moods of France since 1763; the village clustered about the church with its priest; the songs, the folklore, and artisanship of old France; the love of the soil, despite laborious summers and long, cold winters; the many children, the hospitality, the Arcadian indifference to the hustling, material-minded North America about them. There is another side to the picture — remains of illiteracy, less robust children, poverty, intellectual retreat — but these things seem irrelevant to people whose treasure on earth is farm, family, and faith.

Religion and Education.

The largest religious group is the Roman Catholic Church, which claims 42% of the people — in conjunction with the Greek Catholic Church, this reaches 44% — and which enjoys special privileges in the Province of Quebec. About 1.5% of the people are Jews, nearly 54.5% Protestants. Several Protestant denominations have fused in a United Church, but the separate Anglican and Presbyterian churches are still strong.

Illiteracy is rare in the Dominion as a whole, amounting to some 4% among adults. Education is tuition-free and almost everywhere compulsory. In the province of Quebec it is denominational, with separate Catholic and Protestant school commissions, but 95% of the children go to schools controlled by the provinces. Besides 57,000 students of lesser collegiate rank, 48,000 are enrolled in universities, of which some, such as Toronto and McGill, have international reputations. The French-Canadians have two universities, both Catholic: Université de Montréal and Laval Université (in Quebec).

Canadian literature is divided between French and English. The French, written in the standard language rather than the local speech, treats for the most part local-color or confessional material. Though the example of Paris has greatly increased its scope, modernity, and finish, its subject matter remains essentially Canadian. The English literature includes many books widely read in the U.S.A.: its woodlands, trappers, sourdoughs, even its farm people (as in the *Jalna* books) have become part of a continental tradition. Canada is the birthplace of many celebrated American stage and screen favorites. The Canadian Bureau of Ethnology has done much to make Canadian folklore familiar: the fascinating Indian cultures, and the Eskimos, visited and studied by people as different in approach as Boas and Stefansson.

The Nation's Economy

Agriculture. The agriculture is divided into zones: the Maritime Provinces (Nova Scotia, New Brunswick, Prince Edward Island), the Laurentian area, the Ontario area on three Great Lakes, the grandiose grain ocean of the Northwestern Prairie, and the Pacific coastal valleys of British Columbia. These zones differ in products, size of farms, type of mechanization. But a short treatment can report only in general terms on the three basic types of agriculture — field crops, animal husbandry, fruits and vegetables.

There are some 735,000 farms in all (an eighth of the number in the U.S.A.) and 1,262,000 farmers, of whom 993,000 are family workers. About 45% of farm receipts, on the average, come from field crops, 15% from milk products, 23% from farm animals, 5% from fruits and vegetables, and 6% from poultry and eggs.

The gigantic wheat production varies but averages about 250,000,000 bushels, and the annual crop of oats is 480,000,000, of barley, 215,000,000. These grain crops are relatively much greater than United States production, but corn, our largest crop, is scarcely cultivated at all. In mixed farming, the Canadian output is distributed much as is ours: typical crops are potatoes, sugar beets, hay, alfalfa, rye, buckwheat, tobacco (large), and flaxseed. Total production of field crops in 1943 was estimated at $1,100,000,000.

Canadian animal economy is proportionate to ours: cattle number about 9,600,000, swine 8,100,000 (Canadian bacon is famous), and sheep 3,500,000, with a comparatively small wool clip of 6,500 tons. Canada produces about a tenth as much meat as the U.S.A. Fur farming, especially of silver foxes in Prince Edward Island, has flourished.

Of the 1,254,000 square miles of Canadian forests —

about 40% of the entire area of continental U.S.A. — some 300,000 square miles of commercially useful timber are accessible. The pre-war figure for timber production is $213,000,000 a year, for pulp and paper $334,000,000 — about 22% of the world's supply. As a fur producer, Canada has always been in the front rank, from the founding of the Hudson's Bay Company in 1670, through the romantic days of the French *coureur du bois* and his successors, to the present, when she annually sells over 5,000,000 pelts of fox, muskrat, mink, raccoon, beaver, marten, and wolf.

Canadian fisheries, about a fourth of those of the U.S.A. in yield, are relatively more than two-and-a-half times as important in the total economy of the country.

Industry. Canadian industry, long important, has begun to acquire world standing. In 1941 it employed $5,000,000,000 capital and nearly a million workers, and produced goods worth $6,000,000,000 gross. Iron and steel accounted for a fourth (in cash value), non-ferrous metals 12%, wood and paper products about 15%, textiles 11%, chemicals 5%, non-metallic minerals 5%, plant products (canning, processing) 15%, animal products 12%. These are wartime percentages. Also the result of war is the shift in proportion between manufactures and agricultural products, now 55% for industry as against 20% for agriculture, which alters the long-current idea that Canada is a raw materials producer only. That this shift is basically a war phenomenon is shown by the fact that industrial workers were only 12% more numerous in 1939 than in 1926 — an increase roughly equivalent to gain in population — whereas in 1943 they had increased 140% over 1926. Canada is one of the great arsenals of the United Nations.

In a typical pre-war year (1935), Canada's gross manufacturing production was $2,500,000,000, about 5% of our output for the same year, or relatively less for her population. Heavy industry was then a third, whereas today it is 47%, of gross production.

Mining and Fuels. Canada is one of the first three gold producers, supplies more than 8% of its silver, more than 10% of its copper, over 80% of its nickel, 10% of its lead, nearly 10% of its zinc, and 5% of its pyrites, dominates asbestos production, is a large cement producer, may have the largest supply of pitchblende — and offers truly exciting prospects for a variety and abundance of other minerals once her now inaccessible areas are prospected. However extravagant the hopes that periodically sweep in speculative waves over Canadian share markets in mining, they have in large part been fulfilled.

Although Canada has large brown coal reserves, her total coal production is minor ($2\frac{1}{2}$% as much as from American mines). Canadian petroleum production is less than 1% of the U.S.A.'s, though a Canadian petroleum company is active in Colombia and Peru. There are high hopes for petroleum in the Canadian West, where a small supply of natural gas is already available. But Canada is most richly endowed in water-power, which has been developed to 40% of that in the U.S.A. and is thought to be potentially three times its present amount. Most of this power is in the Laurentian and Great Lakes regions; fortunately, it has been developed largely in industrial areas without coal.

Finance. Until 1930 Canada was a debtor country. She owed 15% of her wealth to foreign investment: some of it French, more of it British, and (of late years) still more of it American. She paid out 26% of her national income for imports and payments abroad. She derived 22% of her income (as compared with the U.S.A.'s 8%) from exports; included in this percentage is income from the extensive American tourist trade, which reached considerable proportions during Prohibition and may be expected to continue now that the country's possibilities are known. Hence Canada's prosperity is bound up with world markets for her surplus products. The war and the accompanying expansion of her factory capacity have added a new need.

Largely through that expansion, the war has altered Canada's status as a debtor. She has even been able to present gigantic sums to the mother country as gifts, wisely assuming that such sums can never be paid by usual transfers.

The Canadian dollar is now stabilized at 90¢; probably the main reason why it is not at parity is that parity would disturb the triangular rates of exchange of American-Canadian-British money. Money in circulation has risen from $207,000,000 in 1938 to $633,000,000 in 1942 (more than 3 to 1), but the cost of living has risen only a sixth and wholesale prices somewhat over a third. The Stabilization Board holds all foreign exchange, and for the duration its regulations limit the inflow and outflow of all Canadian money. Canadian credit is high, but some provincial obligations yield more than analogous United States bonds. In Alberta, however, the triumph of the Social Credit Party somewhat diminished confidence on the part of investors.

Canadian bank deposits have risen conservatively, from $3,200,000,000 in 1939 to $4,200,000,000 in 1943. Savings bank accounts are static: most savings have gone into war bonds. Canadian government annuities attract the savings of older people.

The Canadian budget, reflecting the war, has risen from $550,000,000 in peace to ten times that amount in 1944. While the Dominion's foreign debt dropped from $806,000,000 to $450,000,000, the domestic debt has risen from $2,830,000,000 to $8,200,000,000 — the per capita debt is half that of the U.S.A. at comparable periods of the war. But whereas the U.S.A. raises only a third of war costs from taxes, Canada, with taxation at $230 per person, handles half her war costs on a "pay-as-you-go" basis.

In national wealth and income, mechanization, and output on a per capita basis, Canada is second only to the U.S.A.

Foreign Trade. The war has doubled Canada's imports, sent her exports (largely destined for fighting fronts) up 60%. Normally trade is about $157 per capita, with total imports at about $670,000,000 and total exports at about $950,000,000 — four times as high per capita as in the U.S.A.

Of the exports, Great Britain usually took 40%, the U.S.A. 37%, with the rest scattering. Of the imports, 26% came from Britain, 57% from the U.S.A., the rest scattering. Principal exports were wheat, newsprint, gold, nickel, wood pulp, timber, fish, meat, automobiles, copper, furs, and whiskey; principal imports coal, petroleum, rolled iron, fruits, cotton, and sugar.

History: 1914-1944

The Canada of 1914, though warmly attached to the mother country, Great Britain, was in national outlook an almost purely North American commonwealth. The British Governor, the Duke of Connaught, a brother of Edward VII, and his daughter, the Princess Patricia, were extremely popular, but the national spirit of the Canadians was basically North American. The echoes of the American Annexationist Party, led by an Englishman, Goldwin Smith, had not yet died down; and though Canadian nationalism was nascent rather than full-grown, the people's interests were concentrated on the country's amazing internal development. In French Canada, the new Nationalist Party of Bourassa moved increasingly away from French tradition, as France herself became anti-clerical.

Rising nationalism had been discerned in the defeat of Sir Wilfrid Laurier (1911), when he urged tariff reciprocity with the U.S.A. After serving for 16 years as Prime Minister, Laurier gave way to an advocate of protective tariffs, the scholarly Nova Scotian Conservative, Sir Robert Borden. The Liberal Party of Laurier remained basically agrarian, while the Conservatives began to stress Canadian industrial interests. Nevertheless, United States investments in the Dominion had already exceeded those of the British; hence, while Canada grew increasingly national in sentiment, her industrial connections with the U.S.A. deepened.

Canada entered World War I in 1914, and no Dominion could have been more loyal to Britain. Outside of Quebec Province, men volunteered in large numbers, and even there volunteering was quite large. The Canadians suffered immense losses and displayed unsurpassed heroism. The Battle of Vimy Ridge and poems like "In Flanders Field" of Captain MacRae entered into the national legend.

Canada had matured in war. Internally she had been transformed by the far-reaching development of the grain-growing northwest; industrially and in foreign trade she was an advanced nation. Laurier, the beloved "old chief," led the Grits (Liberals) in 1917 in a fight against conscription. He carried 62 out of 65 seats in Quebec, but few elsewhere, and not one west of the Great Lakes! Conscription went into effect, but, as disorders in Quebec showed, the government had to move with prudence in certain areas.

Post-War Reconstruction: 1919–1921. Crowned with victory and glory, the Conservatives seemed assured of continuing in power in 1919. Sir Robert Borden's hold on the country appeared firm. But the return of peace rudely upset these expectations. Despite the death of Laurier, the Liberals neither disintegrated nor disappeared. In western Canada, the proclamation of a Socialist Commonwealth at Winnipeg, accompanied by an eventful though futile general strike, testified to changed social attitudes.

The Progressives under Forke in the west, the Grain Growers Cooperatives in the prairie lands, the rise of a Socialist movement under Woodworth, the strike wave that spilled over from the U.S.A. in 1919, the influence of the American Non-Partisan League in some of Canada's western provinces, and the depreciation of the Canadian dollar — all these developments presaged a modern state, in which the central issue of protection versus free trade, which had separated political parties since 1867, would be relegated to a minor place.

Canada shared in the expansion of world economy in the 1920's. She developed her industries and water-power resources. The formation of a "Pool" among grain-growers led to more efficient results than the older cooperatives had attained. Nationalism simmered in Quebec, but did not explode. The Prohibition era in the U.S.A. resulted in a deluge of American visitors, who came to know and appreciate their sturdy American fellow-nation.

The Liberals in Power: 1921–1923. Casting about for a leader with modern experience, the Liberals chose W. L. Mackenzie King (a descendant of the greatest of Canadian patriots, William Lyon Mackenzie) and began to build their party anew. Sir Robert Borden, the cultured Prime Minister, worn out in his country's service, retired to his home in Grand Pré, the site of Longfellow's "Evangeline." With Laurier and Borden removed from political life, Canada now learned new names.

Mr. Arthur Meighen, Premier of Ontario province, succeeded Borden and insisted on a high protective tariff. The Progressives of the farming west, who had risen in power as the population of the prairie provinces grew, opposed this policy since it entailed a rise in their living costs.

In the 1921 elections, the "dead" Liberals obtained 117 seats, the western Progressives 65, and the Conservative Party in power a mere 51. December 1921 thus marked the ascendancy of western agrarian interests. For while Mackenzie King had a Liberal majority, it was a precarious one, and he needed Progressive support. The victory of a farmer-labor coalition in the Ontario provincial elections appeared to foreshadow radicalism.

The temporary world depression of 1921–23 and the chronic farming crisis in the U.S.A. placed the Liberal MacKenzie King government at a disadvantage. In 1923, the Senate, with its large Conservative carry-over, balked at the government's railway policy. Moreover, the Progressive Party began to splinter into various economic groupings. Although by 1925 business took a considerable upswing, with almost full prosperity in the cities, recovery in the farm areas was spotty.

Hence in the 1925 elections the Conservatives rose to over 100 seats and the western farmers broke away from the Progressives, whose representation fell by two-thirds. King held five-sixths of his Liberal following and sought to continue his government. Losing on a vote of confidence in 1926, he insisted on an appeal to the people. Lord Byng of Vimy, the war hero, now Governor-General, declined to order a second election. Mr. King, insisting that the Crown (through its representative) possessed no such power, prevailed. The elections gave King a small majority; and the constitutional independence of Canada was vindicated.

She was now practically an independent nation, and the Statute of Westminster (1931) later ratified her new diplomatic and constitutional position. Her relationship to the Crown was partly juridical (use of the court functions of the House of Lords and the British Privy Council) and mostly a sentimental expression of imperial unity.

In 1929, after a tremendous boom in stocks similar to that on the New York Stock Exchange, Canadian financial and commodity markets crashed. The resultant crisis and unemployment defeated the King government, with its coalition of Liberals and Progressives, and brought the first Conservative victory since 1917.

The Last Conservative Government: 1930–1935. The Conservative, R. B. Bennett, came to power at the end of 1930, and immediately initiated a high tariff policy. Two years later, however, these duties were modified by a policy of Imperial Preference adopted at the Ottawa Conference, which buttressed British Empire solidarity by encouraging inter-imperial trade relations. But the Ottawa Agreement constituted a serious obstacle to healthy international trade and became one of the chief causes for the rapid growth of economic "autarky."

As unemployment persisted and trade was extremely slack, and with the price of farm commodities falling to disastrous levels, Canada watched carefully the efforts made in the U.S.A. after 1933 to effect recovery. Although Canadian Liberals did not espouse the specific New Deal type of thought, their general orientation approximated that of the Roosevelt administration. The recovery of world prices in 1934 and the boom in Britain improved matters, but not enough to sustain Bennett's high-tariff government.

The Liberal Landslide: 1935–1939. The sharply contested election of October 1935 ended in a Liberal landslide, returning Mackenzie King to power and shattering Conservative influence for many years to come. The appointment of Baron Tweedsmuir (John Buchan, the novelist and historian) as Governor-General proved extremely popular in Canada and coincided with a wave of pro-British sentiment in connection with the Jubilee in London celebrating 25 years of the reign of King George V.

The King government faced a curious Parliament. The stricken Conservatives were reduced to a mere 39 against the Liberals' 177, the widest disproportion ever known in Canada. And there was an entirely new group, with 17 seats, the Social Credit Party. Following the economic theories of Major Douglas in England, this party asserted that the true cause of economic crises and even of poverty was the failure of our present currency system to release purchasing power. Its leader, Aberhart, had won power in Alberta province and was attempting to put his theories into practice. Moreover, the long dormant Socialist movement had begun to revive. The unwieldy Liberal majority permitted all sorts of special groups within its ranks to advance their sectional interests, knowing that they were not imperiling the government by their opposition.

Despite the constant lag in commodity prices, the national economy enjoyed a broad recovery and expanded. It was not until 1939 that the advent of World War II confronted Canada anew with problems similar to those she had so well mastered in 1914–18. But a new industrial alignment (See *Industry*) and new currents at work in Quebec materially altered the political scene.

Canada at War: 1939–1944. Nevertheless, the elections of 1940 revealed few changes. True, the war had not yet emerged from its static phase in Europe, and Canada was only slightly engaged. The Liberals still obtained 173 seats to a mere 38 for the Conservatives; Social Credit fell away to 10 seats; and the mildly socialistic Commonwealth Cooperative Federation (C.C.F.) had 9 seats. Various other elements picked up a few seats here and there, with one member representing a party with growing influence in Quebec, the *Bloc Populaire*. With the Socialist leader, Coldwell, supporting the war, there was but slight pacifist or anti-war sentiment expressed in actual parliamentary representation. In Quebec province, however, and in scattered constituencies elsewhere the situation was not as unified as parliamentary voting made it appear.

The rise of a new leader in Quebec, Duplessis, marked a departure from the old nationalism of French Canada. In Quebec, discontent during World War I had expressed itself primarily as opposition to conscription within the old Liberal Party. True, there were Nationalists, but their one newspaper, *Le Devoir*, and one prophet, Bourassa, grandson of the Canadian patriot Papineau, could not counter the influence of the outstanding Sir Wilfred Laurier.

But in 1940 it was evident that almost half the people of Quebec were following more extreme policies aimed at granting the province its specific point of view within the Dominion. There was a still smaller group of Fascists, under Adrien Arcand, and extreme Nationalists or "Laurentians," who favored an independent French Canadian state. The common sense of the sturdy French-speaking population militated against doctrinaire extremes. Nevertheless, these French Canadians largely embraced particularism; and Duplessis, their spokesman, finally reversed the Liberal majority in Quebec by a narrow margin. He was later overturned, but in 1944 he returned to power, also by a small plurality.

The Dominion, as a whole, moved in the opposite direction. The grant of exceptional powers, similar to the British Defense of the Realm Acts, aided the prosecution of the war. Production, gaining slowly at first, soon assumed gigantic proportions. Volunteering for the armed forces was remarkably high: by October 1942, a third of all males from 19 to 40 had volunteered outside Quebec, and about 13% in that province. Taxation was rigorous, based on the principle that the largest possible revenue should arise from taxation and not from loans. The succession of six war loans was in itself most impressive, when the monies raised were compared to the national wealth.

Canada accepted the British reverses of 1940 with grim resolution and redoubled her efforts. The long neutrality of the U.S.A., even the passage of "cash and carry" resolutions by the American Congress, never diminished Canadian hope of eventual American cooperation. Joint declarations by President Roosevelt and Prime Minister King that the integrity of Canada was a national preoccupation of the U.S.A. proved a pillar of national security; and subsequently, joint conferences bearing on the defense of the Americas were initiated.

The Dieppe raid of 1942, in which Canada's heroic soldiers suffered dreadful losses, spurred on the people's zeal; and the Canadian General MacNaughton insisted that, contrary to popular impression, the Dieppe raid proved the practicability of a "second front." The entry of the Soviet Union into the war (June 1941) led to a relaxation of restrictions against extreme Leftists in Canada, and while censorship of the press caused some flurries between newspaper editors and the government, it never seriously interfered with criticism. Only one diplomatic concession remained: Vichy France was represented at Ottawa long after the British had refused to deal with that authority.

Internally the wretched showing of the Conservative Party led to its reorganization. A new leader, the westerner Bracken, headed the party and its name was changed to Progressive Conservative Party. Its former mentor, Meighen, even suffered defeat at the hands of a Socialist in a by-election for the House of Commons. During the summer of 1944, the Socialists swept the province of Saskatchewan and made impressive gains elsewhere, and the C.C.F., the parliamentary embodiment of Socialist ideas, began to speak of the possibility of winning national power in the post-war elections.

In April 1942 Canada had held a referendum on conscription for overseas service to replace conscription for home defense. The results were: 80% of the population outside of Quebec favored the conscription act, 72% of the Quebec population opposed it. In view of the compact nature of the opposition, the government has implemented the plebiscite with prudence.

Cooperation with the U.S.A. took giant forward strides as the war proceeded. Both countries declared the St. Lawrence Waterways project desirable. The Canol and Alcan Highway projects underlined cooperation in the northwest. The respective legations of the two countries were elevated to the rank of embassies, and there was increasing awareness of the problems of common defense and common economic interests over wide areas. The old French city of Quebec, scene of two significant meetings between President Roosevelt and British Prime Minister Churchill (summers of 1943 and 1944), seemed to consecrate Allied unity.

In the autumn of 1944, the Canadian political situation remained complex: the definite Liberal decline in Quebec, Ontario, and Saskatchewan indicated that King's overwhelming majority might be reduced, but there was no definite indication as to the shape of the next House of Commons. However, it was economic reconstruction rather than political alignments that provided the main subjects of Canadian discussion in 1944.

Stakes in the Peace

Canada will emerge from World War II with a really superb industry, whose capacity to produce is extremely high in relation to the small population of the country. If industrial exports become as vital to Canadian economy as her farm products have been, Canada will be completely dependent for her welfare on world peace and prosperity.

She possesses certain well-defined assets: a model banking system; an intelligent policy of stimulating external trade; a thrifty, orderly, and well-educated people who are members of the far-flung British Commonwealth of Nations and who have, at the same time, the example of America's large-scale industry and unparalleled wealth immediately across their southern border. This fortunate configuration, together with the certainty of increased domestic mineral production, should suffice to ensure that any economic difficulties will be mere interruptions to a definite growth phase.

Canada possesses a lively sense of nationality, but her adhesion to the League of Nations was marked by loyalty and cooperation. Her American orientation has never been closer. Already experienced in three forms of historic cooperation — in the British Commonwealth, in North American fellowship, and in the League of Nations — she should be an ideal affiliate of an international organization. Moreover, she possesses a largeness of views, in international currency problems, for example, and in understanding the necessity of reciprocal economic relations between states, that should aid Canada in her future formulations of policy.

The notion of two peoples within Canada, so dramatized by outsiders, is scarcely as significant as the superficial view might indicate. The industrialization and urbanization of French Canada must create patterns conforming more closely to those of the external world, and the praiseworthy conservation of the traditional speech and manners of French Canada need not always take the political form it has so often assumed in recent years. There have been many decades of intimate collaboration between the English- and French-speaking inhabitants, and happily, in the long cycles of Canadian history, each association has proved progressively firmer.

EIRE

The Land and the People

Eire, the commonwealth that occupies 26 of the 32 counties of Ireland — the other 6 comprising Northern Ireland, a part of the United Kingdom — is chief heir to the legends of pathos and glory which crowd about the name of Ireland. There is a strange thing about the impact of Irish personality on the world: Ireland's great influence has been carried outward from the tiny homeland by the bodily emigration of Irishmen. Since the potato famine in 1846 (almost exactly a century ago), the island's population has fallen from 31% to about 8% of the British Isles, from 4% to 0.8% of Europe's. But the Irish are numerous, and disproportionately influential, in such British cities as Glasgow and Liverpool, in Canada, Australia, and Newfoundland, and above all in the U.S.A., where there are certainly more people of Irish descent than in Eire.

The Irish have been instrumental, among other things, in the preservation and spread of the Catholic faith throughout the English-speaking world. And many powerful families in the Catholic countries of Europe trace their ancestry to émigré Irish gentry of the 18th century, followers of the House of Stuart. Though Eire has remained neutral in World War II, it is estimated that there are 150,000 men from Eire in the British Army alone.

The Land. Eire, as distinct from the whole island, has only one land boundary, that separating her from Northern Ireland — a separation, incidentally, which she considers unnatural and unjust. For the rest, she is bounded by water: on the west, northwest, and southwest, by the Atlantic; on the east by the Irish Sea facing the north of England; on the southeast, by St. George's Channel facing Wales. Eire is Europe's far west: she is even closer to the American continent than is Portugal, being less than 1,900 miles from Newfoundland.

Eire, with an area of 26,601 square miles, is somewhat larger than West Virginia. The island of which she covers the greater part is rimmed by high hills and low mountains along the coasts; the center is a limestone plain. There are wide areas of bog and moorland, impossible to cultivate, but productive of peat (used as fuel). The only mineral deposits are small fields of inferior coal. Only 1.3% of Eire (less than in any other European country) is forested. Most of the island is a land of grass — one vast pastureland. The country has great natural beauty — in the green grasslands, the low eastern mountains, the romantic Lakes of Killarney, the wild and mournful cliffs of Connemara. The lush green of the landscape has given the land her name of the Emerald Isle.

This intense green results from the marine climate, generally cloudy and cool, with a heavy and fairly constant rainfall. Both winters and summers are mild, but the proximity of the ocean subjects the climate to sharp cyclic changes. In the cool phase, crop-yields fall off; in the warm phase, they shoot upward — and in the past the rise and fall of population corresponded startlingly to these cycles of weather.

The People. The Irish are the great Celtic people who in the 7th century were the most advanced group in northern Europe. The long series of invasions which followed the great period of Irish history has left traces of Saxon, Norman, Danish, and English blood in this Celtic people, especially in the east — the old "Pale of Settlement" of the Normans and English — where the people are largely of the same stock as the British. But racial and religious cleavages strike deep into Ireland's violent past: for 200 years before the opening of our century Irish Catholic tenant farmers struggled against British Protestant landlords. Without a knowledge of the deep hatreds thus engendered and still smoldering, the contemporary history of neither Eire nor Northern Ireland can be understood.

Eire, with the rest of Ireland, has suffered during the last century from one of the most drastic depopulations in history. In 1845 there were 6,000,000 people in what is now Eire; there are 2,989,000 today. The birthrate in recent years has been about 19, the death-rate 14. Infant mortality ranges from 66 to 73, about the same as in Scotland. But the increase in population, which should be 5% per decade, has been drained off by emigration. In the U.S.A. alone, in 1930 there were 744,000 persons born in Eire; in 1940, 572,000. And the revenue once derived from this great emigration — payments to shipping and travel bureaus and the remittances from emigrants which sustained many a poverty-stricken family — now play only a small part in Eire's economy.

Religion and Education. More than 90% of the people of Eire are Roman Catholics, most of the others Protestant Episcopalians. Elementary education is tuition-free and compulsory. Part of the instruction must be in the native Gaelic, which is also widely used in ordinary life, especially in the west country around Galway. Most high schools are private, and many are in the hands of the monastic orders. The more famous of the two universities, the University of Dublin (Trinity College), founded in 1591, counts many illustrious men among its alumni.

But Ireland's cultural contribution goes far beyond her formal education. Her folk songs and tales are of haunting beauty. The influence of the Abbey Theater in Dublin has reached around the world. And Irish literature has flourished out of all proportion to Ireland's population: one need only list the names of Swift, Steele, Congreve, Berkeley, Thomas Moore, Oscar Wilde, and in our own day, Synge, Yeats, Shaw, and Joyce. For economic reasons most of these writers settled in England, where their work has been sucked into the stream of another tradition.

The Nation's Economy

Agriculture. The Irish are excellent farmers. Yields per acre for the leading crops are far above the European average; production per man averages $600 annually — less than England's $850 but about the same as in Scotland and France. The leading crops are potatoes (3,500,000 tons), mangels (1,700,000), oats (700,000), wheat (500,000), sugar beets (400,000), and flax (over 6,000,000 pounds). Two-thirds of the people live in rural communities, and over half (52%) are employed in agriculture.

But cattle, pigs, and sheep are more important in the nation's agriculture than are crops. Eire's per capita production of milk and butter is markedly higher than Britain's. Her cattle number more than 4,000,000, sheep 3,000,000, and horses nearly 500,000. Some 4,200,000 tons of hay are harvested yearly to feed the stock. Pigs have declined from 1,000,000 in 1935 to 600,000 today, but they are of first-rate quality. Eire's river salmon are excellent (exported chiefly to England), but sea fisheries are unimportant, employing only 8,000 men.

COPYRIGHT, FIELD PUBLICATIONS

For a long time after its introduction from America in the 1700's, the potato — which is still the staple food of the Irish — formed almost the whole Irish diet. Thus the potato famine of 1846 not only caused widespread starvation but also started the mass emigration that has depopulated the country. Those who stayed at home determined to end the British absentee landlord system, the cause of many of the peasants' woes. Step by step they won their fight, so that today Eire is largely a country of small holdings. What vestiges of this old system still remain appear to be doomed.

Industry. Eire's industry is a case of arrested development. The country has practically no coal and, despite the ambitious Shannon River scheme, insufficient water-power. She must import both fuel and minerals for any large-scale industrial development. About a sixth of the people are employed in industry, but per capita investment in machinery is the lowest of any north European nation (only a seventh of Britain's).

Processed foods and light consumers goods, making use of local (usually rural) products, are the most important Irish manufactures: sugar-beet refining, flour-milling, preparation of (imported) pipe tobacco, and above all, whiskeys and Dublin stout. Next in importance are woolen textiles and clothing, manufactured chiefly at Dublin and Cork.

National Income and Finance. Despite political independence, Eire's economy is of necessity closely linked with Britain's. The unit of currency, the Irish pound, is roughly equivalent to the British pound; both were worth $4.86 in peacetime and have a fixed ratio of $4.04 at present. Furthermore, since practically all her trade (especially during the war) is with Britain, neutral Eire has been obliged to accept Britain's wartime inability to pay cash and has run up in London "blocked sterling" accounts — payable only after the war — to the amount of $593,880,000, five times the amount of money in circulation in Eire. This procedure, of course, makes Eire's financial future dependent on Britain's solvency.

At home Eire has pursued a conservative financial policy. Because there has been no wartime boom, money in circulation has risen only moderately, from $78,376,000 in 1939 to $132,000,000 at the end of 1942. Taxation has risen only from $130,000,000 to $184,000,000. Eire's national debt (about $140,000,000) is only a third of the annual national income, in contrast to Britain's, which is more than twice her national income, because of the war.

The wartime boom in employment and wages has drawn many workers from Eire to England despite blackouts and bombs. In 1941, 35,000 went, in 1942, over 40,000. Yet at the end of 1942 Eire still had 83,000 unemployed, about a quarter of the industrial population.

Foreign Trade. Even in normal times foreign trade is mostly with the United Kingdom (including Northern Ireland), which takes 90% of Eire's exports and supplies over 55% of her imports. This is the central fact in Eire's trade picture. The annual volume of this trade — $134,000,000 in imports and $126,000,000 in exports — is high for the small population, but it must be remembered that most of it, being concentrated on this one neighbor, would have been considered internal British trade before 1922, when Eire achieved independence.

Besides the imports from the United Kingdom, Eire normally receives grain from Canada, Australia, and Argentina; bricks from Belgium; metals and machinery from Germany; and cotton and miscellaneous manufactures from the U.S.A. She also imports corn, coal, textiles, tea, and hops. Her leading exports are cattle, horses, ham, bacon, pork, and butter.

History: 1914-1944

The whole Irish island of 32 counties was part of the United Kingdom of Great Britain when war broke out in 1914. For many decades, however, the mass of the inhabitants of the 26 southern counties (today known as Eire) had voted for "home rule," that is, for a dominion form of government within the British Empire. The majority of Protestants in Ireland and the Conservative party in Great Britain had resisted this demand; but when the war began, the leader of the Irish Home Rule (Nationalist) party pledged Ireland to the support of Britain's war effort.

The more ardent Irish Nationalists, believing that "England's difficulty is Ireland's opportunity," refused to abide by this pledge. Under the leadership of Padraic Pearse, an idealist schoolteacher, and James Connolly, a veteran Socialist, the Irish Republic was proclaimed on Easter, 1916. The British at once suppressed the rebellion, executing many of the insurgents — an act that made the Republicans violent with indignation.

Forming themselves into the Sinn Fein Party (Sinn Fein means Ourselves Alone in Gaelic), the Republicans now increased their demands. They proclaimed the existence of the Irish Republic, naming as President Eamon de Valera, an American-born rebel at that time imprisoned by the British, and as Vice-President Arthur Griffith, sponsor of the revival of Gaelic as the official Irish tongue.

1918-1921. Seventy-three Irish Republicans won victories in the 1918 elections for the British Parliament (81 seats had formerly been held by Irish Nationalists). But the 73 Republicans refused to sit in London; instead, they formed a parliament of their own: the Dail Eireann.

Britain again acted to suppress this latest insurrection, with 60,000 British troops. When these forces entered Ireland, they were opposed by a motley, exalted group of rebels led by Michael Collins. Realizing that regular soldiery could not cope with the guerrilla tactics of the Irish, the British dispatched a special corps, recruited chiefly from non-commissioned officer veterans of the World War, who, because of their costume, were called the "Black and Tans." In addition, the British sent a special élite corps, paid a pound a day, to ferret out rebel "gunmen" and to make raids on suspected Irish civilians.

The struggle deepened in bitterness. The reprisals imposed by the British resulted in a closer unity of the rebels into the Irish Republican Army. British soldiers killed the Lord Mayor of Cork, and his successor, McSwiney, died in the course of a hunger strike in a British jail. After "Bloody Sunday," in 1921, when the British soldiery fired into a football crowd, it became clear that an arrangement had to be concluded.

On July 9, 1921, a truce was offered in London, and on December 6, the Irish Free State was proclaimed. The 26 southern counties of Ireland were embraced in this new area, the 6 northeastern counties remaining within the British parliamentary régime. The Irish Free State was now a British dominion, but it was permitted its own parliament (Dail Eireann) and its independence was almost complete. However, the Dail Eireann ratified the treaty by only 64–57. The Irish Free State was to pay Britain $25,000,000 yearly as compensation for lands ceded by British landlords to the Irish peasantry under the Land Acts of 1870–1909, until $495,000,000 was paid.

Civil War and Parliamentary Boycott: 1923–1927. De Valera opposed the treaty, demanding complete independence and no compensatory payments for the land. A civil war erupted between the Republicans and those who favored the treaty, and the struggle exceeded in ferocity the earlier resistance against the British. In May 1923 the civil war ended, and in the 1925 elections the treaty-supporters gained a majority (63–44) over the Republicans.

But the Republicans refused to sit in Parliament. President Cosgrave strove for conciliation with England and for economic unity with Ireland's best customer, Britain. A businessman's government replaced fervid idealism. Finances were reorganized. De Valera, head of the Republicans, now ordered his followers to take their seats in the Dail Eireann, and from that time (1927) until 1932 the Republicans steadily gained at the expense of the Cosgrave group, whose conservative policies they constantly criticized.

Supremacy of De Valera: 1932–1937. After arriving at an understanding with the Irish Labor party, in 1932 de Valera was returned to power. He proceeded to abolish the Royal veto over legislation, the Oath of Allegiance to the British King, and he ended the transfer of land annuities to England, insisting that these sums be paid into the treasury of the Irish Free State.

England opened up a trade war against the Irish. While both countries suffered, the loss to Britain was small while little Ireland was deprived of $88,000,000 yearly. De Valera countered with a protective tariff in behalf of Ireland's infant industries. He encouraged beet-sugar production, and he made Gaelic (along with English) compulsory in the schools. But Irish agriculture and stockraising could not weather the contest. A trade agreement in 1935 restored Irish prosperity.

The following year de Valera seized the abdication of Edward VIII as the occasion to make the Irish Free State into a veritable republic named Eire, with the British King as merely an external symbol. In 1937 the constitution was adopted. De Valera retained the presidency, which was valid for a seven-year term.

Effective Independence: 1937–1944. In April 1938 relations with Britain reached a stable basis. Eire paid $50,000,000 as a release from land payments; British naval bases in Eire were transferred to the Eire government; and liberal trading arrangements were concluded. However, de Valera insisted that until the 6 northeastern counties were made part of Eire, full economic or political cooperation with Britain would be impossible. The British replied that the 6 counties in question would not agree to incorporation within Eire.

Meanwhile the Irish steered their own course in international affairs. They exhibited a lively sympathy with General Franco in his rebellion against the Spanish Republicans. The Protestant press in the 6 northeastern counties claimed that clerical influences were responsible for Eire's foreign policy; they grew increasingly cold.

When World War II broke out, Eire declared herself neutral. Holding fast to this policy, despite the economic loss involved, de Valera insisted that the Irish people regarded neutrality as the only humane course. Eire protested America's entry into Northern Ireland as an "invasion," and in 1944 de Valera won a clear majority, no longer requiring Labor party support for his control of the Dail Eireann. American involvement in the war has failed to change Eire's attitude of strict neutrality. Britain has insisted on protection from German espionage in Eire which, she averred, was significant.

Foreign Affiliations. Eire has followed a lone path. Though she is economically part of Great Britain, in diplomacy and in spirit she is poles apart. American influence, considered a logical outcome of the large Irish population in the U.S.A., has steadily decreased as Eire has developed her own Gaelic ideals and her own national culture. The large-scale emigration, once characteristic of Irish history, has ceased, except for the groups who have settled in Britain.

If the country's foreign policy shows any orientation, it is in accordance with the attitudes of the Holy See. Since the Vatican proclaims peace as an ideal supreme above all human contentions, its messages have profoundly moved the Irish people, who are overwhelmingly Roman Catholic. The Germans, of course, have labored to exploit Eire's unique international situation, but with indifferent success.

Stakes in the Peace

Eire is a pastoral and agricultural land that depends on British markets. She has a cash balance in London whose repayment depends on future British prosperity. Hence, whatever Eire's political attitudes, the country's future depends on British recovery. Should Britain pass through economic crises, Eire might be compelled to stimulate cottage industries and other forms of industrialization. A consequent impoverishment of the people would not probably debar this action, since the Eire government has shown that it prefers spiritual rewards to material well-being. How long such abnegation can be sustained, is not yet determinable.

Unresolved as a political and economic issue are the 6 northeastern counties. Economically they are an essential part of Ireland, but the religious differences between the two peoples will have to lose their political significance if any satisfactory amalgamation is to be made. So long as Eire regards the predominantly Protestant north as a deprivation, she will probably place her local situation above world affairs.

NEW ZEALAND

The Land and the People

A self-governing Dominion of the British Commonwealth of Nations, New Zealand is one of the most enlightened political and social democracies in the world, with an enviably high standard of living. If she were not so remote in her South Pacific islands, she would probably be known also for the great beauty of her country, as a paradise for vacationists. Doubtless after the war Americans may come to know her better on both counts.

The Land. New Zealand occupies two large islands, North Island and South Island, and a few smaller adjacent ones (103,772 square miles in all), lying 1,200 miles southeast of Australia across the Tasman Sea. Although Australia is the nearest large land-mass — no non-Australian port of any importance is less than 3,000 miles away — the two dominions differ markedly in climate, scenery, economy, and culture, and both Australians and New Zealanders view with a mixture of amusement and annoyance the world's tendency to bracket them neatly together.

A volcanic mountain chain runs through the center of the islands. Earthquakes have been frequent and sometimes severe; the one that destroyed the famous Pink and White Terraces in 1886 was among the greatest convulsions of nature on record. The whole country has a dramatic beauty, abounding in hot springs, rushing torrents and waterfalls, lovely bays, and snowcapped mountains towering over deep-green pasture lands. The moist climate (wholly unlike the Australian) and the lack of a true winter except in the extreme south — New Zealand lies wholly in the south temperate zone — make these islands each as truly an Emerald Isle as Ireland. It is a perfect climate for both health and energy. The Australians find this lovely land a tourist's dream in peacetime — although the good-natured rivalry between the sister dominions scarcely allows them to admit it.

The People. New Zealand is strikingly underpopulated, with 1,541,000 whites and 93,000 Maoris. Even so, immigration is strictly regulated and Asiatic immigration not permitted at all. About half the people live in towns and cities, most important of which are Auckland (population 217,000) and Wellington, the capital (154,000), both on North Island; and Christchurch (134,000) and Dunedin (82,500) on South Island.

The white New Zealanders are of British stock, largely Scotch. Reserved, industrious, liberal-minded yet observant of tradition, they are British not only in race but in character — they are sometimes said to be more British than the British. Certainly their psychology is more British than that of the Australians, despite similar political attitudes. Of all the dominions, New Zealand has the closest cultural ties with the mother country.

The Maoris, the aboriginal Polynesian people, related to the Hawaiians, Samoans, and Tahitians, form the only racial minority. A powerful, belligerent, and intelligent people, they fought hard against the white settlers for decades, but have now been completely reconciled. They are respected citizens, with full rights, and occasionally even intermarry with the whites. Unlike most Polynesian peoples under European dominancy, they have doubled in numbers.

Indeed, both whites and Maoris are increasing, so that New Zealand's population should be well over 2,000,000 by 1980. The birthrate is fairly high: 22.8 per thousand among whites and 44.8 among Maoris. The deathrate for whites is the lowest known, averaging 9.5 and sometimes dropping as low as 8.2. Infant mortality among whites is also the lowest in the world, 30 per thousand. Among the Maoris, both the death and the infant mortality rates are higher (as is the birthrate), the former standing at 20.5, the latter ranging from 87 to 123. Life expectancy among whites again is one of the highest on record, with an average of 65.5 years for men and 68.5 for women.

Religion and Education. About 87% of the people are Protestants, about 13% Catholics. The leading Protestant denominations are Anglican,

Presbyterian, and Methodist, in the order named.

Education is tuition-free and the law making it compulsory is enforced. Secondary education is widely diffused. The excellent University of New Zealand, consisting of four colleges in the four leading cities, enrolls 5,500 students. There is a well-developed system of schools for the Maoris.

New Zealand culture, in literature as in other things, is more British than is the Australian. New Zealanders are serious readers, but in spite of their distinction in academic work, they have not as yet developed a strong native literature. Their great cultural contribution has been in social thought and practice: their strikingly advanced social legislation and their bold resourcefulness in dealing with the problem of a racial minority.

The Nation's Economy

Agriculture. A large part of New Zealand, some 20,000 square miles, is still forest land; pastoral lands sown to grass cover 26,000 square miles; and only some 3,000 square miles are under cultivation.

The products of the pasture lands are most important in the national economy. There are 34,000,-000 sheep (more than 17 per person), 4,500,000 cattle, 2,000,000 dairy cows (one to every person), and about 600,000 pigs.

In proportion to population, New Zealand leads the world in 4 basic commodities, all products of animal husbandry: cheese, of which she produces 6% of the world's supply; milk; butter, 5% of the world's supply; and meat, produced in the enormous amount of 700,000 tons, nearly half lamb and mutton, about two-fifths beef and veal. Not even Australia or Argentina comes near that per capita showing.

The large pastoral holdings of 5,000 acres or over from which these animal products largely come number some 1,050 out of a total of 84,000, and cover 40% of the occupied area. It is on the 53,000 small holdings of under 200 acres, covering only 9% of the occupied land, that the varied subsistence crops are grown. The leading products of these farms are wheat, oats, barley, tobacco, hay, and fruit, for the last of which New Zealand enjoys a good British market.

Industry and Mining. Until recently New Zealand was little industrialized, importing six-sevenths of her manufactured goods. But industry, which increased 57% from 1929 to 1940, has been further stimulated by war needs and the shortage of imports. Now two-fifths of the people live in the principal towns, and the old proportion of 105,000 industrial to 150,000 farm workers has altered in favor of industry. To meet war conditions, the range of manufacture, which used to be fairly well confined to consumers goods and food processing, has been widened. The total value of industrial products is now about $500,000,000 yearly.

Coal mines, on the west coast of South Island, yield about 2,800,000 tons annually, and there is a small production of gold and silver. The abundant waterpower, potentially as great as Switzerland's, is only about 10% utilized.

Finance. The unit of currency is the pound, worth about $3.23. During the war, money in circulation has increased from about $62,000,000 to about $100,-000,000, the price level has risen 50%, and the cost of living 15%. Both commercial bank deposits and savings accounts have mounted steeply, until savings are now over $200 per person.

The budget is divided into four categories: ordinary, social security, public works (a capital investment), and war. The first three have shown a conservative increase; the war budget, naturally, has risen sharply, from about $23,000,000 to about $470,000,000 ($290 per capita). The total debt, foreign and domestic, has swelled from about $978,690,000 in 1939 to about $1,498,720,000, now standing at approximately $900 per person.

Foreign Trade. In peacetime, New Zealand's foreign trade, some $220,000,000 in exports and $213,000,000 in imports annually, showed a per capita rate of $300, the highest in the world — twice Australia's and a third greater than that of so lively a trader as Belgium. Some 93% of her exports come from her dairies and ranches — cheese and other dairy products, meat, and nearly 1,000,000 bales of wool; another 3% is gold. The leading imports are iron and steel, motor cars, textiles, machinery, petroleum, sugar, and tea. This is mostly Empire trade, Great Britain taking 85% of exports, and furnishing, along with other countries of the Empire, 75% of imports. During the war, exports have remained fairly stable, but imports have dropped a third.

History: 1914-1944

New Zealand, geographically remote from world centers, entered into the thick of international affairs in World War I, when she sent her expeditionary forces to the aid of Britain.

In 1912 the Reform party, really a conservative party, had come to power after 21 years of rule by the Progressive Party, which represented the liberal traditions of the Englishman, John Stuart Mill, and the American "single-taxer," Henry George. When the war broke out, the Reform Party gave the Progressives some seats in a coalition cabinet. The latter accepted Reform leadership on patriotic grounds and because of the impressive personality of the Reform leader, Massey.

During the war and for three years after, New Zealand was prosperous, as she had been without serious interruption since 1895 — one of the longest cycles of prosperity in commercial history. But in 1921, while the world at large was in an upward cycle, New Zealand entered a period of depression.

The farmers, entitled by law to 28% more votes than city dwellers for the same population, supported the Reform Party; and since the Arbitration Acts, as they were administered, generally favored Labor, the workers too tended for a long time to favor the Reform party instead of the Progressives.

At the end of the war, New Zealand received a mandate over German Samoa and later took over the mandate of the Pacific island of Nauru, rich in phosphates for fertilizer. But against this, she had a debt of $275,000,000, or over $1,000 for every family. The inflation set in motion by this debt resulted in a boom in land values as spectacular as that in Florida in 1924. When the bubble burst, the farmers owed $700,000,-000, and the entire community trembled on the edge of economic ruin. In addition, land settlement for the returned soldiers cost another $150,000,000. The Progressives, sensing disaster, withdrew from the coalition. They felt that with peacetime taxes — local and national — amounting to over $400 a family, public opinion would turn out the Reform government.

Despite the crash in land values, the elections of 1922 returned the Reform party by a bare majority; but the young Labor party was the surprise of the day, mustering unexpected strength. In 1925 Prime Minister Massey died; a younger Reform leader, Coates, succeeded him.

At the ensuing elections, Coates played upon the public's fear of revolutionary strikes, especially of the port workers. Despite his party's consistent economic failures, he was thus stampeded into power. But once the elections were over, Coates had to face further economic disturbances. For though he made an impressive showing at Imperial conferences and aided actively in British tariff preference schemes, he faced worsening business conditions at home.

In 1928 Australia displayed signs of crisis before the world depression, and New Zealand was soon in a similar plight. In 1931 the Statute of Westminster fortified New Zealand's status as a completely self-governing dominion and soon thereafter prosperity reappeared with British recovery, the first genuine upturn in twelve years. Despite the gradual recovery, unemployment remained relatively high, much higher, percentally, than in Australia.

The older Reform party now called itself Nationalist and in the 1935 elections it confronted the Labor party, which in the previous decade had shown signs of amazing growth. At the polls, Labor, led by M. J. Savage, swept the country with 53 seats in Parliament, compared with 20 for the Nationalists, and 7 Independents. This was the first Labor government in New Zealand's history.

Labor in Power: 1935–1944. The Savage government initiated a far-reaching policy of State Socialism, including an elaborate social security program. In 1938 the voters returned it to power with substantially the same majority.

In view of the growing menace of Japan, both parties, Labor and Nationalist, agreed on an expanded defense program. When War broke out in Europe in 1939, New Zealand immediately joined Britain in a declaration of war on Germany.

In July 1940, Prime Minister Fraser, who had succeeded Savage on the latter's death, announced the formation of a broadened National war cabinet, including two members of the opposition, Hamilton and Coates. The defense of Crete in 1941, largely by New Zealanders under their commander, General Freyberg, focused world attention on the little country's heroic rôle in the war.

The events following Pearl Harbor (December 1941) exposed New Zealand to the grave danger of a Japanese invasion. With the battle of the Coral Sea (1942) this threat disappeared, and with the shift of the Americans in the Pacific to an offensive rôle, New Zealand played a part — the U.S.A. expedition to the island of Tarawa was largely prepared in New Zealand.

As the war went on, socialization also proceeded apace; the Labor-dominated coalition cabinet persisted in its program of progressive State Socialism. Realizing that such a transformation required popular ratification, since otherwise it would seem that Labor was using the war emergency as a cover for basic social changes, the government held elections late in 1943. The results were a setback for Labor; its majority was reduced to 10; only the soldier vote saved it from defeat. The opposition asserted that, as they had a majority of the civilian votes, they should really share power instead of being content with token posts. The Fraser government, however, rejected their demand.

Stakes in the Peace

Although New Zealand, like Australia, has since 1939 advanced industrially with seven-league boots, her basic problems have not changed. Her exports are chiefly to Britain: nothing can replace the importance of exports of lamb, butter, cheese, and other pastoral and farm products in the Dominion's prosperity. Hence her currency and investment policy cannot subsist without an extension of the British market.

Full employment and a rising standard of living, quite unlike the situation in Australia, are vitally bound up with trade with Britain. Perhaps at some remote future date, New Zealand may have other clients, but such new outlets are not her immediate problem.

Internally, the condition of the small farmer can stand considerable improvement. Certainly, a higher level of prosperity among the small farmers would, by increasing their purchasing power, be an important prop to urban light industries. Externally, New Zealand's security can be found only in an international organization. Among her intelligent and forward-looking population, there are no isolationist elements.

[For map of New Zealand, see page 147.]

UNION OF SOUTH AFRICA

The Land and the People

Lying at the southernmost extremity of Africa, this important British Dominion extends over 472,550 square miles — about a sixth the area of the U.S.A. Her administrative capital is Pretoria, her legislative capital, Capetown. Four principal provinces compose the dominion: Orange River and Transvaal, the two former Boer republics (north); Natal (southeast); and Cape Colony (south).

The Union of South Africa is basically subtropical. The *veldt* (a great plateau of plains) in Transvaal and Orange, to the north, includes uplands used for livestock and dairying; but with black soils valuable in mixed farming, subtropical produce is common even here. The crops generally remind one of the "Old South" of the U.S.A.

Bush country prevails in the northwest part of the Union. In the southeast uplands and the fertile, well-watered coastal plain of Natal, the climate is surprisingly like central California's. Capetown, in the extreme south, lies in a coastal plain shut off from the mainland by the ranges and faults of the mesalike Karroos. The climate in the southwest is affected by the Kalahari desert, which is almost as fearful as the Sahara.

Rainfall varies considerably. Less than 10 inches in the southwest desert region, it is from 10 to 25 inches in most of the farming districts, and becomes abundant (up to 40 inches) in the Natal area.

The People. The latest estimate of population of the Union was 10,400,000, distributed as follows: Europeans 2,188,000; Asiatics and mixed races (including some 300,000 East Indians) 783,000; natives (Negroes) 7,250,000. Europeans thus constituted 21%.

The home language of the Europeans varied according to the group. About 56% were Boers (people of mixed Dutch and French Huguenot origin) who spoke Afrikaans, a Dutch tongue altered in the Cape. Some 39% spoke English; 2.5% spoke both Afrikaans and English at home; 1% spoke German; and 1% spoke Yiddish. The farmers are mostly Boers; the industrial, commercial, and financial groups, English-speaking. Europeans largely congregate in the cities: they number 257,000 out of the 520,000 in Johannesburg; 173,000 out of 344,000 in Capetown; and 95,000 out of 260,000 in the capital city of Natal, Durban.

Race Situation. The "race problem" dominates every aspect of life in the Union. Though Europeans are numerous, Negroes number almost 70% and most of the mixed peoples are predominantly Negro. Hence, the laws of the Union are reminiscent of Georgia or Mississippi. However, these Negroes are native and only recently they had their own kingdoms; furthermore, their proportion is greater than anywhere in the American "Black Belt," except for some rare counties. As a consequence, the Negroes and Asiatics have been increasingly insisting upon changes in the system that grants social privileges, social services, and educational positions to the Europeans; that provides wage differentials to the disadvantage of the Negroes; and that protects white labor from supersession by cheaper native labor. No other country has worked out a system so thorough-going, because in no other country are the racial proportions and situations remotely similar. In Brazil the problem was solved by a refusal to admit its existence.

The native populations are powerful, tall, Bantu Negro peoples. There is a small group of Bushmen (remnants of one of the most interesting prehistoric peoples), of Hottentots, and of Zulus. The Asiatics are mostly East Indians, and there are some Arab and Hamite traders.

Most of the whites are Boers, that people who never yielded when the British came but preferred to trek into the interior as national groups in order to safeguard their independence. Though they surrendered to Britain in 1902, by 1910 they were restored to civic domination by the British Liberal party, which regarded their subjugation as shameful.

The mass of the British inhabitants are English as in Australia; — not Scotch, as in Canada and New Zealand. The Jewish element, large and active, was important in developing the leading mining industry; hence, it has pioneer status.

Among the white population of the Union, the "poor white" of the American South has been duplicated. Too poor to engage in farming for himself, he is too proud to work for other white farmers alongside the native Negro. World War II has (temporarily) taken care of this problem by providing urban employment.

The birthrate among the whites was fairly high (25.2 per thousand), the deathrate very low (9.6) and infant mortality only 52. Without taking into account increases by immigration, the forecast for the whites was an increase of 30% by 1970.

Religion and Education. Among the Europeans, over 91% are Protestant, 4% Catholic, and 4% Jewish. The Dutch Reformed Church leads among the Boers, the Church of England among the British. Among the non-Europeans, including Asiatics and Negroes, 40% are Protestant and about 1% Catholic. Buddhists, Confucians, Hindus, Mohammedans number altogether 200,000. Most of the others retain their aboriginal religious practices.

Some 394,000 European children attend school — practically all. Fully 649,000 Asiatic and Negro children also attend school — which, while not comparable in ratio to the whites, is nevertheless high and probably includes most of the children of those natives who are included in the European economy.

The five universities in the Union, all of high rank, enroll 11,000 students. South African scholars are distinguished in economics, and in anthropology, archaeology, and geology they have had every reason to make excellent contributions. Literature flourishes in the Union, but much of it is concentrated on local color and quaint speech, not yet having achieved a mature, national idiom.

See map on page 346.

The Nation's Economy

Mining. For her riches in gold, diamonds, and other metals, the Union of South Africa is one of the treasure troves of the world. Known primarily as a gold producer, she accounts for 40% of the world's supply. Gold mining, with 400,000 employees, provides 30% of the Union's revenues and 70% of her exports. Her 1941 production reached 14,300,000 fine ounces — at U.S.A. buying prices, $500,000,000 — and mining dividends exceeded $100,000,000. Not only is her share of gold production extremely high, but gold production has become increasingly profitable because the price of gold has increased from $20.67 to $35 per fine ounce in the U.S.A. and from 84 to 168 shillings in Britain. Since 1929, gold prices have increased in terms of national currencies, and the war has accentuated this tendency everywhere.

The famous Kimberley diamond field in Transvaal began as a boom in the 1890's and even today the Diamond Syndicate in London controls the world's price and supply on the basis of its South African production. The Union's annual production, $8,000,-000, constitutes 75% of the world output.

The Union is also an important supplier of platinum, chrome, and tungsten. Her antimony (158,000 tons yearly), silver (45,000), copper ore (13,600), steel (314,000), and iron ore (396,000), while of aggregate consequence, are less important than her asbestos (27,300) and coal (20,000,000).

Industry. Because of these mineral riches, capital has been less attracted to industry, though the Union has had a sound basis for its rapid growth, despite small water-power development and the lack of petroleum. Prior to 1930, per capita machine investment was only $3.50. Recently, however, industry has gained swiftly, and it now employs 350,000 (of whom 150,000 are white). There is a new steel industry, pig iron and iron alloys are active, and engineering manufactures amount to $210,000,000 yearly.

In 1933, industry had reached the point where national wealth received $280,000,000 annually as an increment from manufactured goods. The gross production was $555,000,000 and 229,000 were employed. Thus, industrial employment has grown a third in ten years (armaments are minor), and employment in both industry and mining has risen by 63% since 1929.

Agriculture. South African Europeans, however, are on the whole farmers and stockraisers. Whereas mining and industry are more important for export, agriculture and pastoral activity are more important for the internal economy. Corn production averages 2,000,000 tons (a third higher in 1938, but only half in 1941). Cane sugar, especially in Natal, reaches 4,500,000 and more. Potatoes are moderately produced, wine is exported to the British Empire (which gives it needed preference), and wheat is insufficient for domestic needs. In some respects, agriculture is backward, the corn yield being one of the lowest in the world. With 22,500 arable square miles, farming should be able to supply domestic needs. So far as the natives are concerned, however, food production is inadequate.

Livestock is abundant, with 12,000,000 cattle, 38,000,000 sheep, a million goats, a million pigs, and nearly 800,000 horses. The wool clip (which is exported) reaches the huge figure of 125,000 tons — 7% of the world's supply. Meat is abundant, with 190,000 tons of beef and veal, 62,000 of mutton, and 20,000 of pig products. Despite the Dutch origin of most farmers, cheese and butter are comparatively small.

Foreign Trade. The Union is a great trading Dominion: in 1938, exports were $489,000,000 and imports $485,000,000. On a per capita basis (exports $49.00, imports $48.60), she is one of the leading traders of the world. In 1938, gold accounted for 74% of exports, wool 9%, diamonds 2%, hides and skins 2%. Imports, in order of importance, were automobiles and trucks, machinery, hardware, cotton goods, electrical goods.

Britain purchased 85% of the exports. Imports were supplied by Britain 41%, other parts of the British Empire 8%; and among other nations, U.S.A. 18%, Germany 5%, Japan 4%.

Finance. For a long time the position of the Union was unique. In the period ending in the early 1930's, she was the only land that derived as much as 59% of her income from exports or from foreign capital invested in her enterprises, and that paid out 60% of all her disbursements for imports or remittances of funds to the outside world. (Compare this to the U.S.A., whose revenue from exports and capital receipts is only some 8% of the national income, and whose payments for imports and remittances abroad are only 6%.) No other country even approached this proportion.

She was also the only land of which as much as 23% of the national wealth was held by foreigners, and of which over 10% of the whole national income was annually exported to foreign investors as dividends and interest. The capital investment of Europeans in the Union was computed by Prof. Frankel, a South African, as $2,560,000,000 — perhaps the greatest investment on earth for such a population ($250 per capita).

During World War II, the Union could not receive sufficient imports from Britain; thus she reduced her indebtedness from £103,000,000 to £7,000,000 (in other words, the surplus of her gold exports over her few imports from Britain). Thus, the Union's international exchange position has materially changed. Nevertheless, she still depends on the outside world for most of her consumers items.

Comparatively speaking, prices have not advanced greatly during the war. Living costs rose an eighth, wholesale prices a fourth (to the end of 1942). Money in circulation doubled (from £19,300,000 to £39,600,000), but the reserve bank assets of gold and exchange have this issue covered twice over. In 1941, the Union's credit in London was on a 3.18% basis, or first-rate. Bank deposits were $1,000,000,000 in 1941, savings $200,000,000. It is not possible to prorate these figures per inhabitant because of the contrasting economic levels of the blacks and the whites and the difficulty of determining to what extent the native population is part of a money economy.

During the war, the costs of government rose from £49,000,000 to £102,000,000, the internal debt from £278,000,000 to £416,000,000.

Special Race Situation. Since the Union's future is so bound up with the race question, the following data may prove useful. As of 1934, of the 66,000 natives in industries, half received from $2.50 to $3.80 weekly, 43% received from $3.80 to $4.60 weekly, and 7%, in some exceptional cases, received as much as $5.85 weekly. The 20,000 natives in agricultural work for Europeans received about $3 weekly. But European laborers, for example in the building trades, averaged $30 weekly (or $5 more than then prevailed in prosperous Australia). In mining, European laborers received an average $36.50 weekly. The ratio of skilled to unskilled labor in Western Europe was (in wages) about 7 to 5; in the Union of South Africa, the ratio of white to native labor was from 6 to 1 to 8 to 1. Generally speaking, every calculation supports this proportion, whether of income per head or in specific trades.

History: 1914-1944

The Union of South Africa, as part of the British Empire, was an Allied belligerent in World War I. Nevertheless, public opinion in the country was divided, and in 1914 the Boers rebelled under Christian de Wet. The Nationalist party, led by General Hertzog and ex-President Steyn of the former Orange Free State, condoned the insurgents by refusing to censure them. Three years later, this party, now wholly a Boer grouping, again called for an independent republic.

At the close of the war, Hertzog went to Versailles to present his demands. He insisted, as a minimum, that independence be restored to the two former Boer republics: the Transvaal and the Orange Free State. Prime Minister Botha, however, strongly favored the tie with Britain, and opposed Hertzog. When Botha died soon after, Jan C. Smuts, another former Boer general, succeeded him both as Prime Minister and as chief of the pro-British South African party.

Meanwhile, the formation of a Labor party in Great Britain had stimulated South African workers, particularly those of British origin, to form a Labor party of their own. When Smuts called a new election in 1920, he was returned to office by only a slight margin. He proceeded to effect a coalition with Labor and with the Unionists, who favored affiliation with Britain (subsequently absorbing the latter). Smuts' following among the Boers diminished: the dissenters were infuriated at the idea of being associated with an old, outspokenly pro-Empire group, the Unionist party.

The post-war depression affected the center of gold mining, the Witwatersrand, and in 1922 this region witnessed the worst strikes in South African history. When the unrest threatened to develop into a social insurrection, the Prime Minister intervened and pitilessly repressed it. Because of the severity of the repression involving bloodshed, the Labor party deserted Smuts' coalition, and, to avenge their comrades who had fallen in the strikes, joined with the Dutch Nationalists. The Labor party dropped its Socialist platform and the Nationalists their republican demands, so that both could combine against Smuts.

General Hertzog in Power: 1924–1939. In 1924 General Hertzog defeated Smuts at the polls and began a fifteen-year tenure of office as Prime Minister. At first he had some Labor ministers in the cabinet, but the presence of these pro-Britain elements did not prevent him from proclaiming Afrikaans (Cape Dutch) as an official state language. The MacDonald Labor government in Britain assented to this action.

At the 1926 Imperial Conference in London, Hertzog's conduct was mild: his nationalism could not be too truculent because his majority depended on the South African Labor party. In 1929, however, he appealed to the country and made substantial gains, while Labor suffered a sharp decline in votes. Hertzog was now able to reduce the number of Labor men in cabinet posts, and in 1931 the coalition with the Labor party ended. The South African opposition party of Smuts, aware of the growth of Nationalist sentiment among the Boers, based itself increasingly on English support, along with that of the minority Jewish population.

The country was plagued by the recurrent question of the Asiatics (mainly East Indians). In 1924 Smuts had attempted to repatriate them, and now the government enacted "class area" bills for the segregation of Asiatics. When the government of India protested this humiliation of Asiatics, it was ended — temporarily. At the same time, the government adopted conventions with the Portuguese in Portuguese East Africa, providing for the "recruitment" of native labor to work in the ports at transshipping South African products. Forced labor of (Portuguese) Mozambique Negroes and coolie labor of Asiatics became two accessories of South African economy.

In 1931 the Statute of Westminster made the Union of South Africa a completely self-governing dominion within the British Commonwealth of Nations. In the same year, Great Britain suspended the gold standard. The Union of South Africa had been hard hit by the world depression, but when her principal export, gold, rose in price in London from 84 shillings to 112 shillings an ounce, the country boomed again. In 1932 South Africa left the gold standard. When the U.S.A. in 1934 also raised the price of gold by 70%, a speculative mania swept the Johannesburg Stock Exchange.

The example of a National government in Great Britain proved attractive. In 1935 Smuts' South African party and Hertzog's Nationalist party coalesced to form the United party, reducing the opposition to mere fragments. The first fruit of this union was the 1936 Representation of Natives Act, which generally diminished the rights of the native black population and which, by a system of indirect representation permitting the natives to choose only white electors, practically disenfranchised the natives in the Cape Province. Despite an active government policy of segregation, however, the profits obtainable from employing natives (who outnumbered the whites by 7 to 2) at a sixth the wages of Europeans proved too tempting; and fully 560,000 natives were found living outside "native areas." The government made some attempts at land reform in the Transkeian territories, but these were not far-reaching enough to improve the natives' economy.

In the 1930's Fascist groupings, such as the Grey Shirts, arose in the country, and, in the former German Southwest Africa, there were even Brown Shirts of the Nazi type. Antisemitism became rampant, leading to physical assaults on Jews. A cabinet minister, Otto Pirow, formed "Special Service Battalions" on the Nazi pattern, but later when the international situation became threatening, he found it expedient to withdraw his sponsorship.

The Germans exploited the hatred by the more backward Boers of the British, of Labor, of the Jews, of the Negroes, and of the Asiatics, but they did not find the better-educated Boers as responsive as they had hoped. A broad liberal trend was gaining ground. And yet, in Johannesburg some 40% of the police force belonged to subversive, pro-Fascist units. The social situation by no means improved when a panic in gold shares in April 1937 punctured the optimism that had been engendered by excessive prosperity.

Hertzog appealed to the electorate in 1938. The United party won 111 seats; the extreme Nationalists, led by Malan, 27; the uncompromisingly pro-British Dominion party, a mere 8; while Labor collapsed to 3.

South Africa and World War II: 1939–1944. When war broke out in September 1939, Hertzog refused to consider South Africa bound to join with Britain. Smuts, however, insisted on a declaration of war against Germany, and so the United party coalition split apart.

Hertzog was virtually pro-German in his formal speech to Parliament, a fact that may have cost him his majority. A vote was taken, and by the close margin of 80 to 67 the Union of South Africa stood by Britain's side. Hertzog's fifteen-year rule was over, and Smuts became Prime Minister. When the results of the vote were announced, Hertzog, Pirow, and Malan, the Nationalist leaders, pleaded with their followers not to revolt but to maintain their opposition within the framework of the Constitution.

Taking his country into war with so precarious a margin of support, Smuts now performed a miracle. South African battalions covered themselves with glory in the campaigns in Ethiopia and Libya — they were "the bravest of the brave." At home the South African scheme of government corporations for war production took the edge off profiteering and laid the foundation for nationalization. Although the anti-British elements rejoiced when England appeared to be doomed in 1940, they numbered far fewer people than their ringleaders supposed.

Prime Minister Smuts, the architect of national unity, industrial power, and victory, appealed to the country again in 1943. The Nationalist Malan, charging that the nationalized industries were a blind for British financiers, demanded immediate peace and friendship with the Axis. Despite his fulminations, despite sabotage and even overt actions of treason, the elections ended in an astonishing victory for Smuts. The government coalition won 107 seats, Malan 43. The popular vote was 610,000 to 347,000, the greatest victory for imperial unity ever attained.

Regrettably, the government increased the disabilities of Asiatics in 1944, thus provoking protests of liberal opinion in many Allied countries. So far, no important political party in South Africa has officially advocated a more liberal racial policy with reference to the millions of native African inhabitants.

Stakes in the Peace

The Union of South Africa has three unique at-tributes: (1) she is more dependent on foreign trade and investment than any other country on earth; (2) her economy is based on gold, whose primary use is as a monetary standard and reserve; and (3) the disparity in the economic and social rewards accruing to the white and colored populations is most striking.

Recent efforts by Premier Jan C. Smuts to remedy the unbalance in economy and to face up to race relations may, if continued, resolve most South African difficulties, some of which might otherwise be explosive.

The well-defined improvement of the Union's position with regard to foreign creditors during World War II, as well as the sturdy advances made in industrialization, have been a great aid to stabilization.

The race issue, involving native Africans, Asiatics, and even half-breeds, divides the population generally into two main camps. The conservative elements hold that a greater equality in treatment will result in displacement of white European labor and farmers by the natives. The more liberal elements insist that the one sure basis for the continued growth of domestic industry and agriculture is increased purchasing power on the part of the 7,000,000 natives.

Nevertheless, whatever the internal racial situation in the Union of South Africa, she is still basically dependent on the use of gold as the international basis of currencies, and this seems to have been practically assured by the tenor of recent international monetary discussions (especially the Bretton Woods Conference in the U.S.A. in the summer of 1944).

South Africa's stakes in international trade and currency are so decisive that she is well-nigh bound to favor international peace, prosperity, and financial stability.

The Western Hemisphere

ARGENTINA

The Land and the People

The federal republic of Argentina, situated at the extreme southeast of the Americas, recalls the U.S.A. in many striking respects. Among these are the tempo of her industrial and agricultural development, her modernity and her health, and the vigorous belief of her people in their national destiny. Like the U.S.A., Argentina has demonstrated the ability to assimilate and transform immigrant elements and to be transformed by them.

Foreigners who, for the first time, visit the capital, Buenos Aires, are astonished at its enormous amount of traffic — in ideas as well as vehicles and people. Ships from every nation are tied to the modern, ample docks. New skyscrapers, modernistic apartment houses, and dignified palaces dominate the landscape. Four subway systems, whose stations are decorated with murals by the leading Argentine artists, handle the great crowds, which continually shift from the several business sections to the remote, attractive suburbs. Colorful newsstands on the sidewalks and the great book stores running from one street to another, display the latest editions in Spanish, French, Italian, German, Russian, and English. Newspapers center in palatial buildings, where not only the news is edited and printed, but inclusive social and educational programs are carried on for the community. Every day in hundreds of cultural centers — from the exclusive halls of the university to the great labor center, with its 20,000 seats — Argentine and foreign lecturers discuss every conceivable topic related to world problems.

Argentina is so sure of herself that she has coined a word to represent her peculiar strength and profound faith in her future — *Argentinidad*, the unalloyed essence of Argentine life. This is a combination of all that the people believe has made their nation great: the enormous stretch of rich prairies that assure the two fundamentals of physical life — wheat and beef; an overwhelming predominance of the white race, bred from a mixture of the peoples of Europe; extensive estates that ship much of the food that sustains Europe, obtaining in return the machinery and luxury that distinguish the country from her poorer American cousins; modern educational systems and intimate contacts with Old World culture, which give the republic a distinctive place of leadership in world life. It is this distinctive feeling of confidence that makes Argentina especially resentful of any seeming dictation from the outside and that explains, as much as pro-Axis sentiment, why Argentina and the U.S.A. have drawn farther apart during World War II.

Unlike every other Latin American state, save Uruguay, 98% of the population is of European stock, with practically no Indian or Negro admixture. Geographically one of the most remote countries from the great world centers of population and enterprise, she is deeply involved and interested in the fortunes of distant peoples. Indeed, it is the belief of one Argentine school of thought that their country's paramount ties are with Europe, rather than with the Americas.

The Land. Argentina's 1,079,000 square miles (more than a third of the U.S.A.) are bounded in the north by Bolivia and Paraguay, in the northeast by Brazil and Uruguay. From Uruguay she is separated by the giant estuary called the Río de la Plata, fed by the great Paraná and Paraguay Rivers. From Chile, on the west, she is delimited by a 2,000 mile stretch of the Andes Mountains, extending from arid country in the extreme north to the glacier areas of Patagonia in the south. Most of Argentina's east coast, at latitudes south of Africa, faces a limitless sea.

Variety characterizes this large country. The northern climate is semi-tropical in an area filled with scrub forest. The central part, embracing one of the greatest plains on earth, consists of the "humid pampa," to the east and the "dry pampa" to the west. The "humid pampa," with a warm but temperate climate, is an enormously rich granary, dotted with many cities and inhabited by over two-thirds of Argentina's population; the "dry pampa" is an important grassland and cattle country.

Along the Andes in the west extends the famed high Cordillera, with its many green settlements. Southern Argentina, ending in the largely unfertile peninsula of Patagonia and the island of Tierra del Fuego, is much colder. Toward the Straits of Magellan at the extreme southern tip, the country is bleak, storm-tossed, and sparsely inhabited, mainly by aboriginal people. In Argentina, summer comes in January, winter in July.

The land is not rich in mineral resources, possessing only some oil in the south (around Comodoro Rivadavia) and a little coal, gold, antimony, lead, and zinc, mainly in the Andean foothills near Mendoza.

The People. Argentina's rapid population gain in recent years rivals that of the U.S.A. in her pioneer heyday. The 1914 figure of 7,900,000 has today nearly doubled to 13,700,000. What accounts for this striking gain? Basically, immigration — the primary factor in the country's growth for over a century. No other land of comparable importance has based its development on recent immigration. Recent political upheavals in Europe are one explanation of why the more conservative elements have persuaded the government to slow down immigration. Added to this fear of the introduction of radical ideas from abroad, is the desire of the landlords to keep their large estates intact, instead of selling sections to incoming land-hungry foreigners.

The northern, western, and southern regions contain the longest settled population. Many still conserve their indigenous costumes and folkways. Here too there are some *mestizos* (mixed Indian and white) and even a few Indian communities. The Negroes have left almost no trace, though they were fairly numerous at the time of the slave trade.

Argentina entered the 19th century with a tiny population. In 1806 Great Britain made an effort to add the weak country to her far-flung empire. With great heroism, an unprepared people successfully resisted this attack. Four years later they began the long struggle which freed them from Spain. Argentina then began to develop her own distinctive culture. For half a century there was a life-and-death struggle between the untamed *gauchos* (cowboys) of the plains and the more refined *Porteños* (residents of Buenos Aires). During that contest, the dominant figure was Juan Manuel de Rosas, the only long-ruling dictator that Argentina ever had. (Reactionary forces during World War II endeavored to re-create the dictator as an Argentine hero.) The fall of Rosas (1852) was followed by the first of many great waves of immigrant settlers.

Of the present population, nearly one-fourth were actually born in Europe and another half are the children or grandchildren of immigrants. Only one-fourth of the people have lived in Argentina for more than two generations. It is a country of basically Latin stock, a fusion of Spanish, Italian, French, and Portuguese peoples, with the first two contributing an estimated two-thirds of the population. In addition, tens of thousands of Britons have come to Argentina to manage their substantial private investments. There are some 300,000 Germans, counting those born in Argentina of predominantly German descent. Their political and industrial activities heavily outweigh their actual numbers; their pro-Axis efforts before and during World War II are well known. More recent arrivals, Poles and Polish or Russian Jews, have also become a factor in the country. But basically Argentina remains a synthesis of Latin peoples.

What is most astonishing is the rapidity and certainty with which native and immigrant cultures have fused into a genuine and powerful nation. Argentina's decisive economic tradition is that of traders dealing in cattle, grain, and other food exports to Europe, and in the importation of capital, men, and consumers goods from Europe. A powerful social and political influence is wielded by the older Argentine gentry, who still own much of the land and rule their extensive properties in an almost patriarchal manner.

These *estancieros* (proprietors of big estates) spend most of their time in their palatial homes in Buenos Aires or in the hotels of Paris or the Riviera. They have influenced government, for the Conservative party, dominated by them, has been in power during most of Argentine history. In recent years, its control has been challenged by a growing middle class — composed of immigrants with liberal ideas and of the rapidly increasing labor groups, being drawn from the farms to the growing factories and commercial life in the cities. A most effective fighter for the middle class is the Socialist party. Though smaller in numbers, this class has furnished the most distinguished champions of labor, freedom of speech, and the elimination of graft and inefficiency in government.

While Argentina is primarily a pastoral and agricultural land, over 68% of her people live in cities of over 100,000. Buenos Aires, the capital, with some 3,000,000 in its metropolitan area, is the second largest Latin and Catholic city in the world, and the largest city of the southern hemisphere. That Argentina, like Australia, is so highly urbanized for an agricultural country testifies to the relatively small amount of labor required to exploit her farming, her pastoral industries, and her export possibilities.

The cities present sharp contrasts of poverty and wealth. Into their large slum areas are crowded many

See continental map on page 187.

of the recent immigrants, especially those from Eastern Europe. On the other hand, a city like Buenos Aires, with its banks, export houses, stock and commodity exchanges, luxury shops, branches of London and Paris stores, clubs, racing tracks, and polo fields, reminds one of the leading capitals of Europe and America. The growth of sports has been remarkable. A dominant feature of urban life is the numerous elegant clubs with large swimming pools, well-equipped gymnasiums, and tennis clubs. Crowds of 100,000 often gather to watch inter-city or international teams play association football. Such sports are taking the place of racing, except among the wealthy.

The tenant farmers and farm laborers live precariously. Often they drift from country to city. In the cattle country one still sees the descendants of the *gauchos*, the legendary cowboys whose Spanish-derived songs, music, epic cycles, and untamed spirit created a new culture — one of the most original and valid known. The *gaucho* epic, "Martín Fierro," is one of the literary monuments of the world.

The Argentines are a remarkably healthy and well-fed people. The low deathrate averages 10.8 per thousand, with a high proportion of people in the prime of life. The birthrate of 23.9 per thousand indicates a natural increase of more than 13% per decade.

Religion and Education. Roman Catholicism is the prevailing religion. At times subjected to anti-clerical restrictions, as in many other Latin-American countries, the Church has always been able to regain its prestige. A recent decree made Catholic teaching compulsory in the schools of Buenos Aires province. All faiths are freely tolerated. Of the other religious groups, there is a Protestant minority (mostly among the German, British, and United States residents); a minority of Jews, many of them in long-established farm colonies; and small groupings of Armenian, Syrian, and Greek Orthodox Christians.

Figures on illiteracy, not always dependable in Latin-American republics, were 33% in 1929. This has since been reduced by the compulsory, tuition-free educational system. Some estimates put it as low as 12% today. Over 200,000 students attend high schools, fully 60,000 the five universities, one of which (Córdoba) dates from 1613. The University of Buenos Aires, with 20,000 students, is one of the world's great educational centers. As to elementary education, 15% of the population attend these schools, one of the highest proportions anywhere. Thirty years ago less than 9% of the population were in school.

The country has a large and active intellectual class; Buenos Aires particularly enjoys a flourishing literary and scientific life, with many world-celebrated newspapers, periodicals, and book publishing houses. The newspapers have a great cultural range, since the Argentines have a passionate interest in world developments in the arts and sciences. Since the Spanish Civil War of 1936, the Argentine capital has been one of the leading cultural centers of the Spanish-speaking world.

Argentine literature has drawn copiously from the wealth of native folklore and possesses a salty, fresh flavor. The *pampa*, that sea of grass where no tree was seen, developed a powerful yet melancholy strain. The bards wandered over the land, fashioning poetic works like the Arthurian cycles. Later, when the land became urbanized, the popular literary basis remained. The work of Domingo Faustino Sarmiento (1811–88), who used culture as a weapon of political liberation and educational democracy, powerfully impressed the history and social ideas of Argentina.

Modern Argentine writers keep up their emphasis on social questions. A book which won the national prize for literature criticizes the breakdown of national morals, the unfair attitude toward women, the sordid life of the peasants and *gauchos*, and the dominance of the military. Lament is expressed over the disappearance of the *gaucho*, pushed by the oncoming machine age farther into the Chaco hills and sagebrush. Novelists are tackling the problem of the tenements growing around the rapidly developing factories. Economists are keenly aware of the struggle between the old agricultural aristocracy and the modern industrialists, and issue enlightening works on these problems. Argentina produces more books than all other South American countries combined.

The Nation's Economy

Agriculture. Argentina is a fabled "wheat and beef" country. Her yields of wheat per acre surpass those of the U.S.A. by 30%. With only a tenth of our population and less than a fifth of our arable land, Argentina produces a wheat crop of 11,000,000 tons, or four-fifths of the United States total. Similarly, her cattle population, while only half that of the U.S.A., is five times as great per capita.

In arable land, Argentina occupies fourth place in the world (98,000 square miles — 9% of her entire territory). With about 140 persons per square mile of cultivated land, she is relatively underpopulated.

Argentina is a leading export nation, competing with Canada and Australia in wheat, and largely replacing the U.S.A. in corn exports. Barley provides another important export crop. Actually, such nations as Great Britain, Belgium, and the Netherlands would be sorely pressed for grain without imports from Argentina. Yet the quality of Argentine grain is not of the highest; her maize, mostly cattle fodder, does not compare in grading with the United States corn crop, and her wheat rarely reaches the United States or Canadian level of quality. As agriculture advances, however, there is a constant improvement in grain grades and beef quality.

Her animal economy is also extensive, with more than 3,000,000 cattle and 5,400,000 sheep slaughtered yearly. Her *frigoríficos* — or cold-storage plants — are the largest in existence. The annual wool clip, derived from 44,000,000 sheep, reaches the high total of 250,000 tons and is second only to Australia's. In addition, Argentina's pastoral economy includes 10,000,000 horses, 4,000,000 pigs, and 6,000,000 goats.

Her abundant wines, produced mainly for home consumption, have become popular on the foreign market with the cessation of European exports. The country also supplies half the world's linseed oil. Dairy products have markedly increased, notably cheese, which has trebled in a decade. Superb fruits, especially pears, which are now widely grown, contribute to the diversification of agriculture.

But Argentine agriculture faces one very serious disadvantage: its variability. Except for the semi-tropical crops in the north (cane sugar and tobacco), annual crops vary as much as 50% from year to year. And this high variability leads inevitably to huge turnovers in employment. Thus, tenants are easily displaced on the giant estates that dominate the country, and the farm population has little of the stability that generally characterizes agriculture in the U.S.A. Moreover, farm prices, dependent on the quotations in importing centers, fluctuate widely, so that violent extremes of prosperity and depression are frequent.

Industry. Argentine industry, of fairly recent growth, was at first largely the result of British financial investment and penetration. British coal built Argentine industry. The British ships that brought the coal sailed back loaded with grain and cattle, thus reducing freight costs on both voyages to both countries. The British have also been active in developing the meat-packing industry — the well-known British drink, Bovril, comes from Argentina.

British penetration was followed by large capital investments on the part of the Dutch, French, Swiss, Germans, and United States citizens. The Americans have concentrated on industries based on natural resources, mainly meat-packing; the Swiss on breweries and the rayon industry; the French on grain establishments and luxury articles.

Absence or scarcity of essential mineral resources has handicapped Argentina's industrialization. In fuels she is particularly weak. The country has no coal, produces oil only in moderate quantities, and possesses abundant water-power only where it is least accessible and useful. Moreover, Argentina lacks iron and has only a fair-sized output of antimony, lead, zinc, and gold.

These limitations have been swept aside by Argentine energy. The modern trend to industry is aided by extensive local urban markets for factory production. Industry employs some 785,000, with a gross output of $1,300,000,000 — or over $1,500 per worker. The leading divisions are textiles (including rayon), flour milling, tobacco, edible oil, and beer. The State petroleum monopoly is also a large employer of labor. Though the machinery investment per person is well below that of the U.S.A., it is the highest in Latin America, being rivaled only by Chile. Today it exceeds $5.00 per capita.

National Wealth and Finance. The Argentina of 1929 was comparatively rich. Though her wealth per person ($1,060) did not rival that of the U.S.A. ($1,825), she was one of the five leading countries in the world, on a per capita basis, ranking only after Australia and New Zealand among the basically agrarian countries.

Her present position, however, is difficult to assess. Her wealth is greater in absolute amounts but less impressive on a relative per person basis. Her farm lands, at $11 per acre of arable land, are the cheapest of any of the leading agricultural countries. On the other hand, the nation averages one radio set to every eight persons, compared to one to five persons in Australia, and one to two-and-a-half persons in the U.S.A.

At least 12% of Argentina's internal physical wealth was owned abroad in 1930 (not including bonds held abroad). But by this date (the beginning of the world depression) large-scale additional foreign investment had virtually ceased, and since then it has played little part in building Argentine industry, whose recent growth has been based on local investment. On the contrary, the tendency to nationalize foreign properties has gained much ground (since 1940), a typical example being the recent government decree taking over the British-owned Primitiva Gas Company. At present about 50% of the railroads are British-owned, 31% government-owned. (United States and British interests, as of 1939, including Argentine bonds held abroad, were still $800,000,000 for the U.S.A. and $2,250,000,000 for Britain.) Should the nationalization trend be intensified, Argentine economy will undergo some fundamental changes, and new capital for investment will have to be found exclusively in the domestic market — such a trend would materially contribute to the economic independence of the land.

The monetary unit, the *peso*, has a free market value of about 25¢. It has fallen to a third of its 1929 gold parity (considerably lower proportionately than the dollar or pound sterling), but with the outbreak of war in 1939, there was an inrush of foreign money to neutral Argentina, and the country has since accumulated sizable foreign exchange reserves in New York and London. Those in London are mostly in "blocked sterling" accounts, which cannot be drawn upon for the duration of the war.

The price level, sustained for some time by devaluation, has doubled during the war, though money in circulation has increased only moderately (from 1,410,000,000 to 1,850,000,000 *pesos*). The surplus of gold and foreign exchange reserves over the paper money issued, indicates a strong currency. Bank deposits are large (around $1,000,000,000), but much of this represents foreign money seeking a "safe" refuge. Savings at $400,000,000, or $30 per person, are relatively high for Latin America.

The federal government has behaved responsibly in financial matters, even when faced with adverse circumstances. The budget, normally about $375,-000,000, has undoubtedly been greatly increased under recent plans for large-scale military expansion. The total domestic debt of about $1,200,000,000 is equivalent on a peacetime income basis to $20,000,-000,000 in the U.S.A. The foreign debt reaches only $280,000,000, and despite some partial defaults by provincial governments, Argentine credit is, on the whole, high.

Foreign Trade. To understand Argentina's recent political history, one must realize that her prosperity is inextricably bound up with her export of raw materials. World market prices for wheat and beef basically determine her national economy.

Argentina accurately mirrors the trends of world trade. In 1929 her foreign trade represented one of the highest per capita figures in the world (exceeding $125); today that figure has dropped to less than half (about $60). In 1929 Argentina did 3% of world trade, in 1938 only 2%. From 1929–1938 imports fell by 50%, exports by 60%. By 1941 imports had fallen another 22% below the 1938 figure, and though exports remained constant in value, the amounts were actually less in view of the higher level of prices. In 1942 imports remained the same, while exports rose some $75,000,000 over the 1941 figure, making total foreign trade $66 per capita.

Of her exports, animal products account for 60%, agricultural products 25%. Her chief imports include textiles, fuels, chemicals, wood, paper, metals, machinery, iron, and, in prosperous periods, perfumes and silks.

In peacetime, Argentina exported 32% to Britain, 10% to the U.S.A., 6% each to the Netherlands and Belgium, 5% to Germany. She imported 22% from Britain, 15% from the U.S.A., 9% from Germany, 5% each from France and Brazil. During the war, Britain has continued to take one-third of Argentina's exports, while supplying some 18% of her imports. War trade with the U.S.A. has risen sharply, exports reaching 28%, imports 31%, and Argentina has also increased her trade with the other American republics. However, Britain and the U.S.A. still remain the two major suppliers of the Argentine market.

History: 1914-1944

The Argentine republic, a neutral in World War I, provides an outstanding example of the swing to democracy in Latin America during the war epoch. For generations the great influence of the estate-owners had thwarted full democracy, but their power was broken by the electoral law of 1912 which had been sponsored by President Sáenz Peña, and upon which the large urban population had insisted. This law provided for universal suffrage, the secret ballot, and proportional representation. Not even the profits, arising from European war needs, that flowed into Argentina after 1915, could distract an aroused people from their basic political demands. In 1916, for the first time in Argentine history, a government in power was defeated by a majority of the popular vote.

The Radical Supremacy: 1916–1930. The newly elected president, the Radical leader Hipólito Irigoyen, was one of the most remarkable men in South American history. He became the idol of great masses of the people. The impression he made upon politics was so marked that the Radicals, under his successor, Dr. Marcelo T. de Alvear, divided into *personalistas* (that is, his followers) and *antipersonalistas* (those who sought to end his personal domination). Irigoyen acquired his popular hold not through dictatorship but by personal attraction: he was not so much an administrator as he was a democratic agitator. He had given up his estate and lived simply — a new phenomenon in a country in which politics had hitherto been a lucrative career.

The Radicals, his supporters, were the first Argentine party to be based upon the middle classes, hitherto inexperienced in political life. While some of their leaders belonged to the powerful families that had dominated Argentine politics for three generations, the mass strength of the Radicals derived from the newly risen industrial and commercial classes, with the support of the urban workers.

The Radicals had to find their way slowly. The long monopoly of politics enjoyed by the older elements had concentrated statesmanship in a small class, which was quick to criticize the early administrative blunders of the new government.

As a neutral in World War I, Argentina enjoyed a war boom that continued until 1920. Speculation was rife, on the assumption that the "golden age" would last forever. But a depression came in 1921. Irigoyen, however, did not lose his hold on the people. In 1922, when his term expired and he was precluded by law from reelection, he designated his successor, Dr. Marcelo T. de Alvear; and in 1928 when he was again eligible, Irigoyen resumed the presidency.

His government, after 1928, tended toward centralized administration, an always perilous move in a federal republic in which the provinces jealously guard their rights. Irigoyen also refused to delegate his functions, as he grew older, until his self-confidence became a barrier to efficient administration. He did not even trouble to replace vacancies when they occurred. The world depression of 1929, which severely affected South American exporting countries like Argentina, led to a revenue deficit; and this in turn, to a breakdown of government business. When congressional elections were held in 1930, the *personalistas* showed a marked decline.

The Right wing element, which had been absent from government since 1916 and resented the transfer of power to the middle classes, now had its opportunity. Opposition groupings within both the Conservative and Radical parties joined with the army to proclaim a provisional government under a Conservative, General José Francisco Uriburu. On September 6, 1930, Irigoyen was arrested.

But the Conservatives, after seizing power, discovered that they had to deal with a people different from those their fathers ruled. In April 1931 the province of Buenos Aires (not including the capital city) went Radical. The government thereupon decided to delay the legally due federal elections and proceeded to designate its nominees as governors of the various provinces.

In the elections scheduled for November 1931 the Radicals made the mistake of nominating Dr. Alvear, who had been President in 1928 and was therefore disqualified until 1934. The Conservatives, who themselves had reversed a legal government by arms, became indignant at this unconstitutional nomination and excluded Alvear's candidacy. The Radicals then refused to enter the elections. To avoid extreme difficulties, the Conservatives nominated an able *antipersonalista* Radical, General Agustín P. Justo.

The depression was now at its worst point. Prices had fallen disastrously; bankruptcy and unemployment typified the shattered economy; there was a currency and banking crisis. When the Radicals now ridiculed the results of rule by the "experienced" groups, the government countered by declaring a state of siege, which continued through most of the 1933–35 period. It proceeded to wait for the depression to end.

World recovery was slow in improving Argentina's situation, but once the economy picked up, the federal government was punctilious in paying the foreign debt. It so far improved Argentine credit that she was able to refund her bonds at lower interest rates. Her international prestige rose high under the Foreign Minister, Dr. Carlos Saavedra Lamas, who was awarded the Nobel Peace prize in 1936.

The Radicals recovered from the developments of 1930 and triumphed in congressional elections. In 1937, however, the candidate of the government coalition, Roberto M. Ortiz, defeated the Radical, Alvear, who was by now eligible for office. The *personalistas* cried fraud and intimidation, but the new President, though *antipersonalista*, insisted that he was a Radical in political philosophy. Thus he managed to avert difficulties, though he continued to depend on a Conservative coalition for his majority. Soon, however, he demonstrated his radical sentiments by dismissing "National Democrats" (Conservatives) as provincial governors because of their innumerable frauds. By this action, most of the Radicals became united again, for the first time since 1922. Triumphant in 1940, President Ortiz proved to be the first Argentine leader since Irigoyen to enjoy a strong popular ascendancy.

The following year, however, he became very ill and suffered with failing sight. He delegated his power to Vice-president Ramón S. Castillo, a "National Democrat"; but he probably would not have taken the step so soon if he had not been subjected to political pressures within his own administration. Meanwhile Argentina was feeling the effects of World War II. This time there was no sudden spurt in her economy, as there had been in World War I. On the contrary, with Britain blockading the European continent, Argentina had to readjust her commerce.

At the Pan-American Conference held in Rio de Janeiro, in January 1942, it was evident that the Argentine government was not anxious to go so far in abandoning neutrality as were the other American republics. It was with reluctance that she finally agreed to an inter-American resolution recommending the severance of all ties with the Axis powers. While Argentina refused to treat the U.S.A. as subject to the restrictions imposed by international law upon belligerents, the attitude of her Foreign Minister was definitely obstructionist.

When President Ortiz, a dying man, resigned on June 27, 1942, the so-called "neutrality" groups were free to show their hand. These were composed of ultra-nationalists, who resented any United States influence; of admirers of *Hispanidad*, the unity of Argentine and Spanish cultures; of a few believers in "historic dictatorship"; of pro-Germans, pro-Italians; and of a large clique of cold calculators who were interested solely in assuring their own position as exporters and businessmen and who therefore preferred to wait for the outcome of the war so that they could do business with the victors. Whatever the variations, nearly all of these came from the Conservative element in politics.

Death removed not only Ortiz, but also ex-Presidents Alvear and Justo, all of whom had been pro-Ally. But in the elections for the Lower House, Radicals and Socialists outnumbered the government *bloc* by 81 to 68 so that for a time, actions were prudent. The President, Castillo, now limited press and radio, denied the right to discuss the war as imperiling neutrality, and finally declared a state of siege. It was whispered about by the ultra-nationalists that lend-lease was making Chile and Brazil armed menaces to Argentina.

But by-elections showed unmistakably that the people were pro-Ally. The Radicals and Socialists were at the point of forming a *bloc* to overthrow the government coalition (called the *Concordancia*). But before elections could take place, a military *coup* overthrew President Castillo. The public thought this *coup* was pro-Ally. Within three days, General Pedro Ramírez, took over office from the leader of the *coup*, General Arturo Rawson (June 7, 1943). The Ramírez government was quite clearly of an extreme Rightist character.

This régime pursued a fluctuating policy: its spiritual unity with totalitarianism was evident, but it took action against Axis espionage, deported Axis diplomats and subversive agents and severed economic and financial ties with Axis countries. Thus it became difficult to predict the ultimate objectives of its sinuous policy. Actions against labor, Jews, "Communists" (which included lifelong opponents of Communism), and pro-Allies were common, while pro-Nazis were left free to pursue their work. But with inspired demagogy, the government expropriated foreign utilities, raised wages, limited urban rents, nationalized the grain-trade facilities. The homes and property of people of extreme wealth were raided and their possessions impounded. By these ambivalent actions the government thus sapped the opposition — whose social basis lay among the very classes whose sentiments and interests General Ramírez flattered.

Strained relations with the U.S.A. led to Secretary Hull's firm note to Foreign Minister Vice Admiral Segundo Storni. This note led to Storni's resignation, but it fanned the Nationalist flame. Suppression of pro-Ally groups became the order of the day, and men like General Edelmiro Farrell, Colonel Juan D. Perón, and the pro-Axis General Luis Perlinger, became conspicuous. The demagogic policy of Ramírez was abandoned for totalitarian controls of labor. In December 1943 the government dissolved all political parties. Teaching of the Roman Catholic faith in schools was made compulsory, irrespective of the child's religion.

It was known that Argentina had engineered a pro-totalitarian *putsch* in Bolivia and was working to stir up her neighbors, Chile, Uruguay, and Paraguay, to fall in line with her policies. For, while Argentina had broken off relations with the Axis (January 26, 1944), her ambiguous policy steered a tortuous course. Through the repression, the mass of the people remained democratic and pro-Ally, but the dictatorship identified its disliked policies with the basic national pride of the people.

A delicate situation thus arose, requiring diplomatic skill for its resolution. Chile and Bolivia became more refractory to American requests. The Argentine Colonel Perón, who was associated with General Farrell in eliminating Ramírez (February 25, 1944), delivered speeches so bellicose, especially toward Argentina's neighbors, that to explain them away proved a superb scholastic exercise. In July 1944 the U.S.A. recalled her ambassador, Norman Armour. Relations were at the worst point in the history of the two great American republics. In August 1944 the U.S.A. began an economic pressure campaign through the blocking of Argentine gold deposits in the U.S.A. The United States government assailed the policy of the Argentine government in caustic language.

While opposition to the present régime on the part of all of the democratic elements within the country has been felt, it is as yet divided. The position of the government has been strengthened and its control has been prolonged as a result of the strongly nationalistic reaction created because of the general impression that outside pressure was being exerted upon the Argentine nation.

Foreign Affiliations. In her pacific days, Argentina was part of the inter-American group, although she often took her own stand in minor matters. Once she was part of the ABC grouping (Argentina, Brazil, and Chile). Her economic relations tied her to Britain.

It is only recently that American and British influences have not prevailed in Argentina, and they still enjoy the favor of the great majority of this progressive people. Her conservative classes are divided. Some have been close to the Spain of General Franco, a few are outright pro-Germans, but most retain their traditional admiration for Great Britain and France. For a time, Argentina's large Italian population included many who were beguiled by Mussolini and his apparent glories.

Stakes in the Peace

Economically, Argentina has perhaps as complete a stake in freer trade as any country. Her besetting fear is that the British Dominions and the U.S.A. may outdistance her in exports of corn, wheat, and beef, or, at the least, make her exports far more competitive. Some reassurance that these exports will continue to flow in at least average amounts would do much to allay her fears. Since Europe will need to supplement her domestic food supplies for many years, Argentina would find it advantageous to cooperate with the importing states in an international organization.

Internally, the landowning system must be replaced ultimately either by cooperatives or a division into individual holdings on the "humid pampas." These holdings, however, must be of economic size and must have adequate capital.

A true working democracy in Argentina will be assured only after a more equitable division of the land has been carried out; after a more stable economic system, including, especially, a marked increase in industrialization, has been established; and after a political reformation, which guarantees the holding of free elections, has taken place.

BOLIVIA

The Land and the People

Bolivia is a landlocked republic, the great majority of whose inhabitants dwell in areas over 8,000 feet high. She is largely isolated from the main currents of trade and communication in South America. Her predominantly Indian population, poor and exploited, conserve their traditional modes of living to a greater extent than any other South American people, even more than the Indians of neighboring Peru or of Ecuador.

Formed in 1825 out of the Viceroyalty of Peru, Bolivia was named after the liberator, Simón Bolívar. Her ancient capital, Chuquisaca, was renamed Sucre, after another Venezuelan liberator, General Antonio de Sucre. This land that never had to struggle for its independent nationhood has only recently arrived at a true national consciousness.

For a century she was the country of revolutions and military dictatorships, and her gloomy, sanguinary, and tragic history has left a deep impress on the character of her contemporary problems. For a century after independence, her great Indian masses lived as they had lived in the days of the Spanish power, while her small governing class, left to their own devices, became increasingly parochial in outlook. The comparative absence of foreign trade for generations caused the ruling groups to look to the subjugation of their own people as their principal source of income.

Bolivia once possessed a province on the Pacific Ocean: this was wrested from her by Chile, after a long and costly war, and the loss was ratified by the treaty of 1883. For the sixty years that followed, Bolivian policy was largely directed toward regaining her lost sovereign outlet to the sea. This obsession with foreign affairs had other effects: it put a premium on the military class and encouraged the importance of external action, rather than internal improvement as the prerequisite of progress. Her national policy incurred the dislike of Chile. Hence, Bolivia was thought to be always in danger of war, and foreign capital thus grew wary of extensive commitments in the republic. What foreign or local capital did finally enter Bolivia, based its investment exclusively on using the land's rich mineral resources as a means of quick profits by reason of the quasi-slavery of the workers in the mines. The Bolivian governing groups then pursued the policy of repression towards their own people, not only on their landed estates, but also to drive them into the service of the mining companies. Thus, by reason of taxes paid by the mining companies to the government (of which they were the beneficiaries) and their participations in these mining enterprises, the ruling groups profited doubly from the miseries of the indigenous Indian population.

The area now known as Bolivia was, relative to her neighbors, a much more advanced region in the 18th century than today. The youth of the districts that are now called Argentina voyaged to the University of Chuquisaca (Sucre), at that time the center of education for a thousand miles to the south. Here the philosophy of Rousseau and Montesquieu, of Locke and Jefferson, were taught to idealist youths who completed their studies determined to dethrone the Spanish royal power.

In the 16th century, fabled Potosí, in upper Bolivia, the richest paying mine in human history, had produced enough silver to maintain the failing prestige of the Spanish empire — and to this day, to be worth a Potosí, in Spanish, means to be richly endowed. In our time, Bolivia is more accurately termed "the land of tin," being the world's second producer of this essential commodity. Tin overshadows her export trade and affords her principal relationship to the outside world, but it is indeed far from being so significant for the welfare of the mass of her people.

The Land. The landlocked country is bounded by Peru (northwest), Chile (southwest), Brazil (north and east), Paraguay (southeast), and Argentina (south). Her estimated 416,000 square miles, a tremendous expanse, equals Texas and California combined.

Most of the population is concentrated in several clusters: in the productive mining and agricultural land about La Paz (the virtual capital) at 12,000 feet elevation; in the lovely regions, fertile and with a perpetual balmy spring climate, about the charming old capital Sucre and picturesque Cochabamba (averaging 8,000 feet elevation); on the borders of sky-blue Lake Titicaca, with intensively cultivated terraced plots of land and amazing wheat fields (over 10,000 feet high). In the southwestern regions where these clusters of people live, are found nearly all the abundant mineral resources: tin, tungsten, silver, lead, copper, antimony. Petroleum is found in the lowlands.

At the most, only 2% of the Bolivian land is cultivated. Yet, the regions of from 4,000 to 8,000 feet along the incline of the Cordilleras — the celebrated *Yungas* or *Valle*, as they are alternately called — are said to have as great agricultural promise as any region of comparable size in the world. The valleys here are sheltered and fertile and the climate is free from tropical humidity. United States science and aid are now cooperating in developing this relatively neglected area.

To sum up, Bolivia consists, first, of the large mountainous mass of the Andes in the southwest, and among them are found the plateaus and basins of large human settlement (the whole region being known as the *Altiplano*); secondly, the area inclining from the mountain mass into the plain, both to the northeast of the *Altiplano* and to the east, called the *Yungas* or *Valle*; thirdly, the extremely hot and rainy *selva* (tropical rainforest), towards the north, where rubber and cinchona are found. The *Altiplano* is quite cold, and its bleak scenery, stern and imposing; the *Yungas* have the climate of the French Riviera, so much sought after by tourists; while the *selva* districts, and some plains in the extreme south near Argentina, have been characterized by one novelist as "Green Hell."

In the *Altiplano*, pastoral activities are common. In the Sucre district with its Italianate cities, estate farming prevails, and pioneer farming is on the increase in the *Valle*. The natives work at forest tasks in the *selva*.

Rail and road communication, despite intensive developments since 1920, is still quite inadequate and is often uncoordinated. This lack of cheap transport has impoverished the country. The cost of carrying goods to market is so high that production must largely be localized. However, there are several indications of significant change: recent developments of air traffic and improved connection of roads between population clusters; rail, road, and air connections with Brazil and Argentina, on a rapidly increasing scale; several railroads over the Andes to the port of Arica (where Chile has granted Bolivia free port facilities) and to other Pacific outlets — the epoch of isolation is now drawing to a close. Bolivia, once called the Tibet of America, for her inaccessibility and the astonishing elevation of her cities (La Paz is the largest city in the world at over 10,000 feet) is now entering into the comity of nations.

The People. There are said to be some 3,500,000

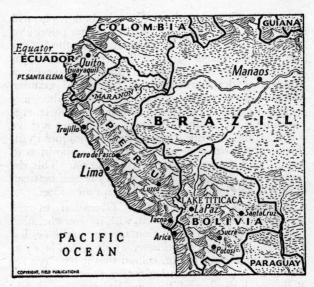

See continental map on page 187.

Bolivians. Official estimates aver that some 54% of the population are pure Indians, that 32% are *mestizos* or *cholos* (of mixed white and Indian blood, but with a marked Indian predominance), that about 12% are predominantly Europeans, though with some Indian traits, and that less than 2% are pure Europeans, mainly of Spanish extraction. There are many Germans especially active in light industries, in jobbing, retailing, and metallurgy.

Most of the predominant Indian population speak two languages, Aymara and Quechua, both of which antedate the Spanish conquest of the 16th century. Spanish is used by the small ruling class in business, industry, government, and social life; it is the official language.

The Aymara Indians, as a rule, live communally in their miserable stone huts in the cold and bleak high mountains. Largely shepherds or subsistence farmers, they speak a rough language with a poor vocabulary. The Quechuas live at somewhat lower altitudes and form the mass of the peons on the large estates. Their language is softer and richer, and their civilization considerably more advanced. Both Indian groups share in poverty, disease, and illiteracy, though unequally. The *cholos*, or *mestizos*, look down on the hardy Aymara; and though the Quechua is not so disdained, he too plays no part in the political or social life of the country. Hence "Bolivia" is a concept that interests, at most, only a fifth of the people.

A few Bolivian families own the very best lands; the lands owned by the Indians are capable of producing subsistence only after heroic efforts, though in certain areas, their resolution and communal application have overcome obstacles. On the large *haciendas*, the peons work from sunrise to sunset and receive in money much less than a dollar a week. The struggle in the mountains against the cold, lack of food, and also the want of oxygen, have made it possible for only the hardiest to survive, and even then at the cost of an astonishing deathrate and after too great a drain on human faculties merely to maintain life.

The development of mining has actually widened the gulf between the classes. The Indian dreads labor conscription into the mines, where he believes he will soon die of lung diseases. Military conscription also falls heavily on these unfortunates. Hence the Indian is suspicious, resents outside influences, and has been intractable to national unity. Lately, however, a number of developments have stimulated genuine national movements. A more conscious labor element has arisen in the towns, and there is now emerging among the youth of all the racial groups a drive for social justice, education, modern techniques in industry and farming — and determined opposition to foreign and domestic mineral exploitation. This rising youth is doing much to diminish the gulf between classes which had so largely followed racial lines.

Education and Religion. Education in the sparsely settled mountain areas, with its overwhelming and resistant Indian population, faces great difficulties. In 1930, illiteracy was estimated at 85%, and lately at 80%, though some optimists hold that it has been reduced to 65%. Recent legislation provides that all Bolivians, including adults, must become literate, but it is not known how effectively this provision has been enforced. About 76,000 children attend elementary schools, that is, about one in seven of school age. Some 5,000 children are in high schools. The University of Sucre, founded in 1624 (12 years before Harvard) has about 1,500 students.

Bolivian literature, as is natural in so challenging an environment, has been extensively concerned with the geology, geography, history, and political problems of the country. But lately, there has been a profound change in content. "Indigenism," or concern with social problems of peoples of Indian origin, has come to the fore. Arguedas' novel, *The Race of Bronze*, depicting the tragic life of the Aymara, has inspired a generation. Historians and polemists are rousing the conscious elements of the people with their brilliant and forthright analyses. Books such as *Pueblo Enfermo (Our Sick People)* are gospels to progressive youth. The historic example of Bolivian leadership in progressive thought before the Bolivarian liberation epoch (1810–1830), is a spur to modern emulation.

Roman Catholicism, recognized by Bolivian law as the established religion, enjoys exceptionally high prestige. The Church is aware of the extent to which pagan survivals dominate among the Indians, and carries on an intensive missionary program. Other faiths are freely practiced, and the Constitution guarantees toleration.

The Nation's Economy

Mining. Mining produces 99% of all Bolivian exports — tin alone accounts for 75%. Three-fourths of this tin production is shipped to British smelters (in Wales), whence it ultimately finds its way to the U.S.A. Unlike the almost pure type that is mined in Malaya, Bolivian tin requires special treatment, since it is a complex mixture of other ingredients. Hence, it is least in demand when Malayan tin is cheap and available, as was the situation before the Japanese occupation of Malaya in World War II. However, in peacetime, the Bolivian tin monopoly enjoyed advantages through the International Tin Cartel, whose price-fixing and quota allocations enabled

Bolivia to sustain her tin exports. The disparity between the income of the mine owners and the wages of the miners is shocking. The cash wages of workers are often 60¢ a week for a 12-hour day.

Bolivia produces certain other minerals. Wolfram (tungsten) accounts for 7.5% of the country's exports, silver 4%, lead and copper 2% each. But other desirable minerals might be exploited and become important. Similarly, the country's water-power resources have been neglected, though they could be made into an important industrial factor. As it is, such industry as exists — flour-milling, brewing — is extremely small.

Communications are critically important for the economy of Bolivia. Foreign trade has been aided by three rail routes to the Pacific and one to the Argentine ports. There is in prospect a railway from Santa Cruz to Santos in Brazil, a distance of about 1,400 miles. Internal highways extending over 3,000 miles have served to open up profitable areas that had formerly been almost isolated.

Agriculture. With only a minute manufacturing economy and only 40,000 wretchedly paid employees in the mines, the overwhelming mass of Bolivians live on small farms, communal lands, or large estates. The unwarrantedly small proportion of the total territory under cultivation (2%) has brought about a population ratio of almost 400 to the arable square mile. The mass of the people live on extremely low subsistence levels. Since only minerals and the high-value crops are worth the cost of transportation to the sea, across passes usually 13,000 feet high, the peasantry produces food crops only for local markets. Indeed, these people would scarcely feel the effects if Bolivia were to lose her entire world trade in tin.

Fortunately, some steps have been taken to relieve the economic misery of the rural population. Corn and potatoes, the two chief food staples, have increased tenfold within the last generation. Largely owing to the Indian population in the high valleys, who have terraced their lands with great skill, the production of cheese, butter, meat, barley, wheat, and rice is rising substantially. Because Bolivian farmers have shown a high degree of application and ingenuity in the land cultivation in the difficult mountain country, it is clear that farming might attain true prosperity if the rich *valle* lands (4,000 to 8,000 feet high) were cultivated with adequate capital and modern techniques. As it is, the nourishment of the people is still far from sufficient.

Tropical agriculture is active. Both cinchona bark and rubber are collected in the equatorial rainforest in the north. Better communications would enhance the possibilities of expanding this activity.

Cattle, though fair in number, are raised in areas too remote from markets, as a rule. The poor roads bring about local consumption and impede the growth of an adequate animal economy. Sheep number 5,000,000 and alpacas and llamas serve as carriers in the remote Aymara regions.

Finance and Foreign Trade. With mining as the chief source of revenue, political issues naturally revolve around the exploitation of mineral resources in Bolivia. The Patiño Mining Company exercises powerful influence, since it dominates the tin industry, producing half of the country's annual output. The Bolivian Patiño family controls this company, but some American and British capital is also invested in the mining industries as a whole.

Money in circulation has risen threefold since World War II. In 1939 Bolivian money was quoted at only 3.5% of its 1929 gold parity; and a 300% increase since that time has seriously aggravated inflation. The domestic debt of around $9,000,000 is outweighed by the foreign debt of approximately $22,000,000, but interest on most of the foreign loans is not being paid now.

Including the Bolivian foreign loan, there is now invested in the country about $100,000,000 of United States interests and $50,000,000 of British interests. Bolivia's annual budget averages $20,000,000. Her currency, the *boliviano*, is worth about 2¢ in the U.S.A.

Usually the average exports of minerals exceed all imports by two to one, a favorable surplus that would be important to the Bolivian financial structure if so much of it did not inure to a single company, Bolivian in origin, but with international financial interests involved. Normally the U.S.A. supplies 30% and Britain 22% of all imports (mainly sugar, wheat, flour, coal, iron, and mining machinery). Recently the share of the U.S.A. has appreciably increased.

History: 1914-1944

From 1913 to 1917 the Presidency of Bolivia was held by a sober and far-seeing statesman, Ismael Montes, who had previously served from 1904 to 1909. In 1917 the government broke diplomatic relations with Germany, and a new President was elected, Gutiérrez Guerra, the leader of the Liberal party that had governed Bolivia since 1898.

President Gutiérrez Guerra followed a policy of conciliation and agreement with Chile concerning Bolivia's lost outlet to the Pacific Ocean, particularly the port of Arica. Opposing this conciliatory attitude, the Republican party ousted him from office by means of an army *coup* (1920). The new designee, Dr. Bautista Saavedra, ruled fitfully. He sought to entrench himself with the people by initiating a lavish policy of foreign loans, economic development, and public works. In 1924, however, a serious rebellion broke out in the eastern part of Santa Cruz province. After mastering the situation he was confronted by divisions within his own party. The *coup* which placed him in power had restricted the vote to members of the Republican party. Thus the intra-party division was the sole legal form in which political opinion could be expressed. The Liberals, now a wing of the Republican party, put forward Dr. Daniel Salamanca as their candidate in 1925. He was defeated, but the election was set aside. After an interim government, a new election was held and another Republican, Dr. Hernando Siles, became President in December 1926.

The new administration was at first quite popular. Bolivia participated in the world-wide prosperity of the late 1920's, and in 1929 she acquired free port facilities at Arica from Chile. But with the arrival of the world depression in 1930, the country began to suffer intensely. Almost at once she found it impos-

sible to pay the interest on her large, newly acquired foreign debt — the interest charges exceeded the shrunken total of her national revenue. The dire economic situation bred popular discontent which erupted in civil war. President Hernando Siles relied on General Kundt, a Germany army officer, to put down the rebellion. (Röhm, founder of Germany's Storm Troops, had served in Bolivia.) But General Kundt was defeated and Hernando Siles fell from power (1930). The numerous exiled politicians now returned to Bolivia and invited Dr. Salamanca, leader of the Liberal wing of the Republican party, to serve as President. Both parties welcomed his election.

The Chaco War and Its Aftermath: 1932-1939. Faced with a catastrophic economy, Dr. Salamanca set to work valiantly to cope with the task of mastering the crisis. Unfortunately, the dispute with Paraguay over the Gran Chaco territory — which had been simmering since 1928 and had led to many border clashes — burst into open hostilities in 1932. Although the country was embroiled in war, the President held firmly to constitutional methods and to constitutional reforms. Bitter military reverses, however, hurt his administration. Most of Bolivia's troops were Aymara Indians, used to living on plateaus 12,000 feet high; they took sick in the swampy, tropical lowlands of the Gran Chaco, in which the Paraguayan soldiers were at home. In 1934, when it became clear that Bolivia would be defeated, a *coup d'état* placed the Vice President, Luis Tejada Sorzano, in power.

Bolivia was in ferment. Her economic miseries were indescribable. The cost of living had risen by 700% during the Chaco war, and the Bolivian currency had lost nine-tenths of its value. The war was a defeat and there was no glory to console her for the losses of her men and her resources. After the armistice in 1935, 30,000 prisoners of war marched home, and 50,000 soldiers, many of whom were Indians, suspicious of all other Bolivian elements, were demobilized. The country was tense with the stirring of social upheaval. In May 1936 a group of army "radicals" overthrew Tejada Sorzano. With the aid of the newly formed Workers Federation, the "radicals" put Colonel José David Toro in power. Apparently, he had the support of General Germán Busch, son of a German physician.

Declaring that the revolution was the triumph of Socialism in Bolivia, Colonel Toro enunciated 53 Points of Socialist policy which he pledged himself to put into practice. His government took steps to confiscate the holdings of the Standard Oil Company — whereupon wealthy mine-owners and local bankers, as well as the conservative landowning elements, took alarm. They instigated a counter-revolution which overthrew Colonel Toro on July 14, 1937.

The new Constitution (1938) served to perpetuate the monopoly of political control enjoyed by the whites and the wealthier *cholos*, by restricting the vote to literate Bolivians whose names were inscribed on a Civic Register.

In May 1938, General Busch assumed power. Pursuing a quasi-radical and quasi-totalitarian policy, he attempted to nationalize the mines, on the one hand; and in order to defeat the type of opposition that had overthrown Colonel Toro, he proclaimed a totalitarian dictatorship (1939). But the army revolted, and before long they announced that General Busch had committed suicide. General Quintanilla, a hero of the Chaco war, was appointed President. However, Bolivia was returning to her constitutional tradition, and Quintanilla gave way (1940) to General Enrique Peñaranda del Castillo, Bolivian Commander-in-Chief during the Chaco war.

World War II: 1940–1944. President Peñaranda at once took measures to protect Bolivia from German influences, which had been using the country as a testing ground. He expelled the German Minister (1941). Following a loyal inter-American policy, President Peñaranda maintained excellent relations with the U.S.A.; Bolivia paid $1,500,000 to American owners of the oil property that had been confiscated. On April 7, 1943, the government declared war on the Axis, although her Congress did not confirm the declaration until December 4, 1943.

President Peñaranda's administration was notable for its intensive road and railway building program. The U.S.A. had assisted in this work with ample credits and engineering facilities. The two republics developed an intimate association in order to study the social situation and the agricultural possibilities of Bolivia and to initiate practical measures for their amelioration and advancement.

In the meantime, disturbances among mine-workers had led to Leftist demands for complete social reforms (1942) — and to the exploitation of these demands by pro-German demagogues. The mine-owners insisted that they were being ruined by a recently imposed export tax on minerals. The increase in tin production (occasioned by the suspension of imports from Malaya) brought about an intensification of political passion: — only a few people (largely foreigners or Bolivians living abroad) benefited from this prosperous activity, while the masses of the people suffered more than ever due to a lack of imported goods. The so-called National Revolutionary party, a quasi-Nazi grouping, waged sharp political war on the old-line Republicans, Liberals, and Socialists. On December 20, 1943, the plotters led by Victor Paz Estenssoro overthrew President Peñaranda and installed Major Gualberto Villarroel as President.

Despite his protestations to the contrary, every American republic except Argentina suspected that Villarroel's régime had been instigated by pro-Axis elements. He was denied recognition. After being diplomatically quarantined for six months, Villarroel finally acted against the movement that had put him in power. He forced many of the pro-Nazi leaders out of the government, and proceeded to allow the free flow of war materials to the United Nations to be resumed. He arrested Axis agents and confiscated the properties of Axis nationals. By the summer of 1944 his consistent record of anti-Axis action enabled the American republics to grant him diplomatic recognition.

Foreign Affiliations. Although for many years she was chagrined over her territorial losses to Brazil and Paraguay, Bolivia's preoccupation has been her passion to recover from Chile a sovereign outlet on the Pacific Ocean. Although Chile granted her free port facilities in Arica (1929), this has not satisfied her conception of her primary need. Hemmed in and poverty-stricken, Bolivia has also recently sought to build highway and railroad outlets to Santos in Brazil and into Argentina, so as to serve her eastern areas.

Stakes in the Peace

Until economic stability and prosperity are assured, Bolivia will continue to stress external demands. Nevertheless, the constant resurgence of liberalism in recent years, after intervals of reaction, shows that Bolivians understand that internal improvement is their country's first necessity.

Bolivia is moving toward a better agricultural basis, tending to develop the limitless possibilities of the Santa Cruz region, with its pleasant climate and rich soil. The Bolivian Development Corporation is aiding cattle-raising and increasing agricultural knowledge, exploiting the newer farming areas, and arranging for rail outlets for their products. Thus, Bolivia's constructive possibilities are being developed, with the help and cooperation of the U.S.A.

Bolivia's political instability has been caused by poverty, by the monopoly of her natural resources by a few, and by the domination of foreign capital. These three circumstances have been aggravated because only a small part of her population has been involved in her political life.

Since the country's large metal production, however impressive in exports, is a fluctuating item and of benefit only to a few, it is essential that Bolivia diversify her agriculture and her industry, so that she can improve the condition of her peasants and workers. To raise to greater human dignity and scope both her Indian population and her *cholos*, the country will have to implement the recommendations of the joint U.S.A.-Bolivian Commission, which stresses the need for much higher wages, improved education, and broader social rights. The vast majority of Bolivians can no longer be so shockingly underpaid, so ill-fed, and ill-housed. They must believe in the prospects for social betterment if they are to become active participants in the life of their republic.

BRAZIL

The Land and the People

Brazil is the fourth largest country in the world. She is also the largest republic on the American continent. Her territory covers half of South America and her 42,000,000 people constitute half of its population. But these data of dimensions do not indicate the more significant respects in which Brazil differs from the other, Spanish-speaking republics.

She was discovered and settled by Portugal, which gave her a slower tempo, a less excitable nature, than that of the Spanish and English colonies. She was the only colony to which the monarch of the mother country came to make his residence. By living nearly fifteen years (1808–21) in Rio de Janeiro, King Dom John VI not only escaped Napoleon, but established Brazil as the real center of his empire. Independence was established (1824) by agreement between the King and his son already in control in Brazil — without the long wars of independence waged by the English and Spanish colonies. Instead of the immediate establishment of a republic, Brazil retained a monarchy for half a century, thus avoiding many internal upheavals experienced by the other republics. Her slaves were freed by proclamation rather than by a long civil war. For half a century (until 1889) Brazil was guided by one of the most enlightened, democratic rulers the world has known, Emperor Dom Pedro II.

Add to these unique experiences, the overwhelming size, physical resources, and beauty of the country, one can understand the prophecy that Brazil is destined to become one of the world's great nations. Two recent developments have heightened this possibility. One is Brazil's great contribution to winning the war by pouring into the United States factories enormous supplies of strategic raw materials, and by opening in the early days of the war the ferry route from northern Brazil to North Africa. The other development is the industrialization of Brazil, which is today proceeding at a rapid rate.

Brazil touches every state and colony in South America except Chile and Ecuador. On the north she borders the Guianas and Venezuela; on the west, Colombia, Peru, Bolivia, and Paraguay; on the southwest, Argentina and Uruguay. At Natal, her easternmost bulge, Brazil faces Dakar on the African continent, a distance of 1,865 miles or about eight flying hours. As a result of this relative proximity, Brazil has had closer relations with northern Africa than have any of her neighbors.

The astonishing diversity of the country, itself a universe, and the feeling of abundant nature, resources, and possibilities, cannot be expressed by formulas or summary characterizations.

The Land. Three-fourths of Brazil is within the tropics, and the climate is warm throughout most of the year, though not quite as hot as is commonly imagined. The coolest regions resemble the piedmont country of Georgia.

The rainfall is from 40 to 80 inches annually for most of the country, but far higher in the Amazonian jungle to the west. Here along the great Amazon River, extending near the Equator almost 4,000 miles (of which 1,700 are navigable), is the *selva*, the largest jungle forest known. Much of this vast hinterland was, until recently, unexplored, though tales of its profuse fauna and flora have been legendary.

The three most southern states of Brazil have a climate like the Carolinas and maintain a flourishing agricultural and stock-raising people, a considerable number of whom are of German descent. They largely retain their German sympathies and many were organized for Nazi propaganda by Hitler. Until the Federal government intervened to prohibit it, German schools, newspapers, churches, choral associations, and sports clubs used exclusively the German language. Travelers who spoke only Portuguese, the language of Brazil, often found themselves unable to communicate with the people.

The State of São Paulo is the most progressive, most densely populated, and pays about a fourth of the taxes of the whole nation. The former dominance of coffee is now rivaled by great cotton farms and rapidly multiplying factories.

North Central Brazil is overwhelmingly a land of dry, treeless plains (savannas) and scrub forests. But she has mountains (notably in the southeast) which, like our Alleghenies, do not exceed 10,000 feet. The map gives a deceptive impression of her peopling, since the bulk of Brazil's population and production is concentrated along the eastern seaboard.

Surprisingly little of the land at present is used for pasture or farming, only 1% (some 38,000 square miles) being under actual cultivation. Though the pastoral areas and the *selva* contribute some food products for domestic consumption, the country basically depends on this relatively small acreage for its staple foodstuffs. Thus, Brazil has over 1,000 persons to every square mile of arable land and if we consider the ratio of population to the area devoted to planted crops, the country is as densely populated as Argentina, with only Mexico and Peru among the Latin American nations equally congested. But the fact is that, like the rest of South America, which averages 14 to the square mile, Brazil is capable of caring for much of the overcrowded population of the Old World.

The development of the Amazon basin offers one of the world's greatest problems and opportunities. This enormous area, a large part of which lies in Brazil, measures 2,700,000 square miles — almost as large as the continent of Australia or about the size of the U.S.A. less Texas. A million square miles of timber await the axe. World War II has started rubber production again, now under scientific direction. Modern medicine and machinery are conquering the old drawbacks to living in the tropics. Difficulties are enormous, but this great challenge beckons to modern man, who is now seriously considering the problem.

Brazil is said to possess practically unlimited mineral resources, including an estimated one-fourth of the world's iron ore reserves. Her iron deposits, just north of Rio de Janeiro (in Minas Geraes) are reputed the largest single concentration on the face of the earth — yet they have scarcely been tapped. In manganese, gold, and diamonds she is world-famous. Due to be exploited are her deposits of copper, lead, zinc, nickel, and chrome, for the most part located in the mountain range running through central Minas Geraes.

Many Brazilian writers insist that the *sertão*, or backland (a thinly peopled marginal territory in the interior) is the "real" Brazil. But the outside world usually thinks of the country in terms of her thriving, modern seacoast cities such as Rio de Janeiro, São Paulo (near the sea), Bahía, and Pernambuco (Recife). Rio de Janeiro, the capital and perhaps the most enchanting of all cities, with its unsurpassed harbor, has over 1,800,000 inhabitants. São Paulo, center of the coffee trade, has grown with the amazing speed of a Detroit or Los Angeles: in 1883, its population was 35,000; in 1907, 340,000; in 1920, 579,000; and today, over 1,500,000. Futurist architects and town planners have found Brazil most hospitable to their conceptions.

The People. Brazil is making one of the most interesting experiments in race relations. Her objective is not a pure white race like Argentina's, a conservation of the Indians, like Mexico's, but a "cosmic race," made up of all kinds of people who want to be good Brazilians. Attacks have been made on this theory and its practice, but the Brazilians have largely succeeded in preventing such efforts. There are no Jim Crow laws against any race. Although in no group is there complete absence of prejudice against class or racial distinctions, Brazil prides herself on keeping down such distinctions and prohibiting them from any legal recognition.

The fundamental racial make-up derives from three stocks — Portuguese, Indian, and African. The intermarriage of these three races has made the Brazilian. Modern immigration, beginning with the Germans and Swiss as early as the 1820's, has brought succeeding waves of colonists, the most numerous being the Italians and Germans.

The product of this racial mixture, the present-day Brazilians, cannot be easily defined. Some estimate that they are 60% Portuguese or other European, 25% mixed with Negro or Indian stocks, 12% pure Negroes, and 3% Japanese and Hindu strains. Certainly, since the slave trade came to its inglorious end, the European proportion has been enlarged by five decades of dense immigration, for Brazil has had 5,000,000 immigrants since 1822, most of them since 1900. Italians and Spaniards followed the early Portuguese, and besides these Latin peoples, who constituted three-fourths of the immigration, there came numerous Germans, Japanese, Russians, Ukrainians, Austrians, and Poles. Most of the 250,000 Japanese live in São Paulo state, where they engage in truck-farming and other remunerative businesses unappealing to Brazilians. Much effort was made, with some success, to assimilate the Japanese; but like the Germans, they were found to have been working against Brazil. The whites are mainly concentrated in the south, the Negroes on the less crowded northern and central coast.

From 1920–41 Brazil's population rose by 36% (compared with 27% in the U.S.A.). The rate of increase has slowed down somewhat, with immigration now limited to 2% per year of each nationality's entrance in Brazil during the last fifty years.

The Brazilian people have revealed color, gaiety, and rhythm. The world knows their dances and is beginning to know their music, but the full cultural impact of this important civilization is not yet appreciated. Patient and tolerant, modern Brazil has never been aggressive. Her boundary disputes with her seven neighbors have been settled by arbitration — favorable to Brazil, for her diplomats are gifted negotiators. They compose more quarrels at Pan-American conferences and lead in more arbitrations than any other South American nation.

Brazilians were not, however, in the past vigorous fighters for social justice. A middle class has been slow in developing. A vigorous labor movement has not appeared to lead in reforms for the working classes. Society is still largely divided between the rich and the poor. The rich own great agricultural estates, and a few well-known families have built up fortunes that would be considered enormous in any country. A very few of these have now begun to organize foundations and charities to tackle the enormous problem of improving the health of the nation. Stray off the beautiful boulevards of Rio de Janeiro into the side streets and you find yourself in the midst of some of the most shocking slums in the world. Walk along the country lanes and visit the sharecroppers on the great farms; and listless, underfed, diseased peasants provide the reason why Brazil, with all the gorgeous life of her great cities, moves so slowly toward human efficiency.

The government has recently devoted much attention to alleviating the suffering of the poor. Social security, minimum wages, free medical attention, and housing programs have been inaugurated. Labor unions, under government patronage, have been strengthened. Foreign firms, sometimes freely, sometimes under coercion, have complied with the labor laws for improved conditions and high salaries more fully than have lesser national firms, especially rural activities far removed from the inspector's vigilance. The white-collar workers including clerks, bookkeepers, school teachers, and a considerable number of less successful physicians and lawyers have a difficult time keeping up appearances and securing anything like a healthful diet.

One answer to this most difficult problem — though certainly not a complete one — is an enlarged nation-wide industrialization, upon which Brazil has now embarked. Another hopeful development is the opening up of the West. Public posters now appeal to people to join the rapidly growing movement to settle the open spaces on the frontier. This offers the same opportunities to build homes, cities, railroads, schools, and fortunes as did the great pioneering adventures on the frontiers of the U.S.A. The settlement of the Western frontier, the development of the Amazon valley, the industrialization of the coastal cities, the enlargement and enforcement of social and health insurance, the opening of schools

See also continental map on page 187

See also continental map on page 187

for all children, are the hopes that animate the Brazilian people.

Religion and Education. Most Brazilians are Catholics, and the Church, though separated from the State since 1889, enjoys great prestige and exerts a strong influence on the national culture. Protestants number over a million, with large Brazilian congregations and influential schools in the cities. German Protestants count some 450,000 members. There are about 100,000 Jews, most of whom have come since the persecutions began in Europe. Shintoists and Buddhists dominate among the Japanese minority; national Christian Churches among 200,000 Syrians and Armenians; and Moslems among the East Indians. They all enjoy religious freedom. An interesting feature of Brazil's religious life has been the widespread diffusion of Positivism, a French rationalist cult, among the intellectuals. Brazil's national motto, "Order and Progress," is a quotation from Auguste Comte, the founder of Positivism.

Education for all the people offers a tremendous problem in a sparsely settled land like Brazil. Its cost per capita in the country districts is extremely high. The public school system provides tuition-free education, but attendance is not compulsory in all states. Illiteracy, once well-nigh universal, has been cut to 60%. About 3 children in 5 receive primary education (1 in 5 in 1916), and 150,000 attend high school. In thickly settled areas education is universal and of high quality. Brazil has 700 commercial and technical institutes, several agricultural colleges, and universities in several capitals, such as Rio de Janeiro, São Paulo, Porto Alegre, and Belo Horizonte.

Prolific and able writers, the Brazilians have surpassed the mother country, Portugal, in the quality and abundance of their work. In poetry, fiction, and drama, Brazilians have restored the Portuguese language to its former distinction. The social problem has recently become the dominant theme in all three fields. Long influenced by Paris, which used to be their cultural capital, they are now drawing on their rich native material. The flowering of art, music, and letters raises the possibility that Brazil may some day rival France for cultural leadership in the Latin world. The distinguished musician Hector Villa-Lobos and the famous painter Candido Portinari have recently been honored in various capitals of the world.

Brazilian literature is of old tradition and distinguished. Novelists like Graça Aranha and Euclides da Cunha have world celebrity. Machado de Assis, the belles-lettrist, was a name to conjure with in Europe. The deeds of the *Bandeirantes*, or daring pioneers, and their frontier descendants, the *Caboclo*, have created a rich historical fiction. Negro life is reflected in myriad facets of prose and poetry. In medical science, special Brazilian situations have fostered original writings.

The Nation's Economy

Agriculture. Coffee, raised mostly in the São Paulo province in the south, furnishes Brazil's leading crop today, its production varying from a high of 1,950,000 tons — 67% of world production — in 1933–34 to a low of 1,100,000 tons in 1940–41. Since coffee is a perennial plant, its cultivation cannot be easily reduced when there is a surplus on the market or immediately expanded in a boom period. Hence its price suffers wide fluctuations; and in the past decade 77,000,000 bags of coffee were burned to prevent a glut on the market. Once 71% of all Brazilian exports, coffee now constitutes only 16% (1942), thus making for a more balanced economy.

Brazil abounds in other important "money crops." She produces most of South America's sugar, and some 7.5% of the world's total. Cocoa yields 146,000 tons yearly, over a sixth of world production. Tobacco, introduced in recent years, now reaches 110,000 tons, by far the highest figure in South America. In cottonseeds, used for cooking oils, Brazil produces 1,300 tons, about 9% of world supply; while in palm kernels, useful for fats and soaps, she raises 10% of the world figure. In 1940 Brazil's extensive cotton crop was a fifth of the U.S.A.'s, in 1941 a sixth. *Yerba maté*, or Paraguay tea, is produced chiefly in the south, and carnauba wax, used for electrical insulation and phonograph records, is a leading specialized product. Original habitat and once the queen of rubber, Brazil is making intensive efforts to cultivate rubber again, but her output is still only 1.5% of world production. Recently rice and oranges have been introduced with success in the southeast.

But Brazil is not self-sufficient in staple foods. In such temperate crops as wheat, potatoes, barley, rye, oats, and even corn, her production is not large. With more than three times the population of Argentina, she yields only 60% as much corn. Hence the population has large segments who are visibly malnourished. But no Latin American country has done more to cope with this, nor has shown better results.

Animal husbandry is extensive: livestock numbers 41,000,000 cattle, 23,000,000 hogs, 6,700,000 horses, 6,000,000 goats, and 4,000,000 donkeys and mules. Hide production is important, though less than in Argentina or Uruguay. Annual production of beef and veal is about 920,000 tons, meat production being about half of Argentina's. But that Brazil could achieve much higher yields of milk and meat from her large cattle population is proved by the experience of Uruguay, which successfully substituted fine European breeds for the "Creole" stock.

The coffee plantations, or *fazendas*, are management holdings, farmed by tenants and belonging to big landowners, many of them absentee owners. But more than in neighboring Argentina and Chile, the trend toward small farms is growing in many branches of agriculture. This change in the pattern of Brazil's farming has been influenced considerably by the Italian, German, and Japanese immigrants. In general the Italians own small plots of land, the Germans usually prefer mixed farming with a variety of crops, and the Japanese engage in truck-farming.

But what has distinguished Brazil's agriculture — and, as we shall see below, her mining — from that of all other nations, has been the speculative manias to which it has given rise. The people have taken up one crop after another: rubber, sugar, cotton, coffee, oranges, and in animal husbandry, cattle — abandoning what they were doing to rush to a new "economic frontier" to "get rich quick." This passion for quick, easy money once burned more intensely in Brazil than even in the heyday of our own American westward expansion. Geographers have termed Brazil a land of "hollow frontiers," that is, a country in which plantations and settlements rise in mushroom style, only for whole areas to be forsaken within a few years, while the population moved onward in pursuit of another glittering promise. This development contrasted markedly with the American "winning of the West" in which each wave of pioneers left a residue of numerous permanent settlements.

But for the future of Brazilian agriculture there are hopeful auguries: the diminishing rôle of coffee (the speculative mania of the 1920's); the increasing diffusion of land ownership; the discouragement of "hollow frontiers"; and the end of monocultures, or excessive reliance on single crops. The last decade has reshaped national directives; long perspectives are replacing immediate gains.

Industry and Mining. As in agriculture, so in mining the Brazilian "get-rich-quick" pattern long played an important, and on the whole, damaging rôle. The gold boom of the 19th century was followed by a diamond boom. And today some Brazilians ask: "Are we now in the iron ore boom?"

Theoretically, Brazil possesses practically unlimited mineral resources. Her iron ore reserves, estimated at 25% of the world's total, scarcely have been tapped. Her gold mines, productive for centuries, remain important, with a yearly output of about 18,000 pounds worth about $8,000,000. Until the entry of the Union of South Africa into the field, Brazil was the world source of diamonds. In manganese, Brazil produces 5% of the world's supply. Other metals, such as copper, lead, zinc, nickel, and chrome, will probably be exploited before long. Mineral production actually rose eightfold from 1930 to 1940.

Unfortunately, Brazil lacks some of the commodities vital to modern industry. Her small coal resources, mainly located in the south, produce an inferior fuel. Though in 1940 a beginning was made in oil production, the country has no large petroleum fields of importance; and her important water-power sources have been inadequately exploited.

Nevertheless, industrialization is now proceeding rapidly, especially in Minas Geraes, aided by an influx of trained technicians (refugees from Central Europe) and by American government cooperation. Production of iron ore and steel, small at present, is expected to rise sharply when Brazil's five-year industrial plan calling for an expenditure of $150,000,000 gets under way. Total industrial production in 1939 was valued at $650,000,000, with some 825,000 workers employed in various industries, the principal ones being cotton weaving, flour mills, machinery, meat packing, paper, and tobacco. Rayon production, about 4% of the U.S.A.'s, already exceeds Argentina's. Industrial production of $900 per capita approximates one-eighth that of the U.S.A., more than half that of Argentina; and while this is not yet a brilliant showing, it registers an impressive improvement over 1930, when per capita production was only a fifth of Argentina's. One positive result has been the elimination of unemployment. The outcome of Brazil's five-year industrial plan and the ambitious scheme for exploiting the Amazon valley will put her rising economy to the test. Once industrialization is achieved, the previous economic history of the land and its difficulties will appear mere prologues.

National Wealth and Finance. The unit of currency, now called the *cruzeiro* (formerly the *milreis*) is worth about 5.15¢ in the free market, about a quarter of its 1929 gold value. Money in circulation rose from $247,000,000 in 1939 to $422,000,000 in 1943, while the cost of living has gone up only 30%. Because of the favorable surplus of exports over imports the currency now has strong backing; and the long period of recurrent currency crises and manipulations may have come to an end.

Brazil's credit position too has improved noticeably, though readjustments have been made in the foreign debt. The feeling persists in some financial circles abroad that Brazil could do better in readjusting her debt, despite recent measures in this direction. The domestic debt stands at $730,000,000, the foreign at about $330,000,000. Tax figures, excluding national defense and public works, amount to $250,000,000 annually, but these two omitted items must markedly increase the tax burden.

The total British financial interest in Brazil is $950,000,000; prior to recent arrangements, that of the U.S.A. was $550,000,000.

An agricultural people, relying heavily on single crops and possessing a relatively small arable area, is not generally a wealthy people. In 1928 the national wealth of Brazil was reckoned at $360 per person, a third of Argentina's. National income was estimated at $31 per person, less than any country in Europe except perhaps Albania, and one-seventeenth the average income of a citizen of the U.S.A. The recent spurt in industrialization does not as yet seem to have altered these basic figures substantially, although in the cities the improvement has been notable.

Of late, Brazil has shown decided gain in domestic savings and accumulation of capital. In 1930 14% of the national wealth was owned abroad, mainly by the U.S.A., Great Britain, and France. While some refugee money has been added to these foreign investments since 1939, the over-all percentage of foreign ownership in Brazil has considerably declined. This new and important phenomenon of domestic savings and significant local investment will increase economic independence.

Foreign Trade. Brazil's foreign trade has been marked by wide fluctuations in recent years. Exports dropped from $470,000,000 in 1929 to $175,000,000 in 1938; imports fell somewhat less sharply. By 1942 exports were $385,000,000 and imports only $238,000,000, giving a favorable surplus of $152,000,000. On a per capita basis both exports and imports usually amount to about $13 a year, about one-fifth of Argentina's. The major products exported, in order of value, are coffee, cotton, cocoa, hides and skins, and meat. Foodstuffs account for 44% of all exports, but coffee, as has been pointed out, has dropped from a position of overwhelming predominance to a current percentage of 16%! In peacetime the U.S.A. took 40% of exports, now it takes 46%; Britain's share has risen from 10% to 16%; and Germany's former share has fallen to Argentina, which now takes 13% of Brazil's exports. The most important items imported by Brazil are machinery and machine tools, wheat (from Argentina, mostly), iron and steel manufactures, coal, gasoline, and chemical products. Before World War II, the U.S.A. supplied 23% of imports, now it supplies 54%; Great Britain, formerly supplying 12%, now supplies 5%. Clearly, the U.S.A. has taken a commanding lead in supplying Brazil. German imports, formerly 20% of the total, have been eliminated.

Diversification of exports indicates a far greater stability for all Brazilian economy; the past shape of Brazilian trade is thus largely historical.

History: 1914-1944

In 1917 Brazil joined the Allies against the Central Powers. Although her participation in the war was largely nominal, her representatives attended the Versailles peace conference, and when the League of Nations formed, she became an early supporter. For some years she held a seat on the Council, withdrawing in 1926 upon the League's decision that her Council position could not be permanent.

Decline of the Federal State: 1918–1930. This country, that early recognized the need for an effective world organization of powers, was herself a loosely federated republic. In 1918 Brazil was not unlike the separate states under the Articles of Confederation which preceded the United States Constitution of 1787. The provincial governors of Brazil's great states were almost as important as the federal president. Since there was insufficient national cohesion the Federal Parliament spent most of its time in trading for advantages among delegates from the several commonwealths.

President Rodrigues Alves, who had served from 1902–06, was reelected in 1918. Too ill to take office, he was succeeded by da Silva Pessoa, who had served as the Brazilian representative at Versailles. Pessoa launched a policy of public works and obtained large foreign loans. However, the world depression of 1921 led to popular discontent, and a new President, Arthur Bernardes, was chosen.

Brazil's economy was slow to recover. In 1924 the coffee growers of São Paulo unsuccessfully resorted to arms against the government. Repeated doses of martial law did not seem a sure prescription for national well-being, and in 1926, the people, anxious for a constructive economic policy, elected Dr. Washington Luiz. He was known to be a strong champion of the coffee valorization policy.

Under this policy, an institute at São Paulo regulated the supply and price of coffee. The institute was authorized to effect borrowings abroad, which the Federal and State governments guaranteed. For three years (1926–1929) the country enjoyed great prosperity, but in 1929 the price of coffee crashed and the valorization scheme, heart of President Luiz's policy, became discredited.

Dr. Luiz nominated another statesman of São Paulo, Julio Prestes, as his successor. This led to intense indignation in Minas Geraes because up to now the states of Minas Geraes and São Paulo had managed between them to alternate the presidency of Brazil. Now that they had been by-passed, the people of Minas Geraes supported the presidential candidacy of General Getulio Vargas, governor of Rio Grande do Sul. However, the Luiz faction counted the votes of the election which showed, according to their figures, a victory for Prestes by over 300,000 (the total vote cast being about 6% of Brazil's population). On October 3, 1930, Vargas declared that he had been defrauded and proceeded to supersede the government. His power still continues (1944).

Vargas Centralizes the State: 1930–1934. The early policy of President Vargas was aimed at welding Brazil into a firm unity. He suspended all constitutional guarantees; dissolved the elected federal, state, and local legislative bodies; appointed his own followers and granted them almost unlimited authority. Before long there was resistance. São Paulo, habituated to supremacy, revolted in July 1932, and in October the President faced other uprisings, which he easily put down. The astonishing mildness with which he punished the defeated factions — a phenomenon rare in Brazilian history — won him a large following, and the next year he ordered a constitutional convention. Brazil held the first secret balloting in her history, and the opposition was allowed fair representation.

The July 16, 1934 Constitution embodied several noteworthy provisions. It granted more power to the Federal government than had been allowed by the Constitution of 1891. With respect to elections, it provided special courts and it gave women the right to the vote; but since the old literacy qualifications remained, most of the people were automatically disenfranchised. The Constitution embodied "New Deal" provisions for social security, yet it made a concession to the "corporate" ideas prevailing in the mother country, Portugal, by allowing a sixth of the deputies to represent labor, the professions, and the like. With respect to foreigners, the new Constitution imposed restrictions on grants of land, minerals, or other resources to non-Brazilians, and it protected the impecunious *intelligentsia* against foreign professional competition. Furthermore, in order to stem the threatening tide of Japanese immigration, the Constitution made certain restrictions

paralleling the United States quota law of 1924. After electing President Vargas to serve until 1938, the Constitutional Assembly concluded its labors. The President proceeded to restore state governments to their respective popular choices.

Divergent Tendencies: 1934–1940. President Vargas soon came into conflict with two large groups. Among the masses, radical ideas had begun to take hold, whereas the youth of both the native middle class and of the German element were aping certain forms of Fascism: wearing green shirts, calling themselves *Integralistas* (that is, followers of a synthetic or "organic" state). Their organizer, Salgado, stressed a mystical approach to politics.

In 1935 President Vargas faced a radical revolt under Luis Carlos Prestes, a young army officer; he suppressed the revolt and Prestes was placed in prison for an indefinite term. The *Integralistas* continued their opposition much longer, but they too were countered without any of the serious disorders that the government had anticipated.

Brazil had defaulted in 1931 on the large foreign debt of her federal and state governments. In 1935 by painfully difficult economy and rigid currency restrictions, the Vargas government managed to resume some payments on the debts.

But the coffee crisis, source of the nation's economic difficulties, did not subside. To maintain prices, a two years' supply of coffee was burned. But this price maintenance system worked out to the advantage of Colombia, El Salvador, and Costa Rica, because unlike Brazil, these nations were not bound to limit their output. Even the world-wide economic improvement (after 1933) failed to reduce substantially the oversupply of Brazilian coffee.

It became necessary to overcome the mood of despair in the country by resolute action. On November 10, 1937, President Vargas suspended the Constitution of 1934, dissolved Congress, and extended his powers to 1943. His proclamation was full of original devices, but in effect, the President was now to have legislative power. Congress was to be primarily a consultative body, while an "Economic Council" was to represent "branches of production." The President had the right to veto the choice of his successor. With state autonomy thus reduced, Brazil progressed still further in her evolution from a confederation into a nation. With respect to the nation's economy, the "peg" on coffee prices was removed and a plan of lesser dependence on coffee exports inaugurated. President Vargas pursued an active policy of "Brazilianizing" the Germans, who were now the largest minority problem, since almost all the Italians had already been truly assimilated. The *Integralistas* considered this policy a provocation. In 1938 they attacked the capital, and were bloodily repulsed.

President Vargas initiated certain additional provisions of a "New Deal" nature. Among them were a minimum wage law and the establishment of a Ministry of Labor. New legislation was also enacted to provide health services and increased rights for women.

The Inter-American Policy: 1940–1944. In 1940 President Vargas, despite his superficial similarities to Premier Salazar in Portugal, showed no ideological unity with the mother country. The fall of France was lamented by Brazilians and it stiffened popular resistance to European totalitarian threats to the Americas. President Vargas based his policy exclusively on friendship with the U.S.A. and he became her champion in inter-American relations. The conference of the Americas, held in Rio de Janeiro in January 1942, was the anchor of Brazilian policy. President Vargas issued a statement that democratic procedures in Brazil would be restored at the conclusion of the war but that the professional politician would be eliminated.

On August 22, 1942, aroused by the sinking of her merchant ships by German submarines, Brazil entered World War II. Under an earlier lend-lease agreement, the U.S.A. was to give Brazil about $100,000,000 in military equipment. President Vargas enforced a strict economic organization and thoroughly tracked down Axis espionage. Economic cooperation with the U.S.A. took the form of rubber projects in the Amazon valley, the equipment of Brazil's heavy industry by the U.S.A., and a number of other helpful arrangements. Presidents Roosevelt and Vargas conferred; and the crucial relation of Brazil to South Atlantic defense led to naval and military conversations between the two countries. In 1944 a Brazilian expeditionary force landed in Italy, the first Latin-American contingent ever to fight on European soil.

Foreign Affiliations. So long as Brazil was an empire (until 1889), she had close ties with Portugal, who was governed by the same royal family. Under the Republic her main political ties have been with the U.S.A., Argentina, and Chile; her financial ties, with Britain; and her cultural ties with France. Recently her political associations with the U.S.A. have been so close as to command admiration, and her jurists and philosophers have been in the forefront of those urging world organization.

Stakes in the Peace

Brazil is proceeding constructively to foster her sound national growth and to replace her "hollow frontiers." The Vargas government has oriented the country toward a diversification in the sources of income, which implies certain basic changes: a lesser dependence on monoculture, such as coffee, and the simultaneous development of a varied agricultural economy; a larger dependence on individual farming instead of the hitherto dominant *fazenda* or industrial plantation type; the rise of industries based on her mineral and agricultural resources; an increased average wealth to replace the excessive poverty of the masses; and the better use of the scrub country. Furthermore, Brazilian cattle must be brought up to the Uruguayan level in quality. With respect to the Amazonian rainforest area, it is possible that with proper hygienic facilities, this *selva* might become an important new area in the economic development of the nation.

Brazil has not lacked foreign capital, but it has been directed toward the production of quick profits. If this same inflow is more intelligently directed, the boundless possibilities of Brazil will begin to be realized.

The increase of centralization will assist this. So long as each state could default at will (and often did), neither federal nor state credit was sufficiently strong to assure more than a hesitant supply of fresh capital after each crisis. When capital did resume its inflow, it was always for quick assured profits, because it was wary of the possibilities of repudiation, once the boom was over.

Brazil's recent industrial understandings with the U.S.A. are a specific indication that the trend of her economy is now directed toward increasing financial stability.

CHILE

The Land and the People

Chile's motto, "By reason or by force," accurately represents her people. A combination of the strongest race of Indians in South America and the most vigorous section of Spanish Conquistadores of the 16th century, the Chileans have used force when the occasion demanded. After achieving independence from Spain, they dominated the life of western South America, and when Spain attempted to reconquer them (1860's), they proved victorious. Force, however, has steadily receded in the life of the nation.

Chile has played a prominent part in Pan-American conferences, the League of Nations, and the Inter-national Labor Organization. She has sent educational and military missions to various other American countries and has opened her doors widely to receive exiled liberals from Spain and neighboring American republics. Advanced social legislation preceded Chile's Popular Front government in 1938, which initiated a new struggle for social justice. Her free vigorous press gives more attention to labor and social questions than does that of any other American republic.

The Land. Chile, long and narrow, is on the Pacific Ocean with a coastline some 2,500 miles long. Geographically, she is perhaps the farthest removed nation from the world's key industrial and population centers, though the Panama Canal has made her far more accessible. With her long "shoe-lace" shape, she is topographically unique among the nations; nowhere more than 250 miles wide, the average distance across her territory is 100 miles. This would be equivalent to a stretch of land from Cuba to a thousand miles north of Montreal, and as wide as the distance between New York and Philadelphia.

In reality, Chile is three countries: (1) the Atacama or nitrate desert in the north, in parts of which rain never falls; (2) Central Chile, where 90% of the people live, a region exquisite both in climate and scenery, an Eden with fertile valleys lying beneath the towering Andes to the east; and (3) the southern country, with broken bays, studded with islands, excessively rainy and densely forested, terminating at Cape Horn in a cold storm belt, one of the terrors of mariners in the days of sailing ships.

In north central Chile the volcanic Andes, the tallest in South America, cover almost half the width of the country. Even the passes through the mountains stand at altitudes of more than 10,000 feet. The active volcanoes often indicate by their eruptions the approach of earthquakes which have so frequently and so disastrously shaken the country. As one goes south, the mountains lie closer to the Pacific, until there is very little land between the ranges and the sea. A series of long valleys intervenes between the Andes and the coastal range that rises abruptly from the sea. For this reason there are few ports in central Chile, Valparaiso being the only one of consequence.

Chile's total area, some 285,000 square miles, is larger than Texas, but her arable land is only 20,500 square miles, about 7% of the country, and nearly all of it lies in the central zone. She shares boundaries with Argentina (east), from whom she is separated by the rugged Andes; with Bolivia (northeast), from whom she took the northern desert in the war of 1879–1883; and with Peru (north, above the Atacama), another defeated and long unreconciled foe (until recent arbitration). Her western boundary is the Pacific Ocean, where it is least dotted with islands. Chile owns two remote island groups: Juan Fernández, home of Alexander Selkirk, the original of Defoe's *Robinson Crusoe*, and the Easter Islands, with their mysterious and awe-inspiring stone sculptures.

The Chilean population is highly centralized. About 4,500,000 of her 5,170,000 people are concentrated in the central third of the republic. There are located the three largest cities: the capital, Santiago (829,830 people); the dominant port, Valparaiso (nearly 300,000); and the city of Concepción (about 100,000).

The great *haciendas* and the owners of these estates who for a century have dominated the government, the economic system, and the culture, likewise are located in the rich temperate zone. The greatest financial returns, however, have come from the barren northern third of the nation, which produced 100% of the world's nitrate before this fertilizer was manufactured synthetically. There also is the world's greatest supply of copper — enough in one deposit to continue the present large output for more than a century. The third division is made up of the southern section, comprising the gorgeous lake region, comparable to Switzerland's in its beauty, and the cold,

rainy, sheep country, extending to Punta Arenas, the most southerly town in the world.

The People. Chile has a fairly high proportion (around 25%) of people of pure European descent, mainly Spanish and these, largely of sturdy Basque origin. *Mestizos* (mixture of Spanish and Indian blood) number around 70%, but the white strain in these persons of mixed race is the dominant element and is said to be higher than elsewhere in Latin America. The native Indians, Araucanians, while not on the same high cultural level as the Incas, were excellent fighters and have impressed their militancy on the national character. The Auracanians fought against the white settlers of Chile well into the 19th century and are not to be compared with the poor, beaten Indians of Peru. One of the longest of Spanish poems, *La Araucana*, by Ercilla, glorifies their resistance to his own people.

Of the foreign population of 105,000, the Germans occupy key positions in the dominant economic class. The German colony in the south near Valdivia numbers some 60,000, including descendants of German immigrants. (Hitler's agents had a more difficult time organizing this group than in some other countries, for many have become devoted citizens of Chile. Fifth Column activities, however, were fostered, which postponed Chile's break with the Axis.) Even the most casual acquaintance with Chile reveals the impressive number of English, Scottish, and Irish names in the front rank of her history, culture, and economics.

In the past twenty years, Chile's birthrate has declined from over 40 per thousand to 33, the deathrate from 31 to 20. The present natural increase is 13% per decade, but the infant mortality of 200 per thousand, while an improvement over the extreme figure of 265 of a generation ago, is still the highest *recorded* deathrate for babies in the world. (Burma's average, unrecorded, may possibly be higher.)

The three geographical sections of the nation might be used to represent three important classes. In the north, the *roto* (the ragged laborer) is dominant. He has been brought by contract from the big estates of the central section where he and his ancestors lived in peonage. In his new job as a miner, he receives higher wages, but in this desert, there is no water, no flowers, no music, only work. Soon the company store of the foreign-owned mining company puts up the prices, his shack grows too small for the rapidly appearing children, the hot sun gets more unbearable, the hours longer, and then comes the periodic shutdown. By now he has a union, which protests his pitiable plight. Social insurance has recently promised him medical aid at the public clinic, higher wages, and improved housing. A few foreign and Chilean employers have volunteered to cooperate in these matters. Improvement comes slowly.

The central section of the nation is dominated by the *hacienda*. The proprietors of these great estates are charming people. They live in large, rambling houses, dispense delightful hospitality, spend much time in Santiago and in Europe. They inherited the right to command and often dominate their house-and-field-servants with a kind, naïve severity, wondering why their patriarchal attitude should ever be criticized. They are accustomed to vote their peons in a block for the candidates who guarantee the continuance of the old order. They accept as a necessary part of life, ugly conditions which Chilean authors are increasingly attacking, including such facts as that 90% of the agricultural land is owned by 7% of the proprietors and the average daily wage for farm laborers is 3 *pesos* (about 12¢). Tuberculosis, illiteracy, and drunkenness condemn the exploited peon to an early death.

The southern third of the country is dominated by German colonists. Along with the German bankers, manufacturers, and merchants in Santiago and Valparaiso, they wield a large influence. This has favored scientific farming, clean hotels, and efficient business. But it has strengthened social rigidity, the military spirit, and the dominance of a self-elected superior class. In the last decade it has meant direct aid to the reactionary nationalists in organizing Fascists and foreigners to fight democracy.

A fourth class, a numerical minority but gradually permeating the whole republic, is composed of school teachers, social workers, employees in social security and other government agencies, university students, labor leaders, writers, and members of women's groups, who give their energies to social reform. These cut across all other divisions and make Chile today one of the most interesting social laboratories in America.

Religion and Education. The Constitution of 1833 provided for a strong association of Church and State. This partnership was protested in the second half of the 19th century and other religious groups were allowed to function, but Roman Catholicism continued in official favor. In the Constitution of 1925, Church and State were completely separated. Anticlerical movements, usually led by university students, periodically challenge the Church's dominance of national life. Complete religious liberty is granted to the Protestant minority, which is made up largely of German settlers, British residents, and converts of Protestant missionaries from the U.S.A., who conduct well-attended schools.

Chile is especially noted for her excellent secondary schools (*licéos*). Foreign educators have always been welcomed. The Argentine patriot, Sarmiento, here founded the first normal school in South America in 1844, the year before the Venezuelan Bello founded the university. German educators began to exert pedagogical influence in the 1880's. During the last twenty years many Chilean students have come to the U.S.A. and methods learned in that country are now influential.

Though education is tuition-free and compulsory, 25% of the adults are still illiterate. Today, 13.3% of the population are in school (the figure was 10% in 1918). Of the five universities, two (at Santiago and Concepción) have high scholastic standing. Normal schools are excellent and her several agricultural and mining schools maintain good standards.

Though Chile cannot compete with wealthier and more populous Argentina as a center of books and periodical literature, her intellectual life is just as active, modern, and stimulating, when population is taken into account. Chileans have written an impressive number of books on economics and geography; and their analytical works on history and literature are almost without a peer in the Spanish language. Their educational life was roused by Andrés Bello (born in Venezuela), one of the great awakeners of civilization.

See detailed map on page 169.

Chilean culture, until about 1910, unlike the Argentine, was predominantly upper class. For all that, it produced a realist, "the Balzac of America," Blest Ganat, whose novels recreated old Chilean society at its prime; but lately style has dominated, as with the novelists Eduardo Barrios and Pedro Pardo, and the futurist poet, Pablo Neruda, the idol of radical Latin American youth. But even stylists are concrete; the Chilean temperament rejects inflation or bombast. In Gabriela Mistral, first poetess of Spanish speech, religion has found a new voice.

The Nation's Economy

Agriculture. Chile is a land of great estates, one of which extends for 400,000 acres. These *haciendas* are veritable small self-contained countries, with fields organized on a comprehensive plan, irrigation centrally arranged, and peasants (the *inquilinos*) living in small clusters. To the outward eye, these estates look idyllic, largely because of the decorative Lombardy poplar trees surrounding the landlords' country houses.

Small farmers play a negligible part in rural economy, unable with their backward methods of cultivation to take full advantage of the rich soil and generally favorable weather. Chile's cultivated land is a third of Argentina's, per capita.

With 40% of the people engaged in agriculture, the main crops, wheat and potatoes, are usually adequate for home consumption. The rice crop is fair, barley, oats, and rye small, and corn deficient for home needs. Homegrown beans and lentils are the chief staples of food. The wine crop, large and of fine quality, competes with the best European wines.

But very little area is planted annually for food crops, most of the land remaining fallow or being used for pasture or alfalfa for the livestock. This emphasis on stock-raising is characteristic of a farm economy in which large estates, rather than small individually-owned farms predominate. The animal population is estimated at 2,500,000 cattle and 6,400,000 sheep. The cattle supply domestic needs almost exclusively, while the sheep give an annual wool clip of 17,600 tons for export. Despite the sizable livestock (for domestic needs), meat production is not impressive, and the output of butter, milk, and other dairy products quite small.

Industry and Mining. Mining, rather than agriculture, makes Chile a factor in the world market. Her copper production, the economic mainstay of the country, is around 20% of the world supply and 90% of the South American output! When copper is in demand, Chile prospers, but when there is a chronic surplus of copper on the world market, Chile suffers. Not only does she produce yearly 510,000 tons of pure copper; she is also the largest South American producer of coal and iron. Coal output (2,000,000 tons) equals half of the continent's supply, and iron production (1,000,000 tons) accounts for two-thirds of South American production. Gold production varies from 13,000 to 22,000 troy pounds per year.

Though the country has no petroleum, the foundations of industry are secure because of ample coal and iron, and extensive water-power resources. Hydroelectric development (now over 500,000,000 kilowatt hours annually) has helped build up the immense industrial centers of Santiago and Valparaiso.

In the north, the principal production of the desert is nitrate, with Chile supplying 100% of the world's natural supply (1,400,000 tons). Before 1913 these nitrate deposits were a world monopoly furnishing $35,000,000 annually to the Chilean treasury. Since then, synthetic nitrogen has been extensively developed in other countries and protected by tariffs. Moreover, the important by-product of nitrates, iodine, once a Chilean monopoly also, must compete with new petroleum processes.

Hence the key minerals of Chile's pre-1918 economy — copper and nitrates — no longer enjoy an unchallenged position. They are subject to world cartels and obstructed by tariffs; and though the war has created a temporary boom for these commodities, no permanent market such as they had in the past is assured them. Chile has therefore sought to use her natural resources to encourage native industry, and she has placed high tariffs against foreign manufactures to aid this process.

Nevertheless, while the index of production has risen from 100 in 1929 to 154 in 1942, employment in industry and mining has not notably advanced. Capital investment per worker is inferior to Argentina's by one-fourth, but output per horsepower-hour is higher. Thus Chilean labor is the most efficient in South America, the nearest to that of Western Europe.

Most of the manufacturing industries are native-owned, though there is some foreign investment, mainly American. In this they differ from the mining industries, which are owned by foreigners, chiefly Americans and some British. The leading industries are: flour milling, brewing, sugar refining, woolen mills, tanneries, wine bottling, shoe factories, and, in the south, furniture. The 300,000 workingmen in the factories now far outnumber the 60,000 miners and 15,000 lumbermen. Though World War II has improved matters, wages in industry are still extremely low, and the health and welfare of the city slum populations is a central political preoccupation. Upon rising industrialization and maturing agriculture are based Chilean economic independence. In a deep sense, the growth of industry is a striving for national fulfillment.

Finance and National Wealth. The outstanding fact of Chile's financial position is that 20% of the national wealth (until recently) was owned by foreigners. One-third of U.S.A. investments in South America are in Chile. Another outstanding fact is the extraordinary concentration of landed property in a small native group. A third is that Chile, considered for generations the most solid financial and industrial nation in South America, no longer occupies that enviable position. As her main export industries have become less dominant, her external financial position has grown more precarious. But the rise of tens of thousands of smaller capitalists, tradesmen, professional men, technicians, based mostly on industrial growth, begins to shape new, constructive possibilities.

This is reflected in Chile's financial history. The *peso*, the national unit of currency, is at about 15% of its pre-1939 gold parity and worth 4¢. There is also an "export" *peso*, used only for foreign trade transactions, worth 3.16¢. Prices have almost doubled between 1938 and 1943; and the cost of living, already high in 1939, has since doubled. Money in circulation (bank notes) has risen from about $20,000,000 to about $75,000,000 in 1942. Currency is covered by only about 10% in gold, but holdings in foreign currency as a result of the surplus of exports over imports probably give the currency adequate backing.

The foreign debt is $72,000,000, the internal debt about the same. Interest payments on the debt run to about $7,200,000 yearly. On the other hand, despite price rises and industrial gains, prices on the stock exchange have actually gone down, probably as a result of the political conflict between the present government and financial circles.

Total United States financial commitments are $700,000,000, British $250,000,000.

Foreign Trade. Copper, nitrates, and iodine have usually constituted more than two-thirds of exports, but most of the profits have gone to the foreigners who have risked their capital to develop these exports. The chief imports are textiles and machinery.

In peacetime, the leading suppliers were Great Britain and the U.S.A., with Germany making rapid headway, and Japan also entering the field. The leading customers were the U.S.A., Great Britain, and Germany, in the order named. The first two nations took more than two-thirds of Chilean exports. Peacetime exports were about $140,000,000, or nearly $30 per person, imports about $100,000,000 or nearly $22 per person.

Prior to World War II, Chilean exports fell (in U.S.A. dollars) by more than the world average from 1929 to 1938 (50% as against an average of 33% for the world).

With a per capita foreign trade of $52, Chile rivals Argentina's figure of $60. As a result of the war, both exports and imports have risen substantially to $177,000,000 and $128,000,000 respectively, with the share of the U.S.A. rising more markedly. The surplus of exports over imports thus bolsters Chilean economy by providing substantial reserves in foreign currency.

History: 1914-1944

During the first years of World War I, there was much pro-German sentiment in Chile among businessmen, educators, and army officers. Disturbances were frequent between partisans of the two warring camps in Europe. Gradually, however, public opinion veered toward the Allies, especially after the entry of the U.S.A. into the war in 1917. But Chile remained neutral, and her economy enjoyed a boom during the last years of the war because of the demand for copper and nitrates.

For nearly a century a few hundred landed families had governed Chile. They had remained as aloof from the rising merchant, industrial, and professional classes as from their *inquilinos* (tenant farmers) or the urban workers, crowded into ugly tenements. With the end of World War I, democratic sentiments asserted themselves. A clever orator and magnetic personality, Arturo Alessandri, emerged in the middle-class Liberal party. He advocated social reforms, democratization, and above all, labor legislation, thereby enlisting labor support for the demands of the middle classes. In 1918, after spectacular successes in the congressional elections, Alessandri became Prime Minister; and two years later he ran for the presidency.

The various Rightist groups, representing the aristocracy, united in a *Unión Nacional* to fight Alessandri. But he defeated their candidate by a single vote in Congress. He faced a divided Congress: the Lower House was Liberal, while the Conservatives controlled the Senate. A great deal of intrigue ensued, blocking most of his moves. He agreed to arbitrate the historic dispute with Bolivia and Peru concerning the Tacna-Arica provinces, but the Conservatives fought arbitration as an affront to the nation. Meanwhile, the country faced a post-war nitrate crisis as the European nations relied heavily on synthetic nitrogen for explosives.

By 1924, having obtained control of both houses of Congress, Alessandri proposed a revolutionary change: payment of salaries to members of Congress. Up to that time, election to this body had been an honor and a privilege coveted by wealthy aristocrats who could afford to pay their own expenses. This proposal meant that representatives of the middle classes would be able to hold office.

Unfortunately for Alessandri, his treasury was in difficult straits, and the army officers had not drawn pay for some time. Stung by his proposal to pay Congressmen while they remained unpaid, the army officers revolted and deposed him (September 1924). A military *junta* of two generals and an admiral governed the country. But the junior officers, soon realizing that they had been used as pawns to preserve the aristocrats' monopoly of Congress, turned on their senior officers. By January 1925, Alessandri was back in office.

Chile then adopted a new constitution by which the President, chosen by direct popular vote, received increased powers, while Congress was stripped of many powers and members of Congress excluded from cabinet posts. The constitution also provided for separation of Church and State. The government instituted a currency reform to cure the now-chronic revenue difficulties.

The Ibáñez Dictatorship and Return of Alessandri: 1926-1936. Alessandri had resigned in November 1925. His War Minister, Ibáñez, succeeded him as Liberal leader and in May 1927 became President. On the plea that impending "class war" demanded emergency action, Ibáñez instituted a dictatorship. He censored the press, jailed or exiled his opponents, and in 1930 was "unanimously" reelected. Despite the unanimity of the election returns, Ibáñez thought it prudent to assure himself of popular support by championing social reforms against the aristocracy.

But the world depression of 1930 caused Chile's entire economic structure to collapse. The government-controlled nitrate monopoly, Cosach, was in grave difficulties; the students and professional classes rose in protest. Though Ibáñez managed to survive the disturbances, he lost the support of the labor unions, who asserted that his reforms inspired no popular confidence. In December 1931, with trade paralyzed and industry at a standstill, Esteban Montero succeeded Ibáñez as President. Meanwhile (1929) the U.S.A. had made her award in the Tacna-Arica arbitration: Peru received the province of Tacna and $6,000,000 from Chile.

For decades Chile had boasted of her sound finances; now she defaulted on her debt. Her currency, which had been fully organized by an American expert, crumbled. Unemployment rose to threatening heights. The army officers, hating the old aristocracy, sulked until July 1932, when they overthrew Esteban Montero. Thereafter, a succession of military revolts shook the country.

A metamorphosis had taken place: Alessandri had turned Conservative. A Leftist officer, Marmaduque Grove, led the radical army and navy officers in revolt. He fulminated against all foreign banks and companies in accents that were the most radical ever heard in Chile. The only person to whom the Rightists could turn to defeat the popular Grove was Alessandri. With a bitter taste in their mouths, they accepted him.

Alessandri abandoned the older parliamentary forms and allowed the formation of a *Milicia Republicana* as a private army to war against Communists and extremists. But, despite the suppression of the Leftist movement, trade revived very slowly. Exports never recovered their pre-1930 levels and unemployment decreased only moderately.

Rise of the Popular Front: 1936-1941. Alessandri's political astuteness had not deserted him. He insisted that the best way to defeat the Leftists was by improving the lot of the *inquilinos* and workers. He placed foreign investments under control but at the same time increased payments on the foreign debt; and he stripped the Cosach nitrate monopoly of power.

But economic recovery was much too slow for large sections of the people. In 1936 the Leftist groups constituted a Popular Front alliance, the moderate Radical Party joining with the Socialists and Communists. Their presidential candidate, Aguirre Cerda, was a Radical. The older Liberal and Conservative parties joined in nominating Ross, a Liberal. Ibáñez entered the campaign as an avowed Chilean Nazi. Just before the elections, he attempted a *coup*, but when his bid for power failed he withdrew from the contest. Aguirre Cerda, candidate of the Popular Front, won the election by a close vote, polling 50.6% to Ross's 49.4%.

Aguirre Cerda became President in 1938. A devastating earthquake, which killed 25,000 people and crippled tens of thousands, made immediate relief more urgent than social reforms. Soon after this tragedy, the outbreak of war in 1939 made further delays necessary. Rifts in the Popular Front appeared: the Communists opened critical fire on the Socialist cabinet minister, Schnake, and the Socialists withdrew from the coalition. And in November 1941 President Aguirre Cerda died.

World War II: 1941–1944. The war made it difficult to find shipping space for Chilean copper and nitrates. Henceforth, every economic difficulty that arose was furiously exploited by pro-Axis groups.

Moreover, an interim Chilean government had to make important decisions at the Rio de Janeiro Conference (January 1942) bearing on Pan-American unity of action. The Chilean delegation played a somewhat ambiguous rôle, at times showing solidarity with Argentina. Chile's eventual policy remained unclear. In fact, when in 1944 some circles urged nonrecognition of the Argentine government, Chile dissociated herself from the U.S.A.

In February 1942 the Radical, Juan Antonio Rios, was elected president, defeating the ex-dictator, Ibáñez, now the choice of the Conservatives. In October, Rios appointed a Leftist cabinet; and in January 1943 the country broke diplomatic relations with the Axis. The government coupled this announcement with the statement that this rupture was "strictly diplomatic," and that Chile owed much of her progress to the peoples of the Axis countries.

Despite Chile's obviously hesitant and fluctuating attitude toward the war, the U.S.A. extended lend-lease in both arms and industrial equipment and made price arrangements for Chilean metals. Popular sympathy was decidedly on the side of the United Nations and the Chilean government kept a close watch on pro-Axis groups, especially the German minority of some 20,000.

Foreign Affiliations. Chile has on the whole been loyal to the Pan-American group of nations. Her friendly political ties with the U.S.A., however, have gone hand in hand with widespread popular resentment over the large invested interests of American corporations, whatever their contribution to Chilean development.

For decades Chile was hostile to Peru and Bolivia and even now difficulties with Bolivia are all too frequent. Since the turn of the century, she has been often associated with Argentina and Brazil as one of the ABC powers, but tensions and disagreements with Argentina have frequently occurred. There is some German tradition in the Chilean army: for years it has drilled, saluted, and marched according to Prussian models.

Stakes in the Peace

Chile's economic life has been based on exports of nitrates and copper. Though her nitrates are the most cheaply produced in the world, most other countries have turned to the costlier production of synthetic nitrogen, so as to be self-sustaining in time of war. Her low-cost copper production is now being challenged by Rhodesia and the Belgian Congo. Nevertheless, if world cartel controls are removed and if the export of nitrates is resumed on a purely economic basis, then Chile's export prospects are bright.

But, should the export of nitrates not be revived in adequate volume, then Chile would have to find alternative sources of income. These would be provided for by a continuation of the astonishing gains in industrialization and by a diversified agriculture. The modernization of agriculture, the intensification of industry, and the basing of the national economy on three foundations: farm, factory, and mine, would produce a more harmonious development and one that would diminish those difficulties that led to political instability for some time.

COLOMBIA

The Land and the People

For centuries the Spanish Viceroyalty of New Granada, Colombia today is one of the most liberal and democratic states of Latin America, the "Republic of Poets," as she is graciously known. This is all the more remarkable because the country is marked by diversities in people, climate, and terrain that are unusual even for South America. Despite many decentralizing factors, human and geographical, Colombians think and act as a nation.

Contemporary Colombia has done a great deal to unify the country through a great network of air routes. The first successful commercial airline in South America was established in Colombia following World War I. It gave splendid service, charged cheap rates, and educated Colombians to be one of the most airminded nations in the world. The journey on the slow boats up the Magdalena River from the port of Barranquilla to the mountain capital of Bogotá, which required from ten days to two weeks, was reduced to a few hours by airplane.

Colombia lies in the northwest corner of South America, fronting both the Caribbean Sea and the Pacific Ocean. Though her 439,828 square miles are larger than some fourteen of our United States, her population, estimated at 9,253,000, is less than Pennsylvania's. She shares land boundaries with Panama (once part of her territory) in the north, Venezuela and Brazil on the east, and Peru and Ecuador on the south.

The Land. The eastern two-thirds of Colombia are tropical lowlands, with very few inhabitants. The western third contains the centers of population, of farming, and of industry. Here are located the country's important mineral resources: gold, petroleum, coal, platinum, emeralds, and salt.

This western third is ribbed by four long ranges of the Andes with long depressions between the mountains. Here one encounters an amazing variety of soils, temperatures, rainfall, crops, and human settlements. Flora and fauna differ widely in these coastal lowlands, high valleys, and lofty mountain ranges. Virtually every kind of crop flourishes here, from the tropical to the Alpine species; from orchids to highland wheat. A startling feature of the landscape in the south of Colombia is the sight of snow-capped peaks rising directly on the Equator.

The Magdalena River is the great water highway to the Caribbean. At its mouth is Barranquilla, with a population of over 150,000, the leading port for oil and other products of the lower Magdalena valley. Nearby is the picturesque port of Cartagena, an ancient fortress of the Spanish Crown in the Western world. Though overshadowed by Barranquilla, it has regained some of its former maritime importance, today numbering over 90,000 people. Bogotá, the cultural and political capital (founded by the Spaniards in 1538) is situated in the center of Colombia, at 8,700 feet above sea level. With a population of 330,000, it is a modern cosmopolitan city with beautiful buildings (many of them built in the 17th century) and an active intellectual life.

The People. Within each of the widely separated and diverse terrains in the western populated third of the country, the people differ markedly in racial composition. It is estimated at: pure whites 31%; *mestizos* (of white and Indian blood, with the Indian predominant) 50%; pure Indian 10%; Negro, mulatto, and *zambo* (mixed Negro and Indian) 9%. The Negro people for the most part inhabit the lowland region on the Caribbean coast.

But these figures do not tell the whole story, for each population cluster in Colombia has its own specific culture. Even among the Indians there are dissimilar

See continental map on page 187.

tribes — from the highly civilized Chibchas in the mountain basins, to backward hunters and fishermen in the lowlands. Negro slaves were introduced in Colombia by the Spaniards in the first half of the 16th century, who also gave the country new domestic animals and plants.

The constant adaptation of plant and animal life to appropriate soils and climates has enriched the population developed in specific autonomous areas like the Cauca valley, the Cundinamarca basin (where Bogotá, the capital, is located), Antioquia, and lower valley districts like Tolima, and the great cluster on the Caribbean Sea.

Perhaps the outstanding group in Colombian history have been the highly developed Antioquians, who settled in rugged mountain country in the northwest and worked out a culture quite distinct from all the other groups. Most of them were dour, unflagging Basques, many of them Jews converted to Christianity to escape the Spanish Inquisition. This small group of people rejected Negro and Indian slavery from the start, remained European in culture, refrained from mixing with either the Indians or Negroes, and maintained a high birthrate (according to some, the highest in the world). Within a century they have increased from 100,000 to 2,000,000 (rivaled only as to growth by the Javanese and the French Canadians). It was the Antioquians who developed high-grade upland coffee, the mainstay of Colombian trade. Their leading city, Medellín, has a population of 150,000 today.

Among those of European stock, the Spanish elements overwhelmingly predominate. The isolation of the Spanish settlers in their several communities led to a preservation of classic Spanish idiom, Spanish customs, ideas, religious traditions, with the least deviations in Latin America. Their Spanish is often said to be the purest spoken in the Americas. In the cities there are some 3,000 Syrian traders and merchants. The total number of Americans and Europeans other than Spanish is under 30,000.

Colombia's birthrate is 32 per thousand, and, contrary to world tendencies, has increased by 20% within two decades. With the deathrate at only 15, a fairly rapid population growth seems assured.

Education and Religion. Illiteracy is about 80% among rural inhabitants, 20% among city dwellers. The over-all government estimate is 52%. Since the bulk of the population live in mountain valleys over

4,000 feet above sea level, difficulties in travel and communications have had an adverse effect on schooling. Traveling schools have been initiated. About 7% of the population receive education.

According to the Constitution, at least 10% of the annual budget must be spent on education, which is free but not compulsory. A feature of the system is its large number (365) of specialized schools and institutions. There are 30,000 pupils in normal and high schools. There are also 4 music conservatories, 2 art academies, 165 night schools for workers, and 5 universities, the most important of which, Bogotá, was founded in 1572.

Bogotá has been called "the Athens of America," and for a long time it was said (somewhat metaphorically) that grand pianos, hauled hundreds of miles over the mountains, were the leading Colombian imports and that from every home in Bogotá floated the sounds of Chopin nocturnes.

Colombian literature is characterized by sensitivity and delicate psychological perception. It has produced brilliant writers. The most polished idyll of the 19th century, "María," by Jorge Isaacs, was Colombian. Silva, the first Latin American poet to introduce modern imagery and rhythm, and the unrivaled linguist, Cuervo, were examples of the culture that flowed from the educated Colombian class, an evolution exactly contrary to the flowering of Argentine culture out of its pampa folklore. Even the first powerful realist, Rivera, in his *La Vorágine* ("The Whirlpool") used poetic inflection to depict the tropical forest and its effect on man. Indeed it is often remarked that poetry is the natural manner of Colombian expression.

The prevailing religion of the country is Roman Catholicism which long determined social and political life. Other faiths are tolerated so long as their tenets are "not contrary to Christian morals nor to the law." In practice, there is full religious freedom.

The Nation's Economy

Agriculture. The principal cash crop for export is coffee. Because of its high quality, it is largely independent of the wide fluctuations in demand for ordinary coffees, from which Brazil has at times suffered. Colombia accounts for 13% of the world's supply of coffee, being second only to Brazil. Bananas, another important crop, are grown in the Caribbean lowlands. Colombia's production of sugar, cotton, tobacco, and cocoa, however, is relatively small, per capita, for a tropical country.

Of the temperate crops, potatoes are produced rather abundantly; wheat, corn, and rice in moderate amounts. Despite 8,000,000 cattle, the country's meat production is insufficient for domestic needs. But valid generalizations about Colombia's foodstuffs are hard to make: in some areas, as in Antioquia, food production is at a very high level and shows a surplus; while in the lowlands to the east, it is produced on a primitive tribal basis and is consequently poor.

Industry and Mining. Industry is still small, having been long confined to local products. However, it is broadening in range and quantity and has begun to employ a fair number of workers in the larger towns. Mining has long played a key rôle in the nation's economy. Gold is found in almost every province — Colombia is the largest gold producer in South America: over 50,000 troy pounds annually. She is also the largest platinum producer in the Americas and was, until Soviet Russia developed the production of this metal, the first in the world. Colombian emeralds are celebrated for their quality, and their production is a carefully controlled government-monopoly. Other important minerals are silver, copper, lead, and high-quality coal.

Colombia's petroleum is rapidly coming to the fore. Though her annual production of 3,700,000 tons does not compare with Venezuela's, oil is second only to coffee as an export product. There are between 5,000 and 10,000 workers in the oil fields and about 25,000 employed in the gold and platinum mines. Considerable capital, chiefly from the United States, is invested in the mines.

Finance. Colombia is a land of conservative finance and remarkably stable economy. Her *peso*, the national currency, now worth 57.2¢ has retained more than a third of its 1929 gold parity, which is a better showing than that of any other South American currency. Money in circulation has hardly increased during World War II (today it is about $13 per capita), while the budget has risen by 50%, a conservative increase for a war period. The cost of living has risen less than 30% and the money is adequately backed by gold and foreign currency reserves. Annual taxation runs to about $6 per person. The national debt is about $60,000,000 domestic and $55,000,000 foreign, and about $3,000,000 is paid out annually for interest and other charges on the foreign debt. Prior to World War II, commitments and investments of United States citizens were $300,000,000 and of Britons, $150,000,000.

Despite her economic stability, Colombia's production is not large, about $66 per capita (twice Brazil's but well below Argentina's). Agriculture accounts for over 40% of this figure, livestock 20%, mining 10%, local industries and commerce, over 20%.

Foreign Trade. Colombia's foreign trade has remained on a remarkably even keel during periods of depression and war boom. In 1938, foreign trade was about $10.87 per capita for exports and $10.28 for imports; in 1941 it remained about the same.

Principal exports are coffee, petroleum, gold, bananas, and platinum, in the order named. Chief imports are textiles, metals, machinery, and automobiles. In peacetime the U.S.A. supplied 40% of her imports, Germany 17%, and Great Britain 15%. The U.S.A. purchased 60% of Colombian exports, Germany 12%, and Canada 6%. In 1942, because of a tanker shortage, oil exports markedly declined. Since coffee and petroleum constitute 93% of exports, this circumstance may have been the major reason why exports did not rise sharply under wartime conditions.

At present, the U.S.A. is clearly the dominant figure in Colombia's foreign trade.

History: 1914-1944

The Conservative party had governed Colombia for a generation prior to 1918, and in that year another of its candidates, Dr. Fidel Suárez, became President. Despite the rigid social basis of this party, which was largely under clerical auspices, a large measure of freedom prevailed, and Colombia's internal history was uneventful. The country's foreign relations, however, occupied the efforts of President Fidel Suárez, who strove to heal the wound that had been inflicted upon Colombia in 1903 when United States troops occupied the Colombian province of Panama.

United States Secretary of State Bryan negotiated a treaty under which the U.S.A. agreed to pay Colombia $25,000,000. The United States Senate, however, refused to approve the treaty because of its statement of regret over the action in Panama. The failure of the negotiations evoked dissatisfaction in Colombia, and President Suárez resigned in 1921. He was succeeded by another Conservative, General Nel Ospina, under whose administration the treaty with the U.S.A. was finally ratified (1922). Both countries displayed tact and wisdom, and cordial relations were at last resumed.

In 1926 another Conservative, Dr. Abadia Méndez, became President. There was a boom in coffee. The Colombian government borrowed abroad extensively, as did many of her provinces and municipalities. Optimism ran high, especially among the Antioquians.

The prosperity period was short-lived, as it proved elsewhere in the Americas; but although Colombia was affected in 1930 by the depression, she suffered none of the disorders that disrupted the peace of the neighboring countries. Liberalism, however, made gains, and divisions appeared within the ranks of the Conservatives. The Archbishop of Bogotá, who usually controlled the Conservative party, wavered between the factions in the face of rising liberalism. As a result, Colombia elected a Liberal President for the first time in forty-five years: Dr. Olaya Herrera, who had been the Minister to the U.S.A.

Under Olaya Herrera's administration, an acute controversy developed with Peru over the boundary question of Leticia. However, the arbitrators awarded the disputed territory to Colombia. President Olaya Herrera faced difficulties in the readjustments of Colombia's foreign loans, but he soon succeeded in restoring internal financial order. In the next election (1934) the Liberals triumphed again, and Dr. Alfonso López Pumarejo became President.

Between 1930 and 1934 the Liberals had been circumspect in ecclesiastical policy. But once their power seemed assured — the Conservatives did not contest the 1934 election — they adopted a new Constitution (1936) which separated Church and State and deprived the Church of its exclusive control of education. The Liberal government even insisted on modifying the *Concordat* with the Vatican, so as to permit civil marriages. The people of Colombia accepted these basic changes in social structure without resistance.

In 1938 the Conservatives reentered party politics,

utilizing the divisions in the Liberal party as their opening wedge. Nevertheless, the Liberal candidate, representing the moderate wing, Dr. Eduardo Santos, was elected President. His term of office was markedly successful. He governed with great moderation but with outstanding constructive vision.

In May 1942, Dr. Alfonso López, leader of the progressive wing of the Liberal party, became President for his second term. The advent of World War II confronted Colombia with a crisis in exports, owing to a shortage in shipping. Strikes occurred, but there were no disorders, and gradually the crisis eased.

Closely linked to Inter-American policy, Colombia declared war against Germany in November 1943. Her chief internal battle was waged against the serious inflation caused by the lack of imports and the high prices demanded for the few goods obtainable. The López government coped with these difficulties through anti-inflation measures similar to those adopted in the U.S.A. after 1940.

Throughout 1943 and 1944, Colombia's trend toward progressivism continued. Some reactionary army officers made an absurd attempt in 1944 to capture President López. Colombia's long history of orderly and increasingly democratic government made such a military adventure appear childish.

Foreign Affiliations. Colombia resented the U.S.A. from 1903 until about 1925 because of what she had considered the despoliation of Panama. This resentment has disappeared, and Colombia is today a sincere and trusted friend of the U.S.A. She has had boundary disputes with Peru, Ecuador, and Brazil, but only that with Peru has led to serious friction. Here and there German influences have been vocal in Colombia, but while they have seemed important at times, they have always receded. Despite her difference in social structure from the Venezuela of dictator Juan Gómez, Colombia's relations with that country were circumspect. Today her neighborly relations are entirely cordial. She is a valued collaborator in inter-American unity.

Stakes in the Peace

Colombia's greatest need is transportation; airplanes in particular can play a tremendous part in this country. She also needs a greater homogeneity in population, in the sense that rich and advanced provinces are too far ahead of poor and retrograde ones.

She is a land of financial conservatism, of increasing democratic maturity, and of broad social foundations in which peonage plays no part. Greater capital, large technical aid, agricultural modernization, and improved transport facilities would serve to develop this country, none of whose possibilities has as yet been truly realized.

COSTA RICA

The Land and the People

See map on page 197.

Costa Rica is the most democratic, the most progressive, and educationally the most advanced of the Central American republics. Her population is unique in the middle American area, for Costa Ricans are predominantly of European blood: four-fifths of them are descendants of independent peasants of northern Spain.

The country is remarkable in other important respects. She enjoys the highest per capita wealth in Central America. She makes the largest per capita expenditure for education. The ownership of her land is more widely diffused among her farmers than in any other Latin American nation, with the possible exception of Uruguay. Her newspapers and periodicals vigorously reflect the free and enlightened life of the country, which is essentially a nation of small farmers — a sturdily democratic land in which suffrage is universal and voting compulsory.

Situated at the narrow section of the isthmus between the Caribbean Sea and the Pacific, Costa Rica (meaning "rich coast" in Spanish) lies south of Nicaragua and shares frontiers with Panama. Her total area is smaller than West Virginia — 23,000 square miles. Both the economic life and the population of the land are oriented toward the Pacific, except for the banana country on the east coast. The latter centers around the thriving port of Puerto Limón, where Columbus landed on his final voyage to the New World.

Costa Rica also owns the strategically located Cocos Island, lying in the Pacific to the southwest.

The Land. The little republic is divided into three areas, grouped according to altitude. The Pacific plain is largely given over to livestock and extensive farming, although it contains relatively fewer large estates than most other Latin American countries. The great bulk of the population — over three-fourths — inhabit the lovely central, temperate highlands, whose average elevation is 3,500 feet. Above the highlands are towering peaks, some 12,000 feet high. This is a country of grass, with fresh winds and a permanent springtime climate. Here the cultivated area, centering about the capital city of San José, extends for a mere 2,000 square miles.

The third region, along the Caribbean, is intensely hot. It may rain 300 days a year, and the annual average rainfall is 263 inches. This is the banana country of Costa Rica.

The People. Unlike any other Central American republic, Costa Rica has an overwhelmingly white population: 80% of her 672,000 people. Unlike the other Latin American descendants of early Spaniards, the Costa Ricans sought to do their own farming instead of using the native Indians for their labor. They built up a small-farm economy which in certain respects reminds one of New England.

Most Costa Rican farmers, living outside the few cities of the land, live simply, work industriously, and with dignity. Painted windows are typical of their adobe dwellings, and colorfulness is a striking feature of their surroundings — from the brightly painted two-wheeled oxcarts of the men to the embroidered shawls and gaily printed flounce skirts of the women.

Almost a fifth of the Costa Ricans are *mestizos* (mixed Indian and white, with whites predominant). Many Negroes, however, live on the rainy Caribbean coast, and, largely English-speaking, work on the banana plantations. This minority is now establishing its own subsistence agriculture.

Costa Rica's birthrate is high: 43 per thousand; and the deathrate is notably low: 17. Thus, a 26% natural increase per decade is indicated. But there is no danger of overpopulation: the 10,200 square miles of grass and 10,000 square miles of uncleared forests in this country could contribute far more to the national economy if there were sufficient population to develop them. Costa Rica is indeed a land of opportunity and pioneering enterprise.

Religion and Education. Roman Catholicism is the state religion. There is complete toleration for other faiths, and the Church itself is here distinguished for liberalism and social vision.

Costa Rica boasts the lowest illiteracy rate in all Latin America, with a full attendance of her school-age children. She has more school teachers than soldiers, and she is *the only American republic* whose budgetary expenses for education exceed those for defense. The country has an excellent national university, a celebrated national library, several colleges, and many specialized institutions.

The capital city, San José, with a population of 76,000, is known for its architecture, its intimate appeal, its music, opera, drama, and generally high cultural level. Costa Ricans are energetic. They are active in sports, particularly soccer, the national enthusiasm of her young men. The high level of education is reflected in political stability, order, and humaneness — in the bullfights, for example, there is no victim.

The Nation's Economy

Agriculture. The principal export crops are coffee and bananas. Costa Rican coffee is raised mainly by small farmers on the highlands; bananas are grown on the Caribbean coast. These, with cocoa, constitute over 90% of the exports of this country that depends heavily on exports for economic survival. Her farmers do not neglect such subsistence crops as corn, beans, and rice, but Costa Rica's supply of cattle does not nearly meet domestic food requirements.

The government, seeking to end the country's dependence on coffee and bananas — both of which are erratic crops as to demand and price — is attempting to encourage subsistence farming, stock-raising, and the utilization of timber resources. There is some gold production, and the country is engaged in developing balsa wood (for airplanes), rubber, and cinchona bark production.

Costa Rica is the seat of a hopeful economic undertaking: the Government of the U.S.A. has collaborated with the other American republics in establishing an agricultural research station at Turrialba, near the Costa Rican capital, to help modernize and transform the entire agricultural system of Latin America.

Finance. The unit of currency is the *colón*, worth 17.8¢. Costa Rica favors governmental regulation of business and social security, insurance, for example, being a government monopoly. Taxes balance at $8,000,000 (or $12 per person), while bank deposits of about $11,000,000 ($16 per person) are fairly high for so small an economy. The country's foreign debt approaches $18,000,000; her domestic debt $8,500,000.

Foreign Trade. For a small Latin American country, Costa Rica does a flourishing trade. In the 1929–1937 period, imports averaged $9,750,000 and exports $11,300,000, or about $33 per capita for all foreign trade. Before World War II, 36% of Costa Rica's exports went to the U.S.A., 30% to Great Britain, and 20% to Germany, but today the U.S.A. takes 81%. In peacetime Costa Rica's imports came chiefly from the U.S.A. (38%), Great Britain (23%), Germany (23%); during the war the U.S.A. has supplied 81%. With World War II, however, imports rose sharply over exports.

Costa Rica's heavy import deficits, totaling about $28,000,000 in the 1938–41 period, are being remedied to some extent, but Costa Rica is excessively affected by world economic cycles. Her depressions and prosperity reflect in an exaggerated manner the unstable character of her markets. The export of bananas has declined from its former ascendancy. Today, owing to the diffusion of landholding among both coffee and cocoa producers, the rise and fall of their trade is almost immediately reflected in the welfare of the whole people.

History: 1914-1944

Since the adoption of her Constitution of 1871, Costa Rica has been an orderly republic. The only exception was the interval of 1917–19 when a reactionary, Frederico Tinoco, after an adverse decision in the very close election of 1917, seized power by a *coup d'état*. The U.S.A. refused to recognize him even though in 1918 he broke diplomatic relations with Germany. The inflexible attitude of the United States government encouraged democratic elements in Costa Rica, who finally overthrew him in 1919.

Julio Acosta, a Progressive, was legally elected President and served until 1924. During his term the country enjoyed financial prosperity, notably between 1922–24. However, the country was severely disturbed by a boundary dispute with Panama. Chief Justice White of the Supreme Court of the U.S.A. made the arbitral award in 1921, but Panama refused to accept it. Armed clashes occurred along the border and the U.S.A. interposed to prevent a major disturbance. While both disputants turned from force, following the counsel of the U.S.A., the difficulties remained unresolved.

Ricardo Jiménez Oreamuno, a former President of Costa Rica, was elected to the office in 1924. This administration contributed an important electoral law in 1925; voting was made secret, direct, free, and compulsory.

Gonzalez Viquez succeeded him as President in 1928. Electric power became a government monopoly in this year, which also saw the height of Costa Rican financial prosperity. In 1929, though the boundary dispute with Panama was still unresolved, the two countries had resumed diplomatic relations.

With the world depression of 1929–33, the economy of Costa Rica was severely shaken. Her receipts from exports sank catastrophically and they did not adequately recover until World War II. Nevertheless, the economic adversity of the country gave rise to no political disturbances, and the people continued in their orderly democratic habits.

President Jiménez Oreamuno was elected in 1932 for his third non-consecutive term. Costa Rica hailed the Good Neighbor policy inaugurated in 1933 by the U.S.A., and cooperated enthusiastically under Presidents Cortés Castro (1936–40) and Calderón Guardia (1940–44). In 1941 Panama and Costa Rica resolved their boundary dispute by negotiation, thus ending by their own offices, an inter-American problem that had persisted for years.

On December 8, 1941, Costa Rica declared war against the Axis. The government of Calderón Guardia confiscated the properties of her Axis nationals, including the German-owned coffee plantations. Economic and military collaboration with the U.S.A. steadily gained in importance.

The Calderón Guardia administration voted several social reforms, among which were socialized medicine and old-age pensions. In 1943 a Popular Vanguard party arose to support this social legislation. Archbishop Sanabria of San José permitted Catholic workers to join with Communists in this Leftist *bloc* and forbade Catholics to become members of Nazi or Fascist organizations. President Ubico of Guatemala, however, denounced these Costa Rican social reforms as "subversive," and refused to permit Archbishop Sanabria to visit Guatemala even in his religious capacity as delegate to a Eucharistic Congress.

In 1944 the elections resulted in a decisive victory for the candidate of the newly formed Popular Vanguard and National Republican party, Teodoro Picado. The present Congress numbers 36 members of the government *bloc* and 9 non-party members.

Stakes in the Peace

Costa Rica is racially distinct from the other Central American republics, with her population of predominantly European origin. She is an exemplary state: popular education is widespread and genuine democracy exists. She is the only American republic whose budgetary expenses for education exceed those for military defense.

However, the undue reliance on two crops — coffee and bananas — is a precarious basis for her ambitious social program, inasmuch as recurrent depressions would result in a demand for retrenchment and economies and hence would jeopardize her social reforms.

Costa Rica's problem is to free herself from excessive rises and falls in the economic cycle. Toward this end, she is striving to vary and intensify her agriculture. The large plantations on her Pacific coast present a problem, but fortunately the predominant upland culture, with wide diffusion of farm ownership, can be adapted to this change.

To preserve and extend their democracy, Costa Ricans would do well to balance their plantation economy with farming, stock-raising, and light industries. Such a development would afford a harmonious basis without which the country's stable welfare and prosperity would be more difficult to envisage.

CUBA

The Land and the People

Cuba, "pearl of the Antilles," one of the richest and loveliest islands on earth, was for centuries the most coveted prize of the New World. Settled by Europeans soon after Columbus' discovery, she has enjoyed for four centuries not only relatively great wealth but the oldest European culture in the Western Hemisphere. The Spanish motherland called her "the ever-faithful isle," but after recurrent, heroic struggles for independence, in 1898, with the help of the U.S.A., Cuba broke away from Spain. The withdrawal of the U.S.A. after the Spanish-American War was gradual: occupation until independence was organized (1902), supervision with the right of intervention (exercised in 1906), and finally today, complete political independence, although Cuban economy is closely aligned with that of the United States.

The Land. Cuba is a long, narrow island (780 miles from east to west, 25 to 120 miles from north to south) lying like a barrier between the Atlantic waters around the Bahamas on the north and the Caribbean Sea on the south. She is a hundred miles south of the Florida keys: Haiti is near her eastern tip, and Jamaica lies to the south. Her land area, 44,164 square miles, is larger than all the other West Indies islands combined.

Forested mountains cover about a fourth of the island, rising to 8,000 feet in the mineral-bearing regions of the southeast, around the celebrated bay of Santiago. There is a small highland area in the south, near Trinidad City, and another one west of Havana. But nearly three-fourths of Cuba is gently rolling country. The flora is one of the richest in the world. Many fine harbors indent the coast. More than half the land is arable: Spanish neglect is evident from the fact that only 3% was cultivated under Spanish rule.

Havana has a mean temperature of 76°; the monthly average is rarely under 70°. The trade winds alleviate the heat, and the dry season is pleasant. Tourists from the U.S.A. are enchanted by its climate, vistas, and incredibly blue waters.

The People. The most common estimate of the racial composition of the Cubans is half whites, a fourth mulattoes, and a fourth Negroes, but some put persons of white or substantially white blood at slightly more than two-thirds. The western third of the island is almost entirely populated by whites; the largest proportion of Negroes being found in the torrid mountain region of the southeast. There is also a small colony of Chinese and other foreigners.

The population is estimated to have risen from 2,048,000 in 1907 to 4,291,000 in 1940, and 4,777,000 in 1943. (The latter figure seems contestable.) Though it exceeds 106 to the square mile, it is not too dense for the resources of the country. Jamaica, Haiti, and Puerto Rico, her neighbors, are much more densely peopled.

Cuba is, above all, the land of sugar, and sugar is the universal topic of conversation. "What date will the government set for beginning the harvest? How many tons of the refined product will be allowed? What is the market in New York doing?" A hundred questions of this kind are eagerly discussed by field hands on the big plantations, waiters and boot-blacks on the city sidewalks, rich planters in their clubs, Congressmen in the gorgeous national capital.

The Cuban people have a reputation for gaiety which is natural for those who live in a country of perpetual sunshine, roses, and palm trees. During the cruel dictatorship of Machado (1924–1933) much thought began to be given to the national ills. University students led in opposition to the dictatorship and took the brunt of the cruel reprisals. About this time, labor also developed an effective organization.

A predominantly urbanized country (about 50%), Cuba has in Havana (population 728,000) one of the show places of the Western Hemisphere. With Madrid, Barcelona, Buenos Aires, and Mexico City, it is one of the five great centers of the Spanish-speaking world. The large immigrant Spanish population, grouped into "circles," according to the province from which they came, have shown remarkable cooperative enterprise. North Americans are active in engineering, in sugar processing, and are generally conspicuous in economic life. The sanitary work that transformed Cuba from a center of yellow fever to a healthy land, she owes to the Americans. The most serious unconquered disease is tuberculosis, which the government is striving to reduce.

Religion and Education. Cuba is predominantly

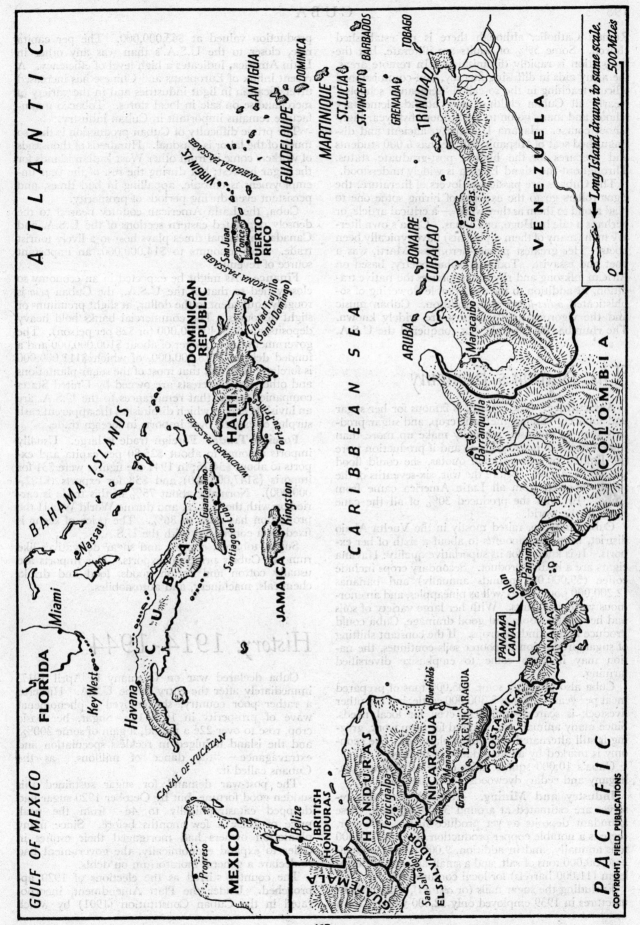

Roman Catholic, although there is no established church. Some 39% of adults are illiterate, but the proportion is rapidly diminishing. In remote areas, the army aids in diffusing literacy, non-commissioned officers teaching in the so-called "sergeants' schools." Nearly all Cuban children now attend elementary school, and many go on to the arduous five-year high-school course. Havana University, ancient and distinguished seat of Hispanic culture, has 6,000 students and prepares for the highest post-graduate status. Throughout the island English is widely understood.

The Cubans are passionate lovers of literature: the cigar rollers go to the expense of hiring some one to read aloud to them as they work — a critical article, or perhaps a tale by Hugo, or Dumas. Cuba's own literary men (many of them diplomats) have typically been poets. Her greatest patriot-hero, José Martí, was a poet and essayist. Today a ballad poetry, based on African folksong and rhythm, expresses the native tradition, in addition to the remarkable flowering of sophisticated *belles-lettres* and erudition. Cuban music and the vigorous native dances are widely known. The rhumba, for example, has conquered the U.S.A.

The Nation's Economy

Agriculture. The country is famous for her sugar and tobacco. Sugar, the basic crop, and sugar products such as molasses, normally make up more than three-fourths of her exports — and if production were not limited by international quotas, she could flood the world market. Before the war, six-sevenths of the sugar exported from all Latin America came from Cuba. In 1938 she produced 30% of all the cane sugar in the world.

Cuban tobacco, raised mostly in the Vuelta Abajo district, normally amounts to about a sixth of her exports. It is known for its superlative quality: Havana cigars are a luxury product. Secondary crops include coffee (59,000,000 pounds annually) and bananas (2,200,000 pounds), as well as pineapples, and an enormous variety of fruits. With her large variety of soils and her gentle slopes and good drainage, Cuba could produce many kinds of crops. If the constant shifting of sugar production to poorer soils continues, the nation may in time come to emphasize diversified farming.

Cuba also produces some 105,000 tons of prepared meat per year. She has 5,300,000 cattle, but her other livestock is scarcely sufficient even for local needs. Since many animals are required for farm work, grazing is still alternated with sugar planting. The economy is marked by an abundance of poultry.

Cuba's 10,000 square miles of forest produce mahogany and cedar, dyewoods, resins, and oils.

Industry and Mining. Although iron ore reserves are estimated at around 3,500,000 tons, these abundant deposits as yet produce little. However, there is a notable copper production of about 151,000 tons annually, and in addition, 9,000 tons of manganese, 50,000 tons of salt, and a small amount of petroleum (11,000 barrels) for local consumption.

Excluding the sugar mills (or *centrals*), Cuban manufactures in 1939 employed only 32,000 workers for a production valued at $63,000,000. The per capita rate, closer to the U.S.A.'s than was any other in Latin America, indicates a high level of efficiency. A recent influx of Europeans and Chinese has increased diversification in light industries and in the variety of merchandise on sale in local stores. Tobacco manufacture remains important in Cuban industry.

The prime difficulty of Cuban production is that so much of the labor is seasonal. Hundreds of thousands of workers come in from other West Indian islands for the sugar harvest; but during the rest of the year unemployment is chronic, appalling in bad times, and persistent even during periods of prosperity.

Cuba, the Latin American country nearest to the densely populated eastern sections of the U.S.A. and Canada, in normal times plays host to a lively tourist trade. This amounts to $14,000,000, an important source of revenue.

Finance. As might be expected in an economy so closely tied to that of the U.S.A., the Cuban *peso* is roughly equivalent to the dollar, at slight premiums or slight discounts. The commercial banks hold heavy deposits, about $140,000,000 (or $28 per person). The government has a budget of about $100,000,000 and a funded debt of $118,000,000, of which $111,000,000 is foreign. The fact that most of the sugar plantations and other large interests are owned by United States companies means that remittances to the U.S.A. are an invisible export which diminishes the apparent cash surplus of exports over imports in foreign trade.

Foreign Trade. Foreign trade is large. Usually imports amount to about $25.80 per capita and exports to about $34.75; in 1941 the figures were $31 for imports ($147,000,000) and $38 for exports ($182,-000,000). Normally about 75% of this trade is carried on with the U.S.A., and during World War II the proportion has risen to 86%. The price of sugar is fixed by a convention with the U.S.A.

Sugar, tobacco, copper, and sugar derivatives like rum are Cuba's principal exports. Her imports are usually cotton and cotton goods, food and drink, chemicals, machinery, and automobiles.

History: 1914-1944

Cuba declared war on Germany in April 1917, immediately after the entry of the U.S.A. Hitherto a rather poor country, she enjoyed a phenomenal wave of prosperity in 1918–19. Sugar, her basic crop, rose to over 22¢ a pound, a gain of some 300%, and the island indulged in reckless speculation and extravagance — "the dance of millions," as the Cubans called it.

The post-war demand for sugar sustained this sudden good fortune, but by October 1920 sugar had dropped catastrophically to 4¢ — from the peak price of 22.5¢ a few months before. Since many plantation owners had mortgaged their estates in order to expand economically, the government had to declare a general moratorium on debts.

The country stirred as the elections of 1920 approached. Under the Platt Amendment, incorporated in the Cuban Constitution (1901) by which the U.S.A. obtained certain supervisory rights over the island, General Enoch Crowder of the U.S. Army was sent to Cuba to ensure free and honest elections. The Conservative President, Mario Garcia Menocal, backed the candidacy of Alfredo Zayas against the Liberal candidate José Miguel Gómez. Zayas won, and despite opposition charges of fraud, assumed office. In view of the economic collapse, General Crowder thought it wisest to permit Zayas to be inaugurated (May 1921).

The government faced an economic crisis unprecedented in severity. Every native Cuban bank had failed; only the foreign banks continued to function. General Crowder insisted that President Zayas reduce the budget, maintain rigid economies, and overhaul the administration. When Zayas appeared sincere in his efforts to restore orderly finances and achieve real reconstruction, an American loan of $50,000,000 was made available (November 1922). But as soon as Zayas had received these funds, he decided against the economic policy he had pledged. The Conservative régime toppled.

Rise of Machado: 1925–1933. At the next election the Conservatives put forward their ablest candidate, former President Menocal, but he was defeated by the Liberal aspirant, Gerardo Machado, who ruled from 1925 to 1933.

During his régime, the Cuban Congress voted constitutional amendments (May 1928), granting universal adult male suffrage and extending the presidential term to six years with reelection prohibited. To buttress his power, President Machado lavishly distributed public offices and rewards and used the national lottery funds as a tool of political influence.

The world depression of 1930 led to the "Chadbourne Plan" to stabilize the price of sugar, and to excessive reliance by the Cuban government on public works to reduce unemployment. Both policies failed to alleviate the deepening crisis and to reduce the misery of the people. When students of Havana University led demonstrations against President Machado, he imprisoned and even executed many of them together with their sympathizers. Machado's repression grew fierce; his secret police tortured prisoners and executed many without the pretence of a trial before a civil court. At this point the U.S.A. proffered the good offices of Sumner Welles, her Ambassador. Cuban underground anti-Machado groups agreed to accept his mediation (1933).

Machado, however, refused to resign from the Presidency. Thereupon (August 1933), a general strike broke out: the people fought the police and the army deserted Machado. To the indescribable joy and relief of the people, Machado fled the country. The Cubans hailed the ABC and the other revolutionary parties as their liberators.

Batista Comes to Power: 1933–1941. The successful groups designated Dr. Carlos Manuel de Céspedes as provisional president. In September, however, Sergeant Fulgencio Batista led a revolt of the noncommissioned Cuban army officers against their superiors. At first a *junta* of five members had undertaken to govern the country, but on September 4, Dr. Grau San Martín, Dean of the Medical School

of Havana University, was chosen by his supporters as the provisional President of Cuba.

What had begun as a revolt within the Céspedes régime, became a revolt against it. For four months there was turmoil, the workers striving to occupy the mills and other factories; and the commercial classes were frightened by their activities. Production sank to a low point. Not until January 1934, when Dr. Grau San Martín resigned and Col. Carlos Mendieta, supported by Batista, became President, was there true governmental authority within the country.

The U.S.A., still acting within the framework of the Platt Amendment, accepted the Mendieta régime as based on popular approval and as exhibiting the ability to maintain public order and production. Some critics in the U.S.A., however, notably the radical press, insisted that the Grau San Martín régime should have been recognized.

After a long period of disorders and widespread unemployment, resulting from interrupted production, Cuban economy began to revive. She could now extricate herself from her crisis which had been aggravated by her default on foreign loans. A United States food credit of $10,000,000 helped her recovery and calmed her people. Finally, on May 29, 1934, a new treaty was concluded with the U.S.A., which abrogated the Platt Amendment, thus endowing Cuba with complete independence. Meanwhile, the U.S.A. arranged quotas for American imports of sugar, reducing the disastrously high tariffs on sugar that she had imposed in 1929, and granted Cuba improved facilities through the Export-Import Bank.

But the return to full prosperity was slow. A radical revolution of students and workers broke out in March 1935. Batista suppressed it and postponed elections. In June 1935 a new constitution was adopted which conferred extensive rights on labor, both rural and urban. Then the Conservatives attempted to regain power under their old leader, Menocal; but he was defeated by Miguel Mariano Gómez, though the real power lay with Batista. Gómez was subsequently impeached on purely political grounds, and in December 1936 Laredo Bru became President.

Batista, aware that no enduring social order could be based on repression, which he had used as a temporary tactic for recovery, and in order to carry out the liberal implications of the June 1935 Constitution, sponsored a constitutional amendment (November 1939) permitting all parties to vote in the elections, even the underground radicals and Communists. In July 1940 the voters elected Batista President for a four-year term.

Cuba and World War II: 1941–1944. Cuba declared war upon the Axis powers immediately upon the U.S.A.'s action. Intimate economic and military relations with the U.S.A. were established, broadening with the popularity of the war against Fascism. The Cuban government has gone to great lengths to sustain Pan-American unity and aggressively to defend democracy. The country has adopted new provisions establishing compulsory voting for all citizens, male and female, above 21, and the direct election of all national and local officials.

The government had obtained 98 out of 138 Congressmen in the 1942 elections. In the summer elections of 1944, the Authentic Revolutionary party (*Auténticos*), led by Dr. Grau San Martín, opposed the Batista government party, which was represented by Carlos Saladrigas y Zayas. Surprisingly enough — for the Grau San Martín party had not been successful in recent elections — Dr. Grau San Martín triumphed. It was considered a hopeful augury that Batista's following, although in control of the army and the police, fully acquiesced in the results of these free elections. This Cuban example gained immense prestige in Central America, where it did much to discredit prevailing dictatorships by proving that in Cuba democracy was compatible with order.

Stakes in the Peace

Cuba's stake in the peace is intimately bound up with that of the U.S.A., with whom she is linked by free, but close, economic relationships. Price rises or falls for sugar and tobacco, or external political events, as they are refracted through the medium of Cuba's leading customer, the U.S.A., are bound to affect the Cuban people profoundly. But this in no way implies a subsidiary rôle for Cuba's national policy.

Her internal problems — such as the need for a greater regularity in the labor supply, increased industrialization to provide for the floating seasonal surplus of labor, greater attention to subsistence crops so as to lower the cost of staple foodstuffs — all these are still secondary to the sale of her two basic products, sugar and tobacco. But with increased mineral production, and with greater diversification of agricultural production, Cuba's dependence on these two commodities will be reduced, and her relations to world economy will be more direct than they have been.

Cuba has always been loyal to international organization. The Republic does not suffer from a parochial point of view, which augurs well for her rôle in future world organization.

THE DOMINICAN REPUBLIC

The Land and the People

"The Cradle of America," the Dominicans call their country. Her capital, named Santo Domingo for more than four centuries, and only recently changed by the dictator Trujillo to Ciudad Trujillo, was the first European city in the New World. The favorite town of Columbus, who there initiated the building of the first Christian church in America, Santo Domingo is reputed to contain his tomb. It was a favorite home of the Conquistadores. The evidences of early American civilization, the first church, the first hospital, the first university, and the houses of early Spanish colonizers, dominate the scene of Santo Domingo and make it the historian's paradise. There are many beautiful tropical landscapes, rich agricultural sections, and forests of mighty mahogany. The people in general, as well as the selected group of scholars and writers, favorably known all over the Spanish-speaking world, are warm-hearted exponents of Hispanic hospitality and culture.

The Dominican Republic (independent since 1844), which shares the West Indies island of Hispaniola with Haiti, stands in vivid contrast to the Black Republic. She is twice as large, occupying the eastern two-thirds of the island, yet has little more than half the population. She is Spanish in culture, largely white in race, whereas Haiti is French in culture, Negro in race. The Dominican Republic is a land of great stock ranches and plantations rather than of small holdings, as is Haiti. She is three times as much affected by world commerce. Before the American occupation of

See map on page 197.

1916, the country had little centralized authority and much internal disorder. The United States Marines occupied the whole island for a considerable period. They left a legacy of modern roads and an improved economy.

The Land. Mountains cover most of the republic's 19,325 square miles, sometimes rising to 10,000 feet. In the west, facing Haiti, there is a large mountain basin. A long narrow plain stretches almost the length of the Republic from west to east (the Cibao) between the northern and central ranges; and in the southeast, separated from the northern plain by mountains, lies the level region containing the capital. Until recently these two leading farming areas had imperfect communications except by sea. The country suffers severely from disastrous visitations of hurricanes.

The estimated 1,768,000 population is thought to be composed of 40% whites, 20% Negroes, 40% mulattoes, but these figures vary widely. Syrians do much of the trading. The birthrate seems to be about 30 per thousand; other vital statistics are mere guesses.

Religion and Education. Although minority religions are tolerated, 97% of the people are reported to be Roman Catholics. The See of Santo Domingo, first in the Americas, was founded at the time of Bartolomeo Columbus, brother of the discoverer. It is highly honored, and its Archbishop is Primate of the Indies — which in the old days meant the Western Hemisphere.

Illiteracy is very high. In 1911 it was some 80%,

but by 1931 some estimates put it at only 55%, attributing the difference to the work of Americans and of President Vásquez. Only about 40% of the children attend elementary school, some 3,000 go to high schools, where English is now compulsory. There are a university (founded in 1538) and a conservatory. At present the franchise is limited to the literate population. However, education has advanced astonishingly from a generation ago, when only one child in ten went to school.

The Nation's Economy

Agriculture. Half the population lives in the long, narrow northern plain, the Cibao, and its famed eastern sections, the beautiful Vega Real. Most of the Dominicans here, independent farmers, raise subsistence crops (corn, potatoes, rice, tapioca) on small, fertile holdings and cocoa beans and tobacco for export. The Cibao area is less than 2,000 square miles. The other half of the population works on the great estates in the mountainous areas and on the southeastern plain, where sugar, the principal export crop, is grown. Coffee production in the Dominican Republic averages 22,000 tons, cocoa 25,000 (about the highest in the Americas). Tobacco production has now reached 25,000 tons.

A high proportion of the nation's land is under cultivation, some 6,600 square miles. Although four-fifths of the people live by agriculture, there is a shortage of farm labor, and 58,000 Haitians have immigrated. (Some estimate the Haitian population as far greater.)

The Republic's livestock economy is fair. There are 920,000 cattle and 850,000 sheep. Prior to 1880, cattle-raising was the predominant economic activity.

Manufacture. Such manufacture as there is consists mostly of processing food and tobacco. Fully 70,000 Dominicans work in the sugar *centrals* which produce about 580,000 tons annually. There is also a small output of prepared meat. A fair number of small factories in the towns produce consumers goods for domestic needs.

Finance. The currency unit, the *peso*, is equal to the dollar. The foreign debt (on behalf of which the U.S.A. supervised Dominican customs until April 1, 1941) is about $14,300,000. The internal floating debt is about $3,300,000.

Foreign Trade. Before World War II, the republic's foreign trade per capita showed $7.17 for imports, $9.44 for exports, as against the 1942 figures of $7.50 for imports and $11.25 for exports ($11,500,000 and $20,000,000 in all). In the latter year, the exports consisted of $7,800,000 for raw sugar, $2,300,000 cocoa beans, $1,400,000 coffee, $1,300,000 molasses, $1,000,-000 yucca starch, with honey and tobacco secondary.

Great Britain has normally taken 75% of the sugar crop of the Dominican Republic, and France 15%. In 1942, however, arrangements made through the United States Commodity Corporation enabled Britain to purchase the entire amount of the sugar export. In the same year, the U.S.A. purchased 51% of the republic's exports and furnished 75% of her imports. The second item constituted a marked increase, since the U.S.A. normally supplies 52% of the goods imported by the Dominican Republic.

History: 1914-1944

The Dominican Republic was a theater of revolutions during the first fifteen years of the present century. In April 1916, Secretary of War Arias assumed control of the government, being the fourth president within two years. The situation remained disturbed, and on May 5, American marines entered the country. Dr. Henríquez y Carvajal was appointed provisional president — but internal disorders persisted. In an effort to stabilize the situation, the U.S.A. formally declared the "Military Government of the United States in Santo Domingo" (November 29, 1916). Although this supersession of domestic authority was stated to be temporary, the feeling grew in Latin America that the U.S.A. would not merely interfere, as in Haiti, but that she would proceed to extinguish national existence when it suited her to plead "disorder."

The United States armed services took over legislative as well as administrative authority and trained a native constabulary. Material improvements followed. Orderly finances replaced chaos, communications were modernized, education advanced, and government became honest and efficient. But internal political demands for liberty and an end to the occupation necessarily mounted. On October 24, 1922, the U.S.A. withdrew her military government. A "Convention of Evacuation" had been arranged in June of that year to plan the orderly diminution of American functions in the country. In 1922 Sumner Welles arrived in the Dominican Republic as the personal representative or Commissioner of the President of the U.S.A. Mr. Welles arranged a treaty whereby, except for an American Receiver of Customs, the independence of the Dominican Republic was fully restored. When General Horacio Vásquez was elected as constitutional President, the Americans left the country.

For six years the Vásquez government enjoyed the fruits of peace and prosperity (1924–1930). But the onset of the world depression was used by reactionaries to end his popularity. In February 1930 he was overthrown by a revolution, and a provisional president, Estrella Ureña, was appointed.

General Rafael Leonidas Trujillo Molina, head of the American-trained constabulary, exploited the costly 1930 hurricane, which had devastated the country, as a pretext for his assumption of dictatorial control in order that the government might thus cope with the emergency. Once endowed with these extraordinary powers, he utilized military support to ensure his election as President in May 1931.

Trujillo became the classic dictator. He had his secret service, permitted no opposition, prohibited political activity, allowed neither free speech nor free press, exiled his enemies, and many assert that his secret police put his opponents to death. Like Díaz in Mexico, Trujillo worked to increase the industry and wealth of his nation, but only on his own terms — and with liberty as the price.

Boundary disputes with the Haitians and a wanton attack by the Dominicans on migratory workers from Haiti (See *Haiti, History*) interrupted Trujillo's program. However, he gained in importance within his country, and he even went so far as to change the name of the capital city, Santo Domingo, to Ciudad Trujillo. He arranged for the election of Jacinto B. Peynado to the Presidency and he later designated Troncoso de la Concha as Peynado's successor.

A new constitution came into force in January 1942. Now Trujillo seemed discontented with indirect rule. In May 1942 he became the sole candidate for the presidency under the new constitution. Prior to his inauguration, the Dominican Republic had declared war on the Axis powers.

Censorship in the Dominican Republic does not permit too detailed a knowledge of her internal history. In her external relations, both the U.S.A. and the Dominican Republic recently raised their legations to the rank of embassies. Prosperity and stability appear to have been aided since 1941 by the subsistence foodstuff program and the sale of her entire sugar crop to Great Britain. There has also been some return to common sense from the self-deification program which Trujillo initiated at one time. Nevertheless, no vestige of democracy exists in the Republic, and the discussion of politics is prohibited.

Stakes in the Peace

Unlike her neighbor, Haiti, the Dominican Republic is underpopulated, even though her population has doubled in the last three decades. Yet she would prefer any permanent immigration to that of the Haitians, who would profoundly alter her national composition once they were admitted for other than temporary harvest employment. Hence the sharp brushes with the Haitians and the summary treatment accorded them. The higher standards of living in the Dominican Republic, owing partly to an absence of population pressure, also acts as a barrier between the two countries.

The Dominican Republic's constant fear of mass immigration in turn tends to strengthen the influence of the military and of strong government within the state.

Indeed, unless some cooperative arrangements replace the present latent hostility to Haiti, the Republic's democratic structure (which can be firmly based only on small holdings in the Cibao plain) will be difficult to erect and maintain. Internal prosperity cannot by itself guarantee the perpetuity of Dominican democracy when it is restored to the people of the Republic.

ECUADOR

The Land and the People

Wedged between Colombia and Peru on the Pacific coast of South America, Ecuador has long fascinated schoolboys as well as scientists and painters. Children are incredulous when they learn in primary school that every day in Ecuador is of exactly the same length, owing to the land's almost precise equatorial location. *El Ecuador* in Spanish means the Equator.

Darwin found Ecuador's Galápagos Islands of immense botanical and zoological value, as his descriptions of their flora and fauna have shown. From his travels in Ecuador, the explorer Humboldt made important contributions to geology and physiography. Painters and explorers have come from far distances to see Cotopaxi and Chimborazo, whose panoramas of high volcanoes are the most magnificent known. For quite different reasons, Ecuador's port of Guayaquil has interested sanitary engineers: once "the pest-hole of the world" because of its endemic yellow fever, it is today a healthy city.

Ecuador's boundaries, long in dispute, are now peaceably adjusted, particularly her Peruvian frontier. If the more extreme claims of Peru and Colombia had been granted, Ecuador would have been left with some 116,000 square miles, instead of the 216,000

which she will probably include. However, the land effectively occupied by Ecuadoreans does not exceed 116,000 square miles, an area about as large as Nevada.

Ecuador, like Bolivia, has suffered much from isolation and from loss of territory to her more powerful neighbors. Since 1920, the now healthful city of Guayaquil has become a port of call for ocean liners, and the new Pan-American Airway service, which gives direct service to the interior mountain capital of Quito, has opened this picturesque republic to the outside world. A newly opened highway from Quito to southern Colombia takes the traveler through the most unique scenery in the world, a veritable avenue of snow-capped volcanoes, placed almost equidistant on either side of the mountain highway nearly 300 miles long like giant trees planted beside a broad boulevard.

The Land. Two high ranges of the Andes form the backbone of the country. Burning upon these thickly forested mountains are thirty volcanoes, culminating in Mt. Chimborazo, over 20,000 feet high. The panoramic beauty of this land at night, when the clouds are lit by crater fires, has never been captured in words.

To the west of the Andes lies the coastal region. Partly swamp and partly hill, this is the location of Ecuador's chief mineral resources — gold, cyanide precipitates, copper, silver, petroleum. It is also the source of her tropical produce: cocoa, coffee, rice, sugar, bananas, rubber, and the many forest products, such as cinchona, tannin, and balsa wood. The mountains farther east are reputed to be an El Dorado in minerals, but thus far little has been done to mine them. Basically, eastern Ecuador is a giant forest.

The two upland basins of Cuenca and Quito are the chief farming and population centers. The richly picturesque capital, Quito, numbers 150,000 people; and despite its equatorial location, the city's climate is cool, for it stands 9,000 feet above the sea. Guayaquil, however, has 180,000 inhabitants, for this port is Ecuador's leading shipping and commercial center. Physically Quito and Guayaquil belong to entirely different areas, and the British accomplished an engineering miracle when they cut through steep mountain passes to link the two cities by rail.

The People. Among the 2,000,000 to 3,000,000 Ecuadoreans — no reliable census is available — the racial composition is varied. Whites of Spanish origin are, however, competently estimated as 14% and *mestizos* (or mixed Indian and white blood, but predominantly Indian) at 29%. The *mestizos* dominate the lowlands. About 56% of the population are pure Indians. Except for a few wealthy families, they constitute practically the entire mountain population. Most of the Indians still speak Quechua, but a great many now speak Spanish. Ecuador is thus basically an Indian commonwealth, whose population is descended from an advanced nation which had been absorbed into the ancient Inca empire, although of different stock.

Some 12,000 foreigners had settled in the country. This estimate must now be increased because of the recent influx of immigrants, largely Jewish middle-class people from Central Europe and numerous Spanish Loyalists. This new immigration has greatly advanced the economic life of Ecuador and stimulated intellectual currents.

The highlanders contrast vividly with the coastal population. They are almost two nations. The political capital, Quito, lies in the predominantly Indian area, in secluded mountains, with a cool climate; these highlanders have little to do with the outside world. On the other hand, the life of Guayaquil centers on foreign commerce and the surrounding hot lowlands produce its export crops. Hence the deep divisions of this imperfectly unified country.

Ecuador's birthrate is nearly 40 per thousand, the deathrate about 20. Infant mortality is high (about 140). On this basis, only an average population gain is forecast for the next generation.

Education and Religion. Most of the people are illiterate, and yet education is legally free and compulsory. A recent survey shows that 50% of the children of school age are now in attendance, as against some 20% a generation ago. About 9,000 pupils go to high school and to the country's one large university, at Quito. There are also three small universities. The intellectual class has largely gone into political life.

Ecuador has consistently produced talented writers. The challenge of nature has sometimes led to a feeling that man is unreal, a transient phantom in an overwhelming panorama. Ecuador is the land of art —

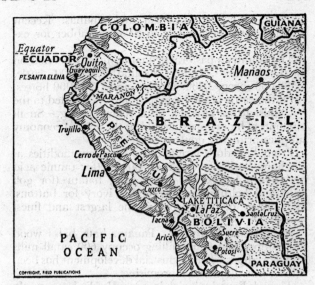

See continental map on page 187.

her architecture, sculpture, woodworking, and painting are distinctive and lavishly ornamental. Her poetry, as with Andrade, is extremely visual. Montalvo, her most celebrated writer, was full of Latin exaltation. Her imagery, too, is that of color and great shapes. Lately "indigenism," or literature centering about the Indian, has found its exponents here as in Peru and Bolivia. Jorge Icaza leads this modern school.

One of the evidences of Ecuador's intellectual expansion is a remarkable group of young writers who have banded together to publish the magazine *América* and to write on social problems facing the nation. Out of this effort have come a number of novelists who today are leaders in Spanish America. Their plots are usually woven around the life of the neglected Indians whose problems are now stirring the people.

Roman Catholicism prevails in this country whose capital has been for centuries an important ecclesiastical center. In the 19th century, Ecuadorean friars were celebrated for their numbers and influence. Other religious faiths enjoy full freedom; there is no longer any state establishment of religion.

The Nation's Economy

Agriculture. Over 90% of the people are engaged in farming, chiefly in the fertile Quito and Cuenca basins. Agriculture is intensive, and despite their low technical level, Ecuadoreans are good farmers. In the highlands, temperate crops such as maize, lentils, and some vegetables and fruits predominate. There are some large estates, but also many small holdings and Indian communal farming in which the land is worked in common. World War II has encouraged crop expansion.

But Ecuador is known much more for the wide range of her tropical products in her lowland areas. She is above all the land of cocoa, which is the chief source of both her exports and revenue and the mainstay of her commercial life. Other leading Ecuadorean products are coffee, rice, sugar, and bananas. Recent attempts have been made to develop rubber for export.

The country's pastoral economy, mostly carried on in the lowlands, centers around 2,500,000 cattle, 3,500,000 sheep, 3,200,000 pigs, and 1,200,000 horses. Even the cattle of the highlands must be herded to the lowlands, to be fattened prior to marketing. Small amounts of hides are exported but the animal economy supplies primarily domestic needs.

From Ecuador's forests come such commodities as cinchona bark (for quinine), tannin (for tannic acid and dyes), kapok (for mattresses), balata (for golf balls and belting), and vegetable ivory for buttons. Her supply of balsa wood is the largest and finest known.

Industry and Mining. Panama hats, balsa wood fabrication, and flour milling occupy 600 small mills and workshops. Thus industrial development has been minor, but the trend is promising.

Though Ecuador is rich in minerals, she has scarcely tapped this wealth. Petroleum output, however, is increasing rapidly; it is now over 95,000,000 gallons yearly. Other leading minerals are copper, silver, gold, and cyanide precipitates used with gold.

Finance. The monetary unit, the *sucre*, is worth about 7¢. Ecuador has conservative and well-administered banking laws, but despite stringent regulations, World War II has considerably forced up prices and living costs. Money in circulation has risen during the war from $10,000,000 to $26,000,000, and commercial deposits are now about $10,000,000. The annual budget, about $11,000,000, is modest, as is the internal debt, $2,500,000. But the external debt of over $29,000,000 is excessive in normal times.

British investments are $5,000,000 and those of the U.S.A. are $10,000,000. Ecuador, in view of her population and potentialities, has not attracted foreign capital to the extent of other American republics.

Foreign Trade. Ecuador's foreign trade in peacetime is usually about $13,000,000 for exports and $10,000,000 for imports. The war has expanded exports to $15,000,000, though imports have remained unchanged. The export surpluses are being used to build up cash reserves abroad. Owing to wartime shipping shortages, consumers goods have become scarce and dear.

Ecuador no longer stakes everything on cocoa, which once constituted 75% of her exports and is now less than 25%. Today her exports are more balanced and varied: they include gold, petroleum, coffee, rubber, Panama hats, bananas, silver, fruit, and nuts, in the order named. Her leading imports are cotton goods, metals, machinery, drugs and chemicals, and foodstuffs.

The principal supplier in peacetime was Great Britain (about 50%), who was also the principal customer (40%). Since the war, Britain has been supplanted by the U.S.A., who accounts for about 75% of Ecuador's imports and exports. The balance is chiefly carried on with Argentina.

Since most of the owners of the cocoa plantations, oil-wells, mines, and railways live abroad, much of Ecuador's revenue is drained from the domestic economy. Fortunately, a growing amount of capital has been lately reinvested within the country.

History: 1914-1944

From 1916 to 1920, under President Baquerizo Moreno, Ecuador concentrated much of her energy on the sanitation of her port city, Guayaquil. In this important task she enjoyed the assistance of the Rockefeller Foundation. This project greatly aided her commerce, which in turn contributed toward her participation in the post-war period of prosperity.

A Liberal administration under President José Luis Tamayo governed the country from 1920 to 1924. Difficulties soon arose with respect to the private banks, which had the right to issue paper currency. When their issues became excessive and inflation grew severe, the consequent economic distress gave rise to riots. Tamayo was denounced as a puppet of the private banks.

His government permitted the election of Dr. Gonzalo S. Córdoba as President, but only on the condition that his administration would not depart too far from the prevailing currency policies. In 1925 Dr. Córdoba was deposed by a *junta*, which gave way to a provisional president, Dr. Isidro Ayora.

The following year (1926) Ecuador set up a Central Bank and reformed her currency. These measures helped to restore prosperity, and in 1929 a Constituent Assembly formally elected Dr. Ayora to the Presidency. But the world depression forced him out in 1931. From that year until 1935 Ecuador had a confusing variety of nine governments, not one of which held power for more than a few months. The country suffered tumults and riots; impeachments and civil wars became usual. In September 1935 the dictatorship of Federico Páez, military overlord, capped the four years of quasi-anarchy.

Páez was an extreme nationalist. He expelled all foreign priests, declaring that the Church itself must be Ecuadorean. He repressed most of his possible opponents by means of a "security law" ostensibly aimed at social revolutionists, and then he "resigned." Páez was succeeded by Alberto Enríquez, whose actions against foreign investors and merchants alarmed business men. He engaged in a lively campaign to win over the urban masses, decreeing minimum wages and annulling foreign concessions. His administration was followed by another period of short-lived governments. Finally, on September 1, 1940, a "liberal and radical coalition" legally installed Arroyo del Rio as President, after an election in which 3% of the population had participated. In the coastal regions, however, the Socialist candidate, former President Velasco Ibarra, had polled the largest number of votes.

President Arroyo del Rio restored the 1906 Liberal Constitution and sought to form a National Union government of all leading parties. In order to cope with shipping shortages (caused by the war) and to control the inflationary rise in the cost of living, his government took on extraordinary war powers (1940). It embarked upon important road-building projects and, with the cooperation of the U.S.A., it initiated a program of economic recovery and development.

In 1941 Peru entered the El Oro region, which had long been in dispute between Ecuador and Peru. The controversy was later resolved by means of a protocol negotiated directly by the representatives of Peru and Ecuador. The representatives of four other American republics, namely, the U.S.A., Brazil, Chile, and Argentina, acted as friendly advisers, urging this direct settlement. In 1942 Ecuador granted naval facilities on the Galápagos Islands and Santa Elena for inter-American defense.

In the late spring of 1944 a revolution broke out in Ecuador. Followers of the Socialist, Velasco Ibarra, overthrew the Arroyo del Rio government, as the Socialist stronghold of Guayaquil led the movement against the upland groupings. The ease with which this popular rebellion succeeded, gave rise to its imitation in many Central American countries.

Foreign Affiliations. Ecuador has generally been on bad terms with her neighbors. Her statesmen have exploited questions of boundary, although Ecuador's population has not as yet fully utilized the much larger undisputed sections of her territory. Recently all the boundary disputes have been resolved. German propagandists have tried to influence the country, but with little success: Ecuador is a firm adherent of Inter-American policy.

Stakes in the Peace

Ecuador is two countries: lowland and mountain, and two peoples: the more prosperous group and the peons. In few other lands — excepting always Peru and Bolivia — is the lot of the native Indian so poor and his subjection so profound. *Aprismo* (See *Peru,*

History) has begun to show its influence in Ecuador, but to a much smaller extent than in Peru. However, the recent formation of a Protective Council for Indians has done much to ameliorate their lot. Fortunately, the development of the lowlands indicates that Ecuador will give rise to a larger commercial and light manufacturing class. With these changes, the reign of politics as the governing passion of the literate, will be reduced.

Ecuador is avid for improvement. Carefully directed foreign investment could easily increase her industrial wealth and also intensify her mining activity. This country, which has perhaps the greatest natural beauty on earth for a comparable area and whose cities are aesthetic delights, ought to enjoy a large tourist trade.

But not until the Indian village, or *commune*, is made into a basis for agricultural well-being, can Ecuador escape the frequent political explosions, which are almost always indicative of an intensive struggle for the few prizes that a poor society can offer. Democracy, to be successful in Ecuador, requires an adequate basis in production, in diffused ownership, and in education among the mass of the Indian people.

With the boundary disputes over, the Ecuadorean people are free of the vicious circle of past generations in which boundary disputes were invariably used for internal party politics — and internal party politics rendered the settlement of boundary disputes impossible. The people of Ecuador can now concentrate on political stabilization internally and the development of their great natural resources.

GUATEMALA

The Land and the People

The most populous of the Central American republics, Guatemala remains basically an Indian country — as she was when the Spaniards first came to her soil in the early 16th century.

The land is for the most part mountain. The Sierra Madre volcanic ranges lie in the southwestern regions, a marked contrast to the tangled jungle in the northern plain of Petén. Buried beneath these semi-tropical forests are the ancient ruins of the Mayan empire — a paradise of archaeologists and a source of many fictions about the Indian white god, Quetzalcoatl. Today the descendants of the Mayas, masters of folk art, gifted in music and crafts, attract foreign tourists to their beautiful land, which has begun to rival Mexico as a mecca for travelers.

The Land. Guatemala covers 45,450 square miles. Washed by both the Caribbean Sea and the Pacific Ocean, she is bounded by Mexico (northwest), British Honduras (northeast), Honduras (east), and El Sal-

See maps on pages 197, 217.

vador (southeast). Her economic life is directed toward the Pacific region, where the mass of her people live. The highland basins are by far the most densely populated sections, for the lowlands near the Caribbean are swampy, and the western areas are dotted with active volcanoes and suffer severe earthquakes. Most Guatemalans live at average elevations of 5,000, where the climate is excellent.

With the scarcity of consumers goods, owing to shipping shortages in World War II, factories have quickly developed in Guatemala. Around these have clustered large numbers of Guatemalans, pressing in from the farms for higher wages. Flour mills and cotton manufactures feature this development, which has also called forth new and fruitful attention to such matters as modern housing, playgrounds, clinics, and schools. Modern dairies, with pasteurized milk and delectable cheeses, are beginning to appear, prophesying a remarkable change from the time when the poor regarded milk as the most dangerous food for children.

These and many other improvements are made possible by the system of modern highways, which are reducing the old isolation of Guatemalans — when the Pacific and Caribbean and the northern and southern sections were practically different countries. An influx of United States government employees, assisting in the development of industrial production, has still further broadened the nation's outlook — an outlook that had already been opened by the increasing tourist traffic.

The People. Guatemala's population of 3,284,000 is the largest of the Central American republics. About 65% of the people are pure Indian and 32% *mestizos* (Indian and white, with Indian predominance). The white population is estimated at from 1% to 2¼%. Most of the European and other white elements inhabit the capital, Guatemala City, which has about 145,000 people.

Nearly all the Indian population live away from the towns, in their own fairly autonomous communities. Unlike other Central American Indians, who participate in national life and speak Spanish, the Mayans of Guatemala retain their own Indian dialects and raise subsistence crops that are virtually unrelated to the commercial life of the country. Mayan women create colorful blankets and textiles, gems of craftsmanship and famous throughout the world. Guatemalan towns are made vivid by the weekly visits of the Indians. Laden with dyestuffs, pottery, cloths, and other products of handicraft, as well as vegetables and fruit, the Indian comes to market to sell his goods — and to create a social life.

Guatemala's natural rate of increase is high. The birthrate is 32 per thousand — a decline from the extreme figure of 52 of a generation ago. The deathrate is 18. Infant mortality, at 102, is lower than both Mexico's and Costa Rica's. These figures estimate that the population should increase by some 15% per decade.

Religion and Education. Roman Catholicism is the established religion, but other faiths are tolerated. Many vestiges of Indian religion are encountered — in folkways as well as material monuments.

In view of the relative cultural isolation of the Indians, who constitute two-thirds of the people, it is not surprising to find that illiteracy is high (80%). About a fourth of the children of school age seem to be receiving elementary instruction, and schools are rapidly being increased. Guatemala has a national university as well. But this picture of education may undergo a drastic change, as a result of the industrial progress in Guatemala brought about in the course of World War II.

Guatemalan literature possesses the originality of an isolated culture. Arevalo Martínez, who has been called a "Latin American Poe," is considered to have fashioned a new literary genre, specializing in bizarre effects.

The Nation's Economy

Agriculture. All plantations in Guatemala have been ordered to produce subsistence crops for the 3,500,000 people (the largest population in Central America). Corn is the major product for domestic consumption, followed by wheat, beans, rice, and plantain. With livestock, except for swine, astonishingly deficient, the meat supply is almost trifling. The amount of milk available per person is only a fortieth of the comparable amount in the U.S.A.

Bananas and coffee, Guatemala's two chief cash crops, constitute 90% of all her exports. Her banana acreage, exceedingly fertile, rivals in size the banana plantations of once-supreme Honduras. Her coffee, of exquisite quality, now furnishes 2.7% of the world supply. Sugar (25,000 tons) lags behind as her third export crop, chicle (used for chewing gum) and henequen lead as export items of the eastern areas.

Coffee plantations were in the hands of two groups: the old families of Guatemala, who produced 36% of the crop, and the Germans, who, until 1941, produced about 64%. The properties of the latter were taken over by the government during World War II.

There has been a rise in such industries as manila hemp, coffee-cleaning, flour milling, pottery, and textiles. The latter two in particular flourish because of their quality, originality, and design; they are highly valued in American art-goods shops. Mining is not extensive; gold and chromite are relatively minor export items.

Finance and Foreign Trade. The unit of currency is the *quetzal*. Guatemalan money is sound, with a cover of 130%. Though money in circulation has risen 50% during the war, it is still only $3.60 per capita. The leading Guatemalan banks show deposits of $2,000,000 — about 60¢ per person. The poverty of the people is intense. Their per capita net income is estimated at $32; that is, about $3 per week per family.

Taxes are about $10,000,000. The internal debt is only $3,800,000, and the foreign debt (on which redemption has been resumed) is £1,500,000.

Foreign trade in peacetime showed an unfavorable balance. Imports were $9.25 per capita, and exports only $7.20. By 1942 this balance was reversed. With $4.50 per capita for imports and $6.50 for exports, there resulted a surplus of deposits abroad that has increased foreign exchange reserves.

In peacetime the U.S.A. supplied 41% of Guatemalan imports, Germany 22%, Britain 10%. Of Guatemala's exports 52% normally went to the U.S.A., 22% to Germany, 9% to the Netherlands, and 6% to Sweden (whose connoisseurs prefer Guatemalan coffee). During World War II, the U.S.A. furnished 70% of all imports and took 90% of all exports.

Guatemalan exports had shifted in 1942: coffee was 48%, bananas 31%, chicle 7%; the percentage of coffee having diminished with the loss of important European markets. Commerce with Mexico is expected to increase now that a new bridge has been completed by the International Railways of Central America. The Pan-American highway, an inter-American project, has proved another aid to commerce.

History: 1914-1944

For some twenty years prior to 1918, Guatemala was ruled by a tyrant, Estrada Cabrera. He mockingly defaulted on debts, opposed amity with other nations, and imprisoned foreigners according to his whims. His merciless reign culminated with his attempt in 1919 to suppress all opposition on the ground that his political enemies were Unionists — that is, they favored a Central American Federation in place of the five, small independent republics.

The following April the Guatemalan Congress, after years of servility, finally dared to impeach Estrada Cabrera. In his place they elected a wealthy merchant and Unionist, Carlos Herrera. With the cause of Federation thus advanced, a Central American Conference met in December 1920 at San José, Costa Rica. A violent controversy erupted over the Bryan-Chamorro agreement between Nicaragua and the U.S.A. (See *Nicaragua*). Nicaragua withdrew from the projected Central American Federation, and Costa Rica, fearful of involvement, soon followed suit.

Guatemala, Honduras, and El Salvador decided to initiate a three-country federation, and they set up a provisional government at Tegucigalpa, Honduras. But an anti-Unionist *coup* in Guatemala, led by General José María Orellana, in December 1921 killed this projected federation. The system of general courts and conferences for Central America, which had been sponsored in the treaties of 1907 by the U.S.A. together with the five republics, fell apart.

In 1923 a new judicial system came into being, with a panel of local and foreign judges to replace the Central American Permanent Supreme Court. A fact-finding committee was established to pass on all disputes and the republics agreed in 1923 that they would not recognize any Central American régime which had been set up by force. However, the resistance of the anti-Unionist Guatemalan government of José María Orellana rendered even these plans ultimately unworkable.

In 1926 Guatemala undertook a thoroughgoing monetary reform. She converted her dilapidated currency into a really sound monetary system, with proper reserves which she was scrupulous to maintain. The following year, however, the foreign relations of the country were disturbed as Guatemala's long-standing boundary dispute with Honduras became acute (See *Honduras*).

In 1930 General Jorge Ubico, an anti-Unionist, seized power. He ruled dictatorially, constantly extending his term of office; but certain noteworthy changes occurred during his régime. Guatemala's peonage system came to an end six years after he had taken power. The new system resulted in an increase in the real wages of the former peons, who were nevertheless still compelled to work their land for a required number of days or else work for others. The country also witnessed a development in her highways and railroad systems.

In December 1941, Guatemala declared war on the Axis nations and confiscated the properties of her Axis nationals. She has collaborated closely with the U.S.A., and the attitude of her Foreign Minister, Dr. Carlos Salazar, contributed much to the success of the consultative meetings of American Foreign Ministers.

The long rule of General Ubico ended in 1944 when a democratic and Unionist movement swept him from power. The highways, railways, and other communications which he had given the nation proved to have contributed to his downfall, for they made possible a diffusion of information and ideas among the people. In the final phase of his rule, Ubico sought to sustain his waning popularity by sponsoring social reforms, such as a minimum wage for workers. His efforts, however, proved of no avail; and the Presidency was turned over to General Frederico Ponce.

Stakes in the Peace

Guatemala appears to have returned to Unionist conceptions; that is, to closer political arrangements, if not outright federation, with her four Central American sister republics. The advocates of Unionism hold that such a grouping would enjoy a much more favorable economic status and prove more attractive as an area of capital investment. The opponents believe that the concrete problems of each republic would become secondary considerations in a Central American Federation.

Guatemala faces the task of abolishing the vestiges of peonage on the land, for they are inseparable from the poverty and political inertia of the mass of her people. The fertile upland region could be made to support three times its present population and on a much higher economic level, if certain facilities were made available; among them, health and education for rural families, modern farming methods, and farm machinery on a cooperative basis.

So long as the vestiges of peonage make labor cheap, machinery is not needed to effect economies; and thus economic improvement lies thwarted. Recent political activities, however, combined with positive economic encouragement from the U.S.A. indicate that Guatemala's plantation system will soon be either profoundly modified or that the vestiges of peonage will be ended.

In external relations, Guatemala has been known for years as an enthusiastic friend of inter-American unity.

THE GUIANAS

Guiana, in the northeastern corner of South America, with the Atlantic to the north, Brazil to the south, and Venezuela to the west, is partitioned among Great Britain, the Netherlands, and France — forming the only European colonies left on the South American mainland. Many Americans became aware of Guiana when, after Nazi occupation of France and the Lowlands, United States troops were stationed in Dutch Guiana as a protective measure.

BRITISH GUIANA

The Land. British Guiana, formerly called Demerara, is the western section of Guiana. It is about as large as Idaho, having an area of 89,480 square miles, with a population estimated at 354,000. The climate is hot and steamy, though the trade winds bring some relief. Nearly all the people live in the lowland along the seaboard, where the capital, Georgetown (population 71,000), is located. The interior of the country is a jungle, with rivers almost impossible to navigate and mountain waterfalls as impressive as any in the world. Much of this wild upcountry is still unexplored.

The People. About 42% of the people are Negroes, descendants of the slaves who worked the great sugar plantations before the emancipation of 1833, and 44% are East Indians, brought over to work on the plantations beginning about 1860; of the rest, 4% are Portuguese, $1\frac{1}{2}\%$ other Europeans (including British), and $8\frac{1}{2}\%$ of mixed races. Some 7,000 aboriginal Indians are thought to inhabit the backcountry. The birthrate is about 36 per thousand, the deathrate only 16; the ravages of malaria and tuberculosis have been greatly reduced.

The Church of England and the Church of Scotland (Presbyterian) are established, but other Christian denominations, such as Roman Catholic and Methodist, receive state aid. The Portuguese and some of the Negroes are Catholics, the mass of the Negroes and most of the other Europeans, Protestants; the East Indians, barring a small number of Moslems, are Hindus.

About 57,000 children — probably more than four-fifths of those of school age — attend government-aided denominational schools. There are excellent government-aided high schools also, and scholarships for England. British Guiana has produced many able people. The study of botany, physical geography, and geology has proved especially attractive in such a setting.

Production. Only some 250 square miles of British Guiana are under cultivation: about 37% in sugar, which yields nearly 3 tons an acre; 38% in rice, a staple food; 12% in coconuts; and the rest in cocoa, rubber, and limes. There is little livestock.

British Guiana is an important source of bauxite (for aluminum), gold, and diamonds. But the mineral production, although large, is a mere scratching of the surface. The forests too should yield more than they do: at present their only important product is balata for elastic.

Trade. Of the export trade, which amounts to $18,500,000 yearly and goes mostly to Britain and Canada, 75% is in sugar, the rest in rum, molasses, rice, timber, balata, bauxite, gold, and diamonds. Most of the $17,000,000 worth of imports — foodstuffs, textiles, and machinery — come from Britain.

History: 1914-1944

Of the history of British Guiana one can say, generally, that the colony has slowly acquired greater governmental autonomy. A trade union assembly met in 1919, despite official obstacles. But with the 1921 depression, its considerable membership declined almost to the vanishing point.

Throughout the 1920's the governor of British Guiana dominated the Court of Policy, as the governing council was termed. However, after an investigation, Great Britain democratized the system. She permitted elections for the Legislative Council, no longer restricting membership in it to officials, and she liberalized voting requirements, though property qualifications remained.

The decline of East Indian immigration continued and finally led to the abolition of the office of Protector of Immigrants, in 1932. Years of unemployment culminated in violent general strikes in 1935. The next year middle-class and labor elements formed a Manpower and Citizens Association. In 1937, trade unionism spread widely, largely as a result of Popular Front movements in the nearby French islands. A Trades Union Assembly, affiliated with the West India Congress of Labor, was constituted.

As a result of recent Royal Commission findings, a new Constitution came into effect in 1943. Elected members now form the majority of the Council. With the influence of the U.S.A. more strongly felt, a general democratic tendency has replaced the rapidly declining influence of the plantation-owners in British Guiana.

NETHERLANDS GUIANA

Dutch Guiana or Surinam was accepted by the Dutch in 1675 as a trade-off for New York — a spectacularly bad bargain based on the assumption that sugar had a brighter future than fur. The country was long a drain on the Dutch exchequer. But it now produces a surplus, and in health, education, and finance the Dutch have made something of their bargain after all.

The Land. Flanked on west and east by British and French Guiana, the colony is 54,291 square miles in area and has 183,730 people, including the aboriginal Indians in the jungle. Its configuration is much the same as the British colony's: rivers flow to the sea, the population lives near the coast, the land rises into a high forest region, and part of the upcountry (near the Brazilian border) is unexplored.

The People. The population, too, is similar: Negroes 46%; Indians (from India) 26%; American Indians 7%; Europeans only 1%; Chinese and persons of mixed blood, less than 1%; the only element peculiar to the Dutch colony is the Dutch East Indians, mostly Javanese, who number 16%. Slavery was not abolished until 1863, and many of the Negroes are the children of former slaves who escaped into the forest. Recent sanitation work has remedied the notorious unhealthfulness of the country, and the deathrate is now only 11 per thousand, against a birthrate of over 27.

Religion is as diverse as the peoples: there are Moslems, Hindus, Roman Catholics, Moravians (Moravian missionaries have been active), and Dutch Protestants. Education is on the upgrade: more than half the children of school age are being educated.

Production and Trade. As in British Guiana, sugar is the leading product and export, bauxite the leading mineral, balata the leading forest product. In peacetime, two-thirds of the exports go to the Netherlands, though the U.S.A. takes the bauxite. The normal average of imports and exports, about $60 per person, is large for the population. But the colony's prosperity varies sharply from boom to depression. At present, it has benefited from the war.

History: 1914-1944

The West Indian disorders of the 1930's failed to shake Dutch Guiana. Elected members of her council (the States) had long been in a majority: thus the people had at their disposal a democratic means of expression. Under the excellent administration of Governor Kielstra, the colony's large deficits were transformed into a surplus during the 1930's.

In 1940, when the Netherlands were invaded by the Nazis, German elements became active in Dutch Guiana; for a time they loomed as a menace to Allied shipping and aviation. But the Dutch authorities counteracted this threat with local forces, and when the Americans gave supplementary aid, the German danger disappeared.

FRENCH GUIANA

French Guiana, or Cayenne, is one of those places known out of all proportion to size and importance. It is not merely that Cayenne pepper is named after it; it is the site of a French penal colony, and a host of novels and movies, not to mention newspaper headlines, have played up its terror and romance — its convict population, the gruesome "dry guillotine," the long affliction of the innocent Captain Dreyfus on Devil's Island, and the unique situation making some black men socially superior to some whites in a world of race prejudice.

The Land and the People. French Guiana, most easterly of the three Guianas, has two sections: the upcountry colony of Inini, where an estimated 6,000

See continental map on page 187.

people are spread over 27,000 square miles, and the coast colony, Cayenne, whose 7,720 square miles (about the area of New Jersey) contain 31,000 people, including 5,600 in the convict colony. The political prisoners in the penal colony, jailed by the Vichy French, have now been released. As for the real criminals — liberal Frenchmen have always recoiled from the dread prison ships that used to leave La Rochelle for Cayenne, but so far the Frenchmen who picture the system as more humane than prison walls have prevailed.

Among the free people of French Guiana, the prevailing religion is Roman Catholic, and education (in the coastal region) is general.

Production and Trade. There is little production. About a third of the people live in the capital, Cayenne, very few in the dreaded upcountry wilderness. The plantations cover only 9,000 acres, and if it were not for gold, balata, and rosewood essence, the colony would be commercially negligible. But its forest resources are admittedly superb. Trade, normally about $2,000,000 annually (about 40% exports, 60% imports), was mostly with France. For a while during the war, while the Vichy régime was in power, the U.S.A. did not permit shipments from American ports to the colony. This was a heavy misfortune while it lasted: most food had to be imported, as the 14 square miles under cultivation can scarcely nourish the people, and it is hard to thrive on prison discipline.

History: 1914-1944

French Guiana has always been a controversial issue in French politics. The Left in France has been ashamed of the penal colony, while the Right has insisted that it is more humane than walled penitentiaries.

In 1936 the Popular Front government canceled the transportation of convicts from France to French Guiana, but the Pétain régime not only restored it but used the colony more extensively than ever. Before March 1943 the Allies declined to permit shipments to French Guiana, but in that month the Free French movement occupied the colony after local revolts had ousted the Vichyites. Political prisoners, jailed for having opposed the Pétain régime, were set free.

The Colonial Ministry in Paris has recently (September, 1944) stated that a serious effort will be made to develop the neglected resources of the colony.

Stakes in the Peace

Possessing untold assets in her interior, British Guiana faces two basic problems: first, to develop communications by river, road, and air into the upland and jungle country; second, to maintain the health of explorers and developers until her mineral and timber wealth is made available. With these two problems solved, the country would no longer depend as it does at present, on an astonishingly small acreage of cultivated land close to the sea.

Dutch Guiana has already altered her economy by emphasis on bauxite production. She has similar assets to those in British Guiana, along with a similar contour; and now that she has been promised dominion status in the coming Dutch Commonwealth, her future seems brighter. Dutch enterprise, never found wanting when commerce is in question, may stimulate development in the country if only to offset the Hollanders' large reliance in recent years on the Netherlands East Indies.

The future of French Guiana turns about the question of the penal colony. If the French do away with the penal colony, the free population of the colony would also fare badly, since at the moment a share of the colony's small economy is bound up with her present social organization. Hence abolition of the penal colony, if effected, must be correlated with some exploitation of mineral resources as well as rosewoods and dyewoods in the interior, especially in Inini. Sanitation, profiting by American example in tropical regions, is another prerequisite to improving the welfare of the colony.

HAITI

The Land and the People

Haiti is a fabulous name to most Americans, bringing thoughts of Henri Christophe's fortress-castle on the rocky mountain-top and of Voodoo drums among the hills. Although some of our notions are really mythical — as the one that most Haitians follow Voodoo in the cinema sense — there is nothing unreal about the romantic history of the Black Republic: her origin as a French sugar-plantation colony, the greatest slave state of her time; her gallant uprising, under the Negro hero Toussaint l'Ouverture, to be the first independent Negro nation in the New World; her long succession of violent and picturesque tyrannies, of which Henri Christophe's was perhaps the most violent and picturesque; her contemporary emergence as a nation with developing civic consciousness.

Haiti is the one American country whose government is of, for, and by the black race. Her independence dates from 1804 (the first republic established in Latin America). With her intellectual ruling class, Haiti is regarded with special affection by the two million Negroes of the British West Indies, the thirteen million in the U.S.A., and aware Negro populations throughout the world.

As an active member of the Pan-American Union, Haitian delegates at inter-American Conferences are heard with special interest, and they also attracted interest in the assemblies of the League of Nations by their oratory and forthright commentaries on imperialism.

The Land. With an area of 10,700 square miles (about the size of Maryland), Haiti occupies the western third of the large West Indies island of Hispaniola, in the Greater Antilles east of Cuba. A mountainous country, it rises to an altitude of 8,000 feet. The ser-

See map on page 197.

ried mountain mass is broken by four large plains and several smaller ones. In the center lies the celebrated Cul de Sac (Blind Alley), a sea-level valley, in which the capital, Port-au-Prince, is located. Along the coast are several excellent harbors.

The People. Over 95% of the people are pure Negroes, 5% are mulattoes with French blood. The upper class, the *élite*, are socially sharply divided from the mass of the population. Such whites as are now in Haiti at all are there as tourists, engineers, priests (many from Brittany, and now, increasingly from the U.S.A.), or employees of commercial houses, banks, or governments. The French influence, for generations so strong that the governing class (which comes from the French-African mulattoes) looked to France for education, trade, and financial connections, and even cable communications, has latterly been giving way to the influence of the U.S.A., although French remains the official language and the people still speak a Creole *patois* based on French. But Haitian popular culture is African rather than either European or American. Even Haitian Catholicism is, in remote regions, modified by African patterns.

The population numbers nearly 3,000,000 (over 90% rural); at the time of the French — and Haitian — Revolution, it numbered only 530,000. The present density, over 290 to the square mile, is four times that of the neighboring Dominican Republic. The population would be robust if better hygienic conditions prevailed; as it is, malaria, hookworm, yaws, and tuberculosis are still too prevalent.

Religion and Education. Haiti is a Roman Catholic country. Although in remote areas some beliefs and practices of ancestral African *vodun* (a folk religion, discouraged by law) have survived in combination with the Christian elements, most Haitians accept and practice a normal Catholicism.

Education is tuition-free and theoretically compulsory, but out of 600,000 children of school age, only 54,000 boys and 33,000 girls attend school — a proportion not likely to speed reduction of the 85% illiteracy rate. Most of these schools are quite defective. Haiti has 4 *lycées* (superior high schools), 15 private high schools, 2 normal schools, and several specialized schools. English is now an obligatory subject. Among so scantily educated a people, the polished Haitian literature (until recently dominated by French modes) cannot find the audience it deserves.

A radical change in educational directives would help advance agriculture and industry. The *élite*, if they turned to engineering, agronomy, forestry, medicine, geology, could rapidly increase the popular welfare. As it is, only literate property owners, that is, the richest tenth of the population, can vote, and government is highly centralized.

The Nation's Economy

Agriculture. Not much of Haiti's territory is arable and a large part of the arable land is poor. Haitian farmers work with the most primitive tools, and the country's once-great irrigation works now lie neglected. Yet on their little garden subdivision patches, a tradition since the days of French domination, the people grow crops of a variety and excellence reminiscent of France. Many of these small farmers belong to cooperatives, or mutual-aid societies. Farm wages are low (about $2 a week), but since farm produce is added to the wage, the rural Haitian is not undernourished as to quantity, though he is often malnourished. All in all, though the country is on a mere subsistence basis, most Haitians are not so poor as West Indians generally, except in terms of cash income — $20 annually per person.

Production. Haiti's leading cash crop is coffee, one of the finest varieties known. Among her other important products are sisal, sugar, cotton, bananas, rubber, cocoa, rum, tobacco, and honey (a superlative variety). Banana production, a new and thriving industry, is dispersed among many individual owners, but marketing is centralized in the Standard Fruit Company. Rubber production has been recently stimulated by a loan of $9,600,000 from the U.S.A.

Haitian urban workers are badly paid and very poor. At present most of them work at sugar refining, rum distillation, tobacco manufacture, and fruit canning. The Haitian American Development Corporation employs some 75,000.

Haiti's extensive mineral resources, as well as her potential water-power, have not yet been developed. However, a plan has been drawn up to stimulate small industries in the republic after the war. The country has been developing public works. Among these are some good roads constructed during the United States occupation (See *History*) and for which Haiti is to repay the U.S.A. $5,500,000.

Finance. The monetary unit is the *gourde*, worth about 20¢; American currency is also used. Although money in circulation has doubled during World War II, the figure is only $1.25 per person, and in the rural districts the people still live by barter. Interest on the nation's debt of $13,200,000 is guaranteed by the U.S.A., which long had a fiscal representative at Port-au-Prince. The annual per capita tax rate is approximately $2, but customs supply about 90% of the revenue and hence internal taxation is only 20¢ a person. The national budget is unfortunately much too small for adequate education and sanitary work.

Foreign Trade. Haiti is not a heavy trader. Before the war, her imports amounted to $2.50 per capita, exports to $2.30. About 40% of her exports went to France, 22% to Great Britain, and only 12% to the U.S.A. World War II has displaced everything. Now 80% of Haiti's exports go to the U.S.A., who also supplies 77% of the imports. (The pre-war average of imports from the U.S.A. was 47% and 17% was supplied by Japan.) She imports chiefly cotton goods, food, petroleum, soap, and machinery.

The per capita rate of both exports and imports has risen (to $3.50 and $3.30 respectively). Although Haiti's best permanent customers are gone for the moment, the country has not lost by the war. Nevertheless she can have no really heavy trade until she produces a greater amount of cash crops; even her sugar and coffee productions are at present small.

History: 1914-1944

In 1915, President Sudre Dartiguenave of Haiti signed a treaty with the U.S.A. under which the latter country was to appoint a financial adviser and a general receiver for customs. In 1916 President Wilson, fearful of the situation in Haiti, sent American marines to the country and declared a technical state of military occupation. The following year Haiti agreed to consult the United States legation before submitting any new laws to her Congress; and the American legation was also empowered to veto any proposed expenditures. These unwarranted measures were assailed not only in Haiti but throughout Latin America.

Considerable friction developed between the American representatives and the Haitians. The U.S.A. sought to remove the old provisions precluding foreigners from owning land in Haiti — a traditional Haitian policy of assuring the Negro republic's independence of white domination. In addition, the American occupying authorities, in pursuing their laudable public works and road building program enforced the *corvée* (or compulsory labor) without paying adequate compensation to the Haitian workers. The people broke out in revolt in the north, but they were suppressed by the American marines.

In 1922, General John H. Russell of the U.S. Marine Corps, the newly appointed High Commissioner for Haiti, initiated a more flexible and generous policy. In the same year, a compliant President, Borno, was inaugurated in Haiti. The Americans floated a loan; they sponsored dispensaries, clinics, and other health services; and they improved irrigation and extended roads into remote areas of the republic. But the Haitian *élite* (mulatto upper classes) resented these American activities. They conducted a nationalist campaign against material improvements, because, as they charged, these were being imposed from without. At the same time, the *élite* failed to offer any program of their own for improving the lot of their poorer fellow-citizens.

In 1930 Sténio Vincent became President. President Hoover made preparations for recalling American marines, and with the advent of President Roosevelt's "Good Neighbor" policy, they were withdrawn in 1934. Haitian customs revenues were still pledged to secure interest on the American loan, but American control was made nominal. Haiti reacquired her National Bank from private American interests in 1934, and seven years later the National Bank was entrusted with the loan service — another step away from American tutelage.

Haiti adopted new constitutions in 1933 and 1935, both of which provided for a more centralized system of government. In addition, the functions formerly undertaken by the army were assigned to the *Garde d'Haïti* (or constabulary) which had been organized by the Americans. This move gave promise of a more stable future, since the army had been a source of disorder and tyranny until the arrival of the Americans in 1916.

In 1937 an event occurred which threatened the peace of the republic. Many thousands of Haitian migratory workers were massacred on the soil of the Dominican Republic. Relations between the two republics became acute, but peace was maintained by outside mediation. The Dominican Republic was finally persuaded to pay a substantial indemnity to the government of Haiti.

Elie Lescot was elected President in 1941. Haiti's attitude toward the U.S.A. was now entirely altered; she was confident that the larger country respected her complete independence. The new spirit of cooperation took concrete economic and political form. She concluded economic agreements with the U.S.A. in 1942 and 1943 (See *The Nation's Economy*), and the

respective legations of the two countries were elevated to embassy status.

Stakes in the Peace

Haiti's main problem is overpopulation. Given sufficient territory and modern techniques, her ample labor supply could make her a wealthy state. Her people could expand naturally into the Dominican Republic or into Cuba, but these latter countries would seek to prevent such mass migration, since it would soon alter their national composition. Perhaps the present population could raise its economic level within a decade or two, but not materially unless its rate of increase declines. In order to obviate this classic Malthusian problem, the U.S.A. is assisting in the development of large plantation economies. But here political tradition — that is, dread of white domination — still stands as an obstacle, although a more cooperative attitude now prevails.

No easy solution can be indicated for the problems of Haiti. Birth control is a chimerical remedy, in view of the prevailing education and social orientation of the people. The development of manufactures based on local production, as with the sugar *centrals* in Cuba, is only one solution. Indeed, any improvement in the Haitian people's condition may, regrettably, prove to be temporary unless an agriculture and industry can be developed sufficiently to absorb the steady increase of her population.

Fortunately, apart from a tiny, though voluble, minority, the Haitian people love peace. They have had enough historical drama to serve ten other countries, and it seems to have satisfied them. Freed from external preoccupations, they can turn to long-term planning and carefully worked out media for better employment and adequate wages.

HONDURAS

The Land and the People

Honduras has been the classic example of the Central American "Banana Republic," in the sense that she depended on her 36,000 acres of banana plantations for economic existence. The variability of a single crop determined whether the country would have a depression or a boom, and Honduras would usually swing from one extreme to the other. A banana disease that cut exports from 29,000,000 stems to 8,000,000 crippled the economy, which recovered when the disease was controlled — only to face a new

See map on page 197.

disaster during World War II, in the form of a shipping crisis.

One of the great foreign corporations interested in the growth and marketing of bananas is now aiding Honduras in the production of other crops, such as abaca to supplant the hemp grown formerly in the Philippines. The United Fruit Company is contributing to this development by the opening of the School of Pan-American Agriculture, 30 miles south of the Honduran capital, Tegucigalpa. This school has modern but simple buildings, a well-selected faculty, and it is free of all expense to the carefully chosen students. It marks a new epoch in the relations of foreign capital with Central America and prophesies a better-nourished people and an improved economy.

Honduras has been aided by air traffic, especially by the remarkably successful TACA, begun by a keen New Zealand pilot with a simple second-hand plane and now covering the remotest corners of the country and other Caribbean areas. The TACA specializes in freight. It asserts that it carries more merchandise than do all the commercial planes in the U.S.A.

The Land. Honduras covers 46,332 square miles — about the area of New York state. She lies east of Guatemala, northeast of El Salvador, and north of Nicaragua. On the Pacific Ocean, she has only a single bay, but on the Caribbean her shores extend the entire breadth of her land. The overwhelming part of Honduran economic life is concentrated in this coastal region, particularly in the hot, humid area some eighty miles wide. Beyond lies a low mountainous terrain, dense forests, and jungles, with high valleys, deep basins, rivers, and some peaks rising to 10,000 feet.

In addition to the banana plantations on the Caribbean coast, Honduras has other resources, though of present minor importance. In the 16th and 17th centuries fair amounts of precious metals were shipped from the land, and the Indians in Honduras still extract some $100,000 worth of gold and silver from the highland rivers. The country's mahogany trees are still abundant. In accordance with native customs, the mahogany is felled during the rainy season, in the wane of the moon, when the tree is said to be richer in color.

The People. Most of the 1,038,000 Hondurans live in the southwestern upland regions. However, the Caribbean coast is well populated, for miracles of modern sanitation have made the hot, sticky region habitable. The country as a whole was marked by relatively self-contained areas, but with the gift of motor roads Honduras is rapidly taking on a sense of national unity.

Some 95% of the people are *mestizos* (mixed Indian and Spanish). The population in the Caribbean area shows a sizable infiltration of Negroes. Not more than 1% of the Hondurans are distinctly white, but these have constituted the most important element in the political life of the republic. A large part of the population still speaks various Indian languages, but on the east coast English prevails. Spanish, however, is the language of government and of instruction.

Religion and Education. The dominant faith is Roman Catholicism, except among the Negroes, who are largely Protestant. Over two-thirds of the people are illiterate. Some 52,000 children go to elementary school, 3,000 attend high school, and 350 are enrolled in the nation's small university. Despite these figures, the education of the people is rapidly improving, and the government is solicitous of education. There are many trade and farm schools, maintaining good standards, in this land of small farmers and of peaceful, hard-working citizens. There can be no doubt that the newly opened School of Pan-American Agriculture at Tegucigalpa will have a stimulating influence upon the educational consciousness of the country as a whole.

The Nation's Economy

The U.S.A. has come to the assistance of this land which has suffered from a sharp decline in her gold and silver production as well as from severe fluctuations in her banana crop. United States loans for public works have helped build the Pan-American Highway in Honduras; a United States financial mission is advising the Honduran government; and agricultural aid and counsel have been extended by the U.S.A.

In addition to bananas, Honduras raises other tropical produce, though it contributes little to foreign trade. For their staple diet the people grow corn and beans, but all crop figures indicate an inadequate supply of foodstuffs.

The enterprising Honduran makes cigar boxes and matches, engages in other light industries, like the manufacture of Panama hats, and tries hard to export fabricated goods. But with customs revenues lower, with imports scarce, with prices rising steeply, and with unemployment high, Honduras, unlike Nicaragua, has proved an economic victim of World War II.

Finance. The currency unit is the *lempira*, worth about 50¢. Taxes are excessive for the country's poor earning power; they reach $6,000,000, or $27 a year per family of five. The public debt is $8,500,000. (In the 19th century, the country was saddled with a nominal debt of $150,000,000!)

Honduras needs a higher level of techniques in agriculture and transportation. Her few railroads (not one reaches the capital!) are owned or leased by the fruit enterprises. Her timber, mining, and grazing resources remain largely undeveloped.

Foreign Trade. Normally, Honduran exports average $8,000,000, and her imports $10,000,000. Bananas usually furnish 67% of the export total (though the variable figure has been as high as 80%); silver accounts for 13%, gold 9%, scrap ores 4%. The U.S.A., which has the largest investment in Honduras, today takes 96% of the exports and supplies 76% of the imports. Even in peacetime, the U.S.A. took 83% and furnished 65%.

History: 1914-1944

Honduras had long suffered from frequent revolutions and local wars. In 1919, however, the Conservative President Francisco Bertrand was overthrown by a revolution led by General López Gutierrez, and the Liberal party regained control of the government.

Relations with neighboring Nicaragua at first were strained, since the López Gutierrez régime was unfriendly to Chamorro, President of Nicaragua. Nevertheless in 1920–21 Honduras strongly supported the program for a Central American Federation. When the project collapsed as a result of controversy over the Bryan-Chamorro agreement (See *Nicaragua*), Honduras, Guatemala, and El Salvador decided to experiment with a three-country federation, and they chose Tegucigalpa, capital of Honduras, as the seat of this union. An anti-Unionist *coup* in Guatemala (December 1921), however, ended this tri-partite project, and Honduras returned to her unfortunate tradition of internal disturbances.

In 1924 the Liberal régime of López Gutierrez was overthrown by the Conservatives, and a protracted civil war began. This destructive conflict normally would have resulted in the recognition of the victors, but under the Central American Treaty of 1923, the five republics had agreed to withhold recognition from any government established by force. Hence, the Honduran régime that had been set up by the *coup* gave way, and Dr. Paz Baraona, a civilian Conservative, became President in February 1925.

In the third year of the Paz Baraona government, the long-standing dispute between Honduras and Guatemala acquired acute importance. The region in question had become valuable for banana cultivation, and no solution was forthcoming. But except for this problem, Honduras seemed to have arrived at political stability. Dr. Paz Baraona served out his full term and genuine elections took place in 1929. A Liberal, Colindres, was made President, and the country appeared to have embarked upon a peaceful constitutional existence. However, Colindres soon faced several abortive rebellions, and in 1932 he was finally overthrown by General Carías Andino, a Conservative.

Carías Andino permitted only one party to function (the Nationalists, who were his followers), and he continually extended his term of office. During his long administration, the difficulties with Guatemala over boundaries were finally resolved by a tribunal of arbitration (January 1933).

Long cooperative in inter-American relations, Honduras followed the U.S.A. in declaring war on the Axis powers in December 1941. Because of the shortage of shipping, the war adversely affected Honduran economy, and the Carías Andino government found itself in need of aid and advice. Elaborate arrangements were soon concluded with the U.S.A. in order to assist the smaller nation.

In November 1943, upon uncovering a plot to assassinate himself and his family, Carías Andino arrested many Hondurans and imposed an absolute censorship. These measures, however, were not too effective, for there were demonstrations against him in July 1944. Carías Andino declared these elements to be sympathizers of Fascism.

Stakes in the Peace

Exploited and plundered by adventurers who inflicted on her the heaviest per capita debt obligation on earth, Honduras has had an unhappy history. The country has often been on the verge of famine because of excessive concentration on a cheap crop requiring extensive shipping, bananas.

More than any other Central American state, Honduras requires deep-seated changes in her grazing areas, an improvement in the quality of her cattle, and modernized farming to employ the mass of the people in the central upland regions. Such changes would not necessarily interfere with the prevailing banana economy on the east coast, provided that the republic did not stake her economic life on the latter.

Honduras has long favored, and even championed, Central American unity, whether political or spiritual. There can be little doubt that, with diffused peasant ownership of land accompanied by cooperative use of farm machinery and intensified education in farm methods, Honduras could within a decade overcome the evils that blight the economic history of this beautiful but unfortunate nation.

ICELAND

The Land and the People

Iceland has been an independent republic only since she dissolved her connection with Denmark in 1944. But her contribution to the democratic tradition goes deep into the past: she has the oldest parliament in the world, established in the 11th century. And though she never formally entered World War II, her contribution to the cause of the United Nations has been considerable. Occupying a highly strategic location astride the great convoy and submarine route across the North Atlantic, she not only furnished invaluable weather data, but consented to British and then American stationing of troops for the duration, to facilitate submarine and air control.

The Land. The island is situated in the middle of the North Atlantic, with its northern tip at the Arctic Circle — a strategic position in both air and sea lanes on which she should be able to capitalize on her own account after the war. The distances to Europe — less than 1,000 miles west of Norway, only 540 miles northwest of Scotland — and the cultural ties to Scandinavia have brought her into the European orbit; but in the new air age, and with Americans made aware of her by the temporary occupation, she should become equally important to America.

With an area of 39,709 square miles, Iceland is nearly as large as Kentucky, but three-fourths of the island is wholly uninhabited, and only 121,600 people live in the remaining 10,000 square miles. The only large town is Reykjavik (Smoky Harbor), with 40,000 inhabitants. About 40% of the people live in rural districts.

Iceland is a land of melodramatic landscapes — volcanoes, enormous lava streams, and geysers (the very name is Icelandic), glaciers and snowfields, gravel and stone basins, deserts, rocky fjords, and desolate uplands. It is a cold land, tolerable only in the extreme south, and shaken by devastating earthquakes. Its land and coastal waters are peopled with spectacular creatures such as reindeer, whistling swans, eider ducks (source of our pillows), seals, and whales. There are delicate fish like the *Gafelsberger*, delight of the gourmet.

The People. The people are as remarkable as their land. Sailing from Norway in the days of the Vikings, they settled in Iceland in 874, and by the 10th century their civilization was far ahead of the homeland's. A hardy people, they have a birthrate of 19 per thousand (it has risen during the war) and the extremely low deathrate of 10, with infant mortality at times even lower than New Zealand's. They are Viking homesteaders, who seem to like cold weather; most of those who emigrate go to Manitoba, in Canada.

In political practice, they are democratic, with their ancient parliament and their direct local self-government like a New England town meeting. In religion 98.6% belong to the established Lutheran church.

But the most striking thing about the Icelanders is their intellectual acumen as a people. Illiteracy is unknown among them, and perhaps no other country has proportionately so many highly educated citizens. There is a university at Reykjavik, and many Icelanders study in Scandinavia. The passion for books and libraries is general among the people.

Icelandic literature has a long and glorious history. Its first flowering was in the sagas of the 12th and 13th centuries, followed in the next century by one of the great poetic outbursts in history, which was itself followed by popular ballads or rhymes. History and biography in and after the Middle Ages continued the cult of heroes, telling of the privations of voyaging to Greenland, the struggle with nature, and adventures on the green Arctic seas. In modern times, the legacy of a thousand years is as fresh as ever. The poetry dominant in the 19th century has been followed by naturalistic prose, especially in the novel. There are in Iceland a theater and a native school of drama. Iceland excels in books of learning and in science. It is a matter of wonder to the outside world how so few and poor a people, with so hard an environment, can hold the place they do in Western civilization.

The Nation's Economy

Production. Six-sevenths of the island is wholly unproductive, and the cultivated area is actually less than 100 square miles. For practical purposes, there are only three crops, turnips, potatoes, and hay. There is just enough hay to feed the few animals: 44,000 horses, 35,000 cattle, 656,000 sheep. The people live on potatoes, mutton — and fish. The yield of the fisheries which furnish both food and livelihood to the people, is enormous — 235,000 tons. In proportion to population, no other country can compare with that showing.

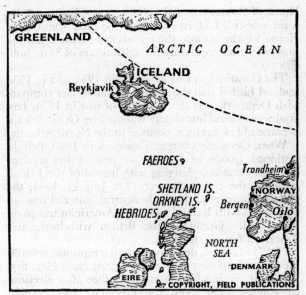
See map on page 113.

Finance. The unit of currency is the *krona*, worth 15.3¢. During the war, expenditures have risen from a normal budget of about $3,500,000 to $4,600,000 (nearly $40 per person). There is, however, a surplus of revenues, and debt remains static at about $8,000,000. During the war money in circulation has increased 600% — a rise explained by the presence of foreign soldiers (with money) and by lavish construction. It may create grave deflationary problems, when the outsiders leave.

Trade. Iceland has to trade to obtain consumers goods and food; thus her chief imports are foodstuffs, textiles, oils, metals, automobiles, and machinery. She exports fish, timber, and wool. Before the war, these exports were distributed among Scandinavia, Great Britain, Germany, and the great codfish-consuming nations, Portugal and Spain; the imports came principally from Great Britain, Scandinavia, and Germany. The per capita trade, though extraordinary, is not comparable to that of nations with a more balanced economy. The pre-war figures for imports are $11,300,000 yearly, for exports $12,700,000; both figures have leaped with the war and the presence of American troops.

History: 1914-1944

Iceland, a possession of Denmark for more than five centuries, was neutral during World War I, as was the mother country. On November 30, 1918, the Icelanders proclaimed their independence and entered into a twenty-five year treaty with Denmark, which stipulated that Denmark was to represent Iceland in foreign affairs and that the King of Denmark was also to be King of Iceland. No other connections remained to limit Iceland's sovereignty.

In May 1920, the country adopted a new Constitution. This document gave broad governing powers to the *Althing*, the oldest parliament in history, established in 930, three hundred years before the English

House of Commons. (The *Althing* has a curious structure: one-third of its members become the Upper House for the session, the remainder constituting the Lower House. And only three Ministers of State hold office!)

The Constitution was amended in 1934 and in 1938 Iceland hinted that she would not renew her compact with Denmark. At the outbreak of war in 1939, Iceland was neutral but closely watched by Great Britain because of her strategic position in the North Atlantic.

When Germany overran Denmark in 1940, Britain stationed troops in Iceland to protect her against German invasion, pledging withdrawal of the British troops at the end of the war. On July 11, 1941, the U.S.A., though still formally neutral, entered into an agreement with Iceland to station American troops on the island. Gradually the British withdrew, and American forces remained.

In 1944 Iceland, declaring herself a republic, severed the last remaining ties with Denmark. Her first President, Sveinn Bjornsson, took office after election. In August 1944, both the President and Foreign Minister of Iceland stated publicly, though in the friendliest manner, that Iceland would not grant permanent bases to other nations when the war ended.

Stakes in the Peace

The economy of Iceland, when American troops are withdrawn from the small island republic, must revert to fisheries as the basis of exports. It is the income from Iceland's fisheries that must pay for practically the entire list of her imports.

Unless sudden new forms of wealth are discovered, such as unsuspected mineral possibilities, her thousand-year history bids fair to continue without any drastic changes. She has passed the era of calamities when she was so remote from communications that plague, famine, and earthquake periodically devastated the island and reduced its population. Today her fishing economy assures her a decent, though scarcely luxurious, standard of living.

Iceland's principal interest is in free trade for her products: without it, her economy would suffer disastrously. So long as Great Britain and the U.S.A. maintain their interest in safeguarding the independence of this strategic island, her future is assured. As for cultural contributions, it is clear that a population so endowed will continue to be a jewel of Western civilization.

MEXICO

The Land and the People

Mexico is a land of contrast, and of revolution. In the central plaza of the capital, examples of vastly different "Mexicos" stand quietly side by side — buildings of ancient pre-Aztec civilizations, Spanish colonial architecture, developments of the early republic, and structures of the most modernistic type. Within a stone's throw of the spot where in 1537 the first printing press in America was set up, there is now a teeming market serving thousands of illiterate Indians, brought from tribal homes by buses made in Detroit. A little farther away is a modern airport, under the shadow of sacred snowcapped Popocatepetl, and nearby the ancient pyramids are swarming with foreign tourists dressed in New York sports clothes. The Indian, who still dominates the countryside and many a city street, moves mutely, an eternal question mark.

The Mexican Revolution, begun in 1910, is one of the most influential events in recent American history. Preceding the Russian Revolution by several years, it attacked the fundamental social, political, economic, educational, and religious problems. It substituted for the white-European-North American-capitalistic régime, a system that emphasized the Indian, the communal holding of the land, and the rights of organized labor. The dominance of the

foreigner and his machine were questioned; native values and government control of industry for the benefit of the common man were emphasized. At the same time a new respect for work, for sports, and for the arts became evident. The earlier enthusiasm which made of the revolution a religion has died down, but its principles are still the guiding power of the nation — part of the explanation of why foreigners find the republic so attractive.

Mexico covers an area of 758,258 square miles, about a fourth the size of the U.S.A. In 1845 these neighbor nations were almost equal in territory, but Mexico lost Texas after 1836; California and the Rocky Mountain areas after her war with the U.S.A. (1848), and ceded southern Arizona and southern New Mexico in the Gadsden Purchase (1853). Altogether, Mexico gave up close to a million square miles.

Mexico has two southern land neighbors: Guatemala and British Honduras. The Gulf of Mexico and the Pacific Ocean wash her eastern and western shores.

The Land. Most of the country towers over 3,000 feet. The uplands run like a spinal column from the northern border to the south, where they rise higher and are more humid. The northern region resembles Arizona, while the southern is cut by deep valleys and crowned by lofty, volcanic peaks. The formidable Sierra Madre Mountains, difficult

to traverse, separate the central plateau from the two coastal areas. The Pacific incline is steeper than that toward the Gulf of Mexico.

The country has three well-defined climate zones: (1) in the south — *tierra caliente* (or rainy tropic lands), sparsely peopled, seat of the ancient Mayan civilization; (2) the higher central region — *tierra templada* (or temperate lands), where tropical vegetation mingles with northern species, and where the bulk of the population is concentrated; and (3) most of the north — *tierra fría* (or cold lands) on the high plateaus. Mexico City, the capital, is located on the elevated plain of Anáhuac; there May is the warmest month and January the coldest.

Poor rainfall distribution, difficult topography, and erratic temperature at present limit the amount of land available for agriculture, so that less than 3% of the national territory (under 20,000 square miles) is actually cultivated. On the other hand, Mexico possesses rich mineral resources — gold, silver, copper, mercury, antimony, lead, zinc, and molybdenum — most of which are found in the northern and north central highlands. Another precious resource, oil, is produced mostly near Tampico, on the Gulf of Mexico, though there are four other important areas of petroleum production.

The People. When Cortés arrived in 1520 he found a population of some 3,000,000 Indians. To this day Mexico remains basically an Indian country, for the Spaniards, though they achieved political domination, never succeeded in uprooting the Indian culture and outlook on life. In 1930 a sixth of the Mexican people still spoke the various Indian languages. Nevertheless, the Spaniards exerted a powerful influence on the outward forms of culture, and Spanish is the dominant and official language.

Some 55% of the people are classed as *mestizos* (of mixed Indian and white blood) and only 30% as pure Indians, but Indian rather than European strains dominate among the *mestizos*. The Indians have produced many of the greatest names of Mexico, such as Benito Juárez. Pure whites number less than 15%, whereas before 1821, while Mexico was still a Spanish viceroyalty, they constituted 20% of the population. The ordinarily tiny stream of European immigration has lately been swelled by colonies of refugees, including 15,000 Spanish Republicans.

A century ago, Mexico's population figure of 8,000,000 as against the U.S.A.'s 20,000,000 represented far less of a contrast than her present figure of 19,653,000 as against our 133,000,000 (a drastic change in ratio from 1:2.5 to 1:6.5). Mexico's high deathrate (23–25 per thousand) reflects the widespread tuberculosis, dysentery, smallpox, and malaria among the people, as well as the inadequate and unvaried diet, based chiefly on corn and beans. The high birthrate of 43 per thousand is in part counteracted by the infant mortality rate of 122. In recent years, economic attractions have stimulated extensive Mexican emigration to cities like Los Angeles and San Antonio, and throughout the southwest of the U.S.A., where Mexicans are estimated at well over a million. At

217

her present rate of growth, Mexico will number about 25,000,000 people by 1970.

About a third of the people live in cities and towns. Mexico City, with 1,800,000 people in the federal district, has increased by 300% in the last thirty years. Among the important urban centers are Guadalajara, Monterrey, Puebla (all above 100,000). Vera Cruz and Tampico are famous ports. Cuernavaca, Toluca, and Taxco enjoy special renown in the world of art.

The Mexicans are more varied in their classification than any other Latin Americans, largely because of the social upheaval of the last third of a century. Previous to 1910, the higher classes minimized their Indian blood and magnified their likeness to European civilization. Since that date, pride in Indian blood, in native products, in national art and music, has become dominant. The Government, through its departments of education, agriculture, and archaeology, has done much to bring the Indian into full participation of national life. It is a difficult task.

There is no racial prejudice against the Indians. A copper-colored skin is as acceptable as a white one and is probably more dominant in government, teachers' associations, scientific societies, and in grand opera and labor conventions. The division, which comes from geographic, linguistic, and economic conditions, is sometimes difficult to establish. Native tribes, such as the Otomi, Zapotec, and some fifty others, numbering around 3,000,000, still live apart in isolated sections, speak their own languages, and live close to the pattern of previous centuries. Other millions, a few degrees nearer modern life, served as peons on the large estates before the Revolution, some of whom today live on the communal lands (*ejidos*). Many have drifted into the towns and cities to become domestic servants, *cargadores* (carrying on their backs anything up to a piano), and laborers in the growing industrial plants. A favorite demonstration of the shifting process shows a photograph of seven unkempt barefooted youths from as many tribes who were brought to the National Indian Institute in Mexico City. Another picture of the same boys taken after two years training, shows them completely transformed into Mexican young men of the middle class. Students in the Institute return to their people as community leaders. The government and the teachers are using many methods to speed up this process.

The *campesinos* (rural people), although many are of almost pure Indian blood, are the next higher group. Their lot is being transformed from practically industrial slaves into free labor and proprietors of small farm properties furnished by the government. The Cárdenas administration (1934–40) distributed 18,511,237 hectares of land to 1,097,579 individuals. This group is largely represented in the *Confederación Nacional Campesina* (Farmers' Union), which has considerable political power. The mere distribution of land, however, does not solve the rural workers' problems, for if he is not trained in farming and marketing methods, he again becomes the victim of exploiters. The Farmers' Union is therefore an important agent in watching the operation of government plans for cooperative irrigation, for machinery, schools, banks, and stores.

The industrial worker is strongly organized in the C.T.M. (Confederation of Mexican Workers), which exerts a powerful influence in government, adult education, and public opinion. The white collar class is legally required to organize, but their interests are more divided and their influence less effective than labor's. There is a marked growth in the participation of women in government and industry.

Nowhere has the social scene shifted more than among the upper class. This is illustrated by various institutions. The National University was formerly attended by the sons of the rich. Today many of its 20,000 students earn their own expenses and belong to labor unions. Chapultepec Castle and Park, former residence of Mexican presidents, from which the poor were rigidly excluded, has now been opened to the common people. The gorgeous white marble edifice built for grand opera for the élite, is now, as the Palace of Fine Arts, crowded by laborers and clerks to attend concerts, lectures, and art exhibits especially arranged for them. The famous families who lent such brilliance to the reign of Porfirio Díaz have largely disappeared or have joined the middle class.

Religion and Education. Catholicism was introduced by the Spanish Conquistadores in the 16th century. Though 90% of all Mexicans are Roman Catholics, few countries have seen such determined and aggressive anticlericalism. No ecclesiastical corporation may acquire property and no religious schools may function. The underlying struggle against clericalism, initiated by Benito Juárez in 1857, continues unabated, despite recent modifications.

The government is resolutely trying to overcome the high rate of illiteracy (45%), but attempts to enforce compulsory education laws do not easily succeed in the northwestern desert and tribal areas, in tropical Yucatán, and on some remote *haciendas*. Expressing her social and cultural ferment, Mexico today shares a general passion for education. There are 22,000 schools in towns and settlements, 12,000 scattered in rural districts, and every large ranch, mill, and mine must maintain one. Education of the *mestizo* population has been a passion of men like Vasconcelos, who insist that mixed races are "cosmic" and have a unique function in intensifying the interplay of cultures. Of the 9 universities, several of them ancient, the University of Mexico City (founded in 1553) has gained the most distinction.

The Mexican people have absorbed a Catholic culture and have produced a distinctive national synthesis. Mexico's mural arts occupy front rank in the world. Names like Orozco and Rivera are known to art lovers everywhere, and their murals serve as a gospel, unscrolling the nation's history to those who cannot read. Her silver ornamentation, church architecture, and private homes blend Spanish with older Indian forms to create an authentic Mexican style. Excellent draftsmen in textiles, leather, and potteries, the Mexicans are imaginative in costume and decoration.

Like the Greek, the Mexican feels that his civilization is ancient. Innumerable tourists have been attracted to the country not only by her scenic beauty but by her colorful popular culture, dances, songs, and festivals. Most important: in the last generation Mexicans have risen enormously in consciousness; they have seen that the U.S.A. has been fascinated by this society that she once misunderstood.

Mexican literature, once subjective, plaintive, grandiose, or ironical, is today social and objective. The writer feels himself to be the custodian of his people's limitless future.

The Nation's Economy

Agriculture. Although Mexico is known for her abundant mineral wealth, most of her inhabitants, crowding the relatively scanty arable land, live from agriculture or stock-raising. Farm economy contrasts sharply with that of the U.S.A., country of the independent farmer. Land ownership in Mexico was at one time highly concentrated even by Latin American standards. Under Spanish rule, 10,000 Spaniards owned the land. In the days of Díaz (before 1910), 90% of the people were landless, possessing not even a garden or vegetable patch. The *hacienda*, or large estate, predominated. With an average size of 8,000 acres (though some were larger than 50,000 acres), the *hacienda* was a kind of community in which people lived, tilled the soil, and made their clothes.

By 1930 the agrarian revolution, begun in 1911, had brought profound reforms to the Mexican countryside. Today less than 50% of the peasantry are landless, about 30% belong to cooperative farms (*ejidos*), and at least 20% own some land. The present régime has favored the *ejido* rather than the small farm (*rancho*). Despite these advantages, a high percentage of the peasantry remain, in effect, peons, tied down to the land by heavy indebtedness.

Mexico's basic crops provide her staple foods — wheat, beans, chickpeas, rice, tomatoes, and potatoes — but none of these is raised in sufficient quantities to provide anything like a well-balanced diet. Wheat production per capita is about one-tenth of the U.S.A.'s, corn, one-fifth. Per acre yields fail to brighten the comparison. These figures alone indicate what modern farming could accomplish.

In crops for export Mexico makes a somewhat better showing. Chocolate, vanilla, chicle for chewing gum, and henequen for hemp and twine (grown mainly in the southern lowlands) are among the best-known products. Mexico produces about half of the world's henequen (in Yucatán), an increasing amount of cotton, and a moderate amount of tobacco, coffee, and cocoa. On the other hand, sugar cane, grown in the tropical areas (particularly in the valley of Morelos) does not suffice even for home needs.

In 1930 Mexico had 10,000,000 cattle, 2,000,000 horses, 700,000 sheep. The production of processed meat reaches only 240,000 tons yearly.

Mining. Minerals furnish the nation's chief source of wealth and the basis of her foreign trade. A leading silver country, she produces 30% of the world supply. Her molybdenum represents 3% of the world supply, mercury 16%, antimony 30%, lead ore 11%, and zinc 8%. Copper production is 6% of the U.S. total, gold about 20%. Many other minerals are produced in fair-sized amounts. Coal is mined in small quantities, but petroleum, although well below the levels reached during the Tampico boom of 1924, still holds an important place, representing 3.5% of U.S. production and taking sixth place in Mexican exports. The petroleum industry has been nationalized, but foreign interests until recently owned about 97% of the metal ore production.

Industry. Mexico is in the throes of extensive industrialization, and Monterrey in the north is somewhat reminiscent of Pittsburgh after the American Civil War. Present plans for industrial expansion contrast sharply with the past. The 1935 census showed $130,000,000 invested in industry, the value of annual output only $175,000,000, and the number of workers engaged 269,000. By 1943 capital invested in industry was estimated at some $500,000,000, but workers had increased to only 332,000, or, to put it otherwise, investment per worker has more than doubled — an infallible sign that modern machinery is replacing workshops.

Industrial production is calculated at about a third above 1929 figures — not a spectacular rise. At the same time, the amount of machinery investment per man is the third-highest in Latin America, only below that of Argentina and Chile. The main industries are textiles, shoes, flour, alcohol, cement, bricks, paper, tobacco, and iron (mainly in the Monterrey region). The districts around Mexico City and Vera Cruz are the only other manufacturing regions of importance, but modern light industries are rapidly changing the aspect of small towns throughout the republic.

National Wealth and Finance. In terms of national wealth, Mexico is still poor. In 1930 her national wealth per person was computed at $310, compared with $360 for Brazil and $1,060 for Argentina. The expansion of Mexico City, and the influx of tourists and foreign residents has increased this figure somewhat; recent estimates, based on 1939 values, give a national wealth of about $7,000,000,000, or $370 per person (about one-seventh the per capita wealth of the U.S.A.).

The monetary unit is the *peso*, worth about 20¢, a quarter of its 1929 gold parity. During the war the cost of living has increased by about 40%; the stock market has risen about fivefold, while commercial bank accounts have swelled to some $175,000,000 (over $8 per capita). Currency in circulation has doubled but the increase of foreign exchange reserves arising out of export surpluses gives a better backing to the currency. On the whole, however, the situation is quite inflationary.

The domestic debt is about $130,000,000. The foreign debt, with a face value of $270,000,000, has been readjusted, but payment of interest on all debt has been cut to $10,000,000 yearly.

Foreign Trade. Normally the U.S.A. supplies 66% of imports, Germany 12%, and Great Britain 6%; while the U.S.A. takes 63% of exports, Great Britain 10%, and Germany 7%. Owing to the war, the United States has become almost the sole customer and supplier. Exports in 1938 were $11.25 per capita and imports $6.63.

Mexican exports stood up far better than the world average from 1929 to 1938.

The chief exports are minerals: silver, copper, lead, zinc, antimony, petroleum, and gold. Other important items are henequen, chicle, chocolate, coffee, and cattle. Leading imports: machinery, metals, textiles, and chemicals.

History: 1914-1944

To understand recent Mexican history, one must begin with 1910 — the thirty-fourth year of the dictatorship of Porfirio Díaz. Under his rule, foreign capital had been invested in impressive amounts and the country greatly modernized. Surrounded by a group of elder statesmen popularly nicknamed *Cientificos* (scientific plunderers), the régime seemed eternal to foreigners. But in 1910 it was overthrown by an idealist landowner, Madero, whose leadership was secondary to the great stirrings of the people. Throughout Mexico there began what the Mexicans still call "the Revolution," an attempt to cancel the social system built up since the Spanish Conquest of 1520. In Morelos, the peasants followed Zapata, a wild, inspired guerrilla; in Yucatán, Socialism was proclaimed by Felipe Carillo a year before Lenin acted in Russia; and in the north, Pancho Villa led bands of rebels against the established system of large estates. Madero had no grasp of the immense social forces beneath his ideological and humane revolt.

In 1913 he began to implement a new land law, when he was treacherously assassinated through the agency of a crafty officer, Huerta, who proceeded to restore the old Díaz order. Though he was recognized by most of Europe, Huerta was regarded as a bloody tyrant by President Wilson, who minced no words. In February 1914 Carranza led a rebellion against Huerta. Aware of the depths of Mexican patriotism, Huerta assailed the American flag at Tampico, which led to American naval action. Even Carranza opposed the American behavior, though he was fighting Huerta.

However, Carranza soon overthrew Huerta. Then cohesive authority disappeared in Mexico, and, once a fully policed and intensely governed state, she dissolved into virtually isolated social units. To most foreigners this seemed a welter of anarchy and a paradise for bandits; to most Mexicans it appeared like the thunder of justice after four centuries of slavery disguised as order. The more moderate Carranza was soon favored by the foreign powers, but the more radical Zapata held his following until he died in 1919, and to this day is the center of legendary song among the peasantry. Villa, determined to assert the position of his supporters, raided Columbus, New Mexico, in 1916, an act which compelled President Wilson to send an expedition to Carrizal in Mexico under General Pershing. However, Villa was adroit, and the impending European war caused the expedition to be abandoned.

In 1917 the German government was stupid enough to promise Texas, New Mexico, and Arizona to Mexico should she join Germany in the event that the U.S.A. entered the war. The Mexicans, hostile to any such involvement, remained neutral. Their anti-American sentiment, then at the boiling point, rested on their belief that the U.S.A. wished to impose an imperialist control over them; the U.S.A. on the other hand, insisted that she wished merely to secure American savings invested at great risk in Mexico, savings which had enriched the sister republic. The British were far more insistent and they openly favored reactionaries like Huerta, whereas the U.S.A. disapproved of internal despotism even to reacquire her capital investments.

The Carranza government called a constitutional convention in 1917, and the document it drew up was then the most radical known. It restored all communal (village) lands that had been enclosed by the great landlords since 1856. It nationalized minerals and subsoil (petroleum) on the ground that these are impermanent assets and subject to national control, for once gone, the foundations of the country are diminished. Social and labor rights, at the insistence of the then radical C.R.O.M. (the trade union federation led by Morones) were stressed as in no other country. The constitution outlawed peonage. The Catholic Church was excluded from primary education, priests were to be controlled as to number in each local area, and the property of the Church was nationalized with no thought of compensation; even French anti-clericalism, until that time the most aggressive, actually paled in comparison with the hostility shown in these measures. However, the Constitution of 1917 remained a promise with but indifferent performance. New social forces were rumbling like a volcano about to erupt. The agreed focus of change was the American oil investment in the Tampico area. Assailing the foreign oil companies, General Obregón began a revolt against Carranza in 1920 and the old President was shabbily assassinated in May 1920.

Obregón went unrecognized by the U.S.A. until 1923. At last an agreement was reached on American properties that had been confiscated. Americans accepted bonds instead of cash and recognition of Obregón followed. A Conservative revolt had broken out under Adolfo de la Huerta, strongly supported by the great landowners and the Church. But the U.S.A., opposed to further disorders in a country torn by 13 years of civil dissensions, freely shipped arms and ammunition to the established government. With this aid, General Calles suppressed the rebellion on behalf of Obregón.

Calles in Power: 1924–1934. Calles, nominally a Socialist, was Obregón's designee for the presidency. He was elected in 1924. Calles enjoyed some popularity in the U.S.A.; within Mexico he faced the most relatively stable situation since 1910. He began to enforce the Constitution of 1917, which until that time had been largely a pious inspiration. A land law really effected some redistribution. In regard to oil and mineral rights, despite previous agreements with the U.S.A., the government ordered the constitution's nationalizing provisions to go into effect.

The Church, determined to face the issue as presented by Calles, stated that it would not obey the constitution and the law. Rioting broke out at the National Shrine of the Virgin of Guadalupe. The government retaliated by ordering all Catholic schools, convents, and monasteries closed. The Catholics resisted. The *Cristeros*, as the rebels were called, evoked lively sympathy from fellow-Catholics in the U.S.A., but they were crushed. A Catholic boycott followed. The Church was now limited to one priest for every 50,000 people; and when one considers the need to say masses alone, this was equivalent to a suspension of the Catholic faith in most localities.

In 1927 the U.S.A. sent a partner of J. P. Morgan and Company, Dwight W. Morrow, to Mexico. At first the radical press in America thought this unwise, for the firm was the archetype of American finance to Mexican radicals. But with a patience that none had shown before, Morrow proved to be the first messenger of goodwill. By kindness, firm but reciprocal understanding, balancing American just claims with Mexican basic needs, and manifesting the greatest of diplomatic equipments, an ability to forget every difference in order to compose those which could most easily be resolved, he changed the atmosphere of Mexican-American relations as much as one man could. By 1928 the 18-year feud was basically over. However, a religious enthusiast had assassinated General Obregón just before he was to succeed President Calles. The real power was with Calles, whose two designees, Portes Gil and Ortiz Rubio rose and fell at his command.

The Rise of Cárdenas: 1934–1940. By 1932 it was obvious that Calles had calmed down in his Socialist passions. True, anti-clericalism remained as insistent as ever and in 1934 it was decreed that all education must be "socialistic." But the Leftist groups were not assured, and they found their champion in Lázaro Cárdenas, almost the god of the Leftists since his accession to power. The Leftists were all-powerful in education, art, music, literature; they were not equally versed in industry, mining, or agricultural techniques, although in the last they showed some enterprise.

Cárdenas quickly undertook land reforms. Up to his inauguration, 19,000,000 acres had been distributed to 750,000 families. These were taken not so much from communally claimed areas as from great estates. Under Cárdenas, another 51,000,000 acres were distributed and another 1,250,000 families received their plots. It was decided that woodland and pasture lands were to be communally used and crop land to be divided, but no one who received an allotment could sell or mortgage his holding. The *Ejido* (or cooperative community) which administered these lands, came to be a central feature of Mexican farming. Conservative elements charged that the *Ejidos* had lowered the average productivity, and that redistribution generally had lowered prospective as well as present production. Cárdenas considered that any limitations were caused by lack of capital and of training, both of which he set about vigorously to remedy.

Labor control now passed into the hands of the C.T.M., rival federation of the older C.R.O.M., and the new leadership of Vicente Lombardo Toledano indicated a firmer insistence on labor demands than before. Toledano was not only a Marxist but a professor at a university for teaching Marxian doctrine. His relations with Communists were sometimes cordial, often strained, but never hostile. The enemies of the government considered him the power behind the throne and made him their target. Toledano, under Cárdenas, could state that labor unions managed railways and utilities, petroleum, sugar mills, textile mills and would soon directly control most industrial and mining production.

Conservative elements, long discouraged, coalesced to fight this trend. A new movement arose to replace the *Cristeros* (rebellious Catholics) and the Fascist *Camisos Dorados* (or Golden Shirts). Neither movement had any great following, apart from devotees, whereas the new movement *Sinarquismo* soon had hundreds of thousands. Based on religion and the family, with a coating of radicalism, its doctrines resembled some of Marshal Pétain's in France. The Cárdenas following declared that it was an offshoot of Falangism in Spain and a Fascist dodge. The *Sinarquistas*, of course, denied the charge, especially since they were extremely active among Mexican immigrants in the U.S.A.

Avila Camacho Succeeds Cárdenas: 1940–1944. In 1940 Avila Camacho, Minister of War in the Cárdenas Cabinet, was elected over Almazán, who opposed the Cárdenas heritage. The election was disputed, and a close vote of Congress decided for Avila Camacho.

Avila Camacho has largely continued the Cárdenas tradition, but with increasing caution. Mexico has been steadily more identified with the U.S.A., joining her as an ally in World War II. A part of Mexico's prosperity arose from the American policy of buying silver above the competitive world price. Under Avila Camacho the stirrings of the Cárdenas group are noticeable. But so long as Mexico follows her present orientation in favor of democracy and Pan-American understanding and unity, the present administration is in a good position. A definitive oil agreement was reached in November 1941 and long-term economic cooperative agreements with the U.S.A. are being worked out. A vigorous opponent of Falangism, Mexico refuses to recognize Franco Spain, and succors refugee Spanish Loyalists. Her social radicalism has in no way lessened cooperation with other American commonwealths of different social faiths.

Stakes in the Peace

Mexico is a country emerging from 25 years of revolution, with some of the objectives of that vast convulsion attained and others still in an unresolved state. The small amount of productive agriculture and stockraising and the consequent appalling poverty of the masses of the people, remain the basic difficulties. The hatreds engendered among Mexicans, partly by foreign influences, make this amelioration of poverty still more difficult. Few countries have had greater talents at their disposal, whether liberators like Hidalgo, native geniuses like Juárez, or unflinching followers of their policy like Cárdenas. But none of these men, however able, has touched more than the rim of Mexican difficulties.

The provision of capital for Mexico would not of itself be too great an aid. Foreign capital poured into the country from 1876 to 1910, but as the subsequent revolutionary era showed, without improving that basis of society which is a precondition of democratic stability. However, as a friend of the U.S.A., Mexico can advance rapidly if her land reforms lead to greater production, if her rising consciousness of democracy among the people is fostered not only by ideas but by actual function, and if the attitude towards the Mexican abroad proves kinder and less patronizing.

The greatest area for capital employment lies in developing Mexico's amazing mineral resources for smelting and metals fabrication; a constructive tendency in this direction is shown in the impressive development of Monterrey. Light industries, largely brought in by refugees, indicate that the Mexican central plateau can also be industrialized; and this could raise the level of prosperity and diminish relative rural overpopulation.

Mexico has demonstrated an excellent Pan-American spirit recently. Firmly opposed to aggressors, she possesses the prerequisites for active membership in a world organization for peace.

NEWFOUNDLAND

During the war, Newfoundland has often made the headlines because of her strategic position for cable communication and air traffic between North America and the British Isles (she is only 1,900 miles from Ireland). She has long been known for the cliffs and deep bays of her coastline, for her Grand Banks of fog, her cod fisheries (focus of her economy), her forests, and the woodpulp they supplied to the London newspapers.

The island of Newfoundland is not part of Canada, but a British colony (once a dominion) now under Commission rule. She is the oldest overseas possession of Great Britain, discovered by the Cabots and settled by fishermen of many nationalities, the English at last prevailing. She exercises jurisdiction over Labrador, the vast wilderness made famous by the devoted labors of Dr. Wilfred Grenfell. Off her coast are St. Pierre and Miquelon, two islands remaining in French possession, the last of their once vast Canadian Empire.

The Land and the People

The Land. Newfoundland (area 42,734 square miles), an island about the size of Pennsylvania, lies off the east coast of Canada. Her dependency, Labrador, stretches over a vast, treeless, and barren expanse (118,000 square miles) along the eastern coast of Quebec and Ungava, facing the North Atlantic and inclining toward Greenland.

The People. Newfoundlanders are of British stock. Their birthrate is about 22 per thousand, their deathrate about 13. In 1935 the population was 289,000. During the war it has risen to 336,000, including American and British soldiers and war-workers stationed for the duration.

Religion and Education. Newfoundlanders are two-thirds Protestant and one-third Catholic. The Church of England leads the Protestant groups, and the Salvation Army claims the allegiance of a tenth of the Protestants. Education is tuition-free and actually compulsory; schools are denominational but supported by the state.

See map on page 151.

The Economy

Production. Newfoundland has only 160 square miles of land under cultivation, with a production of $4,200,000. Nor is there much livestock. Woodpulp from the forests, on the other hand, amounts to some 300,000 tons annually. The pre-war annual production of base metals was $6,600,000 — lead, zinc, copper, fluorspar, and 1,200,000 tons of iron ore.

The mainstay of the country is fisheries. The latest census showed 64% of the employed in cod fishing. Although it has declined during the war, the catch in peacetime was about 56,000 tons, sometimes as much as 68,000. A by-product of the codfish industry is cod-liver oil. Salmon and lobster are other huge catches. The seal catch varies tremendously: 40,000 one year and 5,000 the next is possible.

Finance. Because her finances are involved in the ups and downs of the fisheries, Newfoundland's financial history is as stormy as her coast. In 1944 she was still experiencing a war boom. The country was saturated with war work — war construction, strangers in great numbers and with above-average incomes, to be temporarily housed and catered to. In 1942 tax receipts exceeded expenditures (which were about $17,000,000) by $7,000,000. The large public debt, expressed in Newfoundland dollars — worth about the same as Canadian dollars, 91¢ in American parity — was $88,000,000 foreign and $2,500,000 domestic. But what the end of the war will bring is so uncertain that wartime figures are not of much significance.

Foreign Trade. The pre-war per capita trade of over $280 a year — $26,000,000 imports and $34,000,000 exports — indicates that normally Newfoundland's source of livelihood is exports, her source of subsistence imports. Chief exports are pulp and newsprint, fish, and minerals; chief imports textiles, flour, coal, hardware, and pork. Normally exports go principally to Britain and the U.S.A., and imports come from these countries and Canada.

Labrador. The entire population, consisting of whites and Eskimos, numbers only 4,700, and these are scattered through an area that is over twice as large as Newfoundland. With a population that makes a precarious living by fishing and hunting, Labrador deservedly is referred to as a poorhouse.

History: 1914-1944

Newfoundland, a British Dominion in 1914, actively participated in World War I by the side of the mother country. In the course of the conflict (1917), a National Government was formed in Newfoundland, which included the Fishermen's party. In 1918 William Lloyd became Premier.

While Lloyd was at Versailles attending the Peace Conference in 1919, Coaker of the Fishermen's party withdrew his support of the coalition government. Lloyd resigned his premiership and Michael Cashin succeeded. The 1919 elections witnessed a bitter conflict: Coaker joined with a young lawer, William Warren, to defeat the Cashin government. Then they united under Richard Squires, and this coalition held power for a long period, being reelected in 1923.

In 1923 the government bought out Newfoundland's long-standing contracts with the R. G. Reid interests of Montreal, which controlled railroads, steamship lines, and piers. Since Reid had once dominated the Dominion financially, Newfoundlanders believed that they had at last regained their economic independence. However, the Premier, Sir Richard Squires, was now accused of having accepted money from private interests and as a result of the scandal, the Fishermen's party coalition suffered defeat and fell from office.

The new Monroe government stressed economy, and since conditions were improving even in this hard-hit little country, the new régime carried through its program. In 1925 Prohibition was abolished, and liquor vending became a state function.

In 1927, the Privy Council in London affirmed Newfoundland's claim to Labrador against the claims of Canada, a move which promised to give the country a rich hinterland. But the 1929 depression delivered a hard blow to Newfoundland and her precarious economic foundations proved too weak to weather the storm. She requested aid from the Imperial Treasury; but as such aid was not compatible with dominion status, London suspended the Newfoundland Constitution, withdrew dominion status, and in 1933 entrusted government to a six-man Commission, consisting of three Britons and three Newfoundlanders. In Britain, some official circles expressed anxiety at this innovation, as a poor precedent in Empire affairs.

Recovery was spotty and in 1938 there was a renewed crisis in newsprint and codfish exports.

At the outbreak of World War II, Newfoundland joined Britain immediately in the conflict. In 1941, the U.S.A., by arrangement with Great Britain in accordance with the terms of the Bases-Destroyers Accord, began to build extensive military and naval bases in the island. The war occasioned a marked economic recovery and led to agitation by Newfoundlanders for a resumption of representative government. A delegation of three members of the British House of Commons visited Newfoundland (1943), but they reported that they had not found a clear-cut majority for any given form of government to replace the six-man Commission.

There was a wide variety of suggestions as to the proper course to follow, some even desiring the entry of Newfoundland into the United Kingdom with status similar to Northern Ireland. But no single suggestion won the day, and Newfoundland continued under the makeshift Commission form of government.

Stakes in the Peace

Newfoundland's present political status is humiliating: it is to be hoped that proposed alternatives to the present stopgap Commission government will soon become effective. The recent recommendations of a British parliamentary committee, looking forward to the resumption of a higher status within the British Commonwealth, might, if correlated with directed economic aid, put Newfoundland on a solid basis once again. Diminution of war spending in the colony may make action quite urgent.

This sturdy people have not had the rewards, historically, to which their character entitles them. Their remarkable showing in the Boston area of the U.S.A., to which so many have emigrated, shows their possibilities.

Newfoundland requires fresh capital in her mining and forest exploitation, and a more intensive exploration and use of her potentially rich Labrador hinterland. Recent developments in nearby Quebec, which have transformed the mining economy of that Canadian province, indicate the possibilities of Labrador. Once Newfoundland has some new source of revenue, to supplement the consistently inadequate basis of fishing, she may attain a fair and durable prosperity. Perhaps the large American investments and stimulation during World War II may give just that incentive required to make new departures easier.

NICARAGUA

The Land and the People

See map on page 197.

Nicaragua is a Central American republic whose color, importance, and possibilities deserve to be widely known. She has a fascinating history and social structure.

Rivalries in the middle of the last century between

Great Britain and the U.S.A. led to interventions in Nicaragua. The slaveholding interests in the U.S.A. sponsored the ill-fated filibuster, William Walker of Tennessee, in his attempt to control the little republic (1855–1860). Much later, North American adventurers came to fight in numerous revolutions. These disorders brought about United States interventions from 1913 to 1932. Foreigners deserve much of the blame for the turbulent history of Nicaragua. Their military interventions not only failed to contribute to the people's education and economic life, but they left the Nicaraguans with a deep suspicion of foreigners.

The new Pan-American Highway, the air transportation, and the sanitation programs fostered during World War II by the U.S.A. have served to broaden the outlook and improve the physical welfare of the Nicaraguans. Their capital city, Managua, has been considerably improved. But the country districts, especially the relatively isolated east-coast section about Bluefields, and the territory occupied by the Mosquito Indians, await schools, roads, and public health agencies.

The Land. Nicaragua is the largest of the Central American republics: 57,143 square miles, about the size of Georgia. She is bounded on the north by Honduras, on the south by Costa Rica. Her territory can be characterized as three regions: (1) the plain in the hilly region near the Pacific coast — with its cities and two lakes, Managua and Nicaragua, in a setting of 20 active volcanoes, a land of lava-enriched soil and severe earthquakes; (2) the Mosquito coast on the Caribbean — a hot, moist region with jungles, swamps, and banana plantations; and (3) the highland country in the center of Nicaragua, with peaks 7,000 feet high. Of the three regions, the Pacific inland is the most important: it is the center of Nicaraguan life. Her three chief cities are there as well as three-fourths of her inhabitants.

The waterways of Nicaragua offer possibilities for an interoceanic canal. Lake Nicaragua, 100 miles long and over 40 miles wide, the largest inland body of water between Lake Michigan and Bolivia's Lake Titicaca, is connected with the Atlantic by the San Juan River. Thirteen miles of low, hilly land separate Lake Nicaragua from the Pacific. An interoceanic canal would involve cutting these 13 miles of land and widening and deepening the San Juan River. Such an undertaking would require perhaps a decade to complete — and the waterway would be 180 miles long, over three times longer than the Panama Canal. Nevertheless, Nicaraguans attach great hope to the possibility that this long-discussed project will some day become a fact.

The People. The mass of the people are *mestizos* (mixed Indian and white) with the European strain greatly predominant. On the Caribbean coast the population is composed partly of West Indian Negroes.

Nicaraguan culture is intensely Spanish and national feeling runs high. There has been an acute conflict between the liberal professional class in the city of León and the conservative wealthy landlord group in Granada. The battle of the feudal lord and the burgess, so familiar in English history, is here enacted five centuries later.

The Nicaraguans are lively, gay, and emancipated.

Their national life reflects many North American influences — they have over 200 baseball teams; their drugstores, like ours, are miniature department stores. Though the economy is founded on the soil, the country has been largely one of city dwellers. León is a center of impassioned political opinion and discussion — and of fine old Spanish churches. Granada, 70 miles to the south, is the home of the aristocrats, a stanchly conservative city, notable for its serene beauty.

Religion and Education. The dominant religion of the country is Roman Catholicism. Estimates of adult illiteracy run as high as 50%, but today a large proportion of the children attend school. In striking contrast to the illiteracy figure is the fact that the country has three universities. The trend toward improved education is illustrated by another fact: since 1927 schools have increased by 300%.

The educated classes are actively aware of the modern world. Since the intellectuals play a great political rôle as a group, they take pride in their extensive culture. Among their leading figures was Rubén Darío (1867–1916), the most famous poet of Latin America. His little volume *Azul* changed the content and form of Hispanic verse.

The Nation's Economy

Nicaragua's cultivated area of 1,600 square miles represents a bare 3% of the country's territory. Hence, the arable land is too small for adequate domestic food production. Corn is the largest crop raised for subsistence purposes, and coffee is the chief crop for export. In addition to corn, Nicaraguans live on *garbanzos* (chickpeas), rice, and sugar. Bananas dominate the agricultural activity on the east coast of the country. Among Nicaragua's other farm products are yucca, cocoa beans, plantain, tobacco, cotton, and sesame.

The country's present cattle population is small, but hides and meat are worthy of mention. Another item of consequence is the country's cabinet wood production.

Gold mining has greatly increased in recent years; it has come to displace agriculture as the leading source of exports. The only large local industries consist of coffee-cleaning establishments and some scattered workshops for light consumers goods.

Finance and Foreign Trade. The unit of currency is the *córdoba*, worth about 17¢. During World War II money in circulation has doubled (it is now $3.60 per capita). The national budget is about $6,400,000; the debt, including utilized American credits, about $6,000,000. Nicaragua's cost of living has doubled, and this has created economic strains.

Foreign trade has also doubled since 1935. In 1941 gold exports were $7,300,000, coffee $2,500,000, cabinet woods $400,000, all the rest $1,700,000. In 1942, however, exports of crude rubber exceeded $1,000,000. By 1942 all exports had increased from a total of $11,900,000 to $14,300,000, a clear indication that Nicaragua, once the poorest of the Central American countries in foreign trade, had begun to catch up. Imports, however, fell to $6,700,000, so that although cash receipts from exports were being built up abroad, consumers goods ran short at home. The U.S.A. took 88% of the country's exports and supplied 93% of her imports.

As a result of economic accords concluded with the U.S.A., Nicaraguan rubber planting is to be encouraged. Highway projects employ 10,000 workers. The main hopes of Nicaragua, however, especially of her professional groups, remain fixed on the possibilities of a revival of the project of an interoceanic canal, to supplement the Panama Canal. Consistent and heartfelt inter-American unity characterizes Nicaraguan political and economic orientation.

History: 1914-1944

Nicaragua has unfortunately had the most colorful history of the Central American republics. Various revolutions occurred in the years immediately preceding World War I, and in 1912, at the invitation of President Adolfo Díaz, United States marines entered the country to maintain order. During World War I, under her President, Emiliano Chamorro, the country remained neutral.

Nicaraguan relations with the U.S.A. had long been intimate but difficult. In 1917, the U.S.A. granted her $3,000,000 for the concession of an interoceanic canal project, to supplement the already existing Panama Canal. An agreement in the same year reorganized Nicaraguan finances, limiting monthly governmental expenditures and assuring service on the foreign debt. The plan was to be supervised by one Nicaraguan and two appointees of the United States Department of State.

By 1924, Nicaragua had repaid this debt and had repurchased the shares of her National Bank and National Railway, which had been controlled by a group of New York bankers. Although American financial control had been modified in 1920, the Nicaraguan government requested the bankers to continue to manage the country's finances until 1926 or later.

Meanwhile, Nicaragua's relations with her neighbors had become embittered. President Chamorro of Nicaragua and the United States Secretary of State William Jennings Bryan had concluded the Treaty of 1916 concerning an interoceanic canal. This Treaty had been entered into without consulting the other Central American republics; and the latter declared that it was subject to the authority of the Central American Joint Court. Moreover, both Honduras and El Salvador, as well as Costa Rica, maintained that the Treaty affected their legitimate rights, and their respective territories, without their consent. As a result of these adverse reactions, Nicaragua vetoed the moves of the other republics toward a Central American Federation. However, in 1923 she became party to a treaty that denied recognition to any Central American government established by force.

In the 1925 elections, the Conservative President Chamorro was defeated by a Liberal, Juan Sacasa. Chamorro executed a *coup*, expelled President-elect Sacasa, and declared himself President again. Although his régime was not recognized abroad, the U.S.A. also refused to recognize Sacasa since the latter possessed no *de facto* power. When the Mexican government of Calles recognized Sacasa and gave him arms and supplies, the U.S.A. landed marines in Nicaragua to prevent civil war.

A Liberal revolt erupted on the east coast. United States action forced out Chamorro, but the Nicaraguan Senate named Díaz, and not Sacasa, as President. The U.S.A. dispatched Henry L. Stimson to arrange for free elections and to ascertain the popular will. This move was necessary because of a feeling throughout Latin America that the U.S.A. had dictated the virtual annulment of Sacasa's election.

In the interim, the U.S.A. had recognized Díaz, provided him with a loan, and stationed 2,000 marines at Managua. The rebel Liberals were obdurate. With disorders and acts of brigandage rampant in Nicaragua, Stimson's mission arrived just in time to prevent a formidable explosion.

The 1928 elections returned a Liberal, José Moncada, by an overwhelming margin, but a provincial Liberal leader, General Augustino Sandino, had declined to accept the intervention of the U.S.A. With only a few hundred followers, he attacked American marines in 1928. A guerrilla tactician, he proved difficult to capture because of the ease with which his small force could disappear into the surrounding countryside. The anti-United States parties in Latin America closely followed Sandino's resistance, looking upon him as a liberator in the tradition of William Tell. Without inquiring into the objective merits of Sandino's struggle (in view of Stimson's honorable cooperation with the Liberals), anti-imperialists everywhere championed his cause.

In December 1929 the Liberal Moncada was reelected, but in 1930 Sandino again fought the United States marines as invaders. When in 1931 the marines were withdrawn, Sandino reentered the Liberal fold.

The elections of 1932, held under the supervision of the U.S.A., returned Sacasa to the Presidency. Two years later, as Sandino was leaving the presidential palace, he was assassinated.

President Sacasa continued in office until 1936 when he was overthrown as a result of a *coup d'état* executed by General Anastasio Somoza, Commander of the National Guard. Somoza then became President of the republic. When his political opponents joined forces in a coalition, he exiled their leaders and called a new election (1938). The results showed 117,000 votes for Somoza's group and 1,000 for his adversaries.

A new constitution came into force in 1939 and President Somoza extended his term of office to last eight years. The prevailing Congress numbers 26 Liberals, 9 National Conservatives, and 7 "Traditional" Conservatives.

Nicaragua joined the U.S.A. in the war against the Axis in December 1941. The war brought a boom in exports and close economic and military collaboration between the two countries. While President Somoza adopted a less stringent attitude toward political opponents, he warned the Conservatives against indulging in electoral maneuvers too far in advance of the 1946 elections. In 1944, he declared that he was not a candidate for reelection, nor would he permit his term of office to be extended.

Stakes in the Peace

If the interoceanic Nicaraguan canal becomes a reality, Nicaragua may come to resemble Panama more closely. But unlike Panama, Nicaragua has traditional ties with the other four Central American republics, which make for a potentially richer and more varied future.

Her basic need is an increase in light industries with a consequent rise in trade. This would tilt economic power more in the direction of the Liberal elements, who now have to seek careers in the army, government, or in the professions and thus engage in never-ending intrigues in order to survive as a class. With a new merchant and industrialist group in the cities, increased scope for the intellectual class, and the rise of laboring groups in the canal areas, the small wealthy class would lose its tight hold over some of the peasantry and would thus be compelled to accept a minor rôle in political life.

If these social changes occur, Nicaragua, who has shown astonishing, though often misdirected, energies, should emerge as a leading Central American republic. Her old feud with the U.S.A. is in the limbo of history; and she is now an active "good neighbor." Given a proper economic basis, her advance to full democracy would not be long delayed.

PANAMA

The Land and the People

Panama, on the isthmus of Darien, is noted throughout the world primarily for the Panama Canal, which is the conspicuous feature of the economic life of the republic. This Central American nation was once a territory of Colombia, but she revolted in 1903 and her independence was recognized by the U.S.A. When the operations of the French Panama Canal Company broke down because of political corruption and failure to cope with tropical diseases, the U.S.A. took over the ambitious canal project, and within a decade she connected the 50 miles between the Caribbean and the Pacific — a brilliant triumph of sanitary and physical engineering. Today the republic of Panama is absolutely sovereign and independent; only the Canal Zone is leased to the U.S.A.

The Land. The narrow land of Panama, winding south of Costa Rica to Colombia, is about as large as Maine (34,169 square miles). The Canal Zone is situated near the center of the country, with the city of Colón on the Caribbean and Panama City on the Pacific. These two ports, with their remarkably cosmopolitan atmosphere, contrast sharply with the rest of the country, which is hot, tropical, a region of mountains and jungles with hundreds of rivers and streams.

About half the Panamanian population live in the regions bordering the Canal Zone. The other half inhabit the valleys and carry on agricultural, pastoral, and fishing pursuits. Scarcely fifty miles from Panama City — an ancient center which is today frequented by traders from every part of the globe — live the Indian elements of Panama, whose life does not differ radically from the lives of their ancestors at the time when Balboa explored the land and viewed the water of the Pacific from the isthmus of Darien.

The People. There are 631,000 Panamanians, of whom 128,000 live in and about Panama City and

See map on page 197.

66,000 in and about Colón. Both principal ports are part of sovereign Panama, though situated in enclaves within the Canal Zone. The Canal employs some 40% of the Panamanian population in peacetime. Cristóbal and Balboa are the two important towns in the territory leased by the U.S.A.

The great majority of Panamanians are *mestizos* (mixed Indian and white). In the remote country districts, the Indians retain their tribal organization; they number fully 10% of the population. The pure white element, some 17%, largely engage in commerce in the cities and constitute the landowning class in the country districts. Some 9% of the population are of Negro stock. However, the cosmopolitan appeal of Panama has brought in many Syrians and other trading peoples.

Religion and Education. Under the Constitution of January 2, 1941, the Roman Catholic Church was recognized as the faith of the majority of Panamanians. But freedom is stipulated for other religions.

About 10% of the population attends school, one of the highest ratios in Latin America. There are two colleges, one of which has been constituted as the National University of Panama, and there are many normal, trade, and commercial institutes. The new Inter-American University, founded September 1942 in Panama City, is expected to become a factor in the cultural exchange of the Americas.

The Canal Zone

The Canal Zone, which consists of 5 miles on either side of the waters of the Canal (an area of 552 square miles in all), is leased to the U.S.A. and is administered by her army officials.

Among the Zone population of 51,000, the English

language prevails (as does the Spanish outside the Zone). The population is generally Protestant (whereas most Panamanians are Roman Catholics). Owing to the greater proportion of men, the birth-rate is only 12.4 per thousand; and since most of the men are young, the deathrate is only 6.4.

United States capital investment in the Canal, after depreciation, was $644,000,000 and the net deficit is now over $2,400,000 per year. In peace-time some 5,300 vessels (20,000,000 tons) annually used the facilities of the Canal. With the advent of World War II, United States military needs resulted in a great increase of employment for Panamanians and consequently in augmented payrolls. However, there has been a marked diminution in consumers goods, owing to civilian shipping shortages; and the combination of greater spending power and scarcity of goods has brought about a sharp upturn in prices.

The Nation's Economy

Very few people work the soil of Panama, but de-spite the small cultivated area, the agricultural econ-omy is active. Rice, corn, and beans are raised for domestic requirements, and bananas, rubber (37,000 pounds), and cassava (yielding a nutritious starch) are produced for export. A tendency to emphasize subsistence food rather than export crops has lately been gaining ground — for example, cacao (used for making cocoa and chocolate) has fallen by 60% as an export item. While food crops have markedly in-creased, the wartime shipping shortage has cut banana shipments by half.

Panama's other economic activities are varied. Her cattle and swine have doubled since 1938. Her dense forests give employment to lumbermen; and her pearl-fisheries continue to thrive. In peacetime the tourist and transient trade furnished a really important source of revenue for so small a country.

Finance and Foreign Trade. Panama's mone-tary unit, the *balboa*, is worth a dollar. The country's budgets, exclusive of Canal Zone administration, nor-mally balanced at some $20,000,000 — nearly three times that of neighboring Costa Rica. An interesting curiosity is that 327 ships fly the flag of Panama — one of those juridical quirks, like the astonishing number of American companies registered in the little state of Delaware.

Panama's foreign trade situation has no analogy to any normal country's: with imports of $37,500,000 and exports of only $2,200,000. This apparently incred-ible ratio is not related to Panamanian economy, but to Canal Zone needs, and it becomes easily compre-hensible if placed in the context of the U.S.A.'s intra-national trade. The U.S.A. purchased 97% of Pan-ama's exports, supplied 81% of her imports. Exports were typical products of the tropics: bananas, cocoa beans, gold, coconuts. Imports were gasoline, wheat, flour, perfumes, cosmetics, and some machinery.

History: 1914-1944

The history of Panama differs from that of the other Central American republics in that it so largely con-cerns negotiations with the U.S.A. The independence of Panama was proclaimed on November 3, 1903. Shortly thereafter, the U.S.A. and Panama negotiated a treaty. The U.S.A. guaranteed the independence of Panama, and Panama granted to the U.S.A. the right to build a canal across her central area in re-turn for a cash payment and a deferred annual rental. After one interruption, the Panama Canal began continuous operations in 1915.

In 1918, Panama declared war against the Central Powers. The revival of world trade in the post-war years greatly benefited the economy of the Canal Zone and of Panama generally. The number of com-mercial transits through the Canal rose from 760 in 1916 to 2,892 in 1921 and 5,230 in 1924. Tolls and other transit revenues had increased by 1,000%. The operational deficit in 1916 of $4,400,000 had been succeeded by a surplus of over $16,000,000 in 1924. The great economic advantages of the Canal brought other results as well, notably in the opportu-nity for increased mutual understanding among the peoples on the eastern and western coasts of the Americas.

A boundary dispute with Costa Rica occupied the attention of the two countries in 1921. The question had been submitted to Chief Justice White of the Supreme Court of the U.S.A., but for various reasons, Panama refused to carry out the provisions of the arbitral award. In March 1921 armed clashes broke out along the border. The U.S.A. interposed through diplomatic channels to prevent a major disturbance. Although the dispute remained unresolved, Panama and Costa Rica resumed diplomatic relations in 1928. In 1941 the boundary was finally agreed upon through direct negotiations between the two countries.

As Panama grew in nationhood, she became in-creasingly resentful of certain provisions of the so-called Permanent Treaty of 1903 with the U.S.A. This treaty gave the U.S.A. the right to intervene to preserve order in Panama's two leading cities, and the right to acquire, as she saw fit, any part of the land or water of Panama should the U.S.A. consider this necessary for the protection or maintenance of the Canal. In addition, it gave the U.S.A. a vast number of privileges and powers, proved unnecessary in practice, but increasingly resented by Panamanians. For example, no citizen was permitted to cross from one part of Panama to the other without the consent of the Canal Zone authorities. Furthermore, the goods of the Panamanian merchants were undersold by the commissaries of the Canal Zone, which im-ported articles duty-free.

In 1926, as a result of the violent antagonism which these provisions had created, the U.S.A. un-dertook to negotiate a supplementary treaty with Panama. The Panamanian National Assembly, however, refused to ratify this new treaty, on the ground that it failed to remove the causes of the dif-ficulties and that, in essence, it placed upon Panama more rather than less obligations.

A bloodless revolution broke out in 1931. The U.S.A. declined to intervene, but she proffered her good offices for peace. The new President, Dr. Ricardo J. Alfaro, was succeeded in 1932 by Dr. Harmodio Arias.

In the autumn of 1933, Presidents Franklin D.

Roosevelt and Harmodio Arias issued a joint statement declaring that both governments would agree upon measures that would alleviate the situation existing between the two countries. The following year, negotiations were undertaken, which continued for over a year and a half and finally culminated in the Treaty of 1936.

The new Treaty abrogated all rights of the U.S.A. to intervene in Panama and to seize Panamanian territory; and thus her absolute sovereignty was affirmed. Through a large series of supplementary agreements, the citizens of Panama received commercial privileges previously denied them, and they also were given restricted privileges previously exercised within the Canal Zone by the Canal authorities of the U.S.A. A subsidiary provision increased the annuity payments (from $250,000 to $430,000) to Panama, because of the deflation of the United States dollar. In essence, the Treaty of 1936 and its subsidiary agreements made Panama a partner of the U.S.A. in the protection and maintenance of the Canal. During the difficulties of World War II, Panama has lived up to her obligations scrupulously; and the Treaty of 1936 has become a symbol of harmonious inter-American cooperation.

The internal history of Panama became disturbed in 1940 when President Arnulfo Arias suspended the Constitution and granted himself a long term. Displaying evident pro-Axis leanings, he forbade the arming of Panamanian ships, although several had

already been attacked on the high seas by the Axis. This decree made him extremely unpopular, and he fled the country. It was subsequently charged that he had harbored Axis spies in the Canal Zone.

Ricardo A. de la Guardia became the new President in October 1941. Immediately upon the entrance of the U.S.A. into the war, his government declared war against the Axis powers. The Panamanians have cooperated loyally and actively with the inter-American policies conducive to the success of the United Nations.

Stakes in the Peace

Because she is the passageway between the Atlantic and Pacific oceans, Panama has a unique stake in world prosperity. The increase of interchange among the nations of the earth will not only enlarge the traffic through the Canal but should aid her national economy.

Panama needs a considerable measure of industrialization, so that her citizens can profit from local industries which could help supply the traffic through the Canal. She also needs an intensified development in agriculture and pastoral pursuits — one that could enable her to supply the vegetables, fruits, and meat required by the vessels passing through the Canal.

PARAGUAY

The Land and the People

In a colorful career, filled with the most startling extremes in Latin America, Paraguay has fought long wars with Bolivia, Brazil, Argentina, and Uruguay. At one time (1865–70) the bantam Paraguayans took on a combination of powers outnumbering them by twelve to one. This martial history was climaxed in the Chaco war of 1935 with Bolivia. Paraguay nearly trebled her size when the Chaco area was awarded her (1938) — from 61,647 square miles to 169,000 square miles, roughly the difference between Oklahoma and California.

A landlocked republic, Paraguay extends along the river system that flows into the Río de la Plata. Consequently the country's trade has flowed down the Paraguay and Paraná Rivers towards the mouth of the Río de la Plata at Buenos Aires. There are rail connections to Argentine ports, and recently other communications have diminished the former isolation of Paraguay. The small population of the country and its great distance from populated centers have made transportation costs excessive. These factors have

accentuated Paraguay's tendency to produce for local consumption and to be only slightly interested in commerce with the rest of the world.

The Land. Paraguay is a slightly hilly country with large flat areas, and is almost entirely either forest or grassy plain. The land is swampy, however, in the Gran Chaco to the northwest and along some of the great rivers. Despite her tropical location, the rainfall is evenly distributed throughout the year and never excessive, and the temperature is rarely too hot. These two factors, rare in a tropical lowland area, together with a naturally fertile soil, should have created one of the richest farming districts in the world.

The most productive area is a compact hilly region of some 10,000 square miles close to the Paraná River and tending northwest toward Asunción, the capital, on the Paraguay River. In the thickly forested low, wide plateaus of eastern Paraguay, is found the quebracho tree, source of tannin (used for tannic acid), an important article in world trade. The only important mineral resource is petroleum in the Chaco, and this has not yet been exploited.

Paraguay is said to have the most succulent oranges in the world. But the cost of shipping them to ports is prohibitive. Oil of petitgrain, the concentrated essence of these oranges, commands so high a price that it is economic to transport it: this product has a world market for perfumes. Paraguay also produces the most delicate varieties of *yerba maté*, or Paraguay tea, esteemed by South American gourmets.

The scenery of the country is memorable. A trip on the Paraguay River, a thousand miles from Buenos Aires to Asunción, is an entrancing experience. Orchids, tropical birds, including many colored parrots, monkeys, and crocodiles abound. Gorgeous sunsets startle the traveler. The substantial brick edifices of the old Jesuit missions recall the days when Paraguay was a religious communist society. All along the country roads are seen the hard-working women, smoking long black cigars, carrying great burdens on their heads, or loading oranges into carts, while many of the men — always a minority — often lie in the shade and enjoy themselves. Further along the Paraná River one comes to the overwhelmingly impressive Iguassú Falls, higher and broader than Niagara.

The People. For two centuries the Guaraní Indian population of Paraguay were gathered in mission settlements under the direction of Jesuit priests. They lived in long communal houses and worked collectively in the fields, which were directed by the Jesuits and worked for the benefit of the Indians. Private property in land was nonexistent as was private property in general, and concepts like money and income were unknown.

The Indians, perhaps 300,000, were awakened by the ringing of bells in the morning hours. The converts attended mass, partook of their morning meal, worked in the fields, and took time off for religious instruction. In 1767 the Jesuits were expelled from South America when their order was dissolved by the Pope. The helpless Indians, with no experience of production except as directed by their superiors, fell under the power of the Castilian grandees and became peons.

However, this new order of things had not continued for forty years when Paraguay, along with her neighbors, revolted against Spain. It was at first necessary to protect the independence of Paraguay from the Argentine provinces. In that struggle, a Paraguayan of French descent, Dr. José Gaspar Rodríguez Francia, arose to power. A keen admirer of the French Revolution, he realized that his own people were not so politically mature as the French. Hence he felt that the benefits of the French Revolution must be conferred upon Paraguayans "from above."

He was one of the most ruthless characters of history yet one of the most intellectual. Thomas Carlyle glorified him as the greatest man that had ever lived, and many political thinkers of Europe long regarded him as the greatest political personality ever produced in the Americas. He closed the Paraguay River to international traffic and arrested all foreigners, including diplomats who had endeavored to reach the country. He persecuted and then practically exterminated the upper-class Spaniards who had enslaved the former communal population of the Jesuit missions. He severely controlled the Roman Catholic Church and even toyed with the idea of establishing a native Guaraní religion. (He was himself an atheistic fol-

See detailed map on page 181.

lower of French philosophy.) After destroying the Spanish elements, he distributed the lands to the Guaraní Indians.

The people called him "El Supremo" (the supreme one). Edward Lucas White's novel by that name gives an astonishingly vivid picture of his complex mind and deeds. He was held in such awe that his people turned their faces to the wall when he passed along the street. He was later named "El Perpetuo" (the everlasting one) and after his death, he was referred to for generations not by his name, which no one dared breathe, but as "El Defunto" (the dead one).

Under his successor, his nephew Carlos Antonio López, the country flourished. In 1862 the latter was succeeded by his son, Francisco Solano López. Excited by the material prosperity of Paraguay, this enormously obese man conceived the dream of making Paraguay the imperial power of South America. His aggressive designs compelled the Brazilian Empire, Argentina, and Uruguay, to unite against him. Though they outnumbered him 12 to 1, it took them five years to defeat him. This occurred only after virtually every able-bodied Paraguayan was killed. The five-year war devastated the country. Of the 250,000 males, only 22,000 very aged men and boys under ten survived. The ratio of women to men was 13 to 1.

Handicrafts declined, farming fell into neglect for want of men, and a once literate people, educated by the Jesuits and Francia, soon became illiterate. Paraguay's poverty defied description.

Slowly the country was repeopled, largely by immigration. It took forty years for Paraguay to reach 500,000 population again. And her number today is estimated at between 800,000 and 1,000,000, with a large predominance of females. This population is almost entirely found in the 10,000 square miles that are closely cultivated.

The Paraguayans still have a fiery sense of nationalism. They are nearly all a mixture of Spaniards and Guaraní Indians. The Guaranís are amicable, adaptable, handsome, and quite talented. The Spanish element lives in the capital, Asunción, where it is prominent in administrative life. The mass of the people are wretchedly poor. Within the country there are considerable foreign colonies, the most successful of which are the Mennonites. There are a large number of Germans, who have their own well-attended schools; Italians, who are prominent in commerce; and many Argentines.

Asunción, a city of 100,000, seems far removed from the rush of modern life, although a new airway connecting with Buenos Aires and Rio de Janeiro is introducing the outside world. During World War II a group of health and economic experts have arrived from the U.S.A. and they are cooperating with the government in a program of modernization, and in developing new industries.

Religion and Education. The established faith of the overwhelming majority is Roman Catholic. Other religions have been tolerated, but of late a number of restrictions have been imposed.

Schools have substantially increased, with over 100,000 children now attending primary school (about 60% of those of school age) and about 4,000 are in secondary school. The National University at Asunción is an old, established seat of learning. While illiteracy is declining rapidly in Paraguay, the level of general culture remains quite arrested, except in the large towns. Guaraní remains the popular language, Spanish, the cultural, commercial, and governmental tongue. As might be expected from Paraguay's rich history, her literature is external — that is, historical and geographical, rather than purely literary.

The Nation's Economy

Most Paraguayans are engaged in agriculture, stock-raising, or forestry. The chief agricultural products for home consumption are corn, beans, and fruits. But less than 1% of the land is given to crops, hence there is widespread malnutrition in this bountiful land.

Paraguay nevertheless exports certain agricultural products: tobacco, oil of petitgrain (widely used for perfumes), woods, and yerba maté, or the choice popular Paraguayan tea. Livestock is relatively numerous, the 3,500,000 cattle representing a very high per capita figure; hides and preserved meats are leading exports.

Paraguay has almost no industry save in the usual light consumers goods of typically agricultural countries. The bulk of capital investment is in the extraction of quebracho, cattle stockyards, and canning. These now involve a substantial investment.

Finance. Paraguayan finances have been subject to the most violent fluctuations. The Chaco war drained what little assets were left and the paper peso finally dropped to the rate of 333 to the United States dollar. It was then exchanged for a new unit of currency, the guaraní, at the rate of 100 to 1. Annual revenues are $3,000,000. The national debt of over $22,000,000 approximated the cost of Paraguay's acquisition of the Chaco territory by force of arms. An export tax on yerba maté and hides is reserved to pay interest on the external debt, which is $12,500,000. Paraguay's bank resources abroad have been placed under joint Paraguayan-Argentine control.

Foreign investments in Paraguay are not large: total British commitments are $5,000,000 and those of the U.S.A. are $10,000,000. Banking is on a very small scale. Money in circulation is about $2.50 per capita, deposits in commercial banks about 80¢ per capita. The agricultural economy is little concerned with cash. The nation's economic life has been aided by some 22,000 immigrants, but apparently they have not deposited their internal savings in Paraguayan banks.

Foreign Trade. In normal times, imports (chiefly textiles and machinery) approach $10,000,000, exports $9,000,000. In 1942 the effect of the world war was felt in the decline of imports to $7,600,000 and the rise of exports to $10,000,000. Financial reserves deposited outside the country rose somewhat, but they were used largely to stimulate imports.

The bulk of imports in peacetime came from South America, and the U.S.A. furnished a fifth, and Great Britain and Japan about a tenth each. Paraguay's exports are purchased by Latin America, Great Britain, and the U.S.A., the share of each being about 20%. Paraguay's very small foreign trade may be increased by new arrangements for a customs union with Brazil and Argentina as well as for the right to use Buenos Aires as a free port. The cost of river transport, so high in relation to sea freights, has long retarded Paraguayan trade.

History: 1914-1944

For a generation before 1918 only one president of Paraguay had managed to serve his full term. The term "government" applied to a particular grouping in the Military Club. With the army more powerful than the rapidly changing presidents, Paraguay seemed to fulfill the popular cinema notion of South American politics. For all that, however, railroad and urban improvements, investment, and foreign settlement continued behind the façade of crumbling governments. The long-term effect of the disastrous war of 1865–1870 was over, and a more intelligent and responsible business group in the cities demanded stable government. Thus, from 1924 to 1932 two presidents served out their full four-year terms. A new Paraguay was in the making.

But in 1932 Eusebio Ayala became president and began a border contest with Bolivia. Each country destroyed forts in the Gran Chaco. Efforts by outsiders, including the U.S.A., failed to avert a three years' war that drained the two economically weak opponents. An armistice in 1935 did not reduce the passions of the fiery elements, and peace was not assured until 1938. The treaty of July 21, 1938, made under inter-American mediation, with only slight concessions granted the Gran Chaco to Paraguay.

Paraguay, as so often in her sad history, had again lost far more men than she could afford. Her currency went down by five-sixths. The country declared a moratorium on private debts and suspended salaries of civil servants. In this disturbed situation, a war hero, Colonel Rafael Franco, overthrew President Ayala. Franco sought support for his "economic nationalism" and pledged State Socialism. His military rivals, disquieted, backed Felix Paiva, a "Liberal." Once Paiva came to power he had frequently to cope with counter-revolutionary demonstrations.

In January 1939, General Estigarribia, one of the ablest and most far-sighted leaders Paraguay has produced, was constitutionally elected. A Liberal, he tried to get opposition parties, who had boycotted elections, to participate in politics. In protest, both houses of Congress, which had been elected from only one group, resigned as a body in January 1940. The President ordered a dictatorship and a new constitution. This action, of course, was ratified by a plebiscite. Estigarribia was killed in an air crash just after his full triumph. His successor was General Moriñigo, who exiled or imprisoned Estigarribia's following and imposed a strict censorship. In 1941 several abortive risings were quashed.

Paraguay's only important outlet to the sea has been by way of Argentina. Hence Argentine influence is very strong. President Moriñigo, a natural conciliator, had visited Brazil, Bolivia, and Argentina. Brazil agreed to aid in railway and food expansion programs, so that Paraguay was less dependent on the Argentine outlet for her economic life. Argentina agreed on cultural and economic contacts. Moriñigo also visited the U.S.A. and accepted American military advice in the reorganizing of his military establishment for the purpose of cooperating in inter-American defense measures.

In March 1944 a reconstructed Paraguayan cabinet

excluded the more extreme adherents of the United Nations; the relative strength of the new appointees, as against Pan-American elements, has not yet been tested. Racialism has gained somewhat. Certainly Argentine influence, still significant, has the sympathy of reactionaries.

Foreign Affiliations. For a long period, as a treasured heritage of the 1815–1840 Francia policy of isolation, Paraguay had no external relations. Then she antagonized every neighbor and was long hostile to Brazil, Argentina, Uruguay, and Bolivia after successive wars. Lately she has sought to use her small bargaining powers to assure friendly relations with all her neighbors, a complete reversal of her tragic historic rôle. Argentina has juridical control of some of her finances. Her position is such that she must for some time to come be economically largely dependent on Argentina, although this influence will be modified increasingly as other export outlets become available.

Stakes in the Peace

Paraguay has a salubrious climate, for the most part, which could easily serve the needs of southern European immigrants. Her population possibilities are many times her present small total. The success of the Jesuit missions and of Francia shows that with peace and more capital she can have a constant increase in prosperity.

While the absence of class divisions favors her, Paraguay has not been able to offer sufficient opportunity to her educated youth; as a consequence, most of them have entered the army as a means toward a career. Industrialization is the first requirement. If she could increase her agriculture sufficiently to create an urban middle class to supply farmers' needs, Paraguay would provide more constructive channels for her people's energies.

PERU

The Land and the People

Peru, once a byword for fabulous wealth, was the center of the highly developed Inca Indian civilization which flourished from the 12th century to the advent of the Spanish conquerors in 1531. As the great Viceroyalty of the Spanish Empire at its height in the 16th century, Peru supplied a major share of the precious metals with which Spain flooded Europe, undermining its feudal aristocracy by substituting money for status as the source of power.

Today Peru is only a remnant of her once vast domain; she is a republic of some 482,000 square miles,

slightly smaller than Texas, Arizona, and New Mexico combined. While her population has declined from the days of the Incas, its recent growth is shown by the 1940 census, enumerating 6,200,000, and estimating an additional 800,000.

Having regulated her boundary with Ecuador, her small neighbor to the north, Peru now has a long common frontier with Colombia. On the east she faces Brazil and Bolivia, on the south Chile, and on the west, the Pacific Ocean. Her well-known guano islands off the coast derive their name from a substance widely used for fertilizers. A partial failure of this supply, owing to the shift of the Humboldt current, has led to a plan for producing synthetic fertilizer.

The Land. Topographically, there are three Perus: the coast, mostly a desert; the mountains, culminating in the lofty peaks of the Andes; and the dense, humid forest zone in the east. Half of this land of violent contrasts lies east of the mountains in an area rich in tropical vegetation but difficult of access and thinly peopled. The highlands remain the stronghold of the Indians, as they were before the coming of Pizarro, the Spanish Conquistador, in 1531. In the high Andes, traversed by the deepest canyons in the Americas, the Peruvians have domesticated the llama and the alpaca as beasts of burden and carriers of trade.

Peru still has an astonishing wealth of mineral resources. She has rich deposits of copper, gold, silver, lead, molybdenum, and vanadium, much of them in the mountainous Cerro de Pasco region, northeast of Lima the capital. The mining districts are in many ways a world apart. The same district contains coal deposits (though the product is not high-grade), while the northern region, near the border of Ecuador, holds Peru's oil resources.

Lima, for nearly three centuries the wealthy hub of Spanish civilization in the Americas, lies in an arid belt. The capital's suburban port, Callao, is the country's main shipping center. The northern coasts are dotted with oases, from which short railways extend back into rich valleys where sugar and cotton are extensively produced.

Peru has been transformed by a recent highway building program. Twenty-five years ago a resident of Lima, desiring to go to Iquitos, in the eastern tropical part of the country, often found it easiest to sail to Panama, thence down to Pará, Brazil, on the Atlantic, from there up the Amazon 2,500 miles to Iquitos. Today a thrilling motor ride, crossing the Andes at over 15,000 feet, takes one to Iquitos in two or three days. Cuzco, the ancient capital of the Inca Empire, formerly so inaccessible that most visitors missed its entrancing sights, is now reached by another of these new highways. A part of the system, running from the border of Ecuador to Bolivia (Peru's section of the Pan-American Highway) is completed. Government-built hotels are placed at convenient points to add to the traveler's comfort.

Peru's climate generally varies with altitude rather than latitude. Rainfall, elsewhere a blessing, is a calamity along the arid coast since the warm rain-water disturbs the guano-laying birds and the fish that thrive in colder water.

The People. The mass of the population are Incas, descendants of the Indians who were enslaved and almost exterminated by the Spanish conquerors. These Indians were masters of road-building, masonry, and irrigation. Their immense stone temples and suspension bridges still are a mystery to us, for they did not have wheels and we do not know what tools they used. Excellent potters, weavers, coppersmiths, calculators, astronomers, musicians, and farmers, they were skilled in the art of governing human beings over a wide domain. Under their communal social order, in which income, profit, and private property were unknown, land was held and tilled in common, with the family as the basic unit, but always at the orders of the state.

The Inca descendants of this highly developed people dominate highland Peru ethnically, even though economically and politically they are still ruled by peoples of Spanish descent who constitute the great landowning and governmental class. Pure Indians form half of Peru's population, while the predominantly Indian *mestizos* (of mixed white and Indian blood) contribute a third.

The Indians are extremely poor and live primitively, mostly in stone huts. They are a silent people and have enormous endurance as workers. But they aim only at subsistence, as farmers and shepherds. They are spurred by no incentives other than subsistence, except to accumulate enough money for an occasional celebration — for drink and for coca leaves, the narcotic effects of which they prize. The *mestizos* in the lowlands, however, share largely in the ordinary values of the Spanish-descended population.

The whites constitute about one-eighth of the people, a part of the remainder being Negroes and Asiatics, who live on the coast. The deep conflict of worlds between Indians and those of Spanish descent has persisted, cropping up in social conflicts, in political movements, and in such uniquely Peruvian ideologies as the *Aprista* movement in politics. In 1929 the government consecrated an annual holiday to celebrate Indian achievements.

To narrow the gulf between the Spanish and Indian peoples, two basic plans are offered. One stresses industrialization, improved agriculture and water supply, health measures, better housing, and social insurance for the working classes. Another plan, advocated especially by the influential *Apra* party, is much more radical. It would follow to a considerable degree the pattern of the Mexican revolution. It would rearrange the political divisions of the country to correspond to economic needs, would grant greater self-determination to local communities, and initiate full democratic government. New departments of labor and Indian affairs would stress the solution of these problems. Dependence on Peruvian capital and initiative would be emphasized rather than allowing the former dominance by foreign agencies. There would be national planning and a quasi-governmental control of business.

In the absence of birthrate statistics, we must rely on census figures. These would indicate a high birthrate, for they show over 42% of the population as under 14 years of age (whites under 14 in the U.S.A. are only 25%), and only 15% over 50 (as compared with 21% in the U.S.A.). A rise in population is forecast for the next generation.

Religion and Education. Peru's capital, Lima, was once the seat of the Catholic Church in the Western hemisphere, colonial headquarters of the Inquisition. Today, Roman Catholicism, religion of most Peruvians, is protected by the State. All church edifices, including convents, are state property, and no other religion can be taught in the schools, though the other faiths worship freely.

The elementary schools have over 500,000 pupils, about half the children of school age. In thickly settled areas, education is now universal. The government's recent attempt to substitute largely vocational and practical guidance for classical education and training, has met with some opposition. Though education is tuition-free and compulsory, about half of the people remain illiterate. However, great strides are being made in diffusing education. Peru has 216 secondary schools and 5 universities, one of which, the University of San Marcos in Lima, was founded in 1551, 85 years before the first university in the U.S.A. Its graduates enjoy immense prestige in Latin America.

While Spanish is the official language, fully half of the people speak Quechua, the Inca tongue. The Spanish culture of the upper class has not blended with the Indian culture of the bulk of the people, and as in Mexico, a period of profound social readjustment may be forecast, until the two cultures achieve their inevitable historic synthesis. Recent literature in Peru has lavished attention on the Indian. Ciro Alegría, an *Aprista* exile, recently won a literary prize in the U.S.A. for his novel *Broad and Alien Is the World*.

Peru is far indeed from the polished irony and enchanting nostalgia of her classic writers, like the gifted and original Ricardo Palma. Peruvians today wish to restore the old intellectual primacy of Lima in South America, and they now have a considerable reading public to sustain them. Poets like Chocano have intoned Pan-American chants that rival Walt Whitman's, albeit with classic finish. But all Peruvian literature, however diverse its approach, is richly national. Their numerous histories, essays, and archaeological and juridical treatises are deeply Peruvian. Even philosophy and economic theory have a national flavor. Socialism, elsewhere advocated as an international ideal, is here aggressively local in program. In architecture and music, the successful artists have been those who have sought to merge Spanish and Indian strains. The Inca music's plaintive modes are moving, and their communal chants unique.

The Nation's Economy

Agriculture. With only 5,600 square miles of the country (1.3%) under cultivation, and with four-fifths of her people dependent on crops from this very restricted area, Peru has the problem of nourishing 1,250 people per square mile of arable land. The agricultural economy of this country must be understood in the light of this situation.

Subsistence crops are not limited by altitude. Some items, such as wheat, thrive at incredible altitudes of 12,000 feet, and even sugar cane is grown at 8,000 feet above sea level. The poverty of Peruvian agriculture was accentuated by a long emphasis on export crops, but it has lately shifted to subsistence crops. Even with this new trend, however, the production of sugar (550,000 tons), wheat (118,000), corn (500,000), and rice (110,000) is scarcely adequate for domestic needs — although the large planters use the most efficient methods. Rice has been protected by tariff against the cheaper Asiatic product; nevertheless, it must often be imported into Peru in order to make up the deficit in foodstuffs.

In the remote highland areas, the government has struggled to overcome native resistance to modern farming techniques. In the lowlands, great irrigation projects are being extended. When both undertak-

See continental map on page 229.

ings are successful, the arable area and the productivity of Peru will be enlarged, and domestic food production can be increased toward a basis of adequacy.

Resourceful Peruvian farmers are seeking to diversify agriculture. Flax, for example, is being cultivated increasingly. From the thick equatorial rainforests come such products as cinchona bark, balata, vegetable ivory, and lumber.

The animal economy includes over 13,000,000 sheep, but the cattle population is not large (2,300,000). Alpacas commonly serve as carriers in the Andes area and they also provide a source of fine textiles.

Industry and Natural Resources. Mining continues to be the important factor in Peruvian economy as it has been for centuries. Petroleum production is large: it approximates 2,000,000 tons annually. Coal (of inferior quality) is extensively mined. However, water-power, though it is readily available for industry, remains largely unexploited.

Peru produces 22,000 troy pounds of gold, 500 tons of silver, 48,000 tons of lead, 28,000 tons of molybdenum, and 38,000 tons of copper. Her output of vanadium, the first in the world, is important in ferroalloys and vital to the war effort. Peru is also the world's largest producer of bismuth. In addition, this veritable treasure-house is famed for her substantial deposits of guano, which supplies nitrogen for fertilizers.

Most of Peru's mines, however, are owned by foreigners, chiefly Americans and Britons, whereas the new manufacturing industries are largely native-owned. Though even now, less than 15% of the population is engaged in mining and manufacture, important and varied industries concentrating mainly on consumers goods, are springing up around Lima. The U.S.A. is aiding in the establishment of a 100,000 ton capacity steel mill, among other industrial projects.

The Peruvian government has been keenly interested in material improvements. There are now 16,800 miles of road, suitable for motor traffic, which facilities aid in the diffusion of manufactured goods within the country. Lima, mother-city of Spanish civilization in the New World, with its 600,000 inhabitants as a local market, is beginning to assume importance as a thriving industrial center.

This new industrial impetus in Peru is being felt in dozens of smaller towns which are now transforming their traditional mode of life. It creates a class of industrial owners who are anxious to raise the purchasing power of the people so as to have a market for their factory production. This new class plays a progressive rôle in the nation's politics.

Finance. On the whole, the war has not fundamentally altered Peru's economy, for her trade in agricultural items, such as cotton and sugar, has remained fairly stable, and her big mineral resources have found a continued ready market, especially in the U.S.A. A wide gap still remains, however, between the small group of wealthy residents of Lima and Callao and the mass of poor farmers in the rest of the country.

The monetary unit is the *sol* (meaning sun), which is said to have taken its unusual name from the legend that one of Pizarro's soldiers in a night gambled away the golden image of the sun, sacred to the Incas. The *sol*, now quoted at 15.63¢, is about 23% of its 1929 gold parity.

Money in circulation has doubled during the war to the total of $43,000,000 ($6 per capita). Wholesale prices have doubled, but the cost of living has risen by only 40%.

Peru's internal debt is $73,000,000; her foreign debts total $88,000,000. Interest payments have been suspended on all foreign debts except one issue. Before 1940 total Peruvian commitments of the British amounted to $100,000,000, and those of the U.S.A. were $200,000,000.

Foreign Trade. World War II has not produced any serious dislocations in Peru's foreign trade. Profits from mining and petroleum continue to go almost entirely to foreign companies that have invested heavily in Peru. Exports remain around $77,000,000, imports around $60,000,000. Peru's leading exports are petroleum, metals, cotton, and sugar. She chiefly imports food, machinery, cotton goods, and automobiles.

Normally the U.S.A. supplies 25% of imports, Britain 18%, France 10%. In peacetime 20% of her exports went to the U.S.A., 20% to Britain, 8% to Canada, 11% to Germany, and 8% to France. As a result of the war, the U.S.A. increased her purchases of Peruvian exports to 43% and her supplies to Peru to 62%.

History: 1914-1944

Peru, neutral but pro-Allied during World War I, enjoyed marked prosperity because of the demand for her copper, sugar, and cotton. In 1917 her president, Pardo, member of an old aristocratic family, severed diplomatic relations with Germany.

A small group of aristocrats had dominated the government for so long that they failed to reckon with the rise of a middle class and the emergence of an urban working class. In 1919 these elements, hitherto excluded from power, supported a former president, Leguía. He governed until 1930 and was firmly entrenched so long as the prosperity of the 1920's prevailed. But to ensure his popularity, Leguía relied on an excessive military and police force as well as an ubiquitous secret service, jailing or exiling those who dared to oppose him. He won back for Peru (by arbitration) part of the Tacna-Arica territory lost to Chile in the War of 1879.

But the economic depression of 1930 proved fatal to his power. An army officer, Sánchez Cerro, successfully led an army uprising and Leguía spent the rest of his brief life in jail. Sánchez Cerro had himself named constitutional president.

A quarrel then broke out with neighboring Colombia over the boundary of the Leticia corridor. Both the League of Nations and the U.S.A. interceded to keep the peace, but peace was not restored until mediation had been successfully undertaken by the distinguished Brazilian statesman, Dr. Afranio Mello Franco. On April 30, 1933 President Sánchez Cerro was assassinated and General Oscar Benavides became president.

The Challenge of the Aprista Movement: 1933–1939. The continuing economic crisis gave rise to a movement of revolutionary scope, based on a special philosophy, *Aprismo* (from A.P.R.A. — American Popular Revolutionary Alliance). The founder of the movement, Haya de la Torre, compounded some Marxian deductions with mystic ideas of race and soil. His theory held that, although economic conditions cause changes in history, religion was the social "binder." The Apristas appealed to the Indians and agitated for the destruction of the large landed estates. Their feud with the Socialists was as intense as their hostility to the régime in power.

Aprismo soon challenged the government. For the first time in 400 years, a movement appealing to the Indians for support threatened the position of the dominant class of Spanish descent. In 1931 an Aprista revolt broke out; and when it failed, the government meted out jail sentence, exile, or death to the rebels. Haya de la Torre was not allowed to run for office because, according to the government, his ideas were of foreign origin and only candidates with Peruvian ideas could legally contend for office.

In 1933 the Apristas supported General Benavides, who was elected president. However, he annulled future elections, extended his rule for five years, suspended Congress, outlawed the Apristas, and assumed dictatorial powers.

In 1939 new elections took place with the Apristas barred from participation. Benavides' candidate, Prado, won the presidency with ease — about 5% of the population voted in the election. President Prado later restored wide powers to Congress, and has sought to lead the country back towards democratic practices.

A short-lived controversy with Ecuador over boundaries (1941), which involved armed clashes, was terminated by the Protocol fixing a permanent boundary, signed at Rio de Janeiro in January, 1942.

Peru and World War II: 1939–1944. From the outset of World War II, Peru has been definitely favorable to the Allied cause. In 1942 the Export-Import Bank in Washington opened up credits for Peru, and the U. S. government made agreements with her concerning rubber and quinine. Peru's expanding industries have also received extensive American aid.

Peru broke diplomatic relations with the Axis powers in January 1942 and confiscated Axis properties. She has consistently aided the United Nations.

Foreign Affiliations. Peru's relations with her neighbors, Chile, Colombia, and Ecuador have been stormy; but they have definitely improved as a result of the 1929 border arbitration with Chile, and the resolution of border conflicts with Colombia and Ecuador. Moreover, Peru has shown true cordiality toward Brazil and even greater friendship for Bolivia.

Externally, she was for years closely affiliated with Britain. In American relations, she has shown herself a "Good Neighbor" and a firm supporter of Pan-American policy, despite powerful conservative elements within the country who have close ties with Franco Spain. Recent attempts by conservative interests in Argentina to direct her away from cooperation with the U.S.A. have failed.

Stakes in the Peace

The Indian question dominates Peru: if it is not settled soon, it may pass the point at which it can be easily resolved. The Apristas have appealed to the descendants of the Incas, who may not always remain the abject subjects of the dominant Peruvian groups. The pattern in present-day Peru resembles that in the Mexico of 1910, and a generation of disorders was the price of inflexibility in that nation. All foreign observers, whatever their political views, agree insistently on the need for Peruvian reforms with respect to the Indian question.

Fortunately, the rise of local industry and of a really enterprising and intelligent middle class indicates that this problem will not have to wait for the entrenched feudal groups to unbend. The rising middle class has shown itself aware of Peru's real needs and, what is more, is making impressive progress in production and trade.

EL SALVADOR

The Land and the People

El Salvador, the smallest country in the Western hemisphere, is a republic of vigorous citizens. When the Mexican emperor, Iturbide, planned to annex Central America, this little land appealed to the U.S.A. for annexation; an act of her Congress reading: "Do not deny us our desire; admit us to your Union; grant protection to a people who have long suffered oppression and whose aim is freedom." After this petition was denied, El Salvador became an active participant in the first movement for Central American union (1823). She has subsequently become active in the Pan-American Union, and she has furnished a judge for the International Court of Justice. Her newspapers, businessmen, and public officials are noted for the lively way in which they discuss public issues.

A new kind of revolution occurred in 1944, ousting Maximiliano Hernández Martínez, who had remained in office since 1931. He had cruelly put down various popular efforts to eliminate him, the last one occurring in April 1944. A few days after he had "liquidated" his opponents, the Salvadoran public staged a pacifist strike, refusing to attend public functions of any kind. Schools were vacated, government employees, railroad workers, doctors, lawyers, druggists, newspaper publishers, all refused to work. Priests supported the movement of *brazos caidos* (folded arms). The dictator capitulated. The next month the same technique was successfully used in Guatemala.

See map on page 197.

Coffee production dominates the economic life of El Salvador. In peacetime coffee accounted for as much as 94% of all her exports, and even in the war years it amounts to from 84% to 87% of the export total. But Salvadorans increasingly realize the danger of so great a dependence on one commodity, and they are intelligently and resolutely shaping a diversified economy.

The Land. The 1,829,000 people of El Salvador inhabit an area of only 13,176 square miles — about the area of Massachusetts and Connecticut combined. For Latin America, the density of the population is unusual, being 140 Salvadorans per square mile. Almost all the land is cultivated, even to the mountain slopes, and almost all the people make their living from the soil.

El Salvador faces the Pacific Ocean. She is bounded by Guatemala at the northwest and by Honduras on the north and east. Two ranges of mountains run through this volcanic land, but the valleys and plateaus lying between are rich and verdant. The country has a "summer," or dry season, from November to April, and a "winter," or wet season, for the other six months. The temperature, however, is constant, averaging about 73° throughout the year. Most of the people cluster in the plateaus between the two low volcanic ranges, living on a soil enriched by lava.

The People. Four-fifths of the Salvadorans are *mestizos* (mixed Indian and white). About 19% are pure Indian and 1% pure white. However, the country is free from racial emphases and the compact population possesses a genuine national feeling. Unlike the Mayan Indians of Guatemala, the Indian population of El Salvador participate in the life of the republic and speak its language, Spanish.

The people are self-disciplined, cohesive, and eager to attain a high level of national welfare. The country's leading families have made constructive contributions both to the plantations and the urban settlements. San Salvador, the capital, is a modern city with a distinguished architecture and a virile, aware populace.

Thirty years ago the birthrate reached the phenomenal figure of 50 per thousand. Despite the succeeding decline, it remains very high (42.3 in 1940, 40 in 1941). With a deathrate of 16, natural increase is indicated to be over 24% per decade — in a country whose population density is already the highest in Central America. (Infant mortality is 105 per thousand.)

Religion and Education. The dominant religion is Roman Catholicism. Other faiths are freely tolerated in accordance with the Constitution.

Education is tuition-free and compulsory. However, in the outlying areas, it has not proved easy to implement the educational law in its entirety. El Salvador has begun to cope with a serious illiteracy problem. Special schools have been opened on a large scale to educate adult illiterates. Ten years ago, 1 child out of 8 of school age received instruction; today 1 out of 3 is in attendance.

The country has a good national university and is known for its numerous private high schools. Recent activities of the Salvadorans indicate that their country is on the eve of a great educational expansion. Book sales and periodical literature are showing remarkable advances.

The Nation's Economy

Unlike the countries that neighbor her, in which great estates abound, El Salvador is distinguished by small landholdings. Some 11,000 small proprietors produce the republic's coffee crops in an area of only 300 square miles. And yet this small territory accounts for 3% of all the coffee grown in the world. El Salvador also produces other export items — balsam (in which she leads the world), tobacco, indigo, henequen, and sugar.

Important as are her export crops, the agricultural economy of this smallest land in the Americas also supplies important quantities of food for home consumption. These include 400,000 tons of corn, 16,000 tons of rice, and 16,000 tons of meat. Some 80% of the land of El Salvador is actually cultivated — the highest proportion in Latin America and nearly the highest in the world.

The other economic activities of the republic are overshadowed by agricultural production. Livestock is not extensive, consisting mostly of swine. However, her forests yield cabinet woods of good quality. And although the mineral wealth of the republic is limited, some gold is produced.

Finance and Foreign Trade. The unit of currency is the *colón*, valued at about 40¢. Money in circulation has risen during World War II, from $6,000,000 to $10,000,000, but the gold and exchange backing is over 100%, as a result of increasing reserves abroad. The leading banks have deposits of $2,000,000 of local funds and $1,200,000 of foreign funds. The nation's budget, only $4,400,000 in 1939, has risen to almost $11,000,000. The domestic debt is also small — only $2,000,000. El Salvador has resumed payment of her foreign debt on a curtailed basis; it is about $15,-400,000.

Although the nation is making rapid progress, it remains poor. El Salvador's national production is estimated at only $30 per person, which is 3% of the per capita figure of the U.S.A. Coffee alone accounts for over 30% of national production; agriculture (including coffee) contributes five-sixths, and industrial activity a seventh. There are two railways in the republic, and both are foreign (British and U.S.A.)-owned.

El Salvador's exports in peacetime were about $6.70 per person, her imports $5.60. In 1941, on the basis of a revised population estimate of 1,862,000, exports per capita declined to $6.15 and imports to $4.50. Normally much of this trade — about 60% of exports and 50% of imports — was with the U.S.A. But Central Europe took over 25% of El Salvador's exports, and the country feels the loss of this market during the war.

History: 1914-1944

Beginning with 1913 and for a period of almost twenty years, one family, the Meléndez, and their relatives, the Quinones, governed the people of El Salvador. The repeated popular demands for free elections were disregarded by the family in power, which also paid no heed to the pro-Allied sentiment of the people during World War I. Indeed, the government of El Salvador not merely remained neutral but became even critical of the policy of the U.S.A.

In 1927 Quinones designated Pío Romero Bosque as President; he was to hold office for four years, at the end of which Quinones would again be eligible for the presidency. But in 1931 Romero Bosque refused to comply with Quinones. Instead, he conducted an election which, by contrast with the turbulent ones of the past, seemed orderly indeed. Arturo Araujo became the new President; but he was not in power a year when his ineffectual administration was overthrown by General Hernández Martínez.

Owing to the Central American agreement of 1923 which withheld recognition from any government established by force, the new régime in El Salvador went unrecognized. This diplomatic isolation, however, did not unduly disturb Hernández Martínez, for he was busily engaged in branding all his critics as "Communists" and in suppressing his opponents, some in blood. Before long, Costa Rica, having denounced the Central American Treaty of 1923, recognized Hernández Martínez as the *de facto* President. The other Central American nations followed suit, and after 1933 the U.S.A. accorded recognition.

The Hernández Martínez administration engaged in the construction of public works and in agricultural development. These projects served to mitigate the effects of the world depression upon the country. Nevertheless, Hernández Martínez had found it necessary in 1931 to default on the El Salvador foreign loan of 1922. He made an arrangement with the bondholders in 1936, but the following year it was suspended, and it was not until later that the arrangement was resumed, though on a curtailed basis.

Contrary to her policy of neutrality in World War I, El Salvador instantly aligned herself with the U.S.A. in December 1941, declaring war on the Axis powers. The war brought serious price inflation and a sharp rise in the cost of living — and an increase among the forces opposed to the government. Hernández Martínez suppressed the opposition with a firm hand, inflicting death penalties upon some of the revolutionaries. But the resistance increased and in 1944 it triumphed. The overthrow of Hernández Martínez was the outcome of popular resentment against the clandestine meeting of the National Assembly, which he had held for the purpose of extending his term of office.

Andrés I. Menéndez became President in May 1944. One of the first official acts of the new government was to order free elections for January 1945.

Stakes in the Peace

Although historically the monopoly of governmental influence by two-score powerful families once encouraged authoritarian ideas in El Salvador, the entire evolution of this progressive people is toward political democracy.

El Salvador is ideally situated for a small peasant economy, such as has prevailed in Belgium. Given even more equitable land ownership and scientific farming, this rich region could, with the energy and resourcefulness of her people, produce several times her present food crop.

For a country of so small a population, El Salvador holds high promise. With proper reforms, she could soon rival Costa Rica for first place in progressive democracy in Central America.

THE UNITED STATES

The Land and the People

The United States of America, a federal union of 48 states and one federal district, is the fifth-largest country in the world. The wealthiest and first industrial nation on earth, she is also the largest area of free speech, free press, and free religion.

It is a commonplace to speak of American natural resources as the cause of this nation's primacy in industry and wealth. In area of fertile land, she is surpassed only by the U.S.S.R., India, and possibly China. Forests still cover more than a fourth of her surface. And her vast mineral resources and developed waterpower have made her the industrial leader of the world. But these resources were here when more primitive peoples possessed the land. Hence it must be to the character and culture of the European population, plus the efforts of the African population, that the development of the country is due.

Ours has been the most rapidly expanding economy, the most swiftly peopled land, of any in human annals. The economy, colonial until about 1825, was transformed into a "democracy of expectant capitalists" by free or easily acquired land, which compelled wages in the cities to rival what could be earned by the independent pioneer. High wages made labor-saving machinery necessary to cheapen costs and this in turn, increased productivity; and thus the country of high wages became the country of great profits. The high wages attracted enterprising Europeans, who added wealth of manpower to wealth of machinery. This combination of natural resources, free land, streams of immigrants, high wages, and high mechanization, together with the development of cheap transportation, produced an unrivaled speed of development.

This development was unlimited by rites, customs, or prescriptions. American democracy, by cracking the class structure, made possible a plastic people, among whom economic incentives could function untrammeled. Because industrial growth promoted swift urbanization, distribution of goods was early organized, and life was soon more comfortable than in the capitals of Europe. The great free-trade area of the land made possible standardization and mass production of goods to be sold by salesmanship and advertising to the masses of the people, whose incomes were high by European standards. In contrast to the devotion of European scientists to theory, American scientists, stimulated by the great rewards of enterprise, became celebrated for practical applications. For a long time, too, a small army, inexpensive government, and an almost nonexistent national debt furnished further vivid contrasts to Europe.

Meanwhile the political democracy was taking shape. The *Declaration of Independence* and *The Federalist* were addressed to a politically intelligent people. The Constitution was — and remains — a unique document. Under Jefferson the democratic content was deepened, under Jackson gentility was shelved, under Lincoln the last impediment to free labor was swept aside and the Union made unquestionable.

Freed of excessive sectionalism, industrial development bounded forward. By the end of the 19th
century, the U.S.A. was the wealthiest nation in the
world, and the free speech, free press, and free religion,
correlated with material wealth, inspired European
liberalism.

The area of continental United States is 3,022,387
square miles and that of Alaska 586,400 square miles.
In 1940, 131,669,000 people lived in continental
United States, and 2,476,993 in the other non-con-
tinental territories. Continental United States is thus
somewhat more than a seventeenth of the land surface
of the globe, her population about a sixteenth.

The Land. The U.S.A. is a compact land mass,
contained between the two great oceans, the Atlantic
and the Pacific. Midway between the oceans lies the
Mississippi Basin, one of the largest of the earth's
plains, watered by the greatest of all river systems
used by modern man, the Mississippi-Missouri. The
Appalachian mountain system, between the central
valley and the Atlantic, is of moderate height; the
Rocky mountain system, between the valley and the
Pacific, is among the high regions of the world, although lower than its South American continuation in
the Andes.

Although the country lies entirely in the north
temperate zone, the climate varies from the deep winter cold of the Dakotas in the north to the sub-tropical
climate along the Gulf of Mexico in the south. The
whole Pacific coast is temperate, the southern part
very dry, the northern very rainy. But on the whole
there are no arctic or tropical extremes of either rainfall or temperature, and for an area of her size, the
United States is rivaled only by western Europe in
adaptability to human enterprise.

The People. The people who have made this new
culture came from many lands and many races. The
motto "*E pluribus unum*" — Out of many one — is as
applicable to the American people as to their federal
system of government.

The primary source is the British Isles — and even
here the racial strain is partly Celtic, though mostly
Anglo-Saxon. England supplied the main stream,
her affiliated peoples — the Scots, Scots-Irish, and
Welsh — the secondary stream. The Irish arrived
early enough to be conspicuous in the Revolutionary
Army, and later, after the great immigrations of the
1840's, became a shaping influence in the country's
development.

But the minor streams have been so important as to
make the modern Americans racially as well as culturally a distinct people. The strongest non-British
strain is the Germans, numerous even in the 18th century and highly influential after 1848. The Scandinavian immigration, although it came later and was
generally more local, was nevertheless important.
Older elements such as the Dutch have been small
but conspicuous. The French have left their seal on
Louisiana, in New England the French-Canadians
are numerous, and French influence as a whole is
diffused throughout American society. The Southern
and Central European immigration — Italian, Jewish,
Polish, other Slavic peoples — was the main movement of population to America between 1880 and
1924. Small but distinct contributions have come
from many other European and Near Eastern peoples,
such as the Armenians, Greeks, and Syrians.

The non-white races have also contributed. Negroes, a sixth of the population under George Washington, are today a tenth. The aboriginal Indian,
after declining till he seemed doomed to vanish, is
now resurgent. Chinese and Japanese helped to build
the Pacific region. Many Mexicans have settled in
the Southwest.

The result of all this has been a people made up of
amazingly disparate physical and even cultural types,
but displaying so astonishing a power of assimilation
that a certain national convergence is obvious. American tastes in everything from literature to cooking are
quite unlike those of any given European country.
Whatever the American people accepts from the immigrant — whether Chinese "chop suey" or styles
imitated from the French — it makes a part of the
national heritage. Their great names — whether of
baseball stars, intellectual leaders, or war heroes —
are a mosaic of the world's languages. Although the
basic cultural pattern and language, like the source of
political thinking, remain British, a new people has
been born.

The days of rapid population increase ended with
the ban on unrestricted immigration. The present
rate of natural increase appears to be 6.2%, with a
deathrate varying $\frac{1}{2}$% above or below 10.8 per
thousand, and a birthrate which before the war had
gone down to an average of 17 but has now risen with
full employment. Infant mortality is low among
whites (45), but above average for non-whites (about
74). About a third of the white population is under
20. Although among Negroes it is considerably less,
the life expectancy at birth for whites, which stands at
62 for males and 67 for females, is exceeded only in
Australia, New Zealand, the Netherlands, Sweden,
and Denmark. Whether the population remains
static for the next generation or suffers a decline would
seem to depend on the extent to which full employment
is maintained in the post-war period.

American Groupings. The U.S.A. is a land of
diversified regions, each with special characteristics.
New England (the six northeastern states), lying off
the mainstream of transportation, has a marked regional flavor. Large foreign-born populations inhabit
its manufacturing centers, French-Canadians and
Italians being the most numerous among them. The
Portuguese retain a small minority culture along the
coast, and the Irish element is conspicuous in the urban
centers. The older English stock, prevailing through
New England, has made major contributions to
American letters, erudition, and mechanical inven-
tion; its commercial enterprise has made New Englanders leaders throughout the land.

The Middle Atlantic states are markedly more
diverse in racial origin and in outlook. Since the 18th
century, Dutch and old German elements have contested with the English stock for leadership. New
York, the region's first city, is one of the most polyglot
centers on earth. The largest Negro city in the world,
the largest Jewish city in the world, it would also rank
among the first Irish and Italian cities. In Pennsylvania and in Buffalo, New York, European Slavs,
especially Poles, reach large numbers. The foreign
language newspapers are conspicuous for their large
circulation and influence.

The Middle West, stronghold of the older American
stocks, was settled mostly by New Englanders and

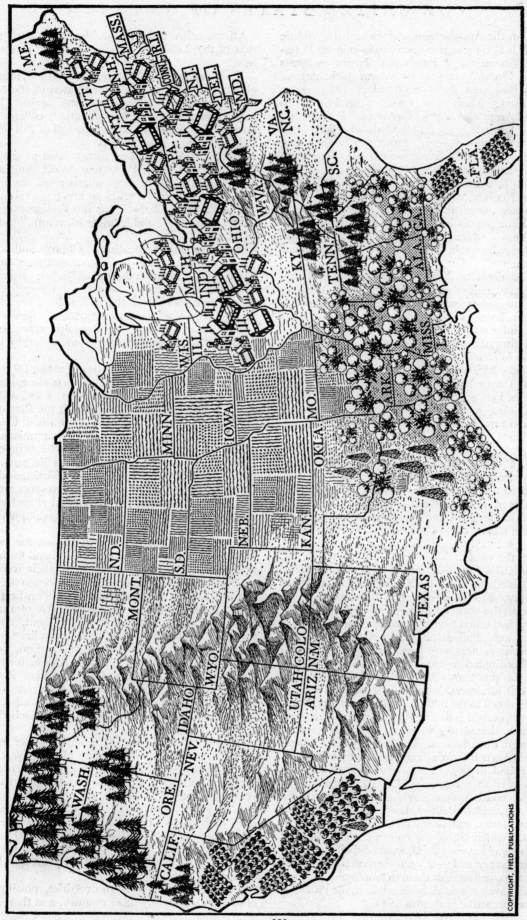

people from the Appalachian regions and the Middle South. It is also the seat of German immigration (especially Wisconsin), of Polish and Negro elements (Chicago, Detroit), of Czechs (about Chicago), of Scandinavians and New Englanders (Minnesota, the Dakotas). Missouri was long a semi-Southern state, with large elements of Germans. Kansas and Nebraska, however, contain elements who arrived in the 1850's to fight slavery. More nearly than any other area, the Middle West typifies the "American approach" as it is conceived by foreigners.

The South, overwhelmingly peopled with English stock and Negroes, divides into various regions. In the tidewater (or sea level) country, the Negroes are about half the population. They are few, however, in the highlands, which are peopled by English and Scotch-Irish who retain vestiges of older British culture in song, dance, and traditional stories. The "New South," particularly Texas, is a rising petroleum, chemical, and cotton empire, with a large Mexican minority to the west. In the Mississippi delta, Louisiana reflects its colorful French-Spanish origins. The peninsular state of Florida, however, has recently seen an influx of northerners, many of whom devote themselves to farming or business.

The Rocky Mountain west is thinly peopled. In it are found the great Mormon settlements, centering in Utah; the half-Spanish state of New Mexico, with a migrant mining population. Scandinavians were long conspicuous among the lumbermen of the northwest, but the rural population is northeastern in origin. California contains large minorities — Mexicans, Japanese, Chinese, Filipinos, as well as indigenous minorities from the Oklahoma "dust bowl" — and many retired middle-class Americans as well as proud descendants of the Gold-Rush population.

As a nation founded and fructified by foreign-born peoples, the U.S.A. cannot be said to have any political basis for a minority problem, yet she has one of the gravest in the world. The Negroes, imported to the country in 1619, were long settled in the South where they remained after the Civil War that freed them from slavery. Nevertheless, large numbers of Negroes have lived in the north for decades — Harlem, in New York City, is the first Negro aggregation in the world, and Pittsburgh, Philadelphia, Cleveland, and many smaller urban centers have large Negro populations.

The subordinated position of Negroes has been characteristic of the Southern states, where legislation has imposed innumerable social and political restrictions, even down to the ballot. While racial outbreaks have often occurred in this South, they were infrequent in the north, though World War II has given rise to several severe disturbances. Particularly has this been true of northern industrial centers to which Negroes have migrated in large numbers as part of the war production effort. Racial difficulties are often explained by housing, recreation, and other social restrictions. Racial hostilities, however, have erupted into costly battles, such as the bloody riot in Detroit in June 1943, which shook the country. The Negroes during the war have made an issue of their restricted position in the armed forces, and when such restrictions have been applied against them in employment, grave difficulties have sometimes followed, as in the Philadelphia transport strike in August 1944.

Of the other minority problems, the most acute is that of the 2,000,000 Mexicans, mostly in the southwest.

The French-Canadians in New England, numbering about a million, are the best treated of the compact national minorities. Restrictions against Jews in matters of residence, club affiliation, college acceptance, and hotel accommodations (all of this unknown to law) are met with widely.

The anti-Catholic movements, such as the Know-Nothings, American Protective Association, and Ku Klux Klan, have by now abated; but for long the Irish felt themselves a religious and national minority. The defeat of a Catholic for the Presidency in 1928, which broke the "solid Democratic South," testified to its survival.

Religion and Education. Church and state are wholly separated in the U.S.A., and freedom of religion is guaranteed in the Bill of Rights. It is difficult to estimate the numbers adhering to the various faiths, for religious censuses in the U.S.A. have been few and the methods of computation various — some denominations claim all born into the faith, others insist on average church attendance or membership in good standing.

Most Americans are Protestants, about 16% Roman Catholic, and 3.5% Jewish. The leading Protestant denominations are nonconformists, such as Baptists and Methodists, who together with the Presbyterians constitute about 60%. The established Church of England (Episcopal) has fewer communicants than the Lutheran. A wide variety of smaller religious sects is characteristic of American religious life, among them the Latter-Day Saints, Disciples of Christ, and Christian Scientists, all indigenous. The Negroes are nearly all Protestants, usually in segregated churches. It is generally held that half the American population attends church.

American churches are well known for extensive missionary work at home and abroad and for hygienic work in stricken lands. Judged by their response to appeals for relief whenever calamity occurs, the American people as a whole are notably philanthropic.

American education is the concern of the states rather than of the Federal government, and even within the states it is largely decentralized. Hence there are wide variations in curriculum, teaching standards, and teachers' salaries. Although education is tuition-free and compulsory everywhere, in at least ten southern states the facilities are less extensive, especially for Negro children. In the advanced states, on the other hand, general education has reached a very high level.

In 1930, about 4,300,000 Americans over ten years of age were illiterate, but many of these were aliens. In that year, of 27,500,000 Americans between the ages of 18 and 44, only 6% had had less than four years of school, fully 21% had been in high school at least a year, more than 19% had been graduated from high school, 12% had spent a year or more in college, and about 3.7% (of persons over 25) had been graduated from college. These are over-all figures; Negroes, for example, showed only 3.1% who had attended college.

The U.S.A. has many universities, possibly more of first rank than any other country, and their relative importance has grown recently because of the suppression of intellectual activity in Fascist and Fascist-dominated countries and the flight of intellectuals to the U.S.A. A notable feature of the American system is the high number of state universities and municipal colleges. Among the many private colleges, some, but by no means all, have standards comparable to those of the European *lycée* or *gymnasium* rather than to those of the European university. The U.S.A. is also rich in institutions of specialized studies, in museums, libraries, and learned societies. The number of persons who have had graduate training is greater in the U.S.A. than in any other country.

Aside from their growing contribution to the age-old arts, Americans have been conspicuous in developing new and frequently popular modes. Thus, for all the widespread enthusiasm for the music of the masters as expressed in the numerous American symphony orchestras, the peculiarly American musical contribution has been the new rhythms and colors in orchestration which have carried jazz and "swing" around the world. American architects invented the skyscraper and other functional designs.

American publishers have lavished great ingenuity, money, and sometimes talent on periodicals with fantastic circulations, and in some magazines, as in the swollen Sunday newspapers, have presented remarkable reviews of current politics, science, sports, and arts. In per capita production of books, however, the U.S.A. ranks far below advanced European countries, except for textbooks. American moving pictures, whatever their artistic merits, dominate the cinema houses of the world. And for the radio, newest and most swiftly developed medium, despite its complex and still only partially explored demands, American pioneer flexibility creates overnight innumerable plays, forums, newscasts, variety programs, concerts, or what you will. New York City is the cultural capital of the country; despite the determined decentralizing efforts of "regionalists," it remains the center of art, music, drama, book production, and the like.

The Nation's Economy

Agriculture. The country's 500,000 square miles of arable land contain over 6,000,000 farms, employing some 7,800,000 family workers and 2,400,000 hired workers. Production in both crops and livestock derivatives, though not notably high per acre, is among the best in terms of *yield per man employed*.

Few countries surpass the U.S.A. in size of yields. Corn, the leading crop, is 58% of the world's supply. Other important yields (in percentages of the world supply) are: wheat 20%, oats 20–25%, cotton (although acreage has recently been halved) 40%, cotton-seed 40%, soybeans (recently developed) 30%, barley 15%, hops 30%, beet-sugar 15%, tobacco 25%, linseed 22%, and peanuts (groundnuts) about 11%. In some crops the U.S.A. is inferior to her population quota, among them: rye about 4%, potatoes about 6%, rice 1%, cane sugar 2%, wine 3%.

Animal products show comparable figures. The meat production of about 9,700,000 tons — almost half pig-products, the rest mostly beef and veal — leads the world in total output though not in per capita rate. The wool clip is about 11% of the world's, mohair about half. The U.S.A. produces about 25% of the world's milk, 12½% of its margarine, some 28% of its butter, and 16% of its cheese. American fisheries usually yield 14% of the world's catch. There are few important crops or food products in which the U.S.A. does not surpass her quota in relation to population.

Livestock on the farms number 74,000,000 cattle, 60,000,000 hogs, and 55,000,000 sheep, besides 14,000,000 horses and mules; the last figure, though low in comparison with other countries, is adequate for an agriculture as highly mechanized as the American.

Recent years have seen considerable shift in the proportion of population to both livestock and crops. In 1890 the U.S.A., with 62,000,000 people, had 60,000,000 cattle, 48,000,000 hogs, 44,000,000 sheep, and 18,000,000 horses and mules. Nor have such basic crops as wheat, corn, tobacco, cotton, oats, and potatoes increased as fast as the population, although others, such as barley and perhaps truck crops, have done so. Yet the consumption of neither meat nor other foods has diminished. The explanation doubtless lies in the decrease of the export trade in foodstuffs, which, though it had begun to recover from the low figures of the 1930's, was still, in 1941, far below its previous high level.

Industry and Mining. American industrial supremacy is uncontested. By whatever measure employed — mechanical investment per man, horsepower used per man, production per man employed or per man-hour worked, value of product — the U.S.A. takes the lead.

Her fuel base is remarkable. American coal production, which has varied between 358,000,000 tons (1932) to 564,000,000 tons (1941), is usually more than a third of the world's; and it is good coking coal and anthracite, excellent for heavy industry. American and American-controlled production of petroleum probably amounts to over 70% of the world supply. The U.S.A. is also the largest producer of natural gas. The energy for American industry comes 54% from coal, 32% from petroleum, 10% from natural gas, and 4% from water-power. American consumption of fuels per person has been estimated (1937) to be 50% greater than Britain's, twice Germany's, and ten times Japan's.

American production of iron and steel, foundation of heavy industry, has been steadily mounting. From a depression low of a sixth of the world's supply (in metal content) in 1932, American output of iron ore rose to an estimated 30% in 1939, and apparently has since risen higher. From 1935 to 1939 inclusive the U.S.A. produced a third of the world's steel. She leads the world in copper output (30%), produces a third of the world's lead and zinc, has been second only to Germany in aluminum production, and (while producing only a third as much gold as South Africa) is the world's second silver producer. Whether in cement or sulfur, phosphates or salt, American resources are exceptional.

In automobile production, the U.S.A. holds a commanding lead. In peacetime her people bought

68% of the world's automobiles. The size and complex integration of the heavy industry that supported this demand was beginning to be rivaled in some of its elements by Germany and the U.S.S.R., but its over-all superiority is too great to be contested in the near future.

In 1939 (the most recent "normal" year), American manufactures employed 7,900,000 workers; during the war the index of industrial employment and production has risen to unheard-of heights. The 1939 factory wage bill was $5,100,000,000, about $1,150 per factory worker; the average individual wage was unequally distributed, varying from $1,325 in California to $680 in Arkansas. The order of industries in number of persons employed was motor vehicles, steel and iron, cotton textiles; in value of total production: motor vehicles, steel and iron, meat packing, petroleum refining.

Wealth, Income, Investments. The national wealth of the U.S.A. has been estimated variously according to the standard used: in Paris a certain amount of building construction may be given a value in francs different from the value in dollars of the same amount of construction in New York. Yet, no matter what the standard, the U.S.A. is always first.

Americans are generally thought to have a fifth or sixth more income per capita than Australians or New Zealanders, a third to a fourth more than Britons, a fifth more than Swiss or Dutch, and even higher percentages of advantage over other countries. In 1928, peak year of pre-war prosperity, American national wealth, about $300,000,000,000 in all, had a per capita valuation of $2,520, as against Canadian $2,100, Swiss $2,000, Australian $1,825, British $1,620, and — for violent contrast — Brazilian $360 and Mexican $310.

Estimates of per capita income in the same year gave the U.S.A. $525, Australia $360, Britain $270, but these statistics are now considered to give the U.S.A. undue advantage; the Chinese figure of $11, however, will serve to point out inequalities of production. In the depression decade 1929–1939 American per capita income fell by 20%.

American investments abroad cannot be perfectly totaled, since much private investment is either unsegregated or unreported. Direct foreign investment totals some $7,000,000,000 (over 28.6% of it in Canada). As this is scarcely 2% of the national wealth, foreign investment clearly has nothing like the decisive importance for the U.S.A. that it has for the Netherlands (23%) or Britain (18%). There are issues of foreign securities floated in New York to be added, but against them must be reckoned the large liquid balances owed to foreigners. At this moment it is not easy to strike a balance between these offsetting claims.

Finance. The American monetary unit is the dollar, unaltered in gold content from 1836 to 1933, but reduced to 59.06% of parity in 1934. Money in circulation has risen steeply during the last decade: $5,536,000,000 in 1934, $7,597,000,000 in 1939, over $22,000,000,000 in 1944. The gold cover rose from $17,643,000,000 in 1939 to $22,726,000,000 in 1942 (exclusive of the currency stabilization fund). The silver cover in the latter year was given as $4,318,-000,000, but the silver was valued at $1.29 per fine ounce, a conventional figure far above market value. In 1942 the U.S.A. held almost three-fourths of recorded central bank reserves.

Between 1938 and July 1944, the national debt multiplied fivefold, from $42 billions to $208 billions. Federal expenditures rose elevenfold, from $9,127,-000,000 in 1939–40 to $104,129,000,000 in 1943–44. Tax receipts rose from $5,387,000,000 to $33,-081,000,000, the deficits being reflected in the gross debt burden. Before World War I, the national debt had been almost nonexistent — before 1913, the U.S.A. had no federal income or inheritance tax. In no other country has there been so profound a transformation — from a central government whose impact on the national income was so slight to one which is involved in half the national income.

Commercial bank deposits, which in 1933 had fallen to $27,851,000,000, by 1938 had recovered to $41,832,000,000. War activity was reflected in their expansion to $83,500,000,000 on June 30, 1944.

In 1939, savings amounted to $13,618,000,000, exclusive of building and loan societies, mutual benefit payments, and equity in life insurance policies. Since 1941, mass subscription to war loans has largely altered the shape of savings.

Prices have advanced from an average of 80.9 in 1939 to 106.0 in 1942 and 104.1 in 1944; the cost of living rose from 81.1 to 98.3 in the 1939–42 stage of the war economy, and to 126.3 in August 1944. These indexes have been challenged as not taking account of alteration in quality or of the "black market."

Stock exchange quotations have been relatively moderate: the indexes fell by a third from 1939 to 1942, and by 1944 had not bettered their best 1939 levels. The yield of U.S. Treasury bonds is only 2%; even prime industrial bonds, with taxable income, yield under 3%.

Foreign Trade. The U.S.A.'s pre-war foreign trade rate of $48 per year per capita — $22.90 exports and $25.10 imports — is well below that of many other nations and indicates considerable self-sufficiency. Her proportion of world trade fell between 1929 and 1938 from 13.8% to 11.3%, in contrast to the British Empire's, which rose from 27.9% to 29.7%.

The most recent reckoning (1930) of dependence on foreign lands shows that the U.S.A. exported only 7% of her home production as against Britain's 25% and Belgium's 51%; she imported only 6% of her consumption, as against Britain's 32% and the Netherlands' 37%.

Since only 4% of American wealth is directly or indirectly invested abroad (as against Britain's 18%), only 8% of American income normally derives from exports and investments abroad. Six percent of the expenditure of the U.S.A. went for imports and remittances and expenditures abroad. Hence, the U.S.A. averages a 2% annual increment in wealth by reason of foreign trade and investment.

American trade is critically important to certain foreign economies. The countries most dependent (in peacetime) on American exports are, in order of their dependence, Cuba, Mexico, Canada, the Philippines, Venezuela, Colombia, Peru, and Japan. Those countries most dependent (in peacetime) on the U.S.A. to purchase their goods are, in order of their dependence, Cuba, the Philippines, Colombia, Mexico, Canada, Brazil, and Peru.

In normal years, the U.S.A. exports far more to western Europe than to all of the Americas including Canada; she exports twice as much to western Europe as to Latin America. Her imports from Latin America, however, equal or surpass her imports from Western Europe.

Before the war, the leading U.S.A. exports were machinery, automobiles, raw cotton, petroleum, iron and steel products, and tobacco. Leading imports were crude rubber, coffee, cane sugar, paper and newsprint, raw silk, woodpulp, vegetable oils, and tin bars.

The leading peacetime customers of the U.S.A., by volume ($100,000,000 or more yearly) were, in order, Britain, Canada, Japan, France, and Germany. The leading sources of U.S.A. imports, by volume ($150,000,000 or more yearly) were, in order, Canada, Britain, Japan, British Malaya, and Cuba.

When one realizes how small a part exports and imports have played in the American economy, it becomes apparent that the economy of the U.S.A. could be materially benefited once the nation found the means of considerably expanding her foreign trade.

History: 1914-1944

At the outbreak of World War I, in 1914, the United States of America seemed a world apart. She had a miniature army, almost no national debt, her federal budget was small, and (until 1913) her taxation had been based on tobacco, spirits, and customs duties. She was the only modern country having neither income taxes nor estate taxes. She was a "debtor" country, owing foreigners $5,000,000,000.

The United States was the exemplar of *laissez-faire*: private enterprise was unfettered. She had recently lowered her tariffs and she interposed no barrier to mass immigration. The "New Freedom" of Woodrow Wilson, her scholarly and idealistic President, stressed the age-old values of Anglo-Saxon civilization. He sought to maintain free competition as against plutocracy, equal opportunity as against privilege. The battle of the commoner against the large financial interests, vivid since the Civil War, seemed definitely to have been resolved in favor of the common man.

Neutrality: 1914-1917. The First World War froze the blood of this liberal people. The notion of a great war seemed archaic and unthinkable for modern man. True, historians and statesmen had multiplied warnings, but the American people, devoted to industry, farming, and education, had not understood the framework of such prophecies. European hatreds were not easily envisaged. The sectional antagonisms of the Blue and Gray had been lost in the unparalleled excitement of a vastly expanding economic life.

The outbreak of war in 1914 led to partisanship in international affairs. The mass of Americans favored the Allies. The assault on Belgium speedily mobilized consciences against Kaiserist Germany and Hapsburg Austria. But although pro-Ally sentiment was paramount in the United States, isolation was the practical choice of her people. It was not until submarine sinkings dramatized the proximity of the war and the interdependence of nations that Americans came to realize that the rising economy of their land was now intertwined with that of the world. It dawned upon Americans that their remoteness from conflict was the illusion of geographical setting and not a ponderable historic fact. They came to believe that tyranny triumphant on a great scale in Europe must soon affect their own cherished liberties.

The War and Its Aftermath: 1917-1921. The United States entered the war (April 6, 1917) after more than two years of neutrality. The adaptability of the country soon astonished the world. A land with almost no large-scale military experience in recent decades, created a mass army, transported it, fabricated matériel on an unheard-of scale, landed millions of soldiers in Europe, created a merchant marine, developed administrative and industrial controls, resorted to new sources of taxation and gigantic financing, all within nineteen months.

When the war was over, the need to ensure an enduring peace led to the sponsorship of the League of Nations by President Wilson, leader of the Democratic party. American public opinion favored the League, but, for a complex of reasons — some personal, some political — the Republican party opposition in the Senate, without necessarily condemning the idea of the League, effectively kept the United States from membership in it.

The end of the war had seen other profound changes, some political and some psychic. Prohibition of intoxicating liquors had been embodied in a constitutional amendment in 1920; the first time in modern history that a moral regulation was made part of the organic law of a nation and not merely provided by statute. Woman's suffrage was also made constitutional (1920). Prices had skyrocketed (1918–20) as a world short of commodities scrambled for the insufficient supply. Land values rose prodigiously because it was thought that high prices for agricultural products would continue forever. Farmers mortgaged what they owned so as to acquire more acreage. In 1920 the inevitable price deflation proved steeper than the rise had been. Business was badly hurt and there was a notable spiritual let-down. A feeling arose that a conservative administration alone could restore prosperity and that the costs of idealism had proved excessive.

The war had left the United States much wealthier, in spite of the subsequent price collapse and economic distress. Her productive apparatus had greatly enlarged. A country that in 1914 had owed Europe five billion dollars found herself in 1920 the world's leading creditor. London now had to share primacy with New York as the financial center of the globe.

Older cultural traditions suffered adversely. The new art of the movies now came to stress glamorous, sensual problems, the very discussion of which had not been socially permitted before 1914. "Modernism" in painting, music, and architecture captivated a mushroom Bohemia, and droves of aesthetic middle-class youths "discovered Europe" and settled there for a period. The "new woman," who had recently entered commerce and industry in large numbers, was now travestied by the "flapper." A new means of communication, the radio, shared with the cinema in diminishing the relative prestige of print and of the isolated platform orator. News was given swiftly, crisply, on the radio; it centered about instant imagery. Academic language gave way to slang and to the "hard-boiled" style. But with all this, there was nothing like the idealism and world-vision that had led the Republic to the heights of 1917–18. In fact, the let-down distressed responsible, far-seeing men.

The presidential contest of 1920 between James M. Cox, the Democratic candidate, and Warren G. Harding, the Republican, was pallid; it was more concerned with domestic disenchantment than specific domestic issues. It registered the fatigue that often follows periods of exaltation, of a desire for internal integration rather than the acceptance of the continued international demands imposed by historic necessity. Harding swept the country and soon gave it the slogan of "normalcy."

"Normalcy": 1921–1925. The eclipse of idealism was instantaneous after the Harding inauguration. In 1921 the triumphant reactionary elements cut the ties of all international interests although they had no warrant from the electorate for this policy. In fact, the Republican party in 1920 had even declared for international organization for peace. The wiser, statesmanlike leaders of the Republican party, Root, Hughes, Taft, found their international point of view ruthlessly disregarded by the isolationist machine politicians, like Penrose. Domestic policies were concerned with the restoration of large businesses and any idea that did not promote this single end was regarded as impractical and even inimical. In finance, Andrew Mellon, Secretary of the Treasury, representing a powerful Hamiltonian tradition, began to shape eight years of economic policy. He was opposed only slightly, by the new farm *bloc* in Congress, composed of representatives from states prostrated by agricultural distress.

Retrenchment was the fiscal foundation. Taxation was to be reduced and the national debt to be paid off as rapidly as was consistent with reduced taxation. The national economy soon easily overcame the depression of 1920–22, largely because of the reconstruction requirements of war-ravaged Europe.

The Washington Conference (November 1921), in which Secretary of State Charles E. Hughes acted for the limitation of naval armaments, despite its defects, was the bright episode of a rather dreary international period. The Nine-Power Treaty aided China and terminated the Anglo-Japanese alliance (1922). In tariff policy, the Republican idea of high protection again dominated. Yet there was a sharp insistence upon Europe's paying both the obligations incurred in the common struggle against the enemy and the funds later advanced by the United States for reconstruction.

This curious administration was soiled by corruption. The reign of the machine politician was at its zenith. In 1923 the "Teapot Dome" Oil scandal shamed the country. Harding died in August 1923 and the Vice-President, Calvin Coolidge, became President.

The elections of 1924 returned Coolidge by a large majority over the Democratic candidate, Davis; but actually the two parties had rarely been less divided on fundamentals. The only unusual feature of the campaign was the independent candidacy of La Follette, the Wisconsin Progressive Senator, whose poll, a sixth of all the votes cast, was the first portent of a dissenting tendency that was later to express itself within the older Democratic party.

Representing an ascetic tradition, Coolidge was abstemious, unimaginative, inhospitable, isolationist, exacting. He was the President during a period of industrial and building boom — accompanied by a permanent crisis in agriculture; of rising stock exchange values — accompanied by thousands of shutdowns of local rural banks; of Prohibition and its zealots — and of bootleggers and hijackers; of a Florida land boom, based on a rising population — and contrariwise, of the Immigration Act of 1924 which shut the doors of the United States in the faces of the peoples of the earth, reversing the policy upon which had been based the amazing population growth of the country.

The Peak of Prosperity: 1925–1929. The second Coolidge administration coincided with the heyday of post-war American and world prosperity. Stock Exchange values rose to unheard-of heights, stock averages having gone up some 500%, and speculation spread to elements of the population which had never before understood its vocabulary. Underneath, there were some dramatic social forces, like the rapid growth of the Ku Klux Klan, which revealed underlays of barbarism; and its swift decline, which showed its impermanence. But this painful episode indicated that racial and religious tolerance, though embodied in the Constitution, required constant vigilance.

By 1926 private American investments abroad had reached $13,000,000,000, mostly in Europe and Latin America. Foreign trade had risen 110% above the 1913 figure, while British foreign trade had risen only 39%. Domestic sales were stimulated by the development of installment selling, centering about durable consumers goods such as automobiles, mechanical refrigerators, and electric sewing machines. Building was never more active. A fantastic number of commercial skyscrapers were constructed, largely in anticipation of increased business. This boom greatly diffused creature comforts and as each requirement was satisfied, it created ever new and expanding demands. By 1928 the familiar culminating point of every boom was seen; that is, the belief spread that in this generation the world had discovered the elixir of permanent prosperity. Economists multiplied treatises to show that the current prosperity had eternal features and even that a new economic science had been born. The warnings of responsible financial experts were ridiculed; they were "superseded" because they "lacked vision."

President Coolidge lent the weight of authority to this optimism. The elections of 1928 centered on such issues as 3.2% mild beer and featured a whispering campaign against the Catholic religion of the Democratic candidate, Alfred E. Smith. Herbert C. Hoover, the Republican nominee, Secretary of Commerce for eight years, was thought to possess those scientific aptitudes now required for the guidance of a complex industrial society. The electorate returned the Republicans by a large majority and the number of ballots cast — 7,000,000 more than in 1924 — registered a revived interest in politics.

The era's belief in magical formulas was exemplified in the Kellogg-Briand Pact by which the signatory nations agreed to "outlaw war" (1928). The Americans were now persuaded that world peace was assured merely by the signature of various countries to a statement that they would not resort to war as an instrument of national policy. As a result, attention was deflected from genuine guarantees against war. Thus the Kellogg-Briand Pact, theatrically ratified by most of the important nations, was to prove ultimately a disservice to the cause of world peace.

The Depression: 1929–1933. In 1929 Herbert Hoover entered upon one of the most distressing administrations in American history. In October the world depression, creeping up from Latin America and Australasia, reached London, and three weeks later, New York. The crash of the New York Stock Exchange was not a mere market débâcle; it was the outward manifestation of the end of an economic cycle. From October 1929 to July 1932 the Dow-Jones Industrial Averages of common stocks sank from 383 to 41, the worst decline in recorded history since the South Sea Bubble of 1720.

The Hoover administration had just passed the Smoot-Hawley Tariff Act, which, by raising protective duties to the highest rates known, aggravated the crisis. There was a wave of bank failures. Unemployment reached staggering proportions. At one time (1932) steel production, the foundation of American industry, fell below 15% of capacity. Building practically ceased. Bond defaults by foreign debtors to American holders were widespread. Three-fourths of Americans who had earned $5,000 a year or more, found themselves among the "new poor," and tens of millions were in need of prime necessities. The price of corn, wheat, and cotton, the lowest in many generations, brought ruin to the farmers, who were already distressed by a decade of difficulties.

To cope with this Niagara of disaster, President Hoover, like most of his fellow-citizens, at first relied on the belief that it was transient — that "prosperity was just around the corner." When it became patent that the depression was basic, he sponsored the Farm Board to arrest the fall in farm prices and he created the Reconstruction Finance Corporation to salvage corporations and banks in temporary distress. The administration resorted to international action, but much too late: the Hoover moratorium of June 1931 on war debts was granted to a Europe in which German economy was already in mortal throes. Veterans of World War I marched on Washington to demand bonuses. The clashes between the U.S. Army and the Bonus Marchers, at Anacostia Flats, inflamed large sections of the country. Only in international affairs, where Secretary of State, Henry L. Stimson, sought world support against Japanese aggression in Manchuria (1931), was there a timely grasp of new and dangerous world tendencies. Regrettably, American international initiative did not meet with proper support abroad.

The country sank to the very depths of the depression in the summer of 1932, when the nominating conventions were held. The Democrats put forth the Governor of New York, Franklin Delano Roosevelt, of patrician origin and democratic passions. President Hoover was loyally renominated by the Republicans, who felt that he had been made the scapegoat for world tendencies. They held that the onset of world recovery (already in the making in Great Britain) portended a second Hoover administration as prosperous as the first had been distressing. The mass of the people, however, believed the Hoover policies had deepened and lengthened the crisis, and he was decisively defeated. The Democratic party also gained control of the Senate and the House of Representatives.

The last days of the Hoover administration were darkened by the complete collapse of the nation's banking system, the last of the 48 states having declared a moratorium the night of March 3, 1933. On March 4, with not a single bank open in the richest land on earth, Mr. Roosevelt was inaugurated. In his inaugural address he uttered phrases that quickened the hopes of men of all parties. There was no questioning the need to act at once if the country was to be saved. For some time, the partisan did not exist: only the patriot was seen in the land.

The New Deal: 1933–1937. President Roosevelt's first step, necessarily, was to reopen the banks and permit the circulation of capital. The export of gold was prohibited and hoarders of gold were compelled to exchange their metal for the greenbacks. By presidential order, the banks reopened: at first a few, then slowly, the great majority. In April 1933 the dollar was divorced from a fixed gold value and it enjoyed an open market until February 1934 when it was stabilized at 59.06% of its former parity, with the reserved presidential right to devalue it to 50¢.

The Roosevelt administration was distinguished for one trait: it sought salvation not in precedent but in innovation. It dared to fail, hoping that it might thus discover empirically the fitting answers to pressing needs. In foreign policy, as in domestic, its variation from previous tradition was at once made manifest. The "Good Neighbor" policy was formulated toward our sister-republics of the Americas: a free association of sovereign states was substituted for the hitherto predominant rôle assumed by the United States. The administration turned its back on the theory that because a nation is rich, industrially strong, and populous, it thereby holds a shred of right to abridge the sovereignty or to diminish the historic dignity of any smaller commonwealth. American foreign investment no longer connoted any right of military interference in any country's affairs. No foreign country's internal régime was again to be subjected to the censorious attitude of the United States.

This new international policy was quickly implemented. In an amazingly short time, considering the historic friction of nearly a century, Latin-American cooperation and trust began to replace the hatred of "Yankee imperialism," "dollar diplomacy," or "Monroeism," as the abuse of the Monroe Doctrine had come to be termed in Latin-American speech.

In European policy, the administration's first efforts were concentrated on common action for world recovery. For this purpose, a World Economic Conference was called in London (1933). It failed of achievement and European criticism unfairly attributed its breakdown to unilateral American decision. President Roosevelt, however, justified the American attitude as based upon absolutely urgent

American internal needs, which had to be served by an independent currency policy.

On a world scale, the Secretary of State, Cordell Hull, of low-tariff antecedents, favored freer trade among nations. He constructively opposed the world tendencies toward "autarky" (self sufficiency), preferential agreements, and trade discriminations of any kind. He was to initiate a series of reciprocal trade agreements, the only counter-manifestation to the world-wide rise of economic nationalism in the 1930's.

Domestically, the character of federal government, both as to scope and functions, profoundly altered. Extra-governmental agencies multiplied. Bank deposits were guaranteed up to $5,000 by a Federal Deposit Insurance Corporation. The Civilian Conservation Corps took care of adolescents and turned their unemployment to social use. The National Recovery Administration ("The Blue Eagle") undertook to establish codes for industry and thus to integrate national production in standards, practices, and prices. The Tennessee Valley Authority was the first attempt to re-create whole backward areas and shape their industrial future and their population by direct government sponsorship and initiative. Great dams were built; not a new departure, but one of far greater range and investment than had previously obtained. The Public Works Administration embodied the belief that inadequate employment in private business should be compensated by public works employment, thus creating purchasing power which would stimulate demand for retail goods, and thus start the wheels of industry. When these public works were found to have only partial effects, the Works Progress Administration began a program of wholly created employment. Although bitterly assailed by conservatives as subsidizing laziness, the W.P.A. was hailed by the administration's advocates as having brought about a renaissance of manhood in those who had despaired, and of having disseminated and stimulated the arts and sciences throughout the country.

The National Labor Board was founded to institute arbitration and to fix bases of remuneration. The Wagner Act, later enacted, was to serve as a charter of labor. The Securities and Exchange Commission was created to regulate finances, to supervise new issues and stock exchanges. This came about as a consequence of important financial malpractices uncovered in the early 1930's. The conservatives charged that the S.E.C. was the principal reason for the almost complete cessation of adequate capital investment; the Roosevelt adherents attributed this lack of private investment to social sabotage.

The country was now markedly divided. By and large, the lower-income groups applauded the administration, whose popularity diminished almost in ratio to personal assets. Not since the Bryan-McKinley contest of 1896 were income groups so clearly reflected in political allegiances.

The farmer, whose problems had not been solved since 1920, was now under the jurisdiction of the Agricultural Adjustment Administration, which paid bonuses for "plowing under" crops and otherwise sought to reduce farm surpluses. There were many jolts in the operation of the A.A.A. and many sections of the country criticized the use of destruction as an instrument of economic recovery.

The principal setback of the New Deal occurred when the Supreme Court voided the N.R.A. in May 1935. Nevertheless, the achievements of the New Deal on the whole survived. Many of the administration's more experimental programs had primarily diplomatic or regional value (such as government purchase of silver at higher-than-market prices, in order to relieve the mining states). But whatever the appraisal of its work, whether it was the author of recovery (already witnessed by 1935) or whether it had impeded what would have been a still greater "natural" recovery, as its enemies asserted, the United States was recognizably a different society in 1936 from that of 1932. Innovations such as Social Security, among many others, passed from being challenged to being accepted in principle by the opposition. Gradually, a large part of the New Deal (though far from all of it) became a general national possession; variations of opinion centered rather on its comparative rôle in the state, on its proper adjustment to free enterprise, on its finance, on its administration, and above all, on the social implications of its operations, rather than on its fundamental human objectives.

This tendency was not yet manifested in 1936 when a sharply contested election campaign revealed the depths of division. The Republican candidate, Governor Alfred M. Landon of Kansas, declared himself a liberal and relied on the historic endowment of Americans to overcome economic crises. The administration overwhelmingly triumphed: President Roosevelt was reelected by a plurality of 11,000,000 votes.

A large factor in his success was the new-found militancy and enormously increased membership of the labor unions. The older American Federation of Labor, based on craft unionism, now had a rival in the Congress of Industrial Organizations. The C.I.O. aimed at organizing great masses of workers, either in the wholly unorganized or in the heavy industries. The triumph of President Roosevelt fortified labor unionism. Soon thereafter the General Motors Corporation and U.S. Steel, among others of the largest corporations, accepted the "closed shop" which they had fought for decades.

The Second Roosevelt Administration: 1937–1939. The first Roosevelt administration had relied on "deficit financing." The plethora of spending or "priming the pump" (in the parlance of the time) was now thought to have been adequate, and the administration insisted on retrenchment. President Roosevelt was immediately accused of "turning to the Right" by numerous Leftist elements. The country soon felt a marked industrial recession, which by the summer of 1938 had become reminiscent of the former depression. Radical elements in the administration attributed the "downturn" to inadequate support of the unemployed; the conservatives pointed out that it was a world phenomenon and would have had no scope had confidence in business not been injured. At any rate, government spending was resumed and by the spring of 1939 a moderate recovery had set in, broadening slowly with the increase of foreign orders for armaments.

The principal domestic issue concerned the privileges of the Supreme Court, whose decisions had largely hindered the innovations of President Roosevelt. The President sponsored Supreme Court reform: this was widely opposed and he failed of his purpose. Later, as vacancies multiplied in the Supreme Court, he was accused of "packing" it with his "favorites," and these justices in turn were accused of following their social philosophies rather than the strict construction of the Constitution and of statutory law. Where once the opposition had held the Court to be sacrosanct, it now held it in disrespect; and vice versa, radical critics to whom the Court had been the embodiment of class prejudice, now rejoiced in its decisions.

But domestic issues were no longer dominant. The shadow of Fascism had darkened Europe. In 1936 the United States (among other nations) declined to send arms shipments to the Spanish Republic, which was facing a rebellion. This ill-advised action led to a greater extension of Fascist influence in Europe.

Upon his reelection, President Roosevelt, sensing the need for intimate inter-American cooperation, journeyed to Argentina. In December 1936 the Inter-American Conference for the Maintenance of Peace was held in Buenos Aires. The principle was formulated that whenever the peace of the Americas is in danger, the American republics shall consult with each other; and also, that every act susceptible of disturbing the peace of the Americas affects every American republic. Hence these two formulations justified the initiation of procedural consultation as provided in the "Covenant for the maintenance, preservation, and re-establishment of peace."

These provisions were the foundations of the defense of the Americas in World War II, and contributed vitally to the security of the twenty-one republics. Congress, in the meantime, had enacted the "Neutrality Act" which greatly impeded American action in behalf of those democracies attacked by Fascist aggressors.

In October 1937 President Roosevelt openly declared that aggressor nations must be quarantined. Despite some timid reactions on the part of even highly placed Americans, this speech translated American belief as to the future path of the democratic defense of the United States.

In 1938 the Czechoslovak crisis led to a plea by President Roosevelt that the powers avoid war by conference. His effort in behalf of European peace was subverted by the four powers at Munich (October 1938) for purposes of their own (See *Czechoslovakia, History*). The American ambassador to Germany was recalled soon thereafter and diplomatic relations between the two countries were reduced to a bare minimum.

Neutrality: 1939–1941. In 1939 the Fascist aggressors unleashed World War II. The United States was again neutral at the outset. Not only was her action limited by the Neutrality Act of 1937, but the prior Johnson Act (1935) prohibited loans or credits to the countries that had not fully met their debts to the United States. Hence Great Britain and France were compelled to sacrifice their assets in the United States so as to buy supplies and food.

They were further burdened by the "cash and carry" Congressional legislation which, in the spring of 1940, seemed almost a device to cripple the Allies by denying them customary private commercial credit privileges and the use of shipping ordinarily granted to belligerents. President Roosevelt made a last effort to ascertain the possibilities of peace by way of the European mission of Under Secretary of State Sumner Welles. The plans of the dictators were too far advanced, and their knowledge of the position of their leading adversary, France, too detailed, for humane reason to deflect them from their criminal path.

The fall of France (June 1940) stunned the United States. The persistent aggressions of Japan in China sickened public opinion. But the resistance of isolationist elements was still not easily overcome. In the summer of 1940, however, the desperate need of Britain to master the submarine sinkings, clearly indicated the necessity for affirmative American action; for if Britain were conquered, the United States would directly face aggression. The arrangement whereby 50 over-age destroyers were ceded to Britain, who in return granted us bases (August 1940) was generally approved by Americans. It provided an invaluable basis for the defense of the Western Hemisphere as well as an aid to the British in their valiant defense of their land. A tripartite agreement among Japan, Germany, and Italy (September 27, 1940), clearly aimed at the United States, pledged their common action against her should she be involved in either European or Asiatic conflict.

The presidential election of 1940 did not turn about foreign affairs; the opinions of Wendell Willkie, the Republican candidate, and of Mr. Roosevelt were similar. Isolationist groupings, not crediting Mr. Willkie's international view, largely supported him, only to be sharply disillusioned when, after his defeat, he became a champion of world unity, and one of the foremost internationalists in the land. Much of the heat of the campaign arose out of the precedent-breaking action of the Democratic party in designating President Roosevelt for the third term.

The presidential contest did not in any way halt the growth of defense. Peacetime Selective Service was introduced for the first time in American history. The government initiated a large-scale defense program whose costliness was not effectively challenged by the opposition.

Soon after President Roosevelt's third inauguration (January 1941) the "Lend-Lease" legislation, so long overdue, opened the possibilities of material assistance to the anti-Nazi forces. After the Soviet Union was wantonly attacked by Germany (June 1941), the visit of Harry Hopkins to Moscow openly demonstrated American interest in significantly aiding any foe of German aggression. This spontaneous action took place although relations with Soviet Russia had not been overcordial because of our government's unmistakable attitude with reference to the Russo-Finnish war of the winter of 1939–1940.

The United States at War: 1941–1944. In his annual message to Congress (January 1941) President Roosevelt enunciated the "Four Freedoms" — freedom of expression, and of worship, freedom from want, and from fear. In August, President Roosevelt and

Prime Minister Churchill, meeting at sea, formulated the "Atlantic Charter," which set forth the basic aims of democratic commonwealths. Increased tension with Japan, one of the most wanton violators of every one of these aims, led the United States to seek to bring Japan to some peaceful solution that would yet defend the integrity of China. In October 1941, however, the advent of the Tojo government in Japan rendered this task unattainable.

After a series of negotiations with Japan in which the Japanese carried out diplomatic conversations as a time-gaining device with which to prepare their treachery, the Japanese Empire attacked the United States at Pearl Harbor in Hawaii (December 7, 1941). The United States was at war with Japan, and within a few days, Germany and Italy declared war upon this country, as did other Axis satellites in due time. The naval setback in Hawaii and the speedy calamitous fall of the Far Eastern countries to Japan led to a dangerous phase of the war in the Pacific. This was overcome in the naval battles of Midway and the Coral Sea (1942), and thus the foundations were laid for converting the war of oceanic defense into a reversal of the direction of the assault. The United States then initiated her plan to conquer the numerous islands lying over extended air and sea routes preparatory to a campaign on the mainland of Asia and those islands within the immediate orbit of Japan.

The war with Germany proceeded according to geographical possibilities: first, by lavish aid to Britain and the U.S.S.R.; second, by the use of Britain as a base for future American operations; third, by the invasion of North Africa (November 1942); fourth, by the invasion of Sicily (June 1943) and of the Italian peninsula (August 1943), culminating in Italian surrender (September 1943); fifth, by the invasion of northern France (June 1944). In the meantime aerial assaults on Germany, vastly augmented, proved important in speeding victory.

Meanwhile, after a series of helpful conferences and arrangements, the Inter-American Conference at Rio de Janeiro (January 1942) led to the common action of the American republics in recommending the breaking of diplomatic relations with the Axis powers; and this was carried out ultimately by all the signatory nations. Many other resolutions were adopted, providing for common economic action against the Axis and, concretely, for constant consultations on post-war problems. The republics also agreed to adhere to the principles of the Atlantic Charter.

Internal Policy: 1941–1944. The war transformed American life. Within a few months the quantity of production of war matériel reached fantastic amounts. Tens of millions of persons engaged either in direct war production or in the making of such commodities as would ultimately serve war needs. Civilian goods diminished in supply, although civilian consumption remained notably high. Unemployment disappeared. The number of persons gainfully employed reached a new high, although some 11,500,000 men had entered the armed services. Women enlisted in the auxiliary branches of the military. New cities sprang into being; many older ones doubled or trebled in population. The supply of labor shifted in wide swings. Hitherto less favored areas of the country, like the South and the Pacific coast, now became intensively industrialized. The government invested tens of billions of dollars in new enterprises. The greatest industries in the land, such as automobiles, steel, rail equipment, came to be almost wholly producers for the military.

Farm prices rose tremendously, thus ending the two decades of halting agricultural economy. On the other hand, price controls kept inflation within bounds, when due allowance is made for the striking increase in national spending power as against the diminished supply of consumers nondurable goods and the nearly total elimination of consumers durable goods. This was a marked contrast to the steep rise in living costs during World War I. American ingenuity coped with such apparently disquieting shortages as rubber and tin. The railways handled the increased freight and passenger loads although their equipment had not been adequately modernized since 1929. In shipping, the country easily surpassed her impressive records of World War I.

As the war progressed, attention shifted from the wonders of achievement to discussions of the widespread collateral effects of this immense effort on the permanent economy of the land. The administration took on a war complexion. The War Production Board was endowed with extraordinary powers. Priorities were established so that the primary war needs would be assured. Controls became elaborate and many critics insisted that they were needlessly vexatious. Whatever the variation of opinion, one fact was indubitable: never before in American experience had private business been so molded by war needs.

The clash of opinion centered rather upon the allegation of the opposition that war necessities and war finances were shaped with the collateral aim of altering the foundation of the social structure. But there was no controversy as to the need for channeling the employment of the people and the direction of capital according to overriding war needs.

At the same time, competent opinion held that the perception of the need for post-war international organization was not as advanced as was the incomparable effort in war production, and above all, the dedication of the armed forces to victory. Isolationist sentiment, although laggard compared to the Copperheadism of the Civil War or the groundswell of resentment in World War I that culminated in "normalcy," was large enough to be disturbing. Fortunately, nearly all responsible opinion went in one direction. The great mass of editorial and radio comment favored international organization. The international affirmations of the Atlantic Charter (1941), of Casablanca (1943), of Teheran (1943), and of Dumbarton Oaks (1944) became guideposts to the future. The presidential contest in the autumn of 1944, between President Roosevelt and Governor Thomas E. Dewey, the Republican candidate, centered primarily about the post-war policy of the nation at home and abroad. Roosevelt triumphed.

Stakes in the Peace

The United States, as the first industrial country of the world, with the greatest diffusion of democracy and welfare among the largest number of people, has a vital stake in world peace and world prosperity.

Her own interests depend upon the maintenance of peace, for it is only in a world at peace that the United States can proceed creatively along the path that she has chosen: to develop her democratic institutions, to raise the standard of living, and to advance the social well-being of her people.

To achieve these objectives, the United States must pursue a consistent foreign policy, implemented by her elected representatives, and without reference to party divisions. She must determine what her true desires are in relation to other countries, and she must ascertain what means she wishes to employ in order that her desires be translated into reality. Once these objectives are understood, they must be pursued without basic deviation.

Two stages are clearly necessary in the course of achieving American purposes: one transitional, the other permanent. The first task consists in defeating, disarming, and rendering harmless the aggressor nations, so that the world can concentrate on providing the minimum prerequisite: security against the recurrence of armed clashes. Once this transitional period has been successfully concluded, the United States will be in a position to carry out her long-range policy of creative concord with the other nations of the world through a permanent international organization.

However, certain supplementary considerations will have to be recognized and acted upon, if the long-range policy of the United States is to be achieved. Among these are: (1) the inter-American system, whereby the welfare and common security of the Western hemisphere can be assured; (2) the continued friendship with the British Commonwealth of Nations; (3) the development of economic relationships and historic friendship with the Soviet Union; (4) the friendship with China and effective aid to the Chinese people — for upon these factors depends the security of the United States as a power in the Pacific; (5) the restoration of democratic France to her former greatness and importance as a nation. Furthermore, the United States must also consider the future of the German and Japanese peoples: she must undertake to influence world trade, investment, and finance in such a manner that these peoples, controlled and disarmed, can embark upon a stable and satisfactory course.

If the United States is to accomplish the objectives implicit in her own productive evolution, she must steer a creative course in economic relations. She must turn from the self-centered tariff policies that have been so costly to world prosperity and shape her own trade policies so that other nations may deal with her. She must, in turn, assure herself equal facilities for trade with other nations, so that mankind may be enriched by the exchange of needed goods and services. The United States must not resist the industrialization of the backward areas of the world, but rather seek to direct her production toward serving this inevitable development. Furthermore, she must make certain that her own people will not be denied access to strategic raw materials, and that other nations also are not so deprived. With respect to currency, the United States must contribute toward stabilization of money through an international bank, so that the chaos of currencies will be avoided. Given good-will and determination, these economic measures should prove readily attainable.

In her Declaration of Independence, the United States created the modern political world; and in her Constitution, she demonstrated that a society without fixed classes can administer a vast continent, develop it at unheard-of speed, and transform it as no other region has ever been transformed, to become the leader in world economic accomplishment. Her demonstrated talent for government and her economic resiliency have not as yet been similarly manifested in foreign policy. When the two areas of accomplishment — domestic and foreign — are equally enlightened, it will be difficult to set bounds to American destiny in a world of free, peaceful, and prosperous peoples.

URUGUAY

The Land and the People

Uruguay is the most socialized country in the Americas. 1903 saw the election of a remarkable president, José Batlle y Ordóñez. He initiated a social program which has since kept Uruguayans intensely interested in bettering their social, economic, and educational life. His motto was "The easing of suffering," and he is gratefully remembered. Today Uruguay has a modern program of social insurance for individuals, state ownership of public utilities, of industries, banks, hotels, and of many other institutions.

Because of its free, democratic, cosmopolitan spirit, Montevideo, the capital, has become a favorite center for international conferences and organizations. Leaders of liberal causes who are expelled from their own lands make their home in this liberty-loving city, as do the literary and philosophically minded, who desire a quiet, stimulating place to work. To the charm of the country, described by W. H. Hudson in his *Purple Land*, has been added recently what is probably the most democratic atmosphere of any South American country, expressed in the words of Rodó, the nation's greatest writer, "to reform oneself is to live."

The Land. Smallest of the South American republics, Uruguay has an area of only 72,100 square miles (about the same as South Dakota) with a population estimated at 2,164,000. Her neighbor to the north and northeast is Brazil; east and southeast of her is the Atlantic; to the southwest and west she is separated from Argentina by the wide Río de la Plata and the Uruguay River.

The Uruguayan landscape would look familiar to the people of our own Eastern states: high hills with granite outcroppings, forested valleys, clear rivers, northern trees and other vegetation, slopes of meadow-grass. The only low flat country is in the west. Entirely in the temperate zone, exposed to southern breezes and sheltered by hills to the north, Uruguay has a mild and equable climate, with winters about like those of South Carolina, and summers somewhat cooler than those of central New York. The Argentines make Uruguay their summer resort. On the seacoast are many government-owned casinos, hotels, and amusement parks, which cater to an extensive tourist trade.

Uruguay is one of the finest grazing countries in the world. For centuries adventurous cowboys roamed her grassy slopes. Only America's "wild West" has seen as picturesque a succession of free-booters, communities of unattached men, and rough-riding cowboys. The cattle raised in those days were useful only for their hides. But after about 1880 British capital and enterprise, directed from Montevideo, became the driving force in the development of the meat trade. Uruguay is now an important source of Britain's meat supply.

There is some mineral wealth in the north — silver, copper, lead, manganese, and gold — but these deposits are not extensively worked.

The People. The 2,000,000 people of Uruguay, like the Argentines, are preponderantly of European stock, with very few Indians and almost no Negroes among them. Spain and Italy were the chief European homelands. The foreign population is large and commercially active and forms an important part of those engaged in agriculture. In the northeast there is a considerable Brazilian minority.

Both the birthrate (20 per thousand) and the deathrate (9.6) are much the lowest in South America, and the deathrate has at times been the lowest in the world. Infant mortality is approximately 86 per thousand, about the same as Argentina's. These statistics indicate a moderately increasing population.

Uruguay is practically unique in that the two largest groups of her population are the urban and the pastoral, taking "pastoral" in the literal sense of "connected with stock-raising." Although in theory almost the whole country is arable, only about 5% of Uruguayans are farmers exclusively. The first settlers, coming from arid Spain, were delighted with the rich pasture land. Roads were easy to build. Holdings were fenced off, the breed of cattle was immeasurably improved both for meat and milk, while sheep-raising also became common. Meanwhile the city-dwellers — which means for the most part the 703,518 people of Montevideo — dressed the meat and prepared the wool for shipment abroad.

In recent years, the industrialization has greatly increased. The workers have crowded into the capital at the expense of the rural areas, where health and educational conditions among the cattle-men are reported as poor. "We talk about industrialization and we enact advanced social legislation," says a student of national affairs, "but we have not yet learned how to get the most out of the resources which nature has provided for a thriving sheep industry."

The state's participation in industry is managed through subsidiary corporations. These are set up and initially financed by the government, but management is in the hands of businessmen and technicians who are instructed that they must make the business pay and render cheap service to the community. These corporations were set up many years before the Tennessee Valley Authority in the U.S.A., but they are organized similarly and for the most part have shown good results. Some of them, like the National Refrigerating Plant, were set up to lower the price of meat processed by foreign packing houses. State corporations include the Bank of the Republic, the Department of Docks in Montevideo, Department of Railroads and Electrification, and the state monopolies of alcohol, petroleum, telegraph, and telephones. To the state manufacture of cement is attributed the magnificent network of national highways, economically constructed.

The system of old-age pensions, minimum hours and wages, payment to labor for time during a strike (if the government arbitrators find the strike justified), health insurance and hospitalization, is a partial explanation of a society remarkably free from class distinctions. There are few notably rich or pitiably poor. Government officials in the high categories receive modest salaries as do managers of the numerous business corporations under state direction. Newspaper editors, university professors, and writers and professional men stand high in the community. Women occupy many positions of leadership and some of them have world-wide reputations in the medical and social fields.

Uruguayans are proud of the care guaranteed to every child: free hospitalization of the mother during birth, nursery care if the mother works, free medical care, and education from pre-kindergarten on through the university until graduation with a professional degree. Not only is this furnished without cost, but if needed, the graduate can then secure a loan from the state to set up his office and support himself while he establishes himself in his profession.

Religion and Education. Uruguay is noted for her wide religious toleration. Church and State were separated in 1917. The Roman Catholic Church is adhered to by most of the people. Protestantism is influential in Montevideo and in a colony of Italian Waldensians; while a considerable number of people term themselves "liberal."

For a century the clerical *Blancos* (White party) have struggled to increase the power of the Church, and the anticlerical *Colorados* (Red party) to decrease it.

On the whole, the *Colorados* (who are liberals, not Communists) have had the upper hand.

Education is tuition-free and compulsory. Illiteracy, though still 35% among adults, has almost disappeared among the young. Over 17,000 Uruguayans go to high school, and some 20,000 — a tenth of all those of college age — attend the celebrated University of Montevideo. In educational and cultural standards, Montevideo is as modern as any city in Europe. Indeed, the cultural standards of the country as a whole (which have been strongly influenced, especially as to philosophical outlook, by French thinkers like Renan) are among the highest in Latin America.

The most revered of South American thinkers, Rodó, was a Uruguayan. His essay "Ariel" has inspired a generation of Latin Americans. The greatest Latin American dramatist, Florencio Sánchez, combined native material with Ibsenian form. The high position of women is shown by the noted poets, Juana de Ibarbourou and Sarah Bollo. One of the founders of French modernist literature, Jules Laforgue, was born in Montevideo.

The Nation's Economy

Agriculture. Uruguayans devote 60% of their land to stock-raising, 20% to stock-raising combined with some farming, and only 6% to farms. Land ownership is widely diffused for Latin America: 44% of the people own their own farms, 40% are tenant farmers (not peons), and 15% manage farms for absentee owners. The population density is only 400 per square mile of cultivated land.

In spite of the low percentage of farmland, the varied food crops are sufficient for domestic needs. The wheat crop is adequate and of high quality and the fruit crop (153,000 tons annually) is large and of excellent quality. Dairy products naturally abound.

In fact, so great is the production of dairy and other pastoral products that the great mass of them must be destined for export. For Uruguay's main source of agricultural wealth is her animal husbandry. Her annual wool clip of 64,000 tons is as great as Argentina's in proportion to population, and the number of her stock — 8,000,000 cattle and 20,000,000 sheep — is even greater per capita.

Industry and Foreign Trade. The stock ranches furnish employment, directly or indirectly, to a high percentage of the people: 24% are engaged in pastoral activities, and 59% in processing and manufacturing, mostly of food products.

Before World War II, the cattle industry, on a decade average, furnished 86% of Uruguay's exports, the sheep industry practically all the rest: live animals, meat, processed meats, wool. The leading crop export was linseed (for paints and varnishes). Uruguay's imports covered the whole range of consumers goods. Before World War II, the country's trade was diffused, with Britain and the U.S.A. leading, and Belgium and Germany trailing far behind. In 1935, Britain took about 30% of Uruguay's exports, the U.S.A. about 15%, while Britain supplied over 20% of her imports and the U.S.A. slightly less.

See maps on pages 169, 181.

Because of the war, trade with the U.S.A., Argentina, and Brazil has partly replaced that with Britain. But wartime restrictions, the scarcity of shipping, and the higher prices prevailing for imports into Uruguay have brought a decline in her total trade. In 1942, imports were $15 per capita as compared with $29.35 in 1938, a decline in volume even greater than in dollar value. Exports in 1942 showed a slight rise in value (from $26.35 to $30 per capita), but because of higher prices, this too represents a smaller volume.

National Income and Finance. For a long time Uruguay was the wealthiest and most progressive nation in Latin America. In the opening years of the century, at the time when Britain was inaugurating her program of social reform, Uruguay adopted advanced social legislation — minimum wages, child welfare laws, unemployment insurance, old-age pensions. So strong was her financial position that at times, the *peso*, national unit of currency, was at a premium over the dollar.

But her economy has suffered for ten years during which her exports commanded low prices. And this period was followed by World War II, with high prices of which she could not take full advantage owing to the shortage of shipping.

The Uruguayan *peso* now stands at about 52.7¢ in the free market. It has, however, been greatly strengthened by a coverage of 130% in foreign reserves — made possible by the excess of Uruguay's exports over her imports.

Money in circulation has advanced slowly (some 17%) during the war. It is now $28 per capita, which is relatively a high figure. Commercial bank deposits and taxes are stable; taxes, at $25 per person, are much lower than in Argentina. The internal debt is about $175,000,000. The external debt (on which interest payments have been resumed) is about $70,000,000.

Prior to World War II, investments of the U.S.A. in Uruguay were about $75,000,000. Despite long association between the two countries, those of Britain were only $25,000,000.

History: 1914-1944

Neutral but unmistakably pro-Allied in World War I, Uruguay broke relations with Germany in 1917. But it is her internal history that commands interest, particularly with the advent of her remarkable President José Batlle y Ordóñez (1856–1929). He initiated a series of sweeping social reforms which culminated in the Constitution of 1917 enacted during the administration of President Viera. This document marked the triumph of the long struggle to establish liberal, democratic government in Uruguay.

To safeguard social gains, Batlle had sought to diminish the power of the President. While the executive retained control of defense, home security, and foreign affairs, all other duties were confined to a National Council of Administration. This body consisted of 9 members, 3 chosen every two years, and one of these three was to be a member of the opposition. The President was to be elected by direct vote, and voting was made compulsory, direct, free, secret, and on a proportional basis. To lessen the domination of urban Montevideo over the countryside, decentralizing measures were effected. Church and State were separated. However well-intentioned, the Constitution provided a system of executive administration which proved in practice to be hopelessly unworkable.

Peaceful Progress: 1919–1939. From 1919 to 1931 three presidents, legally elected, peacefully served out their four-year terms. The old Progressive party, the *Colorados*, divided into two groups: the *Batllistas*, who followed the noted President, and the independents or *Riveristas*; whereas the *Blancos*, now called Nationalists, were reduced to about a third of the total voting strength. This was the heyday of liberal democracy in Uruguay.

The world depression of 1929 struck Uruguay almost immediately. After Dr. Gabriel Terra, a Batllista, became President in 1931, his opponents (the *Riveristas* and Nationalists) joined forces so as to hinder the functioning of the dual authority exercised by the President and the National Council of Administration. It soon became impossible to govern the country.

Terra, defied by Congress, assumed dictatorial powers (1933). In 1934 he abolished the National Council but made cabinet officers responsible to Congress. However, Terra did not interfere with social gains. When his term expired in 1938, Uruguay went peacefully to the polls. Over 21% of the population voted and General Alfredo Baldomir, a *Colorado*, became President.

World War II: 1939–1944. Although the country remained formally neutral, Uruguayan sympathies were with the anti-Axis powers from the outset of the war. In May 1940 the Germans made a bid to seize military control of Uruguay: Brazil rushed aid to the little republic and the U.S.A. dispatched two cruisers.

In January 1942 Uruguay broke off diplomatic relations with the Axis and constructed airfields, which in case of need would be made available for joint inter-American defense. The ultra-nationalist Senator, Luis A. de Herrera (but not most of the other *Blancos*), attacked these moves as a prelude to national slavery, but the government firmly pursued a policy of close cooperation with the U.S.A. and Brazil.

The Argentine militarists have based their hopes on the subversive speeches of the fiery Senator Herrera. To cope with his dangerous tactics, President Baldomir temporarily suspended the Constitution in 1942. However, he soon restored civil liberties and regular elections. Juan José Amézaga succeeded Baldomir as President in 1943.

Faced with an economic crisis because of the loss of European markets, Uruguay obtained substantial lend-lease from the U.S.A. and Britain guaranteed markets for her products. To prevent discontent in the rural regions, the government in 1943 extended social security to herdsmen and farmers, which privileges had hitherto been granted to urban workers only.

President Amézaga (1944) depended on the normal functioning of democracy to sustain Uruguay in her sincere inter-American policy. Pro-Argentine groups and Brazilian *Integralistas*, operating illegally, have exerted pressure, but thus far they have lacked a large popular following.

Foreign Affiliations. Uruguay has never wavered in her friendship for the U.S.A. and Britain. Though her relationships with democratic Argentina and Brazil were cordial, her recent relations with the Argentine régime have been strained. At one point Uruguay was hostile to the U.S.S.R., alleging Soviet interference in her internal affairs; but in recent years Soviet-Uruguayan relations have markedly improved and diplomatic relations have been resumed.

Uruguay has had a difficult path. She is staunchly pro-American but closely bound by economic ties to her neighbor Argentina. Her well-developed hotel industry would collapse without Argentine visitors. On the other hand, she finds the prevailing tone of the Argentine government distasteful and provocative.

Stakes in the Peace

Uruguay is a small state, with an animal economy based on two types of exports: beef and wool. In external relations, she needs, above all, European prosperity; and she would welcome any international settlement that would assure an expanding market for her exports.

Uruguay has, however, for fifty years been in the forefront of progressive governments which have sought world order through cooperative methods based upon effective international organization.

She can be expected to assume the same kind of constructive leadership upon the conclusion of the present war.

Internally, the laggard development of subsistence farming is an economic and political drawback, since it compels excessive reliance on imports of various

foods and keeps rural wages generally low by basing them solely on payments to herdsmen. The prosperity of Argentina and Brazil is a necessity, for Uruguay is the Riviera of South America. Her tourist trade can flourish only in an atmosphere of peace and mutual confidence.

VENEZUELA

The Land and the People

Venezuela is the birthplace of the herald of Latin American freedom, Francisco de Miranda; of the famed liberator, Simón Bolívar; of General Sucre, for whom a grateful Bolivia renamed her ancient capital; and of Andrés Bello, genius of Latin American enlightenment. Venezuela has also been known for her recurrent tyrannies, such as that of Guzmán Blanco, and lately of Juan Vicente Gómez (1909–1935). These contrasts are of the past, as the vigorous and imaginative Venezuelan people now shape their modern, democratic state.

The Land. Though the country is almost as large as Texas, Arkansas, and Louisiana combined, most of her 352,170 square miles are almost uninhabited, and much of the country is unexplored. W. H. Hudson's famous novel *Green Mansions* vividly describes the far southern highlands. The landscape varies greatly from region to region. Half of Venezuela — the Guiana highlands — lies south of the Orinoco River and is still largely unknown. Another third — the *llano* (or plain) — between the Orinoco and the Andes Mountains — is a sparsely peopled cattle-raising area.

Over 90% of the Venezuelans live in a sixth of their land, the 60,000 square miles near the Caribbean, a region of broad highlands, valleys, and coastal lowlands. In this populated region, climate varies with altitude. It is hot and humid along the coast, and delightful in the highland elevated lands of 2,000 feet and over.

The nation's boundaries — British Guiana on the east, Brazil on the south, Colombia on the west — are too remote to play a vital part in the life of Venezuela. Because the population is so highly concentrated near the sea, this coastal region is for all practical purposes the center of Venezuelan life. Nevertheless, the country is defined by her three characteristic areas.

Lake Maracaibo region, lying in the extreme northwest, is economically the most important, since it contains the country's famous oil deposits. Almost uninhabited before petroleum was discovered (in 1920), it has since attracted substantial numbers (including Americans and British) despite the discomforts of its steamy tropical climate. To the east are the spurs of the Andes, rising to a height of 9,000 feet near the sea. Still farther east lies the capital, Caracas, with its

See continental map on page 229.

famed gardens, whose mild climate reflects its altitude of 3,000 feet.

The *llano* (or plain) to the south is chiefly grassland and scrub forest. In the 19th century, when livestock was the basis of the economy, this area was the chief source of Venezuela's prosperity. But during the rainy season (May to October), the vast plains become a series of islands, and the floods severely reduce the grazing area. This feature of the climate explains why the *llano* is sparsely populated. These plains have been the scene of stock-raising ever since colonial days. The cowboys of this district furnished the troops that enabled Bolívar to win Venezuelan independence. From the *llano* and the central highlands arose the plots for numerous stories of typical Venezuelan life — a life that was highly picturesque, with its rich landlords and their peons.

The highland regions, south of the Orinoco River, consist largely of treeless plains, scrub forests, and *selva* (jungle vegetation). For the most part uninhabited and unexploited, this area, fully half the country, is for all practical purposes, wasteland.

The petroleum of the north is today the transforming influence in the life of the nation. Cowboys and farm laborers have been rushing to the Lake Maracaibo section, whose boom has been still further intensified by war demands. They come here to get their share of the higher wages and the new schools and recreation centers provided by the foreign oil companies. This often proves a mirage. With farm labor reduced, there is a shortage of food, and living costs have risen higher than in almost any other country. Dinner in a good Caracas restaurant is about $5, and rents are proportionately exorbitant.

Exclusive of petroleum, Venezuela's mineral resources must be considered of minor consequence. Gold, copper, coal, and mica deposits are scattered in the north. But the fabled wealth of the southern Guiana highlands, the legendary "El Dorado," is yet to be proved — although since the time of Sir Walter Raleigh, the world has sought its wealth.

The People. Statistics vary widely, but of one thing there can be no doubt: Venezuela's more than 3,500,000 people are overwhelmingly *mestizos* (mixed Spanish and Indian blood, with Spanish predominant). They are estimated at from 70% to 85% of the population. Of the other groups, those of pure or predominantly white stock are estimated at some 10%; of Indian stock, from 2% to 10%. Negroes, mulattoes, and *zambos* (mixed Indian and Negro blood) are estimated at 9%. None of these estimates is exact.

There is a strong division between the newly arrived foreigners and the rich Venezuelans who dine at the gorgeous country clubs and palatial residences, on the one hand, and the rural laborers and small farm proprietors who are depressed rather than helped by the new wealth and foreign styles displayed so lavishly in the coastal cities, such as Caracas and Maracaibo. It is a race between the new life born of the petroleum boom, with its modern gadgets, and the older, more permanent agricultural life of the country, plus improved methods and enlarged programs of education, public hygiene, and social justice.

The López Contreras government and its successor have taken steps recently to assure the progress of the rural population by subdividing some of the great estates and by distributing land to the poor, establishing small agricultural banks, improving health, and augmenting educational programs. But these measures, as yet, have affected only a moderate part of the population.

The Venezuelan people were long distinguished for political intensity. In the minds of North Americans, their history has become the proverbial pattern of epochs when the people burst forth in libertarian passion under inspired idealists, alternating with long periods when they were simmering under tyrannies. The absence of a sizable middle class contributed to this shifting pattern. However, with the apparently permanent eclipse of the "aristocracy," a new and active city population has demanded civil order, hygiene, improved roads. The last decade has seen a solid democratic growth, broadening in sober fashion.

There were a million Venezuelans in 1800 and in the ensuing years the population increased at a far lower rate than the average for Latin America. Until oil was discovered, the advance was extremely slow; but the industrial and commercial development of the past twenty years has given rise to a sudden spurt. In 1921–25, the birthrate was 28 per thousand; against declining world birthrate tendencies it is now 36.8. The deathrate is about 17, an important decrease from a generation past, but the infant mortality still reaches the high figure of 122. If the present figures are maintained, Venezuela's population should gain appreciably within the next generation.

Religion and Education. The great mass of the people are Roman Catholics. While this church has long occupied a privileged position, minority faiths are free to develop unhindered.

Between 50% and 60% of the adult population can neither read nor write, but illiteracy during the Gómez dictatorship was estimated at 87%. Few countries have improved so rapidly after a tyranny. The statute books call for free and compulsory education, but only one child in three receives primary schooling. However, here too, Venezuela has made rapid progress: almost 10% of her national budget goes toward education, and adult education for illiterates is now being promoted. Whereas in 1916 only 35,000 children were at school, in 1942 the nation had 5,000 public schools with 260,000 pupils and 5,400 teachers. The Cuban system of using educated army men as teachers where they are stationed, has been widely adopted. Venezuela has three universities, at Caracas, Mérida, and Maracaibo.

The capital, Caracas, with its numerous bookshops, is a lively center of literary activity. Venezuelan culture, like much of Latin America, once had a classic French flavor, fostered in academies of literature and history. But Venezuela has now found her authentic national idiom. Her writers are preoccupied with their country's physical aspects, the actual life of the people, and their destiny. Venezuelan literature is enormous, considering the small reading population. Rómulo Gallegos is as forthright as Zola in his rural novels; Díaz Rodríguez portrays the old time patricians in his novels and has done much to reawaken latent democratic sentiment. In the days when the U.S.A. followed "dollar diplomacy," the volcanic Blanco Fombona fought North American imperialism and his own Venezuelan tyranny with his versatile and powerful writings. His work deeply influenced Latin American literature as a whole.

The Nation's Economy

Agriculture. The principal farmlands lie in the three mountain basins to the west of Caracas, near the older centers of Valencia and its port, Puerto Cabello. Only a fifth of employed Venezuelans are farmers. Corn is widely cultivated as a staple food and coffee and cocoa are produced for export — indeed Caracas cocoa is one of the finest known. But since the soil — except in the land devoted to export crops — is poor and farming methods are primitive, the country must extensively import food for domestic consumption. Even the corn crop is insufficient for the people's needs.

The cattle population is reported to be about 4,200,000. This figure appears to be an understatement, for Venezuela exports some hides, and meat constitutes a fairly large part of the diet. Like agriculture, animal husbandry plays a minor part in the nation's economy. However, the government has recently abolished the monopoly in meat exports, with a resulting stimulus to this promising branch of the animal economy.

Mining and Industry. Petroleum is the great natural resource of Venezuela: her annual production of 37,000,000 tons vies with that of the U.S.S.R. for the second place in the world. On a per capita basis, Venezuela's oil output is the highest known, exceeding even that of the U.S.A. Although this small country supplies about a tenth of the world's oil, only 25,000 people are engaged in this industry.

Venezuela's only other significant mineral is gold; its annual export is valued at $4,800,000. Many tales have been told of the wealth of diamonds and gold in the Guiana highlands, but if these resources exist, they are yet to be exploited. One resource is certainly known: a billion tons of iron ore. These deposits, lying near the surface of the land, will inevitably give rise to a great increase of industrialization in Venezuela. Pearl fisheries off the northern coast are an important minor occupation, and the mining of copper, coal, and mica occupy a similar status in the economy.

Venezuelan industries have developed rather suddenly and under the protection of high tariffs, most of them around Caracas and La Guaira, its port. These "infant industries" — consumers goods such as textiles, glass, cement, and hardware — have been encouraged because the government recognizes the country's present dependence on fluctuating world-market prices for her chief commodities: oil, coffee, and cocoa. The fate of the Mexican oil-fields, which have noticeably run down, has been an object lesson to Venezuela. But variegated industry has hardly advanced beyond its initial stages, and Venezuelans remain on the whole badly nourished and wretchedly poor. However, in the industrialized areas, and in the oil districts, labor is rapidly improving its status, and its social gains enjoy the support of the government.

Finances. Oil revenues have immeasurably improved Venezuelan finances, and the country's foreign debts, long in default, have now been paid off. Taxes are astonishingly high when judged on a per capita basis, but very little of the $96,000,000 of annual taxation is paid by the native citizenry. The oil companies — whose ownership is approximately 50% American and 50% British-Dutch — contribute the lion's share of national income.

Neither prices nor the circulation of money has risen excessively as a result of World War II. The *bolívar*, worth 30¢ as an average, is a soundly backed currency. Although the circulation of money has increased only moderately, the cost of living, in Caracas, for example, was even before World War II the highest in the world and costs of food and rent were exorbitant. Since wages and salaries do not correspond, the lot of the Venezuelans is hard, and these price levels necessarily prevent the needed expansion of retail trade. Also, the mass arrival (in the oil areas) of well-paid foreigners and the example of their homes and tastes have given rise to a demand for living standards beyond the present economic capacity of even the upper middle classes. Automobiles are more diffused in Venezuela than almost anywhere else in Latin America, largely as a result of the availability of oil and excellent highways.

Foreign Trade. Almost 95% of all Venezuelan exports are oil, the remaining 5% consisting principally of coffee, cocoa, and gold. Since 90% of the petroleum resources are owned by American and British-Dutch companies, the principal profit to the Venezuelan government is through taxes. The revenues thus acquired have made possible a large-scale program of public works, especially highways. The surplus of exports over imports is shown by the following figures: exports per capita are approximately $100 compared with imports at $20–$30. There is probably no other country on earth with such a wide span.

Venezuelan oil is shipped chiefly to Curaçao and Aruba (both in the Dutch West Indies) for refining, whence it is trans-shipped mainly to Great Britain, the Netherlands, and the U.S.A. The U.S.A. supplies over 90% of all Venezuelan imports.

History: 1914-1944

The recent history of Venezuela is virtually the history of Juan Vicente Gómez, a remarkable tyrant who took power by a military *putsch* in 1908 and held it until his death at the age of eighty, in 1935. While he appointed several of his followers to serve as presidents, independent action was scarcely expected of them; for Gómez was the government, and the presidents his designees.

His administration took little note of codes of law, nor was honesty an outstanding characteristic. Openly enriching his family and his followers, Gómez did not even resort to the usual devices of concealment. He dominated the cattle industry especially; and his long period of control, which might otherwise have come to an earlier end, was sustained by the abundant revenue arising from the discovery of oil in the Lake Maracaibo basin.

Gómez's cruelty to his political opponents became legendary. In many Latin American countries, especially Mexico, there were colonies of exiles who spent decades hoping for his untimely end. He deprived his people of firearms and built up so elaborate a spy system that his agents knew the names, not only of his critics but also of those who did not praise him with sufficient zest.

Gómez died in December 1935. The pent-up feelings of the people burst forth, as crowds pillaged his mansion and sacked the homes of his many relatives and friends. The Gómez cabinet, however, chose the new President. He was López Contreras, the former Minister of War.

Under the administration of López Contreras, a new constitution was adopted (1936) which swiftly restored freedom to Venezuela. With the right to vote now granted to all males over twenty-one, the people readily adapted themselves to their new way of life. This transition from an extreme dictatorship to a really democratic form of government proved rapid and wholly successful. The outstanding statesmanship of President López Contreras himself was largely responsible for this remarkable achievement.

Radical propaganda was permitted under the new régime: it led to a wave of strikes in 1937. The government deported the agitators (all of whom were foreigners and Communists); but this disorder by no means shook the President's faith in popular democratic expression. His administration made the eight-hour working day obligatory, it authorized collective bargaining, and it required every firm to grant a share in its profits to its workers. However, it placed restrictions upon immigration.

Owing to the constitutional provision concerning re-election, López Contreras was ineligible for office in 1941. His party, however, won the Congressional elections and later, his Minister of War, General Medina Angarita, succeeded him in the presidency.

Venezuela broke off diplomatic relations with the Axis powers in December 1941, after the entry of the U.S.A. into the war. Though not a belligerent, she has consistently supported inter-American action.

The Congress that convened in 1943, under President Medina, contained many members who had been exiles under the Gómez tyranny. President Medina called for a strong party to support the government, but he did not advocate one-party rule, and he declared that the days of the dictatorship were over forever. Medina's outstanding triumph was his successful negotiation of a new contract for oil concessions with American, British, and Dutch interests — which greatly increased the share of the Venezuelan people in the profits derived from their petroleum resources. The foreign oil companies also agreed to build new refining plants after the war; and, in exchange, their concessions were extended for 40 years. At this time, the confiscated estates of the tyrant Gómez reverted to the nation.

Venezuela's serious wartime problem of inadequate food imports has eased as shipping has become increasingly available. Moreover, the government has undertaken an extensive public works program to cope with a possible post-war slump. The U.S.A. has promised the people of Venezuela further financial and technical assistance.

Foreign Affiliations. Apart from a temporary period of truculence in the 1890's, Venezuela has had neither marked foreign antagonisms nor affiliations.

However, her relations with neighboring Colombia are especially close and her ties with the other "Bolivarian nations" — Ecuador, Peru, and Bolivia — are significant. During the last few years, Venezuela has cooperated in inter-American relations, and her relationship with the U.S.A. has become increasingly cordial.

Stakes in the Peace

Venezuela knows that her oil boom, though it may last, may also diminish in relative importance. Meanwhile her chronic shortage of foodstuffs calls for more modernized agriculture in the uplands basins. To assure this advance, only moderate, but not basic, reforms in land ownership are required.

Venezuela must find some solution to the recurrent floods in her cattle country if her pastoral economy is to enlarge. Under no circumstances can she afford repetition of the wasteful methods which under Gómez nearly destroyed the region.

The territory beyond the Orinoco offers a vast opportunity for profitable development. Capital investment will be required but no such development can successfully be carried out unless the Venezuelan government inaugurates an immigration policy which will encourage suitable and desirable emigration from Europe after the war. Unless some constructive plan of this kind is undertaken, Venezuela's economic activity will be largely confined to the 10,000 square miles of fertile land near the coast. Venezuela's economic problems are among the easiest to cope with in all South America.

COLONIAL WEST INDIES

The West Indies are a great congeries of islands which curves from the Bahamas (off the coast of Florida) southeastward, eastward, and southward shutting off the Caribbean from the Atlantic, then from Trinidad curls its tail westward off the north shore of South America as far as the Gulf of Venezuela. The long narrow island of Cuba, Santo Domingo (shared by Haiti and the Dominican Republic), and Puerto Rico — none of which is included in the colonial group under discussion — form a west-east barrier between the Bahamas and the Caribbean. Jamaica lies south of this barrier and with it forms the Greater Antilles. The chain of smaller islands swinging from Puerto Rico around to the Gulf of Venezuela forms the Lesser Antilles.

The West Indies, where Columbus first set foot in the New World, have had a history of violence and exploitation. Most of our pirate lore comes out of them. Even today, if a writer wants a New World setting where anything may happen (as in O'Neill's *The*

See map on page 197.

Emperor Jones), he chooses the West Indies. The charm of the islands lies for us as much in their strangeness as in their beauty. Lately we have begun to think of them in terms of naval bases. Meanwhile, all but the largest of the islands have remained colonial; and to the economists and administrators of the governing nations the West Indies are a nest of all-but-insoluble problems.

BRITISH WEST INDIES

Though France, the Netherlands, and the U.S.A. all have holdings in the West Indies, the leading imperial power there is Great Britain who holds the Bahamas, Jamaica, most of the Lesser Antilles, and Trinidad. Trinidad and Jamaica are the largest and most important of these islands.

Jamaica. Jamaica is a mountainous island studded with cloud-capped peaks that reach an altitude of 7,000 feet. The area is 4,450 square miles, of which only 440 are under cultivation. The rainfall varies greatly: abundant in the north, deficient in the south. Roads are excellent and numerous.

Over 98% of Jamaicans are Negroes. They are largely Protestants. Education is compulsory and school attendance general. But the population is almost intolerably dense — 1,241,000, or 2,800 to the arable square mile — and increasing rapidly (birthrate 30, deathrate 15). Unemployment has ravaged the island, and the only remedy so far found is emigration: to Central America for plantation work, and increasingly, of late, to the U.S.A.

Jamaicans raise a few cattle, and fortunately they are increasing the amount of subsistence farming. But a large proportion of the crops is grown for export: sugar, coconuts, coffee, and above all (since the fall in sugar prices), bananas. From Jamaica also comes the celebrated Jamaica rum. The chief imports are foodstuffs and textiles. Exports average $25,000,000 annually, imports $30,000,000, mostly received or supplied by Britain.

Trinidad. One of the most important of the naval bases recently granted to the U.S.A. in the British West Indies is situated in Trinidad. The island is a broken-off section of South America, 1,980 square miles in area, lying in the path of the trade winds, which make its climate tolerable. A land of asphalt and petroleum, it boasts such marvels of nature as the pitch lake from which asphalt is extracted, and such marvels of economics as the disproportionately large production of 3,000,000 tons of petroleum annually. Both petroleum and asphalt are heavily exported, as are also sugar and cocoa. Trade, mostly with Great Britain, normally shows a favorable balance of about $34,000,000, but has greatly increased during the war.

The 506,000 inhabitants of Trinidad are about 60% Negroes, 33% East Indians, and 7% whites (largely French) or of mixed blood with white predominant. Less crowded and poverty-stricken than the Jamaicans, they face less critical problems. Their College for Tropical Agriculture is a center for the experts of the entire British Empire. Their popular arts — such as the Calypso songs — recently swept America.

Barbados. The small island of Barbados (166 square miles), easternmost of the West Indies, is a central cable station and an old British possession with a population perhaps the most patriotic in the far-flung Empire. The people, 93% of whom are Negroes, number 197,000, and are increasing at a rate of more than 10% a decade. They belong, for the most part, to the Church of England; education among them is general. The population density is 3 to a cultivated acre, with 66,000 acres under cultivation.

The country has an intelligent agriculture, which rotates sugar with subsistence crops, a system that should keep trade stable even after the war. Sugar, molasses, and rum constitute the bulk of the exports, which average $6,000,000 a year, as against $9,500,000 for imports. Most of the external trade is with Canada.

Leeward Islands. Of the Leeward Islands — a chain of little islands forming the northeastern arc of the Lesser Antilles — the best known are Antigua, Montserrat, St. Kitts, and Nevis, birthplace of Alexander Hamilton. Some 91,000 people live in the Leewards. Each of the islands has peculiarities of landholding system, types of produce, rainfall, water supply, altitude, and climate. Some, like Antigua, have a serious labor problem; others, like Montserrat, are self-sustaining. But basically the economy of all is based on sugar, sea island cotton, limes, and tomatoes, and all have had great ups and downs in sugar planting, which resulted in shifts to other crops. All enjoy, from November to May, weather ideal for health and energy.

Windward Islands. The small volcanic islands called the Windwards continue the curving chain of the Leewards in a southerly direction, the British islands in the group interspersed with French possessions. The British Windwards have an area of about 900 square miles and some 270,000 inhabitants. Unlike the Leewards, they are not federated, and the various islands, of which the most important are Dominica, St. Lucia, St. Vincent, and Grenada — have widely different economies. These differences are illustrated by the external trade (which all told, amounts to about $9,000,000 annually, mostly with Britain and Canada): St. Vincent has a world monopoly of arrowroot, Grenada grows cocoa and nutmegs, St. Lucia concentrates on sugar and limes, and Dominica caters to the London cockney's penchant for limes, lime juice, and lime oil. The Dominicans are very poor; the St. Lucians are sharecroppers, but a resettlement scheme is being worked out. St. Vincent is a large estates island, Grenada a small proprietors' island. Unfortunately, the chief similarity among these differing economies is the drastic need for improving the condition of the people.

The Bahamas. Most northerly group of the West Indies, the Bahamas lie in the Atlantic off the southeastern coast of Florida. These islands, most of which are low reefs, form a large group, having a total area of 4,404 square miles and a population of 71,500. The Bahamas have been famous since Columbus discovered the New World by setting foot on one of them, Watling Island.

Blockade runners during the Civil War and bootleggers during Prohibition had their hideouts there, and latterly an abdicated king of England has been their Governor. The islands were once celebrated for their sponges, but in recent years the sponge industry has been suspended until a disease in the sponge beds can be cured. With this loss, exports amount to only $1,200,000 annually, as against $6,000,000 worth of imports; but the difference is made up in peacetime by receipts from the tourists who spend in the Bahamas about $4,000,000, or $60 for every inhabitant. During the war, the tourist trade has of course fallen off, but the loss has been made up by the employment of Bahaman laborers in Florida and the construction of airfields on the islands.

History: 1914-1944

British West Indies. These colonies sent contingents of men to fight for Great Britain in World War I. During the first post-war years, boom conditions prevailed in sugar and tropical produce; but when the crash came in 1921, the poverty of the region became so acute that even the subsequent world revival of trade did little to improve matters.

From 1921 to 1941 the West Indies suffered constant economic difficulties and frequent social disturbances. At first, the outflow of labor to Central America, the Panama Canal Zone, Cuba, and the Dominican Republic afforded some relief. But these countries themselves suffered from the depression after 1929. West Indian labor, particularly in Jamaica, faced deficient nourishment and even near-starvation. Nevertheless, the governing authorities remained fairly casual in their attitude to the problem. Since the franchise was limited in effect to the upper and middle class, mostly whites, the demands of the population, though always recognized in competent official reports, were not genuinely satisfied.

Throughout the 1920's, middle-class and workers' groups, called Representative Government Associations, arose and insisted on a democratic franchise. The fact that in the nearby French colonies, Martinique and Guadeloupe, not only was there manhood suffrage but direct representation in the Paris Chamber of Deputies, made British policy, a relic of plantation days, intolerable to the lower-income groups. British official circles stiffened their resistance to the demands of the Associations and finally reduced their influence. Their success in discouraging middle-class movements had its usual concomitant: the moderate and constitutional groups gave way to the radicals.

In 1919, the trade unions began to develop a sizable movement in Trinidad. In 1921 Major Wood (now Lord Halifax) insisted on reform, and in 1924 the authorities reluctantly granted some power to the middle classes in Trinidad, Dominica, and the Windward Islands. But perfunctory gestures of this type were the only response to Lord Halifax's measured recommendations.

In the 1930's the storm broke. A Labor Party formed in Trinidad in 1932 and before long it numbered 120,000 members. A crippled Negro orator, Uriah Butler, found the Trinidad Labor Party too cautious under its leader, Captain Cipriani, the legendary hero of a cycle of "Calypso" songs. Butler created a rival union, whose demands led to the sanguinary uprisings of 1937, which were duplicated throughout the Antilles.

In 1938, the Jamaican trade unions, formed by the leader Bustamante, promulgated revolutionary demands: many lost their lives and hundreds were wounded and jailed in the subsequent rioting. Sir Stafford Cripps arrived from London as an observer. In the ensuing weeks a Peoples' National Party formed and insisted on extensive reforms.

This state of smoldering civil war induced the British Government to name two Royal Commissions, whose reports (1939–1940) recognized the economic and political needs of the people and offered far-reaching recommendations to the London House of Commons. All these proposals were displeasing to the local magnates on the islands, who had previously fought against the union of Trinidad, Dominica, the Windward and Leeward Islands, and Barbados, because of the proposal to enact manhood suffrage. In Barbados, where the franchise was most extensive, only 3% of the people

voted. Recent constitutional changes in Jamaica, however, show true advances.

By the time World War II had begun, the formation of a West Indies' Labor Congress with a Socialistic program was an accomplished fact. But demands for the products of the islands and the building of American bases led to a rapid amelioration of conditions (1940–43), thus deferring the solution of fundamental problems until after the war.

In the Bahama Islands, these problems have not been so severe because of profits from "bootlegging" during the Prohibition era in the U.S.A. and tourist traffic since then. Moreover, the nomination of the ex-King of England as Governor lent prestige to the islands and enhanced local pride. In none of the West Indies has social unrest in any way diminished British patriotism, and the islanders have loyally aided the mother country in World War II.

On March 9, 1942, the U.S.A. and Great Britain formed the Anglo-American Caribbean Commission, which action constituted a far-reaching and important precedent. Social and economic cooperation was stipulated and a six-member commission was formed to advise both contracting governments on labor, housing, health, education, economics, finance, agriculture, and related matters. Later in 1942, the United States section of this commission was made part of the U.S. Department of State.

FRENCH WEST INDIES

Martinique and Guadeloupe. The French West Indies islands, Martinique and Guadeloupe, are both part of the Leeward-Windward chain that forms the eastern end of the Caribbean Sea. They are famous for the charm and volatile culture of the inhabitants, with their picturesque costumes and *biguine* dances — for the eruption of Mt. Pelée on Martinique in 1902, which buried St. Pierre as Vesuvius buried Pompeii — and for the many famous Frenchmen and Frenchwomen who have been born on one or the other of the islands. For a while during the war, Martinique was a storm center, her strategic position and equivocal relations with Vichy putting her in the headlines day after day. The French are devoted to the two islands as the most important remaining possessions of their once-great American empire.

The position of the natives in French law and politics has been relatively high. The colonies, considered a part of France, elected senators and deputies to sit in the parliaments of the Third Republic, and, in general, cultural relations with the mother country have been extremely close. Most of the people are Roman Catholics. Primary education is general among them, but higher education has been largely confined to the professional classes. In industry, as in the vivacity and charm of their native culture, the people enjoy a reputation higher than that of the British islands. Most of the 260,000 inhabitants of Martinique are mulattoes, only 2% white; Guadeloupe's 310,000 are mostly mulattoes also, although there are many Negroes and more French than on Martinique.

Martinique, with an area of 385 square miles, is owned by a thousand or so families, mostly French, but the mass of the people have subsistence plots on mountain inclines. This rugged island seems to be the home of calamities — hurricanes, earthquakes, volcanic eruptions, tidal waves — and, as the population is more than one to an acre, the margin of subsistence is destroyed by such convulsions of nature. Martinique produces rum (the French consider it the best in the world) and grows sugar, with some bananas and other crops. Before the war there was a lively trade with France, who took nearly all exports and supplied two-thirds of imports. The food deficit was made up by importing large quantities of codfish. Guadeloupe has similar products and problems. Between them, they normally exported $17,500,000 and imported $14,000,000 annually.

History: 1914-1944

The French islands. Martinique and Guadeloupe were generally Radical-Socialist in political complexion, but occasionally a political figure like the Rightist, Leméry, would cause an internal political realignment on the basis of charges of corruption in government. In 1940–43, the use of Martinique as a base for Vichy policies and propaganda in the Americas and the hostile attitude of the governor, Admiral Robert, to the U.S.A. afforded several years of complex political drama, which ended in a victory for the partisans of the United Nations.

NETHERLANDS WEST INDIES

Aruba and Curaçao. The Netherlands West Indies consist primarily of a city, Willemstad, on the island of Curaçao in the Caribbean off the coast of Venezuela, and the oil refineries on Aruba, another little island west of Curaçao. Venezuelan petroleum feeds the refineries, oil being 86% of imports and 99% of exports. Before the war the refined oil (to the amount of $185,000,000 annually) went mostly to Britain, the Netherlands, and other European customers.

As for Willemstad, the capital city, it contains 60% of the 100,000 population of the islands. The Dutch are dominant in trade, government, and society in this old and cherished possession, and there is a considerable white population, both Dutch and immigrant. The mass of the people speak a language so mixed that it is a composite jargon, and they are of almost equally mixed blood. The climate of the islands is dry and the trade winds agreeable, despite the heat.

Stakes in the Peace

The British West Indies have not been neglected in British administrative studies or in Royal Commissions of Enquiry. From 1900 on, whether in Socialist-inspired analyses like those of Lord Olivier or in Lord Halifax's (then Major Wood) excellent suggestions, their problems have been studied competently and thoroughly. All reports have agreed that Trinidad requires a more intensive agriculture, Jamaica a more diversified one, and that it also needs outlets for emigration. All have agreed that the landed system everywhere needs to be overhauled and representative government further advanced.

But no recommendations deny that the islands had been developed historically for other markets, such as the broad European market for sugar, that their economy had been based on slavery, and that they have not yet completely adjusted to the new requirements brought about by the emancipation of the slaves. The use of naval and air bases by the U.S.A. has proved a boon to the islands' economy; but until basic changes of crops, land tenure, and citizens' rights are effected, no reforms will cope with the really disturbing issues that habitually recur in these beautiful islands. Fortunately, the Caribbean Commission is a promise that these difficulties will be mastered.

The French West Indies have been commercial auxiliaries of the mother country to such a degree that no matter what the temporary variations, they depend on the recovery of French prosperity. It is difficult to see what internal changes can greatly aid their economy. In Martinique, profitable land holdings are too concentrated; but in Guadeloupe, where the situation is better, the difference in well-being is not spectacular. Perhaps the future development and prosperity of nearby French Guiana may afford some outlet for the teeming and energetic people of this island realm.

The Dutch West Indies are in a state of marked prosperity as a result of refining Venezuelan oil; but it may be noted that even in the great depression of the West Indies (1870–1915), the sturdy Dutch community of the islands somehow kept their trade active. The commercially-minded Dutch do not down easily.

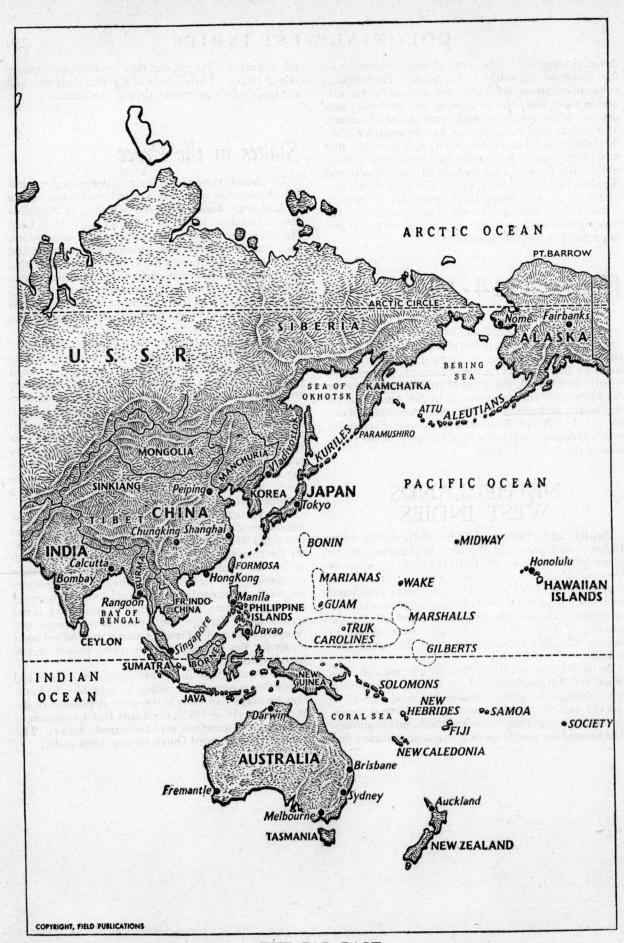

THE FAR EAST

The Far East

AFGHANISTAN

The Land and the People

See maps on pages 281 and 315.

One of the least-known countries, Afghanistan is a mountain stronghold, bordered on two sides by some of the highest mountains on the globe. In the 18th century she owned a vast empire spreading out into Persia and India, which she lost in the ensuing hundred years. Nineteenth-century Afghans, jealous of their independence, tried to prevent foreigners from setting foot on their land. Though today this attitude has changed, the country remains physically almost inaccessible. Three passes, of which the Khyber gateway to India is the best known, are virtually the sole means of entry.

Afghanistan is a monarchy of some 270,000 square miles (as large as Colorado, New Mexico and half of Utah). A landlocked state, she is bounded by the Soviet Uzbek and Turkmenian republics on the north; by Iran (Persia) on the south; and by Baluchistan and the Northwest Frontier Province of India on the south and southeast.

The Land. The country is almost entirely mountainous, and the three chief areas are themselves separated by rugged, almost impassable mountain barriers. South of the Hindu Kush range, facing India, is the region around the capital city Kabul (population 80,000) and Kandahar (60,000), an area containing fruit-growing valleys of surprising fertility. In the west stands a plateau converging on Iran, a fertile, populated region centering about Herat (population 30,000). In the north, a bleak land towers high above the plain of Soviet Turkestan. This region is said to possess rich deposits of iron, lead, coal, gold, silver, and even oil, but thus far there has been no large-scale exploitation of these resources. Sparsely peopled northern Afghanistan has one tongue of land, rising to 24,300 feet: the Pamir Mountains, "the roof of the world." Here human settlements are "low" at 12,000 feet.

With rainfall inadequate, water for irrigation is a key problem in agriculture. Climatic conditions are severe: dust storms are common in the hot summers, and heavy snow and icy cold in the winter, particularly in the north. Daily summer temperatures vary by as much as 30°.

The People. The Afghans are an ancient people, probably of Semitic origin and claiming to be descendants of the Hebrews of the Old Testament. Statistics are not reliable, but the present population is estimated at between 7,000,000 and 12,000,000. In the western part of the country there are some Iranians (Persians). The Afghans are generally tall, wiry, hardy, keen-eyed and bearded, with striking aquiline profiles; and they are usually crack riflemen.

Three languages are spoken: Pushtu (derived from Sanskrit) is the most widespread among the people, especially in the regions nearest India; Persian is the official language of the Court in Kabul and is spoken in the west. In the northern area facing Soviet Asia, the language is a Turkish variant.

Religion and Education. The prevailing religion of the people is Mohammedanism. Most Afghans are Moslems of the Sunni sect, with some adhering to the Shi'iah sect in the west. The *mullahs* (orthodox Mohammedan priests) are extremely powerful, and recent Afghan history has been a stubborn conflict between a few modernizers and this rigid, conservative priesthood.

Numbering some 20,000, the *mullahs* are the judges, teachers, and theologians. Despite their opposition, a few schools have been opened recently and a university has been founded at Kabul. Though no figures are available, illiteracy is extremely high and education primitive. Only in Kabul do secondary schools exist.

The Nation's Economy

Agriculture. Fruit, the staple food of the country, is grown in abundance in the high valleys around Kabul, Kandahar, and Herat. In no other land do fruits play such a preponderant rôle in diet. The leading items are: pears, peaches, apples, quinces, apricots, cherries, plums, pomegranates, grapes, figs, and mulberries. Much of the fruit crop is preserved for winter consumption or marketed as a leading export. There are many nut-bearing trees; and the medicinal products of the asafoetida and castor oil plants are grown for commercial purposes.

Considering the primitiveness of their methods, the inadequate rainfall, and the general rockiness of the terrain, the Afghans are remarkable farmers. In their use of fodder, alternated with barley and carrots, they show a native understanding of the soil, capable of direction along modern lines. But the country's agriculture is not likely to improve until the general level of education materially rises.

In animal husbandry, the fat-tailed sheep is emphasized. Its white fleece is prized for wool and its tail furnishes a grease used as a substitute for butter. The annual wool clip is 6,800 tons.

Mining, Industry, and Communications. The true extent of Afghanistan's mineral resources is unknown. Though oil, iron, coal, copper, and silver exist, none is produced in appreciable quantities. The rare lapis lazuli, here found in its finest state, figures as an export.

Industry is negligible; the state owns the few workshops for matches, boots, and buttons as well as the few factories for small arms at Kabul.

With no railroads, few satisfactory roads, and rivers useful only for sending timber downstream, camels and ponies provide the chief means of transportation. No nation of comparable size and population has such deficient communications.

Finance. One of the poorest countries on earth, Afghanistan has an estimated national income of $22,000,000, or $3 per person. If this figure is correct, China is wealthier per capita, despite her enormous population.

The unit of currency, the *afghani*, is worth 9¢. The Afghan king relies on an annual revenue of about $13,000,000, much of which is contributed by customs duties, and a part by tithes on farms — 5% of gross income on unirrigated and 10% on irrigated farms. Money is not universally used by the people; a large share of these taxes is paid in goods. Since many of the outlying tribes still resent the centralized monarchy, hostages alternate with bribes to force them to continue their contributions to the state.

Foreign Trade. The country trades chiefly with neighboring India, the Soviet Union, and Iran. Chief exports are: fruits, nuts, spices, carpets (expertly woven by craftsmen), wools, and skins. Leading imports are: textiles, machinery, gasoline, kerosene, and sugar. Imports were about $12,900,000 annually, exports $10,500,000 (total trade, $3 per person).

The U.S.A. has begun to take an interest in Afghanistan's economy and is now represented diplomatically at Kabul.

History: 1914-1944

During World War I, Habibullah, Emir of Afghanistan, flirted for a time with German proffers but remained neutral. After his death by assassination in 1919, his nephew Amanullah, succeeded to the throne instead of the late Emir's brother.

To vindicate Turkey, seat of the Caliphate and hence sacred to Mohammedans, Amanullah declared war on Great Britain (1919). The British speedily defeated the Afghans, but in view of the Bolshevik revolution in Asiatic Russia, immediately to the north of Afghanistan, Britain was lenient to the defeated nation. By the Treaty of 1921, the British generously treated Afghanistan as a true sovereign state, but insisted that Russian consulates be withdrawn from areas outside of Russia's "sphere of influence."

The Afghans, loath to antagonize Soviet Russia, carried on subtle and eventually satisfactory negotiations with both sides. Amanullah, now friendly with his two great neighbors, the Russians and the British in India, turned to internal reform.

The example of Kemal Pasha in Turkey inflamed his imagination and he, too, sought to pursue a policy of "westernization." He multiplied diplomatic contacts with the outside world, established telegraph and radio facilities, and began to improve the backward road system. Then he visited Europe, where he realized more keenly than ever the backwardness of his country. The *mullahs* (Moslem priests), however, incited the people to revolt against this modernizer. Amanullah abdicated in January 1929, and before the year was out, the conservative Nadir Shah became Emir. He in turn was assassinated in 1933 and his son, Mohammed Zahir, ascended the perilous throne.

The new Emir faced continual disorders on the northeastern border, but the country was now better organized and its Soviet-trained air force was a new factor in quelling tribal rebellion.

The outbreak of war in 1939 led to ceaseless intrigues by the Axis representatives — the Germans, Japanese, and Italians — who fed the old flame of anti-British sentiment. Throughout 1942 they exploited the joint Soviet-British occupation of Iran as a pretext for stirring up the Afghan tribes. The Court, however, remained pro-British and preserved neutrality in the war.

Nevertheless, until Turkey, her model, broke with the Axis (1944), Afghanistan remained an area to be closely watched; but except for insignificant forays by some hill tribes, no hostile acts took place, even when the Japanese in 1943 advanced to Kohima in northeastern India.

Stakes in the Peace

Afghanistan's poverty, exceptional even for her part of the world, is related to the absence of communications. If this is remedied, most of the roads would lead into Iran and Soviet Russia, so as to serve the most populous regions. Such a project has not hitherto met with British sponsorship.

Since the Teheran Agreement (December 1943), which diminishes national rivalries in that area, and the bilateral Anglo-Soviet guarantee of Iranian independence, the way seems open to a more rapid development of Afghanistan. But not until the power of the *mullahs* diminishes will it be possible to modernize the country. These Moslem priests have seen in nearby Samarkand, in the Soviet Union, that modern techniques in industry and the training of youth in science are serious obstacles to the priesthood's historic primacy.

Hence, the best solution for Afghanistan would seem to lie in (a) the conviction that future dominion status for India precludes imperialist designs on the part of Britain; (b) the realization on the part of the ordinary Afghan that foreign capital is not *per se* inimical to his independence, as shown by the example of Iran's genuine independence and progress; (c) the stimulation of trade with the bordering Soviet Union, without attempts by foreign agents at Kabul to impede this trade.

The slow working of these three factors can stimulate economic progress and thus, by example, refute the retrograde arguments of the *mullahs*. If better communications, increased capital, and more technical knowledge are made available, Afghanistan might reach a high level of economic well-being. With prosperity and a regular state revenue, the passion for arms and armed forays would tend to diminish.

BURMA

The Land and the People

Can't you 'ear their paddles chunkin' from Rangoon to Mandalay?

wrote Kipling, poet of empire — and for a long time about all the English-speaking world knew about Burma was that it was

Somewhere east of Suez, where the best is like the worst,
Where there aren't no Ten Commandments an' a man can raise
a thirst . . .

Then came the drama of the Burma Road, its building, its hopeless defense, its slow re-winning. Even yet Americans tend to think of Burma in terms of "Uncle Joe" Stilwell, Wingate's Raiders, and the road to China, rather than in terms of itself.

The Land. For a long time Burma was considered a part of India, but before the Japanese occupation she had become a separate unit in the British Empire. Burma is bounded on the northwest by India, on the north by China, on the east by China and Thailand (Siam), and on the south and west by the Bay of Bengal. Her strategic position has made the country a chief theater of the Japanese War.

With an area of 261,000 square miles, Burma about equals Texas in size; her population may have reached 17,000,000. Trade moves (in peacetime) up and down the Salween and Irrawaddy rivers, which flow southward to the Bay of Bengal, in particular from Rangoon, the principal port, up the Irrawaddy to Mandalay and thence along the Burma Road to China. Monsoons drench the country with rain from May to October; the rest of the year is dry.

In north Burma mountains alternate with jungles. In the hilly eastern district (called the Shan States), ruled by independent princelings, the little commonwealths nestle in valleys overshadowed by high, forest-clad hills. But most of the people live in lower Burma, where the wide, low river-basins make an ideal rice country. In a small territory to the south are many tin mines.

The People. The Burmese form five-sixths of the population, with Chinese, Hindus (about 1,000,000), and some 2,000,000 Shans making up most of the other sixth. The Shans stand outside the main stream of Burmese culture. For the rest of Burma, the birthrate (32 per thousand) has been about the same as India's; the deathrate, once lower than India's, has recently risen to 23. Infant mortality is enormous — always over 200 and in recent years as high as 223.

The Burmese are a basically Mongolian people, speaking a language allied to the Tibetan, but their darker skin and other variants show that they have absorbed an aboriginal population. They resemble the Indians in nothing — not in origin, speech, or religion — and resent being classified as part of India. They are a mercurial people, with a hairspring base for laughter — or for homicide. Exceptionally refined and courteous, they yet refuse to accept defeat or submit to injustice. In contrast to many Asiatic peoples, they give high honor to women, ranking the statues of bygone queens with those of their consorts. They have an old and beautiful literature, and are gifted in the arts, especially architecture. But their dislike for trade and modern industry has meant that economic dominance in the country has passed to the Chinese and Indians, and of course (before the war) to the British.

Religion and Education. The people are Buddhists: Burma's population is about 84% Buddhist (almost all Burmese). Moslems number 4%, Hindus 4%, Christians over 2%, animists 3%, unknown 3%. The converts to Christianity have been non-Burmese: few peoples have been less hospitable than the Burmese to Christian teachings. Even the usually successful Moslem missionary has failed to dent Burmese Buddhism.

The spiritual head of every village is a monk, and the monasteries are the schools and the centers of communal life. Every town and every hilltop has its pagoda.

The monastery-schools have taught most of the people the "three R's," and about 800,000 children go normally to state-sponsored schools. Burma has also about a dozen institutions of higher learning. The high rate in literacy in Burma contrasts strikingly with the very low rate in neighboring India.

The Nation's Economy

Agriculture. Over 80% of the people are farmers, and 60% of the land under cultivation is sown to rice, of which 9,000,000 tons are produced annually. Other crops — groundnuts, sesame, cotton, and rubber — have been important factors in Oriental trade, and millet and beans furnish Burma herself with secondary subsistence foods. The water-buffalo, the only important farm animal, works in the rich rice fields.

Mining and Oil. British capital developed large mineral and oil resources in pre-war Burma, so that she was producing an annual average of 1,200,000 tons of oil, a sixth of the world's tungsten, 3% of its tin ore, 5% of its lead, 3% of its zinc — the last two percentages being the highest of any in Asia — and various lesser mineral products. Burma also exported teakwood, and was famous for her rubies.

The country's few factories, employing only some 86,000, were largely smelters, oil refineries, and rice-polishing mills — all related to primary production. The chief variegated manufactures are handicrafts.

Finance. The currency unit is the *rupee*, worth about 30¢. Before the Japanese occupation, Burmese budgets called for about $55,000,000 a year. The public debt and most private investments are held in Britain. But the only finance known to the masses centers in the Indian moneylenders.

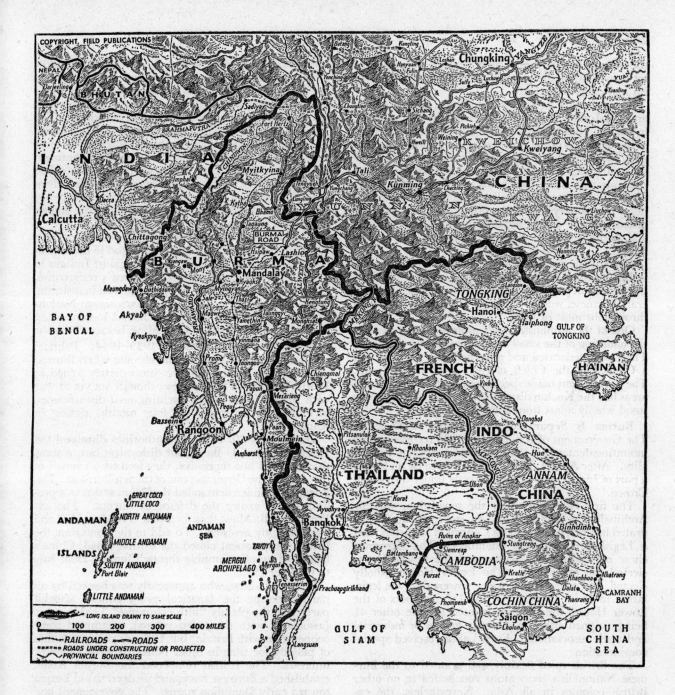

Foreign Trade. In peacetime, Burma was the world's leading rice exporter: a third of her crop was consumed abroad. Her total exports averaged about $160,000,000, her imports about $82,000,000, the two-to-one ratio of exports indicating large payments abroad or reinvestments of trade profits within the country. India took 63% and the rest of the British Empire 32% of the exports, and the Empire supplied 70% of the imports. The Japanese conquest ended most external trade.

History: 1914-1944

During World War I, Burma was administratively part of India, and the Burmese were not greatly involved in the Allied military effort. On the contrary, extensive British and native forces were kept busy pacifying the remote north and northeast hill regions. Unrest was frequent among these native tribes, some of whom practiced human sacrifice well into the 20th century.

By the end of the war, tribal disturbances were overcome, and the country that had been a theater of violence now settled down to orderly administrative life. The Government of India Act of 1919 constituted Burma a full province of India, instead of a sub-province, and in 1922 Sir Harcourt Butler became her first Governor.

Burma's new status, after 1922, permitted the ruling authorities to free themselves of the demands of the Indian Treasury and thus concentrate on purely Burmese requirements. The Government established schools and Rangoon University opened its doors. These improvements helped raise the cultural level of the country in a very short time, yet they were opposed by many Nationalist groups, mainly because the British had originated them.

The resistance to the British in India, led by Gandhi and the Indian National Congress, had repercussions in Burma. But here it assumed a local character, most of the demands of the Burmese being narrowly nationalist, without that supporting economic philosophy that enhanced Gandhi's popularity with the poorer peasants and small merchants of India. (See *India, History*.) Burmese nationalism also had its chauvinist side: reactionary Buddhist priests directed popular resentment as much against the minority Chinese and Indians in the country as against the ruling British.

The British granted a much more liberal franchise in Burma than in India, permitting women, who had the minimum property qualifications, to vote. In general, Burmese women enjoyed a higher status than throughout most of Asia.

One of the administration's most onerous tasks was the handling of the small Shan States in the northeast. These were federated and governed with the advice of a Council of the Chiefs of each small tribal group. The government made special arrangements to control areas like the Kachin districts, whose aggressive people stood wholly apart from Burmese culture.

Burma Is Separated from India: 1937–1939. The Government of India Act of 1935 recognized the mounting demands of the Burmese for separate nationality. After April 1, 1937, Burma was to be no longer a part of India but governed directly under the British Crown.

The first Governor, after the separation, was Sir Archibald Cochrane. The new government, inaugurated in 1937, consisted of a Council of Ministers, and a Legislature with two chambers. The Governor chose one-half of the Senate and the Lower House elected the other half. The Lower House, wholly elected, had considerably wider powers than the legislature in India proper. Of the 132 members of the Lower House, the Burmese elected 91, the other 41 being assigned either to minority groups or industrial and trade associations. Even Labor received special consideration.

The British ruled flexibly and granted to the Burmese Nationalists concessions vouchsafed to no other British colonies in all Asia. Nevertheless, the extreme Nationalists, themselves divided into several factions, triumphed in the elections.

The Nationalist groups regarded British concessions with less enthusiasm than the Indians reacted to their proportionately smaller gains. The sect of Buddhist priests, called *pongyis*, formed into secret conspiratorial groups, their priestly yellow robes cloaking ambitious pro-Japanese schemes. They were reactionaries, resenting, above all, liberal currents such as the Socialist ideas of Nehru in India. The *pongyis* called for a campaign of civil disobedience in which all but a few idealists participated.

The Nationalists now split into (1) Pan-Asiatic groups, who were anti-European but not Burmese exclusivists; (2) anti-Westerners, who were basically anti-British but did not favor collaboration with other Asiatics; and (3) fierce Nationalists, who demanded the expulsion of the Indian, Chinese, and Moslem immigrants from other lands. The Nationalist middle classes, increasingly unruly, enlisted the support of the Burmese laborers, whose low standards of living were, however, higher than those of the Indian workers and who resented the immigration of Indians. The Nationalists also won over the Burmese peasants whose single object of hatred was the alien usurer of whatever race. There was also widespread popular resentment of corrupt native officials, whom the Nationalists called British puppets. Thus Burmese nationalism, riven with factionalism, had little in common with the nationalism of the Chinese Kuomintang or the Indian National Congress.

The Nationalist Premier, U Ba Maw, faced extensive strikes in 1937 in industry, transport, and in the educational institutions. Finally, rioting against Indians in 1938 led to 200 deaths and U Ba Maw's resignation. A compromise candidate, U Pu, succeeded in restoring temporary order, but in 1940 a more insistent Nationalist, U Saw, a man with more finesse in concealing treason than the fanatical U Ba Maw, became Premier.

Burma in World War II: 1939–1944. Political and religious riots had become chronic when Burma, as part of the British Empire, immediately joined in World War II. The Japanese, though not yet at war with Britain, were busy fomenting civil disturbances, including for example, the four months rioting in Rangoon.

On January 20, 1940, the authorities dismissed the Home Minister, U Ba Pe, for disloyalty; but to show that this was not repressive, they formed a council of three to aid the Governor, one of them a Burmese. The Burmese Premier demanded dominion status as a preliminary to assure the defense of Burma. The ex-Premier, U Ba Maw, then formed a "Freedom *bloc*" and was promptly arrested. To add to the confusion, the British Government closed the Burma Road, China's lifeline of supplies running through Burma, from July to October 1940.

Premier U Saw, who apparently was backed by all parties except the fanatical pro-Japanese Miochit party and the plainly "fifth columnist" Thakin party (associated with the *pongyi* priests), attempted some cooperation with Britain; but U Saw's policy was that of playing for time in order better to serve Japanese interests. The British re-opened the Burma Road, established a Burmese navy, and pledged to aid Burma toward early Dominion status. The government had attenuated some of the effects of the war by instituting price controls, checking profiteers, and guaranteeing the export of key products.

But nothing availed to down the swelling chorus of popular criticism. The British spared no effort in flattering Burmese national pride, and the final act of the departing Governor, Sir Archibald Cochrane, was to consecrate Burmese autonomy by unfurling the new national flag (1941). His successor, Sir Reginald Dorman-Smith, manifested considerable faith in the Burmese, even when the British military authorities considered their hostility menacing. In July 1941 the Government, yielding to Nationalist pressure, passed an Indian Restrictions Act, which was so offensive to the Indians as to evoke protests from Gandhi in India.

When the Pacific War broke out in December 1941, the extent of pro-Japanese fifth-column activity in Burma became flagrantly clear. Premier U Saw was arrested in January 1942 for having contact with the enemy. As soon as the Japanese entered Burma, the fifth column betrayed the location of airfields, served as guides to the Japanese, engaged in extensive guerrilla warfare against the United Nations, and murdered and pillaged Chinese, Indian, and British residents. Moreover, they trapped retreating British and Indian troops — their venom against the latter led to frightful massacres.

Progressive Nationalists, aghast at these manifestations, openly espoused the United Nations cause, many of them leaving for the temporary seat of government in Simla in India. Sir Paw Tun, pro-Allied, became Premier-in-exile and surprised the pro-Japanese elements in Burma by his considerable following.

The Japanese inflicted a decisive defeat on the United Nations forces in Burma. The heartbreaking task of evacuating some 40,000 Indian civilians had to be undertaken to save them from the fury of pro-Japanese elements, and this complicated the task of military evacuation. The Commander-in-Chief, General Sir Harold Alexander, stated that the Burmese people as a whole aided the enemy, but the Governor insisted that this was a military impression and not warranted by the facts.

The spring of 1942 saw the full-fledged Japanese occupation of Burma, nearly all of which was speedily conquered by Japanese troops. In 1943 a bitter though indecisive contest raged in upper Burma, while in 1944 the Allied forces in Southeast Asia, now under the supreme command of Lord Louis Mountbatten, won important victories on the Burma-India and Burma-China frontiers. The American General Joseph Stilwell, driven out of Burma in 1942, led a joint Chinese-American force against the Japanese.

Meanwhile, the ultra-Nationalists, who had openly espoused the Japanese cause after December 1941, cooperated freely with the Japanese forces of occupation. U Ba Maw formed a government under Japanese control, similar to the arrangement in Manchuria (Manchukuo). Since his group held only 14 out of 132 seats in the Burmese Parliament, the latter was suspended, and in March 1943, U Ba Maw and his military aides visited the Mikado in Tokyo.

The Japanese "requested" the Burmese to cede two Shan States to Thailand, a request to which they acceded with alacrity (1943). On August 1, 1943, Burma proclaimed her "independence" and declared war on the U.S.A. and Great Britain. The Japanese dissolved the Burmese Independence Army and the Nationalists, disgruntled and surly, soon discovered the value of Japanese promises, as the Japanese Ambassador openly directed their country's policy.

Stakes in the Peace

Burma has lost the British investments of three decades in factories, docks, oil installations, and mining equipment. Plunder, war, and neglect have thrown her back to the days of pre-capitalism. The elimination of the two most enterprising commercial groups, the Indians and the Chinese, has forced her reversion to a primitive agricultural economy. The hatred of Indians and Chinese will make her situation difficult, once the Japanese are defeated.

Burma's dominion status may now lag behind India's since there is no clear evidence as to how much mature support there is for an ordered commonwealth that can cooperate in any Asiatic regional scheme. If the Governor's optimism is warranted, then the liberal and progressive elements in ruined Burma will have a prestige they have never previously enjoyed.

At any rate, the reactionary, fanatical Nationalists will be so discredited in defeat that the progressive Nationalists will have a splendid opportunity to win the confidence of their own people and of the world. If they are successful, they may soon lead this charming and intellectually febrile people to a truly representative government with higher living standards and well-being for the population as a whole.

CHINA

The Land and the People

For thousands of years this vast land nurtured a great civilization and a teeming population. Variously known as the "Celestial Kingdom," "The Middle Kingdom," and "Cathay," China lived for many centuries in self-imposed isolation from the Western world, which as late as 1910 thought of her as an inert, helpless giant. But this giant is now rising, and, once possessed of Western techniques, can look forward to a future of unlimited possibilities. China's emergence as a leading world power in our time is bound to transform the history of Asia and of the world.

In continuous area she is second only to the Soviet Union. China Proper, consisting of 24 provinces, covers over 2,900,000 square miles, almost the size of the continental United States. But if we add the regions known as Outer China, we get a total area of approximately 4,500,000 square miles, 50% larger than the U.S.A. Outer China includes Manchuria (occupied by the Japanese, who call it Manchukuo, 503,000 square miles), Sinkiang or Chinese Turkestan (about 600,000 square miles), and Tibet (about 460,000 square miles). In the following discussion,

China signifies China Proper, unless otherwise stated.

Although there has never been a satisfactory census of China, the generally accepted population figure is about 400,000,000. One human being in every five on earth is Chinese. Adding the estimated 40,000,000 inhabitants of Manchuria, the total Chinese population is the highest on the face of the earth.

In this treatment we shall deal in the main with China as she was before the series of aggressions by Japan which, beginning with the seizure of Manchuria in 1931, have since lopped off large sections of China's national territory. The Japanese rule Occupied China through a puppet government located in Nanking.

Most of China lies in the north temperate zone, only a small portion of the south being within the tropic zone. Northern China has limited rainfall, most of it in summer, and a climate and growing season similar to the northern U.S.A. Much of this area is without grass or trees, and frequent dust storms cause it to resemble the American "dust bowl." The prevailing color of this countryside is brown. The Chinese practice irrigation extensively because of the inadequacy of rainfall. Chief crops are wheat, millet, a sorghum grain called *kaoliang*, and soya beans.

By contrast, the central and southern regions, especially those in the Yangtze river valley and Pearl river delta, are prevailingly green. Rainfall is abundant here, the growing season lasts nine months, gardens and orchards abound, and rice fields lie everywhere — in the lowlands and along the rivers. Here winters are mild, summer humid and quite hot; and here are also the densest centers of population and trade. The Tsin Ling Mountains are generally considered an approximate dividing line between north and south China.

Much of China is hilly or mountainous, so that not more than a seventh of the area of her 24 provinces is cultivable. Four clearly defined agricultural regions exist, each closely connected with fertile river valleys: (1) in the north, the Yellow River basin, where China is most ancient and whence the civilization we now call "Chinese" was diffused to the multitudes of people who have made it their own; (2) the Yangtze River valley, the richest and most fertile of all, center of cotton, silk, and rice cultivation, and culminating in the Nanking-Shanghai area near and on the coast, in pre-war days the most active center of population, industry, and commerce; (3) in the south, the hilly Canton district with a network of rivers, in the valleys of which subtropical products like tea, rice, and choice fruits are grown; and (4) in the southwest, the "red basin" of Szechwan province, a region of silk, cotton, and rice, where the national government is now building cities and industries and fostering agriculture, because this area has remained outside the orbit of Japanese penetration. These four river areas constitute nearly all of economic China (except for the newly developed frontier land of Manchuria, now in Japanese hands).

China is a land of mountains as well as plains and river valleys. Shantung province (northeast) has mountain ranges whose mineral wealth early attracted the empire-hungry Japanese. All through central and south China extend broken or isolated mountain ranges or hills. In the southwest is the remote upland of Tibet, the highest compact area on earth, and the inspiration for James Hilton's tale of "Shangri-La." On the west, in Sinkiang province, the towering Tien Shan mountains divide China from the Soviet Union, while to the north the vast Mongolian steppe contains the Gobi Desert, one of the immense "land oceans" of the world.

Communications over this vast expanse are poor. Railroad mileage is under 10,000 miles, one of the worst showings in the world, slightly more than in little Czechoslovakia and less than 4% of the U.S.A. Roads, too, are undeveloped, with a mileage under 2% that of the U.S.A. Animal and human labor remain the favorite means of transport. Rivers, however, have played a vital rôle for centuries, both as arteries of travel and commerce and as sources of irrigation. Two of China's rivers, the Yellow and the Yangtze, are among the greatest in the world. The Yellow River, called "China's Sorrow," because its frequent changes of course have brought devastation and death to millions, is 2,700 miles long; but it is navigable only by small craft, owing to its silted bed. The Yangtze river, 3,200 miles long, is navigable by sizable ships for over 1,600 miles. Canals, too, are features of the Chinese landscape; and the Grand Canal, built centuries ago to carry grain from Hangchow to Peiping (Peking) over 500 miles away, was one of the marvels of pre-industrial engineering.

China has large cities, but they are not numerous for so populous a country. The chief ones are: Shanghai (population about 3,500,000); Peiping, formerly Peking (1,500,000); Tientsin (1,300,000); Nanking, former capital of Free China and now the capital of the Japanese-controlled régime (1,100,000); Hankow (778,000); and Canton (861,000). The capital of Free China is now Chungking in the southwest, which has increased from 635,000 in 1936 to around 2,000,000. Because of the flight of refugees from the Japanese, similar remarkable population increases have also occurred in other cities deep in the interior, such as Chengtu, Kweilin, and Kunming. In Manchuria the chief cities are Hsinking, the capital (415,000); Mukden (863,000); Harbin (517,000). The seaport of Dairen (formerly Dalny), located on the Kwantung Leased Territory, has over 550,000 inhabitants.

China's mineral resources, though extensive, have not been adequately exploited. The chief coal and iron deposits are in the northern provinces: high-grade coal in Hopei, Shensi, Shantung, and Honan, and iron in Hupeh and Anhwei. Moreover, southern Manchuria possesses some of the richest coal and iron mines in Asia, of which the Japanese have taken full advantage. Other minerals include tin in the southwest (Yunnan province), tungsten in Kiangsi, antimony in Hunan. A little oil has been found in Szechwan in the southwest and Kansu in the northwest, but the total amount seems negligible. Potential water-power is large, but China utilizes less than 1% of these resources. The principal forests are in northern and eastern Manchuria, in the far west beyond Szechwan, and in the hill country of south China. Much of the formerly rich timber-land of central and north China has been completely deforested.

The People. The most striking feature of the

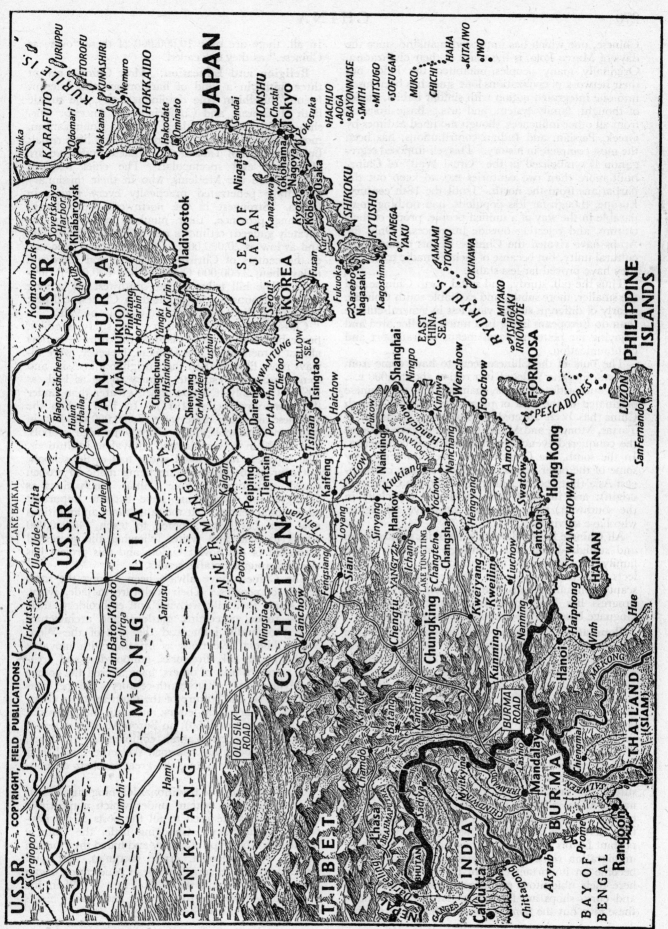

Chinese, one which has impressed mankind since the days of Marco Polo, is the unity of their civilization. Originally many peoples inhabited the land, but their network of civilizations long since has been fused into one integrated nation with similar habits, modes of thought, family system, and arts. Basic isolation from all other influences, though modified at times by Greek, Persian, and Indian contributions, has been the most complete in history. This self-imposed segregation is symbolized in the "Great Wall" of China, built more than two centuries B.C. to keep out the barbarians from the north. Until the 18th century, Europe, though far less populous, had nothing comparable in the way of a unified people, proud of their culture, and rejecting outside influences. Only the Arabs have rivaled the Chinese in this capacity for cultural unity, but because of their nomadic traditions they have proved far less stable.

Thus the tall, sturdy, and stolid north Chinese and the smaller, more subtle, and excitable south Chinese, clearly of different stocks, vary less in general culture than do Europeans living in a much smaller area and enjoying far better physical means of transport and communication.

The bulk of the Chinese seem to have come from the west into the Yellow River region about 3,000 B.C. Some authorities, however, maintain that the Chinese originated in the area of present-day China. North China has been affected by numerous invasions — Tartar, Mongol, and Manchu — but in each instance the conquered eventually absorbed their conquerors. In the south, the Chinese have been influenced by some of the older peoples of Hindu culture in southeast Asia (but not the Annamites, who are Chinese in origin); and in the remote highlands, especially in the southwest, there are some primitive aborigines who have survived.

All Chinese have yellow or olive skin, slanted eyes, and straight black hair. Strongly attached to the family, they regard old age with respect. Many dialects have flourished in this large country with such scanty communications, but in recent years decisive progress has been made in spreading a standard language based on a popular Mandarin dialect.

Population Prospects. It is difficult to assess the rate of growth of China's population because statistics are unreliable. But this much we know: the birthrate is very high and the deathrate, because of poor sanitation, insufficient doctors, widespread diseases, is also very high. The population is undoubtedly growing and will continue to grow in the next generation, despite wars, famines, and floods. Proof of this growth is to be found in the prolific emigration of Chinese: in Manchuria they have been pioneers, both as cowboys and settlers; in Thailand they are active in business and trade; in Malaya they now constitute the largest single group, outnumbering the native Malays; in the Dutch East Indies they have become leading merchants; in many American countries, like Peru and Cuba, they have become important factors in the community and, were it not for immigration restrictions, they would probably have become an important element in the U.S.A. Even here their ubiquitous restaurants, humble laundries, and curio shops are familiar to Americans, though these give but the faintest idea of Chinese versatility.

In all, there are over 10,000,000 of these "overseas Chinese," as they are called.

Religion and Education. Most Chinese accept three faiths in a kind of harmonious and tolerant fusion: Buddhism (the dominant note), the mystic faith of Taoism, and Confucianism. Ancestor worship distinguishes all three faiths. Confucianism, more a code of ethics than a religion, has little ritual; but the rituals of Taoism and Chinese Buddhism are often rich and spectacular. The chief religious minority are the Moslems, who in their missionary zeal have penetrated practically every region in China. Strongest in the northwest, especially in Sinkiang province, their numbers cannot be accurately gauged: estimates run as high as 80,000,000 and as low as 20,000,000. China has long been one of the centers of Christian missions, and there are today about 2,600,000 Catholics and 500,000 Protestants. The hill tribes in the southwest are among the rare groups not assimilated to Chinese culture; and among them pagan nature-worship prevails.

Classical Chinese education — the study of ethics, proverbial wisdom, and classical literature — is now almost a memory. The Chinese, however, were always more literate than their neighbors in Asia, and some authorities estimate literacy to be as high as 50%. Certainly it is now much greater than under the monarchy (before 1911). In 1937, when the Japanese attacked, there were 17,000,000 children in government schools, fully 600,000 in high schools, and 42,000 in universities and equivalent institutions. The Japanese have closed about half of the schools, but courageous attempts are being made to reopen closed institutions in Free China. Such cities as Chengtu and Chungking have become important educational centers. At the same time, an ambitious new plan has been adopted to teach 140,000,000 adults to read and write, following the successful precedent of the Soviet Union, and this project has already brought notable results.

The Chinese have always been among the most artistic of peoples. Their sculpture in jade, ivory, and stone, their silk weaving and embroidery, their prints, robes, porcelains, gardens, and architecture have profoundly influenced the arts of the West. Such Chinese inventions as printing with movable blocks, paper, ink, fireworks, gunpowder, and artillery, among a host of others, have altered the course of civilization. Eighteenth-century Europe was fascinated by the culture of the Chinese, their cities, bridges, fine arts, and letters; and until the Industrial Revolution (about 1760), no European man of letters considered his civilization comparable to theirs. Their lyric poetry has charmed Westerners, and their philosophers rank among the great teachers of mankind.

Chinese worship of traditional learning culminated in the Mandarin system, under which competitive examinations were used to fill the posts of the governing bureaucracy. Changing little, the Chinese wanted no other type of society and hated the "foreign devils" whose alcohol, crude costumes, and loud voices disgusted them as European penetration began to make itself felt in the 19th century. When the West applied science to industry and war, China's ancient isolation was threatened.

Today the once tradition-ridden Chinese are most impassioned for change: the pigtail, traditional dress, and bound feet of women have been abandoned. In hundreds of colleges, factories, and offices, young Chinese men and women seek to be modern. They study the sciences, abandon the abacus for the adding-machine, and turn from a centuries-old rigidity to a maximum of social change. So far these new tendencies have affected only a minority, but their ready acceptance shows how speedily a people can alter.

The Nation's Economy

Agriculture. China is basically an agrarian country, with more than 70% of her people living from farming. It has been said that in China every acre that can possibly yield crops is cultivated. Hill-terracing, extensive irrigation, and tending of the rice-fields have gone on for centuries. But farms are too small: most are under three acres and the entire family must toil all day to make these three acres provide a bare livelihood. In cash, most farm families, averaging 5 persons, earn about $50 a year! Crops are usually marketed through nearby usurers, middlemen, or merchants; or, where the peasant is a tenant or sharecropper, through the local landlords or "gentry."

The total arable land is not large for the immense population: the best estimate gives 400,000 square miles (excluding Manchuria), or about 1,000 people per square mile of cultivable land. But with a yield per acre about 25% less than the American, with scanty communications, primitive farm implements, and poor seed and fertilizer, the Chinese farmer is impoverished. And whenever too much rain falls or dust storms arise, he hovers on the brink of famine. Moreover, taxes and rents are heavy, whether imposed in cash or in kind, and many small farmowners and tenants are victims of moneylenders who charge exorbitant rates of interest.

Though every inch of soil in the arable regions is precious and space for roads or even houses begrudged, the Chinese are not able to raise enough to feed themselves. Food must be imported in considerable amounts, especially rice, wheat, and fish. China's agriculture is still largely feudal in land relations and backward in techniques.

The principal crop is rice which, with millet, is the staple food of the people. In good years rice production has been some 58,000,000 tons, or over 55% of the world crop. Cotton production is high, about half of India's and in good years about a fifth of U.S.A. production. Wheat is increasing and the crop has sometimes equaled the American. Barley production is about a third of wheat, and corn (mostly for fodder) and sugar beets are gaining. In peanuts, China produces a third of the world supply; in soya beans, a sixth of world supply. Including the Manchurian output, China supplies most of this item which is useful for food, fertilizer, and explosives. Tobacco production rivals that of India and the U.S.A., but tea is only one-eighth the figure for India and Ceylon. Most Chinese tea is used for home consumption, since it is the favorite beverage of the people.

Though China's silk production was once almost a world monopoly, as the phrase *crêpe de Chine* implies, today, though silk cultivation remains important, it is a tenth of Japan's. Wool at 60,000 tons is significant; and China is the principal source of human hair that is sold on the market. Tung oil (for paints and varnishes) is a leading item for export, while Chinese fruits, such as ginger, lychee nuts, almonds, tangerines, and blood oranges (Chinese innovations) are abundant.

Industry and Mining. China has the foundations for heavy industry: iron and coal. But political difficulties, poor communications, long distances from the centers of industry, and high transport costs have kept production at fairly low levels. Iron ore production has reached 615,000 tons (only 6% of French production), but the reserves are fair and output could be greatly augmented. The iron industry in Shansi is the oldest in the world.

Iron deposits in Manchuria exceed those in China Proper. Coal output has reached 25,000,000 tons in China Proper and 15,000,000 in Manchuria, most of it good coking coal, ideal for industry. Other products are also expanding: cement is now a tenth of Japanese production; steel, though it reaches only 50,000 tons in China, has been expanded by the Japanese in Manchuria to 450,000 tons. Tin production is about an eighth of Malaya's, the world leader. China normally produces half the world's antimony and more than a third of its tungsten, but the dislocations of the war have reduced these figures substantially. Gold production is very small, oil deposits negligible, and water-power resources scarcely exploited.

For many years China was the least industrialized of the large nations. By every criterion — per capita investment, total investment, hourly horsepower and output per worker — her position was the lowest. Before 1937, about 2,500,000 workers were engaged in industry, most of them in the so-called "Treaty ports" on the coast, where Western nations enjoyed special rights and concessions. The leading industrial center was Shanghai, and the leading industries were cotton spinning, tobacco, and consumers goods for local sale (for example, matches, paper, and shoes). The only sizable industry was textiles, and the figure of 5,000,000 spindles in cotton manufacturing rivaled that in the leading textile nations.

Since the Japanese invasion of 1937, there has been a mass exodus of men and machines to China's west and southwest. Many factories, mostly small workshops with a few employees, have been set up. While their output is small, the variety of techniques learned is remarkable; even complex machine-tools are made quickly and with precision. This development holds promise for China's industrial future, but for some time to come industry must remain in its infancy, with light industry predominating.

Finance and Wealth. Even in her best years, China was wretchedly poor in financial resources. Per capita income in 1930, her most prosperous year, was calculated at $11. The most backward European countries show figures at least five times as large; while the Western nations so far outdistance her that there exists small basis for comparison. And yet China has had a fairly large class of landlords and merchants, some of whom have lived in wealth and luxury. Moreover, in the cities a middle class has been developing for at least three decades. But the backbone of China's population, the peasantry, are victims of an almost unbelievable grinding poverty.

Today, China's economic situation has grown even worse than in peacetime. Perhaps it has never been lower than at present. Currency has collapsed. The official Chinese dollar has fallen to 7% of its gold value; and by the end of 1942, having lost over 95% of its value, its circulation had increased 50 times! This process has continued and even worsened. Were it not for the fact that barter plays so important a part in the economic life of the peasantry, the whole financial structure of Free China would have toppled and a wild runaway inflation would have ruined the country. In Occupied China the situation is almost as bad: by 1941 prices had risen elevenfold in Shanghai. In Manchuria, where the Japanese have exerted stricter controls, prices have risen threefold.

The Japanese occupation has rendered cold statistics useless. Before 1937 Chinese bonds sold abroad to yield a 16% return; today China's credit has to be recreated and propped up by international cooperation. With 200,000,000 Chinese in occupied territory, 50,000,000 refugees in the interior of Free China, large internal armies facing one another, and others facing and fighting the Japanese, guerrilla bands disrupting the enemy's lines of communication, and considerable smuggling occurring between Free and Occupied China, it is manifestly impossible to talk of economics. Production, trade, and finance are all functions of politics in China; and concrete plans for coping with her present plight will be dealt with under *History*.

Foreign Trade. Novels and stories of the sea have popularized the once-famous "China Clippers" of the "China Trade," the pirate-manned junks, and the famous Chinese *compradores* (merchant-middlemen). Apart from tea and silk, however, the China trade was always small, restricted to a few ports and to some caravan routes from Asiatic Russia. The best year for foreign trade was 1929: with a China at peace, both internally and externally, exports reached $439,000,000 and imports $662,000,000 (a total trade of about $2.50 per capita). Exports have remained at this level, but imports into Free and Occupied China have trebled. Manchuria's exports equal China's and her imports are about $250,000,000 yearly.

In normal times China exported mostly to the U.S.A., Britain, and Japan, importing from the U.S.A., Japan, Germany, and Britain. Chief exports were tung oil, raw cotton, raw silk, hides and skins, tea, tungsten, tin, and antimony. Manufactured goods constituted only 3% of exports. Leading imports were machinery and metal goods, finished cotton products, wool, and chemicals. China's participation in the war as a leading member of the United Nations coalition, has, of course, affected the nature of her foreign trade, emphasizing imports of immediate importance to the war effort. But the great promise of the Chinese market still awaits realization.

History: 1914-1944

For over two centuries China had been a monarchy under the rule of the Manchu dynasty. Then in 1911, a revolution swept aside the rulers and a few months later, the first Chinese Republic was proclaimed. One of the leaders of the Chinese Revolution was Dr. Sun Yat-sen, a physician who had spent much of his time abroad enlisting the aid of overseas Chinese in support of his country's national resurgence.

Sun Yat-sen had hoped that the Revolution would usher in a republic with a democratic constitution, but in 1912 power came into the hands of the ambitious Yuan Shih-kai, who established a nominal republic and sought ultimately to make himself Emperor. He failed in his efforts, as did also an attempt to restore the Manchu dynasty in 1917.

During World War I, the Chinese government joined the Allies with a declaration of war on the Central Powers (April 1917). But another nominal ally, Japan, had as early as 1915 made China the subject of threatening demands. Had these "Twenty-one Demands" been granted, China would have fallen effectively under Japanese control.

When the European war came to an end, China was a phantom republic with no genuine central authority. Various military governors maintained provincial armies, levying taxes and enforcing control in several sections of the country. These war-lords were known as *Tuchuns*, hence their period of control is called the *Tuchunate*. Moreover, the year 1918 closed with Japan in occupation of the Shantung peninsula, seized (in 1914) from Germany, who had formerly controlled it, and with provincial armies of the *Tuchuns* looting the unhappy Chinese land.

Formation of a Revolutionary Group: 1919–1923. From the early years of the 20th century there had been a revolutionary current in China. A wave of modernization had swept the country, particularly among middle-class and upper-class youth, resulting in the overthrow of the monarchy and the legal abolition of such long-standing customs as the queue and the binding of women's feet. The "Literary Revolution," which seeks to discard the dead classical language and replace it with the spoken tongue of the common man, was started in 1917 under the leadership of a number of professors at the National University of Peking, and spread rapidly throughout the country. In 1920, the *pei hua* (or the spoken language) was for the first time used in the textbooks of the primary schools.

The capital, Peking, was the seat of the notorious "Anfu clique," who were sustained by the "Nishihara" loans made by the Japanese. In 1920 a struggle broke out between this clique and a powerful war-lord of Manchuria, Chang Tso-lin. Until 1922, other enemies of the "Anfu clique" controlled Peking, leaving Chang Tso-lin independent in Manchuria. Then in 1924, Feng Yu-hsiang, "the Christian general," drove his former friends out of Peking and controlled the north, except for Manchuria, where Chang Tso-lin still held power.

These feudal discords and alternations in power disgusted the more national-minded Chinese in the south. The Kuomintang, "the People's Party," which was then in political control of Canton, now aimed at the political unification of the country. Its leader, Dr. Sun Yat-sen, had hitherto been unable to dislodge the militarists of the south. But by 1923 the newly reorganized Kuomintang, made up largely of the sons of the small landed proprietors, merchants, and professional men, thought the situation ripe for the fundamental transformation of China.

When in 1919 the Allies at Versailles awarded conquered Shantung on a long-term basis to the Japanese, popular Chinese resentment took the form of modern, national patriotism. The Kuomintang, the Communist party, and other political parties rivaled one another in utilizing and in recruiting membership among the youthful students. And, with the rapid development of the factory system in a number of cities, both the Kuomintang and the Communists began to enlist the support of the urban workers as well.

Since British attitudes remained basically those of 19th-century imperialism, Sun Yat-sen and his group turned increasingly to the young Soviet Union, who had voluntarily relinquished all special rights and privileges in China, as their best possible ally. The new ideology of the Kuomintang was radical in internal matters and anti-imperialist in foreign affairs.

The Struggle for the Kuomintang: 1923–1927. In 1923 the Soviet envoy Joffe and Sun Yat-sen entered into friendly relations. Members of the young Chinese Communist party were instructed by the Communist International to join the Kuomintang, and a joint proclamation of Joffe and Sun Yat-sen stated that national unity (to replace the *Tuchunate*) and independence of foreign control were the two goals of the broadened Kuomintang.

In September of the same year, Borodin, a Soviet Russian representative, came to Canton where he speedily revitalized the Kuomintang. The party was to be a severely disciplined one, owing allegiance to principles rather than to the person of Sun Yat-sen, a new party registration was to be held and all deadwood eliminated, and members were to be trained in revolutionary theory and tactics. At the first party congress, held in January 1924, power was delegated to a central executive committee.

Meanwhile, Sun Yat-sen, in his book *San Min Chu I*, formulated his "Three Principles of the People": nationalism; democracy, including initiative, referendum, and recall; and people's livelihood, the essence of which was land reform (inspired mainly by the Single Tax ideas of the American, Henry George). Sun Yat-sen was impressionable and very much influenced by the latest books he read. He was not a vigorous administrator, but he formulated one idea that gripped the imagination of the resurgent Chinese: China was not a colony but a "semi-colony." Hence, to achieve her independence and fundamental reform, three stages were necessary: first, military operations; second, the "tutelage" or training of the people for democracy, under Kuomintang leadership; and third, the achievement of a constitution and a democratic government.

However, the Kuomintang contained deep internal divergences. The Conservatives — merchants, bankers, and landed gentry — were suspicious of and hostile to the radical students, workers, and peasants.

The latter, triumphing at Canton in October 1924, had set about confiscating some property. While internal party dissensions were brewing, Sun Yat-sen undertook a journey to the north to meet with General Feng Yu-hsiang and Chang Tso-lin to effect national unity. Then in March 1925, the spiritual father of the Chinese Republic died.

The death of Sun Yat-sen temporarily cemented the party. All factions paid reverence to him and claimed to be the faithful interpreters of his doctrines. His "Will," the authenticity of which is not absolutely certain, became a textbook on which each side relied for authority.

The Left wing, continuing to control Canton, wielded authority at the second party congress (1926). Many political and social excesses, such as confiscation of property and execution of men branded as "counter-revolutionaries," were committed in the name of the party. The Right wing, alarmed at Russian influence and Chinese Communist participation, drew back: the internal schism deepened. By 1926 a young officer, Chiang Kai-shek, who had returned from Soviet Russia to organize and preside over the Whampoa Military Academy near Canton, was assuming leadership of the Right wing of the Kuomintang.

Chiang Kai-shek took control of the Nationalist army and prepared to lead it in a northern expedition, which set out from Kwangtung in 1926, and almost immediately became irresistible as a new force of revolution against the decadent and reactionary armies of the war-lords. By the end of 1926, the National Revolutionary Armies had conquered the important provinces of Hunan, Hupeh, and Kiangsi.

The shooting of strikers at Shanghai and other cities, and the harsh repression of students demonstrating on their behalf, had evoked an anti-British boycott that nearly strangled the commerce of the British colony of Hong Kong (near Canton). The British were thus singled out because they were held to be the leading Western imperialist exploiters of China.

The Nationalists also instituted boycotts against the Japanese who, after 1922, had for a short time followed a more conciliatory policy in China, largely as a result of the Washington Conference (1922) and the Nine-Power Treaty by which the Nine Powers had agreed to respect the sovereignty, independence, and territorial and administrative integrity of China. (See *Japan, History*). The nine signatories of the pact agreed that Shantung was to be restored to China (finally accomplished in 1929). They agreed, furthermore, that China's two most humiliating disabilities — extra-territoriality for foreigners, meaning the right to be judged by their own, not Chinese, laws and courts; and customs supervision — were to be gradually abandoned.

The Civil War within the Kuomintang: 1926–1929. In this period of exacerbated nationalism, the Left made enormous gains, crushing the war-lord of Hankow by enlisting the peasantry on its side, and spreading Communist ideas on land organization to the peasantry in the Canton region. By 1926 the Kuomintang had occupied Hankow and established its capital there.

Chiang Kai-shek, bitterly opposing these signs of

increasing radicalism, found himself ousted from his post as Commander-in-Chief of the army. Indeed, for a time the Kuomintang Central Executive Committee, controlled by the Leftists and Communists, read him out of the party. But in Shanghai, he obtained the support of the merchants, bankers, and industrialists for the Right wing. Among these was the brilliant financier, T. V. Soong, whose wide knowledge of the modern world aided Chiang considerably. Chiang countered the hostility of the Left by establishing a government at Nanking.

Meanwhile, Chang Tso-lin, the war-lord of Manchuria, had raided the Soviet embassy at Peking, and arrested many Chinese radicals in hiding there, but in Hankow, pro-Communist influence made spectacular gains, which goaded the Right wing to decisive action before it was too late.

Thereupon Chiang joined forces with the "Christian General" Feng, and the situation was speedily reversed. The Left wing suffered a series of defeats, losing one area after another in quick succession. Borodin returned to Russia. The Right wing of the Kuomintang had won the day.

In the winter of 1927–28 Chiang Kai-shek triumphed completely: he crushed the Left wing group in Hankow; and he subdued the uprising in Canton known as the Canton Commune. Nanking now became the capital of Nationalist China.

Now even the northern war-lords trembled: Chang Tso-lin was glad to retire to his fastness of Manchuria. After his death in 1928, his son, the "Young Marshal" Chang Hsueh-liang, accepted the Nationalist flag and became friendly with Chiang Kai-shek.

The Reorganization of China: 1928–1931. Chiang Kai-shek called a party congress of the Kuomintang, excluding the Left wing. The party adopted the "organic law," embodying the Three Principles of Sun Yat-sen, and providing for a "tutelage" period. The government was to consist of five *Yuans*, or administrative bodies: an executive, legislative, and judicial body, as in the U.S.A., and two others, an examination and a control body. On May 12, 1931, the Organic Law was transformed into a People's Provisional Constitution; but all power remained concentrated in the hands of Chiang Kai-shek until the planned end of the "tutelage" period in 1935.

Chiang held effective control only of the richest and most industrialized areas of China. Other provinces were loosely affiliated to him, while in the south discontents simmered and frequently broke out into open revolts. In 1930 the "Christian General" Feng, wearying of his alliance with Chiang Kai-shek, staged a military revolt which was quickly defeated. The age of the war-lord was coming to an end.

These signs of growing national unification forced the Japanese to reckon with a new patriotic spirit in a region they had long considered their special domain. Facing an economic crisis at home, and determined to forestall further unification, the Japanese invaded Manchuria in 1931 on the flimsiest of pretexts, and soon tore that rich area from the Chinese government, renaming it Manchukuo. Chiang Kai-shek, feeling himself too weak to challenge Japanese armed might, reacted only with protests and a general policy of nonresistance. Again the

Kuomintang divided into those who thought it was Chiang's first duty to resist Japan and those who thought Manchuria should go by default in order that Communism be eradicated in China. The Chinese, their patriotic spirit aroused, undertook a boycott of Japanese goods, which led to the Japanese assault on the Chapei section of Shanghai. The Chinese fought heroically in this battle, but hostilities soon gave way to an uneasy truce.

The Campaigns against the Chinese Soviet Areas: 1931–1934. In the southern province of Kiangsi, the Communists had won over the peasantry and established Soviets. In December 1931 Chiang set out to reoccupy the Soviet areas.

He launched a series of campaigns in 1932 and 1933, but none succeeded. The Soviet areas grew, until they comprised some tens of millions of peasants within their orbit, the boundaries of which were fluid and shifting. This spread of peasant revolt reduced confidence in the Nationalist government's finances. To modernize his army and to deal more decisively with the Communist opposition, Chiang called in the former head of the German army, General von Seeckt, who reorganized the Chinese armed forces. The military campaigns against the Reds were stepped up somewhat, but decisive victory still eluded the Nationalist government.

Realizing that so long as he neglected the vital problem of land reform for the peasantry and relied solely on the wealthier classes, civil war might go on and on, Chiang sought an alternative program of agrarian reform, which would wean the peasants away from expropriating the landlords. The Communists were fostering cooperative credit societies, collective irrigation, a cooperative peasant currency, flood control, and progressive land taxes; moreover, the peasant Soviets were making some contact with industrial workers in nearby areas. The challenge was extreme: Chiang felt that unless he reacted vigorously, his own power might be jeopardized.

At the same time the government's Finance Minister, T. V. Soong, had balanced the budget, improved military highways, obtained customs autonomy, and hence a larger national income. The U.S.A. conceded customs autonomy in 1928, and gradually across the years the foreign powers relinquished their rights of extraterritoriality; while a Chinese now sat on the Council of the International Settlement in Shanghai. But these results, foreshadowing an end of the "unequal treaties," admirable as they were, did not make for a solution of the peasant problem.

In 1933, the Japanese moved forward from their puppet state of Manchuria (now called Manchukuo) into the north China area of Jehol. That same year, the Japanese Premier Hirota bade China accept the new status of Manchukuo and cultivate friendship with Japan, in return for which Japan would cooperate in the campaign to eradicate Communism. Chiang Kai-shek refused this offer. Instead, he rearmed the country, hiring Americans and Italians to build up his air force.

Now the Japanese enlarged their demands: they demanded an autonomous North China under their control. In Eastern Hopei province, they established a customs control that permitted extensive smuggling and thus largely nullified T. V. Soong's admirable customs control. These actions roused the Chinese people to demand more vigorous resistance to Japanese encroachments on their homeland.

Chiang's difficulties increased when his 19th Route Army began to show some signs of sympathy with the peasant Soviets. He sought to organize the landlords; and when this effort made no headway, he developed his "New Life" movement, based on classic Confucianism and strongly opposed to Western "materialism." He attempted an economic blockade of the Soviet regions. Finally, in 1934, he broke into these areas and expelled the Communists. But then began one of the most astonishing treks in history.

The Chinese Soviets Move to the Northwest — The National Front Arises: 1935–1937. The Communist armies, forced to relinquish their hold over large areas, broke through the lines of the National government's forces and marched hundreds of miles to the northwest. There, in the much smaller and more primitive areas of the northwest, above the city of Sian, they established themselves anew. Now they were more dangerous to the Japanese, since they were quite near the areas of North China where the Japanese were gaining a foothold.

Once installed in the northwest, the Communists in 1935 appealed to the nation to resist the Japanese invaders. The Japanese, on the other hand, offered to collaborate with Chiang in an anti-Communist campaign if he would agree to Japanese supremacy in North China. He rejected Japan's proposal but persisted in his refusal to accept Communist aid in the anti-Japanese struggle.

Unfortunately he faced a currency crisis, which caused him to abandon the traditional silver basis of China's money in favor of a "managed currency." Badly in need of revenue, he encouraged cooperatives to increase rural production and thus have a wider basis for taxation.

Chiang also faced political opposition. As Japan seized more and more Chinese territory, the desire for resistance spread among all sections of the people. T. V. Soong, Madame Sun Yat-sen, and many other noted Chinese began to question his policy of ineffectual resistance to Japan. But Chiang refused to weaken his internal position by sending troops against Japan. When a revolt broke out in the south, he countered swiftly and the uprising was crushed. Now he seemed to have broken all serious internal opposition, from the former Communist-controlled areas on the Left to the war-lords on the Right.

In 1936 the Communists, stressing that they were anti-imperialists first and foremost, offered to drop their specific social demands and to collaborate unreservedly with Chiang Kai-shek against Japan. They agreed that peasant reorganization should center on small individual ownings and that private merchants and industrial capital should be encouraged in the towns. The spirit of resistance rose throughout China.

In 1936 discussions between the Communists and the National government took place. During the negotiations, Chiang was kidnaped by some young officers under the command of the "Young Marshal" Chang Hsueh-liang (in the famous "Sian incident"). Upon his release, Chiang Kai-shek became the rallying point of the Chinese people; even the Communists,

whom he had sought to repress for ten years, stated that without Chiang Kai-shek, resistance to Japan could not be organized.

The Japanese, sensing the growth of national unity in China, stiffened in their demands, even insisting on having "counsellors" in the Chinese Central government.

Japan Attacks China: 1937–1941. In July 1937, the Japanese began their wanton invasion of China Proper. The bombardment of Shanghai marked a new departure in strategy: the Japanese set out to conquer the rich Yangtze valley. China heroically rallied to defend her independence. Internal differences were sidetracked in this period of wide national unity. The Communist-led military forces were now incorporated into the national army as the 8th Route Army. The Communist-controlled "Border Region Government" in the northwest (formerly the Chinese Soviets) continued to administer its internal affairs.

By December, Nanking fell; and by October 1938, the Japanese had extended their conquests far up the Yangtze to Hankow, and to Canton in the south. Though successful, the Japanese campaigns were expensive and exhausting, guerrilla warfare making their occupation an arduous affair. In the north, the Japanese drove the Chinese south to the Yellow River. North China swarmed with corrupt Chinese who served in puppet governments set up by the Japanese. The unremitting "scorched earth" resistance by the people, however, greatly reduced Japanese plunder and made the war costly.

It was not until March 1940 that the Japanese were able to produce a puppet of some standing: Wang Ching-wei, who had been a vociferous intriguer in the Kuomintang in the old days and who now unashamedly went over to the Japanese. He established a government at Nanking, which enjoyed Japanese "coordination."

Undaunted, the National government of Generalissimo Chiang Kai-shek moved to Chungking in the west, from which it conducted a tenacious war of "trading space for time." Tens of millions of refugees poured west into the interior of China, thus dislocating still further her already precarious economy.

Some reactionary elements within the Kuomintang still urged a renewal of the war against the Chinese Communists, but since Chiang depended primarily on Soviet Russia for armaments and realized that civil war would play into the hands of the Japanese invaders, he was circumspect. As soon as the Burma Road was opened, permitting arms shipments from other countries, the reactionary Kuomintang elements became vocal again. Matters came to a head in November 1940 when the War Ministry asked Generalissimo Chiang to suppress the Communist-led New 4th Army operating against Japan. Civil war threatened; Japan was at the gates; and Great Britain, in a last futile gesture of "appeasement" to the Japanese, had recently closed the Burma Road, China's main supply route (July–October 1940). Fortunately, the danger of internal war at so critical a juncture was averted.

In order to equip the nation for war against the Japanese, many doctrines had to be at least temporarily forgotten. Chiang, the conservative, became the architect of state-controlled enterprise, establishing factories and encouraging some 1,300 industrial cooperatives. The rising costs of war, however, resulted in inflation in 1941, and the peasants in the "rice bowl" area of the Yangtze valley were still being exploited by the local landlords.

But the Japanese assault on the U.S.A. (December 7, 1941) fundamentally altered China's perspective. Japan's victories in China and her control of all vital coastal and river valley centers no longer seemed so decisive. The Sino-Japanese war merged into World War II.

China in World War II: 1941–1944. The opening defeats of the Allies in Hong Kong, the Philippines, Malaya, Burma, and the Netherlands East Indies were immensely discouraging to the embattled Chinese. The Burma Road became useless. Soviet Russia, deeply involved in the European war against Germany, had to reduce shipments of ammunition and supplies.

The Chinese joined the Allies in the Burmese campaign with excellent results, but they had to face repeated assaults by the Japanese who were seeking to consolidate their lines of communication and supply between the Yangtze basin and the Canton area. None of these campaigns, however menacing, proved decisive. But the country's plight became critical late in 1944 when the Japanese armies threatened to "cut China in two."

Regrettably, the old ill-founded suspicion of the Communists kept a substantial portion of Chiang's forces engaged in blockading the area under Communist influence, thus preventing maximum unity against Japan and diminishing China's military potential. Late in 1944, however, it seemed that some progress might be made in allaying these suspicions and bringing the Kuomintang and the Communists, who were still pleading for national unity, closer together. Moreover, strong voices were raised in favor of a more democratic China, like that of Sun Fo, son of Dr. Sun Yat-sen. The meeting of the consultative People's Political Council, held in the summer of 1944, emphasized this growing demand within the Kuomintang itself.

America has taken an active interest in these developments because of the special concern for China shown in the U.S.A. Outstanding Americans have visited Chungking as ambassadors of good-will, while Madame Chiang Kai-shek has reciprocated with an extended tour of the U.S.A.

In November 1943, the Cairo Agreement, signed by President Roosevelt, Prime Minister Churchill, and Generalissimo Chiang Kai-shek, gave China the rank of a major world power, one of the "Big Four." This was a tremendous step forward for a country that twenty years before had been pleading for the gradual end of extra-territoriality!

Foreign Affiliations. The old Chinese Empire was a closed, self-isolated society, knowing little of foreigners and disdainful of the outside world. The New China is extremely sensitive to world opinion and interests. To the merchants and industrialists of China — the rising middle class — the friendship of the U.S.A. comes first, and Great Britain has many traditional ties with important elements in the country. To the Chinese Communists, the Soviet Union has been a lodestone spiritually; but they believe, nevertheless, that their internal policy of peasant democracy and rising industrialism is based exclusively on China's needs, and they place Chinese national interests above any partisan consideration.

The democratic structure of America is the ideal to many forward-looking Chinese; and American generosity in endowing schools, hospitals, and relief work — as well as in using the Boxer indemnity funds for student scholarships — has given us tens of millions of well-wishers in China. Moreover, the rôle played by Americans in stabilizing Chinese finances and fostering industrialization has steadily increased.

In the summer of 1944 American military observers and journalists visited the Communist-controlled areas in the northwest — thus stressing the vital importance of this anti-Japanese group to the success of the United Nations — and lauded their constructive and undogmatic internal reforms.

Stakes in the Peace

Land reform and industrial development are basic requirements of post-war China. To link her scattered resources, special attention must be paid to her woefully inadequate communications. Famine can be prevented first, by roads, reforestation, and erosion control, and then by irrigation.

China's exports have not been such as to interest countries with a surplus of venture capital. This has been a major handicap to industrialization in the past. The U.S.A., for example, has invested very little because this economic basis was wanting. Nor, apart from some ferro-alloys, tung oil, and other minor products, is it yet evident that China can supply much in the way of economic exports.

Hence, China's industrial development, or rather, capital development, may take three forms: (1) the precedent set by Turkey of autonomous development, entailing arrested consumption standards; (2) increased reliance in the economically backward north and northwest on trade links with the Soviet Union, thus reducing the area requiring capital investment by other nations; or (3) outright investment, governmentally sponsored, by advanced industrial nations, with a long-term development of Chinese economy holding out the possibility of ultimate redemption of the sums advanced, by means of exports.

During her "war of resistance and reconstruction," China has perforce followed the first solution, but this will be a long, arduous route to prosperity. On the other hand, the third solution requires international unity and long-range planning.

Whatever the scope of China's present national resurgence, she has for thousands of years followed the tenets of Confucian wisdom, rejecting war and relegating the soldier to an inferior rank in classical Chinese culture. How much of this attitude will survive in a civilization as fluid as is China's today is not easy to assess, but it is unlikely that this peace-loving spirit has been extinguished. Chinese civilization maintained the largest area of peace and peaceful ideals for the longest period that mankind has ever known. In general, modern Chinese youths have shown themselves basically responsive only to the most liberal, progressive, and peace-loving ideals of the West.

Hence, a true psychological mass foundation has been laid for Chinese cooperation in keeping the peace. World organization was long imposed on China in the shape of "unequal treaties," extra-territoriality, and other humiliations. Now it can be implemented on a free and equal basis with an intelligent, receptive, and united people enjoying their sovereignty to the full.

FRENCH INDO-CHINA

The Land and the People

See map on page 265.

Indo-China, France's only important possession in Asia, is, as the composite name shows, a product of the two oldest and most brilliant civilizations in the Far East, the Chinese and the Indian. Conquered in piecemeal fashion by France in the last part of the 19th century, Indo-China is really the collective name given to the realms of Annam, Cochin-China, Laos, Tonkin, and Cambodia, all differing widely in cultural background and physical features. Annam dominates the Pacific seacoast, Laos the interior. The region as a whole has an area of 286,000 square miles (a tenth more than Texas) with a population of over 24,000,000.

The Land. A mountain range running the length of Annam almost parallels the Pacific coast. At the crest and foot of these mountains are two rich rice-producing plains, both in delta areas. In the extreme north lies the delta of the Red River, which flows into Tonkin; in the extreme south, the delta of the giant Mekong River, which pours into the plains of Cochin China. These river valleys occupy less than a fifth of the total area — 13,000 and 40,000 square miles respectively — yet they contain the majority of the population and the chief centers of rice, rubber, sugar, and coffee production.

The leading cities are Hanoi, the capital, in the north (population 140,000); Haiphong, its port (80,000); and Saigon in the south (170,000). Cam-ranh Bay, on the southeast coast, possesses one of the finest natural harbors in the Pacific. Indo-China is connected with China by two strategic railroads: one running from Hanoi in the north to Nanning (Kwangsi province), the other from Hanoi to Kunming (Yunnan province).

Indo-China has a monsoon climate, with extremely hot and humid summers in the south. The north is somewhat cooler in the winter, but the region suffers from devastating typhoons. The rivers, often rising high in summer during the monsoon rains, are not easily navigable. The Laos plateau in the west has a more comfortable climate because of the higher altitude.

Coal is Indo-China's chief mineral resource, reserves are estimated at 20,000,000,000 tons. Extensive deposits of high-grade anthracite lie especially in Tonkin in the north, where there are important veins of tin and zinc.

The People. The population of 24,000,000 is extremely varied, but the most important single group is the Annamites, over 75% of the total. Probably of south Chinese origin, the Annamites show many traces of Chinese culture in their Confucianist religion, arts, language, and social life. The Cambodians in the southwest (some 10%) and the Laotians (under 5%) in the west, though differing among themselves, have both been strongly influenced by Hindu culture, as is shown by their alphabet, Buddhist religion, and customs. The Cambodians are taller, more powerful, and darker-skinned than the slight Annamites; and their civilization is noted for its architectural splendor. The colossal temple of Angkor, erected when Cambodia was a Buddhist kingdom, is considered by some authorities to be the most perfect ornamented construction on earth.

In addition to these main groups, who make up 95% of the population, there is a host of native tribes at varying levels of civilization — the Thais (related closely to the people of neighboring Thailand), the Mois, Chams, Meos, and others, most of whom live in remote, primitive, mountainous areas.

As elsewhere in the Far East, the Chinese are an active minority, engaged in trading, moneylending, retail businesses, and as workers in the coal mines. The French population is under 40,000, chiefly administrators and businessmen.

Religion and Education. The religion of the masses is Buddhism, modified by Confucian rules, but in some regions, such as Cambodia and Laos, there are many vestiges of an older Hindu faith. Under French rule, Catholic missionaries have played an important rôle in education and public health.

French children are educated in government schools modeled after those in the mother country, but not one Indo-Chinese child in ten receives instruction in a government school; the resulting illiteracy is extremely high. There is a small university at Hanoi, but nearly all the young natives who can afford it study in France. Though Catholic missionary schools are numerous, village education is backward and still largely in the hands of *bonzes* (mendicant priests). The French have done much to foster the knowledge of native art and archaeology, some of their institutions in Indo-China combining erudition with excellent taste and imagination; but this specialized learning does not greatly benefit the Indo-Chinese.

The Nation's Economy

Production. Indo-China is *monocultural*: one crop, rice, is 60% of all agricultural produce, 80% of the people's diet, and by far the largest export, In 1939 rice production was almost 8,000,000 tons, more than 8% of the world supply. Next in importance is rubber, averaging about 5% of world output; then come coffee, tea, cinnamon, and sugar in moderate amounts. The meat supply is relatively small, but fisheries, both from the coast and inland lakes, are fairly important as exports.

The leading mineral is excellent anthracite coal, with an annual production of 2,500,000 tons. Production of tin and zinc is on a small scale. Though water-power is available, it is utilized very little.

Under French rule, no heavy industry has been allowed to develop. A few light industries, such as cement, matches, and textiles, have been encouraged and about a million Indo-Chinese work at small handicrafts: weaving, embroidery, and pottery, some of which show a high level of craftsmanship.

Finance. The unit of currency is the *piastre*, equal to 10 French *francs*. Its value is roughly 5 to the dollar, but under wartime conditions this is a mere approximation. Circulation, about $70,000,000 or under $3 per capita in peacetime, doubled between 1938 and 1941, and the issuance of paper money was the monopoly of a French bank. Since Japanese penetration (1941), no figures on finance have been available. The last budget reported (1941) was $30,000,000 and the public debt $50,000,000. The tax system is based in part on a poll tax, which weighs heavily on the Indo-Chinese peasants, who are in general incredibly poor. Most of the productive resources of the country have been controlled by the French.

Foreign Trade. In 1939 Indo-China exported about $88,000,000 in goods and imported $60,000,000. Rice made up at least 50% of the exports, the others being rubber, fish, coal, zinc, and tin. Chief imports were cotton and silk textiles, metal goods, and kerosene.

France took 80% of all exports and supplied 35% of imports, effectively dominating the trade and national wealth of her Asiatic possession; but Japan was growing rapidly as a competitor when she seized control of the country as a stepping-stone to further aggressions in the Far East. The effect of protracted Japanese domination on Indo-China's economy and social life cannot be gauged now with any degree of accuracy.

History: 1914-1944

During World War I, France used 140,000 Annamites from her colony of Indo-China to serve in her armies or work in her labor battalions in Europe. In exchange, the capable French governor, Albert Sarraut, made generous and sincere promises of future benefits and increased autonomy. His popularity was such that with a mere 2,000 French soldiers he kept the country peaceful during those four trying years of war. But when he left in 1920, he had called nationalism into being; and since he had moved cautiously to implement his promises, the situation in the colony became explosive.

His successor, Maurice Long, reverted to the older type of colonial policy, invoking the system of *cadres latéraux*, that is, a native bureaucracy paralleling the French officials. Though wasteful, this system succeeded in training new elements for administrative posts. Moreover, Long displayed some initiative in granting wider native representation and electoral rights in Cochin-China, where the natives had more experience in government.

The next governor, Merlin, anxious to decentralize finances, failed in his efforts and markedly increased the colony's deficits. Upon his inability to deal wisely with the rising nationalist temper, he was withdrawn; and the Leftist government in France attempted an audacious experiment by appointing a Socialist, Alexandre Varenne, Governor-general (1925).

Varenne proved both capable and popular. His efficient administration soon stabilized the country's finances at a time when the French franc itself was in grave danger. He sought to give new life to the Indo-Chinese *communes*, or villages, and thus to train the natives by giving them experience in local self-government. He established popular credit institutions to lessen the rôle of usurers, abolished imprisonment for debt, and enacted several progressive labor laws. But when he enacted decrees permitting natives to compete on equal terms with Frenchmen for civil service posts, a clamor arose among the French. Apart from the question of innate ability, they insisted that native officials were utterly corrupt and had no sense of administrative responsibility.

The natives were partisans of Varenne, but powerful financial, industrial, and governmental elements insisted on his recall. When he spoke of eventual independence for Indo-China, the Centrist government of Poincaré in Paris recalled him (1928). The older colonial elements rejoiced at the appointment of his successor, Pierre Pasquier, an administrator in Indo-China for 30 years.

Indo-Chinese Nationalism: 1928–1940. Despite his previous training, Pasquier was more akin to Varenne than to previous governors. He faced a real crisis, world prices of rubber and rice having collapsed even before the 1929 depression. But whenever he tried to cope with economic problems, Pasquier found himself tied hand-and-foot by tariff or monetary legislation in France, which aimed solely at the welfare of the mother country.

Pasquier cut government salaries and insisted that every French official be fluent in native languages. Installing a Grand Council for economic and financial matters, he sought an administrative compromise between ruinous decentralization and an excessive centralization which would align Annamites against Cambodians or Laotians. But he faced something more serious than the issue of federalism when the nationalist movement swelled into rebellion.

The Annamite nationalists were not fused with the other Indo-Chinese. They were themselves divided into two groups, one revolutionary, the other favoring constitutional reforms. But the slow progress of native rights inclined the balance toward the revolutionaries whose power centered in Tonkin, where they had close connections with Dr. Sun Yat-sen's Kuomintang groups in the south China city of Canton.

The leader of the revolutionaries was Nguyen-ai-Quoc, a man who had studied in Paris and Moscow. Despite his opposition to violence, young hotheads murdered Bazin, the French official in charge of labor impressment. The French police dramatically executed his assassins, after which a mutiny of native troops broke out at Yen-Bay. Its repression was perhaps the most drastic in the turbulent history of Eastern Asia; and the Leftist newspapers in France, excoriating the deeds of Frenchmen in Indo-China, demanded the dismissal of the "bloody and vengeful" Pasquier.

Pasquier replied that terrorists were at work and that this repression was the only efficacious means of maintaining order in an Oriental land. Peasant risings that followed in 1930–31 were rigorously suppressed. The Communists and their nationalist allies then split: the Communists insisting that peasant ownership of the landed estates took precedence over political demands, the other nationalists stressing political independence first.

In 1934 Pasquier met his death in an airplane accident. He was succeeded by Robin, an aggressive functionary who was kept busy suppressing native uprisings. Robin was forced to retire when the Paris press insisted that he connived at brutal treatment of the natives by the Foreign Legion at Vinh, a province that often suffered from famine. Nevertheless, under Robin's administration an impressive economic recovery set in, which endured for several years thereafter.

In 1936 the Popular Front triumphed in the French elections. The new Colonial Minister, Moutet, reviewed the arrests made under Pasquier's governorship and amnestied over two-thirds of the surviving prisoners, hundreds having perished previously in unsanitary prisons. The new governor, Brévié, was a moderate, and a more liberal current made itself felt. Some circles in France accused the Catholic missions of having abused the natives' trust by delivering political prisoners to the police; but this echo of the once-violent anticlerical issue soon faded away.

Indo-China Under Japanese Control: 1940–1944. The intellectually alert and ever-curious French had written first-class books and reports about Indo-China, all of which contributed to widespread improvements in the condition of the natives and to more just treatment by colonial officials.

But this progress came abruptly to an end in 1940. The defeat of France in Europe subjected the broken French power in Indo-China to pressure from Japan and her satellite state, Thailand. The French, bowing to Japan, ceased exports of arms to the Chinese across Indo-China. It was this decision that made the Burma Road all-important as a supply route for embattled China. And when Japan demanded military and naval facilities on Indo-Chinese territory, the French administrators acquiesced.

The French colonial régime, under Admiral Decoux, not only endorsed the Vichy government of Marshal Pétain, but French officers in Indo-China, drawn from the most Fascist-minded elements in France, humiliated French patriots and friends of the United Nations. They went so far as to toast the fall of Singapore to the Japanese, who were already installed in the Indo-Chinese naval base at Cam-Ranh Bay, one of the finest bases in the Far East.

Admiral Decoux, however, continued to be nationalist in his insistence on retaining internal controls and in his economic defense of the colony against the Japanese. The French liberation movement of General de Gaulle promised the Chinese government in Chungking that, after the war, French Indo-China would receive broad autonomy and be governed in a spirit worthy of the principles of the French Revolution.

Stakes in the Peace

Apart from internal economic improvements, such as an increase in communally owned land, better communications, and more efficient administration, Indo-China's prime need is to enter into some arrangement based on her regional position as well as on her affiliation with a metropolitan state like France. Her strategic position with reference to the whole area of southeast Asia was strikingly shown in 1940–42, when she acted as a lever for Japanese conquests.

Indo-China is a close neighbor of the Philippines, Dutch East Indies, the vital Malay Straits — thus she is a keystone in any regional organization for peace and security included within a larger world organization. Inevitably, such a development would more fully satisfy democratic and national aspirations in Tonkin, where the people are close to the Chinese in sentiments, and in Cochin-China, where the native population has matured the most. In Central Annam, mandarin conservatism and remoteness from the nationalist stirrings in the two rich rice-bowl areas, call for a more deliberate and carefully nurtured policy. In any event, the rise of a powerful, democratic China in Asia demands an end to the psychology that prevailed among most French colonial officials in Indo-China, prior to their reorientation of 1936.

France has promised thoroughgoing reforms in Indo-China; and the French have shown in other colonies, such as Martinique and Algeria, that they can inspire deep-seated, even fanatical loyalty. As part of a regional grouping including the Republic of the Philippines, this outpost of the French Republic, lying next to the Chinese Republic, can be turned into a fortress of democratic liberalism against the feudal, courtly groups who have aligned themselves with an ultra-reactionary, militarist Japan.

INDIA

The Land and the People

The East is very old and very wise. And though the wisdom of the East is not the wisdom of the West, the future peace of the world may well depend on our disproving the notion that "never the twain shall meet." Nor could we find a better place to begin an adventure in understanding than India, focal point of so many hopes and fears for the post-war world. For, unless it be China's, there is no voice from the East more significant than "Mother India's."

The Land. India occupies a peninsula so huge that it is spoken of as a subcontinent. It juts southward from Asia between the Indian Ocean and the Bay of Bengal, 1,581,410 square miles in all (more than half the area of the continental U.S.A.). On the northwest the Indus Desert separates India from the Near East. On the north the highest mountains on earth, the Himalayas, shield her from Arctic cold. On the northeast, mountains and jungles divide her from Burma and the Indian-Chinese peninsula. Three great rivers — Indus, Ganges, and Brahmaputra — water the central plain, among the richest and largest in the world. In the south is the mountainous Deccan country, refuge of India's aboriginal inhabitants and first seat of British power.

This great triangle of land knows many climates: the humid heat of the south, the dry heat of the Indus Desert, the sweet cool air of the Vale of Kashmir, the icy heights of the Himalayas; and, most widespread of all, the changing seasons of the central valley, four months dry and pleasant, eight months rainy and hot. Most of the people, industry, and agriculture are in this central valley. The rain upon which the crops depend comes with the monsoon (the southwest wind), from May to September. "The budget of India," goes the old saying, "is a gamble on the Monsoon."

India is divided into two major administrative sections: British India, with 865,000 square miles and 295,308,000 people, governed directly by Great Britain; and the Native states and agencies, with some 716,000 square miles and 93,189,000 people, governed by Indian princes. The best known Native states are Hyderabad (16,000,000 population) and Rajputana (13,000,000). The others vary from tiny realms of a few square miles to such important states as Baroda, Gwalior, Mysore, Punjab, Orissa, and Travancore. Among the many British provinces, the most important are Bengal, Bombay, Madras, United Provinces, British Punjab, Bihar, Central Provinces, Assam, and Sind. The 389,000,000 people of India comprise 18% of the human race.

Before European industry developed, India and China were the richest lands on earth — hence the successive waves of conquerors that have engulfed India. Even Columbus was seeking "the wealth of the Indies."

The People. India is a congeries of peoples becoming a nation. Perhaps no other country has such a variety of inhabitants. Among the many non-Indian peoples, the most notable are the Indo-Chinese in the northeast. The Indians themselves vary greatly in different regions: in the north they are fairskinned; in central India, high-castes are fair, but low castes are commonly darker; in the south almost all are darkskinned. Most Indians have black hair and dark eyes. Their stature varies, from the tall and powerful northern peoples to the rather short folk of the Deccan. The typical features of all, except for the Dravidian population of the south, are markedly similar to the European, with thin finely chiseled nose, thin lips, and high forehead. In fact, most Indians, their swarthiness notwithstanding, certainly come from stock related to the European. It has been argued that the dominant castes are "Aryan" and the low-castes the descendants of aboriginal colored peoples. But so great is the complexity of races in India that any such explanation is suspiciously oversimple.

Whatever the race of the conquerors, most ethnologists consider the Indian caste system a vestige of some long-ago conquest of one race by another. The 2,000 castes and sub-castes fall into four great classifications. At the bottom are the 50,000,000 low-castes or pariahs, politely known as the "depressed classes." The touch of a pariah pollutes a high-caste Indian, nor may the high-caste even touch what the pariah has touched.

India is many-tongued as well as many-peopled. Nearly three-fourths of the people speak Hindustani or Bengali or another of the Indo-European languages related to our own. About a fifth speak Dravidian languages such as Tamil (spoken about Madras), and nearly 4% speak Tibeto-Burman tongues. There are many languages in each of these groupings, some more widely spoken than famous European tongues. India speaks also in many aboriginal and vestigial tongues.

More than 87% of Indians live in the country, only about 12.8% in cities and towns. The largest city, Calcutta, has scarcely 2,000,000 people. The rural population, with rare exceptions, is grouped in villages. Most of these 600,000-odd villages are self-contained. Communication among them is so poor that in time of flood, famine, or epidemic help reaches them with difficulty or not at all — though their isolation has proved no barrier to the spread of cholera or the plague.

The Indian birthrate is high, about 33 per thousand, but the deathrate, which averages 23 or even more, is among the highest in the world. One baby out of six dies. Half the population is under 20 years old, only a tenth over 50. A new-born Indian male (the proportion of males to females is high, 201 to 187) has a life-expectancy of under 27 years, as against 63 for an American — a terrifying difference that needs no commentary. It has been authoritatively estimated that two-fifths of the people of India are poorly nourished, one-fifth very badly nourished.

The fact that Indians require fewer calories than

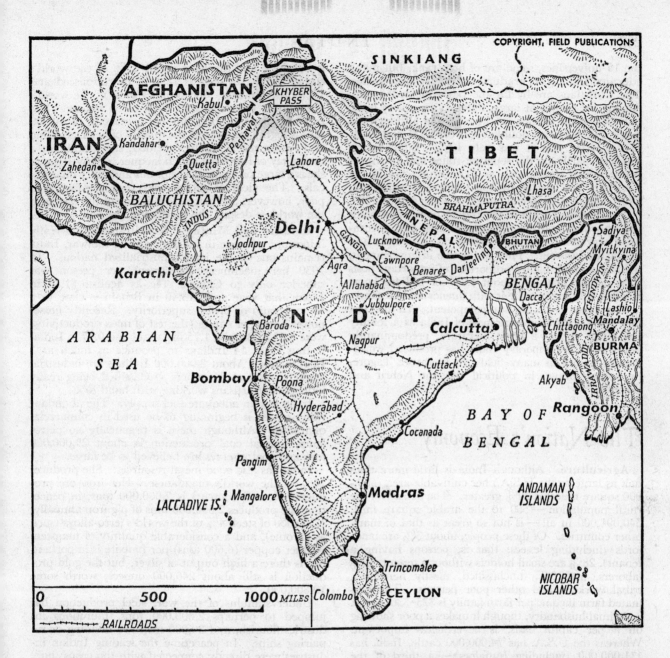

northerners makes the undernourishment and poverty of the people all the more striking.

Religion. Religion interpenetrates every phase of Indian life. Although in the professional classes religious zeal is diminishing, among the people at large everything is still dominated by religion — the crops they grow, the food they eat, the clothes they wear, the houses they live in, the castes into which they are born, even their political attitudes. The religion of the masses is one of the great and ancient faiths of the world. The religious writings of the Hindus form the world's largest body of antique doctrine. Compared to India, both Europe and China are secular civilizations.

The mass of the people, some 255,000,000, are Hindus: polytheists, non-resistants, believers in caste, worshipers in elaborate temples. Of the remaining 134,000,000, some 92,000,000 — largely in the northwest and in Bengal and Bombay — are Moslems; they believe in the unity of God and Man, accept force, and are eager proselytizers. Before the

British came, the Moslems were the dominant political power. Some 18,000,000 Indians follow tribal faiths, many of which, like that of the Todas in southern India, have enriched our knowledge of primitive man and the history of religion. Many others are animists. About 6,000,000 (1.6%) have accepted Christianity. The 6,000,000 Sikhs in the north have their own scriptures and temples and are prominent in the Indian Army. A million Buddhists and a small sect called the Jains make up the rest.

The conflicts of these religions — principally of Hindus and Moslems — have complicated Indian politics and often led to rioting and bloodshed. Indian patriots charge that the British do not want unity among the people; this charge the Raj (Imperial Administration) indignantly denies.

Education. Except in a few areas, education is not compulsory. About 16,000,000 children — only one in four of school age — go to elementary school, about 2,700,000 to high school. Technical and art schools number 300, normal schools over 600. Of the 15 universities, some are of high rank, but many educated Indians are graduates of English universities. The Christians are by far the best-educated group. Among the people at large, illiteracy runs very high: only 5% of the women are literate, and although the general literacy rate doubled between 1931 and 1941, in the latter year it was only 12%. Education is financed partly by the separate states and provinces (some native states, such as Travancore, are in the forefront) and partly by the Central Government, which has an educational budget of about $90,000,000.

The educated tenth of the Indian population holds the franchise, and the professional men and government servants (*babus* and *pundits*) are articulate and politically insistent. They are active in government, holding a much higher proportion of important posts than do the British. About 1.3% of Indians know English, and many write it with fluency and elegance.

The press is hectic but competent. In the last fifty years a growing awareness of India as a totality has given rise to a large literature, predominantly political. Contemporary India has produced world-famous names in many fields: in literature Tagore, in botany Bhose, in political thought Nehru and Gandhi.

The Nation's Economy

Agriculture. Although India is little more than half as large as the U.S.A., her cultivable area (600,-000 square miles) is 20% greater. The density of the rural population — 560 to the arable square mile, 340,000,000 in all — is not so great as that of many other countries. Of these people, about 3% are landlords (including lessees, that is, persons having a tenant), 28% are small holders without a tenant, 35% laborers, and 34% unclassified, mostly herdsmen, tribal workers, and other poor persons. The estimated farm income per farm family is $25–$30 a year.

Animal husbandry, though it makes a poor showing on a per capita basis, is nevertheless important. Whereas the U.S.A. has 74,000,000 cattle, India has 111,000,000 (including buffaloes) — a third of the world's supply. Sheep number 25,000,000, goats 30,000,000, but farm labor has at its disposal only a million horses, a million donkeys, and in the north (for carriers) about 430,000 camels.

The scarcity of meat and dairy products is explained partly by religious taboos: the cow is sacred to most Indians, and Moslems cannot eat pork. There is, however, an 800,000-ton production of clarified butter (or ghee, highly repellent, incidentally, to Europeans), and considerable cow, buffalo, and goat milk is consumed, mostly among Moslems.

The staple foods of the people are rice, millet, and (in bountiful seasons) wheat. The rice-yield varies between 370,000 and 530,000 tons; wheat is about 40% of the American crop. Barley and corn are grown though not extensively. But in production of sugar cane, in which she surpasses even Cuba, and of tobacco, of which she supplies a fifth of the world's crop, India leads the world. All the world's jute (for burlap bags) comes from India. She is second only to the U.S.A. as a producer of cotton (though the quality is inferior), and furnishes about 15% of the world's cotton supply, as well as 18% of its cottonseed and 15% of its linseed. She supplies most of the world's groundnuts (peanuts) and 60% of its sesame. She produces little rubber, but her wool clip of 50,000 tons is highly important; the quality of her Darjeeling and Assam tea is highly esteemed; she has almost a monopoly of lac (from which lacquer is derived); and she is a large producer of castor oils and other pharmacals. The yield of subsistence crops per farmer is poor, however, and per acre it is one of the lowest in the world — despite the promise of the soil.

Industry and Mining. Notwithstanding a really important advance in industry during the war, India remains one of the least industrialized nations. In 1930 her machinery investment per person was superior only to China's: 14¢ as against $1.50 in Japan that year and $13.40 in Britain — close to a 90 to 1 ratio of British superiority. Recently horse-power hours per capita (the test of mass productivity) were 6.65 in Britain, 1.75 in Japan, and 0.47 in India: it thus takes 14 Indians to produce as much as 1 Englishman. About 2,000,000 Indians are industrial workers, most of the others so classified being really independent artisans working with hand tools.

India has an adequate fuel supply. The abundant water-power is beginning to be used in commercial quantities. Although there is practically no petroleum, annual coal production is about 29,000,000 tons and coal reserves are believed to be large.

India has also good metal resources. She produces 16% of the world's manganese. Her iron ore production (metal content) is 2,000,000 tons; in peacetime she produces 2,000,000 tons of pig iron annually, 1,300,000 of steel, 4% of the world's ferro-alloys (such as chrome), and a considerable quantity of tungsten. Neither copper (6,600 tons) nor bauxite is important, nor is there a high output of silver, but the gold production is still about 240,000 ounces, worth some $9,800,000.

Under stimulus of the war, steel production has jumped to perhaps 2,000,000 tons, munitions industries flourish, and 30,000 men are building or repairing ships. In peacetime the leading Indian industries were directly connected with the crops: jute, cotton, and rice mills, sugar refining, cotton ginning and pressing. The great variety of production and diversity of techniques developed under stress of war will undoubtedly speed up India's industrialization, but the assertion often made that India is to be the eighth industrial country in the world is scarcely tenable.

Finance. Formal treatment of Indian finance must give way before two peculiarly Indian institutions: the rural moneylender and the hoarding of precious metals. The country people, nearly all impoverished laborers or tenants with holdings too small to permit good farming, fight a losing battle against declining fertility and meager yields. They must have cash, not only for family needs but for the land tax. And when they go to the moneylender, he charges them such shockingly high interest — 5% *a month* is usual; it is often higher — that, with this added burden, they sink deeper and deeper in debt. The moneylender thus becomes the center of the movement of funds. Yet, though usury is called the true plague of India, the virus that causes it is the desperate poverty due to the land system.

As to the hoarding of precious metals and jewelry, it arises primarily from the sacredness of gold in Indian religious practice, and from the need to provide dowries. Furthermore, the Indian has seen too many conquerors and tax gatherers in 3,000 years to trust anything but the precious stones and metals. Hence figures on the world stock of gold and silver extant must always reckon with the great unknown of Indian hoardings.

Until recently, the custom of hoarding prevented the middle classes and landlords from investing heavily in industry or farm improvement: they preferred tangible wealth to legal claims recorded on paper. The British furnished the initiative in railroad-building, irrigation, and industrialization. Only lately has the pattern of industrial enterprise, starting among the Parsees of Bombay, spread widely among Indian capitalists.

The war has seen a startling reversal of financial relations with Great Britain, the first in 185 years. This reversal is indicated in the assets guaranteeing Indian paper money, of which there is twice as much in circulation as before the war. From 700,000,000 *rupees* (the *rupee* is worth 30.12¢), Indian deposits abroad have risen to 4,900,000,000 *rupees* — so that in less than five years India has been transformed from a debtor country to a creditor. Five years ago, India owed at least 6% of her national wealth to Great Britain and exported 1% of her total production to pay her debts and other disbursements to London. Today London owes India an immense sum, which cannot, of course, be paid during the war, and for which equivalent British investments in India are to be cancelled.

But at home, during the war, over-all prices have trebled and the cost of living has doubled, even according to ultra-conservative official figures. Under this pressure, savings have diminished, despite the increased industrial employment in the cities. Commercial bank deposits, however, have risen, to cope with high prices and the rise of budgetary costs and the national debt.

The rise in the national debt is entirely internal: from 7,000,000,000 *rupees* ($2,100,000,000) to 11,-100,000,000 *rupees* ($3,300,000,000); the external debt, as noted above, has fallen — from $1,400,000,-000 to only $350,000,000 — and it should be extinguished in 1944. Although large exclusions and re-credits have made the budget difficult to interpret, it has doubled during the war, and is about $1,000,-000,000. The Native states, however, levy their own taxes, often severe.

Foreign Trade. In peacetime, India's imports averaged about $550,000,000, her exports about $595,000,000 a year; the per capita figure for trade, $2.85, was among the lowest for a major country. The imports were mostly automobiles and trucks, raw cotton, food and tobacco, metals and petroleum. The chief exports were cotton and cotton goods, tea, jute, grain, nuts, gums and resins from the rich fifth of the country in forest, wool, and raw hides and skins, in which, because of the great numbers of her livestock, India leads the world.

Great Britain took a third of these exports, a fourth going to the rest of the Empire and a fifth to the U.S.A., but Great Britain supplied only a fifth of the imports, as against a fifth from the U.S.A. and two-fifths from the Empire. During the war, exports have risen to $615,000,000, but imports have fallen sharply, to $315,000,000, because the war has forced India's leading suppliers greatly to reduce production of consumers goods.

History: 1914-1944

India contributed generously to British success in World War I: over a million Indian troops fought on various battlefronts in Europe and the Near East. And Indian industry enjoyed a temporary boom during the war years.

With the hostilities ended, many Indians felt that their demands for *swaraj* (home rule) deserved more consideration than the British had previously thought practicable. For a generation the educated classes of India had been represented in an informal consultative body, called the Indian National Congress (founded in 1885). But in the first decade of the present century, more aggressive elements began to insist increasingly on autonomy. As a result, the British enacted the Morley-Minto reforms (1909), creating more opportunities for Indians in the Civil Service and allowing them to participate in legislative councils, though on a very restricted franchise basis. Lord Morley, a true liberal and outstanding philosopher, thought nevertheless that parliamentary government, in the British sense, was not even foreshadowed for India.

But a long campaign by disaffected elements, mostly among the student youth, accompanied by rioting and boycotts, showed that such partial reforms were not adequate. In 1917, the British Secretary of State for India, Montagu, declared that the aim of Great Britain was "the gradual development of self-governing institutions and the progressive realization of responsible government ... as an integral part of the British Empire." In his opinion, however, the scope and timing of any progress depended exclusively on the judgment of Great Britain, who was to assess how far India deserved to advance along this path.

The Montagu-Chelmsford Act: 1919. Reform hung in suspense until the summer of 1919. At that time, rioting broke out in Amritsar, a sacred city of the Sikhs. The British General Dyer ordered his troops to fire on a crowd that had defied his edict against gathering at a given point. Some 379 Indians were killed and 1,208 wounded. Not content with repression, Dyer ordered Indians to crawl on their hands and knees through certain streets. He argued that in acting thus he had prevented rebellion; and at first he was rewarded with a higher command in the then raging British-Afghan war. Later, a wave of criticism both in Britain and India brought censure upon him, but he had already made it extremely difficult for Indian and Briton to speak a common language.

Liberal opinion in England held that the Montagu reforms must now be implemented; and in December

1919, the "Government of India Act," as framed by Mr. Montagu and Lord Chelmsford, became law.

A complex instrument, it provided for an Executive Council (analogous to a cabinet) responsible only to the Viceroy of India. The Central Legislature had two houses: the Council of State, 32 members of which were elected and 26 nominated, and the Legislative Assembly, with 102 out of 141 members elected. The Viceroy had absolute veto powers and could issue decrees without the consent of this legislature. On finance, defense, foreign affairs, and control of the police, the Viceroy's powers were unchecked. Thus the legislature was a consultative body, to record and probe public opinion, but scarcely an assembly able to enact bills into law.

Elections were on a *communal* basis: that is, by religious groups or occupation. Thus Hindus, Moslems, Sikhs in the Punjab, native Christians, and Europeans voted for members of their own groups. Only the very well-to-do exercised the franchise for the upper house, while the franchise for the lower house, though restricted, was much wider and permitted propertied women to vote.

British officers and civil servants in India regretted the reform as being premature, but the Indian Nationalists, still dissatisfied, denounced it as a deception.

The Campaign of Repression: 1919-1921. In 1918 the British government had issued the Rowlatt report, which stated that India was menaced by revolutionary and terrorist conspiracies, that these were immediately dangerous, particularly in Bengal, and required instant action. The authorities passed a Press Control Act and jailed large numbers of people for sedition and conspiracy.

Because of these and other developments, the Indian National Congress boycotted the first elections (1920) held under the Montagu-Chelmsford reform, and only 2,000,000 out of 6,000,000 qualified voters participated. On February 9, 1921, the first Parliament met. It listened to the message from the British King-Emperor, which observed that at last Indians had *swaraj* (home rule) and a "guiding authority" in place of outright authority. The moderates, who were in a majority — since only a third of the electorate had voted — approved this sentiment. But popular resentment persisted. And it erupted at the first opportunity, which came soon, with the visit of Edward, Prince of Wales, to Bombay. He was greeted with widespread rioting.

The loyal Indians in the legislature made their first recommendations: (1) that protective tariffs be imposed so as to enable India to outsell British goods, and (2) that special court privileges for Europeans be withdrawn, so that native merchants would no longer be at a disadvantage in litigation.

The Rise of Gandhi: 1921-1923. Before 1919, Indian nationalism had been advocated by many able Indians, but they were mainly intellectuals or civil servants. None had succeeded in firing the imagination of the people.

A fifty-year-old lawyer, of wealthy origin, who had studied in the Middle Temple of London, soon altered the entire situation. He was Mohandas K. Gandhi, a man who had long fought for Indian rights in the Union of South Africa by pursuing a policy of systematic "non-obedience." Gandhi reflected the oldest Hindu form of thought — passive non-resistance — but by a stroke of genius he had converted it into a positive instrument of struggle instead of mere submission. He shunned European clothing, wore a loincloth and drapes of the very poorest fabric; and his strange, even ludicrous appearance to some Western eyes, made him nevertheless the focus of world attention. Prison did not daunt him, death was no deterrent, and pain apparently was a pleasure. The armies of the British *Raj* appeared to be as powerless against such a man, as the Roman legions had been powerless against the early Christians. At least, his disciples felt so, as by tens of thousands they joined his mass civil disobedience campaigns.

As leader of the Congress party, Gandhi urged India to boycott British goods and to refuse to attend British educational institutions or to recognize British courts, to serve in British-affiliated legislatures, and under no circumstances to enrich the British by working for them. At the same time, Gandhi gave up his considerable fortune to work for his people.

Rich Indians rallied to him. Since he alone had given pride and dignity to a dominated people, they believed that through him it would be possible to bring the British government to compromises. But Gandhi's nationalism sought to unite Indians of all classes. He did not appeal to any class as a class; on the contrary, he tried to unite all strata of Indian society into a powerful entity. And he succeeded in making the mysterious unknown land of fable, India, into a living, urgent political problem in the minds of people in Paris, Cairo, Buenos Aires, and Kansas City. India was no longer a closed preserve for colonial experts and historians.

Gandhi, like most mystics, was a superb politician. He would order shops closed in *hartals* (protests against the British), but when merchants regretted their losses in trade, he would focus on a new method. Yet, despite his strong hold on India's millions, particularly the peasants, he faced real opposition within the country. The native Princes, autocratic rulers, hated him for stirring up the people. The rigidly orthodox caste Hindus, gathered in the *Mahasabha* organization, were loath to deal with a man who associated with the pariahs (Untouchables) and who pleaded their cause. To the distress of the native millowners, he opposed modern industry and pleaded for a return to the spinning-wheel of pre-capitalist village economy. When he told every member of his Congress party to spin 200 yards of cotton cloth a month, they were somewhat taken aback.

For all that, by 1923 the British authorities were compelled to deal with Gandhi as they had never dealt with any Indian Nationalist leader before his time. Whether in or out of jail, Gandhi represented a serious threat to British rule in India.

The Government of India Changes its Policy: 1925-1930. In 1923, the Congress party, breaking away from Gandhi's policy of boycott, decided to participate in the Central Legislature, where they soon became dominant. The Montagu-Chelmsford system of reforms had proved unworkable, and a British tax expert, Sir Basil Blackett, decided that the only way to aid Indian revenue was by doubling the salt tax. The Marquis of Reading, then Viceroy, enacted this suggestion into law, whereupon Gandhi defied the government by leading his followers to the sea and making salt himself at the seaside.

He had just come out of prison, having been arrested as the instigator of the murder of 21 British police officers. Though he had announced the end of the nonresistance movement because it had degenerated into violence, on the issue of the salt tax, he remained adamant.

Continued resistance by Nationalist extremists, however, caused the Government of India to suspend "dyarchy," or dual rule by the executive and legislature, in Bengal and the Central Provinces. Thus, large sections of India reverted to executive power alone, signifying direct rule by the British. As matters stood, taxation and law alike were unenforceable.

Moreover, the religious issue plagued all parties. The Moslems of India wished the British to sustain the power of the Caliphate (religious head of all Islam), which had been abolished in resurgent Turkey (See *Turkey, History*). They wished the shrines of Mecca and Medina saved from the Moslem conquerors of the Wahabbi sect, whom they considered improper guardians of the shrines of Islam. Disturbances raged throughout the Moslem world in the Near and Middle East, with disorders recurring in India's Moslem-populated Northwest Frontier Province, all through the 1920's. Even Gandhi made common cause for a time with these Moslem extremists.

But as the Moslem unrest outside India subsided, the Indian Moslems turned their attention on India and agitated vigorously for their rights within the country. Hindu-Moslem communal clashes were not infrequent in this troubled period.

Yet India took certain forward steps in the 1920's. She was admitted as an independent member of the League of Nations and a full member of the British Imperial Conference (1921–23).

In 1926 the new Viceroy, Lord Irwin (now Lord Halifax, British Ambassador to the U.S.A.), realizing that the age of the Montagu-Chelmsford reforms was over, suggested a commission of inquiry. With a singular lack of understanding of Indian psychology, the British government appointed a commission under the noted barrister, Sir John Simon, with not a single Indian member! Had there been only one or two Indians in the body, the Indian people would have received it quite differently. Here was a committee to inquire into the state of a nation of some 350,000,-000 inhabitants, and it was composed exclusively of Britons!

This impolitic act had portentous consequences. The landing at Bombay of the Simon Commission led to rioting (February 1928). Though certain classes (such as the Untouchables) eagerly seized the opportunity to testify, on the whole, Indian opinion resented the Simon Commission and boycotted it with special fervor. Outbreaks of popular resistance led to shootings in Bengal and the Punjab. The government arrested 29 agitators, 3 of whom were British, and staged the Meerut trials for "mass sedition" (1929).

In 1929 Lord Irwin consulted with the Labor government in London, and an official statement was issued that full dominion status for India was Britain's goal. The Congress party greeted this announcement with derision and disbelief. No longer trusting the British Labor party, extreme Nationalists cited the Meerut trials as proof that all British parties were united on the issue of political repression in India.

The New Congress and the Simon Report: 1929–1932. Gandhi was widely criticized for telling the people to go back to the most primitive weaving and pottery techniques at a time when all industry in India looked to the future. But his critics forgot that by his approach, he had reached the tens of millions of simple peasants and artisans. He had changed the Congress party from a grouping of middle-class and upper-class elements, largely intellectuals, to a mass party of the people. He made it into a functioning political unit in thousands of Indian villages and cities, an organized body with membership dues of 8¢ a year, payable in yarn or money.

Opposed by the Government of India, which denied its political authority, the Congress party increased its membership to a prodigious figure. Hence, when it gave the signal to protest against the Simon Commission and insisted on rapid implementation of the Viceroy's promise of eventual dominion status, it was speaking as the largest organized political force in India.

On January 26, 1930, the Congress party proclaimed India's independence and adopted a national flag. It issued a Declaration of Independence, indicting Britain as having ruined India materially and spiritually. This was, of course, a unilateral declaration, which formulated an aim rather than a program of immediate action. The Congress platform demanded complete and equal adult suffrage; free and compulsory education; state ownership of basic industries, railroads, and public utilities; the right of workers to organize into unions; and freedom of speech and expression (still subject to executive fiat).

The Simon Report, issued in 1930, agreed that there should be responsible provincial government, but not responsible central government for India. It explained its refusal to grant the latter on three main grounds: religious dissensions, primarily Hindu-Moslem differences, the treaty rights of the Native Princes, and the overriding needs of defense. The report met with a generally hostile reception, aggravated by picketing and rent boycotts, the last an unusually significant weapon. In the Northwest Frontier Province, the government faced a rebellion on the part of the Afridi tribesmen, who had gathered in a "Red Shirt" organization.

The Indian government hastily sought to stifle the protest movement by suppressing public opinion and jailing opponents, but it was soon thought wiser to invite Congress representatives to round-table discussions in London. Hence the Working Committee of the Congress was released from jail. Meanwhile, the Indian Princes had come to favor federation, as outlined in the Simon Report, since that would give them a veto power.

On May 4, 1933, Lord Irwin and Gandhi came to an agreement: Gandhi was to cease his civil disobedience campaign and Lord Irwin to grant universal amnesty, except to those jailed for outrages. Gandhi went to London to attend the round-table conferences, but no agreement was reached. Upon his return to India, the new Viceroy, Lord Willingdon, imprisoned him again. The disagreements had centered mainly on finances, British experts insisting that the Indians had shown no capacity in this highly important field. In addition, the police, who had been loyal to the Crown, were loath to accept a system by which they would be controlled by groups that contemned them.

Gandhi was not the only Nationalist to be jailed. By executive order, the government imprisoned 34,500 persons for political offences. However, it gradually released its opponents until there were only 4,700 behind bars.

The Government of India Act: 1935. While a Joint Select Committee was engaged in framing a new Constitution, terrorism spread far and wide in India. For three years Bengal trembled in the throes of upheaval, the Governor, Sir John Anderson, barely escaping assassination. Hindu and Moslem riots increased, and at Cawnpore they attained serious proportions. The Government of India jailed tens of thousands of "suspects."

A shrewd Moslem barrister, Jinnah, now made the Moslem League into a really powerful influence. He began to demand *Pakistan,* or a separate country for Mohammedans in those regions of India where they were most numerous.

In London these stirrings of India added fuel to the parliamentary debates. In the House of Commons, Winston Churchill led the forces that opposed even a slight increase in Indian liberties. Though he was eloquent and forceful in his last-ditch fight, even the Conservative party felt that some reforms were necessary. Hence on December 20, 1935, the British government passed the Government of India Act, the statute under which India has since been governed.

This law makes federation compulsory for British India but voluntary for the Princes in the 562 Native states. However, the provisions for a central government met with such widespread opposition from various quarters that they have never been carried out. Jawaharlal Nehru, the Socialist leader of the Congress party and the rising star of Nationalist aspirations, called the Constitution "all brakes and no engine." But the plan for provincial governments went into effect; and in 1937 provincial parliaments met under the new scheme. With Congress ministries in 8, and non-Congress ministries in 3 provinces (Bengal, Punjab, and Sind), the plan proved quite feasible.

While these matters occupied the forefront of attention, there were two significant agricultural developments. The Lloyd "barrage," a gigantic dam laid across the Indus River in 1932, gave promise of fertilizing some 5,000,000 acres of land. And the Viceroy-elect, Lord Linlithgow, espoused detailed plans for agricultural reorganization.

India and World War II: 1939–1944. The outbreak of the European war in 1939 found India in a curiously divided state of mind. Gandhi counseled civil disobedience, but Nehru, the younger progressive-minded Leftist leader, declared against Fascism. Nehru's constructive international approach to India's problems was marked by modernity and intelligence. He stated that India, as a member of the world community, could be free only if democracy was victorious, however much her own liberties were limited.

The entry of Soviet Russia into the war (June 1941) spurred on this attitude, since Nehru and most Left-wing Nationalists have always regarded Soviet Russia sympathetically because of her enlightened treatment of national minorities and her emphasis on autonomous cultures.

At the outset of the War, the Congress party held majorities in 8 provinces. When by decree of the Viceroy, India was declared at war with Germany, resentment was keen among Indians because the Viceroy had failed even to consult them. The Congress ministries resigned in protest in October 1939. Nevertheless, recruiting for the armed forces continued and eventually the Indian army rose to over 2,000,000. Industry boomed and India became a veritable arsenal of the United Nations in Asia. But there were still 37,000 political prisoners in 1941.

When Japan attacked Britain and the U.S.A. (December 1941), it was confidently expected in Tokyo that India would rise against her British overlords. But Gandhi was in prison, and Nehru, also in prison, took a patriotic stand. The Japanese set up an "opposition" government in Singapore under the leadership of the former extreme Nationalist, Subhas Chandra Bose, now a Japanese quisling, but it had virtually no Indian following.

The Japanese conquest of Burma represented a direct threat to India, but there were no pro-Japanese stirrings in India as there had been in Burma. The Untouchables, now articulate and organized, remained loyal to Britain. Moreover, Japan's record in China, a land for which India felt deep sympathy, was enough to make Indians skeptical and distrustful of the Japanese.

Nevertheless the political deadlock persisted in India and it was clear that the country was not fully mobilized, materially and spiritually, for war. In 1942 the British government sent Sir Stafford Cripps to India, but even this noted Socialist and personal friend of Nehru resisted the demands of the Indians that they be given effective control of their government for the duration of the war. Cripps and Nehru found common ground but when the British offered India freedom only after the war, Congress replied that if Britain entrusted it with real power now, it would fully support the war effort; otherwise it would resort to a campaign of civil disobedience. At moments, it seemed as though the Cripps negotiations would succeed, but in the end they failed. When Congress called a civil disobedience movement, the Government of India once again imprisoned Gandhi, Nehru, and other Congress leaders.

The situation was substantially unchanged in 1944. The weakened Congress party fought on, with most of its leaders in jail. The government was in the hands of a firm executive, Field Marshal Wavell, a distinguished soldier who had succeeded Lord Linlithgow as Viceroy (1943). Among the broad masses of the Indian people, there was active aid for the United Nations cause but little genuine enthusiasm. Indians noted carefully Prime Minister Churchill's assertion that he did not intend to preside over the liquidation of the British Empire and his statement that the Atlantic Charter did not imply the independence of India (an affirmation which Lord Halifax has since interpreted in a quite different fashion).

On the whole, British rule has come through a difficult period of stress better than many persons had anticipated. Vast wartime industrial and trading profits of the manufacturers and merchants were, of course, a factor in holding India in line, though a calamitous famine raged in Bengal and several other provinces during 1943. Indian troops have distinguished themselves in Allied campaigns in North Africa, Burma, Italy, and elsewhere. But the political stalemate continues as the focus of World War II prepares to shift to the Pacific world.

Stakes in the Peace

Underlying all political questions, is the stake of the Indian people in a decisive improvement in agricultural welfare. The fact that there are tens of thousands of Indian villages without means of intercommunication limits production and exchange and makes markets extremely small, far below the country's capacity. With the second largest arable area on earth, India could produce, by even average methods, twice her present crops. By doubling the crops and making urban manufactures accessible to the villages, India would become a true market for imports and thus greatly assist in attaining permanently higher levels of world trade.

Too much of India's improvement has been dictated either by the need for profitable investment or by magnificent projects dear to various Viceroys. But these impulses, though beneficial in modernizing the country, have not touched the heart of India's economic problem: the dire poverty of her people. The development of agriculture and the consequent surplus of farm population, once modern machinery and tools have replaced hand labor, will center people in towns; and when roads radiate from these communities, India will then achieve a level at least comparable to that of regions of agrarian Europe. For

India, this would in itself represent a gigantic economic advance.

Recent tendencies of Moslems and Hindus to come together (Gandhi has lately spoken of a Moslem substate as a reasonable demand and has conferred with Jinnah, the Moslem League leader) are bound to hasten this process. Whether religious differences are as deep as is averred will never be known until a strenuous effort is made to compose these "communal" differences. Only in Bengal and the Punjab do they seem to be major issues: in other areas, the respective religious groups are compactly settled. The rise of urban life, with buses, trains, and tramways, has already begun to work wonders in reducing religious dissension. Even the problem of the Untouchables is far nearer solution today than it was 50 years ago. The experience of working together in the factories in the more modern settlements has done much to undermine the obstacles in the way of common-sense progress.

Despite the resistance of "die-hards" in Great Britain and of vested interests in India, especially some of the Native Princes, India cannot fail to advance to ever-greater autonomy, and at a speed beyond that envisaged in time-delaying "aims at ultimate dominion status." No country is culturally, historically, or spiritually more devoted to peace: India would be an ideal member of a world organization of nations. The rise of a free and self-governing India, taking her place beside a free and strong China, is bound to revolutionize Asia. The rise to a position of power in the Nationalist movement of an enlightened figure like Nehru points significantly in this direction.

The constructive statesmanship of Nehru is concerned not so much with narrowly Indian problems as with the capacities of such a self-governing India to serve as an effective means of stabilizing the Far East in its democratic future. Thus, the Indian National movement, which began by emphasizing its own needs under Gandhi, will, under the guidance of leaders of a more modern type, like Nehru, also serve in the larger framework of a progressive Asia; and thus India will take her proper place in world organization.

JAPAN

The Land and the People

In 1853 a visit by an American naval officer, Commodore Matthew G. Perry, opened up Japan to the modern world after two centuries of feudal seclusion and self-imposed isolation. Within less than a century, Japan had grown from a backward country, without modern industry or a modern army and navy, into a strongly industrialized and militarized State,

swollen with empire. So swift was this ascent that the rulers of Japan, in their attempt at world domination, were emboldened to attack the mightiest nations of the West.

Japan proper is a group of islands in the north temperate zone, extending from 30° to 50° North Latitude off the coast of Asia. The chief islands are Hokkaido, the most northerly, sparsely populated and about the size of Maine; the main island of Honshu, larger than Ohio and Indiana combined, the seat of her great cities, trading and industrial centers; Shikoku and Kyushu in the south, with an important industrial region in the north tip of Kyushu. The total area is 147,593 square miles, about the size of Montana. In addition, Japan has conquered or incorporated into her empire, Formosa, an island off the South China coast, and Korea on the mainland of Asia, increasing the total area to 262,912 square miles. The population of Japan proper, now 73,114,000, reaches 105,226,000 for the empire.

Since her invasion of Manchuria in 1931, especially since the outbreak of World War II, Japan has gained temporary control of another 4,000,000 square miles and subjugated 400,000,000 alien peoples, thus extending her imperial sway to over 500,000,000, second only to the number of inhabitants of the British Empire. But in this treatment we shall consider Japan proper, the island kingdom itself, and not the farflung empire extending to the borders of the Indian Ocean and the northern limits of the waters around Australia.

The Land. Part of a long range of volcanic mountains, the Japanese islands are subject to devastating earthquakes and typhoons. Because of its volcanic origin, the soil, wherever cultivable, is very rich; but only 16% of the total area is fertile, since nearly two-thirds of the country is covered by heavily forested hills and mountains which run down the whole length of the islands. The two most fertile areas are the Kwanto and Yamato plains, in southeastern and southern Honshu. Here, within easy reach of one another are the "six Great Cities," containing almost 20% of the total population: Tokyo (population 6,667,804); Osaka (3,252,340); Nagoya (1,328,084); Kyoto (1,089,725); Yokohama (968,091); and Kobe (967,234).

Tourists have long been attracted by the beautiful Japanese landscape: the long indented coastline with its many bays and inlets, the snow-capped mountains like Fuji rising over the sea, the inland lakes and swift short mountain streams.

The climate resembles that of eastern China in the Yangtze valley, but is more humid and milder, with a more equable distribution of rainfall. In the subtropical south, tea and mulberry trees are cultivated extensively. In the north, in Hokkaido, winters are severe and snowy, much closer to the Siberian climate of the Asiatic mainland. Tokyo, the capital, has a climate like that of Charleston, South Carolina; and southern Japan is often visited by damaging hurricanes and typhoons.

Japan is not well endowed with mineral resources. Moderate coal supplies are available in Hokkaido and in the extreme southwest of Kyushu (near Nagasaki). Meager oil resources exist chiefly on the west coast of Honshu, while iron is scanty, found only in Hokkaido and northeastern Honshu. Iron pyrites, however, are more plentiful in Honshu and Shikoku. While the Japanese mine some copper in Honshu and some gold in Honshu and Hokkaido, total production is small. Water-power resources are relatively large, because of the abundance of rainfall and the mountainous character of the country. Driven by the need to compensate for the lack of other industrial fuels, Japan utilized four-fifths of the developed water-power of the Asiatic continent, though she has less than a twentieth of the total water-power potential of that continent.

The People. Mongolian in origin, the Japanese people probably migrated from the Siberian mainland to the islands of present-day Japan at a historically remote period. This racial stock was largely modified by Malayan or Polynesian strains from the South Pacific area. The original inhabitants of what is now Japan (the Ainus) have practically died out except in parts of Hokkaido island. Centuries of living together on relatively small compact islands have given the Japanese people a high degree of racial cohesion.

Most Japanese are short, with olive or yellow skin-color, and slanted eyes. The outside world, including the world of science, was impressed by their apparent human feebleness until 1894, year of their war with China, and particularly 1905, when their military victory over Russia indicated physical sturdiness and endurance.

The islands of Japan have never been invaded nor have the Japanese ever before been conquered in battle. Yet their culture, though not imposed on them, is largely derivative. They borrowed their language and religion as well as their arts and handicrafts from China and Korea on the Asiatic mainland. And since 1868, the year of Japan's emergence as a modern nation, they have rapidly assimilated the advanced industrial and scientific techniques of Europe and America, while retaining in large measure the social foundations of feudalism. But they are not mere imitators; in their ability to absorb and refract alien cultures without modifying their own national patterns, they have shown remarkable ingenuity and flexibility.

Japanese life is distinguished by an extremely rigid family system. With male authority exalted, women are treated as docile, submissive puppets and the virtual enslavement of women is an important factor in modern Japanese industry. In daily life, most Japanese are profusely courteous. They exhibit delicate taste in gardens, orchards, flower-arrangements, and dwarf gardens, and in the 1870's their accomplishments in the fine arts, especially their decorative prints, strongly influenced French pictorial art and with it that of the Western world. They are eager students: even when Japan was quite small and peaceful, Japanese tourists were everywhere with their cherished cameras and field-glasses.

The Japanese have an active publishing industry, which turns out works in many fields of technology and economics, many of them translated speedily from foreign tongues. But in recent years, persecutions of the advanced intellectual class by the dominant militarists have diminished the rôle and lowered the quality of Japanese scholarship, which in the 1920's rivaled that of the Western nations.

The older Japanese culture was given over to drama (the Nō plays), lyrical poetry, and short stories whose accent was on finish rather than on plot. This older culture was based on a military and feudal way of life, enmeshed in ritual and code. It was this feudal-minded culture that resurrected archaic values like Emperor-worship and proved brutal and sadistic in practice toward subjugated peoples, despite its verbal protestations of chivalry as formulated in the warrior's code of *Bushido*.

The Japanese nation is young in the composition of

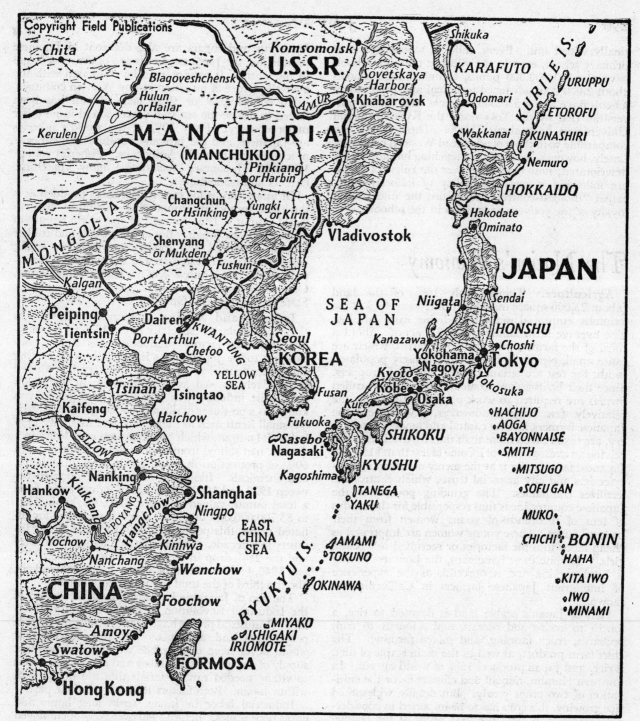

its population, over 45% being under 20. But life expectancy is not high: at the age of 20 Japanese males may expect to live on the average another 40.4 years, compared with the American (white) figure of about 47.6 years. The birthrate fell to 26.3 per thousand in 1939, but has since risen to 29.9, probably because of better wages and full employment under wartime conditions. The normally high deathrate reaches 17.6 per thousand; and infant mortality (at 114) is also high. Between 1935 and 1940 the population increased 5.6%. In 1937 forecasts were made that Japan would have 100,000,000 inhabitants by 1980, but population experts have since lowered their estimates considerably and expect a serious slowing-down in this dramatic rate of increase.

Religion and Education. Up to 1940 there was no official State church and religion was free. In that year the government assumed control over all religious institutions and compelled all Christians, whatever their differences, to be merged into a national church. The great mass of people adhere to various Buddhist sects, of which there are 12, and to Shinto sects, of which there are 13. Shintoism is closely bound up with national and imperial traditions. The priesthood of the two dominant faiths is numerous and there are tens of thousands of Buddhist and Shinto shrines everywhere. Since religion and patriotism are closely interwoven, every manifestation of religious skepticism or lukewarmness inevitably has political implications.

Among the young people, illiteracy has been practically wiped out. Every child of school age is at primary school, even in the villages; the high schools have about 1,000,000 pupils, technical high schools about 2,000,000; advanced technical and professional schools have about 530,000 students, and the six universities (led by the Tokyo and the Kyoto Imperial Universities) have about 73,000. These figures are comparable with those of advanced Western countries. Lately, however, the quality of teaching has noticeably deteriorated; now more than ever the rulers of Japan are following a conscious policy of indoctrination, called "thought-control," to ensure the undeviating loyalty of the younger generation in the schools.

The Nation's Economy

Agriculture. Though only 16% of the land (about 23,000 square miles) is arable, some 45% of the gainfully employed make their living from farming. The average farm family works 2.5 acres. About a third of the farmers own their own farms, which are quite small, especially in the more densely populated south; the rest are tenant farmers and sharecroppers. Since their holdings are so small, most of the so-called owners are required to work part of the time for the relatively few large landowners. Moreover, the Japanese farmers, lacking capital and modern machinery, are taxed much more than the city dwellers. Receiving an average annual income of less than $150, the Japanese farm family is at the mercy of usurious moneylenders and city financial trusts, which control the fertilizer companies. The grinding poverty of the Japanese countryside is thus responsible for the exodus of tens of thousands of young women from their parents' farms. These young women are impressed as cheap labor into the factories or recruited as "geisha girls." Despite these handicaps, the Japanese farmer is hard-working and resourceful, as the experience of immigrant Japanese farmers in California has shown.

Half of Japan's arable land is devoted to rice, a fourth to grains and cereals, and a fourth to fruit orchards, truck farming, and mixed farming. The chief farm product, as well as the main staple of diet, is rice, and Japan produces 15% of world output. In southern Honshu, rainfall and climate favor the cultivation of two crops yearly. But despite widespread rice growing, this crop has to be imported in considerable amounts to meet the food needs of the people. The important grain crops are wheat, barley, and millet (grown more extensively in northern Honshu and Hokkaido). Barley production, calculated on a per person basis, is about half that of the U.S.A.; wheat, despite efforts to stimulate production, about one-seventh. Recently the planting of potatoes and soya beans has been encouraged.

With only 1,500,000 horses for farming, the animal economy is on a low level; in modern Japan human beings often are forced to do the work of farm animals. The extremely small quantity of meat and dairy production is graphically revealed by comparing Japan's production per person with that of the U.S.A.: Japanese meat production is less than 3%, butter one-third of 1%, milk three-quarters of 1%, margarine 2%!

Since fats and sugars are also deficient in Japanese production, the Japanese diet is one of the most frugal in the world. It cannot even be compared with the over-all picture of nutrition in any Western country.

To compensate for these lacks, Japan has been forced to utilize the sea to a degree found in no other major country. Fully 30% of the world's fisheries are Japanese, and the Japanese consume four times as much per capita as do Americans. Fisheries engage 1,500,000 Japanese, including many part-time farmers and tradesmen.

Of money crops for export, silkworm production is the most important, amounting to almost 80% of world output. Ten per cent of the world supply of tea comes from Japan. But cotton, wool, and rubber are not produced and forestry products are small, despite the large forested area in the country. Wood-pulp production is only 8% of the United States figure. Of 50,000,000 acres of forest, 22,000,000 belong to the State or the Imperial family.

Industry and Mining. Japanese industry has risen spectacularly, especially in the 1930's. Seventy-five years ago factory production was almost non-existent; today Japan ranks industrially with leading European countries. Japanese industry has altered qualitatively as well as quantitatively: in the 1920's the textile industry was dominant, and Japan was known as a producer of silk and cotton goods and various small items such as mats, fans, and toys. By 1939 industrial output, which had increased over 100% in a decade, had shifted from light to heavy industry, with 60% of production in metal goods, steel, machinery, and chemicals. Industrial employment doubled between 1929 and 1942; while heavy industry rose from a total output valued at about $700,000,000 in 1931 to $3,700,000,000 in 1940. Even if we allow for inflated prices, this points to a 400% gain in heavy industry in a decade. Despite the shift to heavy industry and the 26% drop in consumers goods between 1937 and 1940, textiles still employ over 1,000,000 workers, about a third of the total industrial population.

The rise of Japanese industry recalls the period of the Industrial Revolution in late 18th-century England. Industrial profits have been fantastically high in percentages and amounts. But this development would never have taken place without an abundant supply of cheap, tractable labor and convenient access to vitally needed raw materials that are not present within Japan. Both factors have played their part.

Industrial labor in Japan works long hours and earns poor wages. Before 1940 over 90% of employed labor received under $7 a week. In the past few years money wages had risen almost 50% (largely because of overtime), but real wages — that is, the actual goods and services that wages could buy — declined strikingly. In peacetime Japanese workers had about a 56 hour week, compared with 35 hours in the U.S.A. and 39 in France. The war has revealed a severe shortage of skilled labor.

An important characteristic of Japanese industry is the amount of small-scale factory production still carried on. Before 1941, more than half the workers were engaged in homework or in small workshops employing less than 5 workers. Female labor predominates in this "household" industry, and these small enterprises often are used as "feeders" for the bigger factories, which allocate work to them, especially in the rayon and cotton industries.

Coal, a leading source of industrial fuel, is found in Japan but it is not well adapted for heavy industry; and Japan's small domestic production of 55,000 tons is supplemented by higher-grade coals from the Asiatic mainland, Manchuria, Korea, and North China. Iron ore production is small, about 2% that of the U.S.A., but it is supplemented by iron pyrites, in which Japan produces a sixth of world output. There is little petroleum in Japan, but 8,000,000 kilowatts of water-power compares favorably with the U.S.A. figure and is a valuable source of power for light industries, such as textile mills.

The sizable local production of copper, silver, and gold is supplemented largely by Korean output. Japan lacks bauxite, the source of aluminum, but obtains it from the Dutch East Indies, and now produces about a sixth as much as the U.S.A. Tungsten for iron alloys is obtained from regions of conquered China, and most of her deficiencies in chemicals are supplemented from conquered territories. Tin and rubber do not exist within Japan, though there is some synthetic rubber industry. Pig iron production in 1939 was about 5% of the U.S.A.'s and steel production 11% of our own. Japan in peacetime was the sixth steel-producing country in the world.

Finance. Japan's financial system is unique: it is a recognized oligarchy. The four large family trusts of Mitsui, Mitsubishi, Sumitomo, and Yasuda — called the *Zaibatsu* — are said to control directly more than 25% of industry, most of the shipping, and 60% of the stocks on the Stock Exchange (total valued at over $3,500,000,000), of which the Mitsui combine alone controls some $1,200,000,000. Members of the *Zaibatsu* are prominent in the war councils of the nation, and since Japan has really been on a war footing since 1931, they have directed their investments toward strengthening the country's war potential. Whatever their disagreements with army and navy leaders, these have revolved around the methods but not the goals of Japanese policy. The Mitsubishi trust, for example, is closely connected with naval circles; Mitsui is identified more with the army.

Together with two other trusts, the *Zaibatsu* controls 57% of all bank deposits, trust funds, and insurance companies' assets. The tendency to financial concentration has continued at a furious pace. In 1940 alone, some $475,000,000 of capital in smaller companies was absorbed by the giant trusts. Cotton spinning, the largest single employer of labor, was reduced to 14 companies and woolen manufactures to 8. The industrial monopolies are also privileged in that they are taxed proportionately only half as much as the farmers of the country.

New rivals have emerged to challenge the powers of the *Zaibatsu*. A horde of war speculators, many of them young men, having enriched themselves in conquered Manchuria and China, have returned to Japan where they continue their financial speculations and receive profitable war contracts. This group of mushroom capitalists are the most vocal imperialists; and in the early stages of the war Tokyo curb markets quoted shares in San Francisco real estate, which they confidently expected to be in Japanese hands in a short time.

Since 1929, investment of new capital in Japan has not been derived from any foreign sources. From 1933 to 1939 new capital issues exceeded $5,400,000,-000, the largest amount of new private capital investment of any country. In 1940 and 1941 it was still about $1,100,000,000 annually. In fact, from the "Manchuria Incident" of 1931 to December 1941 more than $9,000,000,000 in capital was found for industrial expansion. This new capital could have come from only two sources: the plunder of China and Manchuria and the excessive profits based on cheap and sweated labor in Japan.

The government aided this unprecedented expansion with lavish loans and subsidies. Indirect assistance was afforded by the army, for with over $250,-000,000 invested in Manchuria, military expenditures had to be increased to protect the investments. The organization of a "yen bloc" — that is, a system of trading with countries in which no gold payments were required for surplus imports — further heightened financial expansion. In this use of the "yen bloc" Japan preceded Germany in the latter's use of ingenious devices and expedients for trading.

As a result, national income rose from about $2,000,000,000 to almost $6,000,000,000 in the years 1931–39, though the value of the Japanese unit of currency, the *yen*, fell in gold terms by three-fourths. National debt rose from $1,400,000,000 in 1931 to $4,900,000,000 in 1939.

The *yen* is worth about 23.4¢ but fluctuates in value. During the period 1939–42 its circulation doubled, amounting to about $28 per capita. The cost of living is reported as having risen about 30% between 1939 and 1943. Bank deposits clearly reflect wartime inflation, having risen from $3,500,000,000 in 1939 to $8,400,000,000 in 1943; and savings, because of the serious shortage of consumers goods have gone from $1,600,000,000 to $4,500,000,000 in the same period. Peacetime savings were about $23 per person; the wartime figure is about $64.

The war budget has been increased by 400% since 1939, and is now over 50% more than the national income as reported in 1939. The budget figure given for 1943–44, 37,000,000,000 yen (about $8,600,000,-000), is obviously unreliable. Internal debt, now about $15,000,000,000, has increased 300% since 1939; but the external debt, some $345,000,000, is not heavy.

Foreign Trade and Shipping. Japan depends on imports of foodstuffs for home consumption as well as of raw materials for her key industries. To obtain these needed supplies, she had to export actively; and to carry on this trade, the Japanese built up one of the largest merchant marines in the world, fully 6,800,000 tons before December 1941. Though she has suffered serious shipping losses during World War II, her merchant marine is still estimated (June 1944) at about 4,700,000 tons. In peacetime Japan built under 500,000 tons of shipping yearly, but she may have reached this figure now. Although Japan vies with Norway for third place in world shipping, her boats are of a much inferior quality. Nearly 1,000,000 tons are of a pre-modern type and a large part of her modern commercial fleet is old; and she has only six vessels of over 10,000 tons.

Contrary to popular impressions, Japan did not

succeed in flooding the world with cheap goods in the 1930's. In fact, her share of world trade fell from 3.7% in 1929 to 3.5% in 1938. In 1937 per capita trade was far below that of the great trading nations — exports $12.85, imports $15.25. Figures since 1938 are suspect, because in many instances "trade" concealed armament deliveries.

Japan's trade was principally with the U.S.A., Manchuria and Occupied China (parts of the Japanese empire), India, the Dutch East Indies, and Great Britain, in the order named. Fully 32% of her peacetime imports were from the U.S.A. and 21% of her exports destined for America. Of her imports, 32% were raw cotton, 9% wool, 9% iron, 6% petroleum, 4% machinery, over 3% soya beans, and 2% wheat. Her exports were apportioned as follows: cotton goods 19% (she was the world's largest exporter, having replaced Lancashire), raw silk 15%, rayon 5%, machinery 3%, the others scattered fairly evenly among dozens of varied products. Yet her total foreign trade was about the same as that of Belgium, a country having only a ninth of Japan's population.

History: 1914-1944

Japan, nominally a constitutional monarchy but in reality an oligarchy of aristocrats, was an ally of Great Britain and France in World War I. She did very little fighting but used the war as a pretext to obtain the German possessions in China (on the Shantung peninsula); and, by constant intimations that she might leave the Allied camp, succeeded in extorting, by secret treaties, mandates over several groups of Pacific islands north of the Equator.

During the War (1915), Japan made her notorious "Twenty-one Demands" on China, with a view to dominating that country. After the U.S.A. entered the war (1917), the Lansing-Ishii agreement was signed. The U.S.A. construed this as not interfering with the traditional "Open Door" policy permitting all nations to trade with China and guaranteeing China's territorial integrity. Both of these conditions were expressly stipulated. The Japanese, on the other hand, interpreted the text as granting them "special interests" in China and hence justifying their imperialist attitude toward their weaker neighbor.

When the war ended, Japan had reaped all the profits of a neutral and obtained the rewards of a belligerent.

The Epoch of Conciliation: 1919-1927. Nevertheless, the fall of powerful monarchies and the rise of democracy in many parts of the world after the defeat of Imperial Germany, did not fail to influence Japan. Widespread social disturbances — the "rice riots" of 1918-19 — swept the country and challenged the rule of the governing cliques.

In 1918, Hara, leader of the conservative Seiyukai party, became Premier. He was a commoner, the first person of ordinary birth to hold that position, and the gesture appeared reassuring to the West. The impression was given that government by the great feudal-minded clans, and even by the elder statesmen (the Genro) and army leaders, had declined

in favor. The 1920 elections sustained Hara but in 1921 a nationalist fanatic assassinated him. After the usual whirl of cabinet changes, a striking characteristic of modern Japanese history, two of the Genro dictated the choice of Admiral Kato as the new Premier.

Kato was a delegate to the Washington Conference (1921-22), at which the Allied powers agreed on a capital ship ratio of 5 for the U.S.A., 5 for Great Britain, to 3 for Japan. The Allies compensated Japan by a four-power pact, by which she retained the right to unrestricted land armaments, aircraft, and submarines, and which — she assumed — protected her against Western interference in East Asia. Kato based his platform on carrying out the Washington accords, which he interpreted as guaranteeing Japanese freedom of action in the East in exchange for accepting an inferior naval status.

His death in 1923 and the terrible earthquake that devastated Japan in that year, made it necessary to reorganize and reconstruct the nation's stricken economy. A non-party government formed, followed by several governments that included many moderate elements. But in 1927 this short era of liberal ascendancy passed with the rise to power of Baron Tanaka — a militarist, whose memorandum on Japan's aims to conquer the world (the Tanaka Memorial), though officially repudiated, was proved substantially correct by later history. He was the leader of the Seiyukai party, a minority in Parliament.

The army was showing increasing impatience with parliamentary control. Moreover, politicians were greedy for spoil in this period of industrial expansion; party alternations in power seemed blatantly arranged so as to allow each party its turn at contracts and graft. One scandal followed another with almost incredible regularity, so that the army found it easy to exalt feudal honor (Bushido — the code of the warrior) as against the widespread dishonesty of the politicians.

The Road to Imperialism: 1927-1931. The more moderate elements, joining to form the Minseito party, challenged the militarists. In 1930 the Minseito party won a decisive parliamentary majority, 273 to 174. Despite their triumph, they were dislodged from power and the Seiyukai took over, with Inukai as Premier.

World conditions were having their effect on Japan, and the country faced an acute industrial crisis. Demanding drastic action, the militarists decided on the invasion of Manchuria. One of their chief motives was to crush the growing spirit of social criticism and unrest. Universal male suffrage had been initiated in 1925, and now Labor and Peasant parties were forming. The universities had many liberals and radicals, few of whom accepted the pious myths about the Mikado's descent "through ages eternal" from the Sun-Goddess and the mythological trappings involved in Emperor-worship. These Japanese were thoroughly modern in their views on economics, science, and Western thought; and, as the militarists put it, they entertained "dangerous thoughts."

Power had really passed into the hands of General Araki, a feudal-minded militarist, profoundly hostile to Western civilization. During his rule, police repression of advanced thinkers proceeded on a broader scale than in the darkest days of Czarism in Russia. Ultimately, a sizable proportion of the intellectual classes was found in jail, and books and newspapers were slowly reduced to a single, authoritarian formula.

Despite some sporadic guerrilla opposition, Japan conquered Manchuria without much difficulty (1931). After the success of this expedition and the collapse of organized resistance, the reactionaries gained favor and in the next election defeated the moderates by two to one.

China appealed to the League of Nations against Japan's aggression. The report of the Lytton Commission condemned Japanese action in Manchuria, whereupon Japan promptly declared Manchuria "independent"; renaming her Manchukuo, she ostentatiously flouted the Chinese national revolution by appointing the deposed Manchu Emperor of China, Henry Pu-yi, as "Regent" of Manchukuo. Japan then framed a constitution for the state and recognized her. In February 1933, dissatisfied with the strictures of the League of Nations, she withdrew from membership.

The real impulse behind the Manchurian adventure came from the saber-rattling generals of the Kwantung army. It was they who had influenced the elder statesman, Prince Saionji, to nominate Inukai. In spite of their electoral triumph, however, a wave of killings swept the country, largely because the ministers, though nominees of the army, still retained a certain independence.

In one such wave (March 1932) former Finance Minister Inouye and Baron Dan, head of the Mitsui banking interests and one of the most powerful financiers in Japan, were shot. These murders were the work of a "Blood Brotherhood League" formed by a fanatical army lieutenant and a Buddhist priest. This, and other secret groupings, particularly the notorious "Black Dragon Society" of Toyama, were made up largely of sons of the impoverished landed gentry, small merchants, and small industrialists, who had been ruined by the great monopolies. Their embittered heirs formed the backbone of the army, many of them being junior officers; and they resented the power exercised by the giant family combines of the *Zaibatsu*. Their radicalism took a Fascist rather than a Socialist form: that is, they hated the plutocracy but thought that repression of labor and a severely militarized state controlling the monopolies as well as labor would result in a hierarchical, imperialist society, which would conquer vast new territories and thus improve their fortunes and careers.

The "Blood Brotherhood" murderers were, in effect, congratulated, receiving prison sentences usually meted out to those accused only of misdemeanors. The terror culminated in the assassination of the *Seiyukai* leader, Premier Inukai (May 15, 1932).

Whatever the obscure intent of these assassinations, the government nevertheless in the main held to its course. It favored industrial concentration, subsidized monopolies, raised large floating loans to finance its favorite factories and war industries, and rationalized industry, to cut the already cheap Japanese costs of production. By reversing the moderate trend of the 1930's, however, it also increased military and naval expenditures. Thus it

allayed the fears of the younger officers, whose families had been ruined and who saw their salaries jeopardized if disarmament went into effect.

But the condition of agriculture remained fraught with danger. Farmers' taxes rose while industrialists received bonuses. To forestall open rebellion in the countryside, the government encouraged some 5,500,000 peasants to enter farming cooperatives; thus it held agrarian resentment to manageable proportions.

And now a delicate situation arose in the army. Formerly, the Choshu clan had dominated the army, the Satsuma clan the navy. The only way to reconcile the claims of the older clan members with the newer extraclan elements was by extending imperialist conquests to a point where every military man, both in and out of the clans, could be satisfied. But the rise of nationalism in China, with the promise of a unified patriotic China, loomed as a threat to any such expansion, which both the Japanese militarists and industrialists considered imperative.

Pressure on China Grows: 1932–1937. In 1932, Admiral Saito and War Minister General Araki formed a "non-party" government. Despite the supposed purity of the armed services, this cabinet fell over an intolerable financial scandal. Admiral Okada, who succeeded Saito as Premier, continued the reversal of the moderate policies of the 1920's by denouncing the now unpopular Washington Naval Agreement.

On the Asiatic mainland, the Japanese intensified their pressure on China. They proclaimed Henry Pu-yi definitively Emperor of Manchukuo, renaming him Kang Teh; they began to penetrate North China, threatening Peking and Tientsin. Hostilities flared up in Shanghai in 1932, after which the Tangku Truce (1933) was signed between Japan and China, providing for a demilitarized zone south of the Great Wall to the outskirts of Peking and Tientsin, where the Chinese were forbidden to station troops.

In 1934, the Japanese confronted China with a demand for Japanese suzerainty over North China; and a year later, they "invited" China to allow Japanese "counsellors" in the Chinese Central Government. Flushed with these successes in East Asia, the Japanese government called a general election (1936). To its amazement, and despite rigorous police activity in suppressing "dangerous thoughts," the more moderate *Minseito* party defeated the government by 205 to 124, and, in addition, enjoyed the support of the 18 Social Mass party (Labor) representatives. The extremists of the army cliques, backing avowed Fascists, elected only 20 members, or about 5% of Parliament. Clearly, elections were no method of obtaining national support for a program of aggressive imperialism.

Six days after the election, the greatest wave of political murders of our generation (apart from those perpetrated in Nazi Germany), swept Japan. Among the victims were Admiral Saito, Viscount Takahashi, and General Watanabe; the Premier, Admiral Okada, escaped only because the assassins mistook another individual for him. When this mass killing was done, even the Mikado was constrained to notice such untoward events and "regretted" them. This meant punishment of the young officers involved, 17 paying the penalty of their lives instead of receiving rewards and national acclaim.

The army, realizing that control was slipping out of its hands, took steps to reorganize. Hirota became Premier, but the army controlled the War Ministry as usual. Hirota knew that the Chinese situation could not wait. Manchukuo had proved disappointing as a solution of Japan's economic needs, despite railroad development, the establishment of oil monopolies, and attempts at colonization. Japan had purchased from Soviet Russia the Chinese Eastern Railway running through Manchuria; but the double-tracking of the Soviet Trans-Siberian line and the marked industrial expansion in Siberia meant that Japan would have to spend lavishly to keep watch over the Russians on the Manchurian border.

Furthermore, the struggle with "banditry" in Manchuria proved very costly in money and lives, that country remaining virtually as disorderly as it had been under the war lord, Chang Tso-lin before 1928. But though Premier Hirota increased pressure on China, the army extremists hated him for his hesitations; and in 1937 he was overthrown.

The Sino-Japanese War and the Axis: 1937–1941. Hirota had joined the Anti-Comintern Pact in November 1936, aligning Japan with Germany and Italy, but not as yet concluding a full alliance. Signature of this pact was an open provocation to war with the Soviet Union, but despite a campaign of "incidents" manufactured by young Japanese army officers, the Russians were not provoked.

Thereupon General Hayashi formed an even more Rightist government. At the 1937 elections, the people still expressed themselves in rather clear terms against an expansionist policy. The ruling cliques then decided to dispense with the luxury of elections, and the aristocrat, Prince Konoye, formed a nonparty government (May 31, 1937).

In July 1937, Konoye led Japan into open hostilities against China; by August it had flared into large-scale undeclared war, which the Japanese called "the China incident." In October of the same year a National Mobilization Law was passed and gradually applied.

Since 1935 Japanese leaders had proclaimed that Japan was seeking to build a "new order in Asia" and that this was an "immutable objective." A cooperative China must replace the China of Chiang Kai-shek; Western interests, both European and American, must be eliminated; and Soviet Russia forced ultimately to retire west of Lake Baikal in Siberia. The whole area of East Asia was to be a closed *bloc*, for which a new name was coined: "Japan's Co-Prosperity Sphere." In the course of these bellicose adventures, Japanese blood and treasure were drained; and following upon President Roosevelt's "quarantine the aggressors" speech in Chicago (October 1937), Japan came close to hostilities with the U.S.A. when the American patrol ship *Panay* was wantonly bombed by the Japanese in the Yangtze river (1938).

Two "little wars" that raged with the Russians in the summers of 1938 and 1939 on the Manchurian-Siberian and Manchurian-Mongolian frontiers resulted in such decisive Japanese defeats before Soviet artillery that henceforth prudence was substituted for saber-rattling on those frontiers. Even Prince Konoye now proved too moderate for the extremist "wild men." A further move to the Right was indicated, the new Premier being Hiranuma.

No sooner was Hiranuma installed in office than the Soviet-German Nonaggression Pact of August 23, 1939, shook the foundations of Japanese diplomacy. The shock overthrew Hiranuma, and the discomfited reactionaries permitted General Abe, who seemed to have a better grasp of diplomatic negotiations, to become Premier. Abe faced a difficult situation: the U.S.A. denounced the Japanese-American Treaty of Commerce of 1911, which opened the door to a possible embargo, something Japan could ill afford. When General Abe proved ineffectual, and as Japan found her way in the new situation set up by the European war, Admiral Yonai came into power.

No other major nation has changed the personnel of its government more often while at the same time keeping its fundamental objectives unchanged. As the crisis deepened, the government ordered the dissolution of the older parties and entrusted Prince Konoye with the task of forming a totalitarian party to replace them (July 1940).

On September 27, 1940, Japan signed a pact with her Axis partners, Germany and Italy, directed openly against the U.S.A. It was covenanted that if any power not in the European war entered it as an enemy of any one of the three contracting parties, the other two were bound to declare war against that power. By this arrangement, the signatories felt that they had checkmated the U.S.A. in both the European and Asiatic areas. Japan warned that if, for example, the U.S.A. were to protect the Netherlands East Indies, this act would unleash a general war in the Pacific.

Despite the cunning formulation of the tripartite Axis accord, Japanese Foreign Minister Matsuoka went to Soviet Russia to conclude a neutrality pact with her, whether she was at war with Germany or not. The signature of the pact (April 1941) showed that Japan was not yet desirous of challenging all her potential foes.

Repeated assertions by the United States government that it would never consent to the enslavement or control of China went unheeded. As the German armies, seemingly victorious in their sweep into Soviet Russia, approached the suburbs of Moscow, the Japanese sent a special envoy, Kurusu, and delegated Admiral Nomura, their ambassador in Washington, to negotiate with the U.S.A. Then on December 7, 1941, without any previous warning or declaration of war, the Japanese assaulted the Pearl Harbor base in Hawaii.

Their initial successes were great: their freedom from large-scale American naval interference enabled them to sweep on to rapid conquests in the Pacific, particularly inasmuch as they crippled the British fleet by sinking two of its largest warships, the *Prince of Wales* and the *Repulse*, on December 9. Overrunning the Philippines, the Netherlands East Indies, Malaya, and Burma, the Japanese soon acquired the richest colonial territories on earth, containing nearly a fourth of mankind, as their "Co-Prosperity Sphere." The Japanese Empire extended to the northern fringes of Australia and the border of India. The Sun-Goddess seemed to have rewarded the long saga of murders, treachery, and fanaticism with success.

Undefeated for centuries, and never yet successfully invaded, Japan could not believe, after her dazzling successes, that the tide would ever turn. But the tide did turn. The Russians were not defeated. European Fascism was finally placed on the defensive. China, sorely tried, survived. India did not rally to sedition as an accomplice of Japan. Australia remained undisturbed and uninvaded. The U.S.A. won its first victories on the distant periphery of the Pacific fighting; then aimed at strategically vital Japanese positions and passed successfully to the offensive.

Japanese cabinet crises were the usual method of maintaining internal controls. But the elimination of General Tojo, Premier at the time of the sneak attack on Pearl Harbor, and his replacement by General Koiso (spring of 1944), seemed to indicate more than the usual ministerial reshuffling. At any rate, since the summer of 1943, the fortunes of war have gone consistently against Japan, except for some limited but important defensive successes in the campaign against China.

Foreign Affiliations. After her triumph over Russia in 1905, Japan cemented her alliance with Great Britain and received the friendship and sympathy of the U.S.A. She was not yet suspected in Asia and, apart from Czarist Russia, had no enemies.

Today, forty years later, her last associate (but potential rival) is Germany; she has some quislings who do her bidding in China but who would abandon her without hesitation to save their own skins; and she has some friends among the conservative circles in Burma and Thailand. Among her open enemies may be counted China, the U.S.A., Great Britain, and the Netherlands, the leading power in the East Indies. The Soviet Union is unquestionably hostile. The antagonisms between the two nations are deep-seated and of long standing.

Stakes in the Peace

A defeated Japan will emerge with no continental Asiatic possessions. She will certainly be stripped of Formosa, the chain of mandated islands in the Pacific, and possibly the Kurile islands and Southern Sakhalin. Deprived of Korea and Manchuria, two important continental bases of her industry, she will find her industrial basis profoundly altered. She will, of course, be relieved of the burden of maintaining a vast army, navy, and air force. But the social classes from which their officer personnel has been recruited will remain, if the landed gentry continue to dominate the countryside and the ruined middle classes, educated technically but lacking economic outlets, grumble and agitate in the cities. What, therefore, will be done to demilitarize Japan in a long-term sense as well as in the immediate aftermath of the war?

Certain Japanese industries, such as textiles, toys, and miscellaneous cheap articles, may be able to function usefully in peacetime. The agricultural situation may be relieved somewhat by fairer taxation and credits, but it is doubtful if yields can be substantially increased. For Japan, therefore, a large industrial population is a necessity; and it seems clear that the Japanese require considerable foreign commerce to support their teeming, urban millions.

What shall be done to replace Japanese militarism's dream of world domination? Melodramatic views, such as that the Japanese ought to die out or be so weakened and impoverished that they will not matter to other nations, do not survive careful analysis. Expansion of world trade on a freer basis, with a Japan launched on the road of political and economic democracy, may offer a solution. But the benighted servitude of women and the use of an exploited peasantry as factory labor, so as to produce at artificially low costs of production, must be prevented. Moreover, the continued concentration of political power in the hands of small intertwining cliques of the military, the aristocracy, and the giant monopolies of finance and industry would block the road to progress.

The survival of the military clique is, however, barred by the stated policy of the U.S.A., China, and Great Britain which provides specifically for the disarmament and demilitarization of Japan and for the control of that country by the United Nations for an indefinite period, in order that her disarmament will not be circumvented.

Once the Japanese peasantry and working classes are free from the pressure of the militarists and monopolists and the middle class can escape its subsidiary rôle, it is possible that natural economic self-interest will find its normal expression and that industrial Japan will enter a phase of genuinely peaceful competition and political democracy.

KOREA

The Land and the People

For centuries an independent country, and long known as the "Hermit Kingdom" because of her attempts to prevent penetration from the outside world, Korea became part of the Japanese Empire by forcible annexation in 1910. In 1943, the restoration of her independence was guaranteed by the Cairo Declaration, signed by the United States, Great Britain, and China.

Korea (renamed Chosen by the Japanese) is a

peninsula jutting out from the Asiatic mainland into the Yellow Sea and Sea of Japan, at some points only 120 miles from Japan. With an area of 85,228 square miles (slightly larger than Kansas) Korea's only land neighbors are Manchuria and the Maritime Province of Soviet Siberia.

The country is mountainous, with fertile areas chiefly in the west and southwest. In all, 11,000,000 acres are cultivated, 4,000,000 of them given over to rice. The climate in the southwest is pleasant, with adequate rainfall and sunshine; while in the mountainous and densely forested north, it is cold and ill-suited to agriculture.

Korea possesses an abundance of mineral resources: high-grade anthracite coal, gold, graphite, wolfram (tungsten), copper, silver, lead, zinc, molybdenum, iron ore, magnesite, and mica. The chief center of coal, iron, and gold is in the northwest around the city of Heijo (population 185,000); another large coal and iron area is in the extreme northeastern corner above the port of Rashin; while there are other coal deposits in the southeast above Fusan (population 182,000), and gold and coal in central Korea, east of Keijo, the capital (formerly known as Seoul, population 706,000). Extensive water-power resources exist in the north.

The People. The Koreans, who resemble the North Chinese though somewhat shorter in stature, are of the Mongoloid type. They number about 25,000,000 (1944 estimate). Their language is an ancient tongue derived from the Tartar-Mongol family, but containing many Chinese words and strongly influenced by Chinese literary traditions. It is a distinct national language, differing in grammar, construction, and even alphabet from Chinese. It has different locutions for the aristocracy and the common people. The Japanese masters of the country have attempted to suppress Korean in favor of Japanese. At present, about a fifth of the people understand Japanese.

After more than thirty years of rule, and despite strenuous efforts to colonize the country, less than 3% of the population are Japanese, many of whom are in government service or work in a supervisory capacity. There is a small minority of Chinese. Across the border in Manchuria and Soviet Siberia, as well as in Japan proper, Koreans have emigrated in large numbers.

Religion and Education. Chinese religious influences have been strong and most Koreans are Confucianists, devoted to ancestor worship. The Japanese have tried to foster Shintoism and Buddhism, but together these two religions claim scarcely 2% of the population as adherents. Christianity has been spread by missionaries from the West, and over 2% of the population follow the Christian faith. Christian missions have been more important than these figures indicate in stimulating Korean culture. Since the opening of World War II, the Christian missions have been subject to strong Japanese pressure.

Illiteracy is about 60% among the adult population, but many of the younger people have been taught Japanese. Educational facilities, especially of high-school and university level, are extended mainly to Japanese residents, while native Koreans have few opportunities for higher education. Though some elementary schools have been built by the Japanese, many Korean children do not even receive a grade-school education.

The Nation's Economy

Production. Despite her relatively small size, Korea is the fourth rice-producer in the world, supplying one-fifth of Japanese consumption as well as her own needs. The crop averages around 5,000,000 tons but in the last years yields have been smaller. The Korean population has been compelled to reduce its rice consumption by two-fifths so as to supply Japan! In addition to the 4,000,000 acres devoted to rice cultivation, there are 4,000,000 acres given over to barley and millet, staple foods of the poorer people. The remaining acreage — about 3,000,000 acres — is devoted to soya beans, rye, wheat, tobacco, and, in the warmer south, cotton. Silkworm culture employs many farm families, and about 75% of the population are engaged in farming.

In animal husbandry there is a serious lack of horses and sheep, and only 1,700,000 cattle and 1,400,000 swine, with insignificant numbers of livestock. On the other hand, Korea has the world's highest per capita figure in fisheries and supplies about 15% of the world's catch. Her annual output is valued at more than $20,000,000.

Industry and Mining. Until the 1930's Korea was only slightly industrialized. But the rapid development of Japanese heavy industry, especially armaments, created the demand for an industrial base on the Asiatic mainland. As a result, Korean industrial production rose about 400% in money values between 1932 and 1938, when Japanese investments exceeded $550,000,000. As in Japan, the trend was toward heavy industry. Production was valued at about $320,000,000 in 1938 (later figures being unavailable).

The chemical industry, vital for war, now constitutes some 30% of industrial production, with metals and machinery 10%. Altogether, about 1,000,000 workers are engaged in industry, including many working in "household" handicrafts such as woodwork, pottery, and textiles. Korea's heavy industries have been subsidized by the Japanese government to make Japan self-sufficient for war; and most of them are controlled by the *Zaibatsu* (the huge family trusts in Japan) and the newer Noguchi family, whose financial power is based on interests in Korea. The older industries: food-processing, textiles, woodwork, and pottery have remained unsubsidized.

Unquestionably, a basis for heavy and chemical industries has been laid in Korea, though it is impossible to foretell the fate of these industries in a free post-war economy. At the same time, Korea possesses excellent water-power resources, about one-sixth of Japan proper, and more than enough for subsequent industrialization. Most potential water-power, however, is found in the north, somewhat distant from the leading cities.

Korea is extremely rich in mineral resources. Her total coal production is over 6,000,000 tons and includes high-quality anthracite. She produces 3% of the world's gold, 30% of its graphite (though the quality is not high), and supplies half of Japan's requirements of tungsten for ferro-alloys. In addition there is a moderate output of copper, silver, lead, zinc, molybdenum, magnesite, mica, and iron ore. The loss of this mineral wealth would seriously affect Japanese economy, particularly with respect to Japan's food-purchasing capacity, industry, and gold reserves.

Finance. Currency, banking, credit, and trade are all tightly controlled by Japan. Non-Japanese foreign investments are small, and most of these were transferred to Japanese ownership before 1941. An independent Korea would thus require a complete transformation of her financial system.

Foreign Trade. Over 90% of Korean trade is carried on with Japan and Manchuria. In 1939 Korea imported goods worth $300,000,000 and exported $250,000,000, showing a deficit that has continued for years.

Chief exports are rice, silk, soya beans, gold, wolfram (tungsten), graphite, and chemicals. Leading industrial imports are oil, metal products, machinery, and trucks; while sugar, barley, and millet have to be imported to feed the people. Over 16,000,000 tons of shipping entered the country in 1936 and Fusan is the fourth port in the Japanese Empire.

History: 1914-1944

Subjugated by Japan for over 30 years, having been legally incorporated in the Japanese Empire in 1910, Korea, "Land of the Morning Splendor," has a special history by virtue of her continuous resistance to Japanese rule. Japanese arrogance and exploitation have at times driven the Korean people, usually so polite and docile in daily life, into a frenzy of hatred. The prohibition of their language, press, and other expression of national sentiment has given rise to anti-Japanese conspiracies both within the country and abroad. Information concerning its internal history has been veiled by Japanese censorship, but some data have come through.

As part of the Japanese Empire, Korea was nominally in the Allied camp in the war of 1914–18. In 1919, at the funeral of the deposed Korean emperor,

hundreds of thousands of unarmed Koreans rose in revolt. The Japanese suppressed them with sickening cruelty, whipping, torturing, and killing many of the demonstrators in an exhibition of repression virtually unparalleled since the Middle Ages. On March 1, 1919, a Korean group in Shanghai formed a temporary government-in-exile. Koreans abroad who agitated for independence were declared criminals, and the Japanese police trailed them in every part of the world. Yet the Japanese were haunted by their crimes. During the great Japanese earthquake of 1923, the frightened Japanese massacred thousands of Korean residents, who, they felt sure, would take advantage of the catastrophe to rise up within Japan.

Meanwhile a Korean independence movement had begun to operate outside the homeland. Choi Nam Sun, author of the Korean Declaration of Independence, created a Korean literature abroad, while its existence was denied at home. So long as China remained independent of the Japanese yoke, the Korean independence movement centered there. Since the 1930's, however, it has been located in the U.S.A., although the self-designated provisional government remained in China and is now installed at Chungking.

Japan's invasion of Manchuria in 1931 both dampened Korean hopes for independence and, at the same time, provided an area of emigration. China's reverses at the hands of Japan after 1937 temporarily discouraged Korean hopes of liberation, making them seem almost utopian. But the Japanese assault on Pearl Harbor in December 1941 — a move that had been accurately predicted by alert Korean exiles — sent their hopes soaring; and ultimate independence became a certainty after the Cairo Declaration of President Roosevelt, Prime Minister Churchill, and Generalissimo Chiang Kai-shek (November 1943). The United Nations explicitly guaranteed the rebirth "in due course" of a free and independent Korea.

The industrialization of Korea during the 1930's changed the basis of the independence movement. Now large numbers of urban workers as well as middle-class professionals and students are active in the struggle. This change may effect the ultimate social objectives of the new Korea. It is reflected in divergent views of future social policy among exile groups. As they prepare for emancipation, the Koreans have gained some experience in self-government by participating actively in village elections. The exile movement, especially important in the U.S.A., has prepared an elaborate, but realistic administrative and economic program for the coming day of freedom. The two principal Korean groups in exile are the Korean Independence party, under Kim Koo, "Chairman of the Provisional Government," and the Korean National Revolutionary party, led by Kim Kyusik, which is more to the Left. These groups formed a coalition in April 1944 in Chungking.

Stakes in the Peace

The problem of independence must reckon with the fact that the Koreans, an able, homogeneous, and enterprising group, have nevertheless been deprived of experience in national government since 1910; and, in a sense, since 1894. A second fundamentally modifying factor is that the nation's economy has been shaped to meet Japanese rather than domestic requirements. The mining, chemical, public utility, and water-power resources, even rice and fisheries production, have been pressed into the service of Japan, and Korea's foreign trade and financial and corporate basis are now entirely Japanese.

Hence, true independence for Korea implies not only political change but over-all economic recasting and redirecting of markets. For the first few years of independence it will be urgently needful for Korea to accept the guidance of international experts both in the techniques of government and the reorganization of national economy.

The problems are vast, and few countries need so thoroughgoing an overhauling of their economic system. However, this richly endowed land could, within a generation, begin to approach a Western standard of living.

Korea may find her future markets largely in Manchuria and eastern Siberia, to replace the Japanese market. Then she could grant to a demilitarized, chastened Japan such trade as would not help the Japanese to reorganize their militarist system. For one thing must not be forgotten: Japan may be ready to make extraordinary concessions to salvage some part of her large banking and capital investments in Korea.

When the Koreans will have demonstrated their fitness for self-government and its attendant external and internal responsibilities, the Major Powers, who are real friends of the Korean people, will be pleased to see them walk alone.

MALAYA

The Land and the People

See map on page 303.

Malaya, a British possession on the southeastern tip of the Asiatic mainland, became familiar to Americans when tin cans were rationed and rubber tires became scarce. The history of this narrow elongated peninsula, situated just above the Equator, goes back to the 17th century when the Portuguese, then a leading maritime people, seized the narrow Straits of Malacca as the key to trade with the Far East. In the early 19th century an Englishman, Sir Stamford Raffles, saw the possibilities of Singapore, a small island just off the Malayan mainland, and urged his government to develop it as a trading center and naval base.

The Land. Singapore, Britain's "Gibraltar of the East," is one of the most strategically located seaports in existence. In peacetime one-eighth of the world's shipping passes through its waters. This colorful, tropical city of some 750,000 inhabitants has been the scene of numerous stories, novels, and films. Its surrender to the Japanese in 1942 reverberated throughout the world — it was interpreted as a symbol of the decline of Western power in the Far East, and also as a symbol of the spread of Japanese imperialism.

Malaya consists of several administrative units: the British Straits Settlements (of which Singapore is the capital), the 4 Federated Malay States, and the 5 Unfederated Malay States. The latter two groups are ruled "indirectly" by the British, native Sultans being nominally in control. The total area is 53,197 square miles (about the size of Florida), the population 5,365,755.

A mountain chain runs down the length of the Malayan peninsula and only on the west, inclining toward the Straits of Malacca, are there fertile rice-producing plains and good seaports. Most of Malaya is jungle country, but two-fifths have been cleared for cultivation, mainly rubber, which, with tin, is the country's outstanding product. Because of the variety and profuse abundance of her vegetation, wild animals, and species of fish, Malaya is the botanist's and naturalist's dream.

The climate is always hot and humid, with rainfall throughout the year. Until the beginning of the present century, the land was either dense jungle or a number of small piratical states on the coast. But the development of rubber and tin has profoundly altered the country's economic and population structure.

Mineral resources abound, the richest being tin, which is found on the western coast, mainly around Ipoh and Kuala Lumpur, a city of some 138,000. Other important minerals are iron ore, gold, coal, and wolfram (tungsten), most of the iron being in the southeast. Malaya is the largest single center of tin production in the world.

The People. The main feature of Malaya's population is its composite character: The native Malays, some 2,200,000, are only about 40% of the total. The most numerous group is the immigrant Chinese, numbering about 2,300,000; and there are 750,000 Indians. Europeans, chiefly British, number 30,000.

The Malays, a brown-skinned people, related by race and culture to the inhabitants of the Dutch East Indies and the Philippines, work mostly on the plantations and rice-fields and have not the economic importance commensurate with their numbers. Strongly emphasizing family life, they have lost much of their former warlike character (except for a few groups in coastal areas).

The Chinese are employed extensively as laborers in the tin mines, while a few have become wealthy proprietors of rubber plantations. Many Chinese occupy leading positions in the retail trades, commerce, and moneylending and follow keenly affairs in their mother country. The less aggressive Malays have often resented the increasing importance of the Chinese in the country's economic life.

The Indians, both Hindus and Moslems, constitute about 70% of the working population on the rubber plantations.

To the anthropologist, the aboriginal tribes, such as the pygmy Negritoes, Sakais, and Proto-Malays, have been of unusual interest. Many of these upcountry tribes were formerly roving head-hunters or tree-dwellers in the jungle, and the government has taken pains to prevent these aborigines from dying out since their customs and legends may throw valuable light on humanity's remote past.

Native health has improved as a result of government work in public health and the curbing of malaria, leprosy, and hookworm. The birthrate is now around 40 per thousand. The deathrate, which was 36 a generation ago, has now been reduced to 20. Infant mortality, however, still runs high — about 140 per thousand. Malaya's population is growing, but as it grows, the native Malays face the prospect of being seriously outnumbered by the immigrant Chinese, thus becoming a minority in their own land.

Religion and Education. The Malays are devout Mohammedans, the Moslem religion having been brought to that area by Arab traders as early as the 13th century. The Chinese cling to their ancestral faiths — Confucianism, Taoism, Buddhism — while the Indians are mainly Hindus, with a minority of Moslems.

In the Straits Settlements education is tuition-free and compulsory, and 25% of the population there can read and write. Among children, this figure must be even higher because in Singapore every Malay child has had some schooling. In the Federated Malay States there are schools conducted in Malay, Chinese, and Tamil (language of Madras, a province in southern India). Education in the Unfederated States, except for Johore, is far less developed.

The Nation's Economy

Production. Tin and rubber are the mainstays of Malayan economy. Over 35% of the world's natural rubber comes from Malaya, and over 70% of the cultivated area is devoted to that commodity. Only the Dutch East Indies, with an enormously greater area for planting, surpass Malayan production. Malaya also produces about 35% of the world's tin ore and fully 44% of its smelter production of tin.

In addition to tin, the leading minerals produced are: 700,000 tons of coal, useful in re-stocking ships engaged in long voyages; 1,300,000 of iron ore, nearly a fourth of Asia's total output; 700 tons of wolfram (tungsten); and 28,000 ounces of gold. Although industry is very small, the canning of home-grown fruit, especially pineapples, began to enjoy a large British Empire market before the Japanese occupation in 1942; and there are extensive water-power installations for local industries.

The chief subsistence crop is rice, the staple article of diet, but its annual production of 6,000,000 tons is inadequate for home needs, so that the country must import large quantities of rice from her neighbors,

Thailand, Indo-China, and Burma. Malaya also produces nearly 8% of the world's copra (for soaps and fats), and over 11% of its palm oil (for soap).

Finance. About 80% of the capital invested in this British possession is British, much of the remainder being Chinese. The unit of currency is the Straits dollar worth about 47¢.

In view of the elaborate system of administration, with ten local régimes, 7 tariff systems, and several postal systems, financial estimates can only be approximate. Total peacetime expenditures of the Malay States were about £13,500,000 ($65,000,000) and had risen to £16,000,000 in 1941. The total peacetime debt was about £20,000,000 (under $100,-000,000), much of it for public works or loans to the native states. Singapore has important branches of all the large trading banks of the Far East and was served in peacetime by some 80 steamship lines, or about 30,000 ships annually.

Foreign Trade. Few countries have suffered more than Malaya from the economic depression of 1929–1933. Between 1926 and 1933, the price of rubber sank from $1.00 to 5¢ a pound. During the 1929 boom Malayan trade was over a billion dollars, more than $200 per capita. In 1938 exports were $318,-000,000, imports $307,000,000; in 1940, as a result of war, the figures rose to $530,000,000 for exports, $380,000,000 for imports. Pre-war trade was about $115 per person (excluding figures for trans-shipment of goods).

Rubber and tin form the bulk of exports; rice is the leading import. The U.S.A. was in peacetime the ultimate destination of most of Malaya's exports.

History: 1914-1944

As a result of World War I, during which Malaya as a British colony was automatically at war with the Central Powers, the country entered upon a period of almost fantastic growth and prosperity. The rising world demand for rubber coincided with the increased popularity of the automobile. In 1920, however, the world crash in prices reduced the quotations for rubber to one shilling (25¢) a pound; and while this did not impoverish the colony, it was a distinct, though temporary, setback to trade.

The British government then formulated the Stevenson Plan for restricting rubber plantings (1922), which led to protests by the Americans, the principal customers, who now found themselves compelled to pay much higher prices. The price of rubber rose to the peak of $1.14 a pound in 1926 and Singapore was, for these three or four years after 1922, that part of the world where money was made most easily, more easily even than in the Florida land boom or on the New York Stock Exchange in the 1920's. Exports from little Malaya reached $1,300,000,000 in 1925.

But with the collapse of the Stevenson scheme in 1926, the inflated price of rubber collapsed, largely as a result of extensive plantings in the Netherlands East Indies. During the boom, the colonial authorities had instituted some administrative reforms with a view to decentralizing British powers and allowing increased participation of the native Malays and Chinese inhabitants in consultative government.

The Governor, Sir Laurence Guillemard, eager for reform, sought to unite the dispersed sultanates and principalities and to achieve a maximum of local self-government. But during the "easy money" period there was little interest in politics; the social convulsions of the neighboring Netherlands East Indies, of China, and of India were as remote to Singapore as to New York.

In 1927 the new governor, Sir Hugh Clifford, was content to let matters rest: rubber and tin prices were below their peak, but certainly high enough to warrant prosperity. Two years later the bubble burst; and by 1932 rubber was under 4¢ a pound, far below the cost of production on even the most economically run estates. The ruined country watched her exports to the U.S.A. (on which her prosperity was based) fall off by four-fifths.

The Chinese in Malaya Challenge British Policy: 1932–1939. Politics awoke with poverty. Fear of Chinese nationalism dominated the Colonial administrators, some of whom insisted that the Chinese residents — over 40% of the population — cared only for trade and money. Sir Hugh Clifford stated that the native Malay rulers were "sacrosanct," thus barring Chinese control of the Federated as well as the Unfederated Malay States.

In 1930 the British Labor government appointed Sir Cecil Clementi governor. He assumed office at the low point of the economic depression and faced the Chinese, who were now aroused politically by the Kuomintang movement in their mother country. The British-Chinese struggle, with the Malays in the background, dominated the 1930's.

Influential British interests bitterly assailed Clementi for seeking an administrative formula satisfactory to the three major groups. But he followed official British policy in accepting the Ottawa Imperial Preference agreements as to tariffs (1932), which gave Britain an edge over other nations in exports to Malaya, and which thus reversed the century-old policy of Sir Stamford Raffles, founder of Singapore, who had championed free trade as the foundation of its prosperity. The Chinese, intense Free Traders, went into opposition; while the Japanese, whose markets were reduced, also pleaded for free trade, which, of course, they prohibited wherever they were dominant.

Clementi then strove ingeniously for greater uniformity among the Malay States, whose crazy-quilt of administrations, customs, fiscal, and postal systems impeded progress. Thus far the Chinese enthusiastically supported him, but when he urged a customs union in order to limit external free trade, they withdrew their support. To prevent Japanese textiles from flooding the market and ousting imports of British goods, the authorities then introduced quotas on cotton goods. British Empire preference prevailed at last, although, as the Chinese steadily maintained, Malaya was not a British but a world state in her economic involvement, particularly with regard to the United States tire and canning industries.

Malaya and World War II: 1939–1944. The trade revival in the 1930's, with rubber again mounting to 25¢ a pound, greatly aided the more cautious Sir Shenton Thomas, who replaced Clementi in 1934. Though there was a recession in 1937, the construction of the grandiose Singapore naval base, the key to the Far East, stimulated enterprise.

When World War II broke out, the importance of Malaya in British strategy became evident. By 1940, all politics ceased as the colony watched for Japanese aggression. Once French Indo-China was occupied (1940), Japanese intentions were clear.

In December 1941, the Japanese assault on Pearl Harbor coincided almost simultaneously with the sinking off Malaya of the British warships, *Prince of Wales* and *Repulse*, thus crippling Allied naval strategy in the western Pacific. In the ensuing military campaign, the Japanese easily penetrated the Malayan jungle.

The Malays remained passive spectators, while the authorities deliberately refrained from arming the Chinese population, fearing that they would thus gain the upper hand politically. Hence there was no popular resistance to check the swift Japanese advance. Singapore, hitherto deemed invincible, fell easily to the Japanese (February 15, 1942). The fall of Singapore seemed, for a time, to mark the end of the epoch of European supremacy in the Orient.

Once in control, the Japanese ceded four of the Unfederated Malay States to their ally, Thailand. In October 1943, Japan ousted her implacable enemy, the Chinese, from their positions in local government and gave power to the Malays. Throughout 1944 the Japanese, making intensive defense preparations, found it easy to drive into forced labor the mass of the Chinese inhabitants, whose trade had ended and who were now economically helpless.

Stakes in the Peace

Malaya's economy depends on only two commodities: tin and rubber. Rubber now faces competition from synthetic rubber, while tin must compete with substitutes, including other metals, plastics, glass containers, and even paper. Neither is safe from a catastrophic decline: if synthetic rubber is to be produced in many countries irrespective of cost, in order to assure national security, then the Malayan countryside may revert to a wilderness, and the Chinese and Hindu coolie laborers go home. If tin collapses in price, a calamity hitherto avoided on several occasions by an international cartel, then the last foundations of the colony's economy are gone.

On a cost basis, of course, natural rubber is still very cheap, and some of the plantations can make long-term profits with rubber at 7¢ a pound. Most of the smaller plantations, however, would be wiped out in the process. Another factor operating against Malaya is the possibility that the grant of dominion status to the Netherlands East Indies may ultimately raise the level of wages in that area and thus hasten the end of coolie exploitation in nearby Malaya. In that event, synthetic rubber would not be relatively so expensive.

Malaya belongs inherently as much to the international commodities market as to the British Empire alone, except for the strategically located island-base of Singapore, whose importance has largely diminished since February 1942. As such, her salvation rests with the creation of an effective international organization.

NETHERLANDS EAST INDIES

The Land and the People

This cluster of Dutch-owned islands in the Southwest Pacific, which Japan seized in 1942, has been known for four centuries as one of the richest lands on earth. Strategically situated at the gateway to Asia, these "Spice Islands" (as they were called in the 16th and 17th centuries) were coveted by the Portuguese, Spaniards, British, and Dutch for their spices, pepper, cinnamon, tea, and coffee.

The Europeans fought bitterly over these helpless islands. When in 1608 the English were massacred on the island of Amboina, British drama decried the horror to the audience of Shakespeare's day. Spain's occupation of Portugal in 1640 and the Dutch liberation from Spain gave the Netherlands a triple advantage: the Portuguese no longer counted, the Spaniards were weak, and the British had been ousted. The English poet, John Dryden, speaks of the sailors in sea battles between England and Holland for the Indies:

> *Some preciously, by shattered porcelain fall,*
> *And some, by aromatic splinters, die.*

For 300 years, the Dutch held on to this empire and patiently built it up. When the French King Louis XIV threatened them in 1672, the Dutch prepared to flood their own country and to transport their entire population to Java. Many Dutchmen regard the East Indies as their permanent home; others treasure it as an alternate homeland. Indeed some Dutch cities in Java (like Batavia) are several hundred years old.

The spice resources of the Netherlands East Indies that made her important a few centuries ago pale before the enormity of her modern riches: oil, rubber, tin, in particular, and iron, sugar, and cinchona (for quinine). The area's international destiny is inextricably bound up with this immense natural wealth — the storehouse of the Netherlands' colonial riches.

The Equator runs through the Netherlands East Indies, which extends over 3,000 miles from east to west and over 1,000 miles from north to south. Her total area of 735,267 square miles is almost a fourth the size of the U.S.A., her population of 72,000,000 over a half as large. Two-thirds of her inhabitants (48,000,-000) live on the main island of Java (and the nearby small island of Madura) which has the highest population density on record: over 850 per square mile. Sumatra (somewhat larger than Montana) has close to 10,000,000 inhabitants; Celebes, 4,500,000; Bali, the paradise of tourists, 1,500,000; while the other islands, Borneo (part Dutch, part British), the Moluccas ("Spice Islands"), Dutch Timor (near Australia), the western half of New Guinea, and a host of smaller islands — contain the rest of the population.

The Land. Most of the soil is unrivaled — it is the most fertile on the face of the globe. Volcanic mountains run through the islands and the flow of lava in the valleys between volcanic ridges has enriched the earth; in Java, for example, the soil produces three crops of rice a year. Volcanic and earthquake activity has at times been intense: when the peak of Mount Krakatoa erupted in 1883, its volcanic dust was so dense that it colored the sunsets all over the world during the entire year. The climate is tropical and either hot and dry or wet and warm. The mountains, however, afford some relief from the muggy heat.

It is impossible to enumerate the diversity of physical features and vegetation found on these islands. In a sense, they mirror and symbolize the variety and profusion of the much vaster Pacific. Java is famous in botany and zoology for being the zone of Wallace's line — that is, the zone that separates Asiatic fauna and flora from that of Melanesia and Australia; and it was here that the scientist Dubois found the remains of the "Java man," thought by many to be the "missing link" between ape and man.

Physically, Java presents lovely well-irrigated green fields on the coastal plain, towering volcanic peaks, azure sea and skies. On some of the other islands, such as Borneo, Celebes, and Dutch New Guinea, thickly forested jungle land is common. The cities too vary widely: in some, native quarters, Chinese quarters, and modern up-to-date European-style sections are juxtaposed. The chief cities, all in Java, are Batavia, capital of the islands (population 550,-000); Surabaya (350,000), an important seaport and naval base; and Bandung (175,000). The only city of over 100,000 not on Java is Palembang on Sumatra (110,000 population).

Natural resources of this island group are varied and abundant. Oil is exploited on Borneo, Dutch New Guinea, Celebes, Java, and Sumatra, the deposits on the first two islands named having been scarcely tapped. Tin is mined in large quantities on two small islands, Bankga and Billiton, just off Sumatra. Nickel resources on Celebes are extensive, and coal, gold, and bauxite (for aluminum) are found in smaller quantities in western Sumatra. Rubber, grown on large plantations on the east coast of Sumatra and on Java, leads the agricultural commodities for export. Sugar, ranking next to rubber, is grown mostly on Java; and this fertile island is also rich in rice, tea, pepper, cinchona, coffee, tobacco, tapioca, palm oil and coconut products for soaps and fats, sisal (for twine), and kapok. Interestingly, many products were introduced from other continents: rubber, coffee, tobacco, tapioca, and quinine from South America; tea from China and India; and palm oil from Africa.

The People. A storehouse of human types as well as natural resources, the Netherlands East Indies contain well over 125 tribes at varying levels of culture, speaking over 25 different languages. But the principal people are the Javanese, numbering about 50,000,000, a Malayan group with some traces of Mongolian influence. The most widely spoken language is "basic Malay," which is understood by the overwhelming majority of the islanders except among the more remote tribes.

In Sumatra the people are more purely Malay,

with less Mongolian influence; in Borneo there are Negritoes, similar to those in the Philippines; in New Guinea the natives are Melanesians.

The Javanese, usually short and brown-skinned, have delicate features and a remarkable posture. Many artists and physiologists consider Javanese women to have the ideal human form. Their dress, the *sarong* made of exquisitely woven batik, has often been copied and adopted by Westerners.

Many cultural waves have swept over Java. As late as the 15th century the islands were under Hindu domination and one frequently meets traces of Hindu culture, especially in the striking architectural remains of stone temples. But with the Mohammedan conquest, beginning in the 13th century and culminating in the 15th, most of these Hindu influences were pushed into the background, and they survive only in certain customs and tastes in handicrafts. In Bali, however, the Hindu faith and Hindu customs have prevailed down to the present. Throughout the islands the Dutch have preserved the native laws and traits as much as possible; and in many places they rule "indirectly," through native sultans and princes.

The population problem in Java seems to illustrate the Malthusian theory that increase of population tends to outrun the increase in subsistence. Certainly, there has been no comparable population rise elsewhere: Java's population swelled from 5,000,000 in 1816 to 48,000,000 in 1939. There has been no substantial immigration into Java or large-scale industrialization, just more intensive farm cultivation. At present the population density is over 850 per square mile.

In the other islands — called "the Outer Islands" — population is relatively sparse, with some 23,000,000 people in over 680,000 square miles. With population increasing at 1.5% yearly, the islands will have more than 100,000,000 by 1970. To cope with this problem, the Netherlands government in the East Indies laid plans to colonize the sparsely settled outer islands with Javanese. To keep Java down to her present population, 80,000 families must be colonized every year until the year 2000.

Of the non-Indonesian population, the principal minority is the Chinese, numbering about 1,200,000, (or 2%). Many Chinese work as coolies in the tin mines or on tobacco plantations, but they are also active as merchants and moneylenders. In 1940 there were 250,000 Westerners living in the islands, the Dutch numbering 220,000 and occupying key positions in government administration and private enterprise. The Dutch commonly intermarry with the handsome native population and are usually free of the race bias so prominent in other Asiatic colonies ruled by the whites. Many half-castes (of mixed Dutch and native blood) have occupied high places in the Indies' government.

Religion and Education. The Javanese are almost 100% Mohammedan; and throughout the islands well over 90% subscribe to the Moslem faith. The only notable exception is Bali, where Hinduism prevails. Among the Chinese, there are about 1,000,000 Buddhists and Confucianists. Christianity has made some progress, the present number of Christians is about 2,500,000. In the remote areas of Borneo, Celebes, and Dutch New Guinea, most of the native tribes are pagan animists.

Over 90% of the native population is illiterate. About 1% of the people can read and write Dutch. Some 2,300,000 children — about one in seven of school age — go to elementary school for the first three grades. But only about 8,000 attend high school, and though there are some advanced institutions for technical subjects, no university exists. Dutch administration, so enlightened in a number of respects, has not coped adequately with the serious problem of popular education. Less than 10% of the annual budget of the East Indies went for education in peacetime, as compared with 25% in the nearby Philippine Islands.

Native culture in the Dutch East Indies is one of the richest and most fascinating on record. The Malayan language, with its Sanskrit remains, reveals many interesting linguistic influences. In music, the dance, weaving, and other handicrafts, Indonesian culture has reached heights of excellence.

The Nation's Economy

Agriculture. The main crops for subsistence are rice and corn, staple articles of diet. Rice production amounts to about 15% of the world supply, but corn (about 2,600,000 tons annually) does not show unusually good yields. Farming is of two general types: (1) native agriculture — millions of Indonesians own their own small farms, work them on a family basis, and produce just enough for their own needs, or with some surplus for sale or export; and (2) estate agriculture — immense plantations owned and managed by Westerners and worked by native labor. Despite the density of population, the islands produce enough food for home consumption. In the world-famed botanical gardens at Buitenzorg, the development of tropical agriculture was in reality initiated as the result of Dutch enterprise and Dutch scientific ability.

To illustrate the wealth of the archipelago, the Netherlands East Indies produce the following percentages of the world supply of leading commodities: rubber 40% (highest in the world), palm oil (for soaps) 20%, quinine 90%, pepper 80%, kapok 75%, tin 30% (second in the world), copra (for soaps and fats) 33%, sisal 23%, tea 17%, sugar 7% (third in the world), and coffee 6%.

Mineral Production. With an annual oil production of some 8,700,000 tons, about 3% of the world's, the Indies stand fifth among oil-producing nations. Three-fourths of Asia's bauxite (source of aluminum) are here; as well as about 2% of the world's nickel, and some silver, gold, and manganese.

Industry. Apart from factories for processing foodstuffs and oil refineries, industries were not well developed. In 1938 there were about 1,670,000 Indonesians classified as industrial workers but 670,000 (over 40%) were home workers engaged in weaving, spinning, and batik-work. Only 120,000 (less than 10%) worked in the larger factories such as sugar and textile mills and oil refineries. Just before the Japanese invasion the Dutch had drawn up elaborate plans for industrial expansion in iron, chemical, armament, and textile industries, but the war prevented their materialization.

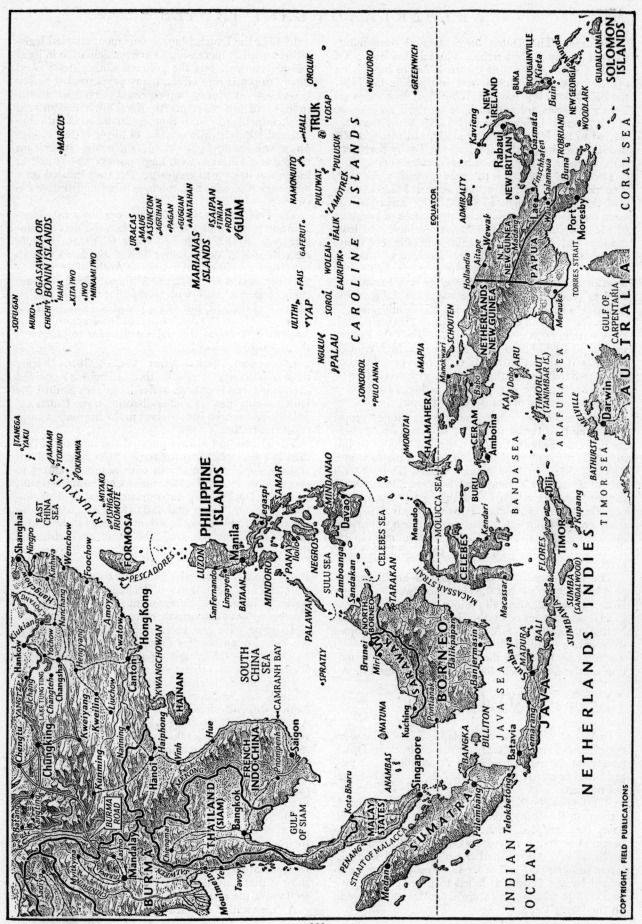

MARCUS

OGASAWARA OR BONIN ISLANDS
MUKO
CHICHI
HAHA
KITA IWO
IWO
MINAMI IWO
SOFUGAN

URACAS
MAUG
ASUNCION
AGRIHAN
PAGAN
GUGUAN
ANATAHAN
MARIANAS ISLANDS
SAIPAN
TINIAN
ROTA
GUAM

OROLUK
NUKUORO
GREENWICH
HALL
TRUK
LOSAP
NAMONUITO
PULUWAT
PULUSUK
PULAP
LAMOTREK
NAMONUITO
GAFERUT
WOLEAI
SOROL
IFALIK
EAURIPIK
FAIS
ULITHI
YAP
CAROLINE ISLANDS

EQUATOR

NGULU
PALAU
SONSOROL
PULO ANNA
MAPIA

BOUGAINVILLE
BUKA
NEW IRELAND
Kavieng
Buin
Kieta
SOLOMON ISLANDS
Wunda
NEW GEORGIA
GUADALCANAL
Rabaul
NEW BRITAIN
Gasmata
WOODLARK
TROBRIAND
Finschhafen
Talamaua
Buna
Lae
Wau
Madang
Port Moresby
PAPUA
TORRES STRAIT
N.E. NEW GUINEA
NETHERLANDS NEW GUINEA
Hollandia
Aitape
Wewak
SCHOUTEN
ADMIRALTY
Manokwari
Merauke
CORAL SEA

Babo
Dobo
ARU
KAI
TIMORLAUT (TANIMBAR IS.)
ARAFURA SEA
MOROTAI
HALMAHERA
CERAM
Amboina
BURU
Kendari
CELEBES
Menado
MOLUCCA SEA
BANDA SEA
Macassar
MACASSAR STRAIT
FLORES
TIMOR
Dili
Kupang
SUMBA (SANDALWOOD)
SUMBAWA
TIMOR SEA
MELVILLE
BATHURST
Darwin
GULF OF CARPENTARIA
AUSTRALIA

Shanghai
Ningpo
EAST CHINA SEA
Wenchow
Foochow
Kinhwa
Nanchang
Kiukiang
Hankow
YANGTZE
Ichang
Chungking
Chengtu
Kunming
Nanning
BURMA ROAD
Mandalay
Lashio
Moulmein
Tavoy
BURMA
THAILAND (SIAM)
Bangkok
GULF OF SIAM
Phnompenh
Saigon
FRENCH INDO-CHINA
MEKONG
Hue
Vinh
Hanoi
Haiphong
HAINAN
Canton
Hong Kong
KWANGCHOWAN
Swatow
Amoy
Foochow
RYUKYUS
OKINAWA
AMAMI
TOKUNO
TANEGA
YAKU
MIYAKO
ISHIGAKI
IRIOMOTE
FORMOSA
PESCADORES
SOUTH CHINA SEA
CAMRANH BAY
LUZON
Manila
BATAAN
San Fernando
Lingayen
MINDORO
PHILIPPINE ISLANDS
Legaspi
SAMAR
PANAY
Iloilo
NEGROS
SULU SEA
PALAWAN
Zamboanga
Sandakan
NORTH BORNEO
TARAKAN
MINDANAO
Davao
CELEBES SEA
SPRATLY
NATUNA
Brunei
Miri
SARAWAK
Kuching
Pontianak
BORNEO
Balikpapan
Banjermasin
BANGKA
BILLITON
JAVA SEA
Batavia
Semarang
Surabaya
MADURA
BALI
JAVA
NETHERLANDS INDIES
SUMBAWA
ANAMBAS
Singapore
MALAY STATES
Penang
STRAIT OF MALACCA
Kota Bharu
Telokbetong
Palembang
Medan
SUMATRA
INDIAN OCEAN

COPYRIGHT, FIELD PUBLICATIONS

Finance. The Dutch have invested tremendous sums of money in their richest colonial possession. Of the $1,600,000,000 estimated (in 1928) to have been invested there, the Dutch were responsible for 75%, the British for 14%, the U.S.A. for 3%. In good years Dutch investors are said to have received an average of 14% on their investments. Large sums were remitted to the Netherlands annually, but much of the profits was reinvested in the Indies. Today perhaps a fifth of Dutch national wealth is invested there.

The unit of currency is the *guilder*, worth about 53¢. The peacetime budget approximated $425,000,000, and the domestic debt $742,000,000. Taxation has been faced with the extremely low income of the mass of the people: 97% — the natives — have the least money and the lowest positions in the economy. Estate agriculture, owned by foreigners, working about a tenth of the soil for export crops, brings the most profits, but native labor receives very low wages. In 1937 income taxes were assessed on 25% of the Europeans (practically every head of a family), on 3% of the Chinese, but only *on one native in 2,000*, although these natives farm most of the land! Thus the bulk of the people (97%) do not have an income high enough to make it subject to taxation. Their poverty contrasts strikingly with the fabulous richness of their land. Most of the wage-earning Indonesians have a per capita income of less than $50 a year.

Foreign Trade. Since they export money crops, the Dutch East Indies are most sensitive to world trade conditions. Exports in 1929 were $581,000,000; but in 1932, during the depression, they sank to under $200,000,000. In 1938 exports totaled $360,000,000 (about $5.50 per capita) and imports $265,000,000 (about $4.50 per capita). The chief exports were rubber, tin, sugar, oil, nickel, bauxite, quinine, pepper, sisal, copra, palm oil, cinnamon, tapioca, nutmegs, tobacco, and tea. Chief imports were machinery, textiles, iron and steel, motor cars, and chemical products.

The Netherlands, of course, played an important part in foreign trade but the Dutch followed an "Open Door" policy, allowing all nations to compete without special advantages or disabilities. In addition to the Netherlands, the U.S.A., Great Britain, and Japan were active in the Indies' foreign trade. In 1944 it was not easy to foresee the effects of Japanese occupation on the finance and foreign trade of these islands.

History: 1914-1944

In World War I, the Netherlands East Indies were double beneficiaries of wartime prosperity: as a Dutch possession they were neutral in the conflict, and they produced commodities vitally needed by the belligerent nations.

But the rise of a local, native *intelligentsia* had become a thorn in the flesh of the cautious Dutch authorities. They therefore decided in 1918 to grant a Constitution and to create a People's Council. But since this *Volksraad* had only limited consultative and no legislative powers, and half of its 48 members were nominated by the Crown, it failed to placate the native nationalists, who by now were articulate and active in all the larger towns.

In 1922 the Dutch home government enacted legislation aimed at increasing native participation in local self-government, but the colonial authorities moved slowly to put it into effect, many years passing before it was even modestly implemented. To assist in the practice of self-government, the Dutch encouraged local councils, to whom they gradually confided more internal administration. The example of the Philippines was annoyingly close: since the Americans trusted the Filipinos with large powers, the Dutch at least must appear to conform. But they insisted on a long period of scientific tutelage in administrative experience.

The *Volksraad* received wider powers by a new Constitution granted in 1925; and when the new legislature met in 1927, fully 38 of its 60 members were elected. But of this number, it was stipulated that 15 must be Europeans, 3 Chinese or Arabs of Dutch nationality, and at least 5 native Malays. The legislature could concern itself with everything except foreign policy and defense, but when it was not in session the Governor-General could issue orders-in-council. A committee of 20 sat throughout the year to safeguard the rights of the legislature.

Indonesian Nationalism: 1927–1938. Despite these significant concessions, the Nationalists remained dissatisfied and began an active campaign against the Dutch authorities. To allay discontent, the Dutch appointed two native Indonesians to the Supreme Council of the Indies.

The Dutch had always pursued the method of "indirect" rule, upholding the native princes and sultans and naming a native regent with nominal powers to accompany every Dutch provincial administrator, who was legally only an adviser. Nationalists, inspired by republican and radical ideas, assailed this ingenious organization based on respect for the native princes and their officials. The Dutch authorities, on the other hand, insisted that the Nationalists were all Communists, carrying out the orders of the Third International. Since the Netherlands was one of the countries in Europe that still declined to recognize the Soviet Union, the government could make these charges without diplomatic complications.

To cope with the increasingly difficult situation, the colonial authorities followed a policy of decentralization, establishing a separate administration for Western Java, and strengthened the secret police. All workers, especially those in the factories, were fingerprinted, and agitators thus detected were jailed. A further difficulty had arisen with the introduction of American moving pictures. The Dutch established a rigorous censorship, allowing only those films that showed the white race in its worthier aspects. But since this sharply reduced the number of films available, the government had frequently to modify its decisions, with even worse results than those it had sought to avoid.

The authorities modernized the regency councils, allowing councils of electors in every village to name the members of these consultative local bodies. The result was that the peasants obtained some measure of representation and, to the general astonishment, showed that radicalism had penetrated to the remotest sections of the countryside.

A "race sense" was aroused and talk of Pan-Asiatic

ideals became widespread. The natives were eager to hear agitators describe the deeds of Gandhi and Chiang Kai-shek. There were some outbursts in the countryside, hardly more than a ripple on the surface, but the Dutch administrators became more vigilant. The *Shakirat Islam*, or Pan-Islamic movement, began to stir among the overwhelmingly Moslem population of the Indies. Then, in 1925–27, a series of wild strikes, new to the islands, broke out in the factories and seaports. The colonial police soon stamped out most of them.

Burdensome taxation, meanwhile, remained a deep source of irritation. Though the prosperity of the 1919–29 decade had controlled discontent, the rise of taxation by 250% in peacetime was an ominous portent. When the world crash of 1929 impoverished the population beyond even their ordinary pauperism, the authorities took steps to economize and to reduce wages, including the pay of the armed services. Despite the mutiny (1932) of the crew of the *Seven Provinces*, the government held firm to its retrenchment policy.

The return of prosperity after 1934 greatly relieved the authorities, bringing to a close a period of seemingly chronic disorders. But as domestic difficulties subsided, the menace of Japanese aggression grew.

Japan and the Netherlands East Indies: 1938–1944. For several years, Japanese statesmen had openly hinted at forcing the Netherlands East Indies to collaborate with Japan in her economic sphere. In 1940, when Germany invaded and despoiled the Netherlands in Europe, Japanese warnings grew more blunt. It was clear by now that the fate of the Netherlands East Indies was central to the peace and security of the Pacific.

In the spring of 1942, immediately after the fall of Singapore, Japan invaded Java. Despite the epic heroism of the small, tragically outnumbered Dutch fleet and the last-ditch fight of the Indies' soldiery and police forces, the archipelago fell to Japan with extraordinary ease.

The Netherlands East Indies fell partly because of Japanese military and naval superiority, and partly because the colonial authorities, distrusting the natives, had failed to equip them with arms. Many of the Indonesians appeared fundamentally indifferent to a change of sovereignty. The Dutch learned the lesson of this tragic defeat, and in December 1942 the Dutch Queen Wilhelmina, in a significant radio broadcast, assured the Japanese-subjugated islanders that in the post-war world the Indies would be an autonomous self-governing part of the Netherlands Commonwealth, and no longer a colonial area.

The Japanese, for their part, pledged an autonomous development of the islands. But owing to serious shipping shortages, they soon abandoned their elaborate sounding plans for "co-prosperity." Japanese-created councils, consisting of the richest natives, at first met with some slight success, and the Japanese have been busily engaged in "conditioning" the minds of the natives with such slogans as "Asia for the Asiatics." Europeans have suffered an eclipse and the Chinese minority have also been humiliated. At this juncture, it is impossible to forecast the social effects of this dramatic change in racial positions.

The day of liberation for the Netherlands East Indies draws near. Native cooperation with the Dutch in the past, whenever they have instituted genuinely liberal reforms, is a good omen for the future Dominion status of the Indies within the Dutch Commonwealth.

Stakes in the Peace

The recent pronouncements of Queen Wilhelmina forecasting a Dutch Commonwealth to replace the Dutch Empire mark the first decisive step in the economic development of the native Indonesians. It is scarcely conceivable that a situation can continue in which the Dutch, Eurasians, and Chinese hold almost all the important and lucrative properties while the mass of the native population is left with small plots of land and almost no cash income.

The next step indicated is the large-scale transfer of Javanese from their island to the large and sparsely populated tracts in the neighboring islands. Such resettlement would not only remedy the over-population of the mother island, Java, and enrich the "outer islands"; it would also inspire a spirit of pioneering enterprise so lacking among the Javanese today.

The democratization of government must proceed rather more speedily than Dutch colonial experts, such as Angelino and other spokesmen for the Netherlands, have envisaged. Japanese occupation, whatever its rigors, has given the islanders a concept of Oriental supremacy. The defeat and expulsion of the Japanese should not leave the Indonesians with the feeling of despair that the natives are permanently inferior to the ever-victorious Westerners.

A painful dilemma will confront the Dutch if resentment of the enlightened Indonesians against the native princelings increases in intensity. A rising republican movement may prove hostile to "indirect rule." For it is doubtful that there is still much native loyalty to these ornamental princes and sultans, who have shown little administrative ability.

An East Indies or Indonesian Federation, in which the peoples of this island-world can exchange their newly gained experience in self-government with neighboring peoples, seems indicated to replace the present situation, in which the islands are divided solely on the basis of their tutelage to remote European states. Various expedients: such as the encouragement of native enterprise, more equitable distribution of landholdings, and the fostering of progressive rather than the slower-moving traditional political attitudes will assist such a natural grouping in assuming some of the functions now allocated to various European empires because of their past investments and past services.

THE PHILIPPINE ISLANDS

The Land and the People

The Philippine Islands are unique among the countries of the Far East. For more than three centuries they have been under Western rule, the Spaniards ruling from the 16th century until 1899, when the U.S.A. acquired them after the Spanish-American War. Hence the Filipinos, Oriental by race and related to the peoples of Malaya and the Dutch East Indies, have been largely westernized in their culture and religious outlook. Moreover, the Philippines are the only colonial possession in the Far East that has been actively prepared for self-government and given a definite date by the ruling country for complete independence. Occupied since 1942 by the Japanese, the Philippine Commonwealth has a government-in-exile functioning in the U.S.A.

The Land. The archipelago of the Philippines, situated in the western Pacific, just above the Equator, consists of thousands of small, scattered islands and islets; but eleven larger islands constitute 94% of the total area of 114,400 square miles. The most important are Luzon, Mindanao, Mindoro, Cebu, and Panay. The group extends over 1,000 miles from north to south and 700 miles from east to west. They are 700 miles southeast of Hongkong, the gateway to South China, 1,500 miles northeast of Singapore, 5,000 miles from Hawaii, and 7,500 miles from the west coast of the U.S.A. — three weeks away by fast ocean liner and a few days by Pacific clipper plane.

The islands are mountainous and volcanic, rising steeply from the Pacific Ocean, and thickly forested. About 50% of the wooded area is government-owned and 10% is scrub or other forest, whose trees are not worth exploiting. There is rainforest vegetation over most of the land, and the people flourish in the well-watered plains between the mountains and the sea. About 26,000 square miles — or some 15% of the total area — are cultivated, though the amount of cultivable land is much higher. The climate is of the monsoon type, with a hot and humid rainy season and a dry, cooler period in the winter months.

The archipelago is rich in mineral resources, especially gold, silver, iron ore, coal, copper, lead, and zinc. The chief centers of mining are around Baguio in the mountains north of Manila, and in the north of Mindanao Island.

Manila, the capital (on Luzon), is a beautiful modern city of some 630,000 inhabitants, with one of the finest harbors in the entire Pacific. Other important cities are Cebu (on Cebu Island) with 155,000 inhabitants, and Davao (on Mindanao) with 103,000.

The People. The Filipinos, though they constitute 98% of the islands' 17,000,000 population, are themselves divided into a bewildering variety of groups. Eight separate races are called Filipinos, and there are in all 43 ethnic groups on the islands, including Malays, Indonesians, the pygmy Negritoes, and the Igorots, who but recently abandoned head-hunting. One group, the Moros on Mindanao, are well known because of their almost fanatic resistance to Filipino rule and their aggressive Mohammedan religion. But almost all Filipinos, except those of Negro stock, are brown-skinned, short, slight of build, and extremely nimble.

The birthrate is 32 per thousand, the deathrate 16.5. Infant mortality (139 per thousand) is still quite high, but a rapid growth of the population is forecast for the next generation. In less than 25 years, the population has increased some 60%.

Among the minority groups, the Chinese, numbering about 120,000, are prominent in retail businesses and trade. Before 1941, there were some 30,000 Japanese around Davao, where they controlled the hemp industry and fisheries. Americans, 4,000, occupied important positions in business and the professions; while the Spaniards (about 5,000) were influential in the professions and invested capital in the tobacco industry and real estate.

There are three official languages: English, Spanish, and the widely diffused native dialect, Tagalog, that was officially adopted just before the Japanese invasion. English is understood by over 2,000,000 people, Spanish by 1,000,000. But throughout the islands at least 8 languages and over 80 dialects are spoken.

Religion and Education. The Filipinos are the only Far Eastern people who have accepted Christianity, a unique development explained by the three centuries of Spanish rule. Today, most Filipinos — about 10,000,000 — are Roman Catholics, but the Philippine National Church, a dissenting Catholic faith founded by Bishop Aglipay in the early years of this century, claims 4,000,000 adherents. There are 500,000 Mohammedans, chiefly among the Moros, and about 200,000 Protestants of various denominations. In the hill country, among the more primitive tribes, there are about half a million pagans, mostly nature-worshipers.

Education is tuition-free and compulsory; and in 1940 most of the children of school age, about 2,000,000, were at school. Almost half the population can read and write today, as compared with a literacy figure of 10% in 1900. Instruction was primarily in English and there were 150,000 students in advanced schools and colleges. The two outstanding universities are the government-supported University of the Philippines in Manila and the ancient University of San Tomas, founded in 1611. American education has done much to raise the cultural level and thus to crystallize the idea of a nation among these peoples who are so divergent in language and racial origin.

Filipino culture, long under alien control, has made forward strides in the face of the acute poverty of most of the people. Many Filipinos have become successful journalists and professional men; and the tradition of José Rizal, writer and fighter for freedom in the late 19th century, is alive in some of the younger Filipino writers.

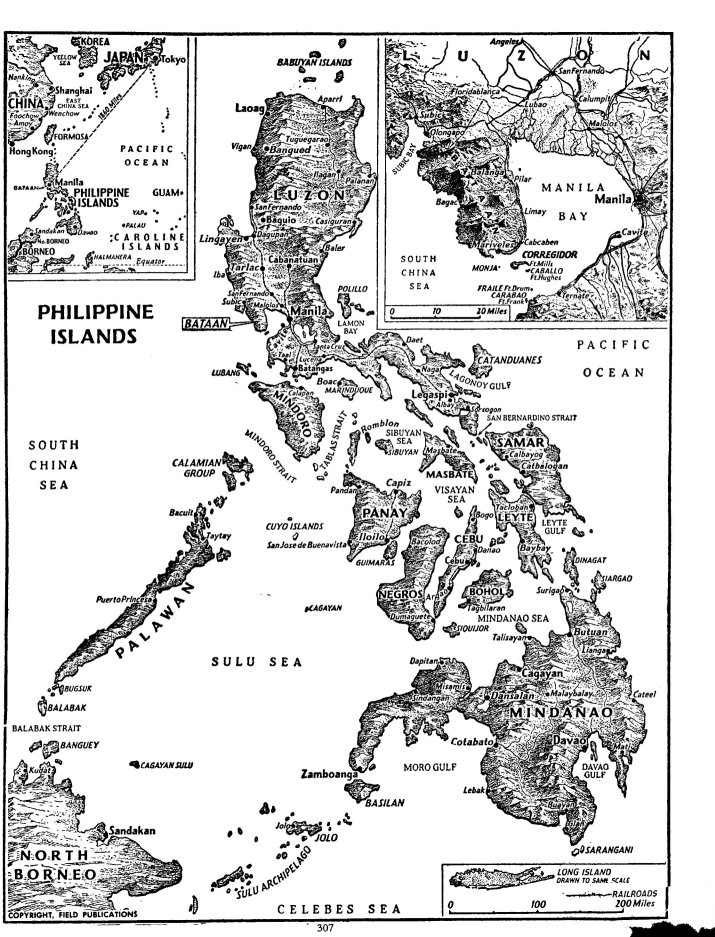

The Nation's Economy

Agriculture. About half the cultivated land is devoted to rice, a staple article of diet, with an annual production of 2,300,000 tons. Corn has also been developed for home consumption. But the chief feature of Philippine agriculture has been the concentration on "money crops": that is, crops which had access duty-free to the U.S.A. These were: sugar cane, over 1,000,000 tons; copra (for soaps and fats), over 600,000; and *abaca* (Manila hemp) over 200,000. Concentration on these "money crops" meant that the islands were not self-sufficient in nourishment and had to import foodstuffs. Of crop values rice was 42%, sugar 25%, coconut products 14%, hemp 4%, and corn 5%. Tobacco, once important, has declined. The pineapple is the outstanding tropical fruit grown. In all, three-fifths of national income is derived from agriculture.

Philippine farming is backward, characterized by widespread tenant-farming or sharecropping, primitive techniques, excessive holdings by big landlords, and large landholdings by the Church. Hence most Filipino farmers, though they are relatively better off than most of the farmers of Asia, are poor in Western terms.

Livestock production was fair: 2,600,000 water-buffaloes (used in the rice fields), 1,700,000 cattle, 500,000 horses and mules, and 36,000,000 pigs.

Mining. Mining was making rapid progress when the Japanese overran the islands in 1942. Gold production was about $38,000,000 annually, and iron ore, much of it used locally, had reached 770,000 tons. Coal, silver, lead, copper, and zinc were among the other minerals exploited.

Industry. Realizing the dangers of a one-sided economy based on "money crops" destined for the United States, the Filipinos sought to increase factory production. In this they were aided by American enterprise and capital. Light industries: sugar refineries, coconut-oil mills, soap, textiles, shoes, cigars and cigarettes, fruit canning, lace and embroideries, and distilleries have developed in the Manila area, but the fate of these "infant industries" under Japanese occupation is unknown. About 40% of the population was engaged in industry in 1939.

Finance. The unit of currency is the *peso*, worth 50¢. In 1940 there were 200,000,000 circulating in coin and paper notes — about $6 per person. The currency was backed 100% by gold or United States securities. The national debt in 1940 was only $36,000,000.

Foreign Trade. As might be expected, the U.S.A. dominated Philippine trade, taking 83% of exports and furnishing 78% of imports. In the years before 1941, Japan made strenuous efforts to penetrate the Philippine market. With annual exports averaging about $156,000,000 and imports $135,000,000, a per capita figure of $17, Philippine trade was brisk for an essentially colonial economy.

Chief exports were sugar and sugar products, gold, coconut products (copra was 36% of the world's share), tobacco, embroideries (most Spanish shawls and mantillas coming from Manila). Leading imports were metals and metal products, oil, chemicals, textiles, wheat, meat, and dairy products.

History: 1914-1944

The Philippine Islands, America's outpost in the Far Pacific, prospered during World War I. Exports of sugar, tobacco, and metals were large and commanded high prices. Though the Islands were at war with the Central Powers, internal politics absorbed much of the people's attention. For in 1916 the United States Congress had passed the Jones Bill, increasing autonomy and plainly stating that independence of the Philippines was an ultimate — and not-too-distant — goal.

Ever since their acquisition in 1899, the Philippines had been a subject of partisan controversy in the U.S.A. Anti-imperialists, led by William Jennings Bryan, had assailed their annexation, and from 1900–1912 every Democratic Party platform condemned both their acquisition and American domination over them. Hence in 1913 President Wilson appointed an avowed partisan of emancipation as Governor-General: Francis Burton Harrison.

The Republican Party, under whose (McKinley's) administration the islands had been acquired, insisted that they remain for a long time under American tutelage. Thus, when President Harding assumed office in 1921, Governor-General Harrison was succeeded by General Leonard Wood, a man of the classic colonial view, that is, that the Filipinos were an admirable people who learned the arts of government with astonishing speed, but that they were far from showing capacity for self-government and might never wholly attain it.

Among the Filipinos themselves, there were conflicting political parties; but all, except for tiny minorities, centered demands on independence. The principal party, the *Nacionalista*, had two wings, one headed by Manuel Quezon and the other by Sergio Osmena. The *Democratas* formed the opposition, while occasionally such national figures as General Emilio Aguinaldo contended for power. Among the irreconcilables was General Ricarte, who nursed his anti-American grudges in Japan.

Succession of Republican Governors-General: 1921–1933. American business interests in the Islands viewed with relief the departure of Harrison in 1921. During his term, the government had sponsored national companies — joint state and private enterprises — which suffered an unhappy fate in the 1921 economic slump, when prices of colonial products fell. Moreover, his administration had favored public ownership of railroads and utilities as well as control of banking — tendencies opposed to the then dominant American philosophy of enterprise.

General Wood, whose rule was based on business efficiency and prosperity, enjoyed the wholehearted support of American business interests. But after two fairly quiet years with the Filipino majority on the Council of State, a quarrel over an American detective, Conley, led to the resignation *en masse* of the Filipinos. Wood used the full powers given him by the Jones

The Nation's Economy

Agriculture. About half the cultivated land is devoted to rice, a staple article of diet, with an annual production of 2,300,000 tons. Corn has also been developed for home consumption. But the chief feature of Philippine agriculture has been the concentration on "money crops": that is, crops which had access duty-free to the U.S.A. These were: sugar cane, over 1,000,000 tons; copra (for soaps and fats), over 600,000; and *abaca* (Manila hemp) over 200,000. Concentration on these "money crops" meant that the islands were not self-sufficient in nourishment and had to import foodstuffs. Of crop values rice was 42%, sugar 25%, coconut products 14%, hemp 4%, and corn 5%. Tobacco, once important, has declined. The pineapple is the outstanding tropical fruit grown. In all, three-fifths of national income is derived from agriculture.

Philippine farming is backward, characterized by widespread tenant-farming or sharecropping, primitive techniques, excessive holdings by big landlords, and large landholdings by the Church. Hence most Filipino farmers, though they are relatively better off than most of the farmers of Asia, are poor in Western terms.

Livestock production was fair: 2,600,000 water-buffaloes (used in the rice fields), 1,700,000 cattle, 500,000 horses and mules, and 36,000,000 pigs.

Mining. Mining was making rapid progress when the Japanese overran the islands in 1942. Gold production was about $38,000,000 annually, and iron ore, much of it used locally, had reached 770,000 tons. Coal, silver, lead, copper, and zinc were among the other minerals exploited.

Industry. Realizing the dangers of a one-sided economy based on "money crops" destined for the United States, the Filipinos sought to increase factory production. In this they were aided by American enterprise and capital. Light industries: sugar refineries, coconut-oil mills, soap, textiles, shoes, cigars and cigarettes, fruit canning, lace and embroideries, and distilleries have developed in the Manila area, but the fate of these "infant industries" under Japanese occupation is unknown. About 40% of the population was engaged in industry in 1939.

Finance. The unit of currency is the *peso*, worth 50¢. In 1940 there were 200,000,000 circulating in coin and paper notes — about $6 per person. The currency was backed 100% by gold or United States securities. The national debt in 1940 was only $36,000,000.

Foreign Trade. As might be expected, the U.S.A. dominated Philippine trade, taking 83% of exports and furnishing 78% of imports. In the years before 1941, Japan made strenuous efforts to penetrate the Philippine market. With annual exports averaging about $156,000,000 and imports $135,000,000, a per capita figure of $17, Philippine trade was brisk for an essentially colonial economy.

Chief exports were sugar and sugar products, gold, coconut products (copra was 36% of the world's share and map?, embroideries (most Spanish shawls and map? coming from Manila). Leading imports were metals and metal products, oil, chemicals, textiles, wheat, meat, and dairy products.

History: 1914-1944

The Philippine Islands, America's outpost in the Far Pacific, prospered during World War I. Exports of sugar, tobacco, and metals were large and commanded high prices. Though the Islands were at war with the Central Powers, internal politics absorbed much of the people's attention. For in 1916 the United States Congress had passed the Jones Bill, increasing autonomy and plainly stating that independence of the Philippines was an ultimate — and not-too-distant — goal.

Ever since their acquisition in 1899, the Philippines had been a subject of partisan controversy in the U.S.A. Anti-imperialists, led by William Jennings Bryan, had assailed their annexation, and from 1900–1912 every Democratic Party platform condemned both their acquisition and American domination over them. Hence in 1913 President Wilson appointed an avowed partisan of emancipation as Governor-General: Francis Burton Harrison.

The Republican Party, under whose (McKinley's) administration the islands had been acquired, insisted that they remain for a long time under American tutelage. Thus, when President Harding assumed office in 1921, Governor-General Harrison was succeeded by General Leonard Wood, a man of the classic colonial view, that is, that the Filipinos were an admirable people who learned the arts of government with astonishing speed, but that they were far from showing capacity for self-government and might never wholly attain it.

Among the Filipinos themselves, there were conflicting political parties; but all, except for tiny minorities, centered demands on independence. The principal party, the *Nacionalista*, had two wings, one headed by Manuel Quezon and the other by Sergio Osmena. The *Democratas* formed the opposition, while occasionally such national figures as General Emilio Aguinaldo contended for power. Among the irreconcilables was General Ricarte, who nursed his anti-American grudges in Japan.

Succession of Republican Governors-General: 1921-1933. American business interests in the Islands viewed with relief the departure of Harrison in 1921. During his term, the government had sponsored national companies — joint state and private enterprises — which suffered an unhappy fate in the 1921 economic slump, when prices of colonial products fell. Moreover, his administration had favored public ownership of railroads and utilities as well as control of banking — tendencies opposed to the then dominant American philosophy of enterprise.

General Wood, whose rule was based on business efficiency and prosperity, enjoyed the wholehearted support of American business interests. But after two fairly quiet years with the Filipino majority on the Council of State, a quarrel over an American detective, Conley, led to the resignation *en masse* of the Filipinos. Wood used the full powers given him by the Jones

Act, and while his opponents charged that he was high-handed, there is no evidence that he exceeded a broad interpretation of his legal powers.

But while Harrison, from 1916 to 1920, had vetoed five bills, Governor-General Wood vetoed 126 from 1921–27, and in some years vetoed an appreciable proportion of all legislation passed. He pleaded that many of these bills were sent him after the adjournment of the Legislature; but the Filipinos resented his action as evidence that he felt his judgment superior to that of the elected representatives of millions of people. President Coolidge, repeatedly insisting on the unwisdom of granting ultimate independence to the Philippines, sustained Wood. But in 1927 ill health caused the latter to leave his post and he died soon after.

His successor, Henry L. Stimson, made friends more easily. By now, the Filipinos had considerable legislative experience, and the electorate, a mere 1% of the population in 1907, had risen to 8% by 1925, despite literacy qualifications. Moreover, the *Nacionalista* Party was now united and formidable. When, after the inauguration of President Hoover in 1929, Stimson returned to Washington, Dwight F. Davis became Governor-General; and in 1932, Theodore Roosevelt, Jr.

The Commonwealth Government Emerges: 1933–1941. In 1933, President Roosevelt appointed Governor Frank Murphy of Michigan, Governor-General of the Philippines. The spirit of Murphy's administration was more akin to that of Francis Burton Harrison, though it was less romantic and displayed a deeper understanding of the grave problems of defense that had arisen as a result of Japanese aggressions in the Far East.

In February 1933, passage of the Hare-Hawes-Cutting Bill laid the basis for wider autonomy and ultimate Philippine independence. But this was soon superseded by the Tydings-McDuffie Act of 1934, under which the Philippines became a self-governing commonwealth as of 1935, with full and sovereign independence to eventuate in 1946.

The grant of independence, however, was accompanied by many restrictions and specifications in tariff policy greatly diminishing Philippine exports to the U.S.A. Opponents of the Nationalist, Quezon, exploited this fact to assert that liberation of the islands was to America's economic advantage, benefiting in particular American sugar- and tobacco-producers.

Nevertheless, by this measure the Philippines became the only self-governing democratic state in the Far East; and for the first time, a colonial country received a precise and formal date for its emancipation. Now Filipinos filled almost the entire Civil Service, and such remnants of American rule as control of the Supreme Court vanished. Manuel Quezon became the first president of the Commonwealth in 1936.

Soon after Quezon's inauguration, the Spanish Civil War broke out. Most of the older Spanish community, centered in Manila, was pro-Franco. This was the first of the pro-Fascist groupings; but others soon gained notoriety. The *Sakdalistas*, a pro-Japanese group with a radical land-program designed to win over the bulk of the poor peasants, had staged an uprising in 1935. Unsuccessful, the *Sakdalista* leaders fled to Japan, but were soon returned to Manila and jailed. Many of them subsequently became active Japanese agents.

Quezon's opposition insisted that he was dictatorial, but his popular support was overwhelming. Among his opponents were Aguinaldo, Bishop Aglipay of the National Church, and a Rightist leader, Sumuolong, who formed a curious united front against Quezon. Meanwhile, the *Sakdalistas* changed their name to *Ganaps* and resumed their activities.

Japan in the Philippines: 1942–1944. Quezon raised the issue of complete independence in 1938 rather than in 1946, thus assuming that his country might be spared Japanese aggression. But when he realized that it would make no difference to an aggressor what the precise political status of the republic was, he acquiesced in the provision of complete independence in 1946.

In December 1941, Japan struck at the Philippines. That same year, President Quezon was reelected for a second term, his inauguration occurring in the midst of the Japanese assault. General Douglas MacArthur had previously been invited by the Commonwealth Government to train the Philippine Army. Commanding the combined American-Filipino forces, MacArthur led his vastly outnumbered troops in the defense of Bataan Peninsula and Corregidor.

Within a few months the Japanese had overrun the Islands. They obtained the support of José Vargas, one-time secretary of Quezon, whom they installed as Mayor of Manila. The Quezon government, unshakably loyal to the U.S.A., continued to function in exile from its seat in Washington, D.C. In 1944 upon Quezon's death, Vice-President Osmena became President.

The Japanese conquerors announced the formation of a provisional government under the presidency of José Laurel, former Philippine Supreme Court Justice, and a new totalitarian party, the *Kalibapi*. On October 14, 1943, Japan proclaimed the Philippines an independent state in the Japanese "Co-prosperity Sphere." The native tongue, Tagalog, replaced English as the official state language.

Meanwhile, the U.S.A. formally pledged that the Philippines would be independent immediately upon their reconquest from Japan. Various American agencies worked with the Philippine government-in-exile on reconstruction plans for the period after the expulsion of the Japanese.

Stakes in the Peace

Tragedy has brought the Philippines nearer to the U.S.A. The contrast between American and Japanese administration will speak for itself. The reality of the war in the Pacific has swept aside former academic discussions.

Philippine independence does not connote isolation; on the contrary, it requires reciprocal guarantees, which not even the largest nations can any longer avoid. National independence will thus take on a 20th century hue, replacing the old absolute view of sovereignty. The position of the Philippines in the Far East is so bound up with that of their neighbors, the Dutch East Indies, Indo-China, and Malaya, that any arrangements with the U.S.A. could best be supplemented with regional agreements for this area of emergent nationalism.

On the economic side, the U.S.A. has imposed a sliding scale of tariffs which gradually reduces the preferences enjoyed by Philippine products exported to the U.S.A. This provision is in accord with American policy of freer world trade, and, at the same time, it allows Philippine economy that reasonable interval during which it can realign its export markets.

THAILAND

The Land and the People

See maps on pages 265, 303.

Lying between Burma and French Indo-China, Thailand (formerly Siam) is the only independent nation in southeastern continental Asia. In the period of European penetration of that part of the world (the late 19th century) Thailand preserved her independence largely by skillfully playing off rival British and French claims.

After the boundary rectification with French Indo-China, imposed by Japan in 1941, Thailand's area measured 200,000 square miles (a fourth larger than California) and her population was estimated at 15,-800,000.

The Land. Thailand is mountainous in the thinly populated north. In the center are grazing lands and dense forests, home of the elephant and tiger. The south-central region, near the capital Bangkok, contains the bulk of the population and the centers of economic importance. Here, in the fertile valley of the Menam River, meaning "mother of the waters," is a region of profuse green vegetation and fertile, well-watered soil, where rice grows in abundance. The southern tip, a thin wedge at the northern end of the Malay peninsula, is largely forest, with some sections devoted to rubber, tin, and wolfram. Other important minerals, including antimony, sapphires, and gold are found in southern Thailand. There are no natural fuels, and even water-power is not extensively available.

The climate is of the monsoon type, wet and excessively humid from May to October and dry and cool in the winter months.

The People. The Thais (Siamese) are thought to have come originally from the north, probably from Yunnan province in China. Though they are more olive-skinned than the Chinese, they are undoubtedly of similar origin and closely related to the peoples of Tibet and neighboring Indo-China. They may have been driven south to their present homeland by conquerors who were later absorbed by Chinese culture.

Thailand's 15,800,000 population contains sizable minorities: some 500,000 Chinese, 500,000 Indians and Malays, and about 60,000 Cambodians. The Thais themselves constitute some 93% of the population, though the Chinese contest this figure, asserting that the number of people of recent Chinese origin in Thailand is as high as 15%. At any rate, the Chinese dominate commerce, retail trades, and the handicrafts industry, ranging from itinerant peddlers to prosperous merchants and owners of rubber plantations. In recent years 10 out of 30 newspapers in the country were written in Chinese.

Religion and Education. Since the 16th century Buddhism has been the state religion of Thailand; and there are over 140,000 Buddhist priests, more than 3% of the adult males. In every town there is a Buddhist monastery that serves as a center of administration, recreation, and education. Even in a truly modern city like Bangkok (population 700,000), temples rise above its hundreds of canals and are mirrored in their waters. In the rural districts, terraced temples loom above the lush green of the rice fields. Buddhism is part and parcel of the country's social and economic life. Because the large estates owned by Buddhist temples and monasteries are exempt from taxation, a heavy financial burden falls upon the peasants.

But the Thais are eager for new knowledge; and in Bangkok the younger generation is keenly alive to world influences, though what effect these modern trends will have on traditional Buddhism is difficult to foresee. Among the minority religious faiths are 50,000 Christians, who have played an important part in modern education.

Education is officially in the hands of the government, but in practice it is in the hands of the Buddhist village priests. About one child in two today attends state-supported schools, so that illiteracy, now estimated at over 60% among adults, is being greatly reduced. Bangkok has two universities.

Thai literature in the Siamese language reflects the relatively high position of women, almost unique in Far Eastern society. It consists largely of love poems and fairy tales, some of which are among the most ingenious and beautiful known. Prior to Japanese domination of the country, the government actively disseminated traditional and historical knowledge among its people.

The Nation's Economy

Production. Thailand, like Indo-China, is *monocultural*, that is, a country of one crop. Rice is the principal food and article of export for the 80% of the people engaged in agriculture. About 5,000,000 tons are produced annually, roughly 6% of the world's supply.

Other important products are tin, fluctuating between 7% and 10% of world production, and rubber, with an annual output of 45,000 tons, only about a tenth of the figure in neighboring Malaya. The chief tropical wood exported is teak, which lends itself to intricate carving. There is almost no manufacturing except for some native handicrafts in weaving, pottery, basketry, and metal work.

Finance. The unit of currency is the *baht*, worth 37¢. During World War II, money in circulation has doubled and is now about $5 per person. Budgets too have risen from $49,000,000 to $104,000,000. Domestic and foreign debts are both small — $8,000,000 and $20,000,000 respectively. Before Thailand fell under Japanese domination, British and Chinese banks predominated — there was only one Japanese bank and one Thai bank. Extensive British interests in Thailand's banking and mining did not, however, prevent Thailand's present close alignment in war with Japan.

Savings accounts in official banks are not much over $2,000,000, but the people, poverty-stricken except in some parts of the Menam valley, resort extensively to borrowing from Chinese moneylenders in the country.

Foreign Trade. In 1938 Thailand exported about $76,000,000, imported $55,000,000. But the outbreak of war in the Far East and the attendant loss of markets caused a subsequent decline.

Chief exports were rice 56%, tin ore 19%, rubber 15%, teakwood 3%. The teak trade was in British hands almost exclusively. Exports went principally to Malaya and India (thence ultimately to Britain in large amounts). Chief imports, mainly from Japan and India were cotton goods, foodstuffs, gunnysacks for packing, and metal manufactures.

History: 1914-1944

In 1914 Thailand (then called Siam), under her absolute monarch King Rama VI, was an Oriental state with court favorites, widespread corruption and intrigues, and a judiciary living on bribes. The country was nominally independent, but there was little popular understanding of or participation in government.

Despite the pro-German leanings of many of her officers, Thailand declared war against Germany in 1917, thus avoiding a joint Anglo-French protectorate that was rumored in the offing. The war brought temporary prosperity to the kingdom; and in 1921 King Rama introduced a spate of reforms, including compulsory education for both girls and boys.

The war-boom soon collapsed, however, and between 1921 and 1925 there was permanent economic crisis, forcing the country to make many foreign loans. Avid for power, Rama ruled with absolutism; at the same time, he was indolent and allowed Prince Devawongse to become regent. As it turned out, this gave the aristocracy, who lived largely on government largess, a dominant representative at the very highest seat of government.

Only one able man rose from the ranks, Chao Phya Youmarej, who by sheer talent became Minister of the Interior, and whose rise presaged social changes. But every cabinet minister was acting independently and there was virtual administrative chaos when Rama died in 1925.

Prajadhipok, the new King, instituted a series of sweeping reforms: a Council of Princes was named to replace the hazardous rule of court favorites, and the cabinet system began to function again. Since the budget was inordinately large, the King reduced the bureaucracy, eliminating the posts of court favorites, and even reducing the decorative royal pages from 3,000 to 300. The educated classes, thriving on state employment, resented these economies.

Visiting America in 1931, King Prajadhipok stated that one day he would grant a constitution. But he insisted that it must come from his regal grace and not from popular demand, and that the political education of the people must proceed slowly and on the basis of prudently accumulated experience. Meanwhile, the economic depression necessitated large expenditures for relief just when state revenues were decreasing; and the Ministries of War and Communications fell into conflict over economies; the War Minister wishing to promote many officers and name others.

The 1932 Revolution and Its Aftermath: 1932-1936. The King celebrated the 150th anniversary of his dynasty in 1932, just as new social forces appeared on the horizon. A middle-class opposition advocated land taxes, which would have injured the landowning aristocrats; immediately, the régime imposed new taxes on the middle classes.

In June 1932 a *coup d'état*, quite orderly and bloodless, occurred. The revolutionists in the newly formed People's Party asked for an end of the absolutist monarchy with its attendant abuses and the substitution of an enlightened constitutional monarchy. The leader of the party, Paris-educated Luang Pradit, drew up the manifesto. The King acceded and a Senate and Council prepared to take over the royal prerogatives. To show that no basic transformation was intended, Phya Mano, an old-time minister, became Chief of State. The demands of the revolutionists with respect to political and tax reforms were quite moderate — almost a perfect replica of those advanced in the France of 1789, when her revolution began.

This change released long-dormant social forces, and there followed a wave of demands from the poorer classes, accompanied by strikes. The government pleaded that it now feared French intervention, since the French in neighboring Indo-China were grappling with Communist-inspired nationalism. In November 1932, a conservative reaction restored most of the King's powers; and the Constitution, as adopted, was quite conservative in tenor.

The only political party allowed to function had two wings: the Conservative, led by Phya Mano, and the Radical, led by Luang Pradit. Army officers asked for permission to form a Nationalist party. When this was refused, they insisted that the ruling People's Party also be dissolved. Now it became plain that they had asked to form a party only as a skillful maneuver to force a dissolution of the People's Party. The Conservatives, doing the Army's bidding, dissolved the Assembly, muzzled the press, and declared that they had saved the country from a social revolution. The British press in the Far East congratulated them, for there had been anxiety as to the fate of the sizable British investments in Thailand.

Emboldened, the Army attempted a second *coup*. In June 1933 they succeeded in installing their friend, Phya Bahol, in power. He was astute enough to enlist the support of the Radical Luang Pradit. Perturbed at this military-radical coalition, the aristocracy rose under Prince Bovara Dej, former War Minister; but they were crushed, and with their failure the princely power suffered an eclipse.

The King, suspected of sympathies with the aristocrats, appointed a regent and went abroad for eye treatments in January 1934. In November, just after the collapse of the aristocrats' rising, an election took place with 10% of the electorate voting. For several years thereafter, there was a varied assortment of plots, conspiracies, and risings, but none proved of serious proportions.

Something more impressive occurred in September 1934 when the Assembly voted down the government. To the amazement of the country, the Ministers promptly resigned without further ado. The Assembly, confident, then passed a bill over the royal veto, authorizing inheritance taxes. Chagrined, King Prajadhipok abdicated (March 1935) and stated that he would live in England. He designated his nephew, a minor studying in Switzerland, to succeed him as King Ananda; the newly formed regency council managed to survive several hostile conspiracies.

Thailand Turns to Japan: 1936–1944. In February 1936 the Western-educated Luang Pradit became Foreign Minister. Japanese commercial and political penetration, using as its lever the hatred of many of the Thai people for the numerous and successful Chinese minority in the country, now made rapid progress. Despite the heightening tensions, elections were held and some 26% of the people voted in an orderly atmosphere.

But when King Ananda returned in 1938, the nation was fervently and vociferously nationalist. The name of the country was changed from Siam to Thailand. Demands arose for the subjugation of the Chinese, and there was agitation against foreigners (Europeans) but not against the Japanese. The British watched warily as Japan negotiated with Thailand to use the Kra Isthmus on the flank of Singapore, the last remnant of old Siam's once-dominant position in Malaya.

In 1940 after the fall of France, Thailand attacked Indo-China to obtain territories in the region of Cambodia to which she laid claim. Accepting Japanese arbitration which favored her claims, Thailand thus became bound to Japan. There were other reasons for these strengthened ties: the untrammeled hatred of Nationalist China on the part of Thailand's ruling groups, and the growing imperialism in the country fostered by the Army and the *intelligentsia*.

By December 1941, when Japan began her assault on the Western powers, Thailand was her accomplice, declaring war against the U.S.A. and Britain in January 1942. The Thais, hoping for territorial acquisitions in Malaya and the Shan States of Burma as well as further concessions in the Laos region in French Indo-China, allowed the Japanese to use their land as a base for the conquest of Burma and Malaya.

Nevertheless, the liberalism that had been so pronounced in the 1930's and that had so profoundly altered her absolutist society was not dead but dormant. An influential minority, both in Thailand and abroad, opposed the alliance with Japan as did, of course, the numerous, enlightened Chinese within the country.

In 1942 Japan flamboyantly awarded parts of Malaya and the Shan States to Thailand, and the latter's régime under Premier Luang Pibul Songgram monotonously endorsed Japanese actions everywhere in Asia and the Pacific.

Stakes in the Peace

Thailand will share in Japan's defeat. Her conquests in Cambodia, the Shan States, and Malaya will be restored. The connivance of the court and government cliques at the destruction by Japan of Chinese independence will leave her dominant groups in an isolated position in the Far East.

On the other hand, however devoted and sincere the democratic elements in Thailand have been, they have not shown sufficient historic maturity to cope with the older reactionary groups. The long struggle between 1932 and 1937 culminated in an easy victory for the Nationalists; and popular indifference certainly played some part in ensuring this victory. The Chinese minority have been articulate in their patriotic anti-Japanese sentiments, but the Thai nobility have fostered intense national hatred of these Chinese residents.

It is to be hoped that the liberal sentiments, which seemed to prevail between 1932 and 1935, can be resurrected. Their triumph depends on the elimination of the landed nobility, corrupt and cynical almost to a man. But the weakening or elimination of this dangerous group, who have jeopardized the safety of Asia, should not mean that power will devolve upon the influential Chinese elements rather than the Thai people themselves.

Until the intellectual classes in Thailand have a function other than government employment, the future of democratic government will be tenuous. But the almost certain triumph of forward-looking elements after the military defeat, and the alignment of a reconstructed Thailand with other nations of southeast Asia into a peace *bloc* will, if accompanied by land reforms, fundamentally transform Thai history.

The Thais form an important part of the great peninsula of southeast Asia, of which they and related peoples constitute the bulk of the population. Some place must be found for them in its structure. Otherwise, the foes of unity and of world organization will exploit Thai disaffection and thus seek to undermine the successful functioning of a regional peace group in southeast Asia.

Near East and Mediterranean Orbit

EGYPT

The Land and the People

Although the Kingdom of Egypt lies in the northeast corner of Africa, it must be considered as an Asiatic country in religion and culture. It is isolated from the rest of Africa by the immense Libyan desert and the wide stretches of Anglo-Egyptian Sudan. From time immemorial, except for some chance contacts with Ethiopia, Egypt's history has focused on the Mediterranean and on the Sinai bridge into Arabia.

Egyptian civilization, the oldest surviving one with which the Western world has had intimate contact, was inundated by the tide of Arab conquests in the 7th century and given a prevailing Arabian cast, though the original people still form the mass of the population. The ancient Egyptians, with the Chaldeans, had given Europeans irrigation, systematic agriculture, laws, architecture, and the state as we know it. At the height of her later power (about 1500 B.C.) Egypt was the center of the Mediterranean world. Alexandria flourished for eight centuries as a capital of world culture and commerce. Egypt is also an ancient seat of Christianity; and, to this day, the Copts (Egyptians faithful to the Cross) retain the oldest patriarchate in Christendom.

But by the beginning of the 19th century Egypt had shrunk in population to less than two millions. Then a man of real genius, however wild, Mehemet Ali, transformed her, and a French engineer, de Lesseps, through the building of the Suez Canal (1869), made her once more a center of commerce, half the world's shipping passing through her gates. The British, despite their bitterly criticized intervention, subsequently brought to the land order, capital investment, science, engineering genius, and irrigation. The population has increased nearly 400% since 1850. Egypt proportionately has grown almost as rapidly as the U.S.A., especially since British control in 1885.

Egypt covers 366,000 square miles but this area is merely an expanse of sand and stone except for the ribbon-like valley of the Nile (really a long, slender oasis) and the delta of the Nile with its deep alluvial soil. If we add the inland oasis of Fayum, the fertile lands make up 13,600 square miles. Hence Egypt is, effectively, about as large as Maryland and Delaware combined. Within that area concentrate 16,680,000 people, more than 1,200 to the square mile. Even in antiquity the fertile regions seem to have been, for those times, densely populated: the story of Joseph shows how, in recurrent cycles, Egypt trembled on the edge of famine.

Along the Nile the rise of the river forms the source of fertility; in the delta the land is always rich. Egypt is a "river land" in a sense no other country can be. The Nile, the greatest river known to the ancients, once worshiped as a god, flows 4,600 miles from the highlands of east-central Africa. Its mysterious increase in volume puzzled men until the end of the last century when its sources were discovered. The strip of land fertilized by the river extends from 2 to 14 miles in width (at Cairo, 10 miles), mainly stretching back from the west bank. Damming and irrigation, practiced from early days, sometimes make possible a yield of three crops a year; and the building of great upcountry dams, like Assuan and still larger projects, has greatly aided the country by making the flow more regular. In the rich delta, alluvium lies 50 to 75 feet deep, a truly fantastic source of crops.

Surrounded by desert in every direction except on the sea, Egypt gets virtually no rain. The sky is almost always blue. Even the winters are warm, sometimes hot, though the nights are often cool. Except on the coast, where north winds bring some relief, the hot, humid delta weather tries European endurance.

The people are usually quite tall, strong, and well proportioned. The oval faces seen in monuments and on mummy cases still prevail among them. From north to south complexions shade from sallow to brown. The women have dark, brilliant eyes, and when young, remarkable carriage. They are famed for the Egyptian nose (had Cleopatra's been shorter a Frenchman once said, the history of the world would have been different). The mass of the *fellaheen* (peasants) and city dwellers exemplify the native Egyptian stock. The Arabs, on the other hand, often own large landholdings or become powerful in politics, though others follow a more primitive nomadic existence. Upcountry and in the western deserts, Berbers (often with some Negroid admixture) prevail. But in Alexandria, Europeans, largely Greeks, dominate as they have done since 300 B.C. Both the birthrate (41.6 per thousand) and deathrate (26.5) stand very high in Egypt, and one baby in six never sees its first birthday.

Religion and Education. Egyptians are 90% Moslems in religion (the legal faith of the realm), 7% Coptic Christians or Greek Orthodox believers, only 1.25% Protestants and Roman Catholics, and 0.4% Jews. In Cairo, a sacred city, flourishes famous El-Azhar, the world's leading Moslem university, drawing students even from remote Nigeria and from an area extending from Morocco eastward to Java. Alexandria is sacred to the Copts.

Arabic is the official language. Fully seven-eighths of the population in 1927 remained illiterate — one child in seven attended school — and we cannot be sure of a radical improvement since that time. Though education has since been made "compulsory," children are taught in *maktabs*, religious vernacular schools of poor grade. The Education Act of 1933 has begun to be enforced, however, and more general and better primary education seems to be gaining. But there are only 70 secondary schools, 10 institutions of higher learning, and one state university. About 20,000 adults attend night schools to acquire literacy. The presence of a large Arabic press (though its journalistic standards have not risen very high) and the reading of periodicals, give evidence, of course, of a definite rise in literacy.

In metropolitan Alexandria the Greek colony lavishly patronizes arts and letters. French taste largely dominated in literary matters until recently

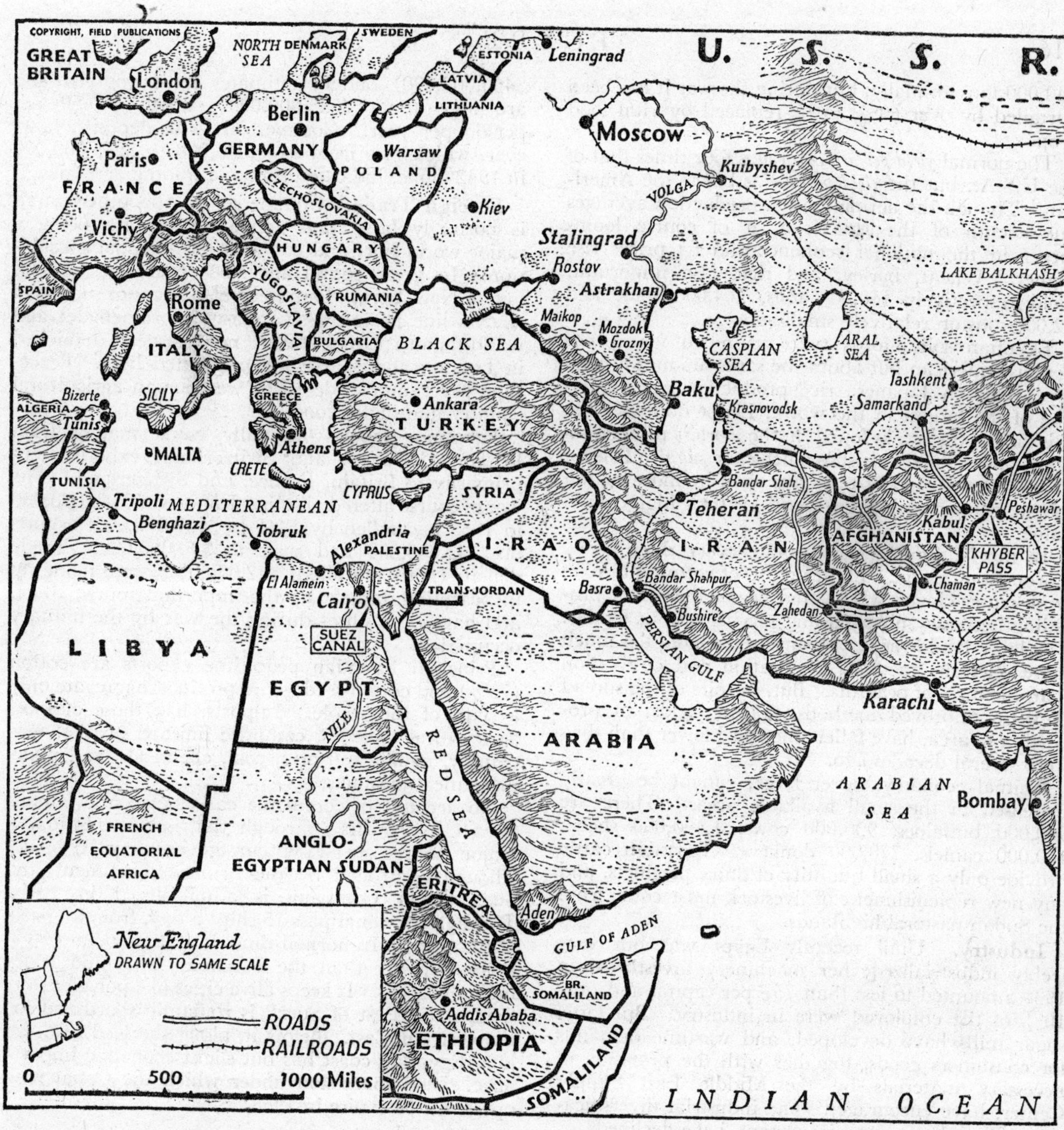
COPYRIGHT, FIELD PUBLICATIONS
GREAT BRITAIN
London
NORTH SEA
DENMARK
SWEDEN
ESTONIA
Leningrad
LATVIA
LITHUANIA
U. S. S. R.
Berlin
GERMANY
Warsaw
POLAND
Moscow
Kuibyshev
VOLGA
Paris
FRANCE
CZECHOSLOVAKIA
Kiev
Vichy
HUNGARY
Stalingrad
Rostov
Astrakhan
LAKE BALKHASH
SPAIN
YUGOSLAVIA
RUMANIA
Rome
BULGARIA
Maikop
Mozdok
Grozny
ITALY
BLACK SEA
CASPIAN SEA
ARAL SEA
Tashkent
Bizerte
SICILY
GREECE
Ankara
Baku
Krasnovodsk
Samarkand
ALGERIA
Tunis
TURKEY
MALTA
Athens
CRETE
Bandar Shah
TUNISIA
CYPRUS
SYRIA
Teheran
Kabul
Peshawar
Tripoli
MEDITERRANEAN
Benghazi
Tobruk
Alexandria
PALESTINE
IRAQ
IRAN
AFGHANISTAN
KHYBER PASS
El Alamein
Cairo
TRANS-JORDAN
Basra
Bandar Shahpur
Chaman
Zahedan
Bushire
SUEZ CANAL
LIBYA
PERSIAN GULF
EGYPT
Karachi
NILE
RED SEA
ARABIA
ARABIAN SEA
Bombay
FRENCH EQUATORIAL AFRICA
ANGLO-EGYPTIAN SUDAN
ERITREA
Aden
GULF OF ADEN
New England
DRAWN TO SAME SCALE
BR. SOMALILAND
ROADS
RAILROADS
Addis Ababa
ETHIOPIA
SOMALILAND
0
500
1000 Miles
INDIAN OCEAN

— very naturally, since the French language, now declining in importance, has been the cultural medium. French influence has also reigned in architecture, as in the modern sections of Cairo and Alexandria, despite the splendid traditional monuments of native Egyptian simplicity.

The Nation's Economy

Agriculture. Egyptian agriculture is being mechanized: though the *fellaheen* retain old methods, the large estates have become quite modern. The immense number of small landholdings has often led to the assumption, true in part, that the intensive cultivation accounts for exceptional Egyptian yields. The great majority of families engaged in agriculture (1,500,000) hold less than an acre of land and must work on shares or as day laborers to eke out a living. All but 1% of the farms fall under 50 acres, but the 12,700 landowners with the largest estates own 40% of the cultivable soil. Thus, though small holdings occur much more commonly than usual in the Orient, they are not major contributors to the crop economy.

Congestion marks all Egyptian life: the great city of Cairo, for example, has more than a million population in its 8 square miles, while even agricultural population in some of the delta areas totals 1,500 to the square mile. Under such crowded farming conditions the small holding merely supplements subsistence.

The principal crop is cotton — the Sakel variety, long staple, for a long time considered the finest in the world, vying with Sea Island American cotton for the quality trade. According to recent reports, however, this high quality has somewhat deteriorated. Cotton ordinarily varies in yield from 400,000 to

440,000 tons annually; but during the war it has been curtailed by over 60%, to be replaced by vital food crops.

The normal *yield per acre* averages four times that of the U.S.A.; but the *yield per man* is below the American. Though the normal cotton production averages one-seventh of the American, it of course looms larger in the national economy and its prices rise higher. Wheat, barley, and rice, also important, yield respectively 150,000 tons, 264,000 tons, and 72,000 tons on relatively small acreage.

Egyptian soil affords twice as much wheat per acre as American but about the same amount of barley. Though Japanese rice production per acre is one of the largest in the world, Egypt doubles even this yield. She ranks fourth in the world's production of cotton-seed and furnishes much cane sugar. During World War II, food crops have risen by more than a fourth, chick-peas being stressed for their high caloric value.

In the Nile delta, crops rotate every three years. Throughout Egypt, summer crops of cotton alternate with winter clover, wheat, and beans, the clover providing necessary nitrogen and serving also as fodder. The large landowners, of course, have adopted much more scientific methods of rotation and cultivation than the mass of peasants. But, in spite of the spread of these improved methods, cotton yields, in proportion to area, have fallen one-third lower than they were several decades ago.

Animal economy, never large, cannot be greatly increased in the small available areas. There are 900,000 buffaloes, 930,000 cows, 1,400,000 sheep, 160,000 camels, 770,000 donkeys. Egyptian cattle provide only a small quantity of dairy products, and any new replenishment of livestock must come from the Sudan pastoral highlands.

Industry. Until recently Egypt was but very feebly industrialized: her machinery investment in 1930 amounted to less than 75¢ per capita, and only 10% of the employed were in industry. But large sugar mills have developed, and wartime demands for consumers goods, together with the provision of necessary materials by the Middle East Supply Center, have encouraged some industrial diversification. Phosphates, once important, have declined.

Finance. The Egyptian pound, quoted at $4.13, commands small gold reserves, but its foreign exchange reserve is up to 80,000,000 pounds, nearly all in "blocked" sterling accounts in London. During the war, money in circulation has almost quadrupled (from 20,800,000 pounds to 75,300,000 in 1942). Per capita circulation now reaches about $20. Most prices are said to have climbed 150% and the total cost of living 100%. Trained economists say that the price indexes are absurd, bearing no relation to the practically universal black markets.

An acute inflation, largely owing to shortage of imports and to lavish spending by the armed forces, has been difficult to control. Boom conditions prevail on the Alexandria Stock Exchange. Nevertheless, savings have diminished by 10%, though money circulates in abundance. Internal bonds now yield only 3.4%, and in London, Egyptian credit is on a better than 4% basis.

Although the public debt stays fairly static (about $460,000,000) budget estimates have doubled and are now about $325,000,000 — about $16.50 per person per year. Commercial bank deposits, however, which rose from $430,000,000 to $575,000,000 in 1942 alone, indicate profitable trading activities.

Foreign Trade. Commerce, on the other hand, is normally large and active, Alexandria being a major world port and center of commercial speculation. Its great cotton and stock exchanges remind one of New York. Hundreds of palaces of successful traders line its impressive sea-wall promenade; and world-famous Greek firms, now largely domiciled in London and Marseilles, originated here. Peacetime per capita trade ($20) was, for an agricultural country, unusually good.

Egyptian imports normally came mainly from Britain, Germany, and Switzerland; exports went primarily to Britain, France, and Switzerland. The war of course altered all this. Imports of $180,000,000 in 1938 had fallen by 1941 to $137,000,000; exports of $142,000,000 had sunk to $90,000,000. Trade deficits (normally about $42,000,000) were made up in peacetime largely by the important tourist trade, and have been offset during the war by the military occupation.

Principal Egyptian peacetime exports are cotton (75%) and cotton-seed; other products aggregate only a sixth of the whole. Imports, like those of most agricultural societies, comprise finished textiles, machinery, metals and ores, coal, chemicals, and pharmaceutical products.

No account of commerce can neglect the famous Suez Canal cutting through the Sinai peninsula, a major source of Egyptian government revenue. Though controlled by the British government, the Suez Canal Company is administered in Paris. Through the canal pass 15 ships a day, from all parts of the world. In normal times it accommodates 50% more shipping than the Panama Canal and levies higher charges. It keeps alive cities like polyglot Port Said, and "East of Suez" is romantic shorthand for the vast Far East. Below it, along the Red Sea, the long Egyptian coast has but slight economic importance. The concession under which the Canal now operates will expire in 1968.

History: 1914-1944

By 1918 Egypt had become involved in World War I as a base for British operations, for in 1914 the British had deposed the old Khedive, Abbas Hilmi, and converted the country into a protectorate. In 1916 Fuad became Khedive with British support; however, the Egyptians demanded full independence when the war ended. The venerated Nationalist leader, Zaghlul Pasha, headed a nearly united people in an independence movement, named the Wafd. In March 1919 nationalist agitation led to bloody revolution. Cairo and other cities were occupied; British residents murdered. Britain thereupon entrusted Lord Allenby, fresh from his conquest of the Near East, to reestablish authority.

After Allenby restored order and exiled Zaghlul, Britain sent a mission under Lord Milner, the veteran colonial administrator, to inquire into the Egyptian problem. It was a maladroit move to include only Englishmen in the mission: their arrival was the signal for boycotts and riots. The Milner report, however, marked a considerable advance. For a protectorate it substituted the idea of a permanent compact between two sovereign states. Moreover, the mission recognized Zaghlul as the representative of Egyptian aspirations.

Pending the acceptance of the Milner report, a moderate, Adli Yeghen Pasha, was made prime minister. But even this moderate could come to no agreement with Foreign Minister Lord Curzon over the question of British military occupation. Adli resigned, and more rioting followed. This time the British sent Zaghlul to prison in the Seychelles Islands. Lord Allenby realized, however, that a nation united in her demands could not be administered by force. He urged a grant of independence.

Nominal Independence: 1922–1931. On February 28, 1922, Britain voluntarily declared Egypt independent. But her declaration included reservations concerning the security of Empire communications, the defense of Egypt, the protection of foreigners and minorities (who were to be exempt from Egyptian taxation and courts). The Egyptians scorned this gift; they were unmoved when the Khedive, to signify approval of Britain's proposals, declared himself King of Egypt in March 1922. British officials were assassinated, and terroristic acts persisted until 1923.

Adli formed an aristocratic party friendly to the Court, but even this party demanded British departure from Egypt and cession of the Sudan. The need for concession was urgent, and in July 1923, the British agreed to retire their officials, while the Egyptians in turn granted their demand for $32,000,-000 as compensation. In August 1923 martial law ended in Egypt.

As soon as the Egyptian king was his own master he rejected the notion of a constitutional monarchy. Forced later by popular pressure, he yielded sulkily and insincerely. Now the Egyptian problem became twofold; to develop democracy against the court clique's resistance, and to make the British grant of independence real instead of nominal. Egypt now adopted a constitution closely modeled on the Belgian. Among its advanced provisions was the system of guarantees of parliamentary supremacy against court intervention.

In September 1923 the popular idol, Zaghlul, was back in the country. In the elections that year, his group, the Wafd, carried 188 seats to 29 for all others, although voting was indirect. The defeated groups — the courtiers, aristocrats, and the old Christian-hating Nationalists — were at a loss to explain away a movement that had polled 85% of all votes. They turned from futile electoral opposition to intrigue. To cope with them, Zaghlul transformed the Wafd into a closely-knit party.

The advent of a Labor government in England in 1924 had kindled hopes among Wafd supporters, but Zaghlul found Prime Minister Ramsay MacDonald adamant against his demands. Though serious crises followed, the British continued to insist that independence agitation was the work of a few extremists who inflamed a simple, non-political people. In November 1924, Sir Lee Stack, head (or *Sirdar*) of

the Egyptian army, was assassinated. Lord Allenby at once demanded $2,500,000, ordered all Egyptian troops out of the Sudan, reduced Egyptian condominium in the Sudan to a shadow, forced Zaghlul to resign, and installed as prime minister the king's friend, Ziwar Pasha. Lord Allenby capped his retaliatory action with a fiat that Britain alone would decide how much of the Sudan could be irrigated by the Nile, thus giving Britain the power of life and death over "independent" Egypt. In England there was widespread feeling that despite the provocation of Stack's murder, Lord Allenby's price was too high for legitimate Egyptian pride and interest.

The Egyptians virtually acquitted the murderers, only one suffering the death penalty. Ziwar Pasha's government, consisting only of the richest nobility, had trouble maintaining its authority. In conservative circles a clever financier, Sidky Pasha, began to replace Ziwar. The government ordered an "election," and despite the arts of the subtle Sidky Pasha, the Wafd won a majority of 125 seats to 85 for all others combined. The king then dissolved parliament and set up a royal autocratic government in disregard of the constitution.

The new British High Commissioner, Lord Lloyd, was a convinced imperialist, a proconsul in the grand tradition. When, soon after his arrival, he witnessed the crushing victory of the Nationalists under Zaghlul, he ostentatiously chose the moderate Adli as prime minister. No such device could long be effective, and in 1927 Adli was succeeded by the temporizing but less pliant Sarwat Pasha. When Sarwat hinted at a reform of the army system, Lord Lloyd ordered warships to Egypt. Of necessity, Egypt yielded. At this time Zaghlul died, and his mantle fell on Mustapha Nahas Pasha.

When the Egyptians hesitated to accept a treaty offered in 1928 by Foreign Minister Sir Austen Chamberlain, Lord Lloyd warned that England's proffer of friendship could not be held so lightly. In April 1928 a third ultimatum from Lord Lloyd resulted in the summoning of British warships from Malta. Egypt's parliament was suspended and the High Commissioner now possessed all effective legislative power. On June 28, the king, grown more bold, threw out the Wafd leader Nahas Pasha by a *coup d'état*, replacing him with Mohammed Mahmud Pasha, perhaps the wealthiest landlord in Egypt. The king declared a dictatorship, accompanied by promises to the *fellaheen* (peasants) and urban workers. When the courts vindicated Nahas Pasha, defamed by the courtiers and accused of corruption, the newspapers were not allowed to print the news of his acquittal. Censorship and terror prevailed. The promised reforms for peasants and workers vanished into thin air.

Lord Lloyd's victories ended when the Labor party came to power in England. With the backing of the Liberals, Henderson, the new Foreign Secretary, abolished the protectorate, offered Egypt a treaty as between equal states, and replaced Lord Lloyd by Sir Percy Lorraine, who stood for more cooperative methods. At the same time, the Conservatives insisted that Lord Lloyd's policy had saved the Empire from a mortal thrust at her most vital point, Suez.

In the Egyptian elections ordered after the negotiations with Henderson, Nahas Pasha and the Wafd again swept the country. A nationalist set of economic demands followed: one for tariff autonomy, another for meeting the cotton competition of the Sudan, and a third for the taxation of foreigners, whose capital had been exempt up to now. During 1930, the king, for the third time, defied the popular will, but now he chose Sidky Pasha as prime minister. A third dictatorship suspended Wafd newspapers and dissolved parliament. Court circles, British economic and governmental interests, and the merchant and banking groups of Sidky Pasha combined, astutely anticipating the fall of Labor power in England. With the end of the Labor government, their power was consolidated. Sidky ordered new elections on a fantastic basis; the Wafd boycotted the elections, and Sidky Pasha, at last, had his majority chosen from the few who voted.

The Era of Cooperation: 1932-1944. After two years of apparent success, serious disorders again swept Egypt and by 1936 it was impossible to delay constitutional reform. The death of King Fuad, succeeded by a minor, Farouk, resulted in an agreement that British forces would quit Egypt, save at the Suez and except when the country was threatened. In 1936, with the country truly independent, Egypt was admitted to the League of Nations. In 1937 she abolished all exemptions from Egyptian law and taxation hitherto enjoyed by foreigners. Attempts of the Axis to win Egypt's support failed after the Italian adventure in Ethiopia and after the decimation of Tripoli's population by Fascist cruelty. Efforts of the Mufti of Jerusalem and the German agent, von Grobba, also failed to shake Egypt, but Nahas Pasha now moved from Egyptian nationalism to Pan-Arab ambitions.

Soon after Egyptian and British relations became cordial, the war broke out. Egypt broke diplomatic relations with the Axis, but would not declare war. However, Britain was permitted to use Egypt as a naval and military base. Throughout the trying days of the Libyan campaign, the first invasion to Sidi Barrani and the second to El Alamein, at a time when the British cause seemed lost, there was no disaffection in Egypt. Nationalist embers stirred but the generous British policy since 1936 had won most Egyptians to passive cooperation. The reconquest of Ethiopia, the loss of Italian possessions, the crackup of German conspiracy in Iraq, all slowly aided the restoration of British prestige. By 1944 Egypt was in the throes of inflation and her internal economics were her first concern. The sore point of the Sudan remained unhealed, but no agitation seemed important while the war continued.

Stakes in the Peace

Egypt is at the crossroads of the maritime world. No international conflict can spare her. British power prevented her occupation, while Axis hopes to win her over shielded her from bombardment. This fortunate combination may not be repeated. Egypt has an acute need for guarantees of world peace. As she is not an industrial nation, her basis of armed power must always be weak. Hence she must rely on world organization.

The internal needs of Egypt are not easily remediable except for a diminution of the ratio of large landed properties to the small fertile area. Nevertheless, the Malthusian tendency of population to rise with every improvement of subsistence does not offer too much hope of large economic improvement in Egypt, for it is difficult to think of the soil yielding much more by any means of cultivation. The development of diversified factories in the larger cities may be the only effective means of draining the surplus rural population.

ANGLO-EGYPTIAN SUDAN

The Land and the People

An immense territory to the south of Egypt, the Anglo-Egyptian Sudan lives under joint British and Egyptian sovereignty. Under the leader "Mahdi" (Divine Guide), the inhabitants humiliatingly defeated the famous General Gordon at Khartoum (1885), and only Kitchener's crushing of the dervishes at Omdurman (1898) finally quelled native resistance. The British made an immediate agreement with Egypt for joint Anglo-Egyptian administration, for the Sudan vitally concerns Egypt: the headwaters of the Nile are controlled in Sudan and Sudanese live-stock is a critical source of replenishment for the Egyptian supply.

Some idea of the vastness of the country may be suggested by the fact that its 960,000 square miles approximate one-third of the U.S.A. Once populated by some 8,500,000 before 1883, it later declined to 1,800,000; but present estimates claim some 6,300,-000. The population is composed of mixed Hamitic, Semitic, and Negro peoples, chiefly nomads who follow the Moslem faith; some Negro peoples in the south, however, have never embraced Islam. Educational facilities are slight, only one child in twenty receiving any schooling.

The country is bounded on the east by the Red

Sea, Eritrea, and Ethiopia; on the south by Uganda; on the west by French Equatorial Africa. The northern frontier fades into Egypt whose actual claim to the Sudan has been opposed by Britain.

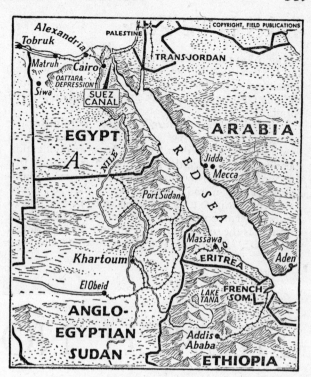

See map on page 315.

The Economy

The land is prevailingly agricultural, with hot, dry climate in the cultivated central areas. The Sudan raises cotton extensively (about 91,000 tons), but her gum arabic, 80% of the world's supply and valued at over $3,000,000, is better known. The people raise their basic food, millet, which is also used as fodder and poultry food. Livestock number 2,700,000 cattle, 2,500,000 sheep, 2,000,000 goats, and as many as 420,000 camels. The country's forests are valuable, and the upper Nile area produces papyrus.

Before the war exports reached about $28,000,000, imports about $30,000,000. Ginned cotton, cotton seed, gum arabic, millet, sesame, hides, and skins constituted the major exports — and about half went to Britain and a good percentage to Egypt. Imports were textiles, iron and steel wares, and motor cars, mainly from Britain, Egypt, and Japan (fully 20%). The war increased Sudan's exports to about $36,-000,000.

Since the British entered the area, they have invested some $125,000,000. Sudan herself has recently assumed the debt on a new investment of some $33,000,000. And the coming years may witness even larger investment sums, for the country has two great potentialities: her highland soil, in competent hands, might become one of the great cultivated areas of the world; her water-power resources are among the greatest on earth. Modern engineering has already prepared a foundation with dams and other structures, and the hydroelectric future of the country may well become of extreme importance in the economy of the African area.

History: 1918-1944

In 1918 the Anglo-Egyptian Sudan was a condominium of Great Britain and Egypt, governed with the aid of a Council. When the Egyptians agitated for complete independence from Britain, the fate of the jointly controlled Sudan territory became uncertain. Lloyd George stated in 1922 that whatever might be the effect of Egyptian independence, no new arrangement would be permitted which might jeopardize Britain's heavy investments in the Sudan.

In 1924 a delegation of Sudanese and Egyptians resident in the Sudan prepared to go to Egypt to request unification with her, but the British authorities intervened. At Khartoum the Sudanese White Flag society demanded unity with Egypt, but its influence was nullified by government order. Some time later, military cadets at Khartoum mutinied in a demonstration for affiliation with Egypt. It was only the northern Sudan that was affected by the agitation for union with Egypt; the south was wholly different in tradition and interests.

The advent of a Labor government in England raised expectations of Sudanese unification with Egypt; but Ramsay MacDonald declared in October 1924 that Britain would insist on fulfilling her obligations to the Sudanese. Egypt, he agreed, was entitled to have a voice in economic matters and in the amount of Sudanese territory to be irrigated by the Nile, and Britain was to concern herself solely with the actual administration of the Sudan. The murder in 1924 of Sir Lee Stack, Governor-General of the Sudan, provoked the British to impose virtually complete control.

The Sudanese government, however, had much more to consider than Egyptian interests. Forays from the southern tribes were common; slave-dealing was rife along the turbulent Ethiopian frontier. The Sudan broke up the slave-trading rings, but from 1928–1933, Ethiopian tribes persisted in sheltering the slave-traders. In 1935–36 the border was actively patrolled during the Italian invasion of Ethiopia. (In the late 1920's, too, the Sudan had an epidemic of *Mahdis*, or divine messengers, and their fanatical followers, who raided villages and required stern repression.)

During the 1930's the government instituted anthropological surveys and undertook extensive education of sons of leading tribal families. The educated class now numbers about 12,000, mostly resident at Khartoum and Omdurman.

During the 1930's Egyptians protested repeatedly against paying nearly $4,000,000 a year into the Sudanese budget. Egypt also chafed at advancing large loans for development work in the Sudan, since she had practically no voice in the disposition of these funds. As yet, this relationship has not been altered.

Stakes in the Peace

Anglo-Egyptian Sudan has immense agricultural and pastoral possibilities. She is one of the few large remaining areas for future expansion of production, and she could easily support many times her present population.

The British have poured money, administrative talent, and engineering genius into this land; and they have substituted order for chaos as civilization speedily pushed back the frontiers of barbarism. But the long and acrimonious dispute between Anglo-Egyptian Sudan and Egypt indicates that the Egyptians will continue to desire some voice in a region to whose government budget they contribute and which commands the source of their economic life: the waters of the Nile. During the war the controversy has been quiescent, but never forgotten. A *modus vivendi*, reconciling Egyptian needs and British functions, is within the province of cooperative statesmanship.

The primary physical needs of Anglo-Egyptian Sudan are order, the training of a large native population in modern farm techniques, and the transformation of nomads into a stable population. Furthermore, the economy of the southern areas near Ethiopia and Kenya require improvement to the level of the comparatively advanced areas near Egypt. Road building is a prerequisite to the success of this latter policy.

The Sudanese can become prosperous through an intensive development of their animal economy, for which the teeming population of Egypt offers a ready market. Such a development would not only aid the Sudan; it would raise the living standards in the entire delta and valley of the Nile.

FRENCH NORTH AFRICA

The Land and the People

French North Africa, a richly endowed area, is strategically situated, as World War II has clearly shown. Recent landings at Algiers and Casablanca, as well as the early historic exploits of Stephen Decatur against the Barbary pirates, have made this area somewhat familiar to Americans. In ancient times it included the seat of the Carthaginian Empire; with Sicily, it formed the leading granary of the Roman Empire. In the time of St. Augustine it was an important part of Christendom. But after the Arab conquest made its religion and culture increasingly strange to European Christians, it gradually forfeited many of its former ties with the continent to the north. So long as the Moors held Spain and Sicily, however, northern Africa was usually considered European, as today Algeria, with her three *départements* in the French republic is considered, in part, a section of metropolitan France.

French North Africa, the area of the so-called "Barbary States," forms a geographical unity that has been artificially divided into three countries. Part of the Mediterranean basin, it hardly "belongs" to the rest of the African continent. Throughout history its ties have been with Europe or Asia rather than Africa, save for rare contacts with Negro societies to the south by way of caravan routes or the coastal passages towards Senegal. The old Arab geographers, indeed, called it the "Western Island" because it is bounded on the north by the Mediterranean, on the west by the Atlantic, and on the south and east by the vast sand and stone ocean of the Sahára, which cuts it off from the rest of Africa more effectively than would the sea.

Algeria, Tunis, and Morocco are under French dominion. Morocco has technically the status of an independent Sultanate and Tunis, under its Bey, that of a regency. Algeria's status is special: she is administered by a French Governor-General, but three of her departments (Oran, Algiers, Constantine) send representatives to the French Parliament in Paris. French intervention in Africa began in 1830 in Algeria, in 1881 in Tunis, and, for all practical purposes, about 1905 in Morocco. Conquest remained incomplete, however, until the late 1920's under the famous Marshal Lyautey.

The Land. If we exclude desert and the sparsely peopled mountains on the Saharan border, the effective areas appear as follows: 153,870 square miles for Morocco, 222,206 for Algeria; and 48,362 for Tunis. Additional administered territory, more than 700,000 square miles, supports mainly nomad Berber, Tuareg, and Arab tribesmen.

A small Spanish Zone exists also in Morocco, roughly coincident with the wild Riff territory in the extreme northwest (in recent years known for the rebellion of the tribes under the ill-fated Abd el-Krim). Spain also seeks, by unilateral acts, to assimilate the former international zone of Tangier. But the economic importance of both the Riff and Tangier are slight compared to French North Africa.

The mountainous systems incline southwestwards from northern Tunis to southwestern Morocco. Not far behind the Mediterranean and Atlantic coasts this formidable wall rises for a length of 1,500 miles. The northernmost range, the Riff, is the counterpart of the Sierra Nevada mountains about Granada in Spain, across the Strait of Gibraltar. The easternmost ranges, broken by the sea, emerge in Sicily — really a detached part of the Barbary States; the westernmost mountains dip into the Atlantic and emerge as the Canary Islands, culminating in the

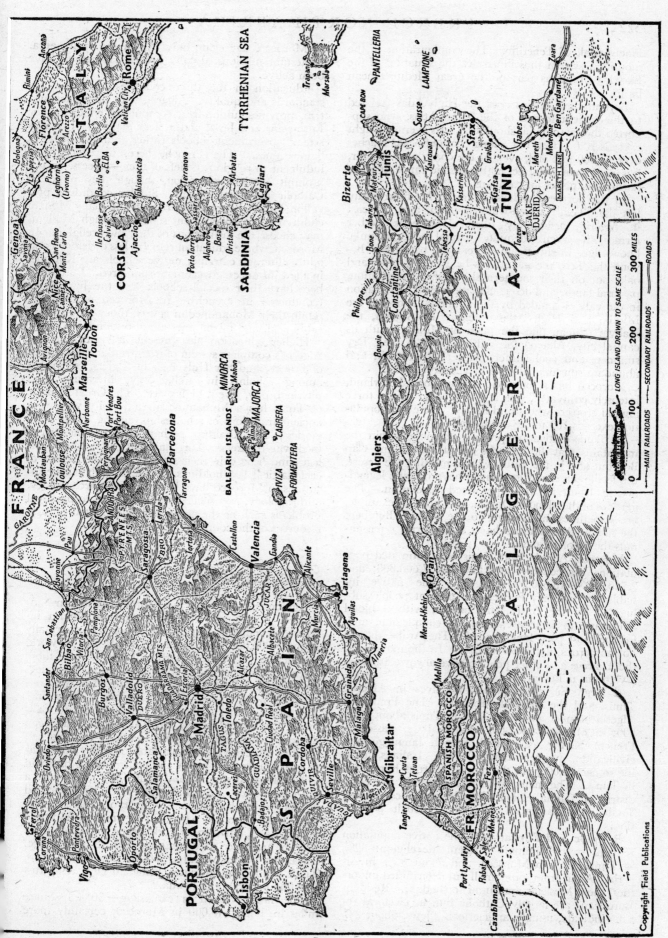

ITALY

Rimini
Ancona
Bologna
Arezo
Florence
La Spezia
Pisa
Leghorn (Livorno)
Vatican City
Rome
ELBA

Genoa
Savona
San Remo
Monte Carlo
Nice
Cannes
Marseille
Toulon

Bastia
Ile Rousse
Calvi
CORSICA
Ajaccio

Porto Torres
Sassari
Alghero
Bosa
Oristano
SARDINIA
Terranova
Arbatax
Ghisonaccia
Cagliari

TYRRHENIAN SEA

Trapani
Marsala
PANTELLERIA
LAMPIONE

CAPE BON
Bizerte
Tunis
Sousse
Sfax
TUNIS
Graiba
Gabes
Ben Gardane
Tuara
Medenine
Mareth
MARETH LINE

FRANCE
Avignon
Montauban
Montpellier
Narbonne
Toulouse
Port Vendres
Port Bou
Perpignan
ANDORRA
PYRENEES MTS.
Pau
Bayonne
GARONNE
EBRO

Barcelona
Tarragona
Tortosa
Lerida
Zaragossa

BALEARIC ISLANDS
MINORCA
Mahon
MAJORCA
Palma
CABRERA
IVIZA
FORMENTERA

Philippeville
Bone
Tabarka
Mateur
Hairouan
Kasserine
Tebessa
Tozeur
LAKE DJERID
Garsa
ALGERIA
Constantine
Bougie

San Sebastian
Pamplona
Bilbao
Santander
Oviedo
Vitoria
Burgos
Valladolid
DUERO
SPAIN
Castellon
JUCAR
Valencia
Gandia
Alicante
Murcia
Cartagena
Aguilas
Almeria

Algiers
Oran
Mers-el-Kebir
Melilla

Salamanca
Avila
GUADARAMA MTS.
El Escorial
Madrid
TAGUS
Toledo
Alcazar
Albacete
Ciudad Real
Cordoba
GUADIANA
GUADALQUIVIR
Seville
Granada
Malaga
Badajoz

Ferrol
Coruna
Vigo
Pontevedra
Oporto
PORTUGAL

Lisbon
Gibraltar
Algeciras
Ceuta
Tetuan
Tangier
SPANISH MOROCCO
Fez
Meknes
Sale
Rabat
Port Lyautey
FR. MOROCCO
Casablanca

LONG ISLAND DRAWN TO SAME SCALE
0   100   200   300 MILES
LONG ISLAND
MAIN RAILROADS ——— SECONDARY RAILROADS
ROADS

lonely peak of Teneriffe. The configuration of the mountain system thus illustrates the situation of the Barbary States as part of the great Mediterranean basin.

Beyond these chains rises the High Atlas (related to the ancient legend of the Titan Atlas, who supported the earth on his shoulders). Its average height exceeds 10,000 feet, but a long chain of peaks reaches over 12,000 feet and, even at the coast, near Agadir, it is more than 6,000 feet high. A solid range, it offers hardly any passes for caravans.

In the northern valleys, near the Mediterranean, lies the "Tell," a well-watered plain, and, at least in Algeria, assiduously tilled. Here the Berber farmer, if given adequate capital and scientific knowledge, might create an earthly paradise. Beyond the Tell, the mountains bear cedar, pine, and oak; but on their southern slopes scrub vegetation, pastoral lands, and desert climate prevail. Irrigation in the valleys is aided by the abundant snows of the Middle and High Atlas ranges. In Algeria, the Kabyle plateau and the plain of Mitidja (with its capital city, Algiers) form the centers of life. Dry summers and cool winters with alternate rain and abundant sunshine afford a privileged climate.

Morocco has a long but narrow coastal lowland, intensely cultivated, yielding, at favored points, three annual crops of wheat and barley. Here the population exceeds 100 to the square mile.

In Tunis cultivation prevails not only within the mountains that dip into the sea at Bizerte and Cap Bon but also in the south, where, meeting the desert, the fertile oases and grasslands have become legendary in Islam for their perfumed vegetation. The gardens of the island of Djerba, off Tunis, for example, are sometimes intoxicating to the senses. But here the *sirocco* (the Saharan desert sand storm) often annuls the labors of man.

Morocco, Algeria, and Tunis have estimated populations, respectively, of 8,000,000; 7,600,000; and 2,700,000 — 18,300,000 in all. The native inhabitants, basically Berbers, an ancient people subjugated by the Arabs, are brunet, with a blond admixture in some areas, fair in complexion, and, for the most part, long-headed. The Arabs, though not numerous, dominate socially. In the mountains, the Tuaregs and other peoples have always displayed a vigorous militancy.

A large European population lives in Algeria, Tunis, and the cities of Morocco. The French in Algeria number about 800,000; in Tunis about 150,-000; in Morocco 250,000. Native Jews, classed as French, having assimilated French language and civilization, number about 500,000. Italians, totaling some 170,000, are the most numerous Europeans in Tunis. The many Spaniards center in the Oran district of Algeria. None of the largest cities, Algiers, Tunis, and Casablanca, exceeds 300,000 in population.

Religion and Education. The native population remains overwhelmingly Moslem in religion: 89% in Tunis, 94% in Morocco, and about 83% in Algeria. Apart from some small but determined minorities, these Moslems are Sunni (orthodox). Resident Europeans are largely Catholic but, as electoral results indicate, usually anticlerical. Jews, about 2%

in Morocco, aggregate only 3% in the entire area. Protestant missions, usually French Huguenot, have been active.

Education in the three countries lacks uniform standards and quality. Algeria, with its French system, provides tuition-free, compulsory education for Europeans and Jews; and a clear majority of natives attend government schools rather than Moslem religious ones. The French, here, as everywhere, indulgent to religious beliefs of their subjects, do not prohibit Moslem education, though they proscribe Catholic parochial schools. Similar conditions prevail in Tunis where both European and many Moslem children go to government schools, though Moslems may choose the institutions of their own religion. In Morocco, where education remains less developed and adult illiteracy extreme, native schools are Koranic, in a few instances, government-sponsored. Europeans here have their special schools, and the Jews theirs (conducted in French). In Morocco natives also retain their Mohammedan courts, though European, rabbinical, and mixed ones are also found.

Higher education also presents a varied picture. Algeria's complete system of *lycées*, ranking with those of France, and her University of Algiers, celebrated among scholars in archaeology, literature, and physiography, give it high place. The Great Mosque of Tunis has a Mohammedan university with very ancient traditions of scholarship, among whose chief glories is Ibn Khaldun, perhaps the most modern of medieval thinkers. This university and the 8 colleges and *lycées* gain their support from the income of ecclesiastical landholdings. Some French higher institutes in Morocco have been active in archaeology, anthropology, and special studies related to practical problems such as the great, still unexploited natural resources of the country.

The Economy

Agriculture. In the last century, agriculture advanced greatly and the population of Algeria increased sevenfold. Barley, the major crop, normally about 3,800,000 tons annually, totals 8% of world production. The three Barbary lands produce more wheat in proportion to total population than does the U.S.A.: 2,700,000 tons. The output of wine, already 36% of that of France herself, is increasing. The wines, rather coarse and not dissimilar to California "ordinary" types, have almost driven cheap domestic wine out of the French working-class market.

Olive oil, everywhere a variable quantity from year to year, ranks well below the contributions of Spain (40% of world supply) and Italy (25%), but over a ten-year period, French North Africa has averaged 8% of world production. Other crops include walnuts, figs (there are 6,000,000 fig trees in Morocco alone), dates, citrus fruits, cork, beans, and chick-peas. Market and spice gardening has risen to importance: coriander, cummin, and artichokes are typical crops. Tunis yields pomegranates, pistachio nuts, alfa grass (for fine papers), and henna.

The land worked is extensive — 30,000 square miles in Tunis; 40,000 in Morocco; certainly more than 25,000 in Europeanized Algeria — with 500 people to the cultivated square mile. Yet, despite several crops per year and favorable land and climate, the production cannot feed the population; food must be imported.

Animal economy bulks large. About 22,000,000 sheep yield a wool clip of 35,000 tons. Though cattle do not abound, the people raise many goats (12,000,-000) and camels (500,000). Fisheries are extensive, supplying luxury markets abroad — especially with tunny fish and anchovies. Except for mutton, meat is not plentiful. North African cuisine centers, in fact, on mutton, barley, and beans.

Mining. Among the three primary sources yielding 88% of the world supply of phosphates, North Africa just about equals average American production and surpasses Russia's. Algeria, Tunis, and Morocco together yield 32% of the world's supply. These, their leading mineral exports, have long assured the French farmer the continued fertility of his land. A production, also, of 2,500,000 tons of iron ore forms a considerable addition to that of France, herself Europe's largest producer. The coal workings remain small. Ferro-alloys, greatly aiding French heavy industries, include 2.8% of its antimony, and 1% of its molybdenum. French North Africa also produces 2% of the world's lead.

Local Industries. Industry, while in a state of growth (as, for example, flour mills and cement works), remains largely in an artisan stage, though sometimes it is centered in large workshops. Traditional handicrafts still prosper. Moroccan leather used in fine book bindings has long been world-famous, and Moroccan copper goods, intricately wrought, are widely admired. Tunisian pottery, leather embroidery, carpets, and slippers also enjoy high distinction. The arts and crafts of this area have, in fact, long won recognition as among the finest artisan accomplishments of mankind.

Finance. Although the three states have separate issues of money, all currency, tied to the French franc, is now stabilized at 50 francs to the dollar. During the war Algerian money in circulation has trebled and Moroccan currency quintupled. Moroccan notes are covered 60% by gold and foreign exchange, but present Algerian exchange reserves cannot be determined exactly. At the present parity, monetary circulation in Algeria stands at $170,000,000 ($22 per capita), Morocco at about $70,000,000 (less than $9 per capita).

Ordinarily the budget of Algeria has been in deficit. Great new networks of roads in both Algeria and Morocco, though very helpful to the areas, have proved extremely costly.

The Moroccan debt (nearly all for productive purposes) seems to be about 3 billion francs (now $60,-000,000). A large part of Algerian debt has been integrated with that of France, however, and thus cannot be segregated. Though French North African taxation has been heavy, yet it is illuminating that French Morocco, for example, does not pay a third the per capita tax demanded in the Spanish Zone.

Foreign Trade. In 1938 exports of the three Barbary lands together totaled $243,000,000, imports $247,000,000 (about $28 per capita). Algeria was the most active in this commerce. France was,

of course, the principal user of Barbary commodities and principal supplier of its imports. She supplied, for example, 60% of Morocco's imports and took 40% of her exports in 1938; and similarly for Tunis. But Algeria trades 80% with France, Algiers and Marseilles being really sister-cities.

Principal exports include grains, wine, phosphates, sheep, and wool; principal imports: textiles, machinery, automobiles (mainly low-powered French models), sugar, coal, iron, and coffee.

ALGERIA
History: 1914-1944

During World War I, Algeria furnished France with 172,000 troops; and in 1918 the grateful mother country ended virtually all discrimination against the natives of Algeria in criminal law and abolished similar discrimination in taxation. The French granted citizenship to natives who chose to give up such Moslem rights as polygamy.

A series of economic crises from 1920–27 overshadowed political issues. Exports failed to advance in value sufficiently to compensate for the depreciation of the French franc, and thus Algeria was unable to import enough food for her people and enough raw materials for her industry. The agricultural yield, furthermore, suffered from frequent droughts.

A four-year recovery followed the restoration of prosperity in the mother country (1926) and the construction of large irrigation works in Algeria by the French helped; but by 1931 Algeria suffered an economic crisis even more acute than that of 1920–27. The government had done nothing to cope with the speculative agricultural basis of Algeria, particularly in wine. (By contrast, Tunis and Madagascar escaped the depths of economic crisis, because of their balanced economies.)

A complex situation now developed in Algeria. Radicalism spread among French farmers and workers there, nationalism gained in Arab circles, wild disorders occurred among Berbers, and outright Fascism and terrorist leagues grew up among wealthy French interests. The latter used antisemitism as a rallying point, especially under the Abbé Lambert, Mayor of Oran. There, Spanish immigrants of the *Falange* type were used to aid Fascism. Italians were similarly used in the mountain stronghold of Constantine, where pogroms and mass murders took place in 1934. Algeria was in an agitated state, close to civil war.

The Paris government dispatched a M. Régnier to make an official enquiry. Upon his declaration that the economic miseries of the Algerian peoples required immediate remedy, the Paris government formulated relief programs. Although funds were lavishly granted, the natives insisted that the French in Algeria got the lion's share and that they did not materially benefit. In 1936 Algeria supported the Popular Front régime in France; most of her deputies were Radicals. Trade unions soon dominated the ports and industries in Algeria; they became common even among native farm laborers. By 1939 internal conditions had considerably improved. Then the war in Europe intervened.

1939-1944. Following the collapse of French military power, it was expected that Algiers would be made the temporary capital of metropolitan France. When Vichy was made the new capital of France, Britain requested the naval authorities at Oran to guarantee that the French fleet there would not be permitted to return to the ports of metropolitan France. When this request was not satisfied, a battle broke out on July 4, 1940, at Mers-el-Kébir, which was to poison British-French relations for a long time.

The grip of the French collaborationist Vichy régime was firmer in Algeria than in Morocco and Tunis because of more direct governmental relations. The rights of Jews were revoked despite the "Crémieux" decrees which had conferred these rights in 1871 (as a reward for their loyal acceptance of French sovereignty and culture). Numerous European refugees in Algeria were handed to Nazi Germany for execution; and tens of thousands were killed or crippled in the construction of the Trans-Saharan Railway, upon which the Germans insisted, since they expected it to aid the extension of German military power to Dakar!

The invasion of North Africa, by the forces of liberation, in 1942 sealed the fate of the Algerian area, which was soon occupied by Allied troops. Admiral Darlan, temporarily in Algiers, accepted American terms; but since he had been a Vichy leader, a storm of controversy arose, which suddenly ended with his assassination. The French National Committee of Liberation, headed at first by Generals Giraud and de Gaulle was then constituted, with Algiers as the provisional capital of France and the seat of a temporary National Assembly. In 1943 this new régime liberated refugees and political prisoners, ended the racial and repressive laws of the Vichy government, raised to citizenship 600,000 Moslems who could read French, and extended other rights and powers to Moslems in Algeria.

MOROCCO

History: 1914-1944

The French had established a protectorate over the Sultanate of Morocco in 1912. When World War I forced France to transfer a large number of her troops from Morocco to Europe, the French Governor of Morocco, Marshal Lyautey, found himself under the constant threat of uprisings of rebellious native chiefs. Once Germany had been defeated, Lyautey could draw on full French military power. He undertook four grand campaigns against the rebellious chiefs and by 1923 had conquered all of Morocco that was of economic significance.

Spain's wretched showing against Abd-el-Krim in the Riff Mountains had so damaged European prestige that the French felt compelled to help Spain defeat the native warrior. In May 1926 Abd-el-Krim surrendered; he was exiled to Madagascar. But French public opinion was resentful of the long wars in Morocco and the expensive rescue of humiliated Spanish arms. Hence, in September 1925 the Leftist government in France recalled Lyautey; the task of pacifying Morocco was turned over to civilian auspices.

The French changed the face of the Moroccan land. They developed modern cities, motor highways, reservoirs, hotels, and the tourist trade. Marshal Lyautey had the vision to retain intact, and without modernization, the ancient Moorish cities such as Fez, Meknès, and Marrakech. New and modern settlements were built outside their limits. Steeg, Lyautey's successor, had to consolidate the economic changes. French settlers or French companies took over communal lands and introduced modern agricultural techniques. The French swiftly exploited the country's mineral resources. As Morocco became a treasure trove, her various companies grew important on the Paris Stock Exchange.

By 1930 only two remote Moroccan areas remained unpacified, but in 1933 natives rebelled in many areas, and it took two years of combined French and Spanish operations to quell these uprisings.

Under the Popular Front government in France (1936–38) Morocco became an intensely disputed issue. The Leftists insisted that Peyrouton, its governor, was creating a reactionary group in the colony for the purpose of undermining French liberties, just as General Franco had used the Spanish zone in Morocco as a base for revolt against the Spanish Republican government. The Moroccan question smoldered until 1940 when, at the fall of France, General Noguès (Governor of Morocco) at first wavered and later openly espoused the Pétain government. Noguès relentlessly arrested de Gaullist sympathizers, and the large Jewish population felt the full weight of antisemitic decrees.

In November 1942 the brilliant American military landings put an end to the Noguès régime. Soon Casablanca witnessed the historic conference (January 1943) at which Roosevelt and Churchill formulated their "unconditional surrender" policy and Allied plans to invade southern Europe. Now adhering to the French National Committee of Algiers, Morocco dismissed the Vichy collaborationists.

TUNIS

History: 1914-1944

A Sultanate under a French Residency, Tunis in 1914 was still technically a part of the Turkish domain, for Turkey had reserved protectorate rights over the country. But for all practical purposes only French control counted during World War I, when Turkey and France were antagonists. Tunis supplied the Allies with soldiers and workers, and she beat off an Arab invasion officered by Turks. With the end of the war in 1918, the French insisted that Turkey abandon even her nominal connection with Tunis.

The most important difficulty was with the Italians and the Maltese. These two large immigrant groups, who outnumbered the French, were permitted in 1923 to retain their original nationality (even Maltese and Italians who had been born in Tunis). Italy always insisted on special privileges under a convention made in 1896. While Italy formally accepted French control of the Sultanate of Tunis in a treaty of 1929, Fascist-inspired agitation demanded Italian occupation of the country. Border rectifications between Tunis and Italian Tripoli failed to satisfy these Fascist demands, since the areas ceded Italy were worthless for agriculture.

The French found it more difficult to handle Tunis than either Algeria, long under direct rule, or Morocco, where the sword was recognized as their warrant. Hence in 1922 and 1925 France decided to grant increased local powers to the natives. Although these concessions took on the classic colonial form of largely consultative powers under European majorities in the councils, they averted a dangerous attitude on the part of Tunisian nationalists. However, the Sultanate, kept up for its showy and traditional elements, became a center for Italian intrigue and had constantly to be watched by the French.

The fanatical leader of the Nationalist cause was Sheik Taalbi, whose book *Tunis the Martyred* became the scripture of revolt and led to the growth of the *Destour* (or independence movement). However, as Tunis remained prosperous while Algeria suffered economic crises, this nationalist movement was kept within bounds. A world revival of trade from 1927 to 1930 turned Tunisian prosperity into a boom. But as soon as the world economic crisis and the still sharper deflation of prices came about (owing to France's rigid adherence to the gold standard), there were disorders and mass shootings; the new trade unions organized strikes in the ports and among the utilities. In June 1933 the French outlawed the Nationalist party; and from 1934–35 they sternly repressed a series of manifestations against their power. However, the rise of the Popular Front government in France (1936) conciliated the Tunisians; and by 1938 an apparent loyalty had replaced years of strife.

When France collapsed in 1940, Tunis was less certain of her fate than were the other colonies. The Italians would have moved in but the French Mareth Line in the south was too much for their feeble land forces, while Bizerte was invincible by sea. Thus, though Italian intrigue seduced the Sultanate and some of his Court, and though the Italian population was active, Tunis was held for France by the vigorous policy of General Weygand. In November 1942, however, the Germans got to Tunis before the Allies moved in from Algeria. Several months later (April 1943), the bloody Tunisian campaign, with breathtaking fluctuations of fortune culminated in a great rout of the Axis forces. The pro-Italian sovereign fled to Rome. The privileges enjoyed by Italy in Tunis since 1896 were soon canceled by the Committee of National Liberation in Algiers.

Stakes in the Peace

Although Algeria, Morocco, and Tunis have quite different problems, in fundamentals they have similar stakes in the peace.

The French Provisional Government has proposed still greater grants of local powers and citizenship to Algerians, a more rapid spread of tutelage in Morocco, and almost complete self-rule for Tunis. In all three regions, the problem of agriculture stands first. With a large European population, agricultural techniques could be made available to the mass of native farmers within a generation.

For a France biologically weakened by four years of tyranny, colonization is not the issue. Instead, France now has a direct interest in increasing native well-being. In most areas the yield of crops can be doubled, not only by a moderate increase in agricultural knowledge but also by a comparatively modest addition of up-to-date tools and machines. Once these lands are self-supporting, agricultural wages will rise, and with them the possibilities of French exports to the area will develop. As matters now stand, most of the demand for consumers goods comes from people who are either Europeans or assimilated to European culture.

The foundations of prosperity have been laid in roads, rail, and port developments, in extensive modernization, and the unfolding of Trans-Saharan projects. The native Arabs and Berbers have seen to their amazement competitive success in agriculture and industry by a sizable body of European settlers, a phenomenon rarely encountered in colonies. Their first expression was one of resentment; but this war has shown fundamental cooperation, and the educated natives have moved away from merely negative nationalism, and are now paying more attention to industrial and agricultural development.

If the French ride this wave, they will solve one of their acute political problems and at the same time enrich their empire. The general colonial philosophy of the new French government favors spectacular advances in this area. There is undoubtedly a gulf between stated aims and their realization; but if France has her expected rebirth of energy, French North Africa should, in twenty years, rival South European regions in per capita wealth and production.

IRAN (PERSIA)

The Land and the People

Iran is one of the many states that at one time or another had the largest empire in the world. Persian power was at its zenith for two centuries until 331 B.C., when its rival world-conqueror, Alexander the Great, destroyed it. Though later, as the Parthian Empire, Persia again rose — this time to be the single unconquered rival of Rome — her power melted like snow before the Arabs, who shaped her into an important Moslem state (about 640 A.D.). For a time subject to the Mongols, Iran at last emerged independent.

Not only have the Persians had a long and fascinating history, but they have made remarkable contributions to civilization. They have been excellent farmers and horticulturists, and their literary and plastic arts claim a distinctive place. The poets Hafiz and Omar Khayyam stand among the great names. Philosophy produced Sufi and Baha Ullah (founder of Bahaism); and Zoroaster is a great religious tradition. Their "Passion plays," perhaps superior to the European, have been admirably described by Matthew Arnold. Even school children catch some intimation of their epic cycles through the story of Sohrab and Rustum. Firdusi won a lasting fame in originating romantic fiction — a prolific literary genre in our later times.

Though she had long been important as the fourth largest petroleum producer in the world, during World War II, Iran drew wide popular attention as a main route by which American lend-lease goods moved into Russia. Military engineers transformed the Trans-Iranian Railway into an adequate artery of shipment. They erected new port facilities, they built new roads with modern filling stations, truck and bomber assembly plants, and a very large gasoline refinery. Americans engaged in these ultra-modern undertakings saw about them the life of another century — nomadic herders in their tents, settlements of mud-huts, and the camels and donkeys of traders' caravans like those of the Middle Ages.

The Land. With an area of 628,000 square miles, Iran is about a fifth as large as the U.S.A. Northward lie the U.S.S.R. and the Caspian Sea; eastward, Afghanistan, a turbulent neighbor, and Baluchistan in British India; southward and southwestward, the Indian Ocean and the Persian Gulf; westward, Iraq and Turkey. Iran's capital, Teheran, recently became world-famous when President Roosevelt, Prime Minister Churchill, and Marshal Stalin conferred there in 1943.

Most of the country is a high plateau which culminates in the Elburz mountains in the northwest near the Caucasus section of the Soviet Union and the Ararat area of Turkey. Here large volcanic ranges rise, the source of northern Iran's severe, periodical earthquakes. Desert running diagonally from northeast to southwest, separates the country's two fertile highland regions. The Iranian plateau slopes in the southwest into the valley of the Tigris and on the southeast into the valley of the Indus, while the central highlands rise into the Hindu Kush mountains of Afghanistan. Above Teheran, mountains rise to 18,600 feet.

The region is hot near the Persian Gulf — infernally hot, in fact at Bushire. In the north, winter and summer differ by 40° in temperature, and extreme day-by-day variations occur. Although even in the north summer temperatures exceed 80°, the nights are cool on the high plateau.

Iran includes both many wide waste areas and also remarkably fertile regions whose abundant fruit trees and luxuriant green, contrasted with the clean white of the houses, have inspired painters and poets for centuries. Except in the extreme south, flora much like the European prevail. But basically, most of the country has scanty vegetation: the green areas are not extensive. Most of the arable land, even in the well-watered mountain valleys, requires some irrigation.

The People. Estimates of the population generally stand at 15,000,000, a fifth of them nomadic herders of sheep and goats. Ancient Persians were esteemed handsome, and the people remain fairly tall and muscular. Their origins appear to be multiple: the older stocks were comparable to those who dominated northern India, while the Parthians, who opposed the Romans, seem to have had a Turanian strain. But the original stock ("original," that is, within historical times) still defines the masses of the people.

Important racial minorities number about a sixth in all: about 720,000 Turks; 675,000 Kurds; 260,000 Arabs; some 234,000 Lurs (originally Persians with Arab admixture); many Gypsies, Leks, and Baluchis (from neighboring Baluchistan); and several minor groups.

Religion and Education. The ancient religion of Persia, Zoroastrianism, is almost abandoned today, except among the Persian Parsees in India, who are still sun-worshipers. The mass of contemporary Persians follow the (Mohammedan) Shi'iah faith; they are therefore heretics from the orthodox Moslem point of view and often maltreated at Mecca as unworthy of the name of Islam. They reject the body of doctrine and canon law elaborated since the Koran, and they differ also on the apostolic succession from Mohammed: thus their priesthood rejects that of other Moslems. The Shi'iah is all-powerful, or was until modernization: few countries have more land allocated to religious revenue, more shrines, more religious passion, and, until recently, a more thorough priestly monopoly of education.

Moslems form 98% of the population. Apart from a group of Sunni Moslems in the west, religious minorities include the 50,000 Armenian and 30,000 Nestorian Christians, 40,000 Jews; some Bahai, followers of the *Bab* (or "Gateway") who was martyred by the Shi'iah priesthood; and a few foreign Protestants and Catholics. Complete religious tolerance rules in the large towns, but in some rural districts the non-Moslem needs his discretion.

Education of children still lies largely in the hands of the priests who teach small hedge-and-sidewalk schools and who, of course, stress the faith. In the large towns, however, government instruction leads, and more than 200,000 urban children attend modern schools. The state makes valiant efforts to train all these children in more advanced European studies.

There is an active popular press, most of whose journalistic inspiration and style and more literary features derive from France. But the Soviet Union has recently bestowed great attention on every aspect of Persian culture, with the result that today the advanced youth look increasingly to Russia, where so much is done to further knowledge of the Persian past and to resurrect its glories.

The present Persian language, like English, combines several streams; hence, like English, it is rich in synonyms and is a plastic literary instrument. Again, like English, in grammar it tends to be analytical rather than inflected. The Persians excel also in the arts of miniature painting and manuscript illumination and in carpet weaving, calligraphy, pottery, textiles, metal working (their exquisite scrollwork, for example), and architecture — in which their fusion of color and style has been the despair of all rivals.

The Nation's Economy

Agriculture. More than 80% of the people are farmers or stock-raisers; and food production, per person, far exceeds that of most Asiatic countries, even the richer ones. On the small amount of cultivable soil, basic foods, barley, wheat, and rice, annually yield about 1,000,000, 1,800,000, and 400,000 tons, respectively. Cotton, raisins, and dates also provide large crops, and raw silk is produced. Persian wines are abundant and widely known for their flavor. The prevalent gardening crops are ample, vegetables being more popular than usual among Moslems. But Iran really excels in her varied fruits and berries, her exceptional melons, and her succulent stone fruits. Flowers grow in profusion in some regions — the roses of Isfahan are legendary.

The principal meat supply comes from sheep, of which there are 16,000,000. The wool clip reaches about 13,200 tons, and the famous Persian lamb skins command exceptional prices. Apart from sheep, pastoral production does not loom large in terms of population. There are 6,000,000 goats, 1,000,000 oxen, and 1,000,000 cows; but horses and donkeys are numerically inadequate for a country with so small a motorization.

Industry. The principal industry, petroleum, with a normal yearly output of 6,700,000 to 8,700,000 tons, is the fourth largest production in the world. The British own the concession, and their Anglo-Persian Oil Company (which greatly aided the conversion of the British Navy from coal fuel to oil) has become the dominant influence in Iran's economy.

Principal minerals, none present in important

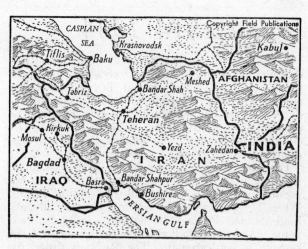

See map on page 315.

quantities, include coal, copper, iron oxides, and rock salt. After petroleum, carpet weaving retains its old supremacy: Iranian carpets command special esteem and excellent prices in all the world's finest markets. In the four famous carpet centers, all workers weave by hand. Cotton and wool spinning have become interesting but not yet very large. Other industries, such as beet-sugar, jute, and matches, are either owned or sponsored by the government.

Finances. The lion's share of government expenses of about $100,000,000 a year (over $6 a person) comes out of the oil revenues. Monetary circulation has risen from about $50,000,000 to $100,000,000. An American financial expert, formerly an advisor in the U.S. State Department, Dr. A. C. Millspaugh, now Administrator-General of the Finances of Iran, wields wide powers. He holds the reins of official economic control and has done much to impose order and to curb both waste and corruption. Such an arrangement is not unprecedented: an American, Mr. W. Morgan Shuster, was appointed before 1910 to reorganize finances, but the move was not approved by the then supervisory governments.

British influence predominates in Iran's banking, but the Russian bank finances the Soviet trade.

Foreign Trade. The world of commerce knows Iran first as a petroleum producer. Petroleum, carpets, and some Persian lambs are the staple exports; others are scattering. Most exports go to Russia (more than half), and then to Britain, India, and Egypt; most imports come from Russia and Britain. Like the British ownership of oil wells, the 1907 division of spheres of influence between Czarist Russia and Britain left its mark on trade. Though the south produces the bulk of petroleum, the north includes the larger population: hence the greater emphasis on Russian imports on the northern border.

In peace years imports averaged about $4.40 per head; exports, $11.40. Declining during the war, imports reached $1.70, and exports also sank, though less radically. But the U.S.A., usually absorbing only 10% of exports and furnishing only 12% of imports, has more recently improved these figures; and the numerous military personnel stationed in Iran now prove a primary factor in economic activity.

History: 1914-1944

Persia was an absolute monarchy until 1906, when she adopted a constitution and chose a Parliament (or *Majlis*). The following year, Britain and Russia agreed to delimit their respective spheres of influence in Persia — a step which the Persians regarded as dismemberment. While the British were more circumspect in the south, the Russian Empire acted as though northern Persia were its possession.

German intrigue during World War I skillfully took advantage of the Persians' hatred of Czarist oppression and of their deep distrust of the British. When Turkey entered the war as a German ally, the road through Persia to India was opened for Germany. And although Persia was legally a neutral, she became a battleground. The Russians drove the pro-German party out of Teheran, and the British finally prevailed after bitterly fought campaigns. By 1918 Sir Percy Sykes, the experienced British soldier and negotiator, had succeeded in making Britain's position paramount. Meanwhile, the Soviets had taken power in Russia — a new reality that Persian and British policy had to take into account after 1918.

Last Years of the Qajar Dynasty: 1918-1925. In 1919 Great Britain concluded an agreement with Persia which gave her undisputed primacy and deliberately excluded the Soviet Union. The people answered with an uprising, led militarily by a Persian head of a Cossack division, Riza Khan Pahlevi. He seized power with the aid of the leading editor in Persia (Saiyid Zia, whom he was later to force out of office).

Taking over the reins of government from the young Shah, Ahmad, within a few years Riza Khan had organized an army and gained firm control over the entire country. And he invited an American expert, A. C. Millspaugh, to consolidate Persia's finances. Riza Khan made the life of the young Shah unendurable; and in 1923 Ahmad fled. Two years later the Parliament was asked to overthrow the celebrated Qajar dynasty, in power since 1794, and to make Riza Khan Pahlevi the Shah and endow his family with hereditary royal power. Once his new dynasty was established, Riza Khan obtained the end of the "capitulations" or privileges to foreigners (1928). Not only was Persia's long period of subordination to the Great Powers over; she even acquired a seat on the Council of the League of Nations.

Modernization of the State: 1929-1939. Riza Khan had no old family tradition to hamper him. Though he proved cooperative with Britain rather than with the U.S.S.R., he sharply contested the renewal of the Anglo-Persian Oil Company concession, which he regarded as over-liberal to the British. The concession was arbitrated and finally renewed.

He proceeded to disarm the tribesmen and jail their venerated chiefs — a supreme affront to the older form of social organization. With next-door Turkey demonstrating how easily the Moslem priesthood could be reduced to obedience, Riza Khan dared to limit the power of the Shi'iah *mullahs* — and

he succeeded. Transforming much of his country, he expanded rail, air, and road communications, deepened military control, and intensified feelings of nationalism. In 1935 this new nationalism was symbolically expressed when the name of Persia (an innovation since 538 B.C.) was changed to Iran — a still older designation, but untainted by 2,500 years of novelty.

The World War: 1939-1944. During World War II, Riza Khan's attitude proved extremely ambiguous. The press in Teheran hinted that Russia was about to invade Iran to control her rich oil fields. In the spring of 1941, when the Arabs rose against Britain in Iraq, the watchful waiting of Riza Khan in nearby Iran gave the British cause for concern. Hence, when Germany invaded the Soviet Union in June 1941, the security of the entire Near East hinged on Iran. Pressure compelled Riza Khan to abdicate; on September 16, 1941, he was succeeded by his son, Mohammed Riza.

British and Soviet forces entered parts of Iran, stating that their occupation was for the duration only, and was not to be construed as a threat to Iranian integrity. In April 1942 Iran formed a cabinet friendly to Britain and Soviet Russia, and in July 1942 a Treaty of Alliance was signed. The country became a leading base for United Nations supplies. At the end of 1943, the Teheran declaration of President Roosevelt, Prime Minister Churchill, and Marshal Stalin heightened Iranian confidence in the certainty of their national independence.

Stakes in the Peace

The recent binding bilateral guarantees of Great Britain and the Soviet Union should allay the last vestiges of a resentful nationalism, since Iran's independence is now certain. Hence the residues of decades of British and Czarist Russian intrigue, and of Iranian suspicion of foreign capital, should now disappear.

Her national revolution under Riza Khan Pahlevi has shown a passion for modernization triumphant over the conservative Shi'iah priesthood. Recent improvements in roads and airports are the first step to a really impressive industrial development. American capital may find Iran grateful, as she has been grateful to two Americans who reorganized her finances.

Ultimately the remarkably generous D'Arcy oil grants to Britain will have to be still further modified so as to increase Iran's state revenue. Trade on the northern frontier with the Soviet Union can follow only upon an increased productive capacity in the U.S.S.R. herself, which is a long-term prospect in view of the destruction wrought in southern Russia by the Nazis. But Afghanistan and India on the east, and Turkey and Iraq on the west and southwest, hitherto indifferent customers, could easily absorb the first light industrial products of awakening Iran. Iranian workers might produce many of the miscellaneous products formerly made in Japan, since Iran possesses the prerequisites for manufacturing these small articles.

But first in importance for Iran's economy is irrigation, with improved methods in intensive vegetable- and fruit-raising. The country's farm products, although of prime quality, are still deficient in quantity.

An end to governmental corruption and widespread education of the eager urban population, with more emphasis on scientific and commercial techniques, would soon enrich this most promising country. The grave losses caused by former nomad raids and disorders in unpoliced areas have markedly decreased. The establishment of civil order will cheapen costs of production by increasing general security, and thus put an end to the levies and plunders of primitive tribes, that were a disgrace for a nation whose general civilization is so advanced.

IRAQ

The Land and the People

Iraq, or Mesopotamia, the "Blessed Land" of Scripture and the legendary seat of the Garden of Eden, is today an Arab monarchy affiliated with Britain. On this soil, centuries before the Christian era, three of the greatest empires rose and died: the Chaldean, on the banks of the Tigris, the Babylonian, on the Euphrates, and the Assyrian in the north. Centuries later, the storied city of Bagdad served as the seat of the Caliphate, under whose rule Mohammedan civilization rose to its zenith. Today the Moslem faith is still preponderant, Arabs constituting 80% of the population.

Iraq is bounded by Turkey (north), Iran (east), the Persian Gulf (south), and Saudi Arabia, Kuwait, Transjordania, and Syria (west). It covers an area of 116,000 square miles, of which two-thirds are desert lands partly useful for grazing. In the upland regions to the north, inhabited by the once-fierce Kurds (16% of the population), lie the oil fields of Mosul, whose reserves are held to be extremely important. The rest of the country is a flat, alluvial plain that culminates in the delta port of Basra on the Persian Gulf. The ancient city of Bagdad is still the capital of the land, but its many modern buildings have given it a contemporary aspect.

Religion and Education. Some 93% of the population are Moslems (both Sunnis and Shi'iahs) — the holy city of Karbala, in the north, is the shrine of the Shi'iah sect. About 3% of the people are Jews, and 4% Christians, a large number of whom belong to the Nestorian, Armenian, and Maronite confessions.

Primary education, though tuition-free, is not compulsory; and minorities like the Turks and Kurds retain the right to their own language schools, though on the primary level only. All other schools are conducted in Arabic. About 50,000 boys and 17,000 girls attend government schools, 17,000 go to private schools. Thus one boy in seven and one girl in twenty receive primary education. Several technical schools and higher institutes exist, but more advanced education has not progressed very far.

See map on page 315.

The Nation's Economy

Agriculture and Industry. Iraq is the land of dates: fully four-fifths of the world's crop come from her trees. The soil is extremely rich when irrigated by canals; and vast irrigation projects, mainly British, have transformed the river basins. Barley, wheat, and rice, important in the economy, annually yield 600,000, 450,000, and 350,000 tons respectively. The principal animal product, wool, affords a clip of 5,000 tons. Cotton culture now produces 25,000 bales.

Considerable peace-time tourist trade prevails, and Bagdad has become a leading airport for traffic between western Europe and the Far East. Pilgrimages to Karbala have long been a further source of revenue.

But all other means of income seem beggared by comparison with petroleum. The normal yearly production of 4,000,000 tons, 1.2% of world supplies, has been greatly reduced, however, during the war. Closed pipe lines, especially to the French mandate of Syria, have diminished the flow of Iraq petroleum to 1,700,000 tons. But great reserves, rather than present production, make Iraq important in the oil economy of the Near East.

Some industrial improvement has taken place. The port of Basra on the Persian Gulf has been modernized also, and the demand for flow of war matériel to the Soviet Union has made American engineers active in road improvements. Since most of the pipe lines terminate in the Mediterranean, the petroleum industry has not been a stimulus to the ports of Iraq.

Finance. During the war, as usual in the Near East, money in circulation has risen inordinately: from $5,200,000 to $20,700,000 in 1942 — about fourfold. But exchange resources abroad have increased sufficiently to cover the augmented issue of money. London controls both the banking system and the issue of money, and the Iraq *dinar* equals the British pound in value.

Price increases have inspired anxiety and occasioned attempts at severe controls. Government budgets, about $17,000,000 in peacetime, have risen to about $44,000,000, of which oil royalties yield some 30%. The national debt is $23,000,000.

Foreign Trade. Bagdad and Basra have had their rich traders from time immemorial (one of the merchant families legendary in the East, the Sassoons, originated in Iraq). In contemporary commerce, imports exceed exports by about $13.30 per capita to only $7.75. This chronic deficit of foreign trade is compensated by receipts from tourists and pilgrims and by some capital investment.

Normal imports, from Britain, Japan, Iran, and India, were mainly textiles, machinery, sugar, and tea. Exports ostensibly destined for Syria and Palestine move ultimately to Britain, the U.S.A., and India. After a fall in trade (imports having sunk to $27,000,000 and exports to $16,000,000), wartime imports have recently swung back to more than $46,000,000.

History: 1914-1944

Before World War I, Iraq was that section of the Turkish Empire called Mesopotamia. It was composed of three provinces: Mosul, Bagdad, and Basra. The victorious British army was stationed in this region when the Allies defeated Turkey in 1918. In conjunction with the French, the British issued a proclamation assuring the establishment of native governments, whose power would depend only on the consent of their peoples.

But the failure to implement these promises by 1920 made the Arabs in Iraq impatient. Having been proclaimed King of Iraq at Damascus in Syria, Feisal, son of the King of the Hejaz, set out to assert Arab rights in Iraq. When in May 1920 the League of Nations awarded Great Britain a mandate over Iraq, the Shi'iah Moslem priesthood urged the natives to revolt, but Sir Percy Cox quelled the rebellion and established a native Council of State.

The Emir Feisal, having been expelled from Damascus by the French, again offered himself for the prospective crown; and in 1921 a plebiscite showed that 96% of the voters favored his ascent to the throne. He was crowned on August 23, 1921, and thus Bagdad, once capital of the Mohammedan world, again saw a native Moslem monarchy. The most articulate elements in Iraq apparently approved the British mandate, while the Kurds, in the north, were granted minority rights.

The infant kingdom passed through difficult opening years. The French disliked Feisal; the Turks were hostile, resenting Iraqui control of the rich Mosul oil fields; and the family of Feisal hated the successful King Ibn Saud, ruler of Saudi Arabia. Feisal, however, was undaunted; and though beset by enemies, he declined to accept the mandatory position of Great Britain, requesting an alliance as between sovereign states.

In October 1922, after serious nationalist agitation had been mastered, a twenty-year treaty of alliance was signed by the two countries, but the agreement was not executed until 1924. During those two years the situation altered greatly. Though the Turks had been driven out of northern Iraq, their power had grown elsewhere, and Turkish (and hence Moslem) prestige stiffened the resistance of the Shi'iah priests who boycotted Feisal's elections. As a result, the treaty was reduced to a four-year compact.

The British, who realized the harmful effects of their tortuous policy on the Arab world, hastened to effect arrangements between Feisal and Ibn Saud, and by 1925 Iraq was at peace with all her neighbors. Elections took place and the "organic law" (constitution) was completed.

Iraq Achieves Independence: 1930–1944. Protracted treaty negotiations continued, with the Iraq government patiently striving to achieve completely independent status and Great Britain insisting on proofs of its capacity for defense. In 1930, a new treaty stated that Iraq was an independent state, and that Britain would sponsor her application for membership in the League of Nations. Upon her admission to the League in 1932, Iraq's independence became effective, and the mandate was at an end. In 1935 King Ghazi succeeded his father, Feisal, to the throne.

Nationalist elements, despite this honorable consummation of the mandate, were not satisfied with Iraq's military alliance with Great Britain, particularly the provision whereby Britain was entrusted with the air defense of the kingdom. In October 1936 the army staged a *coup d'état*, forming the ultra-nationalist Sulaiman government. But as administrators these nationalists proved failures, and so in December 1937 the exiled moderate, Nuri-es-Said, who had negotiated the treaty of independence with Great Britain, returned to power. In April 1939, Feisal II, a four-year-old boy, succeeded to the throne, with his uncle, the pro-British Emir Abdul-Ilah, as Regent.

During World War II, anti-British intrigues multiplied in Iraq as the Nazis threatened to break out of Europe and Africa into the Near East. In April 1941 a *coup*, led by Rashid Ali al-Gailani, put the pro-German elements in power and exiled the Regent. This seven weeks' rebellion was the gravest threat of the war to Allied security in the Near East, but the British easily mastered it and restored to power the pro-British Regent and the faithful and statesmanlike Nuri-es-Said. The Iraq government then extended broad military privileges to the British for the duration of the war.

In January 1943, Iraq had the distinction of being the first Mohammedan state to declare war on the Axis. While there were a few sporadic incidents of anti-British terrorism, the country seemed never to have been so calm and so united as in 1944.

Stakes in the Peace

Iraq has two economic foundations: dates and petroleum. Excessive dependence on dates is a result of the somewhat arrested development of agriculture in the upcountry, which causes emphasis to be placed on the easily raised date-palm in the hot river valleys. Irrigation projects, when extended, will help to bring this monoculture to an end. Moreover, increased education and orderly progress in the formerly dangerous mountain country around Mosul, where the Kurds made both life and property insecure, will be a boon to agriculture in that promising district. A higher yield of barley is fundamental to national well-being, and is easily attainable, as British experts have demonstrated.

Large-scale port improvements at Basra and Bagdad should greatly increase Iraq's carrying trade; while railroad and bus extensions, replacing the antiquated, costly caravan trade in the back country, will cheapen the cost of goods and make them more accessible to the population. The increasing prosperity of Iran and other Shi'iah Moslem areas may make the pilgrim trade to the shrine at Karbala more profitable than when those countries were poor.

In the sphere of politics, the present dynasty may be counted on to insist on the independence of Iraq, for it would scarcely yield to the Saudi dynasty that wishes to incorporate all Arab-speaking lands into a common federation. The speed with which Rashid Ali al-Gailani's rebellion collapsed in 1941 indicates the power and popularity of the present British-backed dynasty.

Since parliamentary experience is gaining in Iraq, and education is on the upgrade, a full-fledged parliamentary system (really popular, in the sense of a large and articulate middle class) is in the making. The need to defend Iraq's sovereignty against the immoderate ambitions of neighboring Moslem states is a guarantee of her genuine loyalty to some type of League of Nations.

PALESTINE

The Land and the People

Palestine, the Holy Land, source of the religions of Europeans, has been a British mandate since 1920. Bible history centers in Palestine, and for millenia the Jews have regarded it as their sacred land, to which their Messiah would one day recall them. Christians also venerate Palestine as the land in which Christ redeemed mankind. To Moslems, Jerusalem is the third Holy City. For 1900 years Palestine has been a center of pilgrimages, and the Crusades were fought for two centuries to regain the Holy Land. No other country can compare with her in sanctity for so many faiths.

The Land. Palestine's small area, about 10,250 square miles, approximates that of Maryland. Palestine faces Syria on the north; Transjordania, the Jordan river, and the Dead Sea on the east; the Sinai area belonging to Egypt on the south; and the Mediterranean on the west — boundaries have altered little from the Biblical ones ("from Dan to Beersheba"). A narrow populated coastal plain soon rises to a block of mountains. On the plateau, life centers in the city of Jerusalem. Southward lies the Sinai desert; southeastward, the desert about the Dead Sea, whose borders lie 1,300 feet below Mediterranean sea level.

The coastal plain is highly fertile, the slope from the highland to the plain grateful to the tiller, and the hill country (the "high places" of the Bible) favorable to town life. In the lowlands and valleys, however, swamp areas abound and breed widespread malaria. Jewish colonization has flourished in Carmel and the plain of Esdralon, and in the citrus lands about Nablus. Northward extend the Sea of Galilee and its hilly environs, almost 4,000 feet high. Haifa in the north and Jaffa in the midlands afford good harbors. Near the latter stands the new Jewish city of Tel Aviv.

Coastal climate is Mediterranean, but cold winters often visit the plateau. Since summer rains are deficient and much of the soil porous, Palestine requires irrigation on a large scale; the small total of irrigated land is being increased. Even in Biblical times, cultivation seems to have been slight; Palestine was then primarily pastoral.

Ratios of population have been changing with great rapidity in Palestine through the continual immigration. As late as 1942 the total figure seems to have been about 1,605,000, of whom 987,000 were Moslems — mostly Arabs; 126,000 Christians — most of them Arabs; and 478,000 Jews, almost all of European origin. The last figure is in dispute: some estimates give over 500,000 Jews; even 700,000 has been advanced as the true figure. Jews have of course come to Palestine mainly within the last quarter-century.

Arabs and Jews form almost two distinct nations — and two widely different cultures — within the same boundaries. Certain figures underline great differences. Arab birthrate (49.2 per thousand) remains steady; the Jewish (20.7), like that of most

Europeans, constantly declines. Arab deathrates (about 21.4 per thousand) are much higher than Jewish (only 7.9), though it must be remembered that the Jewish population, largely recruited from among young adults, is dominated by age groups in which the deathrate is lowest. The natural increase of the Jews, by births, shows only 12% as against 27% of the Arabs. Infant mortality among the Jews (56) is less than half of the Arab figure (122). Though the Jews tend to agglomerate in cities like Jerusalem (about 60% of the city — 86,000 persons), Haifa (50% — 57,000 persons), and Tel Aviv (wholly Jewish — 140,000 persons), nevertheless they and certain old colonies of German Unitarians do the greater part of the modern farming.

The Jews came to Palestine mainly in four waves. First came the now older, more religious Jews, then those who answered the call of the international Zionist movement. These, however, were not comparable in numbers to the "pioneers" (*Chalutzim*) who arrived in the 1920's after World War I, or to the large middle-class emigration in the 1930's from western Europe fleeing the Nazi terror. The Christians include mainly old settlers or native peoples: for centuries religious foundations have kept up their numbers, even under the disfavor of the old Turkish régime. It may even be said that the medieval crusaders left some lasting traces.

The presence of opposed cultures, the Arabian and the Jewish, at utterly different social and historic levels, has, of course, led to much friction. Despite a history of dissension and even, at times, bloody strife, some elements among both peoples feel that common interests can eventually prevail, given sufficient goodwill and an adequate material basis for its continuance, once established. Jewish immigration, about 12,000 annually, has been restricted to satisfy Arab demands, and more recently the gates of Palestine have even been closed to the Jews, at least temporarily, except for a small number of refugees who are still permitted to enter the country under exceptional circumstances.

Education and Religion. Though education has not been made compulsory, the Jewish population is 100% literate, except for a small colony from Yemen (southern Arabia). Of the Arabs, about 70,000 children now attend the schools, about one-third those of eligible age. (A generation ago education had reached a fraction of this figure.) The Jewish cultural life typifies that of a period of national awakening: symphony orchestras, theaters, libraries, and literary and scientific production abound. A Hebrew university, largely American-endowed and of the highest rank, flourishes in Jerusalem. Arabic and Hebrew are the official languages; English prevails in administrative life. The Hebrew press maintains high standards; and the Arabic press is rapidly growing.

Three Christian patriarchs and several bishops are domiciled in Jerusalem. The Moslems have their Grand Mufti (See *History*), and the Jews two high Rabbis for the celebration of the Sephardic and Ashkenazi rites. Though the war interrupted the great flow of pilgrims, the shrines will soon again attract worshipers of these three religions from every part of the world.

The Nation's Economy

Agriculture. The agriculture is on two technical levels: the Jewish, which is modern, productive, and based on adequate capital; and the Arabian, which is traditional, primitive, and low in yield. Jewish agriculture is typified by cooperative communities, Arabian by small family farms aiming at subsistence and not at export. An American expert, Dr. Lowdermilk, has paid tribute to the imaginative Jewish reclamation projects that have arrested erosion, conquered malaria, greatly increased the arable area, and augmented fertility.

Agricultural Palestine long followed a basic monoculture of citrus fruits. During the war this proved calamitous, for shortage of shipping space cut exports from 15,000,000 cases to practically nothing. Then they rose slowly to 2,500,000 cases, insufficient to sustain the basis of agriculture. The government has been forced to vote subsidies to keep the citrus farmers going and, at the same time, has encouraged subsistence farming to prevent a recurrence of collapse. Subsistence farming is now common among the large numbers of Jewish cooperative farmers.

Recently food crops have shown improved figures: wheat 112,000 tons; barley 122,000; olives 62,000 (to the value of $11,000,000); olive oil 9,500; and corn fully 74,000. Livestock production remains small; but here too the Jewish farmers, trained under European consumption of dairy products, have tried, by cross-breeding, to adapt European livestock to local conditions of survival. Under the stimulus of Jewish example and government aid, the hitherto backward Arab cultivation shows gradual but marked improvement. Palestine nevertheless has not become self-sustaining in food production, though half the people live on farms.

Industry. An industrial boom hit Palestine in the last decade. The sudden injection of European and American savings and contributions, together with the arrival of tens of thousands of skilled artisans, mechanics, engineers, and scientists, has transformed the land. Cement, potash, and sulfur have risen to importance: the Dead Sea has become a great chemical asset. Power installations have utilized the Jordan and the short but turbid streams hitherto running to waste in the hills. A wide range of consumers goods, of good quality, shows the vigor of manufacturing industries, though costs of production still remain high.

Factories to the number of 1,300, representing Jewish capital investments of $70,000,000 and employing 30,000 workers, function energetically. A large oil refinery has been built. Chemicals, including complex pharmaceutical products, usually provide employment to German exiles. The apparel trades, led by experienced immigrants from New York, are active. Viennese expatriates specialize in bonbons and fine textiles. The diamond-cutting trade, almost everywhere Jewish, has been almost bodily lifted and transferred from Antwerp and Amsterdam to Palestine, where the busy exiles work in thirty plants.

Finance. Palestine's banking usually affiliates with London, and her pound stands now at a premium over the British. Currency in circulation has risen from a pre-war 7,800,000 pounds to 22,600,000 pounds in

1943. Its cover, based on London deposits, is about 56%. Bank deposits of about $90,000,000 — 80% by the European and American population — average (for them) $200 a head. Savings in cooperatives, mutual benefit societies, and building associations have grown extensively also; and the Jewish population contributes, as well, to an old-age pension Fund. As elsewhere, wartime prices have soared distressingly.

Foreign Trade. Foreign trade perennially shows a great surplus of imports. Before the war these were $70,000,000; exports, only $28,000,000. In 1941 exports had sunk to a mere $5,500,000, while imports stood at $46,000,000. Continual deficits of some $400,000,000 a decade were normally compensated by capital investment and tourist traffic. Thus Palestine exemplifies a country in the deficit-investment stage of development.

In pre-war days, imports of wheat, sugar, and textiles flowed predominantly from Britain, Egypt, and the U.S.A. Exports then centered on citrus fruits, soap, and wine; more recently they have featured apparel, polished diamonds, and chocolates. In 1942 they rose slightly, to over $7,000,000 (excluding Dead Sea chemicals). Recent export goods, sent to Egypt and Syria, usually were ultimately destined for Britain. The expenditures of the army and the services of the Middle East Supply Center during the war have largely modified destinations of manufactured goods. Oil from Iraq and Arabia is transshipped mostly to Britain.

History: 1914-1944

Before 1914 Palestine was a *sanjak* (or sub-province) of the Turkish Empire, which fought on the side of Germany in World War I. In 1918 Lord Allenby, the British Commander, wrested Palestine from the Turks.

Lord Balfour, on behalf of the British government, had declared in 1917 that Britain viewed with sympathy the establishment of a national home for the Jewish people in Palestine. This declaration immediately raised the prestige of the Zionist movement among Jews throughout the world. Zionism had been formulated by Theodore Herzl, a Viennese journalist, as a necessity for the Jewish people. It contemplated an independent state in Palestine, ancestral home of the Jews. From 1896 Zionism had commanded a large following, though Jewish sentiment was by no means undivided on this issue.

The Zionists greeted the Balfour declaration with enthusiasm, but in their eagerness they failed to inquire into its extremely careful and cryptic wording. At the time it was not known that both McMahon, British representative to the Arabs, and the romantic adventurer T. E. Lawrence, had made commitments to the Arabs which seriously modified the apparent intent of the Balfour statement. Almost at once scholastic distinctions were made as to the meaning of a "national home." Did that phrase signify full independence, or a reserved area, or merely a sponsored settlement with a measure of religious or local autonomy? The population of Palestine in 1920 suggested the difficulties of the case: there were over

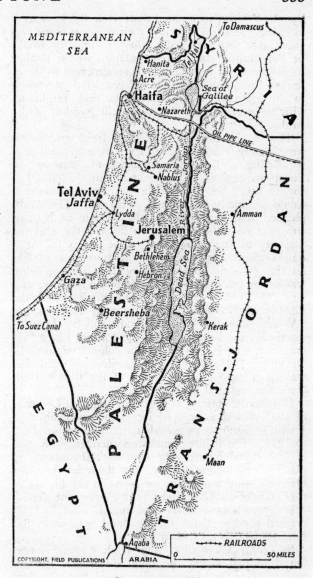

See map on page 315.

60,000 Jews, some 660,000 Arabs, of whom an eighth were Christians.

For two years the British military administration was not incautious enough to proclaim the Balfour declaration. Pan-Arab sentiment had been fanned during the war. The Zionists, for their part, wished Palestine to include portions of Syria, Transjordania, and sufficient elbow room to convert the country into a valid economic area, not a small historic museum. Britain considered this impracticable, and in 1920 Palestine began her career as a British mandate in an area much too small for the realization of her economic potentialities. But the Jews, animated by ideals that transcended material aims, began a settlement that has amazed the world.

In 1920 the British appointed Sir Herbert Samuel High Commissioner. Hebrew was proclaimed one of the official languages of the country. Following riotous demonstrations among Arabs against the Jewish immigration and status, Winston Churchill, then Colonial Secretary, issued a White Paper affirming British recognition of the Zionist organization.

PALESTINE

But the White Paper stated that, while the Jews were in Palestine by full right and their national home was guaranteed internationally, their nationality would be Palestinian; the Arab population would neither be displaced by Jews nor made subordinate to them. Jewish immigration was to be restricted according to the interests of the inhabitants, and, implicitly, with some regard for the numerical position of the Arabs.

The Arabs insisted that their legal guarantees were merely nominal, since they were a colonial people facing a European immigration possessed of European capital. They pointed out that the European could buy land while the impecunious Arab would gradually lose control of his soil. The Arabs pleaded that Article 22 of the League of Nations covenant on self-determination favored them as the majority of the inhabitants. The policy of Arab non-cooperation persisted, as did murderous attacks on the growing Jewish settlements. The agitation was led by the Husseini, a family of the nobility, who demanded union with Syria. On July 24, 1922, the League of Nations formally granted Palestine an "A" mandate, but both the Arabs and the Jews insisted that the British treated the country like a "B" mandate, that is, one of inferior colonial status. In November 1923, as a result of disorders, all legislation was concentrated in the hands of the British High Commissioner and British officials.

Despite the clamors of the Arab National Congress of 1925, Palestine enjoyed increasing tranquillity as Jewish emigration exceeded immigration from 1925 to 1927. The British diminished their garrison, and in 1928 Lord Plumer dispensed with the army, replacing it by a constabulary. But the following year, bloody rioting broke out, the worst in the history of the mandate. The plight of the innocent Jewish colonists, whose industry and imagination had recreated the life of the stricken land, was such that their protection became urgent.

Sir John Chancellor, the High Commissioner, found himself facing the usual dilemma. Britain, with stakes in the Mohammedan world, had to reckon with Arab policy; at the same time, the Jews were a useful bulwark of European influence and civilization. The fanaticism of the Mufti of Jerusalem, later a Fascist traitor, made impossible any negotiations with this Moslem dignitary. The Jews now numbered 17% of the population and dominated economic life. The British government studied the dire situation and in a White Paper endorsed the report of a British expert, Simpson, who thought the country did not permit of much expansion. The White Book of 1930 had such an anti-Zionist tone that in 1931 a corrective supplement had to be added. There was dismay among Jews that so great a Socialist intellectual as Lord Passfield (Sidney Webb) in the Labor government in London was also unsympathetic.

Palestine and the Advent of Nazism in Europe: 1933–1944. In 1933, Nazi persecutions of European Jewry altered circumstances. Highly trained and wealthy Jews were now added to the stream of idealists who had so valiantly built up the Jewish homeland. Capital flowed into Palestine. Immigration restrictions, which had been based on the assets of immigrants, were a barrier against millions of poor Jews, but not against this active, industrial group. The Arab now saw an industrial and urban development he had never even conceived of. This led to renewed anti-Jewish rioting, but now the Jews were a far larger proportion of the population, more confident and better organized.

A Royal Commission under Lord Peel recommended in 1937 the partition of Palestine into independent Jewish and Arab areas, with the Holy Places under an international mandate. This proposal satisfied nobody. In Jerusalem, Dr. Magnes, head of the Hebrew University, suggested that the Jews and Arabs form a state in friendship, within a federation, to include Syria and Transjordania and thus give Palestine genuine economic scope. Though this view gained many adherents, it has not prevailed against insistent nationalisms.

The Peel report was not acted upon until 1939, when the celebrated White Paper limited Jewish immigration so stringently that it brought about the cessation of legal immigration by making it subject to Arab approval. World War II caused the collapse of Palestine's export trade (the war's economic effects have been described under *Production*). Certain humane waivers were now made to permit the immigration of Jewish refugees, but the White Paper restrictions remained the basic law, despite vigorous protests, especially from the U.S.A.

The Arabs were inflamed by Axis propaganda, and, when that ebbed, by Saudi Arabian and Indian Moslem nationalists. Britain denied the Jews the right to form a Jewish army within the British ranks, even for service in the Libyan campaign. They were singled out for concealing arms, while the Arabs were not imprisoned. Polish officers, garrisoned with the British Army, were permitted to search Jewish homes for deserters. The state of tension had not much abated by the summer of 1944.

Stakes in the Peace

Palestine has an importance disproportionate to her small population. The Holy Land is the shield of the Suez Canal, the terminus of petroleum supplies for Britain and other lands, the bridge from Asia to Africa. The country may become the focus of Pan-Arab disturbances; at the same time, her brilliant colonization by the Jews is in constant jeopardy.

Many people support the proposed solution of a Jewish-Arab cooperative state, but only as a local area federated with larger, predominantly Arab countries. Under such conditions the Jews could not be regarded as a force sufficient to dominate Arabs, compared with whom their numbers are small, and yet their Palestinian accomplishments would be secured and their numbers advantageously increased.

Arab agitation is partly inspired by powerful feudal families who see modern civilization as sapping the sources of their exploitation of their fellow-Arabs. But even Jewish labor unions have not taken the Arab worker into fellowship, so that there is ample room for greater toleration on both sides. The British mandate has secured property development by imposing order, sound finance, international security. But, as in Syria, a higher international stewardship will ultimately have to replace British control.

SAUDI ARABIA

The Land and the People

Foreigners fascinated by her life, poetry, and culture have given Arabia a colorful place in their literatures. The best accounts in English are still Burton's *Voyage to Mecca and Medina*, Colonel Lawrence's famous *Revolt in the Desert* (whose political aspects have been challenged), and Doughty's great *Arabia Deserta*. All three writers have found in the country inspiration favorable to unusual beauty of style.

But the great peninsula of Arabia, a third as large as the U.S.A., has extraordinary historical as well as literary associations. The economic fact basic to an understanding of its record is that its arid, sterile land cannot without widespread irrigation and agricultural development adequately support the people. They have therefore hurled themselves on the outside world, breaking through once (in the 7th century) to sweep like one of their own furious desert storms before subsiding again. They carried their new faith, militant and fanatical Islam, throughout four-fifths of the old Roman Empire — as far as Tours in France — subjugated Spain, reduced the great Byzantine Empire to a mere appendage, preempted the then fairest Christian lands (Palestine, Syria, Asia Minor — every place indeed where St. Paul had preached except Rome itself), blighted Africa and Egypt, smashed almost in a night the ancient fire-worshiping empire of the Persians, and established sway over the Brahmins of India.

Following this gigantic effort, these swarthy conquerors who had swept over the earth on their magnificent horses, setting up military and civil rule that was one system, settled into luxury and gave the world arithmetic, algebra, and astronomy; developed historical theory; revived ancient philosophy; distilled alcohol; advanced medicine; gathered the fables of the East into the *Arabian Nights*; and then gradually fell back into the rearguard of human development.

The Land. The Arabian peninsula that produced these people of such extremes of energy and stagnation embraces over a million square miles. Its water boundaries are the Red Sea (west), the Indian Ocean (south), and the Persian Gulf (east). Iraq lies to the northeast, Syria and Lebanon to the north. The Arabian peninsula is easily three-fourths a sandy or stony desert waste, but numerous oases emerge from the vast expanse.

It is one of the intensely hot sections of the world, except for winters which are often intolerably cold on the rocky plains. Westward the peninsula becomes a high plateau, southward it rises to mountainous heights. Except in the southeastern Sultanate of Oman, whose mountains reach 10,000 feet, it slopes gradually eastward into the Mesopotamian plain and the Persian Gulf. Rainfall is practically unknown outside the extreme southeast and southwest, though there are some poor grasslands (steppes) that support pastoral activity. In sum, if we except the fertile regions of Oman (southeast) and Yemen (southwest), Arabia is a land of enormous steppe desert, sandy waste, and mountainous wilderness.

The People. Experts variously estimate the Arabian population at from 7,000,000 to 10,000,000. The people are Semites (the Midianites of Scripture). Their ancient tongue, Arabic, is the principal Semitic language, Hebrew being a secondary branch of the same family.

The people differ in their modes of living: tented nomads predominate, but others lead polished, sedentary lives in the oasis towns. Inordinate pride of family rules among them; Burton pointed out that even humble Arabian folk can tell of scores of ancestors for generations back. Princely families thus have a great hold on their jealous, warring tribes, which sometimes coalesce into large, powerful confederations.

Though in an industrial age the Arabians seem far removed from the center of things, their language still dominates Mohammedan life and serves as the vehicle of trade over a large part of the world. One dare not underestimate their rôle. To this day, the Arab Mohammedan missionary in Africa makes five converts to the Christian's one, and his converts hold to their faith. French and British colonial policy in the Near East recognizes and is much affected by this fact.

Religion and Education. Though some Christians remain among them despite 1300 years of pressure, and though Jews are active in some of the towns, nearly all Arabians hold the Moslem faith. The position of the Jews has been made difficult by the Zionist movement in Palestine, since Ibn Saud, monarch of Saudi Arabia, is its avowed foe. The Moslem sects, the Wahhabi and orthodox Sunni, dominate the peninsula, but the northwest includes many who subscribe to the hated Shi'iah faith that is more common in Iran and Iraq. Education remains in the hands of the priests.

SAUDI ARABIA

The peninsula includes many states, some of which — Iraq, Syria, Palestine Mandate — are treated on other pages of this volume. The present chapter proceeds by dividing the area into Saudi Arabia and the minor Arabian Peninsula States about her.

The peninsula is really controlled by Saudi Arabia, a central dual monarchy consisting of Nejd and Hejaz, covering 700,000 square miles and inhabited by some 3,000,000 people. Ibn Saud rules this dual kingdom in which the Wahhabis, a unitarian and puritanical sect, are dominant.

Saudi Arabia's known ambition to weld a powerful Pan-Arab Federation including Egypt, with herself at the center, has made itself an object of diplomatic attention. Saudi Arabians regard themselves somewhat as the Prussians did when they slowly expanded their little Brandenburg into Germany and dreamed of expanding it to the dimensions of the globe. The

Pan-Arab Federation would embrace 33,000,000 people, control the fourth-largest petroleum deposits in the world, hold sway over Suez and the routes to the East, and bring to a focus once more the enormous forces of Mohammedanism. Such a dream must be of more than passing interest to the rest of the world.

But though this may seem a remote fantasy, Saudi Arabian economic policy, today realistic and long-range, takes strictly into account the present industrial feebleness of the area and bases itself on needs of tax-payers rather than of nomads, and on the need for sufficient oil rather than on horse-raising, on the importance of consumers goods (especially textiles and motor cars), and on the imperative need for diminished economic reliance on income from religious pilgrimages.

Saudi Arabian Economy. A pastoral economy basically rules the land, as in the central Nejd desert (550,000 square miles, twice the size of Texas, and the ancestral home of most of our race horses). Though the oases yield dates, wheat, barley, fruit, wool, hides, ghee (clarified butter, staple of the East), the people produce, above all, sheep, camels, and the celebrated Arab steeds. The automobile, however, has radically affected animal exports: the basic economy perforce must be shifted. Fortunately, petroleum has been discovered near the Persian Gulf, with a production of 800,000 tons. Recent negotiations with Ibn Saud for an eastern pipeline emphasize the importance of this source of oil.

The production in the western area is unimportant. Here the annual pilgrimages of the faithful to Mecca and Medina normally have sufficed to sustain these two ancient oasis cities. During the war, however, the revenue has dwindled nearly to the vanishing point.

MINOR ARABIAN STATES

The following constitute the minor states of the peninsula: (1) Yemen, a kingdom to the southwest, with 3,500,000 people; (2) Oman, a sultanate to the southeast, largely populated by Baluchis (from northwest India) and Negroes; (3) Aden, a British crown colony with an important airport, a marine refueling station, and one of the most strategic ports in the world, since it commands the entrance to the Red Sea and eventually to the Suez Canal; (4) the nearby British protectorate of Aden; (5) Trans-jordania, a northwestern kingdom whose ruler heads the Hashimite family, which is exalted even in this region of commonly illustrious ancestors; (6) Kuwait, adjoining Iraq; (7) some formerly piratical states to the southeast (the Trucials); (8) the Bahrein islands in the Persian Gulf; and (9) the island of Socotra, a sultanate, which child readers of Kipling will remember as "in the pink Arabian sea." In most of these small states British political agents reside.

Economic Factors. Yemen includes Mocha, from which came the original coffee still used in blending because of its fine bouquet, but only a small export today. Yemen is the ancient land of Sheba, whose beautiful queen visited Solomon. Today about its gray-walled cities spread fields of coffee, barley, millet, wheat, and pastoral lands whose people live by producing hides.

Oman is known for her pearl fisheries, though dates and pomegranates predominate in production. The economy of the other states has only picturesque interest for the world at large.

The Bahrein islands, however, are important for their petroleum, producing 936,000 tons yearly. Though this Arab state is independent, it is under British protection; the oil, however, is owned by American interests. The Arabs know the Bahrein islands for quite other reasons — for their boats, sails, mats, and white donkeys for show-riding.

History: 1914-1944

Prior to World War I, most of the permanently settled areas of Arabia were ruled by Turkey. She controlled Syria and Palestine, large regions east of the Jordan river, Hejaz with its two Moslem Holy Cities of Mecca and Medina, the western rim of Arabia along the Red Sea, including Asir and Yemen and to the border of Aden. In the northeast, Turkey also ruled the lands that are now Iraq. However, the desert areas inhabited by nomadic Arabs, were controlled by Ibn Saud, head of the Saudi family. His people were Wahhabis, the most puritanical and zealous of Moslems, whose every campaign is, by definition, a Holy War against unbelievers — including fellow-Moslems of other sects. The Wahhabi tribes were consolidated into a powerful social system, having abandoned traditional tribal divisions, wars, and blood feuds. They had concentrated on unity in support of their religious beliefs.

When war broke out in October 1914 between Turkey and Great Britain, the importance of the Arabs became critical. With her large Moslem populations in India and the Sudan, Great Britain realized that Turkey's spiritual hegemony in the Moslem world constituted a serious danger to the British Empire. Since Turkey was the seat of the Caliphate, it was almost impious for Moslems to oppose her. Not only did she hold dominion over the Moslem Holy Cities, but she enjoyed some legal jurisdiction over Egypt and some vestigial rights in Tunis. The Moslem population of Afghanistan, who anxiously followed the fortunes of Turkey, might at any time prove a danger to Britain on her Indian frontier. In November 1914, German agents sought to direct Turkish armies into the depths of Persia in order to effect a junction between Turkey and Britain's Moslem subjects in India.

The British at once undertook to enlist Arabian support against Turkey, for Arabian resistance against Turkey would keep her occupied in defending her Arabian possessions and her nearby frontiers. In order to implement their policy, the British approached the two rising princely families of Arabia, who, however much they might be impressed by the Caliphate within Turkey, respected their own family traditions and ambitions far more. Skilled British negotiators were dispatched in an effort to utilize the possibilities.

Captain W. H. I. Shakespear undertook to persuade Ibn Saud, the ruler of the Wahhabis, to attack the Arab principality of Jebel Shammar. Only a few years earlier, Ibn Saud had humiliated the Turkish army, and Jebel Shammar had taken up arms in be-

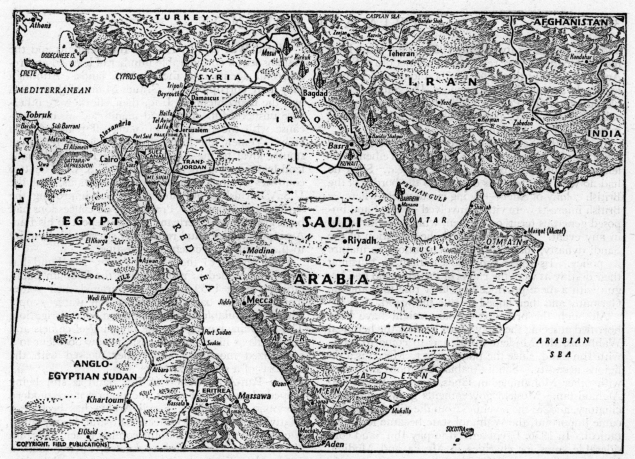

See map on page 315.

half of the Turks. The British had additional reasons for approaching Ibn Saud. Since his subjects, the Wahhabis, regarded the pilgrimages to the Holy Cities as idolatrous, the British believed that Ibn Saud would have no scruples about assailing Turkey. Hence, Ibn Saud was in a position to shatter the power of the Turks in the Arabian peninsula. Captain Shakespear persuaded him to attack Jebel Shammar. But in 1915 the fighting proved indecisive and Captain Shakespear was killed. Ibn Saud decided not to pursue the war.

The British turned their attention to Husein Ibn Ali, the *Sharif* or Viceroy of Hejaz and the Emir of Mecca. In June 1916 he revolted against Turkey. Not only did he deprive her of Mecca, but he cut her communications along the Red Sea and down to Yemen. The following year, the British agent, Col. T. E. Lawrence, now associated with Husein, captured Aqaba, which left the Turks with only a precarious hold on Medina. Turkey's day in Arabia was over.

Husein's victories inflamed his imagination, and he proclaimed himself King of all the Arab countries. Ibn Saud, resenting Husein's self-arrogated dominion over him, watched carefully for the first sign of weakness. Husein seized Khurma, a village on the boundary between his domain of Hejaz and Ibn Saud's domain of Nejd. Ibn Saud made no counter-move, but he held the Khurma incident in mind as a pretext for war against Husein when such would suit his plans.

In 1918 General Allenby triumphed in Palestine and General Marshall conquered Iraq. Turkey surrendered to the Allies. Believing that Britain's interest in the Arab regions was now diminished, Ibn Saud

proceeded to threaten Husein, using the latter's earlier seizure of Khurma as his pretext. Husein appealed to Britain to support his claims to Khurma. The British Foreign Minister, Lord Curzon, warned Ibn Saud (1919) that Britain sustained Husein and threatened to cut off his annual pension of $300,000 paid by Britain. While this warning was being transmitted, Ibn Saud annihilated a Hejaz army led by the second son of Husein. But Ibn Saud did not exploit this crushing victory, since he preferred never overtly to antagonize the British.

In a series of brilliant campaigns against Arab princelings (1920–22), Ibn Saud proceeded to build up his desert empire. By 1922 he had conquered the whole of inner Arabia to the borders of Hejaz and Yemen. In the meantime, Britain had placed two of Husein's sons on the thrones of Iraq and Transjordania, to the humiliation of Ibn Saud. Desiring peace in the peninsula, the British government arranged a conference at Kuwait between the two rival Arab powers, but without success.

Ibn Saud decided to strike, having waited nine years for the proper moment. He hurled his Wahhabi legions against the Hejaz kingdom. The Wahhabis fought with the fire of religious fanaticism that had long ago subsided in the polished and wealthy Mohammedan circles of the Holy Cities. Within a year Ibn Saud won Mecca and Medina and the whole of Hejaz. In December 1925 Husein fled and Ibn Saud proclaimed himself King of Hejaz.

The principality of Nejd now became his other kingdom. Great Britain recognized his boundaries and title by the treaty of May 1927. Five years later his two kingdoms were renamed the Kingdom of Saudi Arabia. Shortly thereafter the boundaries were permanently arranged. Furthermore, Ibn Saud secured his outlet on the Persian Gulf, thus altering the so-called "British Lake" policy of absolute British control in regions of the Persian Gulf.

In 1934 Ibn Saud conquered the large territory of Asir. In the same year the Kingdom of Yemen challenged his authority, but fell in quick defeat. Since he had no wish to extend his domain to the border of the British colony of Aden — being circumspect wherever British interests were vitally involved — Ibn Saud imposed generous terms on Yemen, which was his vassal in any event. Thus culminated the evolution of the Saudi dynasty, that had taken generations to mature its policy. Its rulers proved as patient in pursuing their destiny as were the rulers of Prussia, who had begun with a mere province and later rose to dominate Germany and then hoped to rule the world.

Although the orthodox Moslem might have been horrified at seeing the Holy Cities held by the heretical Wahhabis, the Moslem world had to come to terms with Ibn Saud, since the pilgrimage to Mecca is a religious necessity. Saudi Arabian relations improved with other Mohammedan lands, such as Egypt and Afghanistan. Moslem governments grew more conciliatory, and, as the revenues from the pilgrimages became important, the Wahhabi state became less puritanical. In 1936, Egypt agreed to pay Ibn Saud considerable sums for charities in Mecca and Medina. It was a religious duty for pious Egyptians to sustain these charities — which also greatly aided the Saudi treasury.

World War II. In 1940–41 the Germans and the Italians sent a considerable number of learned and resourceful agents into the Arabian lands. Although they had corrupted the Grand Mufti of Jerusalem and the malcontents in Iraq, their efforts were otherwise unsuccessful. Ibn Saud manifested his common cause with the Allies by breaking off relations with Italy. Yemen, the focus of Axis intrigues, remained stoutly loyal to the Allies. In 1943 Ibn Saud made lend-lease arrangements with the U.S.A. The two countries entered into diplomatic relations, and the U.S.A. furnished aid and advice for improving the agricultural economy. Previously, oil concessions had been granted to Americans. With respect to his Pan-Arab policy, Ibn Saud repeatedly stressed his hostility to the Zionist movement in Palestine.

With regard to the nomad Arabs, Ibn Saud has largely succeeded in transforming the Bedouin population. Since 1939 he has encouraged their settlement in large oases, improving the water supply wherever available and developing modern irrigation. The Bedouin, having lost the breeding of camels and fine steeds as his economic basis, is now obedient to a centralized monarchy and rather pleased with the comforts of a settled existence.

The Pan-Arab policy of Ibn Saud is still being shaped along secular paths and upon a more modern economic foundation. Saudi Arabia has become a relatively orderly and industrious realm, keenly interested in the dispositions of the coming peace. Certain of her attitudes are already known, among them a marked hostility to the Zionist movement in Palestine, which Ibn Saud has stated repeatedly and with deliberate emphasis.

SYRIA AND LEBANON

The Land and the People

Syria and Lebanon, two mandates granted France by the League of Nations, have proclaimed their independence within the mandates. Lands of ancient civilization, they lie today off the beaten track of modern development. But rich associations will always cluster about the land of the cedars of Lebanon, whose long valleys carried Greek and Lydian, Assyrian and Babylonian, into Palestine and Egypt. All Christian countries remember the conversion of Saint Paul on the road to Damascus.

Once the exchange center of the world and the land bridge between Orient and Occident, Syria lost her 3,000-year strategic position when the Suez Canal cut through the Sinai peninsula (1869). East and West no longer meet to barter in the oasis cities of Damascus and Aleppo. The ports of Tyre and Sidon (old Phoenicia, the cradle of maritime commerce)

have given way to Beyrouth as the leading harbor in modern times.

These lands extend between Turkey (north), Iraq (east), Palestine (south), and the Mediterranean (west). Syria's area of 72,650 square miles added to Lebanon's of 3,470 about equals the combined size of Ohio and Indiana. Within Syria, Latakia (known to most Americans for its tobacco) and Jebel Druze form semi-autonomous territories. Rising steeply from the Mediterranean, the country reaches heights of about 11,000 feet and then dips into the Arabian desert on the east. On the Mediterranean, climate resembles that of Greece or southern Spain; on the desert it approximates that of more hospitable sections of Arabia; in the mountains, winters are often severe.

With Latakia and Jebel Druze, the reported population, including nomads, now totals 3,700,000 — 2,500,000 in Syria, 800,000 in Lebanon. The ancient Syrians ranked among the important Semitic peoples and kingdoms. Although the old Semitic (Aramean) stock survives, no one knows to what extent Greek, Arab, and Kurd have altered its basic proportion in a land so long the crossroads of the Near East. As far back as Roman times, mixing of racial strains was common. At present Kurds predominate in the northeast mountains; the Arabs, in the desert.

From every point of view, complexity rules in the relations of the peoples. Arameans with Arabian and other intermixtures dominate, and Arabic prevails as the chief language. But the dialects are diverse, not compact. National minorities (seven peoples) assume large proportions — in addition to the 28,000 Europeans (largely French).

Religion. Though the Moslem religion enlists a majority of the people, the antagonistic sects often clash; and one of them, the valiant Druses, has often had to flee from Moslems who insist that they do not truly belong to the faith. Large Christian minorities, about a fourth of the population, are also diverse, including Maronites, Greek Orthodox, Armenians, Melchites, and Protestants, whose relations have not always been cordial.

Inability to consolidate into one homogeneous people makes Syria, in fact, in many respects a kind of miniature India. A large number of upland Syrians subscribe to the program of Pan-Arabism.

Education. Both public and private elementary schools exist, and missionaries (especially Americans) have long been active in education. Thus a majority of children of primary-school age (about 275,000) can attend some kind of school. Many vocational institutes and some French, American, and Arabian colleges continue education beyond the lower levels. With widespread, growing literacy, the vernacular press has risen in importance. But these conditions do not prevail in the mountainous northeast or on desert and steppe, where a low level of education rules almost universally.

The Nation's Economy

Since the cultivated area extends to only about 5,000 square miles, food production cannot be large. Obviously, about 468,000 tons of wheat, 203,000 of barley, and 72,000 of millet are insufficient to feed the population. Minor products include olive oil (about 15,000 tons), cotton (5,000), and cotton-seed (15,000). Wine, grapes, citrus fruits, and silk are also produced in commercial quantities.

Animal economy has never been large: 2,600,000 sheep and 500,000 cattle just about meet local needs. The wool clip comes to 2,500 tons. Camels, once numerous, have decreased since the French popularized the automobile. Minerals are inconsiderable. Industry remains confined to minor enterprises satisfying local consumer needs.

Finance. The Syrian and Lebanon pound now equals 20 French francs (fixed at 2¢ a franc). Peacetime government receipts reached about 12,000,000 pounds — at figures then prevailing, about $6,000,000. But there are two budgets: one for "common purposes" of the four areas, one for local disbursements. Since Syria lives in part upon her past, tourist

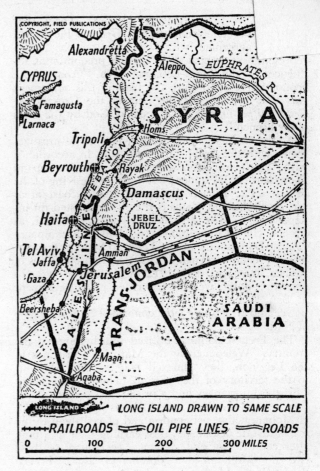

See map on page 315.

traffic normally contributes considerably to the national income.

Foreign Trade. In 1938 imports totaled $40,000,000 in contrast to a mere $16,000,000 of exports. The large transit traffic, however, especially in petroleum, for which Syria acts as a terminus for Iraq, helps through service payments to make up the chronic trade deficit. Principal peacetime exports are silk, wool, textiles, and fruits — chiefly to Palestine, Iraq, and France. Principal peacetime imports — meats, vegetables, cotton goods — for the most part come from France, Britain, and Japan.

The Syrians seem to be born peddlers and traders. They have brought consumers goods to remote areas in 12 South American republics; they prosper in ladies' underwear trades in New York; and there are few large cities in the world that do not house an active, industrious, enterprising Syrian colony that has taken over the heritage of the ancient Phoenicians, who carried trade to the remote corners of the known world. (Incidentally, remittances from these emigrant Syrians have afforded considerable revenue).

History: 1914-1944

Syria and Lebanon were provinces of the old Turkish Empire, which fell apart after its defeat by the Allies in 1918. During the First World War (1916) a French Commissioner, Georges Picot, had made an agreement with Colonel Sykes, the British representative, which gave France predominant influence in the Syria-Lebanon area. Apart from economic considerations, the basis of this agreement was that France was the heir of the Crusades — *Gesta Dei per Francos*, "the deeds of God by the arms of the French."

At the same time, the British had made arrangements with the Arabs during the war, in accordance with which an Arab government was set up in Damascus (1920) under Feisal, son of the King of the Hejaz. The French dominated the seacoast areas but on the inland plateaus the Arabs insisted on independence. The arrival of General Gouraud, as French High Commissioner, resulted in a campaign against Damascus that put Feisal to flight and established French supremacy (1920). The aspirations of France, who had since 1912 unflaggingly sought to penetrate Syria, were underwritten in an agreement at San Remo (1922), which gave her mandatory power and which was later confirmed by the League of Nations.

The French skillfully utilized the divisions of the country. Welcomed by the Maronite Christians in the Lebanon, they annexed only enough Moslems to the territory of the "Grand Lebanon" to assure Christian supremacy and a pro-French policy. Then they rescued the small sect of Alawis who were fearful of Mohammedan persecution and placed them in the seacoast state of Latakia, thus earning their gratitude after centuries of enslavement. In control of these two non-Mohammedan dominated areas, France then split the Moslem states into two, each revolving around the rival commercial cities of Damascus and Aleppo. In this variegated mosaic of sects and subsects, peoples, languages, and types of culture, the French achieved a maximum of complexity and political gerrymandering.

A national constitutional convention of the people met and agreed to a decentralized state, but one that was still basically Arab. General Gouraud issued an ultimatum and crushed all opposition. But he had to keep 60,000 troops in Syria, and disorders were endemic.

However, their Moroccan campaign (1924) compelled the French to reduce their garrison. The now small French force could not cope with Arab riots, Turkish raids into Alexandretta (a border region claimed by Turkey), and, finally, a full-scale rebellion by the Druses in the remote southeast. In 1924 the second French High Commissioner, General Weygand, tried to organize a federation to cope with the unrest, but his policy of Christian supremacy served only to aggravate the situation.

Arab and Druse resentment burst into flame just as General Sarrail, a free-thinker with no pro-Christian bias, became High Commissioner. Sarrail saw that the seemingly adroit French policy was really unworkable. The Syrians, who felt themselves a nationality whatever their religion, resented the confessional basis of representation. Considering it wise to reverse the tactics of the "clerical generals," Gouraud and Weygand, Sarrail sought to impose secular schools on a religious people. This, too,

proved a mistake, and soon he was faced with a true national uprising.

The Era of Repression: 1925–1936. The French had allies, but not enough of them. Maronites, Alawis, over 100,000 Armenian Christian refugees, and most other Christians supported them, but some Christians and all the Moslems and Druses were opposed. The rebellion swept over most of Syria and penetrated Damascus itself. Sarrail bombarded the city and destroyed a part of it, leading to anguished protests throughout the world. He triumphed and followed up his victory with ruthless pacification, pleading in extenuation the brutal murder of some 10,000 Christians by the rebels. The Leftist government then in power in France was unsympathetic to repression: Sarrail was recalled. A League of Nations inquiry openly held the French administration at fault.

The French then sent a civilian, Senator de Jouvenel, to Syria to study the situation. His report, emphasizing the complexity of the Syria-Lebanon area, made the usual proposals for long tutelage in self-government. Ponsot, the next High Commissioner, attempted to work with the Syrian political parties; and in 1928, after civil liberties had been restored, an elected assembly framed a constitution. But when the Assembly insisted that the French had unduly extended Lebanon and stood firm on ultimate independence for Syria, Ponsot dissolved the body. He bided his time, but the French authorities knew that they must soon grant Syria a republican constitution. In the Lebanon their problem was more manageable, as most ministries were pro-French.

In 1931 nominally independent Syria elected a Mohammedan president. But popular struggles against these makeshift devices persisted. The first parliament of Syria proved refractory to cooperation with the French and after a year of disputes, the authorities dissolved it (1933). However, the attempt to govern without parliament proved more difficult than to govern with a hostile one.

The Thorny Path to Independence: 1936–1944. In 1936 the French tried to imitate the successful policy of the British in Iraq by offering Syria a treaty of alliance as an independent nation; but the military alliance was hedged about with restrictions favoring French supremacy (as was the British treaty with Egypt). Every concession led to even sharper controversy, and the Syrians rejected the treaty. The Popular Front government in France, dismayed at this rebuff to its overtures, permitted the older colonial policy to continue, while assuring both Syria and the Lebanon that they would be independent in 1939.

At the outbreak of war in 1939, Syria, in ferment, was occupied by General Weygand with a large and excellently equipped French Army of the Orient, curiously kept out of the European conflict. Since the needs of France were primary, the grant of independence was deferred. The French collapse in 1940, with Weygand back in Europe, caused many French to hope that Syria would remain pro-Allied; but the swift diplomatic recognition of the Pétain régime turned over power to the Vichy nominees.

Britain warned that Germany, whose intrigues had met with some popular support, would not be allowed to occupy Syria directly or by way of Vichy collaboration. Of the French force in Syria, 6,000 officers and men crossed into Palestine to join the United Nations. The situation was further complicated by the Italians, who were conspiring to take over the country, and by the Turks, who, having received the Alexandretta region from France in June 1939, now grew actively interested in the area.

The pro-Axis orientation of General Dentz, the Vichy-appointed High Commissioner, compelled the British and Free French forces to liberate Syria. The Free French guaranteed independence, and the U.S.A. appointed a diplomatic agent who has since been elevated to the rank of Minister.

In 1943, however, Free French Commissioner General Catroux was confronted with Lebanese and Syrian demands for immediate independence. This insistence led to the imprisonment of the Lebanese President and Premier; but world protests, both popular and diplomatic, caused Catroux to grant the two states complete independence as of June 1, 1944. but the mandate question remained unresolved.

Stakes in the Peace

Having distrusted all the European states as intriguers, Syria has an overriding psychological stake in the peace. It will take some time for her to recover confidence in international justice, but once she does, the talents of her remarkable people are bound to raise the country to a much higher economic level.

Since many Lebanese and Syrians possess a European level of technique, the provision of capital for that area should prove remunerative. Modern methods could double the yield of orchards and intensively cultivated vegetable farms. Air transport could make berries and other early spring produce salable in prosperous countries with a cold climate. Syria has many possibilities that have enriched the French Riviera, and ultimately the tourist business could be greatly enhanced.

The initiation of cooperative measures among Syria, Lebanon, Palestine, and Transjordania, for irrigation and power development, correlated with a customs and currency union for the entire area, would enrich these regions and materially improve the living standards of their inhabitants.

Had the French concentrated on this development, instead of committing innumerable administrative errors, they would by now have faced a prosperous and friendly nation. Given effective world organization, and active Syrian participation in it, the time is not too late, even for the hitherto unwelcome French, to draw upon the reservoir of centuries of friendship with the peoples of Syria and Lebanon.

TURKEY

The Land and the People

Long a kind of veiled bride of her past, Turkey in recent years has commanded the attention of the world by a phenomenal transformation of her customs and ways of life and thought, under Ataturk (Kemal Pasha), the father of the new republic and a great force in her social and economic reorganization. This land is the remnant of a great empire that once made all Europe tremble — an empire that reached to Vienna, included the Balkans, Hungary, the Ukraine, and Tripoli, exacted tribute from Tunis and the Arabian chiefs down to Aden, and held sway over Egypt and Mesopotamia. Subject peoples made up that great empire; modern Turkey, which lost 3,000,000 square miles in the last two centuries, reaching very much its present proportions in 1918, is now almost entirely composed of native Turks.

The names of Turkey's principal cities arouse legendary and historical associations. Istanbul, earlier called Byzantium and Constantinople, from 300 A.D. to 1453 the wealthiest and most populous city in the world, had reputedly, in 1204, amassed riches beyond those of all Europe combined. Smyrna, the second city, has been a leading mart of commerce since the 6th century B.C.; and Ankara, on the plateau of Asia Minor, now commands interest as the new capital and third city of the republic. Most of present-day Turkey is the region long known as Asia Minor. Because of her strategic location and her recent remarkable cultural and economic transformation, Turkey has real international importance.

The Land. Turkey-in-Europe is bordered by Bulgaria and Greece on the west. Turkey-in-Asia faces the Black Sea (north), Soviet Russia (northeast), Iran (east), and Iraq (Mesopotamia), French mandated Syria, and the Mediterranean (south). Only 4.5% of Turkey lies in Europe (13,012 square miles): 286,324 square miles are Asiatic. Between the two sections flow the Bosporus, the Sea of Marmora, and the Dardanelles, connecting the Black Sea with the Mediterranean.

The core of Turkey, a high plateau, slowly subsides into foothills (except in the east) that end in valleys facing the sea or, southeastward, in the plain leading to Arabia. The coast, with rare exceptions, is bush country for about 75 miles inward. Cultivated land lies mainly in the west. Most of the wealth and population centers in this area (including Istanbul) and from Smyrna to the territory facing Rhodes. In Istanbul and on the "Pontic coast," although winters are not exceptionally severe, climate is affected by cold winds blowing from Russia across the Black Sea; on the plateau winters are bitter, summers dry and hot. Mediterranean climate prevails in the fertile southwest. Mountain ranges in the northeast culminate in the mass surrounding Mt. Ararat, about 17,000 feet high — in the Book of Genesis, the resting place of Noah's ark.

There are 550 Turks to every arable square mile whose total is about a tenth of the land (32,000 square miles). Nevertheless four-fifths of the people live by agriculture and stock-raising. In mineral resources Turkey is extremely rich though these were scarcely touched under the Sultanate. The striking manner in which they were developed under the rule of Ataturk is presented under our discussion of industry and mining.

The People. The 1940 census showed a population of 17,869,000, equivalent to New York's and New Jersey's combined. These people called Turks are not a "race"; certainly the major part of the population does not come from the steppes and highlands of central Asia from which the language spread. The term "Turkish" is a linguistic, not an exact ethnological word, though some ethnologists consider the Turks examples of an Armenoid people related to the Armenians whom they have so relentlessly persecuted. Most of the people seem to be of old Lydian stock settled here before the Greeks, but the Moslem cultural pattern, thoroughly imposed upon them, made zealous adherents of them for a very long period. The speed of their recent acceptance of European ways indicates how cultural change may occur without marked population change.

The older peoples of Asia Minor showed brilliant statecraft in their kingdoms, and the Lydian and Pontic monarchies (the legendary Amazons too, if they may be included) displayed warlike qualities. But a "Turkish" admixture must have been present; and the long history of the Turkish Empire, which absorbed Greeks, Albanians, Persians, and Slavs, and brought myriads of unfortunate, handsome Caucasian women to its harems, greatly affected the character of the people. Turks of today, a people of average height, muscular, fair-skinned, are no more uniform in physical characteristics than is their architecture, a mass of eclectic borrowings.

Religion and Education. Since the transfer of populations to Greece, the once numerous Christians do not bulk large and the population is about 98% Moslem. Nevertheless American missionary colleges like the famous Robert College, outside Istanbul, remain a noteworthy experiment in educational internationalism.

The new governmental order, despite the dangers involved, has been violently opposed to old Moslem ways. It separated Church and State, substituted Turkish for Arabic in the ritual, prohibited the fez, prescribed European dress, took education away from the priests, discouraged women's use of the traditional veil, prohibited polygamy, and interdicted clerical garments as street wear. The Turkish language was transposed into Latin characters. Christians were placed under civil law rather than their church authorities.

Almost nonexistent under the Sultanate, education for the masses has been made compulsory. Though 55% of adults were still illiterate in 1935 (as compared with fully 90% under the last Sultan), today almost everyone under thirty can read and write. Proficiency in Latin characters, confined to 20% of the people in 1935, now stands considerably higher. About a million children attend primary schools. There are 95 secondary schools, 26 *lycées*, 23 higher and professional schools. Turkey has clearly turned her back on her old past, to march with the modern world.

The Nation's Economy

Agriculture. In a land where 80% of the people live by agriculture and stock-raising, Turkey's recent gains in these categories seem the more phenomenal. Land banks have given large aid. Peasant methods have been extensively modernized. Agricultural planning has been directed by the government, the various yields being provided for carefully. A rise of 300% in cotton production, for example, was planned and carried out; but when war came and cash crops were partly abandoned for food crops, cotton declined.

Wheat and barley bulk largest among the crops, wheat having reached about 3,000,000 tons in 1942 and an estimated 4,400,000 in 1943. Barley, normally about 2,500,000 tons, yielded 1,560,000 in 1942 (a poor year). But these impressive figures (a wheat yield as large as France's and 5% of the world's barley) cannot tell the whole story. The average wheat and barley crops, as of 1939, have more than doubled the figures of 1925–29. No other large country in the world has more than doubled its basic plant food in ten years. Corn, though still a small crop, gained almost 90% in the same period. Rice production doubled. Potatoes went up fivefold, beet-sugar threefold. Tobacco, less phenomenal, still gained about 35%. Wine increased. Olive oil advanced 50%.

In animal economy the figures are equally startling. The wool clip rose in ten years from 12,000 to 37,000 tons. Cattle now number 7,600,000, Angora goats (for mohair) 3,700,000, other goats 8,000,000, sheep 17,200,000, buffaloes 700,000, mules, 1,300,000. Since 1924 Angora goats have increased by 150%. Since 1926 sheep have gained by 31%, cattle 50%, buffaloes 40%. Turkey today stands out as a really rich pastoral and agricultural land. The rest of the world must continue to watch with great interest her amazing progress.

Industry and Mining. A planned industrialization program, carefully determined upon and then financed without foreign capital, has made considerable strides. Though not socialized, this program of a planned industrial economy closely followed the Soviet model in other respects. Mining was first increased. Coal was raised from about 1,700,000 tons to 2,700,000. Copper rose phenomenally, from

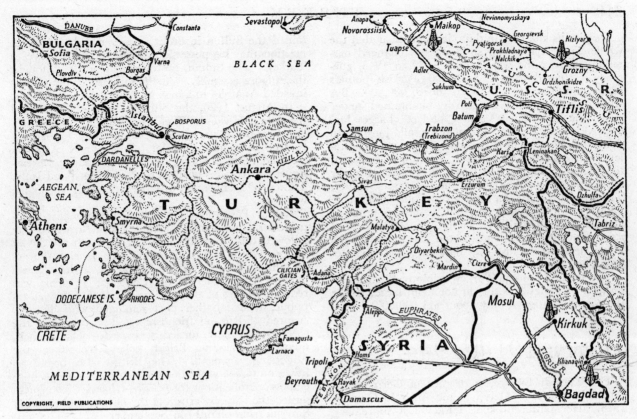

See map on page 315.

600 to well over 11,000 tons. The abundant abrasive, emery, increased from 7,400 to 11,900 tons. Chrome was stepped up until it provided 20% of the world's supply. Meerschaum, mainly a Turkish product, was doubled, manganese trebled.

All this success in minerals led to modernization of mechanical industry. After 1934, once mining had been pushed to necessary levels, capital was directed into machinery. A five-year industrial plan concentrated not only on furthering mining but on producing textiles, paper, and glass. Some $8,000,000 were voted for electrification. In 1936, however, though 256,000 were employed in industry, concentration had not developed and shops averaged only 4 employees each. But the new plan has certainly resulted in greatly increased production of cotton yarns (30,000 tons), woolen yarns (9,300), paper (10,500), glass (8,200), and cement (about 200,000). New steel mills, flour mills, soap factories, sugar refineries, chemical plants, canning plants, tanneries, and power installations have arisen in favorable localities. Though total figures remain unavailable at present, there can be no doubt that Turkish industry has been significantly transformed.

Commerce and Finance. The war has, of course, hurt foreign trade: 1940 was the last reported year, showing heavy exports to the British Empire. The steady decrease of trained exporters, largely because of discriminatory taxation (they were predominantly Armenians, Greeks, and Jews), has injured trade; and, since the Sultanate had so long discouraged the pursuit of commerce by native Turks as beneath the dignity of the Osmanli, the new régime has been compelled to train a young generation of modern merchants.

Principal exports include tobacco, mohair, wool, carpets, hazelnuts, cotton, and raisins; main imports, cotton goods, iron and steel products, machinery, tea and coffee. Minor specialties are also exported — meerschaum, canary seed, opium (to Holland, for pharmacals), and silk. Three-fourths of Turkish imports enter through Istanbul, but only half that proportion of exports leave from the same port since production centers are nearer Smyrna.

Before the war imports averaged about $5.65 and exports $6.80 per capita, yielding a good trade surplus. Germany loomed as the principal source of imports (45%), Britain and the U.S.A. supplying less than 10% each. Germany was also the leading customer (52%), the U.S.A. taking but 11% and Britain 5%. Trade ties with Germany have been very strong indeed, even before the Nazis imposed their barter pressures. Such facts as these, as well as diplomatic commitments and internal considerations, must be taken into account in studying the history of Turkey's recent, precariously maintained neutrality.

Under the Sultanate, taxation laid a heavy toll on the people, earning for Turkey a distinction of being the classic example of rapacious government. The new régime has also been forced to tax heavily, though it uses the proceeds mainly for constructive purposes rather than, like the Sultans, for sheer luxury and corruption. Expenditures of about $40,000,000 burden the poorer peasantry, though in American terms the amount may not seem large. These ordinary expenditures nearly trebled during Turkey's neutrality in World War II, and the tax-gatherers collect 8% of the gross value of a peasant's crops. Domestic public debt stood at about $29,000,000 in 1939; the foreign debt at about $17,000,000.

Despite lack of certain data, it seems clear that the whole Turkish financial situation has changed materially during the war. From 1939 to 1943, currency increased from 281,000,000 Turkish pounds (their pound equaling $.0725) to 757,000,000. But with a million men necessarily maintained under arms, the government's secret budget charges had created a large deficit. When price inflation rose to dangerous proportions, the state imposed a capital levy as a combative measure. Foreigners protested this action, charging that it was a disguised transfer of their property to the Turks who were let off lightly. They raised the cry of a return to the old inhospitable habits of the Sultanate, which had made alien property insecure and precarious. Thousands of them faced ruin. But the government insisted that they were the most burdened because they had the largest share of liquid assets.

The leading bank in Turkey is jointly English and French. Savings deposits do not loom large; before the war they stood at only about $11,000,000.

History: 1914-1944

The Turkish Empire, a partner of Germany in World War I, surrendered to the Allies in October 1918. Her power broken, Turkey lost supremacy over the Arabian peoples; she no longer controlled Syria, Palestine, Mesopotamia, and the holy cities of Mecca and Medina. For some time the actual status of the nation was ill-defined; her boundaries were unclear, her powers dubious. With the rise of Greek imperialism, the fall of Czarism in bordering Russia, and a hopeless confusion as to the future of the Sultanate and the far more important Caliphate in Constantinople (religious center of the Moslem world), it appeared that chaos might long prevail.

Mustapha Kemal Pasha and the Resurrection of Turkey: 1919–1923. Aware that their land was doomed to partition and subjugation, the progressive elements and young army officers began to organize the apparently hopeless country. The defeated Sultan, whose one desire was to preserve his life and wealth, bowed to repeated foreign humiliations. To subdue the activities of nationalists he named as military inspector general Mustapha Kemal Pasha, who immediately went over to the nationalist groups himself. In June 1919, under the leadership of Kemal Pasha, the nationalists issued a proclamation denouncing both the Sultan and the victorious Allies. A national congress assembled in Asia Minor in July 1919, Kemal Pasha presiding. The Sultan, realizing that temporizing would not avail against these determined men, permitted the formation in 1920 of a national parliament dominated by the nationalists.

The new parliament insisted that all areas predominantly Turkish in composition should belong to Turkey. The Allies proceeded to arrest the parliamentary leaders, but many escaped to Angora (later called Ankara) in Anatolia. There a national assembly met, announcing itself the sole authority for Turkey. While continuing to treat the Sultan as the nominal monarch, it divested him of power by declaring him a prisoner. The assembly formally retained the Sultan in order to preserve the excellent position that his possession of the Caliphate gave to Turkey. The Sultan, however, still pro-Ally, fought the Angora assembly. At the same time, the Greeks invaded Anatolia to annex all of western Asia Minor.

In August 1920, the Sultan's representatives and the Allies signed the Treaty of Sèvres. Turkey lost her European areas and retained only ambiguous control of Constantinople. Greece and Armenia received large portions, and the remainder was assigned as "spheres of influence" to France and Italy. Turkey had effectively disappeared; only the name was left.

Kemal Pasha now launched a nationalist campaign which ended in the conquest of Armenia. He followed this by concluding a treaty with the Soviet Union, whose international status was also that of an outlaw nation. By the fall of 1921, when Russia had become master of the Caucasus, Armenia was redefined; part of the territory became a Soviet republic, while another part remained with Turkey. Assured of Russian friendship and successful in the east, Kemal now turned westward. The French, quickly abandoning British policy, recognized the Angora government. The British also began to frown on Greek aspirations, which seemed to promise endless complications (See *Greece, History*). The Turks settled the issue by crushing the Greeks and entering Smyrna triumphantly in September 1922. The city was promptly burned, but the Moslem quarter, by the purest of accidents, remained unharmed.

The Turks abolished the Sultanate and Mohammed VI fled to a British warship, thus ending a dynasty of seven centuries. Holding on to their religious power at all costs, the Turks conferred the Caliphate on another prince, Abdul-Mejid; however, once the country was reorganized, older religious sentiments quickly dimmed. In October 1922 the Allies came to an understanding with Kemal Pasha, and by the Treaty of Lausanne (July 1923) Turkey entered the family of nations as a new commonwealth.

The Administration of Ataturk: 1923–1938. Every aspect of the old state was dead, from its "capitulations" or special foreigners' rights to its rooted domestic ideas. Turkey became a republic with Kemal as President and his close friend General Ismet Inonu as Prime Minister. In March 1924 Kemal dared to do something that shook Islam to its foundations: he abolished the Caliphate (which had the relative rank of the Papacy in Christendom). The government declared that education was to be secular. Nationality replaced religion as the country's guiding star. To overcome the anticipated opposition of the pious country people, the astute Kemal freed them from religious tithes which had impoverished them for centuries; no one wanted to revolt for the privilege of paying tithes to the priesthood.

In 1924, irked by opposition, Kemal proclaimed a dictatorship, although nominally observing republican forms with punctilio. He suppressed the ever-rebellious Kurds and the ever-critical opposition. Using every pretext to introduce his reforms, he abolished monasteries because they "abetted rebellion." Women were unveiled and polygamy prohibited. Kemal, under League of Nations auspices, shifted the

Greek and Turkish populations into their respective
countries, thus ending, despite temporary hardships,
the national minorities problem that had frequently
burst into conflict.

In 1926 Ataturk (or The Turk, as Kemal was now
called) cruelly punished all opponents. While curbing opinion more firmly than any other despot, he
modernized Turkey; he assailed popular superstitions,
Arabic script, and Islam as the official religion, and
he prohibited the use of old titles of honor like Pasha
and Bey. He sought to industrialize Turkey in a
single generation.

Ataturk relied on Soviet Russia for technical and
moral aid, disregarding the world's opinion of Russia
and of himself. Wringing continuous concessions
from the Allies, he obtained the fortification of the
Dardanelles once more; the 1936 Convention of
Montreux, which restored this privilege, was his
culminating triumph. He had obtained loans from
Britain (to whom he swore fealty), from Germany
(to whom he pledged friendship), and from France
(to whom he was positively brotherly despite a family
quarrel over the Sanjak of Alexandretta in Syria
which he claimed). This astonishing individual died
on November 10, 1938. He was succeeded by Ismet
Inonu, his friend and one-time Premier.

Turkey in World War II. When war broke out
in 1939 Turkey almost immediately displayed a pro-
British attitude. She soon made a pact with Britain
by which she received subsidies and armaments.
Turkey also made trade pacts in the fall of 1940.
Nevertheless, she was at no time unequivocally in
the United Nations' orbit. Germany sent von
Papen to "condition" Turkey; trade arrangements
with Germany, centering on chrome, encouraged
Turkey's calculated neutrality.

When Germany overran the Balkans (1941) and
reached the Caucasus (October 1942), Turkey's
inaction was excused on the ground that her neutrality, as a persistent threat to Germany, would be more
useful than her belligerency. However, as German
influence waned in 1943, the inspired press of Turkey
abandoned the ambiguous style with which it had
alternately annoyed, wheedled, and baffled both
camps: it now veered toward the United Nations.
In May 1944, following Churchill's severe strictures
against aid to Germany, the Turkish régime changed
its policy of receiving the maximum aid while granting the minimum of facilities or assurances. Turkey
stopped Germany's large chrome supplies, and then
ended diplomatic relations with her.

Stakes in the Peace

Turkey has come a long way in achieving industrial and mining autonomy with a minimum of
foreign investment. The limits of this type of economic development have not yet been ascertained.
Profitability is not a limiting factor, any more than
in the Soviet Union, if the specific deficits of any one
state-sponsored enterprise can be met by revenues
diverted from another source. However, Turkey's
diminishing yield of taxation and her really wretched
showing in savings, indicate that, unlike the Soviet
system, one cannot attempt to socialize the national
economy without certain basic changes in property
relations. Hence Turkey must soon choose either a
more usual type of capitalist activity, so that her individual capitalists may accumulate profits, or accept
outright socialization.

Turkey is in an economic dilemma. Kemal
Pasha stimulated her economy, when capital was
scarce, by non-profitable (state) enterprises with an
attendant low level of consumption. Today, she
can continue in his path, or she can seek sufficient
capital for profitable enterprises with a higher level
of consumption. Will she choose the former "economic statism" or capitalism?

It is this dilemma that largely explains Turkey's
bizarre and unheroic history during World War II:
she requires subsidies and yet is afraid of expenditures,
since she has already reduced consumption to pay for
industrialization; and she has few resources left to
tap for war.

Politically, Turkey must always seek the favor and
friendship of the Soviet Union. She may be friendly
to whom she wills, but she cannot afford to be inimical to Russia. Strained relations between the
two nations would not necessarily lead to armed
conflict, but it would make foreign capital timid and
cause a recession in internal economy. As yet,
Turkey does not act like a state that once possessed
a well-established merchant tradition: she still lacks
the feeling for international trade and international
relationships that characterizes more advanced economies.

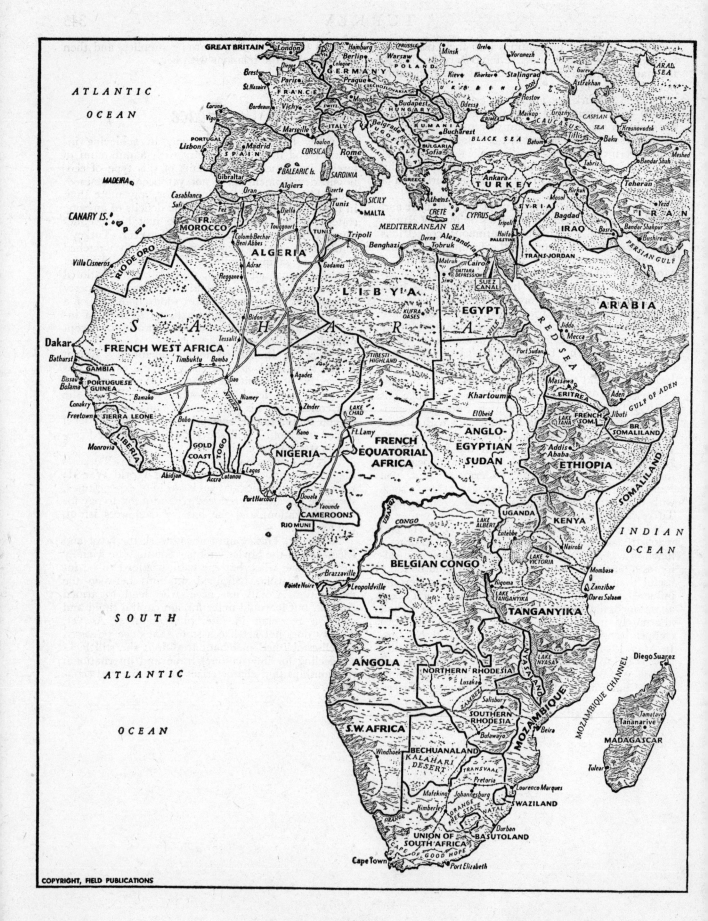

Africa

THE BELGIAN CONGO

The Land and the People

This immense equatorial country emerged during World War II as a veritable treasury of strategic materials urgently needed by the Allied nations. Until the late 19th century, it had been for ages "Darkest Africa." As the famous Congo Free State, inaugurated in the days of vivid interest in the country after Stanley's dramatic rescue of Livingstone, the area was entrusted in 1889 to the control of King Leopold II of Belgium, as his personal domain. His brutal administration of the area horrified the world. In 1908 it became a Belgian colony, and since that time the Belgian government has striven to obtain first rank among imperial nations in the benefits extended to a native population. The Congo became a colony in 1908 and has since been directly administered by the Belgian Ministry of Colonies.

The Land. The 902,082 square miles (about 30% of the U.S.A.) compose the very heart of the equatorial rainforest area of Africa. One of the great river regions of the world, the country is watered by the broad Congo, which is navigable for 8,000 miles. Westward lies French Equatorial Africa; eastward the Sudan, Uganda, and Tanganyika; southward Northern Rhodesia and Portuguese Angola. In the west the land extends toward a very short coast line on the South Atlantic.

The abundant rainfall varies little throughout the year; and humid, hot weather is the rule, though temperatures do not rival the highest summer figures of New York City. Living in the Congo region has been so great a problem for Europeans largely because of the consistently hot and humid weather. But in new cities like Leopoldville and Stanleyville surprising relief has been attained by intelligent building, living habits, and proper diet.

Communications are gaining in this land, with over 8,000 miles of navigable river, at least 20 good river ports, 50,000 miles of usable highway (where once only head-porterage by natives was possible), 350 miles of railways, and a new network of airways.

The Bantu Negroes dominate the Congo population of 10,363,000. Hamitic and Semitic intermixtures, elsewhere common, hardly exist here, and the southern Bushman or Hottentot does not modify the basic stock. Except in settled areas, especially the mining districts, tribal organization retains its age-old grip upon the people. The Belgian Congo is, in short, the closest approximation in actuality to the conventionalized, popular Africa of the cinema and the best-seller.

Most of the Negroes are forest dwellers, living on shifting cultivation and often in shifting settlements. The tsetse fly, carrier of sleeping sickness, which attacks livestock as well as people, sometimes forces the people to turn from region to region in search of food. Much of the native population moves up and down the long reaches of the Congo river, whose great estimated water-power reserves may some day transform the primitive forest into a region of great wealth.

The European population numbers only 33,000, of whom two-thirds are Belgians.

Religion and Education. Missionaries have converted only a small part of the population from the native religions, which are roughly classified as "fetishisms," and still practiced as for centuries in the past. The few Europeans are mainly Catholics.

Both government and religious missions are active in education. The 5,200 schools have enrolled 265,000 — an eighth of the school-age population — a remarkable proportion if we recall that a generation ago hardly any received education. But schooling is contingent on the health and survival of the children; and the unremitting struggle against disease, conducted through hygienic and laboratory stations, has still a long way to go. Medical science has reduced the tsetse fly plague but tuberculosis remains a severe threat, particularly in the mining areas. Transportation and general advancement have, however, reduced famine.

The Economy

Mining. The native agriculture is changing from mere scratch to a plantation basis; but minerals are the real wealth of the Congo. Production figures can do no more than suggest the great resources of the mines and mineral treasuries of a land in which exploitation has been so recent. The Belgian Congo furnishes abundant uranium (the source of radium); some 168,000 tons of copper ore (about 8% of world output); 15,000 of tin ore; 6,000 of zinc and an equal amount of lead; 2,000 of manganese; 1,800 of cobalt. In addition, there are many lesser-produced minerals (including coal), gold (37,000 pounds) and diamonds (5,500,000 carats).

Agriculture. Agricultural production, impressively increasing, shows figures like the following: rice 66,000 tons; coffee 25,000; cotton-seed 100,000; cotton 45,000 but gaining fast. The forests produce 17,000 tons of copal (used for lacquers) and one-eighth of the world's palm oil and of its palm kernels. Products raised largely for export are coffee, sugar, cotton-seed, groundnuts, palm oil and kernels, cotton, rubber, bananas, corn, cocoa, rice, and tobacco.

Finance. The astonishing agricultural and industrial advances of the Belgian Congo required large capital. A figure of $715,000,000, mainly from Belgium, invested before 1935, has probably risen now to exceed a billion dollars. Even the first sum would mean an average stake of $450 in the Congo for every Belgian family (assuming five people to a family). This suggests something of the crucial importance of the territory for a small nation like Belgium and the reasons behind the fact that Belgian colonial universities and institutes rank among the finest in the world. Publications on the Congo by Belgian experts are distinguished in every field from ethnology to engineering.

In 1938 only about 410,000,000 francs (approximately $13,000,000) were in circulation. Later figures are unavailable. Foreign exchange reserves built up by the surplus of exports, without remittances to Belgium as a counterpart, must have mounted greatly in recent years. Budget figures formerly stood at about 1,100,000,000 francs ($36,000,000), and the debt at 5,800,000,000 francs ($193,000,000). But if the franc is stabilized at 44 to the dollar, as has recently been assumed, the debt and budget figures would appear smaller. There seems every reason to believe that Belgium, with her gold and exchange reserves, will retain a high parity for the Congo franc.

Foreign Trade. Peacetime trade showed a high preponderance of exports ($88,000,000) over imports ($33,000,000). During the war the figures have been even larger: exports, $108,000,000; imports, $50,000,-000. In 1941 the gold miners transferred to tin, and exports in general took on a more wartime character.

Normally 75% of exports go to Belgium, the remainder to Germany and Italy, and to Mozambique and Angola for trans-shipment. Ivory, once so noteworthy, is no longer important. Imports of machinery, textiles, metals, metal wares, automobiles and trucks, and coal came mainly from Belgium (38%), Britain (14%), Japan (13%), and the U.S.A. (8%).

History: 1914-1944

During World War I, the Belgian Congo was a military center for Allied action against the German colonies in Africa. Belgium assisted the French in conquering the Cameroons, aided the British in the defense of the Rhodesias, and at last, avenging German violation of her neutrality, invaded and conquered a considerable part of the colony of German East Africa. In 1919, at the conclusion of the war, Belgium received a mandate over Ruanda-Urundi, a rich cattle country east of the Congo.

The development of copper in the Katanga area was so promising that the authorities made it into a separate province (1926) under its own governor; and it became general policy to give considerable autonomy to any governor in areas that required special attention. Thus a policy of decentralization began, though on a modest scale. In September 1927, Belgium concluded a treaty with Portugal by which she gave up a large territory in the Congo in exchange for a right of way to the sea across the Portuguese colony of Angola.

The officials in the Belgian Congo found that their policy of compelling Negroes to cultivate their soil or else aid in plantations, mines, or industrial enterprises adversely affected the social basis of Negro life. Hence in the 1930's they reversed this policy and sought to reconstitute the scattered elements of the Negro tribes, so that the Negroes might recover their natural setting.

Despite the fact that the Congo native had better medical care, more numerous and higher grade schools, and was better nourished than the native in the British and French possessions, he enjoyed neither the benefits of British "indirect rule" nor the French grant of steps toward citizenship. Late in the 1930's, the Belgians allowed the natives to have consultative assemblies, but these were of smaller scope than those in British-controlled areas.

On June 18, 1940, after the Germans had overrun Belgium, Dr. Vleeschauwer, Minister of Colonies in the Belgian cabinet, assumed direct power over the four Congo provinces. He enlisted 30,000 Congo troops in the conquest of Ethiopia from the Italians and (an innovation) allowed the natives to take white Italian generals as their prisoners.

Meanwhile, the influence of neighboring French Equatorial Africa increasingly oriented the Belgian government-in-exile toward granting wider native rights. In 1940 Protestant missionaries protested vigorously against the educational policy of colonial officials. Despite government denials of discrimination, the dispute remains unresolved.

In May 1943 the Belgian authorities sent Congo troops to the Near East to aid the United Nations. At the same time, there were extensive transfers of native labor to new tin-mining areas, to enable the Allies better to cope with the shortage of tin, which had resulted from the loss of Malaya to Japan.

Stakes in the Peace

The Belgian Congo has advanced so rapidly under Belgian tutelage that it is in the extension or rather intensification of Belgian policies that her future is to be sought. The first problem is the extension of sanitation and public hygiene, which alone can add enormously to the colony's human and physical resources. The second is the increased education of the natives in agriculture, so as to end the curse of "shifting cultivation," which many authorities consider the prime cause of their poverty. The third is the intensification of the campaign to exterminate the tsetse fly, not only to end the human lethargy caused by its poison, but to make pastoral lands more steadily productive. In the adjacent Belgian mandate of Ruanda-Urundi, where the beasts are free of the tsetse fly, there is abundant food for the population.

The fourth need is the continued development of local consumers goods industries, such as cotton prints, which would make these cheap products available to the rising demands of the natives. It might be wiser for Belgian cotton-spinning capital to concentrate less on selling from Ghent and to invest part of its surplus in the Congo.

The fifth requirement lies in adequate use of potential water-power resources, partly to supply air-conditioned homes and offices which would encourage Europeans to live in comfort in the Belgian Congo and thus place their technical knowledge at the disposal of the awakening natives.

Finally, the British system of "dual government" could be spread over a wider area. Given more sedentary settlements, the natives would have permanent rather than transient interests in any given area and might show surprising aptitudes for self-government.

These are all vital problems of the colony itself. They do not bear on the question of the extent to which an international administration of colonies might prove of auxiliary value to national administration of the Congo, that is, if a future international organization is charged with such tasks.

BRITISH EAST AFRICA

The immense domain of British East Africa — which includes Kenya, Uganda, Tanganyika, and Zanzibar — is not an administrative unit. It is, however, a customs and currency union under British control, the East African shilling being the unit of exchange (roughly 25¢). The four main regions are discussed individually:

KENYA

This colony is about as large as the American Middle Atlantic states — 224,690 square miles. An area abounding in big game, Kenya lies south of Ethiopia, west of Somaliland, faces the Indian Ocean, and is bounded by Uganda (south) and Tanganyika (west).

Natives number 97% of the 3,534,000 people. Largely Hamites, Nilotes, and a mixture of Negro peoples, Kenya's native population is the most diverse in Africa. The Europeans in the colony number only 24,000; the East Asiatics, 44,000; and the Arabs, 15,000.

Kenya is largely a steppe, with a plateau (mostly of lava) from 5,000 to 8,000 feet high, and mountain peaks rising to 17,000 feet. Though the Equator passes through the center of the region, and the climate is tropical in the lowlands and near Lake Victoria, many highlands enjoy pleasant weather. But heat and malaria, often present even in the highlands, have made Europeans concentrate only on the most favored locations — such as Nairobi, the capital, which has a fair English population.

Economy. Though Kenya is well suited for an animal economy, cattle-raising is still small, and Kenya is known chiefly for her coffee and her pyrethrum (a base of insect powders). Her other exports include gold, tea, and sisal. (See *Uganda, Finance.*)

History: 1914–1944. Long designated by the British government as a promising region for white settlement, the East African protectorate witnessed a change in internal composition during World War I. With the departure of large numbers of white residents for the battlefronts, the Indians and other Asiatic inhabitants grew increasingly prominent and influential in commerce, and came to outnumber the whites by a wide margin. Hence, when a new constitution, adopted in 1919, deliberately gave the Europeans (whites) local governmental supremacy over the Asiatics, the relations between the two population groups became hostile.

In the meantime, many British war veterans had emigrated to the East African protectorate and founded prosperous farms in the highlands. European settlement was vigorously encouraged, but Asiatics continued to pour into the protectorate in even larger numbers. The Indians grew bitterly resentful of their subordinate position under the 1919 constitution; and their protests were sustained by the Government of India, which insisted upon equal rights for its subjects. The European residents rallied under Lord Delamere, who talked truculently of rebelling against the local government if the demands of the Indian residents were sustained.

In 1920 the entire region, except for a coastal strip, was transformed into a British Crown colony. Its name was changed to Kenya and its former currency, the Indian *rupee*, was supplanted by the East African shilling. An important change occurred with respect to labor: natives were no longer compelled to work for white employers.

With the sharpening of the hostility between the Europeans and the Asiatics, the British government issued a White Paper (1923). This document declared that although the interests of the native population were of first consideration, nevertheless white immigrants were to be given preference over Asiatic immigrants. Disturbed by the implications of European supremacy in the White Paper, both the Asiatic and native populations grew increasingly bitter. For their part, Europeans also resented the White Paper, for it declared that native interests were more important than prospective European settlement. Despite these discords, Kenya progressed economically, particularly after the government adopted a new policy regarding native reserves (1924). Not only were the natives assured of the right to inhabit the areas designated for their residence, but these reserves were declared to be inviolate, irrespective of the demands of European inhabitants or of future mineral discoveries on the reserves.

Fearful that the natives might receive even greater consideration, the Europeans rallied against the administration's proposal to grant representation in the government to the natives ("West Africanization"). Nevertheless, there were now clear indications that the natives would be given increasingly liberal treatment, for the governorship of Kenya was in the hands of Sir Robert Coryndon, whose administrative record in Uganda was known for its extension of rights to the native population. In 1926 Lord Delamere opened his campaign for an elected majority of Europeans in the Colonial Council. His followers clamored for supremacy on the ground that only the whites had had the vision to invest in and develop the colony, whereas the Asiatics had risked their capital only after European enterprise had blazed the way.

In the meantime, the prohibition of compulsory native labor (1920) had resulted in a labor shortage for the white employers. Natives were being encouraged to build up their own economy on their reserves; only those natives not so engaged were now available to the whites for their farms and plantations. Sir Edward Grigg, who succeeded Governor Coryndon (upon the latter's death in 1925), suggested that the Europeans focus their efforts on pastoral enterprises, since these require the least amount of labor for the value produced. The Europeans now began to agitate for a federation of all the territories of British East Africa, believing that such an arrangement would give them the enlarged economic scope they required. But the resistance of Uganda to this proposal, and the manifest impossibility of converting the League of Nations mandate, Tanganyika, into a permanent part of a

British imperial federation, rendered this scheme impossible.

In 1927 the European residents of Kenya were declared to be joint trustees, with the British imperial government, of the native population. Finally in 1934, a new constitution gave the Europeans complete governmental supremacy, both as to elected and nominated members of the lower house, over all other elements in the population combined. (The upper legislative chamber was composed exclusively of British officers.)

Gold was discovered at Kavirondo, on the native reserves, and contrary to the governmental provisions of 1924, these mineral areas were transferred to Europeans. A Native Lands Trust bill was passed in 1938 in order to make secure the rights of the natives to their reserves. Furthermore, the pressures exerted by the native population blocked the enactment of the demand most cherished by the European groups: that all of the desirable highland territory be reserved for their exclusive use.

UGANDA

This land of 93,981 square miles (about as large as New York and Pennsylvania combined) was penetrated by the British in 1894, and made a British protectorate in 1924. It is prevailingly a high steppe country, with a climate resembling that of the mild Ethiopian plateaus; but there are also hot and humid lowlands that abound in jungle vegetation. The great Lake Victoria, really an inland sea, forms part of the southern boundary.

Uganda is a land of Pygmies, Bantu Negroes, and an aristocracy of tall Hamitic Negroes who are a fourth white. With 3,800,000 inhabitants, Uganda is three times as densely populated as Kenya.

The native Bantu Negroes organized the most advanced culture of any Negro people in history, without recourse to foreign aid. (Roscoe's fascinating study of the Bagandas is famous.) Even today the native kings and their ancient institutions are carefully respected.

Uganda has made strides in education: about half of the children of school age receive instruction, and the educational system has begun to spread a knowledge of English. Both Moslem and Christian have made deep indentations into the tribal faiths, many of which center in elaborate animal totem clans.

Economy. Uganda's economy differs from that of Kenya, particularly in organization: Kenya follows the private-property system, Uganda practices communal landholding and production. But there are other differences as well. Uganda has a rich cattle economy, whereas Kenya's is still undeveloped. Furthermore, Uganda has emphasized cotton crops to such a degree that today cotton forms 75% of her exports. Coffee is less important than in Kenya: it amounts to 10% of Uganda's exports.

Finance. In figures for investment, trade, and budget, Kenya and Uganda are usually presented as a unit. Their combined exports are $24,000,000, imports $40,000,000. British investments in both regions are large, some $230,000,000. Their combined budget ($10,000,000) is also large, in relation to the level of culture, as well as their debt ($14,000,-

000). Although we cannot break down these figures with respect to each region, there can be no question that the territorially smaller Uganda, with her heavily loaded railways, is a far more productive possession than the Kenya colony.

History: 1914–1944. During World War I, Uganda demonstrated her loyalty to the mother country by supplying 10,000 troops for action against German East Africa and by placing 160,000 men at the disposal of the British for auxiliary work in the campaign. At the end of the war, a severe famine struck Uganda (1919) and from the following year until 1927 the protectorate suffered from the serious decline in prices commanded by colonial products. This succession of misfortunes was finally mastered by the British governor, Sir Robert Coryndon, with the aid of an eminent native statesman, Sir Apolo Kagwa, Prime Minister of the largest of the native states, Buganda. The Coryndon government carefully planned the agricultural economy and constructed roads from regions possessing food surpluses to those suffering from chronic shortages. Excellent railways arose, culminating in a direct route to the coast of Mombasa (1928). The government formed a native council, gave local jurisdiction to tribal councils, and constantly extended the administrative scope of the native princes.

Uganda had become the most progressive area of British East Africa in terms of economic and educational development. Eager to preserve her autonomy, she declined the proposal of the council of governors (1926) for an East African federation, and two years later rejected the recommendations of the Hilton Young Commission, which envisaged a greater East Africa. Uganda preferred to devote her energies to developments within her borders.

The formation of a parliament, in which native chiefs participated with British officials, resulted in truly effective control of internal affairs. Legislation proved competent and the British Colonial Office rarely found it necessary to veto the acts of this parliament. With the spread of education, the literate natives came to demand a House of Commons to represent them in the same way that the native chiefs were represented in the parliament. Although these political demands have not yet been fulfilled, the administration has responded to other requirements of the population, prominent among which are the trade schools and the university. In general, the British have taken emphatic steps toward modernizing both the economic and cultural life of Uganda.

TANGANYIKA

Formerly German East Africa, Tanganyika has been a British mandate since 1919. The area is large, 374,000 square miles, roughly an eighth of the U.S.A., and much greater than Kenya and Uganda combined. The 5,291,000 inhabitants are almost all Bantu Negroes, with some 38,000 Asiatics, and 6,000 Europeans (of whom 40% are German).

Tanganyika is the land of wild fauna, lion, leopard, rhinoceros, and of milder beings like zebras and chimpanzees. The highest mountain in Africa, Kilimanjaro (19,320 feet), rises in the north of the region. The coast is hot and humid, and in the whole of the mandate there are only two small areas climatically fit for European settlement.

Compared to Uganda, Tanganyika neglects education. Tribal Negro faiths are practically universal, though Moslem influence is considerable along the coast.

Economy. Tanganyika is a great cattle country, with over 5,600,000 head, and with millions of sheep and goats. Were it not for the tsetse fly plague, she would export far more hides and skins. Her exports of about $28,000,000 yearly consist chiefly of sisal, gold, cotton, coffee, and hides. Her imports are only $18,000,000.

The territory has had a rocky economic history, with some tremendous reverses; but it is today on the way to stability. Though Germans and British have invested fully $260,000,000, only recently has Tanganyika investment begun to pay.

History: 1914–1944. At the end of World War I, the League of Nations assumed jurisdiction over Tanganyika, formerly German East Africa. The League gave the southern area to Portugal and assigned two mandates: (1) to Belgium, the rich cattle country of Ruanda Urundi (in the west), and (2) to Great Britain, the rest of the territory of Tanganyika. The German settlers were required to leave the region and their estates were sold (mostly to Greeks and Indians).

Owing to the problems of readjustment from German to British administration, the economic condition of Tanganyika remained poor; not until 1924 were exports equal to the 1913 level. By 1925, the European population of Tanganyika was only 3,500 as against 5,500 in 1913. Desirous of developing the area, the British permitted experienced German settlers to return in 1925; and they soon constituted a third of the European population.

The British planters held the view that so long as its future political status remained nebulous, it would be impossible to develop the mandate or to make large investments in the territory. In 1926 the British Minister of Colonies, Amery, declared categorically that Great Britain held Tanganyika under the Treaty of Versailles as of right, and that the future of Tanganyika within the British Empire was as assured as any other part of British East Africa. This unwarranted announcement gave rise to agitation for incorporating the mandate into the empire. The Tanganyika League formed for this purpose, and was soon actively assisted by "White Supremacy" groupings in Kenya. Much of the mandate's history consisted in the struggle between punctilious British civil servants anxious to conform strictly to the terms of the mandate and the white planters impatient to convert Tanganyika into a British colony and to exploit the natives without regard to the stipulations of the mandate.

The essential struggle was economic. The natives were far better off under the mandate rule than they had been under the Germans. Mandate officials, for example, introduced "indirect rule," which permitted the natives to hold important posts in consultative assemblies. Recognizing that such an administrative trend made compulsory native labor impossible, the white colonists instituted a campaign of ridicule against the officials. Since the Asiatic settlers were also protected by the administration, the controversy between the government and the European population became even more intense.

In 1924 the administration permitted the natives to restore their former tribal organizations, an act which the white planters firmly opposed. The administration also sponsored the formation of large rural cooperatives among the natives. Fully 25,000 native coffee planters in time succeeded in establishing a giant marketing mutual organization. The white planters insisted that this development spelled disaster for all their efforts in behalf of Tanganyikan economy.

The German Consul-General in Kenya attempted to exploit the discontent of the German planters in Tanganyika for purposes of anti-British action. When World War II broke out, however, very few Germans in the mandate were found to be dangerous. Apparently Nazi propaganda had met with greater responsiveness among the more reactionary British planters. The natives, however, proved intensely loyal, undoubtedly as a result of the farsighted policy of the mandate officials. During World War II rubber plantations were introduced into the economy, and they proved of signal assistance to the prosperity of Tanganyika.

ZANZIBAR

This Sultanate and British protectorate — two islands off the coast of East Africa — was once a mighty state — until the Portuguese attacked in 1505. Today the land area is only 1,020 square miles and the population 235,000. The people are a veritable museum of ethnology: every variety of African and Asiatic seems to be there, and with every possible intermixture. Zanzibar's architecture is also well known for its examples of the Arabian style. But the land's contemporary fame has a more mundane base: Zanzibar is the center of cloves, producing nearly the entire world supply. Clove and clove oil exports are 75% of Zanzibar's total trade. And this is so important that her per capita commerce is $40 — astonishing for the area, and many times that of nearby lands.

Stakes in the Peace

The prospects for the three areas of British East Africa vary according to the respective internal situation. The uplands of Kenya can be impressively developed if there is a diminution in the arrogant attitudes of the white settlers. Uganda, on the other hand, undoubtedly will give rise to a greatly advanced industrial and political population within a generation. As for Tanganyika, there is need for large capital investment in order that the plantations, and particularly the native cooperatives, measure up to Ugandan levels. The recent wanderings of the tsetse fly eastward in Tanganyika present a danger that can be countered only by a colossal sanitation campaign.

The future of British East Africa depends upon some international organization — one that is founded upon native interests, that is constructively related to world economics, that eschews imperialism, and that regards itself as the temporary custodian of power until the democratic potentialities of the populations can be effectively developed.

BRITISH WEST AFRICA

British West Africa consists principally of three colonies: Nigeria (including part of the Cameroons mandate), the Gold Coast, and Sierra Leone. All three are "colonies" in their coastal areas and "protectorates" in the upcountry. Their importance to Britain may be gauged by the fact that when she was beleaguered in 1940 and 1941, they supplied 40% of her fats: without these, Britain might not have survived.

NIGERIA

The subject of an abundant literature on administration, peoples, and resources, Nigeria has been held by the British since 1879; in 1903 the territory became fully British. Nigeria is an immense country — 372,600 square miles, an eighth of the U.S.A., with a population exceeding 21,040,000. Most of the land lies on the hot, damp Guinea coast, a tropical rainforest; but the upcountry is mostly savanna. Crossed by 21,700 miles of roads, 2,700 miles of railway, and linked to the Trans-Saharan system and to roads that reach East Africa, Nigeria is actually a giant communications center.

The southern section is principally peopled by the Yoruba, a Sudanese Negro group; the northern section, by the Hausas, a mixed Sudanese Negro and Arab grouping whose language has spread throughout the area as a trading Esperanto. The Yoruba are fetishists; the Hausas, Moslems; and Arab and Berber cultures have largely replaced the Sudanese Negro civilization among them.

Nigeria is the most advanced of West African lands in every positive accomplishment, from education to administration. Fully 543,000 children attend school — an extraordinary number for this West African region. Nigeria is a showplace of the British Colonial Office.

Economy. The land is important as a producer of 40% of the world's supply of palm kernels, 30% of its palm oil, and 14% of its cocoa. It is also a large producer of groundnuts and ginger. The livestock economy — 3,000,000 cattle and 2,000,000 sheep — provides some 8,000 tons of hides and skins. Gold, silver, tin, and coal are also found; and during the war cotton lint and rubber have become prominent.

Trade. A large part of the exports are handled by the giant Unilever companies of Britain and the Netherlands, which dominate the world's soap and margarine trade. Exports in all total $45,000,000 and imports $50,000,000.

Nigeria's large debt, about $125,000,000, has been spent on constructive work, which has assisted her remarkably alert and virile native population to a higher economy. British investments exceed $375,-000,000. But every year Nigeria sends Britain over $10,000,000 for debt service and pensions for British officials, and in addition the official emoluments are $5,000,000, two-thirds of which are remitted to British officials when on leave.

Natives of British West Africa fought actively on the side of Great Britain in World War I. At that time Sir Frederick (later Lord) Lugard served as governor of Nigeria, and it was during his term of office that British colonial policy in Africa made its most significant departure from precedent.

History. "Dual government" — by the Colonial Office with the collaboration of native groups — and "indirect rule" originated under Lord Lugard. By these policies, tribal authorities became in a sense the vehicles of administrative decisions. In Nigeria too the Lugard plan initiated the policy of Upper Houses, composed of colonial officials, and Lower Houses, partly elected and partly nominated, with consultative powers and some native representation. Moreover, Lugard promoted the policy of dividing colonial possessions into colonies in the more advanced, and protectorates in the more primitive areas.

In many ways Nigeria came to be the model colony of Great Britain, with the rise of a native officialdom and education for the sons of native notables. Sir Hugh Clifford, who became Governor of Nigeria in 1919, implemented the Lugard reforms, and by 1923 the first elections were held.

THE GOLD COAST

One of the most lucrative of British possessions, the Gold Coast produces more than a third of the world's ordinary cocoa — its port, Accra, is the "world capital of cocoa."

Although the land is attractive for great wealth and variety of resources, the seacoast is one of the unhealthiest parts of the world; the jungle is lush and dangerous. However, a superb road system of 6,600 miles of motor highway, enables produce to be swiftly and cheaply trucked. In view of the high export figure — higher than Nigeria's though population and area (91,000 square miles) are considerably smaller — the importance of these communications can scarcely be overstated.

Sudanese Negroes constitute most of the nearly 4,000,000 population. They include the famous Fuzzy Wuzzy of Kipling's poem, who "broke a British square," and these Ashantis have been respectfully treated ever since their remarkable showing as warriors. Religion has made some progress among the natives, and many Christians are found among them today. About one child in ten goes to school. Recently the Gold Coast has been made the center for a West African Institute of Arts and Sciences.

Economy. Production is extraordinary for so small an area and so few people. Even in the 18th century, the region attracted Europeans, because of its abundant gold dust and the American slave-trade. Today, the Gold Coast not only produces a third of the world's cocoa (inferior in quality, however, to the Ecuador and Venezuela product), but she possesses rich gold fields and has become an important source of diamonds and manganese.

Gold Coast exports are normally $53,000,000, imports $38,000,000 (though during the war the latter have fallen to $22,000,000). The export trade consists of cocoa 50%, gold 30%, and the rest mainly diamonds and manganese. Half of these totals go to Britain, 15% to the U.S.A., and in peacetime 10% to Germany and 5% to the Netherlands. The British furnished most of the colony's imports.

The combined British and Dutch investment is about $175,000,000. Government expenditures cost $25,000,000 and the Gold Coast debt is $50,000,000.

History. Material prosperity rather than administrative reforms was emphasized on the Gold Coast. But although the authorities did not introduce the elective scheme of Nigeria, natives sat on nominated councils and the chiefs were increasingly consulted in local administration. The Gold Coast history is that of a boom, the volume of cocoa exports having quintupled from 1916 to 1936, while other exports of colonial produce fell off by three-fourths. The premium on gold exports after Britain devalued her currency in 1931 compensated for the fall in cocoa prices in that period. Hence the Gold Coast at no time suffered from economic crisis, even though it abandoned all but four exports and neglected diversified production. In 1937–38 the Governor stated that, despite twenty-five years of unbroken prosperity, he feared for the colony's future, based as it was only on cocoa and gold.

SIERRA LEONE

This western neighbor of Liberia was, like Liberia, begun as a refuge from the slave trade. British philanthropists founded Sierra Leone in 1788, antedating the Liberian establishment; hence the name of the capital, Freetown. It should be noted, however, that although the coast was a slave refuge, the uplands as late as 1927 were based on slavery.

The 1,773,000 people who inhabit the 30,000 square miles of land are practically all Negroes. Those on the coast, descendants of refugees, are mixed; and while the population includes many Moslems, most of the people have remained pagan.

With an average rainfall of 168 inches at Freetown, Sierra Leone has been called "the White Man's grave," but the white man has nevertheless been interested in the region's economy. Of the total exports of $11,000,000, some 40% were palm kernels, 30% diamonds, 15% gold, and 12% iron. Imports were $6,500,000. About half the trade was with Britain. It must be recorded of Sierra Leone that during the 1928–1938 decade, when exports throughout the world severely declined, her exports actually rose.

History. The Sierra Leone colonial authorities, following the example of Nigeria, made provisions in 1924 for elections to a council and gave the native chiefs wide powers in the Legislative Council. Here the principal issue was the abolition of slavery, which was not final until 1928, when the expected resistance of the native chiefs failed to materialize.

In the 1930's British West Africa saw some interesting innovations. Christian missionaries were instructed to educate and proselytize among the pagan natives, but enjoined from interfering with Mohammedan areas where the local Emirs agreed to government schools. In the Gold Coast, higher education was actively fostered with the establishment of a college at Achimota; while in Ashanti, the restoration of its royal dynasty, repressed for 35 years, indicated the British desire to intensify native loyalty.

In Sierra Leone, the colony's Legislative Council on the coast received powers to develop the protectorate in the interior, thus training native members in colonial administration at second remove, so to speak.

When World War II began, British West Africa actively aided the mother country. The 1940's saw increased shipments of fats to beleaguered Britain; the development of air fields, especially at Lagos; and the linking of Nigeria to French North Africa by the Trans-Saharan route, thus augmenting the importance of the Northern Protectorate of Nigeria. In the Gold Coast, despite the added war burdens, the authorities continued the task of making it the cultural center of West Africa.

Stakes in the Peace

The problems of the three important colonies of British West Africa differ considerably.

The Gold Coast views the undue emphasis on its cocoa production as potentially dangerous, nor does the record of constant profits and increasing prosperity beguile its administration from the dangers involved.

In Nigeria, the development of roads and river transportation, and the astonishing rise of great trading centers like Kano in the north and Lagos in the south, indicate that the colony is merely at the beginning of its incalculable possibilities.

Sierra Leone requires the gradual development of the upcountry, with truly communal agriculture to replace the shattered production relations brought about by emancipation of the native slaves.

In Nigeria, of course, the basic economy cannot be diverted away from fats and minerals, except for more active encouragement of subsistence agriculture. Emphasis on tribal councils, far from reducing native initiative and training in self-government, seems to have stimulated these phenomena.

The huge surplus of exports from these three colonies has given them a call on large assets in London and may assist in supplementing their still limited capital investment. But most promising of all is the development of West African education. In Nigeria it bids fair to rival that in Uganda in the near future; and although critics, particularly among the Fabian group in London, regret the emphasis on advanced rather than primary education on the Gold Coast, when one contrasts the efforts made in the last 20 years with the attitude of naked exploitation prior to 1900, the progress is strikingly impressive.

ETHIOPIA

The Land and the People

Aside from Liberia, founded as a slave refuge, Ethiopia alone among African countries retains independence, after the short-lived interval of Italian domination under Mussolini (1936–1941). Formerly termed Abyssinia, the country has not been important in world history, though in early times she was closely associated with Egypt, sometimes under the same rulers. The Mohammedan conquest of Egypt in the 7th century isolated the Abyssinian Christians, as Gibbon says, "for near a thousand years, forgetful of the world, by whom they were forgotten." European exploitation and penetration began in the latter 19th century.

The land area approximates 350,000 square miles, about the size of the three American Pacific Coast states. An undetermined population has been variously estimated, usually at 5,500,000; but the Italians in 1937 announced the figure as 7,600,000. Eritrea and the Somalilands separate Ethiopia from the Red Sea to the west; Sudan, Uganda, and Kenya intervene to the south and west.

In so largely mountainous a land, with good rainfall, climate is more tolerable than in the Sudanese area to the west or on the hot Somali coast to the east. The lowland areas, with many hot, humid savannas, are peopled by poor nomads. In the highland varied crops and stockraising prevail, and the population is denser than in the Sudan.

With a sheltering highland on the border between desert and equatorial forest and an intermediate zone for flora, Ethiopia could be truly fertile and prosperous, given better methods of cultivation. The Soviet botanist Vavilov maintains that most of the plants used in European farming originated here; certainly coffee did.

Two peoples, the Ethiopians (about 30%) and the Gallas (about 50%) dominate this land of mixed racial origins. Originally a Hamitic people, the Ethiopians show a large Semitic infiltration and, most of them, some Negro blood. The Gallas are Hamites. Other tribes are the Danakils, fanatical Mohammedans, and the Falashas (most interesting to anthropologists, Hamitic-Negro Jews). Armenians, Syrians, and Arabs, mainly traders, are numerous in the towns; and the European population, especially under the Italians, has been large.

The French railway to Jibuti in Somaliland on the Red Sea, built under great difficulties in the last century, offers the only important egress from Ethiopia; but the leading Ethiopian and Galla peoples have at least this connection with the outside world, whereas the Negroes, largely in the southwest, remain very much self-contained. Leadership has not yet fused the Ethiopian peoples; their government is a loose feudatory superstructure somewhat resembling the European monarchies of the 12th century.

Addis Ababa, the capital, has often been spotlighted in the news in recent years along with its monarch, Haile Selassie. Harar, the great market in the east, is also well known.

Religion and Education. The proportions of various religious groups are difficult to determine exactly: Christians are perhaps 40%, Mohammedans 40%, and the followers of native religions much of the remainder. The Christians, of the Coptic order, accept the Patriarch of Alexandria, and their church holds a large share of land and supports a priesthood of perhaps 100,000, including monastics. Mohammedanism, however, spreads more rapidly than Christianity among the natives, supplanting fetishism. Jews (Falashas) total no more than 100,000. Among the Europeans, the Greek and Armenian churches predominate.

The few government schools and the missionary institutions with their foreign teachers and books have not gone far in supplanting the fixed control of the priests in education. Among peoples of comparable arrested levels of material culture, Ethiopia has, therefore, on the whole, one of the lowest levels of education.

The Nation's Economy

The only commercially important crop, coffee, stands at about 20,000 tons annually. Cattle, sheep, goats, and the small but strong and handsome Abyssinian horse form the basis of animal economy.

The Italians, during their brief control, listed the resources of the country in iron, potash, cabinet woods, gold, and many other products; but they have not yet been exploited. Almost no industries have arisen.

Finance. The people still use the Maria Theresa dollar, coined in Vienna in the 18th century. But, since their currency is now in suspense, pending reorganization, British East African money has come into temporary use. The Bank of Ethiopia holds about $1,900,000 in paid-up capital. Its issue, called the *thaler*, has been stabilized at 39¢. In 1942 the British came to the aid of the country's finance with a loan of $12,500,000 for two years.

Before the Italians arrived, government revenues totaled about $5,000,000 to $7,000,000 — largely, however, paid in kind. State toll-gates, formerly an important source of revenue, have now been abolished to aid in diffusing trade. The government thus seems eager to build a modern consolidated country, and the Allied nations have given some assistance in the form of machinery and educational aid. European interest has also served somewhat to stabilize administrative and fiscal affairs.

Foreign Trade. Exports of hides and skins, coffee, wax, civet, and clarified butter move not only by the French railway but also by six caravan routes, which better roads may soon supplant with motor transit. (The Italians established many of the needed new roads, though building them mainly of earth and gravel. Only 65 miles of macadamized roads existed in all Ethiopia in 1937.) The people import mainly gray sheetings, cotton goods, some gasoline, sugar, glass, and soap. Their foreign trade, mainly by barter, follows systems very complex in determination of equivalents, indicating commercial development well beyond the primitive level. Under the Italians, however, money economy spread rather widely.

Trade cannot be estimated: caravans sell largely to the neighboring native peoples, and the railway statistics are insufficient guides. Britain, however, buys $900,000 worth of goods from Ethiopia, and sells her about $45,000 worth.

History: 1914-1944

Ethiopia was neutral in World War I, but during the end of the conflict the feudal lords successfully revolted against the emperor (Lej Yasu) who had himself usurped the throne from Empress Zauditu. One of these feudal lords, Ras Tafari, later Emperor Haile Selassie, became regent of the kingdom, with the Empress as the nominal ruler, under his control.

With royal authority thus divided, the feudal lords exploited their opportunity to make themselves almost independent. Ras Tafari pursued two policies: he increased central power at home and in order to secure independence, he struggled for and eventually obtained membership in the League of Nations (1923), despite British opposition.

Following his protest (1925) against a British-Italian agreement for spheres of influence in his country, the Italians sent the Duke of Abruzzi to treat with him. In 1930 the Empress died and Ras Tafari was finally crowned Emperor (Haile Selassie), after fourteen years of effort. He consolidated the state, suppressing rebellion through provincial governors. With strong faith in the League, he ignored Italy's excessive demands.

Italy, however, used an obscure border incident at Walwal as a pretext for invading the country in 1934. Flouting the findings of the League, the Italians executed their premeditated plan to conquer the country, after a short campaign (October 1935 to May 1936). While the League condemned Italy as an aggressor, it imposed only limited and ineffectual "sanctions" and gave *de facto* (not *de jure*) recognition to the Italian conquest. Italy proceeded to annex Ethiopia to King Victor Emmanuel's empire.

During the Italian invasion, the British and French foreign ministers (Hoare and Laval) had granted partition rights to Italy, but an aroused British and French public opinion prevented the implementation of their plan.

Emperor Haile Selassie, an exile in England, waited for the coming of justice.

In 1940, following the outbreak of war between Britain and Italy, the Italian régime in Ethiopia fell after a rapid Allied campaign. Haile Selassie regained his throne, and two years later concluded arrangements with Britain, which gave her many special privileges in the redeemed land.

Stakes in the Peace

Not only has her independence been restored, but Ethiopia is now assured of active British interest in her development. Military exploration and the construction of a network of roads since 1940 have almost put an end to the independent chieftains and their power. And on the Sudan frontier, slave-trading, the plague of the region, has almost vanished.

If the Ethiopian highlands are given the added irrigation they require on the fertile slopes, the wealth of plant life, both in variety and hardiness of type, can lead to a favorable agricultural development. The consistent British policy of building up two neighboring lands, Kenya and the Sudan, should give Ethiopia a promising local market for her hides and skins; and as motor transportation slowly replaces caravans, the opportunities should enlarge.

The development of Ethiopia would greatly assist sedentary agricultural life throughout the adjacent area, since the activities of her nomadic groups have long prevented settlement in many border districts of Kenya and the Sudan. Moreover, the present extremely small trade has prevented the growth of a sizable merchant class, a prerequisite for a stable society in the early stages of industrial development.

Both the Gallas and the Abyssinians have shown themselves quickly adaptable to modern ideas, nor is the Coptic priesthood now a barrier to progress, since they have before them the successful example of their coreligionists in Egypt, who have profited by modernization. During the period of their rigorous rule, the Italians failed to develop the country constructively (apart from building roads), but they did accomplish one thing: they made detailed studies of the land, which indicate its far-flung possibilities.

FRENCH EQUATORIAL AFRICA

The four colonies — Chad, Gabon, Ubangi, and Middle Congo — of French Equatorial Africa cover an area equivalent to 32% of the U.S.A.: 959,000 square miles. The population numbers 3,500,000; and if we include the Cameroons mandate (formerly German, today mostly French), the total reaches 5,800,000. Not more than 5,000 French people live in the entire area.

The Negroes in the north are Sudanese, in the south Bantu. While Mohammedanism has been effective in the lands near the Sahara, the center and south remain pagan. Until recently, education was neglected — only 15,000 children attended school.

The southern regions are typical equatorial rainforest, with some 300,000 square miles of forest abounding in fine cabinet woods. The rainfall is heavy and the water-power potential, owing to the system of large rivers, is so great that some authorities estimate that this land may one day be the first in the world in this development. At present, however, the region is limited to the usual tropical economy, with palm kernels, palm oil, coffee, ivory, cocoa, cotton, and cotton-seed produced for export, as well as some recent amounts of rubber.

The northern country is largely savanna; hence a pastoral economy dominates, with cattle, sheep, donkeys, camels, and ostriches prominent in an extensive caravan trade. Legendary Timbuctoo to the west and other centers are decaying, as new administrative and trading points develop in the colony itself.

Trade is small ($3 per capita), with exports at $7,700,000 and imports at $8,500,000. With the new network of roads built to connect Allied military operations and with hundreds of miles of new railways, commerce should develop.

French Equatorial Africa has been the stepchild of France. Abuses led to their correction at the hands of the gifted Savorgnan de Brazza, one of the noblest figures in colonial history. Regrettably, the work of this French explorer was not followed through, and the region remained an unimpressive contrast to British Nigeria and the Belgian Congo. In 1940, however, the colony electrified the world when Félix Eboué, Governor of the Chad, proclaimed the Free French Republic.

History: 1914-1944

As part of the French Empire, French Equatorial Africa was involved in World War I, especially in the campaign to reconquer the German colonies in Africa. But the census of 1921 showed such a marked ten-year decline in population that, after making all allowances, reform became urgent. The French government acted to end the "concessions" to private companies, the last of which was to expire by 1936, but this program was never fully realized. The authorities introduced and vigorously pushed the policy of conscription, thus leading to further depopulation.

Nevertheless, the French, as always, concentrated on the education of a native élite, who were to be the carriers of French influence and at the same time separated from tribal influence. In the Cameroons mandate, where the Germans had been severe to the natives, French influence was a liberating force. Successive governors strove to find a workable substitute for the diminishing concessions and the temporary device of forced cooperatives. But the obviously better physical conditions of the Negroes in the Belgian Congo, next door, showed that purely political expedients would not help. Yet not until 1940 were there any dramatic changes.

When France fell (1940) the colonial empire accepted the Vichy government. One man refused: Felix Eboué, Governor of Chad, a Negro born in Cayenne, South America. At Fort Lamy in the Chad Region he raised the flag of Free France (August 29, 1940), and from him dates the national resurrection of French resistance in Africa, as in Europe from General Charles de Gaulle. With the able assistance of General Jacques Leclerc, Eboué converted the colony into a Free French base, establishing radio facilities at Brazzaville, and granting to the United Nations air fields, port facilities, and important raw materials.

Internally, Eboué replaced the régime of concessions by true (not forced) cooperatives, and whatever now survives of the concessions is in the process of liquidation. Granting greater civic and council rights to the native population, he brought about a remarkable upsurge of loyalty and an increase in physical productivity. The results astonished the diehard colonial authorities in the areas faithful to Vichy, where production showed a decline.

Eboué died in 1944, emancipator of the region and an example of the loyalty that France could inspire because of her racial liberalism, a liberalism surpassing that of other European colonial powers.

Stakes in the Peace

The example of the late Felix Eboué has stimulated this lush country, and its new local governors are eager to improve it along the lines of the Belgian Congo. Since the area lacks the rich Katanga copper fields of the Congo region, its possibilities are limited to two main developments: the first, timber in the equatorial rainforest; second, pastoral economy, which most experts think can be enormously expanded, both in quality and quantity, in the Sudanese districts.

The country suffers sharply from "shifting cultivation" and here, as in French West Africa, the forced associations of producers have caused the natives to produce only what was required. But the democratic wave in this area, the development of trading facilities at Libreville and of light industries at Brazzaville and surrounding regions, and the emphasis on radio as a medium of instruction as well as amusement in the native villages, have given a life and enthusiasm to this region in three years that far surpass the efforts of previous decades.

The encouragement of native cooperation is an avowed aim: if their education in their responsibilities is correlated with an increase in their functions in administration and economy, the country may yet see a harmonious development that will accelerate progress toward native self-government. Although detailed figures are not available, this promise seems already reflected in impressive increases in production and trade.

FRENCH WEST AFRICA

French West Africa includes Mauretania, Senegal, Dakar, the Ivory Coast, Dahomey, French Sudan, and Niger — an immense territory of 1,815,000 square miles, more than 60% of the U.S.A. The population, however, is only 15,800,000, including the inhabitants of the French mandate in Togoland.

The region includes Senegal, an ancient French possession, taken in the days of Louis XIV and used as a base for the slave trade with the rich French sugar plantations in the West Indies. Dakar, as a central naval and air base, became celebrated during World War II, its importance for American security having been frequently stressed.

Most of French West Africa divides into two zones: the excessively hot, rainy area of the Guinea coast and the hot, dry, almost desert lands about Senegal and Dakar on the Atlantic. The country consists mainly of lowlands, though toward the Guinea coast, there are large highland blocks, broken by grandiose river basins; and here the population is densest.

Except for some 25,000 Europeans, three-fourths of whom are French officials, missionaries, or traders, the 15,800,000 people are mostly Negroes, speaking Sudanese tongues. Where they border the Sahara, the native populations show some Berber and Hamitic influence. The religion is fetishist, but Mohammedanism has made inroads in the Sudanese regions, though not to any extent on the Guinea coast. The Negroes include once-powerful empires, like that of Dahomey, and their people have long been celebrated for complex administration, military organization, penal codes, ingenious agriculture. Their sculpture, both in masks and fetishes, has influenced Futurist art, especially in Paris and Berlin.

Few regions favor European survival less than the Guinea coast, nor is the climate tolerable to Europeans anywhere in French West Africa. Though sanitary services are fairly well organized, a great deal remains to be done.

Education varies in the many provinces. It is extensive in Senegal and Dakar, following French models; in other regions the educational system aims at integrating urban, rural, and itinerant schools. On the whole, there has been great progress. All schools must teach French and must remain secular. While the French emphasize trade and farming schools, their principal concern is to build up an educated native group which will be French in culture and whose future lies in administration.

Economy. With corn and rice as the main subsistence crops, the agriculture produces palm kernels and oil, cotton-seed, cotton, coffee, tobacco, sesame, and cocoa for export. Hides and skins are also important. The forests are rich in beautiful cabinet woods, such as ebony, and in gums, whose commercial output is large. French West Africa also produces about 130,000 ounces of gold.

Native industries are active for domestic needs, being mostly on a handicraft basis. Some light industries, however, have grown up in the ports and trading centers.

Production is not voluntary. The natives are grouped forcibly into Sociétés de Prévoyance (mutual aid societies), which also market the production. With millions of members, practically all adult males, these societies constitute the entire economic organization of the area. They are related to the native social structure, either of tribe, family, or community, and are headed by local notables. The French have not tried to interfere with their internal administration, even though the bias of French rule, as contrasted with the British, has been to replace the concept of the tribe by that of the citizen.

Trade. Exports in peacetime amounted to 1,400,-000,000 francs (then worth about $42,000,000); imports, 1,600,000,000 francs (then about $48,000,000). The per capita trade was $6, an extremely low figure.

The principal exports, in addition to the items listed above (under *Economy*) included recent shipments of fruit and rubber. Textiles and also petroleum, machines, foods, and beverages constituted the imports. France supplied 60% of the imports and purchased 80% of the exports in peace-time.

Finance. The Federation of Colonies separates its budget into common and local, but the total seems to have been less than $25,000,000 yearly. Though the government expense is small, the capital investment of the French has been quite small as well — only $17 per native (not much less than in British Nigeria). The significance of this figure appears when it is compared with the Belgian investment of $66 per native in the Congo.

History: 1914-1944

In World War I, French West Africa sent over 100,000 Senegalese troops to Europe, where they fought against the Central Powers. At the close of hostilities, the French concentrated on building up the naval and aerial facilities of their West African colony. They improved the port of Dakar and made the regular air-mail route of the *Aéropostale* Company into an important link between France and South America. Certain pilots, like Saint-Exupéry, have immortalized this South Atlantic air run.

Senegal, an old French colony, granted full French citizenship to all literate natives. Her deputy in the French Chamber, Diagne, a Negro, served a term as French Minister of Colonies. Local assemblies received full power but, although Negroes in Senegal nominally enjoyed full rights, the fact that debates had to be conducted in French proved in practice to be a limiting factor. In 1924 the French withdrew judicial powers from the native chiefs.

By 1939, the French had fostered a really large Negro élite class, and in areas like Dahomey, the natives became important in administrative posts.

When World War II broke out, the port of Dakar in the African "bulge" loomed as a strategic prize; and after the fall of France in 1940, it became an obvious cause for concern to the British. They therefore accepted the project of General Charles de Gaulle to take Dakar and use it as the base for French colonial revival. The attack (September 1940), which was bitterly resisted and finally abandoned, seriously injured British prestige and dealt an almost mortal blow to de Gaullist aspirations. The failure gave a fillip to the prevailing sentiment that whoever was championed by Britain in those dark days was doomed. Nevertheless, the fleet of the Vichy French was badly hurt, and Dakar's repairing facilities proved of little value. The only result of Vichy control was that the Nazis received *sub rosa* opportunities to send their submarines prowling in the South Atlantic and to hunt down political refugees throughout West Africa. Production, however, declined in the entire area.

United Nations forces regained Dakar in 1942, the United States government stating clearly that American security was closely bound up with the status of that port. At the time, some French circles raised the question as to what this attitude signified for post-war French sovereignty over the area. However, the Dakar natives have undoubtedly been among those most loyal to France, as witness the distinguished record of the Senegalese troops in World War I, and recently in metropolitan France.

In 1943, the provisional Algiers régime of de Gaulle promised increased native rights on the Ivory Coast, Dahomey, and other areas in which "forced cooperatives" were no longer consistent with "the new colonial policy."

Stakes in the Peace

This immense domain possesses important potentialities, both in human and natural resources, and they are of a type that can be developed within a fairly short period. The Guinea coast area has lagged far behind nearby Nigeria and the Gold Coast, but with an additional per capita investment of only $10, it should rival these other colonies. Export of timber is the first obvious resource, and the French government is aware of the possibilities.

A second step indicated is to increase the voluntary aspects of the *Sociétés de Prévoyance*, so that they are consulted as to plans and initiated into new techniques. Their long-demonstrated ability in matters of production and marketing augur well for a future increase in the scope of their activities. Another material help would be the abolition of inter-colonial tariffs.

In the 19th century, the Guinea slave was so skilled and resourceful that his Portuguese master in Brazil utilized his talents as an overseer; this proven ability might well be utilized in his country of origin. In the river valleys of the Guinea coast, subsistence crops can be increased substantially, especially in the neighborhood of large trading centers. On the more arid Atlantic coast, light industries, particularly those connected with local products such as oil-seeds and groundnuts (peanuts), could be augmented.

There can be little doubt that France will favor an extension of political rights for the natives, even outside their old parliamentary bailiwick of Senegal, which has representation in Paris. Moreover, an expansion of trade schools is forecast, by which the celebrated native skills in handicrafts can be applied to more complex industrial processes. This will be a welcome supplement to the development of a native élite, trained only for administration. Thus, the small per capita trade now obtaining could begin to rival that in the prize possessions of West Africa; and France would find herself indirectly enriched by this commerce.

LIBERIA

The Land and the People

The Negro republic of Liberia has a special interest for Americans. It was founded by American idealists who, in 1817, thought that Negro slaves should be bought from their masters and then settled in West Africa, and that by this means slavery would gradually disappear in the U.S.A. The few freed slaves were settled on the Guinea coast and the town established there was named Monrovia after James Monroe, then the American president. In 1847 the settlement became a republic. Monrovia, her capital, is today a town of 10,000.

Recently Liberia signed a treaty with the U.S.A. for the duration of the war, and President Roosevelt declared that the welfare and defense of the land are vital to American interests. Since Liberia faces the bulge of Brazil across the narrowest stretch of the South Atlantic, the country has extraordinary potential strategic importance.

With a coast line of some 350 miles in one of the wettest parts of the world, Liberia stands southeast of the British colony of Sierra Leone (also established as a slave refuge), west of the French colony of the Ivory Coast, and south of French Guinea. An area of about 43,000 square miles, she extends inland 200 miles; but the effective territory really controlled by the government amounts to considerably less. Most of the land lies at less than 1,000 feet above sea level; all of it, within the equatorial rainforest belt.

About 2,500,000 people live in Liberia. Those on the coast — 12,000 of American descent, centering in Monrovia (offspring of those for whom the enterprise was begun), and about 60,000 native Negroes who participate in their culture — are the dominant population. Their government has gradually gained some authority over the northern tribes and the numerous pagan Kroos. There are also some six other fairly numerous native peoples, many of them Mohammedans. The Negroes of the interior retain their native arts and sculpture, much admired by experts, and illustrative of the African influences which have recently impressed art circles of the West.

The electors of the Liberian republic must be Negroes and property holders; thus governmental power really lies in the hands of a small coastal group of descendants of American slaves, who have established a tutelage over part of the population. The "True Whig" party that runs the country has often been described as an oligarchy; but recent economic developments may eventually extend democratization.

The coastal people are almost all Protestants, conducting their services in the official language, English. But paganism prevails among the mass of the people, while Mohammedanism is strong in the north, gaining there as everywhere throughout the Sudan and Equatorial regions. American Protestant missionaries have worked for a century in Liberia. Since the mission schools number 121 and the government has established 51 others, education has made a modest beginning.

The Nation's Economy

Though productive, the soil had been neglected until recently. Its leading products have been coffee, palm oil, palm kernels, and cocoa; but both the extraordinary plant possibilities and the rich forest resources offer far more than the people have yet known how to utilize. The undoubted mineral resources remain untouched, except for a small gold production.

A transformation occurred during the war. A 1926 concession of a million acres of rubber lands to the Firestone Company of Ohio has now been cultivated up to 77,000 acres, yielding 18,000,000 pounds of dry rubber. An astonishing upswing has resulted. Whereas in peacetime Liberia, exporting but $570,000 worth of goods (coffee, palm oil and kernels, cocoa, and fibers for mats) and importing $1,100,000 worth (mainly cotton goods, spirits, and tobacco), floundered in chronic financial difficulties, imports had trebled by 1941 and exports had multiplied by eight (to $5,000,-000). The "permanent" deficit has become a surplus.

Estimated exports for 1942 stood at more than $7,300,000. Rubber has been the magic wand behind these startling transformations, and the U.S.A. has become virtually the sole nation figuring in Liberian trade. But communications remain a problem: though there are coastal roads, practically none penetrate the interior, where head-porters are still needed to carry packs through the forest. No railway exists and no good harbor.

Finance. In 1926 Liberia received a private American loan, secured by a lien on customs and a headtax, and agreed to accept an American fiscal supervisor to segregate revenues for its servicing. The bonded debt approximates $1,400,000, the internal debt a mere $160,000. Debt history has been fluctuating, with periods of arrears. The Liberian dollar is now worth about 84¢.

History: 1914-1944

Liberia entered World War I in 1917, soon after the U.S.A., and was a signatory of the Treaty of Versailles. Her delegate to the Peace Conference, Mr. C. D. B. King, was elected President in 1920 and served three terms until 1932, when Edwin Barclay succeeded him. Both Presidents represented the True Whig Party. Barclay was reelected in 1936 for 8 years.

In 1926 the government granted the Firestone Rubber Company of America a concession of 1,000,-000 acres for 99 years; and a financial loan for the country was arranged.

The Germans had been influential in the colony, especially in trade, and from 1911 to 1917, when they had nearby colonies, Liberia had a good many difficulties with them. It was therefore natural for her actively to aid the United Nations cause during World War II, and to enter the war against the Axis (1944).

In 1942 the United States stationed American troops in Liberia, where they aided in the construction of roads and airfields. On his return from the Casablanca Conference (January 1943), President Roosevelt visited Monrovia, capital of Liberia, and the Liberian President Barclay subsequently visited Washington, D.C.

The True Whig candidate, William V. Tubman, succeeded Barclay as President after the 1944 elections, the entire Senate and House belonging to the same party.

Stakes in the Peace

Liberia must ever be a cultural obligation of the U.S.A., whose citizens conceived of her existence, fostered her origins, and have since sought to enrich and advance her.

The "True Whigs" on the coast clearly lack the means to develop the hinterland or to raise the educational and production levels of millions of natives in the hinterland. Outside of the Firestone concessions and recent war-inspired activities, capital investment in Liberia compares most unfavorably with that in European colonies nearby. Hence, the provision of at least as much investment as obtains in the nearby Gold Coast, for example, is a prerequisite of development. The opening up of the interior and the improvement in health and general welfare of the natives will benefit the groups of American culture on the coast, who have exercised a historic, but rather sterile domination.

So long as the development of Liberia permits increasing democratic participation in government and genuine national independence, foreign investment can be only beneficent. The attempts of both the British and French since 1918 to gain political and economic control of the republic have not been successful. On the other hand, the years of World War II have witnessed a quickening interest in Liberia on the part of Americans. And there are indications that the little country will be the scene of constructive American investment in the future. Doubtless, such foreign capital as will be made available to Liberia will be primarily American, although the U.S.A. has never made any official move that might be even remotely construed as sponsorship, except for the statement that Liberian security is of vital concern to the U.S.A.

MADAGASCAR

This large island 240 miles off the east coast of Africa, in the southern part of the Indian Ocean, is about an eighth larger than her mother country, France — 241,094 square miles. The land centers on a large, high plateau, with mountain ranges rising from the block. Steep cliffs descend to the coast, where there are narrow plains, lagoons, and a regular shore. One of the few bays, Diego Suarez, affords an excellent harbor.

Pleasantness of climate depends on altitude; though the coasts are hot and humid, Europeans can live fairly well in the mountainous center. Even the highlands are subtropical, and it is not yet certain that European children can thrive on this island.

Madagascar is the one great ethnological surprise of the world. Separated from the Malayan areas by thousands of ocean miles, and still farther from the Melanesian areas of the Pacific, Madagascar has a population and language unmistakably derived from those regions. How the people migrated over a stretch of water that would have taxed European sailing ships of the Middle Ages, is not yet known. East Indian coolie, Arab trader, and African Negro are found on the coast; but the leading races, especially the dominant Hovas, are Malayo-Polynesians, whose speech is beautiful and poetic. Of the 4,000,000 inhabitants, only 25,000 are French and 13,000 other Europeans.

The French have tried to absorb the more advanced Hovas, using radio broadcasts and newspapers to spread the French way of life. Education is universal and compulsory — the language of the Hovas prevails in elementary instruction, but French is used thereafter. Furthermore, a large section of the Hovas have adopted Protestantism, the French Huguenots having achieved their greatest missionary triumph in this island. The people may be described as lively, ingenious, good farmers and artisans, and possessed of excellent taste. Women enjoy high status, owing to a long line of female sovereigns. Though the religion is communal pagan, the absence of a native priesthood has been a help to French administration.

Economy. Rice and corn are grown for subsistence, but the export crops are typified by variety — coffee, tapioca, groundnuts, for example. Vanilla, clove oils, and essential oils, however, are important. Vanilla amounts to $2,000,000 in export, and the essential oils, over 18,000,000 pounds, largely destined for the French perfume industry, are factors in world economy. Recently a group of light industries have grown up, especially in Tananarive, the modern capital city of 125,000 inhabitants.

Before the war, three-fourths of the trade was with France, who bought coffee, vanilla, canned meats, hides, and perfume oils. All exports amounted to $23,000,000; imports, $16,500,000. Hence, per capita trade was twice the figure of French West Africa or French Equatorial Africa. During the war, trade fell off sharply, but since the Inter-Allied Commodity Services undertook marketing, Madagascar trade has begun a swift recovery. Internal trade is facilitated by fully 15,000 miles of good roads as well as canals that connect the leading ports.

History: 1914-1944

Madagascar had been ruled by the French under a new colonial policy implemented before World War

I by Marshal Galliéni (known in 1914 as the "savior of Paris"). His régime dealt with the natives in terms of their special national peculiarities, with each area of native culture under local rather than centralized jurisdiction. Galliéni really consulted native notables and gave them some joint powers. Resisting the demands of greedy colonial adventurers for quick-profit plantation products, he insisted on a diversified economy based on the natives' security. His policy was later brilliantly vindicated: from 1918 to 1931, despite the erratic fluctuations of the franc, Madagascar not only avoided crises, but enjoyed slow and steady economic growth.

Many of the inhabitants, however, lamented their Queen, Ranavalona II, deposed by the French, who had died in exile. Secret societies had sprung up during World War I to overthrow the French. The alarmed governor, Picquié, tried to foster French nationality without interfering with native faiths, and thus he opposed religious education by the Europeans in the island. But the French Protestants had made many converts and their struggle with Picquié in favor of their mission schools ended in victory for them. Though they improved the health of the people, which had seriously declined, most schools remained secular — a contrast with the situation in other French colonies, where religious instruction largely prevails. Olivier, appointed governor in 1924, ably extended the Galliéni tradition.

The world depression hit Madagascar in 1931, though not too severely, and three years later the government decided to make Diego Suarez into one of France's leading naval and commercial bases. Owing to lack of labor, this project for what the French call "the finest harbor on earth" was barely begun.

Two years later, the Polish government, contemplating the forcible exile of much of its Jewish population, sent commissions to Madagascar to examine the possibilities of Jewish settlement there. Upon ascertaining that the climate was insalubrious for whites, the commission recommended that Jews be sent to the island. This recommendation met with French obstacles, although the new governor, Cayla, was a man of obvious Fascist sympathies.

A liberal governor, de Coppet, succeeded Cayla, only to be dismissed by Marshal Pétain. But when Cayla returned to the island, a British ultimatum sent him packing. He was succeeded by Annet, who in 1940 had delivered Dahomey to the Vichy régime. Annet met with the unremitting hostility of the Free French settlers and many of the natives. Two years later, however, Britain stationed troops in the island on behalf of the United Nations to protect it from Japan who had long studied its possibilities as a strategic air and naval base. At once the British turned Madagascar over to the Free French, while retaining the right to station garrisons there for the duration of the war.

Stakes in the Peace

Madagascar has two basic needs: first, the development of her cattle economy and of a European level of farming in her highland zones; second, the conquest of malaria and other tropical diseases by proper sanitation in the lowland lagoon areas. Once these improvements are made, this talented people should attain a level of national income much greater than that which now prevails. With the spread of education, Madagascar could easily become a showplace of French tutelage. The French have promised a grant of wider home rule and should soon implement this pledge.

From the world point of view, there can be little doubt that the superlative strategic position of Madagascar makes her almost the ideal point from which international controls throughout the vast Indian Ocean area can be exercised. French cooperation in this task would enrich the island, enhance its security, diminish the costliness of present local defense, and set the island in the direction of world trade, rather than retaining it as a mere feeder of French import firms. These French commercial interests would soon find that they had not made a bad exchange in thus enlarging and diversifying the trade of Madagascar.

PORTUGUESE AFRICA

Portuguese Africa consists principally of two ancient possessions of the Portuguese crown: Mozambique in the east and Angola in the west. Vestiges of an empire that from Vasco da Gama to Albuquerque dominated the South Atlantic, both in Africa and America, these lands held the key to Arabia, India, and China, and with more enterprise the Portuguese could have taken

Australia. Camoëns' epic *The Lusiads* commemorates this period, as does Meyerbeer's opera *L'Africaine*. The reality today is more prosaic. Portugal has invested some $335,000,000 into these lands, as part of her imperial economy — an immense sum which, in terms of her resources, would be equivalent to a $10,-000,000,000 investment for the British.

MOZAMBIQUE

Northeast of the Union of South Africa and bordered by the Rhodesias and Tanganyika, Mozambique is a large area — larger than Montana and New Mexico combined: 297,000 square miles. All the 5,080,000 inhabitants are Negroes (mainly Bantu), with the exception of some 27,000 Europeans and East Indians. Until recently, much of Mozambique was governed by a chartered company, whose postage stamps, with their giraffes, delighted philatelists the world over. Today the administration is united under the Portuguese Ministry for Colonies.

Mozambique has a long coast line, part cliff and part swampy lowland. Four months of the year the climate is hot and rainy, five months it is cool. Although the coast is malarial, the interior plateau is healthful and most of the land high and rolling. The two main centers, Lourenço Marques and Mozambique, are port cities on the Indian Ocean.

Education is notably undeveloped — about one child in eleven attends primary school (conducted mostly in Portuguese). The entire colony of over 5,000,000 has only one high school, and the entire enrollment in trade schools is only 4,000 pupils. Although Catholicism has made some progress, the mass of the people have remained animist.

Industrial development is similarly backward, despite good roads and railways — one aspect of which, the railway bridge over the Zambezi River is an engineering marvel.

Economy. Ravages of the tsetse fly have hindered agricultural and pastoral expansion in otherwise promising areas. Cattle, for example, number 560,000 and sheep 70,000 — there should be millions.

Agriculture, mostly at primitive levels, centers on export crops, such as groundnuts, sesame, copra, sisal, cotton, and sugar. The principal trade, however, is in trans-shipment from the Union of South Africa, and the chief "exports" are the natives forced by the Mozambique government to work the mines in Transvaal (to the west).

Trade. Trade is in the hands of the European and East Indian groups. During the war, imports fell from $22,000,000 to $18,000,000, and exports — chiefly agricultural products — from $11,700,000 to $8,000,000. The principal customers are Portugal, the Rhodesias, Union of South Africa; principal suppliers: Portugal, Britain, and the U.S.A. (Though the Portuguese is the official currency, most business is transacted in South African pounds.)

Portuguese Africa, like the mother country, was at war with the Central Powers in 1914–1918.

History. The decade of the 1920's witnessed repeated attempts to implement trans-shipment agreements with the Union of South Africa. The compact provided that Mozambique was to handle $47\frac{1}{2}\%$ of all Transvaal imports, but in exchange was to furnish much-needed labor in the gold-mining areas of the Transvaal. With the colony's economic base thus secured, the Portuguese did little to improve it. Nevertheless, the British insisted in 1926 that the type of quasi-slavery in effect within Mozambique be ended.

Lourenço Marques in Mozambique is the Riviera of South Africa and a tourist paradise. As a result of Portugal's neutral position in World War II, it became a notorious center of Axis spies. The Nazis openly established headquarters there, under the direct supervision of Berlin.

During the war, the activities of German agents, who fomented rebellion among German residents in their former colony of Southwest Africa and who spied on shipping for German and Japanese submarines, led to a cooling of relations between Mozambique and the Union of South Africa. When the Allies occupied neighboring Madagascar (1942), Lourenço Marques lost much of its significance for the Axis, and gradually its importance as a base for espionage diminished.

ANGOLA

Angola, on the west coast of Africa, is almost a sixth of the U.S.A. in area: 498,000 square miles. Although the coastal plain is barren and unhealthy, the plateau averages 5,000 feet high, and rises in beautiful terraces: healthfulness increases with altitude. The terraces are thick with vegetation, but the upland hills are mostly bush country. The entire region enjoys a cool season four months of the year, including the southern area, which is largely desert.

The population — only 3,738,000 — is overwhelmingly Negro (Bantus chiefly), though Bushmen inhabit the remote areas. A mulatto population of some 28,000 are active in the towns, Luanda and New Lisbon, and the 44,000 Europeans (mainly Portuguese) control the colony. The neglected natives suffer from malaria, hookworm, smallpox, leprosy, and even goiter and elephantiasis.

Education is neglected: there are only 73 primary schools, 2 high schools, and 13 trade schools. Since Angola has been a colony since 1482 (ten years before America's discovery), this points to no obsession on the part of Portugal with the intellectual development of her subjects. The recent example of the Belgian Congo, however, has stimulated the younger colonial officials.

Economy. Agriculture remains small, though manioc (used in tapioca) is an important export crop, and sugar, coffee, palm oil, are produced in fair quantities. Diamonds and wax also appear among the export items, as well as the principal subsistence crop, corn.

The mineral output centers upon diamonds and salt, with brown coal in fair amounts. Although native artisan work in iron and copper is esteemed, these ores have a small production. Compared with the Rhodesias and other neighboring British areas with similar possibilities, Angola's production is surprisingly small. And yet her roads are excellent and numerous.

Trade. Portugal nearly monopolizes the colony's trade, importing about $15,000,000 from Angola and exporting to her some $10,000,000, chiefly in textiles and foodstuffs. The currency unit, the *angolar*, is worth about 4¢. Angola's budget is only $11,000,000 and her debt, $40,000,000, is almost all owed to Portugal. The colony is governed by Portuguese "corporations" along Fascist lines.

History. Persistent criticism by the Anti-Slavery Society of London finally led the Angola authorities in 1921 to abolish compulsory native labor for private employers. However, the Portuguese arranged another system (which they also used in Mozambique): they imposed heavy taxes on the natives. The latter, not having any money, had to work out these taxes, usually in the Union of South Africa. When they returned, customs officials stripped them of their earnings to pay the arrears of back taxes, plus interest and other charges. In 1928 Angola dropped the mask and again instituted forced labor.

Missionary complaints multiplied against the Portuguese prohibition of printing books in native languages, a ban that prevented diffusion of the Bible. Just before Salazar took power in Portugal, the ban was relaxed to permit the printing of books in native languages, provided that the opposite page contained an authenticated Portuguese translation.

In the "corporate government" period, Angola officialdom became increasingly Fascist in outlook, and the propinquity of the former German Southwest Africa impelled Britain and Belgium to watch the borders and ports unceasingly. As for the people of Angola, nothing was done to remedy their lot: Angola remained, in the expressive words of Lord Hailey, the "Cinderella of colonies."

Stakes in the Peace

The Portuguese, realizing that it is no longer possible for the older type of colonial government to continue, have sought to exploit their colonies in a more modern fashion. In Mozambique, of course, the development is overshadowed by that of the Union of South Africa, for which the colony is an *entrepôt* or trade outlet. South African banking and commercial influence is so powerful that, save for political control, Mozambique can scarcely be considered entirely Portuguese-ruled. The development

of Mozambique's pastoral and agricultural reserves is a crying need; but thus far, the example of what all her neighbors have accomplished in this respect has had slight effect.

In Angola, Portuguese neglect of their possession contrasts sharply with the recent expansion of nearby Belgian Congo. Here too, the rich terraces one meets as one approaches from the sea are capable of rich agricultural yield. Portuguese investment of capital is not lacking, for on a per capita basis it has rivaled that in the French colonies and minor British possessions of the region, all of whom have made more progress. Nor can it be ascribed to a want of interest in Lisbon. On the contrary, the Portuguese have an abundant literature in colonial studies and have devoted constant attention to colonial policy. What then is wrong? Up to a few years ago, the greed of the trading companies was an obstacle, and since then, "corporate" control by the Portuguese government seems to have been spectacular rather than efficient.

It is hard to say whence amelioration can come, unless it be some international provision of new capital, or some investment capital from Lisbon (which it has, in abundance), accompanied by a progressive policy like that of Lord Lugard in Nigeria, which would rouse the natives to cooperation. The abolition of forced labor (which rarely is fully productive) would undoubtedly improve conditions; but as matters now stand, these Portuguese colonies are the most poorly administered of all European possessions in Africa.

The possibility of Angola as a new homeland for European refugees is very great. It would indeed be desirable for the new international organization to reach an agreement with Portugal whereby European refugees can be given security in Angola and, by international action, an amount of financial help sufficient to enable them to become self-dependent in that region.

THE RHODESIAS

The Land and the People

Northern and Southern Rhodesia, two countries named in honor of the empire-builder Cecil Rhodes, were governed by his chartered company from 1889 to 1924. Northern Rhodesia, a British colony, is larger than Texas and almost twice as large as Southern Rhodesia, which has near-British Dominion status. The Rhodesias lie north of the Union of South Africa, with the Portuguese colonies to the west and east, and Tanganyika and the Belgian Congo to the north. Their aggregate land area numbers 440,000 square miles; their aggregate population, 2,828,000

Bantu Negroes and 83,000 Europeans. Because of their differences, the two countries are discussed separately.

SOUTHERN RHODESIA

Southern Rhodesia (larger than Montana) is a great plateau and most of the towns are situated on the divide between the Zambezi and Limpopo river basins. The country is hilly, the populated sections rising almost 4,000 feet. During the dry season, the weather is often cool, especially at night. Southern Rhodesia is well forested; whole areas are beauty spots, especially because of the giant evergreens. She is the great antelope country. Victoria Falls is the scenic wonder of the country.

Though the colony's economic development is important, tourists are fascinated by the archaeology. Gigantic shaftings of copper and gold mines worked either in prehistoric or ancient days extend over 200,000 square miles. (The mining industry today follows the track of these ancient workings.) A host of theories attempt to explain their origin. Hundreds of Bushmen rock paintings testify to a high prehistoric culture. A city of ruined stone buildings has also stimulated acrimonious controversy with respect to its significance for man's past history. One thing, however, is certain: for thousands of years, Southern Rhodesia has been a central point in the various important civilizations.

Education is universal for European children and more than one native child in three attends school. The inhabitants of the bush country, however, enjoy no such educational facilities. Missionary efforts have been small and unremarkable, the natives persisting in their animistic faith.

Agriculture. The European population (70,000 compared with 1,456,000 Bantu Negroes) has gone in for mixed farming and pastoral activity. Corn and wheat, cotton and tobacco, peanuts (groundnuts) and fruit, are the leading articles, especially citrus fruits. The cattle population, some 2,700,000, is on the increase. Dairying, however, is already important.

Mining. The mining industry holds primary importance for the export economy. Annual gold production exceeded $30,000,000 and assorted base metals $15,000,000. Southern Rhodesia is second only to Canada in asbestos production, and her new bauxite discoveries, combined with her water-power, should make her a leading aluminum producer. The country has ample coal for local manufacture, and there is already a thriving infant light industry in its up-to-date towns whose 43,000 workers produce about $50,000,000, gross.

Finance. The colony has a large external debt (about $50,000,000); nevertheless, she advanced the mother country $15,000,000, interest-free, to aid in the war effort. Britain's investment in both Rhodesias has amounted to some $510,000,000.

Foreign Trade. Southern Rhodesian commerce is brisk, with exports about $70,000,000 and imports $50,000,000. These figures indicate prosperity for the dominant European population. Southern Rhodesia has proved far more rewarding to the white immigrant than Kenya, for example.

History: 1914-1944

Since 1926 Southern Rhodesia has pursued the South African policy of segregating the natives. To get about, the natives must have "passes," though some of them are allowed to do skilled work, which is not permitted in the Union of South Africa. The government ordered the tribal society retained, and divided available land among the tribes. The 50,000 Europeans received 48,000,000 acres of ele-

vated areas and the 1,100,000 natives (grouped in tribes) received 28,000,000 acres.

The British Crown in 1923 bought out the rights of the chartered company. The colony adopted a Constitution providing for autonomous government and extending the vote to all qualified British subjects. The local legislature, and not the British Colonial office, took over the control of native affairs.

Local politics has turned on the issue of federation with South Africa and Northern Rhodesia. Some favor one or the other as alternatives, while some advocate that both Southern and Northern Rhodesia should enter into the Union of South Africa. Sir Godfrey Huggins, Unionist party leader, who has dominated political life for a decade, has insisted on the unity of the two Rhodesias after the war.

The government, in October 1937, fostered native councils in the segregated native areas under British supervision; hence "dual sovereignty" exists among these natives. Direct legislative power (in the lower house) resides only in the whites. In 1943 the legislature had 23 members of the Unionist party and 7 Laborites. On the question of policy toward the natives, their differences have not been wide.

NORTHERN RHODESIA

High hills and depressions alternate through 290,000 square miles of Northern Rhodesia. Far more tropical in climate and vegetation than Southern Rhodesia, the colony has her full share of tropical diseases in the lowlands. The 1,372,000 Bantu Negro population hold to their primitive animist faith. Educational facilities are available to children of the 15,000 European inhabitants, and many mission schools and some state schools serve the native children.

Economy. Northern Rhodesia is primarily a copper producer. Her yearly output of 250,000 tons is most of Africa's and over a ninth of the world's supply. She has a good production of zinc, but other metals are not important except cobalt alloy.

The farm economy of the Europeans, in a formative stage, is not yet profitable, but tobacco and oilseeds are important export crops. There is practically no manufacturing in this colony whose mineral, water-power, and timber resources have barely begun to be exploited.

Foreign Trade. Northern Rhodesian exports, including transit shipping, reaches $50,000,000. Copper is, of course, the principal commodity — her copper is one of the most important export factors in the world. Her copper interests are among the leading shares quoted on the London Stock Exchange.

History: 1914-1944

In 1924 the colony of Northern Rhodesia was transferred directly to the British Crown from the chartered British South Africa Company. The company, having incurred great losses in administrative expenses, was conceded extremely profitable mineral royalties. Under the Crown's direct government, the native population increased by 50% and the number of European immigrants trebled. Exports multiplied by 25, imports by 8. And practically all trade was based on the enormous development of the three great copper companies: Rhokana, Roan Antelope, and Mufulira.

There has been a conflict between the Europeans, who wish to federate with Southern Rhodesia, and the natives, who oppose federation because they now enjoy greater rights than do the natives of Southern Rhodesia. Within the colony there has also been a struggle between two projected policies: the Union of South Africa policy, that segregates natives and assigns them a low status, and the policy of dual control, far more considerate of native rights, which was originated by Lord Lugard in Nigeria (See *Nigeria, History*).

As yet, no native sits in the Legislative Council of Northern Rhodesia. White labor, mostly engaged in supervisory work, sides with the white community as a whole against native labor — especially since it is paid about ten times as much. Nevertheless, the white settlers are hostile to the copper companies, which, they assert, pay out too much in dividends abroad and reinvest too little in the colony. These white settlers also attack the profits of the old chartered company, which receives generous compensation from the copper companies.

In 1940 general strikes of the natives broke out in the mines. These were suppressed with some bloodshed. The local opposition in the Legislative Council has since charged that the copper companies despite war needs have restricted output in order to reduce their payments of excess profits taxes.

A lively agitation exists among devoted British civil servants for some special services that will help improve the appalling condition of the natives, as revealed by investigating commissions.

Stakes in the Peace

Southern Rhodesia's stake in the peace will depend on her future affiliations. If the Rhodesias are united and given autonomy, Southern Rhodesia will have the largest say in administering the immense copper production of Northern Rhodesia; but she will have to deal with a thorny native problem. If she federates with the Union of South Africa, she also enters an area in which native policy is even more important than within her local boundaries.

So far, these considerations have prevented the expansion of Southern Rhodesian jurisdiction. Apart from tariff agreements, it is difficult to see what she would gain from any expansion of her area. She is one of the few remaining countries ideally suited to European settlement, with a climate, natural beauty, and wealth of resources making her one of the most promising lands of the twentieth century. What she needs is a large number of European immigrants, well-trained in agriculture, and possessing a fair amount of initial capital. Given these, she could have a European population of some 5,000,000 within thirty or forty years. Here, certainly, is one of the pioneer fields of humanity in the post-war era.

Northern Rhodesia is in a wholly different situation. If anything (and were her name not Rhodesia), she would seem to be linked to the Tanganyika and Nyasaland areas; and she may eventually gravitate into that regional grouping, as several British economic experts have recommended. But she can score no significant advances until the key problem of the grinding poverty of her native population is dealt with, at least as competently as in the Belgian Congo. This country does not seem destined for European settlement and farming, but rather for stable native agriculture, with European direction of mining and transportation. Even in that case, European labor seems destined only for supervisory tasks; but if the problem of tuberculosis and tropical disease is coped with, the better-nourished natives will gradually develop a more advanced culture.

International Organizations

THE LEAGUE OF NATIONS

The League of Nations was formed by virtue of a Covenant incorporated in the Treaty of Versailles (1919). The Covenant, consisting of 26 articles, stipulated conditions of membership, procedures for settling disputes, and the use of sanctions to punish any member-state who disregarded its rulings.

Article 10, a key provision, guaranteed every member against external aggression as follows: "The Members of the League undertake and preserve as against external aggression the territorial integrity and existing political independence of all Members of the League. In case of any such aggression or in case of any threat or danger of such aggression the Council shall advise upon the means by which this obligation shall be fulfilled."

The Covenant also contained expressions of the need for disarmament, disallowed secret treaties, and introduced a system of mandates for certain areas (principally those colonies formerly held by Germany and Turkey). The Mandate system, created under Article 22 of the Covenant, divided the mandated areas into three classes: Class A, Class B, and Class C, varying in accordance with the conditions of each territory; and it pledged the mandatory powers to undertake their work "as a sacred trust of civilization," with "safeguards in the interests of the indigenous population" and without deriving any benefit "from such trusteeship."

The Covenant was formulated by a commission (authorized January 20, 1919) under the presidency of Woodrow Wilson, with ten Great Powers and nine smaller nations represented by their most distinguished statesmen.

The legal existence of the League of Nations began on January 10, 1920. A permanent organization was set up, its seat at Geneva, Switzerland. The League consisted of an Assembly, or "lower house," and a Council, or "upper house." It was contemplated that the Assembly would meet every year, the Council every three months. On the most important decisions, the League required unanimity.

The original membership numbered 29 countries. But the U.S.A., after a historic national debate of far-reaching consequences, decided not to join. Eventually, the League's membership rose to 60 countries; and at one time, the Soviet Union and the U.S.A. were the only important non-member nations. The Soviet Union, however, joined in 1934.

The first three years of the League were marked with many successes. It regulated a number of minor disputes between countries with auspicious results. But in 1923, when Italy bombarded the Greek island of Corfu, the League's decision in effect rewarded the aggressor, and after that date its prestige declined.

In the Saar region and the Free City of Danzig, which it supervised, the League did its work admirably. It handled refugee problems well, including difficult exchanges of populations — for example, between Greece and Turkey (See *Greece, History*), and advanced loans to aid these unfortunate migrants. In minor administrative tasks, its achievements were superb: improving public health, regulating the drug traffic, banning white-slave trade, providing passports for people without a state, combating "forced labor" in the colonies, wiping out colonial slavery, and working for intellectual cooperation among the peoples. Its statistical and economic documentation was unrivaled, and its influence in the International Labor Organization (I.L.O.) and other supra-national institutions that must supplement national bodies, proved invaluable.

The first Permanent Secretary of the League was an Englishman, Sir Eric Drummond (now Lord Perth), who resigned in 1933 to be succeeded by a Frenchman, Joseph Avenol.

In 1932 the League had to grapple with the vital problem of the Japanese invasion of Manchuria. Unanimously it condemned Japan as an aggressor, whereupon Japan resigned. (See *Japan, History*.) Shortly thereafter, Germany ostentatiously withdrew (1933) and was followed several years later by Italy (1938), who resisted the League's partial sanctions in her aggression against Ethiopia. It was during this period that the U.S.A. moved toward international cooperation by adhering to the International Labor Organization.

By 1937, the calculated and ever-truculent blackmail of the Axis powers, Germany, Japan, and Italy, and the inability of the League to deflect them from their course of aggression, diminished the League's importance until it became little more than a consultative assembly. Nevertheless, in that year only 8 sovereign nations were not members: the U.S.A., Brazil (who had resigned her membership when deprived of a permanent seat on the Council), Egypt, Costa Rica, Paraguay, Saudi Arabia, and the two aggressor states, Germany and Japan.

In 1938 it was evident that the important issues of aggression and territorial adjustment, whether in Austria, Czechoslovakia, or even League-supervised areas like Danzig and Memel, would no longer be settled within the League. Soon a number of nations — Albania, Chile, Guatemala, Honduras, Hungary, Italy, Nicaragua, Peru, Spain, and Venezuela — quit the organization, either on ideological grounds or because they objected to payments to what they felt was not a sufficiently effective international organization.

The outbreak of World War II in September 1939 saw the League reduced to virtual impotence. In December of that year it expelled the U.S.S.R. from membership as an aggressor in the Soviet-Finnish War (1939–1940). By the spring of 1940, the German occupation of a large part of France made it prudent to decentralize the League's functions: the Economic and Financial Bureau was installed in Princeton, New Jersey; the Opium Board in Washington, D.C.; and the International Labor Organization in Montreal, Canada; a reduced staff remained at the central offices in Geneva. Governments under Axis influence, such as Vichy France, Finland, and Rumania, left the organization, while Austria lost her membership when German annexation was accepted as an accomplished fact.

During the war, the League, whose organizational weaknesses and functional shortcomings had driven even many of its most convinced supporters to despair, again proved to be the nucleus of international organization, once the original concept of its powers was revived and even extended. It is rather as a frame of reference or point of departure than as actually constituted that the League of Nations has value for the future. The lessons of League succe\ since 1920 will, if objectively analyz\ salutary to the higher and more eff\ world organization destined to emerge in\ world.

UNIVERSAL POSTAL UNION

The Universal Postal Union represents the first and as yet the most indicative and wholly successful example of international cooperation over a long period. Formed in 1875 by 22 countries, it has gradually extended to include the whole world.

The Union is based on a convention declaring that its members agree that for the purposes of postal communications, there is only one country: the whole world. Every nation has the unlimited use of the communication facilities of every other nation for the conduct of the mails; and every signatory country must grant to the others the full use of any improvements in its postal service communications. Rates, weights, and the nature of services are internationally uniform for international services.

The agreement on ordinary mail was soon extended to registration of letters and then to money-orders and parcel-post, though these latter have not been made completely uniform. Many supplementary services have been arranged, and always on an amicable basis.

Postal conventions are held every 5 years when practicable, and every member state, whatever its size, has an equal vote. The Union clears accounts among its signatories, which requires the most extensive bookkeeping, since it must keep track of the 50,000,-000,000 letters that annually crisscross over 114 postal jurisdictions. The International Bureau is now located at Berne, Switzerland.

The Union has managed to function through many wars and it has successfully adjusted to "blocked currencies." It is a sixty-year-old demonstration that when international cooperation *must* override "absolute national sovereignty" — and there is no other workable alternative — cooperation functions smoothly.

INDEX OF MAPS

NEW ZEALAND

TASMANIA

Melbourne

Auckland

Sydney

Brisbane

NEWCALEDONIA

FIJI

SOCIETY

SAMOA

NEW
HEBRIDES

CORAL SEA

Darwin

AUSTRALIA

Fremantle

JAVA

INDIAN
OCEAN

SOLOMONS

NEW
GUINEA

SUMATRA

BORNEO

Singapore

CEYLON

EQUATOR

GILBERTS

TRUK
CAROLINES

Davao

PHILIPPINE
ISLANDS

MARSHALLS

GUAM

Manila

FR. INDO-
CHINA

BAY OF
BENGAL

Rangoon

Bombay

HAWAIIAN
ISLANDS

WAKE

MARIANAS

Hongkong

BURMA

Calcutta

Honolulu

FORMOSA

INDIA

MIDWAY

BONIN

Shanghai
Chungking

TIBET
CHINA

SINKIANG

Tokyo

Peiping

MONGOLIA

JAPAN

KOREA

Los

San Francisco

PACIFIC OCEAN

Portland

MANCHURIA

Seattle

KURILES

Vladivostok

PARAMUSHIRO

ATTU ALEUTIANS

Sitka

SEA OF
OKHOTSK

KAMCHATKA

U. S. S. R.

Juneau

BERING
SEA

ALASKA

SIBERIA

Fairbanks

Nome

ARCTIC CIRCLE

PT. BARROW

ARCTIC OCEAN